INDUSTRIAL WORK AND LIFE

LONDON SCHOOL OF ECONOMICS MONOGRAPHS ON SOCIAL ANTHROPOLOGY

Managing Editor: Charles Stafford

The Monographs on Social Anthropology were established in 1940 and aim to publish results of modern anthropological research of primary interest to specialists.

The continuation of the series was made possible by a grant in aid from the Wenner-Gren Foundation for Anthropological Research, and more recently by a further grant from the Governors of the London School of Economics and Political Science. Income from sales is returned to a revolving fund to assist further publications.

The Monographs are under the direction of an Editorial Board associated with the Department of Anthropology of the London School of Economics and Political Science.

INDUSTRIAL WORK AND LIFE

AN ANTHROPOLOGICAL READER

Edited by Massimiliano Mollona, Geert De Neve
& Jonathan Parry

LONDON SCHOOL OF ECONOMICS MONOGRAPHS ON SOCIAL ANTHROPOLOGY

Volume 78

Oxford • New York

English edition
First published in 2009 by
Berg

Editorial offices:
First Floor, Angel Court, 81 St Clements Street, Oxford OX4 1AW, UK
175 Fifth Avenue, New York, NY 10010, USA

Berg is the imprint of Oxford International Publishers Ltd.

Library of Congress Cataloging-in-Publication Data

A catalogue record for this book is available from the Library Congress.

British Library Cataloguing-in-Publication Data

A catalogue record for this book is available from the British Library.

ISBN 978 1 84788 076 5 (Cloth)
        978 1 84788 074 1 (Paper)

Typeset by SAGE India.

Printed in Great Britain by the MPG Books Group, Bodmin and King's Lynn

www.bergpublishers.com

CONTENTS

PART 5: THE INDUSTRIAL WORKING CLASS?

20. Bourgeois and Proletarians   395
    Karl Marx

21. Perspectives on the Politics of Class   405
    Rajnarayan Chandavarkar

22. Class Structure in the Classic Slum   415
    Robert Roberts

23. Community and Class Consciousness   427
    Jane Nash

24. Learning to Protest in Japan: Class Consciousness, Solidarity,
    and Political Action   437
    Christena Turner

    Appendix of Sources   463
    List of Series   467
    Index   475

PREFACE

Though two of us now hold posts elsewhere, our collaboration on this volume stems from the fact that we have all been closely associated with the Department of Anthropology at the London School of Economics, all developed an interest in the study of industry during our time there and have all taught courses on the anthropology of industry in our respective institutions. This collection brings together some of the readings which we have found most helpful in that teaching. It would have been easy to put together a volume on any one of the sets of issues covered by the five different sections into which it is divided, but we have opted for a wider coverage on the calculation that this would be more useful to students new to the field. Each of the section introductions refers to other relevant literature and is followed by a short list of 'recommended further reading' intended for those who would like to pursue the issues it raises.

While all three editors are social anthropologists by training, and many of the chapters in our collection were authored by anthropologists, almost as many were written by social historians, sociologists and others. As the general Introduction to the volume explains, this is because we believe it essential that the study of industry and industrial life is inter-disciplinary and broadly comparative. Rather than an 'anthropological' perspective, what we have privileged is an 'ethnographic' one – broadly conceived as one that stresses the value of an on-the-ground 'field view' of society that focuses on everyday processes. That perspective, we believe, is of real value to students of industry across the whole range of social science disciplines and it is to a general social science audience that we hope this volume will appeal.

The selection of readings and the editing of excerpts was done collaboratively by the three editors. Mollona has contributed the general Introduction to the volume and, though the other two editors had an input at an earlier stage, Parry takes responsibility for the final form of the section Introductions (which at some points rely heavily on his general review article on 'Industrial work' in J. Carrier (ed), *A handbook of economic anthropology*, Cheltenham: Edward Elgar). It was Charles Stafford who originally suggested a volume of this kind and we gratefully acknowledge his encouragement as well as his patience. We also thank Camilla Griffiths for her extremely efficient (and also patient) administrative assistance at various stages of this project.

Massimiliano Mollona
Geert De Neve
Jonathan Parry

GENERAL INTRODUCTION

Massimiliano Mollona

This collection juxtaposes a series of ethnographic accounts of industrialization and industrial life in various Western and non-Western societies, and its aims are broadly comparative and interdisciplinary. Most of its chapters are by social historians, anthropologists or sociologists, but we hope that it also speaks to a wider audience of students and colleagues with an interest in industry across the social science disciplines. All three editors are by training social anthropologists, and one of the main objectives of the volume is to demonstrate to others the value of the ethnographic method for the study of industry (or at least of a worm's eye 'field view' of industrial work and life). More parochially, a second objective is to suggest to colleagues of our own discipline that the study of industrial transformation should be placed higher up their agenda than it is at present. Among anthropologists who have traditionally specialized in the study of *other* non-Western cultures or who supervise graduate students who do so, only a very small proportion work on industry; this implies that they have not yet quite woken up to the fact that many of these economies are now significantly industrialized.

The Reader is divided into five parts: industrial time and work discipline; shopfloor organization, with special reference to skill, control and consent; the relationships between the workplace and the home and the way in which the division between these spaces is gendered; teleological models of industrialization that suppose that industrial societies tend to converge on a common design, and on working-class consciousness. Each part has its own introduction and a list of suggested further readings from amongst the sources referred to in the text. In each part an opening chapter raises general issues and problems then discussed in the section as a whole. The subsequent chapters in the section are intended as 'case histories' which bear on these.

In choosing broadly 'ethnographic' pieces, we want to privilege what Roberts calls 'the factuality of first-hand experience' and what Thompson termed the 'human actuality'. Industrial ethnographies reveal the interplay between analytical and experiential dimensions of work and the tensions between 'the economy' as a 'substantive'

xii   GENERAL INTRODUCTION

field of practices, and 'economics' as a set of prescriptive models and theories. Thus, they open up the field of economic theory to different critical and empirical perspectives, allowing new inter-disciplinary discussions and collaborations. Indeed one of the objectives of this reader is to encourage scholars and students from a range of social science disciplines who are critically engaged with 'Economics' to consider the importance of the kinds of data anthropologists collect. Anthropology is not the only discipline to rely on ethnographic methods. Sociology has produced some of the most vivid shopfloor ethnographies so far, especially in the early traditions of the Chicago School (Hiller 1928; Roy 1952) and the Harvard School of Industrial Relations (Roethlisberger and Dickson 1939). More recently, in the fields of industrial relations (Delbridge 1998), management (Knight and Wilmott 1989; Ezzamel and Willmot 1998) and accounting (Ahrens and Mollona 2007) ethnographic studies in different institutional settings have shed new light on the tensions between managerial models and ideas of work, on the one hand, and the workers' practices and culture, on the other hand. They have shown, for instance, that abstract political theories and models of activism shared by trade union leaders and politicians (and some academics) very rarely inform the workers' actions, which are instead pragmatically entangled in their every day activities, worries and struggles on the line (Durrenberger 2002). Industrial ethnographies lead us to question the assumption, central in much sociology of work, that managerial re-organizations always stifle workers' resistance. Rather, they show that these processes sometimes have unintended negative consequences for the employers. For instance, models of Total Quality Management (TQM) and teamwork may actually create resistances from line workers and middle-management on the line, because they infringe their sense of professionalism and autonomy (Ezzamel et al. 2008). In other instances re-organizations deeply fragment industrial workforces, as in the Sochaux Peugeot automobile plant described by Beaud and Pialoux (2001) where the implementation of a Japanese merit system fragmented the workforce into older 'mates' who opposed it and the younger more educated and individualistic 'scabs' who supported it. Similarly, in Mollona's (2009) ethnography of the steel industry in Sheffield, the management's promotion of different organizational subcultures fragmented the workers' understanding of and resistance to restructuring and team-working.

But this Reader proposes more than a mere endorsement of the participant observation methodology; in fact, we argue that ethnography is central to understanding the radical socio-economic changes of the last twenty years, including the current financial 'crisis', which, if anything, shows the gap between models and reality in the economy. Ethnographies of work often challenge the universalistic and ethnocentric assumptions that constitute the core of 'economics', in particular its view of society as a field comprising rationalizing and individualistic actors in mutual competition for scarce resources. By revealing the human dimension of work – the importance of self-realization, creativity, collaboration and solidarity – and plurality of forms of livelihood, ethnography opens up alternative economic visions and political possibilities.

Flexible production has radically affected people's experience of work in time and space (Harvey 2003). The hyper-mobility of capital, modular technology and extensive labour deregulation have rendered the mechanistic times and spaces of industrial capitalism obsolete. Today capital does not attach itself to any specific or fixed location but fluctuates between nodes in global production chains. Open to international speculation and arbitrage, labour is just another variable and temporary factor of production and work is precarious, insecure and geographically dispersed.

Post-industrial guru Daniel Bell (1973) predicted the disappearance of the manufacturing industry and of a manual working-class in the wake of technological innovation, mechanization of labour and the advent of the service economy. The inclusion in this volume of traditional pieces of industrial ethnography reflects our belief that the 'old fashioned' world of industry and the working class has not disappeared but rather has taken on new spatial and temporal reconfigurations. Industrial ethnographies are central to an understanding of the contemporary context for two reasons.

First, the South can no longer be associated with the world of the 'peasantry'. The emergence of China, India and Brazil as major industrial powers signals not only the end of American hegemony (Arrighi 2005) but also the existence of working-class histories, lived experiences and patterns of industrialization that differ from the trajectories of industrialization and proletarianization in the North. These call for ethnographic investigation. The industrial ideologies of Taylorism and Fordism might no longer be current in the North, but they are central in the economic development of the South. Today, China's industrial might is based on the 'old fashioned' bureaucratic and hierarchical system of mass-production rather than on lean manufacturing. The fact that the new world economic powers combine flexible production with the 'old fashioned' Fordist system poses a fundamental challenge to the Western dogma of the superiority of the 'lean economy'.

Secondly, contrary to much conventional wisdom, 'old processes' of class stratification are central also in the 'post-industrial' North. Braverman (chapter 5) shows that white collar workers are subject to the same process of labour standardization, deskilling and alienation as the Fordist manual workers. Indeed, studies on the service economy cast data processing workers, software engineers and other 'creative labourers' as modern 'cyberproletarians' (Huws 2003) (rather than skilled professionals). During much of the post-Second World War period the industrial working class in the North was homogenous in terms of gender, ethnicity and political background. The workforce of the new service and manufacturing firms, on the other hand, is far more heterogeneous, and increasingly characterized by young women from minority ethnic backgrounds, with little previous experience of work and of trade-union activism. Capital and labour deregulation led to a new regime of tax relief and exemption from the duties of workers' welfare and union representation for small firms and to the spread of small subcontractors employing migrant and ethnic labour, often illegally and in conditions of semi-slavery. The 'modern' system of flexible production is built upon a network of Victorian sweatshops hidden beneath the post-industrial façade of shopping malls, highways and leisure centres (Mollona 2009). The dislocation of the Fordist factory and of the male, white and skilled manual worker has brought to the fore issues of ethnicity, gender and kinship, informal production and household economies, which are central in the ethnographies of work discussed in this Reader. If class is dead as a universal concept, it reemerges in specific contexts in different forms, languages and practices that need to be documented ethnographically.

Much contemporary sociology is unable to capture these changes and, operating from within the classical sociological tradition, assumes that the working-class in the North has been either 'bourgeoisified' or wiped-out by the 'Washington consensus' – a series of anti-labour policies followed by most neo-conservative governments in the North that systematically and relentlessly attacked industry and the working class, causing the latter's extinction.[1] The theory of working-class 'embourgeoisement' goes back to the classical 'affluent worker' project (Goldthorpe et al. 1968). In the post-war years the British working class benefited from relatively high salaries, secure pensions and comfortable homes, and had incomes and lifestyles comparable to the middle-class. Some considered them the 'new bourgeoisie'. In this context, the study by Goldthorpe et al. revealed an instrumental and individualistic attitude among the workers of the new car factories in the South-east that differed from the solidarity which characterised the world of traditional working-class communities. They discounted the hypothesis that the working-class held the same values as the bourgeoisie and showed that instrumentalism was more a form of political activism than of quiescence. Nonetheless they also demonstrated that the working class had shifted its political focus onto a 'merely' economic terrain. Sociologists taking a more ethnographic perspective criticised this typological and industry-based approach to workers' consciousness, arguing that perceptions of work could not be assumed to be homogenous within the same industry and that indeed they vary even within the same factory (Beynon and Blackburn 1972). Against the 'culturalist' framework of the affluent worker project, sociologists of labour claimed that workers' motivations were largely the effect of managerial 'indoctrination' (Lupton 1963), shop floor organization (Burawoy, chapter 7) or mechanization (Beynon, chapter 6). They linked rapid working-class decline to technological improvement and repressive industrial policies instead.

Unfortunately, anthropology also subscribed to this sociological view of the death of class and industry in the North, underestimating patterns of industrialization and class formation in the South, as well as the emergence of new class inequalities in the North. Breaking away from traditional studies of industry and inequality, the anthropology of the 'New Economy' has, with some sophistication, questioned the de-humanizing and de-personalizing effect of the forces associated with 'stock market capitalism'. For instance, Zaloom (2003) shows that skilled knowledge and trading practices among brokers of the Chicago stock exchange shape 'from below' global commodity and financial flows. In conflict with the dominant view that associates the economy with the realm of rationalization and finance with self-interest and algorithmic abstraction, scholars have stressed the peculiar imagination associated with financial circulation (Li Puma and Lee 2002) and described finance as a space of religion (Guyer 2007), reciprocity (Maurer 2008) and even 'hope' (Miyazaki 2006). Similarly, the excellent business ethnographies in the volume *Frontiers of Capital*[2] (2006) show how risk leveraging, securitization, Information and Communication Technology (ICT) and other techniques associated with 'fast-capitalism' have paradoxically, increased trust and personal networks rather than impersonal and alienated social relations. These contributions reflect a critical awareness of the complex web of technologies, institutions, knowledge and actors of late capitalism. But in focusing on what is 'New' in the 'New Economy', they have left out – or at least relegated to the background – the old questions of inequality and class stratification. Based on multi-sited, multi-scalar and interpretative fieldwork much scholarship on the 'New Economy' has ignored the other side of fast-capitalism: the slow, monotonous grind of making a livelihood for the majority of people stuck 'on the dark side' of globalization. For instance, most ethnographies of fast-capitalism discuss brokers, technocrats, computer programmers and members of the financial elite, but fail to look at the impact of financialization on the working-class. Unlike these, Blackburn's *The Fourth Dimension* (2006) shows that securitization, leverage and other techniques of financial speculation have emerged thanks to the proliferation of micro-finance, workers' pensions funds, sub-prime loans and other imaginative forms of expansion of working-class credit (read 'debt'). The consequences of the current 'trust failure' in the financial system impact unevenly along the social spectrum. The shattered hopes of Japanese brokers described by Miyazaki do not compare with the immediate struggles of repossessions, bankruptcies and redundancies faced by the working-class worldwide. Today the unemployment, home repossessions, pensions' write-offs and family bankruptcies that have followed the collapse of the financial system are making the reality of class painfully evident again. Most of all, the myths of the disappearance of the industrial working class – an inverted version of the myth of its making – reflect an ethnocentric understanding of society and history that is deeply flawed and outdated.

The everyday experience of work is affected by four factors: factory organization, trajectories of industrialization, industrial and welfare policies (or ideologies) and occupational identities or sense of class belonging. These four dimensions of work exist in all capitalist societies but they take different forms in different historical, cultural and geographical contexts. By showing different historical and cultural instances through which factories, industries, state ideologies and working-class consciousness affect the 'world of work', the chapters in this Reader make it clear that there are no general laws of capitalist development, despite the persistence in time and space of inequalities and exploitation.

In spite of technological innovation, factory closures and gentrification, industrial labour is still one of the main forms of livelihood in most societies. But industrial work patterns and identities are in a constant state of flux and change, blurring the boundaries, between North and South, class and identity, town and countryside, factory and society, too often taken for granted in traditional social science. I suggest that this new complexity of the contemporary world of work puts anthropology at the centre of a renewed *critical* 'Political Economy' (Roseberry 2002; Robotham 2005) that looks at labour as the central locus of human value – that is, of self-realization, exploitation and emancipation. Reflected in the multi-disciplinary structure of the Reader, is the belief that an understanding of the spatial and temporal fluidity of contemporary factories, industries and workforces requires collaboration between anthropology, sociology, history and industrial relations and a dialogue between 'models' and 'ethnography' (Narotzky 2007). Below, I discuss the four dimensions of factory labour, industry, state ideology and class consciousness. For each of them, I offer a suggestion about how the ethnographic perspective challenges some taken-for-granted assumptions of mainstream social theories, and highlight some potential theoretical developments.

(A) THE SOCIAL EMBEDDEDNESS OF FACTORIES

The first proposition is that the factory is a social space and not, as following some sociological and managerial theories, merely a technological and productive one.

This first proposition might seem bland, but many managerial theories of firms still discuss 'work' as material input and the labour process as a process of transformation of scarce resources into valuable outputs. This process is mainly informed by technological factors. Even some orthodox sociologists still emphasise how technology and divisions of labour on the shopfloor are the main determinants of the experience of work under capitalism. These perspectives fail to explain the social embeddedness of capitalist forms of livelihood. Unlike them, industrial ethnographies show the fragmented experience of work under capitalism and how these fragmented perceptions of work lead to different subjectivities and political consciousness. Harry Braverman's classical sociological enquiry on the nature of industrial alienation (chapter 5) argues that the 'scientific division of labour' invented by Taylor, based on standardization of tasks and the supervision and mechanization of labour, reflects the capitalist imperative of extracting surplus labour within the amount of time (the working day) set in the capitalist contract. For the workers, the deskilling of their labour on the shopfloor implies more than boredom. The capitalist division of labour creates an artificial separation between 'planning' (left to the management) and 'execution' (the task of the workers) and therefore de-humanizes their productive activity. Without control over their actions industrial workers under capitalism are deprived of the human power of imagination and, ultimately, of political consciousness.

Burawoy's celebrated ethnography of 'Allied' (chapter 7), an engineering factory in Chicago, departs significantly from Braverman's analysis. It suggests that the workers consent to produce as long as they can turn production into a kind of game through which they can overcome boredom at work. Paradoxically, the extraction of surplus value operates through the workers' very informal culture and subjectivities. If the workers described by Braverman are coerced into production by a hostile and de-humanizing apparatus of production, the workers of Allied consent to produce because of their control of the production line. Braverman emphasizes capitalism's apparatus of coercion; Burawoy argues that consent is its driving force. Burawoy's ethnography demonstrated with clarity that line workers have greater control and knowledge of the production process than managers and supervisors, anticipating the current managerial trends of TQM, teamwork and horizontal co-ordination that increase productivity by extending the workers' control of the line. But both studies relate the workers' consciousness or experience of work to divisions of labour on the shop floor and discount the relevance of cultural factors (i.e. gender, ethnicity, age or religion) that the workers bring to the shop floor.

Some of our ethnographies show that *gender* is central in the experience of wage labour. Sometimes gender-based forms of identification lead to successful strategies of workplace resistance. For instance, Westwood's (1984) ethnography of 'StitchCo', a garment factory in the British Midlands, and Elizabeth Dunn's (2004) monograph on Alima-Gerber, a recently privatised Polish baby food factory, show how women workers challenge the dehumanization of work through feminine rituals and narratives that domesticate and resocialize their labour and workplaces. In the case of 'Anarchomex', the middle-sized Mexican electric factory described by Salzinger (chapter 10), the 'macho' display of the young, unskilled male workforce became a form of workers' self-organization. *Ethnicity* is a central theme in China's current wave of industrialization, which is based on the exploitation of migrant labourers from the provinces who are kept in a constant state of job insecurity through restrictive migration and ethnic policies (Pun Ngai 2005). Industrial ethnographies of contemporary Brazil reveal that the Brazilian working class is profoundly fragmented along racial and ethnic lines in spite of the country's dominant myth of racial democracy. Guimarães et al.'s (1995) ethnography of the petrochemical industry in the state of Bahia, shows how the traditional fragmentation between skilled (*tecnicos*) and unskilled (*peões*) labourers reproduces both regional distinctions between urban and rural workers and racial ones between black and white workers.

The ethnographies in the Reader show that the experience of work under capitalism is more complicated, rich and socially embedded than would appear from traditional sociological and managerial theories, which often underplay the interconnections between the social relations at the factory level and the workers' personal background. The ethnographies highlight the 'dual nature' of work, one connected to the workers' personal – racial, gender, generational, ethnic and religious – background and the other impersonal, based on bureaucratic and productive norms. The fact that work does not belong to the autonomous sphere of production means that in-dustrialization does not follow the universal logic of optimal allocation of scarce resources. In the next section I discuss universal models of industrialization as 'ideological projects'.

(B) GLOBAL CONVERGENCE?

My second proposition is that industrial paths do not converge towards a single Western or 'core' model but take different and uneven trajectories between world 'cores' and 'peripheries'.

The 'modernist' myth that industrialization would lead world societies into their final stage of development was not only a capitalist one. Kotkin (1997) describes how Stalin's development of Magnitogorsk in the middle of the Ural Steppe, at the time the biggest industrial steel complex in the world, served as a powerful symbol of Socialist modernity. Throughout the twentieth century, industrialization was a colonial project aimed at forcing the ideas of modernity, progress and democracy upon the world peripheries. In a fascinating piece of social history Cooper (1992) demonstrates that the proletarianization and de-casualization of the Mombasa dock workers in Colonial Kenya was more an issue of political control than of economic development. In some contexts industry as a colonial project encountered little re-sistance. Gluckman's piece (chapter 15) on the 'Industrial revolution' in colonial Rhodesia in the 1960s shows how easily class and the authority of the trade unions overtook tribalism and the elders at the periphery of the Empire. In the postcolo-nial context modernization theories legitimated further industrial expansion in the South through developmental projects and programmes of structural adjustment. In some contexts these projects had devastating impacts on the local agrarian popu-lation (Harriss and Harriss 1989). In others, they encountered local resistance, sub-versions and failures. Discussing the way in which industry is represented by villagers who live on the edge of a company town in contemporary central India, Pinney (1999) shows how resistance against the new industrial regimes is more likely to come from high caste landowners than from people at the bottom of the village hierarchy. Ong's (chapter 4) ethnography of labour in a microelectronic Japanese factory in Malaysia's Free-Trade Zone demonstrates how young rural female factory workers rebel against the foreign management by becoming possessed by malevolent spirits on the shopfloor and slowing down and disrupting production. The fragility of post-colonial industrial development is further unveiled in Ferguson's (chapter 16) power-ful description of the urban decline, poverty and demoralization that followed the collapse of the colonial economy of the Zambian Copperbelt in the 1980s.

Today, the myth of Western industrial modernity is crumbling on two fronts. First, the new spatial reconfiguration of trans-national capitalism makes the traditional

distinction between the 'industrialized' North and the 'underdeveloped' South problematic. Secondly, yesterday's developing countries are today's industrial powers. At
this moment the lives of many workers at Jaguar-Land Rover in the Castle Bromwich
plant in the United Kingdom who are facing the prospect of mass redundancy depend
on decisions taken by the company owner, Tata Group, in India. Besides, industrialization in the South does not conform to the Western model of 'shareholder capitalism',
based on short-term financial returns rather than on 'good administration'. The idea
that the world is converging towards a Western model of industrial development is
increasingly problematic.

The world 'peripheries' have developed their own models and 'varieties of capitalism' (Hall and Soskice 2001) that differ from the narrow Anglo-Saxon model. This
is also the point made by Dore (2000) who sketches the main differences between
the Anglo-Saxon 'stock-market' capitalism (with a short-term goal of maximizing
returns on shares, low workers' involvement and a managerial bonus culture) and the
'stakeholders' capitalism of Japan (with a long-term emphasis on profitability and
good administration, workers' participation and community involvement). More
recently, the 'Japanese model' – problematically branded as 'Confucian capitalism'[3] –
has been adapted to the requirement of global capitalism, but in many cases industrialization in the South diverges from the Western type of flexible capitalism. For
instance, the top world steel corporations in India and Brazil are run like family businesses rather than as financial enterprises, with their 'old fashioned' conglomerate
structures protecting them from economic downturn. In Brazil, partly as a consequence of its late industrialization, companies do not conform to the trend of corporate
restructuring and flexible and lean capitalism of the North and are organised like 'big'
diversified businesses (Goldstein and Ross-Schneider 2004). These firms internal-
ize credit and financial services instead of 'buying them' and are therefore insulated
from the current failure of financial markets. Against Thompson's famous discussion
of the rigid discipline associated with industrial capitalism, Parry's (chapter 3) vivid
industrial ethnography presents a relaxed and loose industrial discipline, characterised
by absenteeism, flexible time keeping and socialising on the shopfloor of the Bhilai
Steel Plant (BSP) in central India. BSP is an important economic player with a viable
financial profile, even if public. This hybrid form of state capitalism, where 'peasant
time' is incorporated into the factory premises and boundaries between state control
and free market are blurred, does not seem to hamper India's role as the leading world
steel producer. Breman's (2004) description of the closure of the Ahmedabad textile
mills (in Gujarat) and Chitra Joshi's (chapter 17) monograph on Kanpur's vanishing
textile mills (in the north Indian state of Uttar Pradesh) from the 1980s onwards show
how fragile industries in the South can be when confronted with economic liberalization policies, market competition and the growing demands of flexibility.

Another important current trend is that of miniaturization of economic forms
and the emergence of Petty Commodity Production (PCP) and Small and Medium-
sized Enterprises (SMEs) as nodes in global commodity chains. Challenging the

'small is beautiful' mantra that echoed among liberal economists in the 1990s, some anthropologists[4] have argued that these forms of micro and 'flexible' capitalism act as transmission belts between global capital and local forms of livelihood. Suspended between independence and self-exploitation, the family and the factory, the community and the market, petty capitalists struggle to reconcile an increasingly mobile capital at the global level with increasingly fragmented labour at the level of the community. For instance, Frances Rothstein (2006) provides a vivid account of the small-scale garment industry in San Cosme, Mexico, which developed as a consequence of free market policies and the industrial recession of the 1980s. Under constant pressure from powerful international retailers and manufacturers, petty capitalists share the insecurity and uncertainty of their workers. But in sustaining local forms of flexibile labour and entrepreneurship they reproduce the power of global retailers. A similar scenario is contemplated in the ethnographies of Kondo (1990) and Gill (chapter 14) that unveil the spread of despotic small family firms and daily labourers forced to work in conditions of semi slavery in the urban spaces of post-depression Japan. Pun's (2005) ethnography shows the diverse and contradictory industrial landscape of contemporary China with unskilled workers (*damgomei*) ruthlessly exploited in the new private capitalists' sweatshops standing side by side with the skilled aristocracy of labour (*gongren*) of the ultramodern socialist factories. Chinese factory workers are 'floating people', suspended between the rural and the urban, the modern and the backward, and the individualism of Western capitalism and the collectivism of Chinese socialism. Paralleling the 'miniaturization' of production, the increasing informalization of the economy is another important recent phenomenon. But rather than being a tool of subaltern empowerment as some anthropologists argued in the 1970s, informality and micro-enterprises seem to reproduce neo-colonialist relations between North and South (Roitman 2005; Elyachar 2005) or even between different parts of the European Union (Smith 2006).

Anthropological studies of work and industry show a differentiated and contradictory global economic landscape that cannot be captured through conventional dependency or developmental models based on clear-cut spatial and temporal divisions. From Shenzhen to Delhi or London, 'global cities' display similar 'dystopic' landscapes, made up of factories, global corporations and invisible sweatshops, slums and gentrified neighbourhoods, and of affluence and extreme poverty. Thus, the agenda for an 'anthropology of the global factory' is to go beyond socio-economic dichotomies – such as North/South, formal/informal and core/marginal – and to look at industry and work as spatially complex, relational and 'total' facts open to mutation, change and transformation. In particular the study of industry must focus on *inter-connections* rather than on specific sites or issues. On the inter-connections between the labour-intensive work that takes place in temporary, localized and marginal 'micro' sites of production and the capital-intensive, secure, formalized and 'public' work performed in global corporations; between conspicuous consumption (for instance of fashion items) and sweatshop labour; and between the corporate world and the State. For instance, Dore's and Gill's ethnographies of work, contained in Part 3, show two radically different forms of industrial work in contemporary Japan. On the one hand, the work of the 'family men' of Hitachi generates stable salaries, secure pensions and lifelong employment. On the other hand, we have the precarious work of the 'men of uncertainty', daily labourers who live in temporary accommodation and are constantly on the move like modern hunter-gatherers. Yet, as Marx pointed out, these two forms of labour are indissolubly linked. My sugges-tion is that anthropologists of the 'global factory' must look at the spatial and temp-oral interconnections between the visible, stable and 'respectable' labour at the core and the precarious, invisible and degrading labour at the margins.

In summary, whatever else it might be, industrialization is an ideological project rooted in the twentieth century 'modernist' – capitalist and socialist – imagination. In line with much contemporary neo-institutional economics, we need to problematize the idea of a global convergence towards a western type of corporate capitalism, and to be aware of the many 'varieties' of capitalism and industrial developments that challenge that model. The fact that industry is an ideological space as much as an eco-nomic one leads me in the next section, to consider the role of states in articulating such ideologies.

(C) THE END OF INDUSTRIAL DEMOCRACY?

My third proposition is that the end of a totalizing ideology of modernization also entails a crisis of the Western ideal of industrial democracy.

The contemporary relationships between the state and the economy challenge the assumption of a global convergence towards western-style democracy due to market pressure, self-regulation or structural adjustment. In particular, the idea that indus-trialization and the spread of the market economy in the South would lead to both more democratic and 'leaner' states proved wrong. First, the Western hegemonic form of the 'nation-state', if it ever existed, is undergoing a radical transformation. Since the 1980s the waves of restructuring, privatization and decentralization of the old 'Keynesian state' in the North has led to the devolution of state powers to lower level regions, local governments and 'global cities' operating as semi-autonomous and public-private subjects. Able to set their own economic and fiscal policies, these localities are increasingly part of the competitive advantages of global firms who locate where fiscal exemptions, cheap land and flexible labour are made available. As a consequence of the 'rescaling' of the state at the local level (Brenner 2004), global corporations are increasingly powerful local actors, impacting on the life of com-munities through voluntary and community activism, urban planning and develop-ment, philanthropy and tax transfers. Ramalho and Santana (2006) argue that, in the southern region of Rio de Janeiro, 'localism' has led to empowering experiments of participatory democracy between municipalities, workers and civil society. In con-trast, states must negotiate their power at various supranational levels, with regional constituencies, international financial, juridical and political institutions, trade blocks and continental partners.

Second, the emerging powers in the developing world have centralized, nationalized and regulated economies. Here factories are ruled more through state ideology than through the laws of the market. For instance, Rofel's (chapter18) ethnography of women workers in a state-run textile factory in contemporary China shows how the socialist state, in its various historical transformations, rewrites the workers' identities through ideologies of productivity and modernity cast along gender and generational lines. With the Shenzhen Labour Service Control (LSC) denying rural workers the status of permanent residents (*hukou*), the *damgomei* described by Ching Kwan Lee and Pun are kept in a state of transience and forced to accept low wages and precarious work. Thus, it can be argued that, under Hu Jintao's market socialism, China's modernity and progress are built on the despotic treatment of rural migrant labourers. Alliances between global corporations and anti-union paramilitary forces question the assumption of the separation between the state and the economy and of the democratizing forces of industrialization. For instance, in Colombia, Coca-Cola employed the right-wing United Self-Defence Forces (AUC) for anti-union repression (Gill 2007) and it is widely reported that various large companies with steel and mining interests, such as Tata and Essar, have colluded with the Chhattisgarh state government to sponsor a vigilante paramilitary organization (known as Salwa Judum) that has displaced many tens of thousands of 'tribal' villagers from their land in the name of counter-insurgency operations against the (Maoist) Naxalite movement (Parry 2008). The current economic crisis sparked waves of bank nationalizations, protectionism and nationalism in Britain and US too, bringing to the foreground the regulatory power and popular appeal of nation-states. As with the economic landscape, the political landscape of late capitalism is varied, complex and contradictory so that the regulatory power of states is increasingly indistinguishable from the regulatory power of private corporations. Industrial relations are repressed through private militias, migration laws are set according to the needs of the labour market and different corporate constituencies and local development are progressively entangled in the global trajectories of Corporate Social Responsibility (CSR). This blurring of the divide between the public and the private, state democracy and state violence, corporate responsibility and citizens' activism goes together with the fading of the partitions between 'cores' and 'peripheries' described above.

The ethnographies discussed challenge two pillars of the Western idea of industrial democracy: 1) that successful market economies are free from state intervention; and 2) that the spread of the market economy leads to greater democracy. Today, states and economies are indissolubly linked, but industrial development and industrial democracy often diverge. In the case of China, industrial power is achieved through state despotism, whilst in Brazil industrialization triggers new forms of participatory democracy.

(D) THE POLITICAL POSSIBILITIES OF CLASS

My fourth proposition is that the absence of fixed political and economic cores and peripheries highlighted above leads to new forms of class stratification and to new political 'possibilities'.

The earlier sections of this volume look at different social forms (gender, ethnic, religious or generational) through which class relations are reproduced. They suggest that class is much more diffused and varied a phenomenon than is argued by mainstream sociology. The chapters in the final section further question the universality of Western notions of class. In his fascinating history of the labour movement in Bombay, Chandavarkar (chapter 21) argues that the 'working class remains silent in Indian history' and shows how problematic it is to apply the Western idea of class in the Indian context. In spite of their political activism the Bombay millworkers were internally differentiated along lines of caste, ethnicity and kinship and did not conform to Marx's idea of a universal homogenous proletariat. But against the culturalist bias of many anthropologists, Chandavarkar argues that the strength of the 'primordial loyalties' of caste, kinship and religion, vis-à-vis class consciousness of the Indian labour force, is not a pre-industrial heritage, but mirrors contemporary capitalism. Robert Roberts' (chapter 22) classic ethnography of Engels's Salford slum reveals the deep fragmentation of the working-class community at the height of Britain's industrialization. Fragmented along occupational, gender and generational lines the working-class of Salford resembles more a 'caste system' than the modern proletariat imagined by Marx and Engels. The interaction between caste and class is also central in Miranda Engelshoven's (1999) 'Diamonds and Patels', which explores the absence of class conflict and union militancy in the diamond ateliers of Surat (western India). Whilst anthropologists normally stress how cultural factors prevent the formation of a working-class consciousness, the ethnography of June Nash (chapter 23) shows the powerful mixture of class and culture in the political consciousness of the Bolivian tin miners. Similarly, Kearney (1996) discusses the articulation of 'class' and 'identity' in the mobilization of the people of San Jeronimo, in Oaxaca, Mexico. The migrant workers of San Jeronimo have fluid identities being at the same time peasants in their town, informal labourers in Californian agro-businesses, urban migrants in the Mexican shanty town and proletarians in American cities. Based on their mixed – class and indigenous – identities the Oaxaca peasants develop effective anti-capitalist strategies by combining class-consciousness with indigenous human rights and ecological consciousness. Indeed Nash and Kearney's excellent ethnographies provide a critical counterpoint to Marx's theory of class consciousness. They ask the following question: 'How do industrial workers develop a common political consciousness, given their social fragmentation in the capitalist labour process?' Their answer is that 'class for itself' cannot emerge outside the framework of a wider political consciousness, whether religious, ethnic or racial, that both encompasses and outstrips class identity. The conclusion that seems to emerge from Nash and Kearney is that political movements purely based on class are doomed to fail.

In arguing that culture fosters revolutionary consciousness among wage-workers and that a narrow class focus increases social fragmentation, Kearney and Nash turn classical Marxism and its idea that class and not culture is the basis of workers' consciousness upside down. Pushing this point further, 'subaltern' and 'New True Socialism' (NTS)[5] scholars argue that those non-class-based and subaltern political formations in the South dislocated by post-Fordism are the agents of a new revolutionary politics. Subaltern studies reject the totalizing and Eurocentric narrative of progress, industrialization and class consciousness, and emphasise the ethnic solidarities, tribal consciousness and moral economy of the peasants in India and Latin America. In line with this view, contemporary industrial relations scholars emphasise how labour movements in the South have articulated anti-productivist radical politics, which move away from class based and factory-bound notions of labour and activism and articulate new democratic political identities across society. For instance, the *Kilusang Mayo Uno* (KMU) trade union in the Philippines[6] or the Brazilian Central Workers Union[7] (CUT) rapidly rose to power in the 1980s because they were supported by social forces outside the traditional labour movement including church organizations, women, squatters, intellectuals and human rights activists protesting against military rule. The revolutionary role attributed by some anthropologists to subaltern and new peasant movements in the South is paralleled by sociological analyses that show that workers in the North are trapped in bourgeois apathy, 'militant particularism' (Hayter and Harvey 1993), sectionalism (Beynon 1972) or shopfloor pragmatism (Durrenberger 2002).

But in the light of the spatial conflation between 'North' and 'South' and the cultural diversity of class stratification discussed above, the opposition between the 'bourgeoisified' working-class in the North and revolutionary peasant movements in the South, if it ever existed, is now obsolete. Furthermore, workers' mobilization always entails a combination of class and identity politics; discourses and practices of class do not exist in a social vacuum. For instance, Turner's ethnography of class activism shows how the emergence of political consciousness among engineering workers in Japan entailed a tension – both personal and within the trade-union – between hierarchical, universal and class-based ideas of activism and the communitarian ideals of 'love' (*aij*), 'mutual obligation' (*giri*) and 'human feeling' (*ninjo*). Similarly, Massey and Wainwright's (1985) in-depth discussion of the British miners' strike in 1984, a 'typically' male, white and socially conservative section of the working-class, demonstrates how traditional forms of labour activism (strikes, pickets and lockouts) by the mining community were combined with open campaigning styles of women, CND and ethnic urban movements. Mollona also suggests[8] that it is problematic to draw boundaries between community unionism and factory-based activism in the case of the labour movement in UK. Moreover, the 'forces of labour'

(Silver 2003), like the forces of capital, operate on a transnational scale and labour activism is increasingly shaped in the form of social unionism, community activism and North-South networks (Fantasia 1989; Fine 2005; Anner 2003).

In conclusion, contemporary ethnography reveals the transient and spatially dispersed nature of contemporary factories, states and workforces, and challenges the myth of convergence towards single models of work, industrialization and activism propagated through various forms of colonial and postcolonial projects. But the contemporary context of blurred boundaries between 'the economy' and 'society' does not entail the 're-embeddedness' of the former into the latter, but new (some would say, worse) forms of inequality and stratification. The central legacy of Marx's philosophy is the idea that labour is not mainly a material, individualistic and egoistic activity, as some economists still would argue, but a social and collective process of imagination, creativity and self-valorization. Ethnographies of labour show the 'other' side of work – pluralistic, imaginative and human-centred – that is hidden underneath the bureaucratic, normative and alienating experience of work that prevails in most contemporary societies. In so doing, ethnographies open up new possibilities of alternative, imaginative and equalitarian forms of livelihood

NOTES

1. Zolberg (1995).
2. Fisher Melissa and Greg Downey (2006).
3. For a critical assessment of the notion of Confucian Capitalism, see Greenhalgh (1994).
4. Rothstein Frances and Michael Blim (1992) and Smart Alan and Josephine Smart (2006).
5. According to Meiksins Wood (1986), amongst the 'NTS' theorists are Andre Gorz, Ernesto Laclau, Chantal Mouffe, and Nico Poulantzas.
6. Scipes 1992.
7. Ramalho and Santana, 2001.
8. Mollona, forthcoming.

REFERENCES

Ahrens, Thomas and Mollona, Massimiliano. 2007. 'Organisational Control as Cultural Practice – A Shop Floor Ethnography of a Sheffield Steel Mill', *Accounting, Organisation and Society*, 32: 305–31.

Anner, Mark. 2003. 'Industrial Structure, the State, and Ideology: Shaping Labor Transnationalism in the Brazilian Auto Industry', *Social Science History*, 27(4): 603–34.

Arrighi, Giovanni. 2005. 'Hegemony Unravelling', *New Left Review*, 33: 83–116.

Beaud, Stéphane and Pialoux, Michel. 2001. 'Between "Mate" and "Scab": The Contradictory Inheritance of French Workers in the Postfordist Factory', *Ethnography*, 2(3): 323–55.

Bell, Daniel. 1973. *The Coming of Post-Industrial Society: A Venture in Social Forecasting*, New York: Basic Books.

Beynon, Huw and Blackburn, Robin. 1972. *Perceptions of Work. Variations within a factory*, Cambridge: Cambridge University Press.

Blackburn, Robin. 2006. 'Finance and the Fourth Dimension', *New Left Review*, 39.

Breman, Jan. 2004. *The Making and Unmaking of an Industrial Working Class: Sliding Down the Labour Hierarchy in Ahmedabad, India*, Amsterdam: Amsterdam University Press.

Brenner, Neil. 2004. *New State Spaces. Urban Governance and the Rescaling of Statehood*, Oxford: Oxford University Press.

Cooper, Frederick. 1992. 'Colonizing Time: Work Rhythms and Labour Conflict in Colonial Mombasa', in N. Dirks (ed), *Colonialism and Culture*, Ann Arbor, MI: University of Michigan Press.

Delbridge, Rick. 1998. *Life on the Line in Contemporary Manufacturing*, Oxford: Oxford University Press.

Dore, Ronald. 2000. *Stock-Market Capitalism: Welfare Capitalism*, Oxford: Oxford University Press.

Dunn, Elizabeth. 2004. *Privatizing Poland, Baby Food, Big Business and the Remaking of Labor*, Ithaca, NY: Cornell University Press.

Durrenberger, Paul. 2002. 'Structure, Thought and Action: Stewards in Chicago Union Locals', *American Anthropologist*, 104(1): 93–105.

Elyachar, Julia. 2005. *Markets of Dispossessions: NGOs, Economic Development and the State in Cairo*, London and Durham, NC: Duke University Press.

Engelshoven, Miranda. 1999. 'Diamonds and Patels: A Report on the Diamond Industry of Surat', *Contributions to Indian Sociology* (new series), 33(1): 353–77.

Ezzamel Mahmoud and Willmott, Hugh. 1998. 'Accounting for Teamwork: A Critical Study of Group-Based Systems of Organizational Control', *Administrative Science Quarterly*, 43(2): 358–96.

Ezzamel Mahmoud, Willmott, Hugh and Worthington, Frank. 2008. 'Manufacturing Shareholders Value: The Role of Accounting in Organizational Transformation', *Accounting Organization and Society*, 33: 107–40.

Fantasia, Rick. 1989. *Cultures of Solidarity: Consciousness, Action, and Contemporary American Workers*, Berkeley: University of California Press.

Fine, Janice. 2005. 'Community Unions and the Revival of the American Labor Movement', *Politics & Society*, 33: 153–99.

Fisher, Melissa and Downey, Greg (eds). 2006. *Frontiers of Capital*, Durham, NC and London: Duke University Press.

Gill, Leslie. 2007. 'Right There with You': Coca-Cola, Labor Restructuring, and Political Violence in Colombia', *Critique of Anthropology*, 27(3): 235–60.

Goldstein, Andrea and Ross-Schneider, Ben. 2004. 'Big Business in Brazil: States and the Markets in the Corporate Reorganization of the 1990s', in Edmund Annan and Ha-Joo Chang (eds), *Brazil and South Korea. Economic Crisis and Restructuring*, London: Institute of Latin American Studies.

Goldthorpe, John, Lockwood, David, Bechhofer, Frank and Platt, Jennifer. 1968. *The Affluent Worker: Industrial Attitudes and Behaviour*, Cambridge: Cambridge University Press.

Greenhalgh, Susan. 1994. 'De-orientalizing the Chinese Family Firm', *American Ethnologist*, 21(4): 746–75.

Guimarães, Antonio Sergio, Agier, Michel and Araujo, Nadia. 1995. *Imagens e Identidades do Trabalho*, São Paulo: HUCITEC.

Guyer, Jane. 2007. 'Prophecy and the Near Future: Thoughts on Macroeconomic, Evangelical and Punctuated Time', *American Ethnologist*, 34(3): 409–21.

Hall, Peter and Soskice, David. 2001. *Varieties of Capitalism: The Institutional Foundations of Comparative Advantage*, Oxford: Oxford University Press.

Harriss, John and Harriss, Barbara. 1989. 'Agrarian Transformation in the Third World', in D. Gregory and R. Walford (eds), *Horizons in Human Geography*, Basingstoke: Macmillan.

Harvey, David. 2003. *The New Imperialism*, Oxford and New York: Oxford University Press.

Hayter, Teresa and Harvey, David. 1993. *The Factory and the City: The Story of the Cowley Automobile Workers in Oxford*, London: Mansell.

Hiller, Ernest. 1928. *The Strike: A Study in Collective Action*, Chicago: Chicago University Press.

Huws, Ursula. 2003. *The Making of a Cybertariat*, New York: Monthly Review Press.

Kearney, Michael. 1996. *Re-conceptualising Peasantry: Anthropology in Global Perspective*, Boulder, CO and Oxford: Westview Press.

Kondo, Dorinne. 1990. *Crafting Selves. Power, Gender, and Discourses of Identity in a Japanese Workplace*, Chicago: The University of Chicago Press.

Knight, David and Wilmott, Hugh. 1989. 'Power and Subjectivity at Work: From Degradation to Subjugation in Social Relations', *Sociology*, 23(4): 1–24.

Kotkin, Stephen. 1997. *Magnetic Mountain: Stalinism as a Civilization*, Berkeley, CA: University of California Press.

Li Puma, Edward and Lee, Benjamin. 2002. 'Cultures of Circulation: The Imagination of Modernity', *Public Culture*, 14(1): 191–213.

Lockwood, David. 1966. 'Sources of Variation in Working-class Images of Society', *Sociological Review*, 14(3): 249–67.

Lupton, Tom. 1963. *On the Shop-floor*, Oxford: Pergamon.

Massey, Doreen and Wainwright, Hillary. 1985. 'Beyond the Coalfield: The Work of the Miners' Support Group', in Huw Beynon (ed.), *Digging Deeper: Issues in the Miners Strikes*, London: Verso.

Maurer, Bill. 2008. 'Re-socialising Finance? Or Dressing it in Mufti? Calculating Alternatives for Cultural Economies', *Journal of Cultural Economy*, 1(1): 65–78.

Meiksins-Wood, E. 1986. *The Retreat from Class. A New 'True' Socialism*, London: Verso.

Miyazaki, Hirokazu. 2006. 'Economies of Dreams: Hope in Global Capitalism and its Critiques', *Cultural Anthropology*, 21(2): 147–72.

Mollona, Massimiliano. 2009. *Made in Sheffield. An Ethnography of Industrial Work and Politics*, Oxford: Berghahn.

Mollona, Massimiliano. Forthcoming. 'Community Unionism vs. Business Unionism. The Return of the Moral Economy in Trade Union Studies', *American Ethnologist*.

Narotsky, Susana. 2007. 'The Project in the Model: Reciprocity, Social Capital and the Politics of Ethnographic Realism', *Current Anthropology*, 48(3).

Parry, Jonathan. 2008. *The Anthropologist's Assistant. A Story*. Unpublished Paper.

Pinney, Christopher. 1999. 'On living in the kal(i)yug: Notes from Nagda, Madhya Pradesh', *Contributions to Indian Sociology* (new series), 33(1): 77–106.

Pun, Ngai. 2005. *Made in China Women Factory Workers in a Global Workplace*, Durham, NC and London: Duke University Press.

Ramalho, Jose Ricardo and Santana, Marco Aurelio. 2001. 'Tradição Sindical e as mudanças econômicas dos anos de 1990', in J.R Ramalho and M.A. Santana (eds), *Trabalho e Tradição Sindical no Rio de Janeiro. A Trajectória dos*, Porto Alegre: Traça.

Ramalho, Jose Ricardo and Santana, Marco Aurelio. 2006. *Trabalho e Desenvolvimento Regional*, Rio de Janeiro: MAUAD Editora.

Robotham, Dom. 2005. 'Political Economy', in James Carrier (ed.), *A Handbook of Economic Anthropology*, Cheltenham: Edward Elgar.

Roethlisberger, Fritz and Dickson, William. 1939. *Management and the Worker*, New York: Wiley.

Roitman, Janet. 2005. *Fiscal Disobedience. An Anthropology of Economic Regulation in Central Africa*, Princeton, NJ: Princeton University Press.

Roseberry, William. 2002. 'Understanding Capitalism – Historically, Structurally, Spatially', in David Nugent (ed.), *Locating Capitalism in Time and Space*, Stanford: Stanford University Press.

Rothstein, Frances. 2006. 'Flexibility for Whom? Small-scale garment Manufacturing in Rural Mexico', in Alan Smart and Josephine Smart (eds), *Petty Capitalism and Globalization*, New York: State University of New York Press.

Rothstein, Frances and Blim, Michael (eds). 1992. *Anthropology and the Global Factory*, New York: Bergin and Garvey.

Roy, Donald. 1952. 'Quota Restriction and Goldbricking in a Machine-shop', *American Journal of Sociology*, 57(3): 427–42.

Scipes, Kim. 1992. 'Understanding the New Labour Movement in the Third World. The Emergence of Social Movement Unionism', *Critical Sociology*, 19(2): 81–102.

Silver, Beverly. 2003. *Forces of Labour*, Cambridge: Cambridge University Press.

Smart, Alan and Smart, Josephine (eds). 2006. *Petty Capitalism and Globalization*, New York: State University of New York Press.

Smith, Gavin. 2006. 'When the Logic of Capital is the Real Which Lurks in the Background: Programme and Practice in European "Regional Economies"', *Current Anthropology*, 47(4): 621–39.

Westwood, Sally. 1984. *All Day, Everyday: Factory and Family in the Making of Women's Lives*, London: Pluto Press.

Zaloom, Caitlin. 2003. 'Ambiguous Numbers: Trading Technologies and Interpretations in Financial Markets', *American Ethnologist*, 30: 258–72.

Zolberg, Aristide. 1995. 'Response: Working-class Dissolution', *International Labour and Working-class History*, 47: 28–38.

Part 1:
Industrial Time and Work Discipline

SECTIONAL INTRODUCTION

It is a truism that England's early Industrial Revolution broke with household-based cottage industry by centralizing production in factories. A new kind of differentiation between workplace and home, and between 'work' and 'leisure', was created. A sharp temporal division overlaid the spatial one. The argument of E.P. Thompson's much-cited essay, around which the other readings in this section are grouped, goes further. Factory production led to the diffusion and institutionalization of a new attitude to time and demanded a new form of work discipline. In the (for Thompson 'more humanly comprehensible') pre-industrial world, work is task-orientated, and governed by the rhythms of nature and the religious calendar. It is the tide that determines when the fisherman puts to sea; the weather and season that determine when the harvest is gathered. The working day expands or contracts according to the task in hand, and life is not rigidly compartmentalized into work and leisure, or ruled by the clock. Bouts of intense labour alternate with long periods of idleness. True, the Puritans had delivered endless homilies on time, which must be spent wisely for the sake of one's soul. True also that wage labour makes a significant difference to the way in which time is regarded. When wages are paid, time is money and employers have an interest in ensuring that workers don't waste it. But the revolutionary change is brought about by large-scale machine production. The working day becomes increasingly regular and repetitive, and is increasingly governed by the clock. So pervasive would the new work discipline become that its ethic is sometimes applied to leisure pursuits (Moorhouse 1987).

Though he emphasises the historical specificity of each case, for Thompson industrialization everywhere requires workers to accommodate themselves to the discipline of the clock, and the implication is that this will almost inevitably cause friction. Factory production demands a new kind of time discipline because, Thompson stresses, it requires the elaborate synchronization of tasks: a requirement that becomes increasingly insistent with increases in scale and in the division of labour. Technology seems to be key, consistent with which he notes that 'factory time' was stubbornly slow to take root in the English potteries, which lacked 'the aid machinery to regulate the pace of work on the pot-bank'. What is at issue in his essay, however, 'are not only changes in manufacturing techniques which demand greater synchronization of labour and a greater exactitude in time regimes in *any* society; but also these changes as they were lived through in the society of nascent capitalism'. The context of '*industrial capitalism*' is underlined by his title; and, though not made explicit, the taken-for-granted background is presumably the compulsion to return a profit and to keep the plant in constant operation in order to yield a dividend on the enormous capital invested in it. In what measure technology is determinant and in what measure the capitalist market, is not however explored. Are the bitter conflicts over time reported from some industrial settings in planned economies, for example Haraszti's (1977) account of a socialist-era Hungarian factory, principally the consequence of tendencies endemic to *industry*, or of the intrusion (in that instance palpable) of *market* incentives and principles?

Subsequent writers have pointed out that the imposition of clock time was less than Thompson might lead us to suppose (e.g. Whipp 1987; *see also* Parry, this volume). In fairness, however, it should be acknowledged that he was clearly aware of variation between industries, drawing explicit attention to its early introduction in textile mills and engineering workshops, and to the irregular rhythms of work that long persisted in the docks and potteries (one of Whipp's main examples). He also considered the possibility, on which Pun Ngai (2005) recently elaborated, that the sexes might be differentially attuned to clock time. A related criticism is that Thompson supposedly accepts too easily the omnipotence of capital and the extent to which it is able to control labour and inculcate a new attitude towards time (especially in craft workers used to self-regulation). Roberts's (1992) discussion of drink and industrial discipline in nineteenth century Germany shows how the bosses' ability to impose their will was in fact rather limited; while Gutman (1988) argues that in the United States the transition to an industrial work culture was more prolonged and problematic than Thompson implied.

Though one reading of Thompson would identify machine technology as that which necessitates a new work discipline, it may be the other way round: technological and organizational innovation is sometimes the result, not the cause, of a desire to discipline labour. The Ford assembly line is an instance (Beynon 1984: chapter 1; Miller 1992). That was a business decision, but the impetus behind the introduction of a new work regime on the Mombasa docks in colonial Kenya was, Cooper (1992) shows, political and ideological. No interest was ever taken in whether it was economically more efficient. In the early days, dock labour was flexible but relatively well paid casual labour that could be hired and fired as demand fluctuated and was largely recruited from the rural hinterland. It still had one foot in the agricultural economy and was relatively independent. In time, this system came to be identified with labour indiscipline and political subversion. Above all it challenged the colonialist's conception of what a modern industrial labour force should be like and their idea that 'work should be steady and regular and carefully controlled'. The solution was to de-casualize dock labour and ensure that it became fully committed to the *urban* economy. Dockers would only be properly disciplined when they feared loosing livelihoods that exclusively depended on well paid, relatively secure employment and the housing that went with it. De-casualization was above all about producing a predictable and pliant labour force; its consequence was the creation of an enclave of secure, highly paid and industrially disciplined workers cut off from the rest of the workforce. The result was the dualism found in many Third World settings between an aristocracy of labour and the labouring poor.

The two chapters that follow Thompson's address the stark contrast it draws between pre-industrial and industrial work regimes. In the (pre-1868) Tokugawa period, Smith tells us, Japanese 'peasants' already had an acute and morally loaded sense of time as something fleeting and precious, of which good productive use should be made. Peasant agriculture (like Thompson's factory) required an elaborate synchronization of tasks and farming manuals enjoined the painstaking planning of agricultural operations. Crops had to be carefully matched to the soils of particular fields, and this demanded meticulous scheduling to ensure that crucial labour intensive operations did not overlap. Diary evidence suggests a work regime of great regularity, rather than Thompson's 'alternating bouts of intense work and leisure'. These pre-existing notions about the value of time, Smith argues, and the routinized work discipline to which peasants were already inured, allowed neophyte Japanese factory workers to adapt without much friction to the factory regime. Time discipline never became the bone of contention that it did elsewhere.

The chapter by Parry relates to a more contemporary world: an industrial urban complex in central India that has grown up on a green field site around a gargantuan public sector steel plant. As his informants see it, the fields were never so happy, nor the mills so dark and satanic, as Thompson's picture suggests. Agricultural labour is now so deeply disliked that even *unemployed* youngsters, for whom it is emblematic of the benighted world of their illiterate "thumb-impression" fathers, determinedly avoid it. Even their elders agree that factory work is preferable to the back-breaking toil of ploughing the fields, and transplanting the paddy in the monsoon rain. In terms of time discipline, a job in the steel plant is hardly exacting. Time keeping is flexible, tasks are intermittent and there is plenty of opportunity to socialise. Though some jobs are extremely demanding, the proportion of the day spent on them is not, rarely more than two or three hours in a shift, often much less, and then one's time is effectively one's own. Manning levels are sufficiently generous, and the disciplinary powers of management sufficiently constrained, that workers have wide latitude to organise their own informal duty rosters and some are persistently absent. The tyranny of the clock is not so oppressive, and 'industrial time' is not experienced as qualitatively different from 'peasant time'. That's the Indian public sector, many would say; but Parry's comparison with private sector factories suggests that the difference is not always so marked as is popularly supposed. Much industrial production inevitably proceeds in a stuccato fashion and continuous work-flows are difficult to sustain. Different types of industrial process are associated with different intensities of labour and impose work disciplines of different degrees of rigour. Thompson's stark contrast between work in the fields and the factory tends to homogenize both in a misleading manner.

Discussing the way in which industry is represented by villagers who live on the edge of another company town in central India, Pinney (1999) points to the paradoxical fact that it is 'those who do not clock-on in the factory that are most concerned with its dreadful consequences'. These are mainly high caste landowners whose antipathy to industrial development is not unconnected to their present difficulties in obtaining agricultural labour, the higher rates they must pay for it, and the shorter hours (now governed by the distant sound of the factory siren) for which it works. Those who experience the factory personally, who were at the bottom of the old village hierarchy, have a rosier view. The wages are better, the work is easier, and the job has liberated them from the subservience and repression of the old rural order – a judgement that is not significantly qualified by the demands of the factory clock.

In a now classic monograph, Ong (1987) offered an analysis more in tune with Thompson's contrast. Her study was of young female factory workers of rural origin employed by multinational factories in Malaysia's Free-Trade Zones; and her focus was on the periodic epidemics of spirit possession on the shop floor that disrupted production. In the traditional village, Ong reports, the labour of young women in the fields went largely unsupervised by men, was task-orientated and paced by the Muslim calendar, and lightened by the camaraderie of the female work group. The spirit possessions of the factory she interprets as a kind of 'ritual of rebellion', 'a weapon of the weak' which these young women deploy against the time regime and disciplines of industry administered *male* supervisors, mainly ethnically alien Indians and Chinese. Put differently, pre-capitalist beliefs and values provided workers with the tools for a critique of the dehumanizing aspects of modern manufacture. Nash (chapter 22) and Taussig (1977) had earlier drawn attention to this ideological potential, the latter decoding two key pieces of Columbian plantation worker folklore as a critical commentary on capitalist relations of production and on the mystery of capital accumulation, an analysis from which Ong was concerned to differentiate her own. For her, the problems of which these spirit afflictions are symptomatic are not capitalism and class, but rather the inhumanity of factory work and the inequalities of gender. This picture is, however, qualified by other South-east Asian ethnography that convincingly argues that young female factory workers do not experience a sharp disjunction between work in the fields and the factory, that they see an industrial job as the best option open to them and that such jobs provide them with a new sense of self-worth (Wolf 1992).

Originally published one year after her monograph, Ong's chapter in this volume shifts the analytical emphasis. Though it does not explicitly evoke the world of peasant agriculture, nor single out the oppression of factory *time*, spirit afflictions continue to be understood as an unconscious protest against industrial discipline (of which time discipline is one important component). Now, however, possession episodes seem less subversive. On the evidence provided, it might equally be argued that rather than a rejection of male control and the factory regime, they might possibly be a somatization of workers' guilt at escaping proper male authority at home (Parry 2005). What is clear is that by becoming possessed women 'prove' their own inferiority (since demons are only attracted to the spiritually weak and physically polluted), and that possession allows management to re-present the real problem (objective conditions in the factory) as the psychological problems of individual workers. Ideas about spirit possession, Ong concludes, become part of a 'hegemonic' discourse (in Gramsci's sense) that secures the acquiescence of society at large to the ideas of the dominant class. This reading thus provides a bridge to Part 2 where one central theme is how consent to the factory is manufactured.

RECOMMENDED FURTHER READING

Cooper, F. 1992. 'Colonizing time: Work Rhythms and Labour Conflict in Colonial Mombasa', in N. Dirks (ed.), *Colonialism and Culture*, pp. 209–45, Ann Arbor, MI: University of Michigan Press.

Gutman, H.G. 1988. 'Work, Culture and Society in Industrializing America, 1815–1919', in R. Pahl (ed.), *On Work: Historical, Comparative and Theoretical Approaches*, pp. 125–37, Oxford: Basil Blackwell Ltd.

Moorhouse, H.F. 1987. ' "The work ethic" and "leisure" activity: The hot rod in post-war America', in P. Joyce (ed.), *The Historical Meanings of Work*, Cambridge: Cambridge University Press.

Ong, A. 1987. *Spirits of resistance and capitalist discipline: Factory women in Malaysia*, Albany, NY: State University of New York Press.

Pinney, C. 1999. 'On living in the kal(i)yug: Notes from Nagda, Madhya Pradesh', *Contributions to Indian Sociology* (new series), 33(1): 77–106.

Roberts, J.S. 1992. 'Drink and industrial discipline in nineteenth-century Germany', in L. R. Berlanstein (ed.), *The industrial revolution and work in nineteenth-century Europe*, pp. 102–24, London: Routledge.

Whipp, R. 1987. 'A time to every purpose': An essay on time and work', in P. Joyce (ed.), *The historical Meanings of Work*, pp. 210–36, Cambridge: Cambridge University Press.

OTHER WORKS CITED

Beynon, Huw. 1984. *Working for Ford* (2nd edition). Harmondsworth: Penguin Books.

Haraszti, M. 1977. *A Worker in a Worker's State: Piece-rates in Hungary* (trans M. Wright). London: Pelican.

Miller, G.T. 1992. *Managerial Dilemmas: The political Economy of Hierarchy*, Cambridge: Cambridge University Press.

Parry, J.P. 2005. 'Industrial Work', in J. Carrier (ed.), *A Handbook of Economic Anthropology*, pp. 141–59, Cheltenham: Edward Elgar.

Pun, Ngai. 2005. *Made in China: Women factory workers in a global workplace*, Durham, NC: Duke University Press.

Taussig, M. 1977. 'The Genesis of Capitalism among a South American Peasantry: Devil's Labour and the Baptism of Money', *Comparative Studies in Society and History*, 19: 130–55.

Wolf, Diane. 1992. *Factory Daughters: Gender, household dynamics and rural industrialization in Java*, Berkeley, CA: University of California Press.

CHAPTER ONE

Time, Work-Discipline, and Industrial Capitalism

E.P. Thompson

Tess . . . started on her way up the dark and crooked lane or street not made for hasty progress; a street laid out before inches of land had value, and when one-handed clocks sufficiently subdivided the day.   *Thomas Hardy.*

I

It is commonplace that the years between 1300 and 1650 saw within the intellectual culture of Western Europe important changes in the apprehension of time.[1] In the *Canterbury Tales* the cock still figures in his immemorial rôle as nature's timepiece: Chauntecleer –

> Caste up his eyen to the brighte sonne,
> That in the signe of Taurus hadde yronne
> Twenty degrees and oon, and somwhat moore,
> He knew by kynde, and by noon oother loore
> That it was pryme, and crew with blisful stevene . . . .

But although "By nature knew he ech ascensioun/Of the equynoxial in thilke toun", the contrast between "nature's" time and clock time is pointed in the image –

> Wei sikerer was his crowyng in his logge
> Than is a clokke, or an abbey orlogge.

This is a very early clock: Chaucer (unlike Chauntecleer) was a Londoner, and was aware of the times of Court, of urban organization, and of that "merchant's time" which Jacques Le Goff, in a suggestive article in *Annales*, has opposed to the time of the medieval church.[2]

I do not wish to argue how far the change was due to the spread of clocks from the fourteenth century onwards, how far this was itself a symptom of a new Puritan discipline and bourgeois exactitude. However we see it, the change is certainly there. The clock steps on to the Elizabethan stage, turning Faustus's last soliloquy into a dialogue with time: "the stars move still, time runs, the clock will strike". Sidereal time, which has been present since literature began, has now moved at one step from the heavens into the home. Mortality and love are both felt to be more poignant as the "Snayly motion of the mooving hand"[3] crosses the dial. When the watch is worn about the neck it lies in proximity to the less regular beating of the heart. The conventional Elizabethan images of time as a devourer, a defacer, a bloody tyrant, a scytheman, are old enough, but there is a new immediacy and insistence.[4]

As the seventeenth century moves on the image of clock-work extends, until, with Newton, it has engrossed the universe. And by the middle of the eighteenth century (if we are to trust Sterne) the clock had penetrated to more intimate levels. For Tristram Shandy's father – "one of the most regular men in everything he did . . . that ever lived" – "had made it a rule for many years of his life, – on the first Sunday night of every month . . . to wind up a large house-clock, which we had standing on the back-stairs head". "He had likewise gradually brought some other little family concernments to the same period", and this enabled Tristram to date his conception very exactly. It also provoked *The Clockmaker's Outcry against the Author*:

> The directions I had for making several clocks for the country are countermanded; because no modest lady now dares to mention a word about winding-up a clock, without exposing herself to the sly leers and jokes of the family . . . Nay, the common expression of street-walkers is, "Sir, will you have your clock wound up?"

Virtuous matrons (the "clockmaker" complained) are consigning their clocks to lumber rooms as "exciting to acts of carnality".[5]

However, this gross impressionism is unlikely to advance the present enquiry: how far, and in what ways, did this shift in time-sense affect labour discipline, and how far did it influence the inward apprehension of time of working people? If the transition to mature industrial society entailed a severe restructuring of working habits – new disciplines, new incentives, and a new human nature upon which these incentives could bite effectively – how far is this related to changes in the inward notation of time?

II

It is well known that among primitive peoples the measurement of time is commonly related to familiar processes in the cycle of work or of domestic chores. Evans-Pritchard has analysed the time-sense of the Nuer:

> The daily timepiece is the cattle clock, the round of pastoral tasks, and the time of day and the passage of time through a day are to a Nuer primarily the succession of these tasks and their relation to one another.

Among the Nandi an occupational definition of time evolved covering not only each hour, but half hours of the day – at 5-30 in the morning the oxen have gone to the grazing-ground, at 6 the sheep have been unfastened, at 6-30 the sun has grown, at 7 it has become warm, at 7-30 the goats have gone to the grazing-ground, etc. – an uncommonly well-regulated economy. In a similar way terms evolve for the measurement of time intervals. In Madagascar time might be measured by "a rice-cooking" (about half an hour) or "the frying of a locust" (a moment). The Cross River natives were reported as saying "the man died in less than the time in which maize is not yet completely roasted" (less than fifteen minutes).[6]

It is not difficult to find examples of this nearer to us in cultural time. Thus in seventeenth-century Chile time was often measured in "credos": an earthquake was described in 1647 as lasting for the period of two credos; while the cooking-time of an egg could be judged by an Ave Maria said aloud. In Burma in recent times monks rose at daybreak "when there is light enough to see the veins in the hand".[7] The Oxford English Dictionary gives us English examples – "pater noster wyle", "miserere whyle" (1450), and (in the New English Dictionary but not the Oxford English Dictionary) "pissing while" – a somewhat arbitrary measurement.

Pierre Bourdieu has explored more closely the attitudes towards time of the Kabyle peasant (in Algeria) in recent years: "An attitude of submission and of nonchalant indifference to the passage of time which no one dreams of mastering, using up, or saving . . . Haste is seen as a lack of decorum combined with diabolical ambition". The clock is sometimes known as "the devil's mill"; there are no precise meal-times; "the notion of an exact appointment is unknown; they agree only to meet 'at the next market'". A popular song runs:

> It is useless to pursue the world, No one will ever overtake it.[8]

Synge, in his well-observed account of the Aran Islands, gives us a classic example:

> While I am walking with Michael someone often comes to me to ask the time of day. Few of the people, however, are sufficiently used to modern time to understand in more than a vague way the convention of the hours and when I tell them what o'clock it is by my watch they are not satisfied, and ask how long is left them before the twilight.[9]

> The general knowledge of time on the island depends, curiously enough, upon the direction of the wind. Nearly all the cottages are built . . . with two doors opposite each other, the more sheltered of which lies open all day to give light to the interior. If the wind is northerly the south door is opened, and the shadow of the door-post moving across the kitchen floor indicates the hour; as soon, however, as the wind changes to

the south the other door is opened, and the people, who never think of putting up a primitive dial, are at a loss . . . .

When the wind is from the north the old woman manages my meals with fair regularity; but on the other days she often makes my tea at three o'clock instead of six . . . .[10]

Such a disregard for clock time could of course only be possible in a crofting and fishing community whose framework of marketing and administration is minimal, and in which the day's tasks (which might vary from fishing to farming, building, mending of nets, thatching, making a cradle or a coffin) seem to disclose themselves, by the logic of need, before the crofter's eyes.[11] But his account will serve to emphasize the essential conditioning in differing notations of time provided by different work-situations and their relation to "natural" rhythms. Clearly hunters must employ certain hours of the night to set their snares. Fishing and seafaring people must integrate their lives with the tides. A petition from Sunderland in 1800 includes the words "considering that this is a seaport in which many people are obliged to be up at all hours of the night to attend the tides and their affairs upon the river".[12] The operative phrase is "attend the tides": the patterning of social time in the seaport follows *upon* the rhythms of the sea; and this appears to be natural and comprehensible to fishermen or seamen: the compulsion is nature's own.

In a similar way labour from dawn to dusk can appear to be "natural" in a farming community, especially in the harvest months: nature demands that the grain be harvested before the thunderstorms set in. And we may note similar "natural" work-rhythms which attend other rural or industrial occupations: sheep must be attended at lambing time and guarded from predators; cows must be milked; the charcoal fire must be attended and not burn away through the turfs (and the charcoal burners must sleep beside it); once iron is in the making, the furnaces must not be allowed to fail.

The notation of time which arises in such contexts has been described as task-orientation. It is perhaps the most effective orientation in peasant societies, and it remains important in village and domestic industries. It has by no means lost all relevance in rural parts of Britain today. Three points may be proposed about task-orientation. First, there is a sense in which it is more humanly comprehensible than timed labour. The peasant or labourer appears to attend upon what is an observed necessity. Second, a community in which task-orientation is common appears to show least demarcation between "work" and "life". Social intercourse and labour are intermingled – the working-day lengthens or contracts according to the task – and there is no great sense of conflict between labour and "passing the time of day". Third, to men accustomed to labour timed by the clock, this attitude to labour appears to be wasteful and lacking in urgency.[13]

Such a clear distinction supposes, of course, the independent peasant or craftsman as referent. But the question of task-orientation becomes greatly more complex at the point where labour is employed. The entire family economy of the small farmer

may be task-orientated; but within it there may be a division of labour, and allocation of rôles, and the discipline of an employer-employed relationship between the
farmer and his children. Even here time is beginning to become money, the employer's
money. As soon as actual hands are employed the shift from task-orientation to timed
labour is marked. It is true that the timing of work can be done independently of any
time-piece – and indeed precedes the diffusion of the clock. Still, in the mid-seventeenth
century substantial farmers calculated their expectations of employed labour (as
did Henry Best) in "dayworkes" – "the Cunnigarth, with its bottomes, is 4 large
dayworkes for a good mower", "the Spellowe is 4 indifferent dayworkes", etc.;[14]
and what Best did for his own farm, Markham attempted to present in general form:

> A man . . . may mow of Corn, as Barley and Oats, if it be thick, loggy and beaten down
> to the earth, making fair work, and not cutting off the heads of the ears, and leaving the
> straw still growing one acre and a half in a day: but if it be good thick and fair standing
> corn, then he may mow two acres, or two acres and a half in a day; but if the corn be
> short and thin, then he may mow three, and sometimes four Acres in a day, and not be
> overlaboured . . . . [15]

The computation is difficult, and dependent upon many variables. Clearly, a straight-
forward time-measurement was more convenient.[16]

This measurement embodies a simple relationship. Those who are employed experience a distinction between their employer's time and their "own" time. And the
employer must *use* the time of his labour, and see it is not wasted: not the task but
the value of time when reduced to money is dominant. Time is now currency: it is
not passed but spent.

We may observe something of this contrast, in attitudes towards both time and
work, in two passages from Stephen Duck's poem, "The Thresher's Labour". The
first describes a work-situation which we have come to regard as the norm in the
nineteenth and twentieth centuries:

> From the strong Planks our Crab-Tree Staves rebound,
> And echoing Barns return the rattling Sound.
> Now in the Air our knotty Weapons Fly;
> And now with equal Force descend from high:
> Down one, one up, so well they keep the Time,
> The *Cyclops* Hammers could not truer chime . . . .
> In briny Streams our Sweat descends space,
> Drops from our Locks, or trickles down our Face.
> No intermission in our Works we know;
> The noisy Threshall must for ever go.
> Their Master absent, others safely play;
> The sleeping Threshall doth itself betray.
> Nor yet the tedious Labour to beguile,
> And make the passing Minutes sweetly smile,

> Can we, like Shepherds, tell a merry Tale?
> The Voice is lost, drown'd by the noisy Flail. . . .
>
> Week after Week we this dull Task pursue,
> Unless when winnowing Days produce a new;
> A new indeed, but frequently a worse,
> The Threshall yields but to the Master's Curse:
> He counts the Bushels, counts how much a Day,
> Then swears we've idled half our Time away.
> Why look ye, Rogues! D'ye think that this will do?
> Your Neighbours thresh as much again as you.

This would appear to describe the monotony, alienation from pleasure in labour, and antagonism of interests commonly ascribed to the factory system. The second passage describes the harvesting:

> At length in Rows stands up the well-dry'd Corn,
> A grateful Scene, and ready for the Barn.
> Our well-pleas'd Master views the Sight with joy,
> And we for carrying all our Force employ.
> Confusion soon o'er all the Field appears,
> And stunning Clamours fill the Workmens Ears;
> The Bells, and clashing Whips, alternate sound,
> And rattling Waggons thunder o'er the Ground.
> The Wheat got in, the Pease, and other Grain,
> Share the same Fate, and soon leave bare the Plain:
> In noisy Triumph the last Load moves on,
> And loud Huzza's proclaim the Harvest done.

This is, of course, an obligatory set-piece in eighteenth-century farming poetry. And it is also true that the good morale of the labourers was sustained by their high harvest earnings. But it would be an error to see the harvest situation in terms of direct responses to economic stimuli. It is also a moment at which the older collective rhythms break through the new, and a weight of folk-lore and of rural custom could be called as supporting evidence as to the psychic satisfaction and ritual functions – for example, the momentary obliteration of social distinctions – of the harvest-home. "How few now know", M. K. Ashby writes, "what it was ninety years ago to get in a harvest! Though the disinherited had no great part of the fruits, still they shared in the achievement, the deep involvement and joy of it".[17]

III

It is by no means clear how far the availability of precise clock time extended at the time of the industrial revolution. From the fourteenth century onwards church clocks and public clocks were erected in the cities and large market towns. The majority of English parishes must have possessed church clocks by the end of the sixteenth century.[18] But the accuracy of these clocks is a matter of dispute; and the sundial remained in use (partly to set the clock) in the seventeenth, eighteenth and nineteenth centuries.[19]

Charitable donations continued to be made in the seventeenth century (sometimes laid out in "clockland", "ding dong land", or "curfew bell land") for the ringing of early morning bells and curfew bells.[20] Thus Richard Palmer of Wokingham (Berks) gave, in 1664, lands in trust to pay the sexton to ring the great bell for half an hour every evening at eight o'clock and every morning at four o'clock, or as near to those hours as might be, from the 10th September to the 11th March in each year

> not only that as many as might live within the sound might be thereby induced to a timely going to rest in the evening, and early arising in the morning to the labours and duties of their several callings, (things ordinarily attended and rewarded with thrift and proficiency) . . . .

but also so that strangers and others within sound of the bell on winter nights "might be informed of the time of night, and receive some guidance into their right way". These "rational ends", he conceived, "could not but be well liked by any discreet person, the same being done and well approved of in most of the cities and market-towns, and many other places in the kingdom . . .". The bell would also remind men of their passing, and of resurrection and judgement.[21] Sound served better than sight, especially in growing manufacturing districts. In the clothing districts of the West Riding, in the Potteries, (and probably in other districts) the horn was still used to awaken people in the mornings.[22] The farmer aroused his own labourers, on occasion, from their cottages; and no doubt the knocker-up will have started with the earliest mills.

A great advance in the accuracy of household clocks came with the application of the pendulum after 1658. Grandfather clocks begin to spread more widely from the 1660s, but clocks with minute hands (as well as hour hands) only became common well after this time.[23] As regards more portable time, the pocket watch was of dubious accuracy until improvements were made in the escapement and the spiral balance-spring was applied after 1674.[24] Ornate and rich design was still preferred to plain serviceability. A Sussex diarist notes in 1688:

> bought . . . a silver-cased watch, wch cost me *31i* . . . This watch shewes ye hour of ye day, ye month of ye year, ye age of ye moon, and ye ebbing and flowing of ye water; and will goe 30 hours with one winding up.[25]

Professor Cipolla suggests 1680 as the date at which English clock- and watch-making took precedence (for nearly a century) over European competitors.[26] Clockmaking had emerged from the skills of the blacksmith,[27] and the affinity can still be seen in the many hundreds of independent clock-makers, working to local orders in their own shops, dispersed through the market-towns and even the large villages of England, Scotland and Wales in the eighteenth-century.[28] While many of these aspired to nothing more fancy than the work-a-day farmhouse longcase clock, crafts-men of genius were among their numbers. Thus John Harrison, clock-maker and former carpenter of Barton-on-Humber (Lincs.), perfected a marine chronometer, and in 1730 could claim to have

> brought a Clock to go nearer the truth, than can be well imagin'd, considering the vast Number of seconds of Time there is in a Month, in which space of time it does not vary above one second . . . I am sure I can bring it to the nicety of 2 or 3 seconds in a year.[29]

And John Tibbot, a clock-maker in Newtown (Mon.), had perfected a clock in 1810 which (he claimed) seldom varied more than a second over two years.[30] In between these extremes were those numerous, shrewd, and highly-capable craftsmen who played a critically-important role in technical innovation in the early stages of the industrial revolution. The point, indeed, was not left for historians to discover: it was argued forcibly in petitions of the clock- and watch-makers against the assessed taxes in February 1798. Thus the petition from Carlisle:

> . . . the cotton and woollen manufactories are entirely indebted for the state of perfec-tion to which the machinery used therein is now brought to the clock and watch makers, great numbers of whom have, for several years past . . . been employed in inventing and constructing as well as superintending such machinery . . . .[31]

Small-town clock-making survived into the nineteenth century, although from the early years of that century it became common for the local clock-maker to buy his parts ready-made from Birmingham, and to assemble these in his own work-shop. By contrast, watchmaking, from the early years of the eighteenth century was con-centrated in a few centres, of which the most important were London, Coventry, Prescot and Liverpool.[32] A minute subdivision of labour took place in the industry early, facilitating large-scale production and a reduction in prices: the annual output of the industry at its peak (1796) was variously estimated at 120,000 and 191,678, a substantial part of which was for the export market.[33] Pitt's ill-judged attempt to tax clocks and watches, although it lasted only from July 1797 to March 1798, marked a turning-point in the fortunes of the industry. Already, in 1796, the trade was com-plaining at the competition of French and Swiss watches; the complaints continue to grow in the early years of the nineteenth century. The Clockmakers' Company alleged in 1813 that the smuggling of cheap gold watches has assumed major pro-portions, and that these were sold by jewellers, haberdashers, milliners, dressmakers, French toy-shops, perfumers, etc., "almost entirely for the use of *the upper classes of society*". At the same time, some cheap smuggled goods, sold by pawnbrokers or travelling salesmen, must have been reaching the poorer classes.[34]

It is clear that there were plenty of watches and clocks around by 1800. But it is not so clear who owned them. Dr. Dorothy George, writing of the mid-eighteenth century, suggests that "labouring men, as well as artisans, frequently possessed silver watches", but the statement is indefinite as to date and only slightly documented.[35] The average price of plain longcase clocks made locally in Wrexham between 1755 and 1774 ran between £2 and £2 15s. od.; a Leicester price-list for new clocks, without cases, in 1795 runs between £3 and £5. A well-made watch would certainly cost no less.[36] On the face of it, no labourer whose budget was recorded by Eden or David Davies could have meditated such prices, and only the best-paid urban artisan. Recorded time (one suspects) belonged in the mid-century still to the gentry, the masters, the farmers and the tradesmen; and perhaps the intricacy of design, and the preference for precious metal, were in deliberate accentuation of their symbolism of status.

But, equally, it would appear that the situation was changing in the last decades of the century. The debate provoked by the attempt to impose a tax on all clocks and watches in 1797–8 offers a little evidence. It was perhaps the most unpopular and it was certainly the most unsuccessful of all of Pitt's assessed taxes:

> If your Money he take – why your Breeches remain;
> And the flaps of your Shirts, if your Breeches he gain;
> And your Skin, if your Shirts; and if Shoes, your bare feet.
> Then, never mind TAXES – *We've beat the Dutch fleet!*[37]

The taxes were of 2s. 6d. upon each silver or metal watch; 10s. upon each, gold one; and 5s. upon each clock. In debates upon the tax, the statements of ministers were remarkable only for their contradictions. Pitt declared that he expected the tax to produce £200,000 per annum:

> In fact, he thought, that as the number of houses paying taxes is 700,000, and that in every house there is probably one person who wears a watch, the tax upon watches only would produce that sum.

At the same time, in response to criticism, ministers maintained that the ownership of clocks and watches was a mark of luxury. The Chancellor of the Exchequer faced both ways: watches and clocks "were certainly articles' of convenience, but they were also articles of luxury . . . generally kept by persons who would be pretty well able to pay . . .". "He meant, however, to exempt Clocks of the meaner sort that were most commonly kept by the poorer classes".[38] The Chancellor clearly regarded the tax as a sort of Lucky Bag; his guess was more than three times that of the Pilot:

Guesswork table

Articles	Tax	Chancellor's estimate	Would mean
Silver and metal watches	2s. 6d.	£100,000	800,000 watches
Gold watches	10s. od.	£200,000	400,000 "
Clocks	5s. od.	£3 or £400,000	c. 1,400,000 clocks

His eyes glittering at the prospect of enhanced revenue, Pitt revised his definitions: a *single* watch (or dog) might be owned as an article of convenience – more than this were "tests of affluence".[39]

Unfortunately for the quantifiers of economic growth, one matter was left out of account. The tax was impossible to collect.[40] All householders were ordered, upon dire pains, to return lists of clocks and watches within their houses. Assessments were to be quarterly:

> Mr. Pitt has very proper ideas of the remaining finances of the country. The *half-crown* tax upon watches is appointed to be collected *quarterly*. This is grand and dignified. It gives a man an air of consequence to pay *sevenpence halfpenny* to support *religion*, *property*, and *social order*.[41]

In fact, the tax was regarded as folly; as setting up a system of espionage; and as a blow against the middle class.[42] There was a buyer's strike. Owners of gold watches melted down the covers and exchanged them for silver or metal.[43] The centres of the trade were plunged into crisis and depression.[44] Repealing the Act in March 1798, Pitt said sadly that the tax *would* have been productive much beyond the calculation originally made; but it is not clear whether it was his own calculation (£200,000) or the Chancellor of the Exchequer's (£700,000) which he had in mind.[45]

We remain (but in the best of company) in ignorance. There were a lot of time-pieces about in the 1790s: emphasis is shifting from "luxury" to "convenience"; even cottagers may have wooden clocks costing less than twenty shillings. Indeed, a general diffusion of clocks and watches is occurring (as one would expect) at the exact moment when the industrial revolution demanded a greater synchronization of labour.

Although some very cheap – and shoddy – timepieces were beginning to appear, the prices of efficient ones remained for several decades beyond the normal reach of the artisan.[46] But we should not allow normal economic preferences to mislead us. The small instrument which regulated the new rhythms of industrial life was at the same time one of the more urgent of the new needs which industrial capitalism called forth to energize its advance. A clock or watch was not only useful; it conferred prestige upon its owner, and a man might be willing to stretch his resources to obtain one. There were various sources, various occasions. For decades a trickle of sound but cheap watches found their way from the pickpocket to the receiver, the pawnbroker, the public house.[47] Even labourers, once or twice in their lives, might have an unexpected windfall, and blow it on a watch: the militia bounty,[48] harvest earnings, or the yearly wages of the servant.[49] In some parts of the country Clock and Watch Clubs were set up – collective hire-purchase.[50] Moreover, the timepiece was the poor man's bank, an investment of savings: it could, in bad times, be sold or put in hock.[51] "This 'ere ticker", said one Cockney compositor in the 1820s, "cost me but a five-pun note ven I bort it fust, and I've popped it more than twenty times, and had more than forty poun' on it altogether. It's a garjian haingel to a fellar, is a good votch, ven you're hard up".[52]

Whenever any group of workers passed into a phase of improving living standards, the acquisition of timepieces was one of the first things noted by observers. In Radcliffe's well-known account of the golden age of the Lancashire handloom weavers in the 1790s the men had "each a watch in his pocket" and every house was "well furnished with a clock in elegant mahogany or fancy case".[53] In Manchester fifty years later the same point caught the reporter's eye:

> No Manchester operative will be without one a moment longer than he can help. You see, here and there, in the better class of houses, one of the old-fashioned metallic-faced eight-day clocks; but by far the most common article is the little Dutch machine, with its busy pendulum swinging openly and candidly before all the world.[54]

Thirty years later again it was the gold double watch-chain which was the symbol of the successful Lib-Lab trade union leader; and for fifty years of disciplined servitude to work, the enlightened employer gave to his employee an engraved gold watch.

IV

Let us return from the timepiece to the task. Attention to time in labour depends in large degree upon the need for the synchronization of labour. But in so far as manufacturing industry remained conducted upon a domestic or small workshop scale, without intricate subdivision of processes, the degree of synchronization demanded was slight, and task-orientation was still prevalent.[55] The putting-out system demanded much fetching, carrying, waiting for materials. Bad weather could disrupt not only agriculture, building and transport, but also weaving, where the finished pieces had to be stretched on the tenters to dry. As we get closer to each task, we are surprised to find the multiplicity of subsidiary tasks which the same worker or family group must do in one cottage or workshop. Even in larger workshops men sometimes continued to work at distinct tasks at their own benches or looms, and – except where the fear of the embezzlement of materials imposed stricter supervision – could show some flexibility in coming and going.

Hence we get the characteristic irregularity of labour patterns before the coming of large-scale machine-powered industry. Within the general demands of the week's or fortnight's tasks – the piece of cloth, so many nails or pairs of shoes – the working day might be lengthened or shortened. Moreover, in the early development of manufacturing industry, and of mining, many mixed occupations survived: Cornish tinners who also took a hand in the pilchard fishing; Northern lead-miners who were also smallholders; the village craftsmen who turned their hands to various jobs, in building, carting, joining; the domestic workers who left their work for the harvest; the Pennine small-farmer/weaver.

It is in the nature of such work that accurate and representative time-budgets will not survive. But some extracts from the diary of one methodical farming weaver in 1782–83 may give us an indication of the variety of tasks. In October 1782 he was still employed in harvesting, and threshing, alongside his weaving. On a rainy day he might weave $8\frac{1}{2}$ or 9 yards; on October 14th he carried his finished piece, and so wove only $4\frac{3}{4}$ yards; on the 23rd he "worked out" till 3 o'clock, wove two yards before sun set, "clouted [mended] my coat in the evening". On December 24th "wove 2 yards before 11 o'clock. I was laying up the coal heap, sweeping the roof and walls of the kitchen and laying the muck miding [midden?] till to o'clock at night". Apart from harvesting and threshing, churning, ditching and gardening, we have these entries:

January 18, 1783:   "I was employed in preparing a Calf stall & Fetching the Tops of three Plain Trees home which grew in the Lane and was that day cut down & sold to John Blagbrough."

January 21st: "Wove $2\frac{3}{4}$ yards the Cow having calved she required much attendance". (On the next day he walked to Halifax to buy a medicine for the cow.)

On January 25th he wove 2 yards, walked to a nearby village, and did "sundry jobbs about the lathe and in the yard & wrote a letter in the evening". Other occupations include jobbing with a horse and cart, picking cherries, working on a mill dam, attending a Baptist association and a public hanging.[56]

This general irregularity must be placed within the irregular cycle of the working week (and indeed of the working year) which provoked so much lament from moralists and mercantilists in the seventeenth and eighteenth centuries. A rhyme printed in 1639 gives us a satirical version:

> You know that Munday is Sundayes brother;
> Tuesday is such another;
> Wednesday you must go to Church and pray;
> Thursday is half-holiday;
> On Friday it is too late to begin to spin;
> The Saturday is half-holiday agen.[57]

John Houghton, in 1681, gives us the indignant version:

When the framework knitters or makers of silk stockings had a great price for their work, they have been observed seldom to work on Mondays and Tuesdays but to spend most of their time at the ale-house or nine-pins . . . The weavers, 'tis common with them to be drunk on Monday, have their head-ache on Tuesday, and their tools out of order on Wednesday. As for the shoemakers, they'll rather be hanged than not remember St. Crispin on Monday . . . and it commonly holds as long as they have a penny of money or pennyworth of credit.[58]

The work pattern was one of alternate bouts of intense labour and of idleness, wherever men were in control of their own working lives. (The pattern persists among some self-employed – artists, writers, small farmers, and perhaps also with students – today, and provokes the question whether it is not a "natural" human work-rhythm.) On Monday or Tuesday, according to tradition, the hand-loom went to the slow chant of *Plen-ty of Time, Plen-ty of Time*: on Thursday and Friday, *A day t'lat, A day t'lat*.[59] The temptation to lie in an extra hour in the morning pushed work into the evening, candle-lit hours.[60] There are few trades which are not described as honouring Saint Monday: shoemakers, tailors, colliers, printing workers, potters, weavers, hosiery workers, cutlers, all Cockneys. Despite the full employment of many London trades during the Napoleonic Wars, a witness complained that "we see Saint Monday so religiously kept in this great city . . . in general followed by a Saint Tuesday also".[61] If we are to believe "The Jovial Cutlers", a Sheffield song of the late eighteenth century, its observance was not without domestic tension:

> How upon a good Saint Monday,
> Sitting by the smithy fire,
> Telling what's been done o't Sunday,
> And in cheerful mirth conspire,
>> Soon I hear the trap-door rise up,
>> On the ladder stands my wife:
>> "Damn thee, Jack, I'll dust thy eyes up,
>> Thou leads a plaguy drunken life;
>> Here thou sits instead of working,
>> Wi' thy pitcher on thy knee;
>> Curse thee, thou'd be always lurking.
>> And I may slave myself for thee".

The wife proceeds, speaking "with motion quicker/Than my boring stick at a Friday's pace", to demonstrate effective consumer demand:

> "See thee, look what stays I've gotten,
> See thee, what a pair o' shoes;
> Gown and petticoat half rotten,
> Ne'er a whole stitch in my hose . . .".

and to serve notice of a general strike:

> "Thou knows I hate to broil and quarrel,
> But I've neither soap nor tea;
> Od burn thee, Jack, forsake thy barrel,
> Or nevermore thou'st lie wi' me".[62]

Saint Monday, indeed, appears to have been honoured almost universally wherever small-scale, domestic, and outwork industries existed; was generally found in the pits; and sometimes continued in manufacturing and heavy industry.[63] It was perpetuated, in England, into the nineteenth – and, indeed, into the twentieth[64] – centuries for complex economic and social reasons. In some trades, the small masters themselves accepted the institution, and employed Monday in taking-in or giving-out work. In Sheffield, where the cutlers had for centuries tenaciously honoured the Saint, it had become "a settled habit and custom" which the steel-mills themselves honoured (1874):

> This Monday idleness is, in some cases, enforced by the fact that Monday is the day that is taken for repairs to the machinery of the great steelworks.[65]

Where the custom was deeply-established, Monday was the day set aside for marketing and personal business. Also, as Duveau suggests of French workers, "le dimanche est le jour de la famille, le lundi celui de l'amitié"; and as the nineteenth-century advanced, its celebration was something of a privilege of status of the better-paid artisan.[66]

It is, in fact, in an account by "An Old Potter" published as late as 1903 that we have some of the most perceptive observations on the irregular work-rhythms which continued on the older pot-banks until the mid-century. The potters (in the 1830s and 1840s) "had a devout regard for Saint Monday". Although the custom of annual hiring prevailed, the actual weekly earnings were at piece-rates, the skilled male potters employing the children, and working, with little supervision, at their own pace. The children and women came to work on Monday and Tuesday, but a "holiday feeling" prevailed and the day's work was shorter than usual, since the potters were away a good part of the time, drinking their earnings of the previous week. The children, however, had to prepare work for the potter (for example, handles for pots which he would throw), and all suffered from the exceptionally long hours (fourteen and sometimes sixteen hours a day) which were worked from Wednesday to Saturday:

> I have since thought that but for the reliefs at the beginning of the week for the women and boys all through the pot-works, the deadly stress of the last four days could not have been maintained.

"An Old Potter", a Methodist lay preacher of Liberal-Radical views, saw these customs (which he deplored) as a consequence of the lack of mechanization of the pot-banks; and he argued that the same indiscipline in daily work influenced the entire way-of-life and the working-class organizations of the Potteries. "Machinery means discipline in industrial operations":

> If a steam-engine had started every Monday morning at six o'clock, the workers would have been disciplined to the habit of regular and continuous industry. . . . I have noticed, too, that machinery seems to lead to habits of calculation. The Pottery workers were woefully deficient in this matter; they lived like children, without any calculating forecast of their work or its result. In some of the more northern counties this habit of calculation has made them keenly shrewd in many conspicuous ways. Their great

co-operative societies would never have arisen to such immense and fruitful development but for the calculating induced by the use of machinery. A machine worked so
many hours in the week would produce so much length of yarn or cloth. Minutes were
felt to be factors in these results, whereas in the Potteries hours, or even days at times,
were hardly felt to be such factors. There were always the mornings and nights of the
last days of the week, and these were always trusted to make up the loss of the week's
early neglect.[67]

This irregular working rhythm is commonly associated with heavy week-end
drinking: Saint Monday is a target in many Victorian temperance tracts. But even the
most sober and self-disciplined artisan might feel the necessity for such alternations.
"I know not how to describe the sickening aversion which at times steals over the
working man and utterly disables him for a longer or shorter period, from following his usual occupation", Francis Place wrote in 1829; and he added a footnote of
personal testimony:

> For nearly six years, whilst working, when I had work to do, from twelve to eighteen
> hours a day, when no longer able, from the cause mentioned, to continue working, I
> used to run from it, and go as rapidly as I could to Highgate, Hampstead, Muswell-hill,
> or Norwood, and then "return to my vomit" . . . This is the case with every workman
> I have ever known; and in proportion as a man's case is hopeless will such fits more
> frequently occur and be of longer duration.[68]

We may, finally, note that the irregularity of working day and week were framed,
until the first decades of the nineteenth century, within the larger irregularity of the
working year, punctuated by its traditional holidays, and fairs. Still, despite the triumph of the Sabbath over the ancient saints' days in the seventeenth century,[69] the
people clung tenaciously to their customary wakes and feasts, and may even have enlarged them both in vigour and extent.[70] But a discussion of this problem, and of the
psychic needs met by such intermittent festivals, must be left to another occasion.

How far can this argument be extended from manufacturing industry to the rural
labourers? On the face of it, there would seem to be unrelenting daily and weekly
labour here: the field labourer had no Saint Monday. But a close discrimination of
different work situations is still required. The eighteenth- (and nineteenth-) century
village had its own self-employed artisans, as well as many employed on irregular
task work.[71] Moreover, in the unenclosed countryside, the classical case against
open-field and common was in its inefficiency and wastefulness of time, for the small
farmer or cottager:

> . . . if you offer them work, they will tell you that they must go to look up their sheep,
> cut furzes, get their cow out of the pound, or, perhaps, say they must take their horse to
> be shod, that he may carry them to a horse-race or cricket-match. (Arbuthnot, 1773)

> In sauntering after his cattle, he acquires a habit of indolence. Quarter, half, and
> occasionally whole days are imperceptibly lost. Day labour becomes disgusting . . . .
> (Report on Somerset, 1795)

> When a labourer becomes possessed of more land than he and his family can cultivate
> in the evenings . . . the farmer can no longer depend on him for constant work . . . .
> (*Commercial & Agricultural Magazine*, 1800)[72]

To this we should add the frequent complaints of agricultural improvers as to the
time wasted, both at seasonal fairs, and (before the arrival of the village shop) on
weekly market-days.[73]

The farm-servant, or the regular wage-earning field labourer, who worked, unre-
mittingly, the full statute hours or longer, who had no common rights or land, and
who (if not living-in) lived in a tied cottage, was undoubtedly subject to an intense
labour discipline, whether in the seventeenth or the nineteenth century. The day of
a ploughman (living-in) was described with relish by Markham in 1636:

> . . . the Plowman shall rise before four of the clock in the morning, and after thanks
> given to God for his rest, & prayer for the success of his labours, he shall go into his
> stable . . . .

After cleansing the stable, grooming his horses, feeding them, and preparing his
tackle, he might breakfast (6–6-30 a.m.), he should plough until 2 p.m. or 3 p.m.;
take half an hour for dinner; attend to his horses etc. until 6-30 p.m., when he might
come in for supper:

> . . . and after supper, hee shall either by the fire side mend shooes both for himselfe and
> their Family, or beat and knock Hemp or Flax, or picke and stamp Apples or Crabs, for
> Cyder or Verdjuyce, or else grind malt on the quernes, pick candle rushes, or doe some
> Husbandly office within doors till it be full eight a clock . . . .

Then he must once again attend to his cattle and ("giving God thanks for benefits
received that day") he might retire.[74]

Even so, we are entitled to show a certain scepticism. There are obvious difficulties in the nature of the occupation. Ploughing is not an all-the-year-round task.
Hours and tasks must fluctuate with the weather. The horses (if not the men) must
be rested. There is the difficulty of supervision: Robert Loder's accounts indicate that
servants (when out of sight) were not always employed upon their knees thanking
God for their benefits: "men can worke yf they list & soe they can loyter".[75] The
farmer himself must work exceptional hours if he was to keep all his labourers always
employed.[76] And the farm-servant could assert his annual right to move on if he disliked his employment.

Thus enclosure and agricultural improvement were both, in some sense, concerned with the efficient husbandry of the time of the labour-force. Enclosure and
the growing labour-surplus at the end of the eighteenth century tightened the screw
for those who were in regular employment; they were faced with the alternatives of
partial employment and the poor law, or submission to a more exacting labour discipline. It is a question, not of new techniques, but of a greater sense of time-thrift

among the improving capitalist employers. This reveals itself in the debate between advocates of regularly-employed wage-labour and advocates of "taken-work" (i.e. labourers employed for particular tasks at piece-rates). In the 1790s Sir Mordaunt Martin censured recourse to taken-work

> which people agree to, to save themselves the trouble of watching their workmen: the consequence is, the work is ill done, the workmen boast at the ale-house what they can spend in "a waste against the wall", and make men at moderate wages discontented.

"A Farmer" countered with the argument that taken-work and regular wage-labour might be judiciously intermixed:

> Two labourers engage to cut down a piece of grass at two shillings or half-a-crown an acre; I send, with their scythes, two of my domestic farm-servants into the field; I can depend upon it, that their companions will keep them up to their work; and thus I gain . . . the same additional hours of labour from my domestic servants, which are voluntarily devoted to it by my hired servants.[77]

In the nineteenth century the debate was largely resolved in favour of weekly wage-labour, supplemented by task-work as occasion arose. The Wiltshire labourer's day, as described by Richard Jeffries in the 1870s, was scarcely less long than that described by Markham. Perhaps in resistance to this unremitting toil he was distinguished by the "clumsiness of his walk" and "the deadened slowness which seems to pervade everything he does".[78]

The most arduous and prolonged work of all was that of the labourer's wife in the rural economy. One part of this – especially the care of infants – was the most task-orientated of all. Another part was in the fields, from which she must return to renewed domestic tasks. As Mary Collier complained in a sharp rejoinder to Stephen Duck:

> . . . when we Home are come,
> Alas! we find our Work but just begun;
> So many Things for our Attendance call,
> Had we ten Hands, we could employ them all.
> Our Children put to Bed, with greatest Care
> We all Things for your coming Home prepare:
> You sup, and go to Bed without delay,
> And rest yourselves till the ensuing Day;
> While we, alas! but little Sleep can have,
> Because our froward Children cry and rave . . . .
>
> In ev'ry Work (we) take our proper Share;
> And from the Time that Harvest doth begin
> Until the Corn be cut and carry'd in,
> Our Toil and Labour's daily so extreme,
> That we have hardly ever *Time to dream*.[79]

Such hours were endurable only because one part of the work, with the children and in the home, disclosed itself as necessary and inevitable, rather than as an external imposition. This remains true to this day, and, despite school times and television times, the rhythms of women's work in the home are not wholly attuned to the measurement of the clock. The mother of young children has an imperfect sense of time and attends to other human tides. She has not yet altogether moved out of the conventions of "pre-industrial" society.

V

I have placed "pre-industrial" in inverted commas: and for a reason. It is true that the transition to mature industrial society demands analysis in sociological as well as economic terms. Concepts such as "time-preference" and the "backward sloping labour supply curve" are, too often, cumbersome attempts to find economic terms to describe sociological problems. But, equally, the attempt to provide simple models for one single, supposedly-neutral, technologically-determined, process known as "industrialization" (so popular today among well-established sociological circles in the United States)[80] is also suspect. It is not only that the highly-developed and technically-alert manufacturing industries (and the way-of-life supported by them) of France or England in the eighteenth century can only by semantic torture be described as "pre-industrial". (And such a description opens the door to endless false analogies between societies at greatly differing economic levels). It is also that there has never been any single type of "the transition". The stress of the transition falls upon the whole culture: resistance to change and assent to change arise from the whole culture. And this culture includes the systems of power, property-relations, religious institutions, etc., inattention to which merely flattens phenomena and trivializes analysis. Above all, the transition is not to "industrialism" *tout court* but to industrial capitalism or (in the twentieth century) to alternative systems whose features are still indistinct. What we are examining here are not only changes in manufacturing technique which demand greater synchronization of labour and a greater exactitude in time-routines in *any* society; but also these changes as they were lived through in the society of nascent industrial capitalism. We are concerned simultaneously with time-sense in its technological conditioning, and with time-measurement as a means of labour exploitation.

There are reasons why the transition was peculiarly protracted and fraught with conflict in England: among those which are often noted, England's was the first industrial revolution, and there were no Cadillacs, steel mills, or television sets to serve as demonstrations as to the object of the operation. Moreover, the preliminaries to the industrial revolution were so long that, in the manufacturing districts in the early eighteenth century, a vigorous and licensed popular culture had evolved, which the propagandists of discipline regarded with dismay. Josiah Tucker, the dean of

Gloucester, declared in 1745 that "the *lower* class of people" were utterly degenerated. Foreigners (he sermonized) found "the *common people* of our *populous cities* to be the most *abandoned*, and *licentious* wretches on earth":

> Such brutality and insolence, such debauchery and extravagance, such idleness, irreligion, cursing and swearing, and contempt of all rule and authority . . . Our people are *drunk with the cup of liberty*.[81]

The irregular labour rhythms described in the previous section help us to understand the severity of mercantilist doctrines as to the necessity for holding down wages as a preventative against idleness, and it would seem to be not until the second half of the eighteenth century that "normal" capitalist wage incentives begin to become widely effective.[82] The confrontations over discipline have already been examined by others.[83] My intention here is to touch upon several points which concern time-discipline more particularly. The first is found in the extraordinary Law Book of the Crowley Iron Works. Here, at the very birth of the large-scale unit in manufacturing industry, the old autocrat, Crowley, found it necessary to design an entire civil and penal code, running to more than 100,000 words, to govern and regulate his refractory labour-force. The preambles to Orders Number 40 (the Warden at the Mill) and 103 (Monitor) strike the prevailing note of morally-righteous invigilation. From Order 40:

> I having by sundry people working by the day with the connivence of the clerks been horribly cheated and paid for much more time than in good conscience I ought and such hath been the baseness & treachery of sundry clerks that they have concealed the sloath & negligence of those paid by the day. . . .

And from Order 103:

> Some have pretended a sort of right to loyter, thinking by their readiness and ability to do sufficient in less time than others. Others have been so foolish to think bare attendance without being imployed in business is sufficient. . . . Others so impudent as to glory in their villany and upbrade others for their diligence. . . .

> To the end that sloath and villany should be detected and the just and diligent rewarded, I have thought meet to create an account of time by a Monitor, and do order and it is hereby ordered and declared from 5 to 8 and from 7 to 10 is fifteen hours, out of which take $1\frac{1}{2}$ for breakfast, dinner, etc. There will then be thirteen hours and a half neat service . . . .

This service must be calculated "after all deductions for being at taverns, alehouses, coffee houses, breakfast, dinner, playing, sleeping, smoking, singing, reading of news history, quarelling, contention, disputes or anything forreign to my business, any way loytering".

The Monitor and Warden of the Mill were ordered to keep for each day employee a time-sheet, entered to the minute, with "Come" and "Run". In the Monitor's Order, verse 31 (a later addition) declares:

> And whereas I have been informed that sundry clerks have been so unjust as to reckon by clocks going the fastest and the bell ringing before the hour for their going from business, and clocks going too slow and the bell ringing after the hour for their coming to business, and those two black traitors Fowell and Skellerne have knowingly allowed the same; it is therefore ordered that no person upon the account doth reckon by any other clock, bell, watch or dyall but the Monitor's, which clock is never to be altered but by the clock-keeper . . . .

The Warden of the Mill was ordered to keep the watch "so locked up that it may not be in the power of any person to alter the same". His duties also were defined in verse 8:

> Every morning at 5 a clock the Warden is to ring the bell for beginning to work, at eight a clock for breakfast, at half an hour after for work again, at twelve a clock for dinner, at one to work and at eight to ring for leaving work and all to be lock'd up.

His book of the account of time was to be delivered in every Tuesday with the following affidavit:

> This account of time is done without favour or affection, ill-will or hatred, & do really believe the persons above mentioned have worked in the service of John Crowley Esq the hours above charged.[84]

We are entering here, already in 1700, the familiar landscape of disciplined industrial capitalism, with the time-sheet, the time-keeper, the informers and the fines. Some seventy years later the same discipline was to be imposed in the early cotton mills (although the machinery itself was a powerful supplement to the time-keeper). Lacking the aid of machinery to regulate the pace of work on the pot-bank, that supposedly-formidable disciplinarian, Josiah Wedgwood, was reduced to enforcing discipline upon the potters in surprisingly muted terms. The duties of the Clerk of the Manufactory were:

> To be at the works the first in the morning, & settle the people to their business as they come in, – to encourage those who come regularly to their time, letting them know that their regularity is properly noticed, & distinguishing them by repeated marks of approbation, from the less orderly part of the workpeople, by presents or other marks suitable to their ages, &c.

> Those who come later than the hour appointed should be noticed, and if after repeated marks of disapprobation they do not come in due time, an account of the time they are deficient in should be taken, and so much of their wages stopt as the time comes to if they work by wages, and if they work by the piece they should after frequent notice be sent back to breakfast-time.[85]

These regulations were later tightened somewhat:

> Any of the workmen forceing their way through the Lodge after the time alow'd by the Master forfeits 2/-d.[86]

and McKendrick has shown how Wedgwood wrestled with the problem at Etruria and introduced the first recorded system of clocking-in.[87] But it would seem that once the strong presence of Josiah himself was withdrawn the incorrigible potters returned to many of their older ways.

It is too easy, however, to see this only as a matter of factory or workshop discipline, and we may glance briefly at the attempt to impose "time-thrift" in the domestic manufacturing districts, and its impingement upon social and domestic life. Almost all that the masters *wished* to see imposed may be found in the bounds of a single pamphlet, the Rev. J. Clayton's *Friendly Advice to the Poor*, "written and publish'd at the Request of the late and present Officers of the Town of Manchester" in 1755. "If the *sluggard hides his hands* in his bosom, rather than applies them to work; if he spends his Time in Sauntring, impairs his Constitution by Laziness, and dulls his Spirit by Indolence . . ." then he can expect only poverty as his reward. The labourer must not loiter idly in the market-place or waste time in marketing. Clayton complains that "the Churches and Streets [are] crowded with Numbers of Spectators" at weddings and funerals, "who in spight of the Miseries of their Starving Condition . . . make no Scruple of wasting the best Hours in the Day, for the sake of gazing . . .". The tea-table is "this shameful devourer of Time and Money". So also are wakes and holidays and the annual feasts of friendly societies. So also is "that slothful spending the Morning in Bed":

> The necessity of early rising would reduce the poor to a necessity of going to Bed betime; and thereby prevent the Danger of Midnight revels.

Early rising would also "introduce an exact Regularity into their Families, a wonderful Order into their Oeconomy".

The catalogue is familiar, and might equally well be taken from Baxter in the previous century. If we can trust Bamford's *Early Days*, Clayton failed to make many converts from their old way of life among the weavers. Nevertheless, the long dawn chorus of moralists is prelude to the quite sharp attack upon popular customs, sports, and holidays which was made in the last years of the eighteenth century and the first years of the nineteenth.

One other non-industrial institution lay to hand which might be used to inculcate "time-thrift": the school. Clayton complained that the streets of Manchester were full of "idle ragged children; who are not only losing their Time, but learning habits of gaming", etc. He praised charity schools as teaching Industry, Frugality, Order and Regularity: "the Scholars here are obliged to rise betimes and to observe Hours with great Punctuality".[88] William Temple, when advocating, in 1770, that poor children

be sent at the age of four to work-houses where they should be employed in manufactures and given two hours' schooling a day, was explicit about the socializing
influence of the process:

> There is considerable use in their being, somehow or other, constantly employed at least
> twelve hours a day, whether they earn their living or not; for by these means, we hope
> that the rising generation will be so habituated to constant employment that it would
> at length prove agreeable and entertaining to them . . . .[89]

Powell, in 1772, also saw education as a training in the "habit of industry"; by the
time the child reached six or seven it should become "habituated, not to say naturalized to Labour and Fatigue".[90] The Rev. William Turner, writing from Newcastle in
1786, recommended Raikes' schools as "a spectacle of order and regularity", and
quoted a manufacturer of hemp and flax in Gloucester as affirming that the schools
had effected an extraordinary change: "they are . . . become more tractable and
obedient, and less quarrelsome and revengeful".[91] Exhortations to punctuality and regularity are written into the rules of all the early schools:

> Every scholar must be in the school-room on Sundays, at nine o'clock in the morning,
> and at half-past one in the afternoon, or she shall lose her place the next Sunday, and
> walk last.[92]

Once within the school gates, the child entered the new universe of disciplined time.
At the Methodist Sunday Schools in York the teachers were fined for unpunctuality.
The first rule to be learned by the scholars was:

> I am to be present at the School. . . a few minutes before half-past nine o'clock. . . .

Once in attendance, they were under military rule:

> The Superintendent shall again ring, – when, on a motion of his hand, the whole
> School rise at once from their seats; – on a second motion, the Scholars turn; – on a
> third, slowly and silently move to the place appointed to repeat their lessons, – he then
> pronounces the word "Begin". . . .[93]

The onslaught, from so many directions, upon the people's old working habits
was not, of course, uncontested. In the first stage, we find simple resistance.[94] But, in
the next stage, as the new time-discipline is imposed, so the workers begin to fight,
not against time, but about it. The evidence here is not wholly clear. But in the better-
organized artisan trades, especially in London, there is no doubt that hours were
progressively shortened in the eighteenth century as combination advanced. Lipson
cites the case of the London tailors whose hours were shortened in 1721, and again
in 1768: on both occasions the mid-day intervals allowed for dinner and drinking
were also shortened – the day was compressed.[95] By the end of the eighteenth century

there is some evidence that some favoured trades had gained something like a ten-hour day.

Such a situation could only persist in exceptional trades and in a favourable labour market. A reference in a pamphlet of 1827 to "the English system of working from 6 o'clock in the morning to 6 in the evening"[96] may be a more reliable indication as to the general expectation as to hours of the mechanic and artisan outside London in the 1820s. In the dishonourable trades and outwork industries hours (when work was available) were probably moving the other way.

It was exactly in those industries – the textile mills and the engineering workshops – where the new time-discipline was most rigorously imposed that the contest over time became most intense. At first some of the worst masters attempted to expropriate the workers of all knowledge of time. "I worked at Mr. Braid's mill", declared one witness:

> There we worked as long as we could see in summer time, and I could not say at what hour it was that we stopped. There was nobody but the master and the master's son who had a watch, and we did not know the time. There was one man who had a watch . . . It was taken from him and given into the master's custody because he had told the men the time of day . . . .[97]

A Dundee witness offers much the same evidence:

> . . . in reality there were no regular hours: masters and managers did with us as they liked. The clocks at the factories were often put forward in the morning and back at night, and instead of being instruments for the measurement of time, they were used as cloaks for cheatery and oppression. Though this was known amongst the hands all were afraid to speak, and a workman then was afraid to carry a watch, as it was no uncommon event to dismiss any one who presumed to know too much about the science of horology.[98]

Petty devices were used to shorten the dinner hour and to lengthen the day. "Every manufacturer wants to be a gentleman at once", said a witness before Sadler's Committee:

> and they want to nip every corner that they can, so that the bell will ring to leave off when it is half a minute past time, and they will have them in about two minutes before time . . . If the clock is as it used to be, the minute hand is at the weight, so that as soon as it passes the point of gravity, it drops three minutes all at once, so that it leaves them only twenty-seven minutes, instead of thirty.[99]

A strike-placard of about the same period from Todmorden put it more bluntly: "if that piece of dirty suet, 'old Robertshaw's engine-tenter', do not mind his own business, and let ours alone, we will shortly ask him how long it is since he received a gill of ale for running 10 minutes over time".[100] The first generation of factory workers were taught by their masters the importance of time; the second generation formed their short-time committees in the ten-hour movement; the third generation struck for overtime or time-and-a-half. They had accepted the categories of their employers and learned to fight back within them. They had learned their lesson, that time is money, only too well.[101]

. . .

NOTES

1. Lewis Mumford makes suggestive claims in *Technics and Civilization* [London, 1934), esp. pp. 12–18, 196–9: see also S. de Grazia, *Of Time, Work, and Leisure* (New York, 1962), Carlo M. Cipolla, *Clocks and Culture 1300–1700* (London, 1967), and Edward T. Hall, *The Silent Language* (New York, 1959).
2. J. le Goff, "Au Moyen Age: Temps de L'Eglise et temps du marchand", *Annales, E.S.C.,* xv (1960); and the same author's "Le temps du travail dans le 'crise' du XIVe Siède: du temps médiéval au temps moderne", *Le Moyen Age*, lxix (1963).
3. M. Drayton, "Of his Ladies not Comming to London", *Works*, ed. J. W. Hebel (Oxford, 1932), iii, p. 204.
4. The change is discussed Cipolla, *op. cit.*; Erwin Sturzl, *Der Zeitbegriff in der Elisabeth-anischen Literatur* (Wiener Beitrage zur Englischen Philologie, lxix, Wien-Stuttgart, 1965); Alberto Tenenti, *Il Senso della Morte e l'amore della vita nel rinanscimento* (Milan, 1957).
5. Anon., *The Clockmaker's Outcry against the Author of . . . Tristram Shandy* (London, 1760), pp. 42–3.
6. E. E. Evans-Pritchard, *The Nuer* (Oxford, 1940), pp. 100–4; M. P. Nilsson, *Primitive Time Reckoning* (Lund, 1920), pp. 32–3, 42; P. A. Sorokin and R. K. Merton, "Social Time: a Methodological and Functional Analysis", *Amer. Jl. Social.*, xlii (1937); A. I. Hallowell, "Temporal Orientation in Western Civilization and in a Pre-Literate Society", *Amer. Anthrop.*, new ser. xxxix (1937), Other sources for primitive time reckoning are cited in H. G. Alexander, *Time as Dimension and History* (Albuquerque, 1945), p. 26, and Beate R. Salz, "The Human Element in Industrialization", *Econ. Devel. and Cult. Change*, iv (1955). esp pp. 94–114.
7. E. P. Salas, "L'Evolution de la notion du temps et les horlogers à l'époque coloniale au Chili", *Annales E.S.C.,* xxi (1966), p. 146; *Cultural Patterns and Technical Change*, ed. M. Mead (New York, UNESCO, 1953), p. 75.
8. P. Bourdieu, "The attitude of the Algerian peasant toward time", in *Mediterranean Countrymen*, ed. J. Pitt-Rivers (Paris, 1963), pp. 55–72.
9. Cf. *ibid.*, p. 179: "Spanish Americans do not regulate their lives by the clock as Anglos do. Both rural and urban people, when asked when they plan to do something, gives answers like: 'Right now, about two or four o'clock' ".
10. J. M. Synge, *Plays, Poems, and Prose* (Everyman edn., London, 1941), p. 257.
11. The most important event in the relation of the islands to an external economy in Synge's time was the arrival of the steamer, whose times might be greatly affected by tide and weather. See Synge, *The Aran Islands* (Dublin, 1907), pp. 115–6.
12. Public Rec. Off., W.O. 40/17. It is of interest to note other examples of the recognition that seafaring time conflicted with urban routines: the Court of Admiralty was held to be

always open, "for strangers and merchants, and seafaring men, must take the opportunity of tides and winds, and cannot, without ruin and great prejudice attend the solemnity of courts and dilatory pleadings" (see E. Vansittart Neale, *Feasts and Fasts* [London, 1845], p. 249), while in some Sabbatarian legislation an exception was made for fishermen who sighted a shoal off-shore on the Sabbath day.

13. Henri Lefebvre, *Critique de la Vie Quotidienne* (Paris, 1958), ii, pp. 52–6, prefers a distinction between "cyclical time" – arising from changing seasonal occupations in agriculture – and the "linear time" of urban, industrial organization. More suggestive is Lucien Febvre's distinction between "Le temps vécu et le temps-mesure", *La. Problèms de L'Incroyance an XVIᵉ Siècle* (Paris, 1947), p. 431. A somewhat schematic examination of the organization of tasks in primitive economies is in Stanley H. Udy, *Organisation of Work* (New Haven, 1959), ch. 2.

14. *Rural Economy in Yorkshire in 1641 . . . Farming and Account Books of Henry Best*, ed. C. B. Robinson (Surtees Society, xxxiii, 1857), pp. 38–9.

15. G.M., *The Inrichment of the Weald of Kent*, 10th edn. (London, 1660), ch. xii: "A generall computation of men, and cattel's labours: what each may do without hurt daily", pp. 112–8.

16. Wage-assessments still, of course, assumed the statute dawn-to-dusk day, defined, as late as 1725, in a Lancashire assessment: "They shall work from five in the morning till betwixt seven and eight at the night, from the midst of March to the middle of September" – and thereafter "from the spring of day till night", with two half hours for drinking, and one hour for dinner and (in summer only) half hour for sleep: "else, for every hour's absence to defaulk a penny": *Annals of Agriculture*, xxv (London, 1796).

17. M. K. Ashby, *Joseph Ashby of Tysoe* (Cambridge, 1961), p. 24.

18. For the early evolution of clocks, see Carlo M. Cipolla, *Clocks and Culture, passim*; A. P. Usher, *A History of Mechanical Inventions*, rev. edn. (Harvard, 1962), ch. vii; Charles Singer *et al* (eds.), *A History of Technology* (Oxford, 1956), iii, ch. xxiv; R. W. Symonds, *A History of English Clocks* (Penguin, 1947), pp. 10–16, 33; E. L. Edwards, *Weight-driven Chamber Clocks of the Middle Ages and Renaissance* (Altrincham, 1965).

19. See M. Gatty, *The Book of Sun-diales*, rev. edn. (London, 1900). For an example of a treatise explaining in detail how to set time-pieces by the sundial, see John Smith, *Horological Dialogues* (London, 1675). For examples of benefactions for sundials, see C. J. C. Beeson, *Clockmaking in Oxfordshire* (Banbury Hist. Assn., 1962), pp. 76–8; A. J. Hawkes, *The Clockmakers and Watchmakers of Wigan, 1650–1850* (Wigan, 1950), p. 27.

20. Since many early church clocks did not strike the hour, they were supplemented by a bell-ringer.

21. *Charity Commissioners Reports* (1837/8), xxxii, pt. I, p. 224; see also H. Edwards, *A Collection of Old English Customs* (London, 1842), esp. pp. 223–7; S. O. Addy, *Household Tales* (London, 1895), pp. 129–30; *County Folk-Lore, East Riding of Yorkshire*, ed. Mrs. Gutch (London, 1912), pp. 150–1, *Leicestershire and Rutland*, ed. C. J. Bilson (London, 1895), pp. 120–1; C. J. C. Beeson, *op. cit.*, p. 36; A. Gatty, *The Bell* (London, 1848), p. 20; P. H. Ditchfield, *Old English Customs* (London, 1896), pp. 214–41.

22. H. Heaton, *The Yorkshire Woollen and Worsted Industries* (Oxford, 1965), p. 347. Wedgwood seems to have been the first to replace the born by the bell in the Potteries: E. Meteyard, *Life of Josiah Wedgwood* (London, 1865), i, pp. 329–30.

23. W. I. Milham, *Time and Timekeepers* (London, 1923), pp. 142–9; F. J. Britten, *Old Clocks and Watches and Their Makers*, 6th edn. (London, 1932), p. 543; E. Bruton, *The Longcase Clock* (London, 1964), ch. ix.

24. Milham, *op. cit.*, pp. 214–26; C. Clutton and G. Daniels, *Watches* (London, 1965); F. A. B. Ward, *Handbook of the Collections illustrating Time Measurement* (London, 1947), p. 29; Cipolla, *op. cit.*, p. 139.

25. Edward Turner, "Extracts from the Diary of Richard Stapley", *Sussex Archaeol. Coll.*, ii (1899), p. 113.

26. See the admirable survey of the origin of the English industry in Cipolla, *op. cit.*, pp. 65–9.

27. As late as 1697 in London the Blacksmith's Company was contesting the monopoly of the Clockmakers (founded in 1631) on the grounds that "it is well known that they are the originall and proper makers of clocks &c. and have full skill and knowledge therein . . .": S. E. Atkins and W. H. Overall, *Some Account of the Worshipful Company of Clockmakers of the City of London* (London, 1881), p. 118. For a village blacksmith-clockmaker see J. A. Daniell, "The Making of Clocks and Watches in Leicestershire and Rutland", *Trans. Leics. Archaeol Soc.*, xxvii (1951), p. 32.

28. Lists of such clockmakers are in F. J. Britten, *op. cit.*; John Smith, *Old Scottish Clockmakers* (Edinburgh, 1921); and I. C. Peate, *Clock and Watch Makers in Wales* (Cardiff, 1945).

29. Records of the Clockmaker's Company, London Guildhall Archives, 6026/1. See (for Harrison's chronometer) F. A. B. Ward, *op. cit.*, p. 32.

30. I. C. Peate, "John Tibbot, Clock and Watch Maker", *Montgomeryshire Collections*, xiviii, pt. 2 (Welshpool, 1944), p. 178.

31. *Commons Journals*, liii, p. 251. The witnesses from Lancashire and Derby gave similar testimonies: *ibid.*, pp. 331, 335.

32. Centres of the clock and watchmaking trade petitioning against the tax in 1798 were: London, Bristol, Coventry, Leicester, Prescot, Newcastle, Edinburgh, Liverpool, Carlisle, and Derby: *Commons Journals*, liii, pp. 158, 167, 174, 178, 230, 232, 239, 247, 251, 316. It was claimed that 20,000 were engaged in the trade in London alone, 7,000 of these in Clerkenwell. But in Bristol only 150 to 200 were engaged. For London, see M. D. George, *London Life in the Eighteenth Century* (London, 1925), pp. 173–6; Atkins and Overall, *op. cit.*, p. 269; *Morning Chronicle*, 19 Dec. 1797; *Commons Journals*, liii, p. 158. For Bristol, *ibid.*, p. 332. For Lancashire, *Vict. County Hist. Lancs.* (London, 1908), ii, pp. 366–7. The history of the eighteenth-century watch trade in Coventry appears to be unwritten.

33. The lower estimate was given by a witness before the committee on watchmakers' petitions (1798): *Commons Journals*, liii, p. 328 – estimated annual home consumption 50,000, export 70,000. See also a similar estimate (clocks and watches) for 1813, Atkins and Overall, *op. cit.*, p. 276. The higher estimate is for watch-cases marked at Goldsmiths Hall – silver cases, 185, 102 in 1796, declining to 91, 346 in 1816 – and is in the *Report of the Select Committee on the Petitions of Watchmakers, PP.* 1817, vi and 1818, ix, pp. 1, 12.

34. Atkins and Overall, *op. cit.*, pp. 302, 308 – estimating (excessively?) 25,000 gold and 10,000 silver watches imported, mostly illegally, per annum; and Anon., *Observations on the Art and Trade of Clock and Watchmaking* (London, 1812), pp. 16–20.

35. M. D. George, *op. cit.*, p. 70. Various means of time-telling were of course employed without clocks: the engraving of the wool-comber in *The Book of English Trades* (London, 1818), p. 438 shows him with an hour-glass on his bench; threshers measured time as the light from the door moved across the barn floor; and, Cornish tinners measured it underground by candles (information from Mr. J. G. Rule).

36. I. C. Peate, "Two Montgomeryshire Craftsmen", *Montgomeryshire Collections*, xlviii, pt. 1 (Welshpool, 1944), p. 5; J. A. Daniell, *op. cit.*, p. 39. The average price of watches exported in 1792 was £4: *P.P.* 1818, ix, p. 1.

37. "A loyal Song", *Morning Chronicle*, 18 Dec. 1797.

38. The exemptions in the Act (37 Geo. III, c. 108, cl. xxi, xxii and xxiv) were (a) for one clock or watch for any householder exempted from window and house tax (i.e. cottager), (b) for clocks "made of wood, or fixed upon wood, and which clocks are usually sold by the respective makers thereof at a price not exceeding the sum of 20s . . .", (c) Servants in husbandry.

39. *Morning Chronicle*, 1 July 1797; *Craftsman*, 8 July 1797; *Parl. Hist.*, xxxiii, *passim*.

40. In the year ending 5 April 1798 (three weeks after repeal) the tax had raised £2,600: *P.P.*, ciii, Accounts and Papers (1797–98), vol. xiv, 933 (2) and 933 (3).

41. *Morning Chronicle*, 26 July 1797.

42. One indication may be seen in the sluggardly collection of arrears. Taxes imposed, July 1797: receipts, year ending Jan. 1798 – £300 Taxes repealed, March 1798: arrears received, year ending Jan. 1799, £35,420; year ending Jan. 1800, £14,966. *P.P.*, cix, Accounts and Papers (1799–1800), li, pp. 1009 (2) and 1013 (2).

43. *Morning Chronicle*, 16 Mar. 1798; *Commons Journals*, liii, p. 328.

44. See petitions, cited in note 32 above; Commons Journals, liii, pp. 327–33; *Morning Chronicle*, 13 Mar. 1798. Two-thirds of Coventry watchmakers were said to be unemployed: *ibid.*, 8 Dec. 1797.

45. *Craftsman*, 17 Mar. 1798. The one achievement of the Act was to bring into existence – in taverns and public places – the "Act of Parliament Clock".

46. Imported watches were quoted at a price as low as 5s. in 1813: Atkins and Overall, *op. cit.*, p. 292. See also note 38 above. The price of an efficient British silver pocket watch was quoted in 1817 (*Committee on Petitions of Watchmakers, P.P.*, 1817, vi) at two to three guineas; by the 1830s an effective metal watch could be had for £1: D. Lardner, *Cabinet Cyclopaedia* (London, 1834), iii, p. 297.

47. Many watches must have changed hands in London's underworld: legislation in 1754 (27 Geo. II, c. 7) was directed at receivers of stolen watches. The pickpockets of course continued their trade undeterred: see, e.g. *Minutes of Select Committee to Inquire into the State of the Police of the Metropolis* (1816), p. 437 – "take watches; could get rid of them as readily as anything else . . . It must be a very good patent silver watch that fetched £2; a gold one £5 or £6". Receivers of stolen watches in Glasgow are said to have sold them in quantities in country districts in Ireland (1834): see J. E. Handley, *The Irish in Scotland, 1798–1845* (Cork, 1943), p. 253.

48. "Winchester being one of the general rendezvous for the militia volunteers, has been a scene of riot, dissipation and absurd extravagance. It is supposed that nine-tenths of the bounties paid to these men, amounting to at least £20,000 were all spent on the spot

among the public houses, milliners, watch-makers, hatters, &c. In more wantonness Bank notes were actually eaten between slices of bread and butter": *Monthly Magazine*, Sept. 1799.

49. Witnesses before the Select Committee of 1817 complained that inferior wares (sometimes known as "Jew watches") were touted in country fairs and sold to the gullible at mock auctions: *P.P.*, 1817, vi, pp. 15–16.

50. Benjamin Smith, *Twenty-four Letters from Labourers in America to their Friends in England* (London, 1829), p. 48: the reference is to parts of Sussex – twenty people clubbed together (as in a Cow Club) paying 5s. each for twenty successive weeks, drawing lots each for one £5 time-piece.

51. *P.P.*, 1817, vi, pp. 19, 22.

52. [C. M. Smith], *The Working Man's Way in the World* (London, 1853), pp. 67–8.

53. W. Radcliffe, *The Origin of Power Loom Weaving* (Stockport, 1828), p. 167.

54. *Morning Chronicle*, 25 Oct. 1849. But in 1843 J. R. Porter, *The Progress of the Nation*, iii, p. 5 still saw the possession of a clock as "the certain indication of prosperity and of personal respectability on the part of the working man".

55. For some of the problems discussed in this and the following section, see especially Keith Thomas, "Work and Leisure in Pre-Industrial Societies", *Past and Present*, no. 29 (Dec. 1964). Also C. Hill, "The Uses of Sabbatarianism", in *Society and Puritanism in Pre-Revolutionary England* (London, 1964); E. S. Furniss, *The Position of the Laborer in a System of Nationalism* (Boston, 1920: repr. New York, 1965); D. C. Coleman, "Labour in the English Economy of the Seventeenth Century", *Econ. Hist. Rev.*, 2nd ser., viii (1955–6); S. Pollard, "Factory Discipline in the Industrial Revolution", *Econ. Hist. Rev.*, 2nd ser., xvi (1963–4); T. S. Ashton, *An Economic History of England in the Eighteenth Century* (London, 1955), ch. vii; W. E. Moore, *Industrialization and Labor* (New York, 1951); and B. F. Hoselitz and W. E. Moore, *Industrialization and Society* (UNESCO, 1963).

56. MS. diaries of Cornelius Ashworth of Wheatley, in Halifax Ref. Lib.; see also T. W. Hanson, "The Diary of a Grandfather", *Trans. Halifax Antiq. Soc.*, 1916. M. Sturge Henderson, *Three Centuries in North Oxfordshire* (Oxford, 1902), pp. 133–46, 103, quotes similar passages (weaving, pig-killing, felling wood, marketing) from the diary of a Charlbury weaver, 1784, etc., but I have been unable to trace the original. It is interesting to compare time-budgets from more primitive peasant economies, e.g. Sol Tax, *Penny Capitalism – a Guatemalan Indian Economy* (Washington, 1953), pp. 104–5; George M. Foster, *A Primitive Mexican Economy* (New York, 1942), pp. 35–8; M. J. Herskovits, *The Economic Life of Primitive Peoples* (New York, 1940), pp. 72–9; Raymond Firth, *Malay Fishermen* (London, 1946), pp. 93–7.

57. *Divers Crab-Tree Lectures* (1639), p. 126, cited in John Brand, *Observations on Popular Antiquities* (London, 1813), i, pp. 459–60. H. Bourne, *Antiquitates Vulgares* (Newcastle, 1725), pp. 115 f. declares that on Saturday afternoons in country places and villages "the Labours of the Plough Ceast, and Refreshment and Ease are over all the Village".

58. J. Houghton, *Collection of Letters* (London, 1683 edn.), p. 177, cited in Furniss, *op. cit.*, p. 121.

59. T. W. Hanson, *op. cit.*, p. 234.

60. J. Clayton, *Friendly Advice to the Poor* (Manchester, 1755), p. 36.

61. *Report of the Trial of Alexander Wadsworth against Peter Laurie* (London, 1811), p. 21. The complaint is particularly directed against the Saddlers.

62. *The Songs of Joseph Mather* (Sheffield, 1862), pp. 88–90. The theme appears to have been popular with ballad-makers. A Birmingham example, "Fuddling Day, or Saint Monday" (for which I am indebted to Mr. Charles Parker) runs:

> Saint Monday brings more ills about,
> For when the money's spent,
> The children's clothes go up the spout,
> Which causes discontent;
> And when at night he staggers home,
> He knows not what to say,
> A fool is more a man than he
> Upon a fuddling day.

63. It was honoured by Mexican weavers in 1800: see Jan Bazant, "Evolution of the textile industry of Puebla, 1544–1845", *Comparative Studies in Society and History*, viii (1964), p. 65. Valuable accounts of the custom in France in the 1850s and 1860s are in George Duveau, *La Vie Ouvriere en France sous le Second Empire* (Paris, 1946), pp. 242–8, and P. Pierrard, *La Vie Ouvrière à Lille sous le Second Empire* (Paris, 1965), pp. 165–6. Edward Young, conducting a survey of labour conditions in Europe, with the assistance of U.S. consuls, mentions the custom in France, Belgium, Prussia, Stockholm, etc. in the 1870s: E. Young, *Labour in Europe and America* (Washington, 1875), pp. 576, 661, 674, 685, &c.

64. Notably in the pits. An old Yorkshire miner informs me that in his youth it was a custom on a bright Monday morning to toss a coin in order to decide whether or not to work. I have also been told that "Saint Monday" is still honoured (1967) in its pristine purity by a few coopers in Burton-on-Trent.

65. E. Young, *op. cit.*, pp. 408–9 (Report of U.S. Consul). Similarly, in some mining districts, "Pay Monday" was recognized by the employers, and the pits were only kept open for repairs: on Monday, only "dead work is going on", *Report of the Select Committee on the Scarcity and Dearness of Coal*, P.P., 1873, x, QQ 177, 201–7.

66. Duveau, *op. cit.*, p. 247. "A Journeyman Engineer" (T. Wright) devotes a whole chapter to "Saint Monday" in his *Some Habits and Customs of the Working Classes* (London, 1867), esp. pp. 112–6, under the mistaken impression that the institution was "comparatively recent", and consequent upon steam power giving rise to "a numerous body of highly skilled and highly paid workmen" – notably engineers!

67. "An Old Potter", *When I was a Child* (London, 1903), pp. 16, 47–9, 52–4, 57–8, 71, 74–5, 81, 185–6, 191. Mr. W. Sokol, of the University of Wisconsin, has directed my attention to many cases reported in the *Staffordshire Potteries Telegraph* in 1853–4, where the employers succeeded in fining or imprisoning workers who neglected work, often on Mondays and Tuesdays. These actions were taken on the pretext of breach of contract (the annual hiring), for which see Daphne Simon, "Master and Servant", in *Democracy and the Labour Movement*, ed. J. Saville (London, 1954). Despite this campaign of prosecutions, the custom of keeping Saint Monday is still noted in the *Report of the Children's Employment Commission*, P.P., 1863, xviii, pp. xxvii-xxviii.

68. F. Place, *Improvement of the Working People* (1834), pp. 13–15: Brit. Mus., Add. MS. 27825. See also John Wade, *History of the Middle and Working Classes*, 3rd edn. (London, 1835), pp. 124–5.

69. See C. Hill, *op. cit.*

70. Clayton, *op. cit.*, p. 13, claimed that "common custom has established so many Holydays, that few of our manufacturing work-folks are closely and regularly employed above two-third parts of their time". See also Furniss, *op. cit.*, pp. 44–5, and the abstract of my paper in the *Bulletin of the Society for the Study of Labour History*, no. 9, 1964.

71. "We have four or five little farmers . . . we have a bricklayer, a carpenter, a blacksmith, and a miller, all of whom . . . are in a very frequent habit of drinking the King's health . . . Their employment is unequal; sometimes they are full of business, and sometimes they have none; generally they have many leisure hours, because . . . the hardest part [of their work] devolves to some men whom they hire . . .", "A Farmer", describing his own village (see note 77 below), in 1798.

72. Cited in J. L. and B. Hammond, *The Village Labourer* (London, 1920), p. 13; E. P. Thompson, *The Making of the English Working Class* (London, 1963), p. 220.

73. See e.g. *Annals of Agriculture*, xxvi (1796), p. 370 n.

74. G. Markham, *The Inrichment of the Weald of Kent*, 10th edn. (London, 1660), pp. 115–7.

75. Attempting to account for a deficiency in his stocks of wheat in 1617, Loder notes: "What should be the cause herof I know not, but it was in that yeare when R. Pearce & Alce were my servants, & then in great love (as it appeared too well) whether he gave it my horses . . . or how it went away, God onely knoweth". *Robert Loder's Farm Accounts*, ed. G. E. Fussell (Camden Soc., 3rd ser., liii, 1936), pp. 59, 127.

76. For an account of an active farmer's day, see William Howitt, *Rural Life of England* (London, 1862), pp. 110–1.

77. Sir Mordaunt Martin in *Bath and West and Southern Counties Society, Letters and Papers* (Bath, 1795), vii, p. 109; "A Farmer", "Observations on Taken-Work and Labour", *Monthly Magazine*, September 1798, May 1799.

78. J. R. Jefferies, *The Toilers of the Field* (London, 1892), pp. 84–8, 211–2.

79. Mary Collier, now a Washer-woman, at Petersfield in Hampshire, *The Woman's Labour: an Epistle to Mr. Stephen Duck; in Answer to his late Poem, called The Thresher's Labour* (London, 1739), pp. 10–11.

80. See examples below, notes 126 and 127, and the valuable critique by Andre Gunder Frank, "Sociology of Development and Underdevelopment of Sociology", *Catalyst* (Buffalo, summer 1967).

81. J. Tucker, *Six Sermons* (Bristol, 1772), pp. 70–1.

82. The change is perhaps signalled at the same time in the ideology of the more enlightened employers: see A. W. Coats, "Changing attitudes to labour in the mid-eighteenth century", *Econ. Hist. Rev.*, 2nd ser., xi (1958–9).

83. See Pollard, *op. cit.*; N. McKendrick, "Josiah Wedgwood and Factory Discipline", *Hist. Journal*, iv (1961); also Thompson, *op. cit.*, pp. 356–74.

84. Order 103 is reproduced in full in *The Law Book of the Crowley Ironworks*, ed. M. W. Flinn (Surtees Soc., clxvii, 1957). See also Law Number 16, "Reckonings". Order Number 40 is in the "Law Book", Brit. Mus., Add. MS. 34555.

85. MS. instructions, *circa* 1780, in Wedgwood MSS. (Barlaston), 26. 19114.

86. "Some regulations and rules made for this manufactory more than 30 years back", dated *circa* 1810, in Wedgwood MSS. (Keele University), 4045.5.

87. A "tell-tale" clock is preserved at Barlaston, but these "tell-tales" (manufactured by John Whitehurst of Derby from about 1750) served only to ensure the regular patrol and attendance of night-watchmen, etc. The first printing time-recorders were made by Bundy in the U.S.A. in 1885. F. A. B. Ward, *op. cit.*, p. 49; also T. Thomson's *Annals of Philosophy*, vi (1815), pp. 418–9; vii (1816), p. 160; Charles Babbage, *On the Economy of Machinery and Manufacturers* (London, 1835), pp. 28, 40; E. Bruton, *op. cit.*, pp. 95–6.

88. Clayton, *loc. cit.*, pp. 19, 42–3.

89. Cited in Furniss, *op. cit.*, p. 114.

90. Anon. [Powell], *A View of Real Grievances* (London, 1772), p. 90.

91. W. Turner, *Sunday Schools Recommended* (Newcastle, 1786), pp. 23, 42.

92. *Rules for the Methodist School of Industry at Pocklington, for the instruction of Poor Girls in Reading, Sewing, Knitting and Marking* (York, 1819), p. 12.

93. *Rules for the Government, Superintendence, and Teaching of the Wesley an Methodist Sunday Schools, York* (York, 1833). See also Harold Silver, *The Concept of Popular Education* (London, 1965), pp. 32–42; David Owen, *English Philanthrophy*, 1660–1960 (Cambridge, Mass., 1965), pp. 23–7.

94. The best account of the employers' problem is in S. Pollard, *The Genesis of Modern Management* (London, 1965), ch. v, "The Adaptation of the Labour Force".

95. E. Lipson, *The Economic History of England*, 6th edn. (London, 1956), iii, pp. 404–6. See e.g. J. L. Ferri, *Londres et les Anglais* (Paris, An xii), i, pp. 163–4. Some of the evidence as to hours is discussed in G. Langenfelt, *The Historic Origin of the Eight Hours Day* (Stockholm, 1954).

96. *A Letter on the Present State of the Labouring Classes in America*, by an intelligent Emigrant at Philadelphia (Bury, 1827).

97. Alfred [S. Kydd], *History of the Factory Movement . . .* (London, 1857), i, p. 283, quoted in P. Mantoux, *The Industrial Revolution in the Eighteenth Century* (London, 1948), p. 427.

98. Anon: *Chapters in the Life of a Dundee Factory Boy* (Dundee, 1887), p. 10.

99. *P.P.*, 1831–32, xv, pp. 177–8. See also the example from the Factory Commission (1833) in Mantoux, *op. cit.*, p. 427.

100. Placard in my possession.

101. For a discussion of the next stage, when the workers had learned "the rules of the game", see E. J. Hobsbawm, *Labouring Men* (London, 1964), ch. xvii, "Custom, Wages and Work-load".

CHAPTER TWO

Peasant Time and Factory Time in Japan

Thomas C. Smith

In "Time, Work-Discipline and Industrial Capitalism", E. P. Thompson describes how factories changed the time-sense of English common people, concluding that the "first generation of factory workers were taught by their masters the importance of time".[1] Workers of that generation brought to the factory an inappropriate inner sense of time which Thompson, following others, calls "task-orientation" and identifies by three characteristics. First, the peasant or labourer pursues an accustomed round of activity that appears to be a necessity imposed by nature's rhythms. Secondly, social intercourse and labour intermingle, blurring the division between "life" and "work,"; there is little distinction between labour and "passing the time of day", and life alternates between bouts of intense effort and idleness. Thirdly, this attitude towards labour appears wasteful and lacking in urgency to men used to living by the clock.[2]

To illustrate, Thompson quotes descriptions of task-orientation in non-market societies. Evans-Pritchard is quoted on the Nuer of the Sudan: "The daily timepiece is the cattle clock, the round of pastoral tasks, and the time of day and the passage of time through a day are to the Nuer primarily the succession of these tasks and their relation to one another".[3] And Pierre Bourdieu on the Algerian peasant:

> Submission to nature is inseparable from submission to the passage of time scanned in the rhythms of nature. The profound feelings of dependency and solidarity toward that nature whose vagaries and rigours he suffers, together with the rhythms and constraints to which he feels the more subject since his techniques are particularly precarious, foster in the Kabyle peasant the attitude of submission and nonchalant indifference to the passage of time which no one dreams of mastering, using up, or saving.[4]

Over the centuries task-orientation had been modified in England, but not so far as to avoid a severe conflict over time when industry developed. The struggle to impose time-discipline on English working people began in the domestic manufacturing districts long before the appearance of the factory. Nevertheless it was in the textile mills and engineering workshops, where time-discipline was most rigorously imposed, that the contest became most intense. Victory came hard; it took employers a generation of fines, money incentives, bells, preachings and schoolings to teach workers the importance of time.[5] Nothing less was required than the creation of "a new human nature upon which . . . incentives could bite effectively".[6]

Thus the struggle over time-discipline reveals with special clarity and economy the deep cultural conflict Thompson sees in the industrial revolution in England. The English transition to modern industry was peculiarly protracted and fraught with difficulty. England's was the first industrial revolution – there were "no Cadillacs, steel mills, or television sets to serve as demonstrations as to the object of the operation" – and all cases of industrialization are unique.[7] Yet Thompson appears to see in time-discipline a universal element of conflict, illustrating at length that "what was said by the mercantilist moralists as to the failures of the eighteenth-century English poor to respond to incentives and disciplines is often repeated . . . of the peoples of the developing countries today". He concludes: "Without time-discipline we could not have the insistent energies of industrial man; and whether this discipline comes in the forms of Methodism, or of Stalinism, or of nationalism, it will come to the developing world".[8]

This seeming prediction of universal cultural conflict over time-discipline describes Japanese industrialization poorly. Although early Japanese factories were deeply troubled by strife between workers and management, difficulties over time do not appear to have been particularly acute. Tokugawa peasants, who by Thompson's reckoning should have been the most task-oriented of people,[9] and whose progeny provided a major part of the early factory labour force, had a lively appreciation of time. Not, of course, of clock time: that would have required the habit of timing critical work independently of night, day and weather – impossible in farming, with or without clocks. Nevertheless time was regarded as fleeting and precious, and great moral value attached to its productive use. Farmers made elaborate efforts to co-ordinate work and to stretch nature's constraints by the skilful use of early and late varieties, between-row planting, straw-covered planting beds, fast-acting fertilizers,[10] and other time-saving devices. None of this ingenuity, however, was for the benefit of individuals. Time was not a personal possession but belonged primarily to families and, through them, to kin, neighbours and villages.

These two aspects of Tokugawa peasant time – the economic value placed on time and the social value placed on its group control and use – call into question the implicit assumption that all pre-industrial people have so casual a sense of time that they must be taught its value. They also suggest that a high economic evaluation of time need not be accompanied by its individualization but may instead be combined with a high degree of time-socialization. This combination in Japan not only sur-vived the coming of the factory but became the basis of a formidable time-discipline within it. Indeed, it appears that time-thrift in the Japanese factory was not imposed unilaterally by management but was a joint creation with workers.

I. PLANNING TIME

If the farm family would escape poverty, it must treat time as precious [kōin oshimubeshi].
By rising early and shortening the daily rest period, two additional hours a day can be worked. That is seven hundred and twenty hours a year: the equivalent of sixty days:
two months when no food is consumed, no wage paid, no oil required for lighting . . .
Thus can the farm family escape the pain of poverty, raise itself up, illuminate the deeds of ancestors, and confer blessings on descendants.[11]

Basic to task-orientation is the given sequence of work set by nature's rhythms so that "the day's tasks . . . seem to disclose themselves, by the logic of need".[12] The only urgency is to do the task indicated; no one need pay close attention to time or to plan it. It bespeaks a certain attitude towards time, therefore, that one of the earliest Japanese books on farming – the *Hyakushō denki* [Farmers' Tales], a compilation of current knowledge of crops, soils and farm management, dating from about 1680 – insisted on the necessity of planning:

Things that must be done during the year ought to be planned and prepared for at the beginning of the year; otherwise everything will bunch up at the end and cause trouble. What must be done during the month should be planned on the first day . . .
If each moment of each day is not properly used, the peasant cannot escape a lifetime of poverty.[13]

If the author is not quite saying that time is money (as in fact he seems to be), he as-serts unambiguously the need for planning. The assertion is not unusual; many of the several score of Tokugawa farm manuals that have been published strike the same theme. They warn the farmer to start preparing for the spring planting immediately after the New Year: to make straw mats and rope, repair tools, see that the animal gear is in order, clear ditches and weed paths, cut wood, trim wind-breaks, make home repairs so that time need not be taken for such work later, and select and treat planting seed to be put away carefully and intermittently exposed to the sun to keep dry.[14] A much-quoted proverb advised, "Plan for the year in the first month; for the day, in the morning".[15] Some purists recommended planning the day's work the night before, making ready any special food and gear that might be needed. Characteris-tically, the advice is detailed. The *Saizōki* [Saizō's Record], a book written about the same time as the compilation just cited, stated that:

If five people are to go the next day to cut grass on the mountain, sickles and carrying poles should be prepared the night before so as to be ready in the morning. Matters should be arranged so that the group can work the upland fields as it returns, and spades should be carried to the fields to be ready . . . Thus each day's work should be planned the night before with great care.[16]

Time horizons were by no means limited to the year. Peasants were exhorted to economize at all times, and especially to save in bumper years for the inevitable bad years, when even the wealthy peasant could lose his land, see his family driven on to the highways by destitution, and find himself another man's servant.[17] There was much discussion by farm writers of measures to improve soils (a notoriously long process), and many crops were held to do best at intervals of some years.[18] "If you grow egg-plant, do not grow it again on the same field for five or six years. It dislikes short intervals and languishes if repeated within two or three years".[19]

From the eighteenth century on, writers of farm manuals were enthusiastic advocates of sericulture, vaunting its profitability and citing cases of whole villages and districts transformed by its adoption.[20] But silkworms were delicate creatures requiring constant and expert care; the beginner could not hope to master the art of raising them for some years, and in the mean time there would inevitably be losses from disease and poor-quality cocoons.[21] Since sericulture required special equipment, a major reallocation of time, and often a reallocation of land for mulberry as well, peasant households were not likely to take it up without thought of the long term. But many did take it up, since there was a dramatic spread of sericulture to new districts in the last half of the Tokugawa period.[22]

Like other Japanese, peasants thought of the family (*ie*) as a corporate entity with a transgenerational life of the highest moral value. Writers of farm manuals were overwhelmingly concerned with the details of farming, but amid the discussion of soils, tools and plant varieties they often touched on themes of larger significance. An eighteenth-century farmer from Hokuriku – who wrote on farming, in order (as farmer-authors often said) "to hand on [his] knowledge of agriculture to [his] descendants" – closed discussion of the rice harvest with instructions on the rituals to be performed. Make a *torii* of bamboo in the field, he advised, and celebrate the Gods of the Five Grains; then husk the rice left over and present it to the ancestors of the family.[23]

Comments on the relation of the family to farming were sometimes more abstract:

> The farm family consists of the fields, wealth and heirlooms handed down from ancestors. This property does not belong to us, the living members of the family. We must not imagine it does, even in our dreams. It belongs to the ancestors who founded the house; we are only entrusted with its care and must pass it on to our descendants . . . There may be events beyond our control, such as flood, fire or illness, as a result of which the sale of property becomes unavoidable. In that case, we must make every effort by saving and planning to recover what has been sold, make the property whole again, and pass it on undiminished to our children and grandchildren.[24]

II. LAND FORMS, CROPPING DECISIONS AND PLANNING

Cropping decisions raised difficult problems of work scheduling, which were in some degree different for each farm family. The idiosyncratic nature of such problems resulted mainly from land forms and patterns of land transfer over long periods of the past. By Tokugawa times, farms were typically composed of a number of small and scattered fields, usually on uneven terrain, where even adjoining fields (according to one writer) were likely to be different in respect to soil, drainage, sunlight, access to water, or exposure to wind. Consequently most farmers grew a mixture of crops and crop varieties, and the mixture tended to differ from neighbour to neighbour. Manual writers insisted that the most important factor separating the quality of one man's farming from another's was skill in matching crops and varieties to the growing conditions of individual fields.[25]

And cropping decisions required anticipation of work-flow. Each crop[26] entailed a number of narrowly timed tasks: seed treatment, soil preparation, planting (and often transplanting), repeated and numbered weedings and fertilizations, and so on. Hence cropping decisions set a work schedule for an entire growing season.[27] Since most families had few adult workers and little or no access to work-animals, careful thought had to be given to the scheduling implications of crop choices. Critical and labour-intensive tasks could not coincide or overlap too broadly;[28] otherwise a planting would be ten days late, a weeding skipped, a fertilization half done.[29] Since there was no way of controlling the weather, scheduling problems were likely to be serious even with the best of planning, and some manual writers gave advice on which tasks to skip in specific cases of time-conflict.[30]

The co-ordination of work on crops grown during the same season was complicated by the widespread practice of double-cropping. Winter and summer crops tended to overlap and crowd one another. A standard problem in manuals was how to get winter wheat planted early enough to stand the onset of cold weather, but not so early as to interfere with the autumn rice harvest. Authors universally advised staggering the autumn harvest by a mixture of early, middle and late rice varieties;[31] however, doing that complicated the summer work schedule and at times required compensatory changes in other crops.[32] Another technique for summer-winter combinations was to start the new crop between the rows of the maturing crop, which changed work schedules by advancing planting dates, and raised an additional delicate problem. The new crop had to be up, firmly rooted and clearly visible by the time the old crop was ready to harvest, but not yet of a size to interfere with harvest work or suffer damage from it.

Planning strategies must have been standardized to some degree, but for a variety of reasons routinization was limited. Fields frequently changed hands through purchase, foreclosure and rental, and each transfer changed the labour requirements and cropping possibilities of two farms. Cropping rules themselves decreed year-to-year changes. Rice varieties were not supposed to be planted continuously to the same land, and crop records in fact show frequent changes of variety on particular fields.[33] A surprising number of common crops required rotation intervals of more than one year: safflower two years, egg-plant five, peas six, Chinese yams seven.[34] Then there was always the wild card of weather, upsetting the most carefully laid plans and forcing complex readjustments. The farm diary of the Noguchi family of Kyushu, running from 1847 to 1865, is a saga of struggle against the weather. Far from being entranced by nature's rhythms, the Noguchi were ever fighting to over-come its irregularities – flood one year, drought the next, too much rain early in the summer, too little later.[35]

Many authors insisted on record-keeping as an aid to planning – otherwise who could remember how long it was since yams had been grown on "front field"? – and some authors had very exacting standards of the art. In his treatise on cotton, Ōkura Nagatsune advocated standardizing time for recording yields: "After picking the cotton each day, return immediately to the house, weigh the cotton and enter the results in a notebook at so-called picking-weight, since the weight will vary later on".[36] No doubt record-keeping was exceptional, but farm records none the less survive in considerable numbers and from widely scattered places. The Noguchi family diary gives rice yields annually for each field, and records the average yield per *tan* of land for each variety.

III. TIME IN THE ISHIKAWA FARM DIARY

We get a realistic, as opposed to a theoretical or cautionary, view of the use of time in the diary for 1867 of the head of a family named Ishikawa,[37] who lived in the hilly country west of Edo, where farming was less commercial and technically advanced than in some parts of the country. For every day of the year, Ishikawa notes his activities, though not what others in the family did, and unfortunately his notations are terse – "worked wheat", "went to market" – often leaving the reader with an imperfect idea of what he did. Yet the 354 entries, accounting for every day of the lunar year,[38] give us as close a view of the actual use of time by a Tokugawa farmer as we are likely to get. There is also a helpful year-end summary of crop yields, attesting to Ishikawa's interest in productivity, and to the fact that the family grew twelve crops and also raised silkworms. To coordinate so many operations took expert timing, and it was not unusual for Ishikawa to go from cutting one crop, to seeding another, milling a third, then back to threshing the first, on successive days.

In Ishikawa's case, co-ordination was complicated by status. As a low-ranking samurai and a man of importance in his village, he was obliged to spend thirty-nine days during the year on public and ceremonial functions, some of which by their nature could not have been timed for his convenience. The remaining 315 days were distributed broadly among 222 outside workdays, 35 inside workdays, 2 market-days, 38 mixed workdays (part inside and part outside, including 16 part-day trips to market) and 18 rest-days. What was meant by "inside work" is uncertain but evidently not "rest", which was named separately. In addition to the usual chores rec-ommended for slack seasons, such as rope-making, tool repair and the treatment of seeds, inside work may have included help with the silkworms, for which the women of the family were responsible, and the record-keeping necessary for the year-end summary of yields. Outside work is invariably specified, providing the diary's most detailed information on the use of time.

Three things stand out in these detailed entries: the extraordinary variability of tasks from day to day, the steadiness of work-flow, and the general infrequency of rest-days. One hundred and twenty-seven different field tasks (many frequently repeated) are recorded during the year. Often two or three appear in a single day, and each day's tasks tend to vary from those of the previous day. The entries give an imme-diate impression of this variability, but it is made clearer by some simple counting. If we classify each of the 260 outside workdays (including 38 mixed workdays) by the degree of correspondence between the work done on that day and the work done on the previous outside workday, we get the following breakdown: tasks completely different, 158 (60.7 per cent); tasks partly different, 61 (23.4 per cent); and tasks the same, 41 (15.7 per cent).

Such variability does not necessarily mean continuous and radical improvisation. Within broad limits, the round of work was implicit in the cropping pattern. But the cropping pattern itself was not a given; it was a considered plan to which there were possible alternatives, as is clear from the important changes in cropping on the Ishikawa holding between 1720 (for which there is a year-end summary) and 1867. At the same time, with so many crops and tasks the detailed and final ordering of work on many days must have waited until the last minute. Unforeseen events also occa-sioned adjustment in plans: village celebration of much-needed rain in the eighth month; trips to market (possibly linked to price movements); emergency construc-tion that required several days of timber-cutting, followed by irregular visits from a carpenter who had to be assisted. There is some indication of agricultural rhythms in the tendency of public work to fall early in the year, before the spring planting. But some duties continued at regular intervals during the year, and rest-days show little seasonal variation. The most rest-days in any month is five in the first; and astonish-ingly, no month after the third has more than one, except the seventh month with three. The alternating bouts of intense work and leisure that Thompson emphasizes are not easily discernible, but the Ishikawa family may have been exceptional.

. . .

IV. CONCEPTS OF TIME AND PRODUCTIVITY

Where farmers had to ponder the duration, order and potential interchange of tasks, they were not likely to find difficulty in thinking of time abstractly relative to their work. This occurred, in fact, before the shift of land from large to small holders was far advanced. The earliest Japanese book on farming, the *Shimmin kangetsu shū*,[39] dating from the first half of the seventeenth century, lists the man-days per unit of

land required for various farming operations on both paddy and upland.[40] Such estimates were a standard feature of later farm manuals and became more refined with
time. They soon included not only man-days per unit of land for all the major crops
of a district, but an increasingly detailed breakdown of labour time for each crop by
task, requiring figures in tenths of man-days, with adjustments if the work was done
by women or children.[41]

In addition to yields and labour requirements, the manuals often listed for the
major staples the cost per *tan* of land for fertilizer, tools, wages, animal hire, taxes,
and so on. The difference between yields and these costs may be taken as the return
on family labour. (Costs were sometimes cited in kind but could be readily converted
to money at market prices.) Thus the monetary return on family labour on a man-
day basis was theoretically calculable for major crops.[42] Rough estimates of this kind
must have informed shifts in cropping when farmers, in great numbers and often
against the law, took significant amounts of land out of rice to grow cotton, mulberry, indigo, sugar, tobacco, and rush for *tatami* mats.[43]

V. TIME, FAMILY AND COMMUNITY

Time was one of the two major productive resources of Japanese peasants; and like its
counterpart, property, it belonged to the family, a condition reflected in law. Families
were punishable for the transgressions of individual members, and were therefore
expected to control them. In population registers – the basic documents of administrative and legal control – individuals were always entered by family membership,
never autonomously, though sometimes of necessity they were listed as one-person
families. The right to sit in the village assembly, to draw water from the irrigation system, to participate in the management of the shrine, even to reside in the community:
all were lodged in families, never in individuals. If all living members of a family died,
the family's name and rights (*kabu*) in the village would continue to exist if there were
property to inherit; relatives or the village itself would then appoint an heir, whether
kin or not, to inherit the family name, house, ancestors and tax burdens.

The primacy of the family over its members is seen in the language of farm manuals.
If by "farmer" we mean an individual man or woman managing a farm, agricultural
writers had no equivalent. Of course they had several common words for peasant –
nōmin, hyakushō and *nōfu* – but none that necessarily suggested a managerial role.
When they had need to express the idea of a decision-making agent in farming, they
used the word *nōka* or farm family. Thus the *nōka* was said to ponder, decide, plan,
harvest, succeed or fail, and to have ancestors and descendants.

Some manual writers were concerned with how to ensure the high degree of individual compliance with *nōka* decisions that this required. The need for compliance
was urgent, since it was a "principle [*ri*] always to be kept in mind" that the *nōka*
could not move in unison (*sorotte*), hence farm successfully, without "a complete
harmony of wills". The utmost care should be taken, therefore, to raise children not

to be self-willed (*wagamama*) or self-indulgent (*hoshiimama*), so that they might grow up to be frugal and forbearing and "modestly give way to others":

> Children must be warned from an early age against extravagance and wilfulness and self-indulgence. The clothing and other articles they use must be kept below the family's status and means. If, out of too much love, children are indulged with fine things, they will come to love extravagance, and this extravagance will grow with age. Restraint becomes difficult if it is not taught early.[44]

Time, which belonged to the family, also belonged through it to the village and neighbours on whom the family depended for access to water, common land, the village shrine and mutual aid. Villages laid down complex rules on the use of time: the proper number of days' mourning for family members of different status; the kind and number of courses to be served guests at weddings and funerals, and hence the time spent preparing them; the occasions on which sake could be brought to the fields and served during work-breaks; whether villagers could leave the village for work outside.[45] Many villages set standard wage rates for various kinds of farm work, by sex, at various levels of skill.[46] Leaving work for New Year's greetings, except between parents and children, was forbidden in some villages.[47]

As the by-laws of village youth groups (*wakashū*) show, the communal regulation of time was by no means a strictly utilitarian concern. These documents are moral protocols having little or nothing to do with procedural matters within the group. They enjoin frugal, decorous, sober and industrious behaviour, which is identified with filial piety and winning the favour of the "Gods of Heaven and Earth" (*tenchi kamigami*). They illustrate and warn against self-indulgence, avarice, licentiousness, quarrelsomeness, and other kinds of immorality associated with the misuse of time. Spending "leisure with young friends may result in untoward events and unfiliality towards father and mother".[48] Thus members are warned never to miss a meeting of the youth group (where they were under the sway of elders); always to be present in the group on festival days; to rise early, work fiercely, and devote themselves single-mindedly to family occupations; to spend their spare time studying, reading and writing; not to leave the village for entertainment or festivals, not to drink or gamble, not to sing popular songs; not to play the samisen or use slang. To disobey such injunctions would disgrace parents and the village and invite the punishment of the gods.[49]

No doubt because the village was considered a single moral sphere, efforts were made to monitor and improve the use of time in the community. A youth group in Wake county in Bizen province felt impelled to designate certain days only that could be observed as holidays in the village, and to mete out punishment (*ishu-gaeshi*) to evil persons violating this dispensation. The *Hōtokusha*, a society inspired by the teachings of the late Tokugawa agrarian moralist Ninomiya Sontoku, gave much attention to the proper use of time and to the abolition or curtailment of singing, dancing and theatrical performances in villages. A certain follower of Ninomiya, named Furuhashi, made up a time schedule (a "work/rest table") and exhorted fellow villagers to follow it; another made the rounds of the village each morning wakening people to the sound of a wooden clapper.[50]

The language of Tokugawa agriculture was rich in vocabulary expressing work in a context of obligation to others. *Suke* was labour given by a dependent to a protector in return and gratitude for benefits such as the loan of land, animals and a house.[51] *Yui* was an equal exchange of like labour such as mutual help in transplanting rice. *Hōkō* was service while living as a servant and quasi-member in another's family. There were numerous words for work apart from social relations, but these refer to the physical act or effort of work (*shigoto, hataraki, kasegi*). It is difficult to find any word that suggests work in a social context without carrying a sense of obligation to others.

After the Meiji Restoration in 1868, this limitation of vocabulary became an inconvenience. None of the words mentioned could properly be used for factory employment, which in both theory and law was held by the new westernizing government to result from a contract freely entered into by autonomous and equal parties. So foreign to social experience was this notion, however, that no satisfactory general term for worker was found until the 1930s.

Meanwhile the word *shokkō*, coined in middle Meiji, became the standard word for factory worker. From the beginning it was marked by the stigma of poverty and unattached status. It soon became a term of opprobrium, and workers vigorously objected that its use branded them as outcasts. Companies responded by coining new words for worker in company documents; but none came into general use. *Shokkō*, despite its heavy pejorative overtones, continued to be the usual word for factory worker until the 1910s. The long and unsuccessful search for a satisfactory word suggests the great difficulty of combining in the same word both the idea of honour and the idea of working for oneself without respect to social obligation, an uncongenial combination to Tokugawa peasants and early industrial workers alike.

VI. TIME AND MODERN INDUSTRY

Two general propositions have been advanced in this paper: first, that late Tokugawa peasants had a lively, morally rooted sense of the preciousness of time; and secondly, that they thought of time as socially rather than individually controlled. This is, of course, a matter of degree. Tokugawa peasants were more sensitive to the value of time than populations who have been described as task-oriented, but they were no doubt less so than modern Japanese factory workers.[52] In addition, a wide variation in attitudes must be assumed in so large a population. Nevertheless, owing to the near universality among peasants of family farming, the importance of labour intensity to successful farming, and the frequent movement of farm families up and down the landholding and social scales of their villages, it is difficult to think of any large part of the farming population as casual about time or its social control.

Tokugawa peasants did not, of course, go into modern factories in any significant numbers, and their children and grandchildren, who did, had different formative experiences. Farming itself changed remarkably little from the grandparents' time to the grandchildren's. The structural features of agriculture of the previous century – small farms, overwhelming dependence on family labour, integration of farming and by-employment – persisted beyond the Second World War. But during this time, the environment of farming was transformed, and in few ways so remarkably as by the spread of schools, railroads and public offices, all of which increased the awareness of clock time among country people. It was a slow process, however. Until 1900 a significant proportion of children did not attend school, especially in country districts, and at that date, even in the largest and most modern factories, the vast majority of blue-collar workers had had four years of schooling or less. The influence of the railway came yet more gradually. Tokyo was not joined to Osaka by rail directly until 1889, to Aomori in the north of Honshu until 1891, and to Shimonoseki in the extreme south until 1901.[53]

The first two generations of Japanese factory workers, covering roughly the years 1880 to 1920 (when Tokugawa influence would have been most direct and discernible), were marked by troubled and occasionally violent labour relations. Problems, moreover, were clearly most intense in large and heavily capitalized enterprises, where the regulation of time was strictest. Yet time does not seem to have been a critical issue between workers and managers. Neither group spoke passionately of problems of time; indeed, government statistics show that relatively few labour disputes before the Second World War originated in part over working hours, and even fewer primarily over them.[54]

The workers' relative lack of interest in a shorter working day may partly reflect the Tokugawa peasant preference for income over leisure, up to a level near the limits of physical endurance. In 1889, when the Tokyo tramcar workers demanded a ten-hour day, they did not ask for a reduction in the eighteen hours they worked, but only for "proportional" overtime pay after ten hours. Many observers noted the eagerness of workers to work overtime. Yokoyama Gennosuke in 1897 wrote that, despite a normal working day of twelve to fourteen hours, most workers did several additional hours of overtime daily. Masumoto Uhei, an engineer with many years of factory experience, said in 1919 – when the regular working day was ten to twelve hours – that workers judged the attractiveness of a factory by the amount of overtime available in it, and that employers stole skilled workers from one another with promises of overtime. In the early 1920s letters from workers to the plant newspapers at the Yawata steel works complained about favouritism in the assignment of overtime, stating that senior workers got all the overtime. No worker letter complained of excessive overtime.[55]

Equally important in easing early problems of time in industry was the worker conception of the employment relationship as properly governed by hierarchical ethics. Worker criticism of employers was couched in moral language calling for loving concern for workers and condemning its absence as cruel and unrighteous. Even in labour disputes entailing work stoppages before 1918, workers put their demands to management in the form of a "petition"; and in talks to settle disputes they co-operated with management to avoid even the appearance of a negotiation between equals.[56] Workers clearly observed these forms in order to preserve the integrity of their moral claim to hierarchical justice. They may have been similarly constrained from making prime issues of working hours, holidays, and fines for tardiness by the belief that to do so would call into question the moral basis of the relationship.

On the understanding that the employment relationship was not or ought not to be strictly impersonal, managers often tolerated a certain tardiness and absenteeism. In some factories there was a customary leeway between official and actual starting times.[57] Punishments for tardiness, set out in company regulations in the early part of the century, do not seem particularly harsh, and efforts to discourage absenteeism placed more emphasis on bonuses for attendance than on penalties for absence. As late as 1900 the Yokosuka naval arsenal did not automatically discharge a worker for absenteeism until three weeks had gone by without word from the offender.[58] Commonly, after the settlement of work stoppages, and after workers apologized for their actions, employers granted pay to workers for the time lost in striking – gestures on both sides aimed at healing a breached moral relationship.

Managers felt free, on the other hand, to demand workers' time whenever and in almost whatever amounts required. Even the most firmly established holidays were routinely cancelled when work-flow was heavy.[59] Daily working hours were only nominally fixed, and in busy periods work began well before the prescribed hour and continued long after finishing time. Company rules commonly provided for occasions on which workers would work an entire night of overtime following the regular working day.[60]

How alert and energetic workers could have been during such marathons is doubtful, but they rarely complained loudly. In fact, no time-related issue seems to have aroused worker indignation as much as the appearance of favouritism in promotions and rises, and invidious distinctions between white-collar and blue-collar workers. *Rōdō sekai* [The World of Work], a turn-of-the-century magazine promoting unions, complained: "Don't our workers know the value of work time?".[61] In 1914 *Yūai shinpō* [Friendly Society News], the official organ of a nascent trade union, ran an editorial purporting to voice what workers demanded of "capitalists". Included were demands for treatment with parental love (*oyagokoro*), profit-sharing, equal treatment with white-collar employees, promotion based on ability (*jitsuryoku*) and character (*jinkaku*) rather than on personal connections (*enko*), and bonuses for outstanding performance – nothing about working hours, pace of work, holidays, or penalties for tardiness.[62]

Significantly, the spread of discussion among employers in the 1910s about shortening working hours was based not on worker demands but on the growing belief, supported by experimental evidence, that excessive working hours lowered labour productivity and so undermined Japan's competitive position in the world.[63] Workers themselves cited this argument in letters to the press, claiming that shorter hours would permit them to work more efficiently and make a larger contribution to the nation's industry.[64] Another worker argument for shorter hours had a similar thrust, namely that excessive working hours hampered the educational and moral development of workers to the detriment not only of themselves but also of industry and society.[65] Rarely, if ever, did workers argue for shorter hours on explicitly selfish grounds. Their insistence on seeing issues of time in the context of social and moral relations is suggested by their reaction to the call of the Paris peace conference in 1919 for world-wide reform of working conditions. Japanese employers were alarmed at the inclusion in the call of a demand for the eight-hour day, claiming compliance would raise their labour costs prohibitively. Japanese workers, on the other hand, paid less attention to the eight-hour issue than to the provision that labour was not a commodity.[66] Workers took this as international validation of their demand for recognition of worker *jinkaku* (moral personality), and hence for the improvement of their status, both in companies and in society generally.

Still, time-discipline in Japanese factories in the early twentieth century was unquestionably lax by present standards, and laxness was not overcome for some decades.[67] The gradual improvement was, in part, the result of a more finely calibrated sense of time that came with the increased use of clocks and watches generally, and from cumulative experience with factory time. But more important than either was the gradual legitimation of the factory through company reforms which raised worker status, increased job security and real wages, gave some measure of protection against sickness, injury and old age, shortened working hours, and institutionalized worker-management consultation. From the beginning there had been a certain presumption in favour of the factory's legitimacy because of its seeming parallel to family and community authorities. However, employers' and managers' behaviour undercut the hopes stirred by this parallel, demoralizing and angering workers. But as the treatment of workers slowly improved, so did their time-discipline. Workers may not have been always happy with the resulting disposition of their time (and may not be today), but they came to recognize its legitimacy.

This acceptance of factory time seems to be a result not of the transcendence of the pre-industrial time-sense, as Thompson suggests took place in England, but of the more or less untroubled adaptation of the older time-sense to the requirements of the factory. Let me suggest three reasons for this view. (1) Something like the revolution in time-sense of which Thompson speaks had already taken place. No doubt elements of task-orientation remained, as they do today, but it seems unlikely that they were so pervasive as to pose a major obstacle to modern industry. (2) If they had posed such an obstacle, early Japanese industry would have been accompanied by an ideological attack on workers' time behaviour, and there is little evidence of anything of the kind. (3) The feature of pre-industrial time most closely linked to social processes – the notion that in significant social relationships time does not belong unconditionally to the individual – not only survives today but has become a central element in time-discipline in Japanese business and industry.

It is well known that workers' restriction of output was a major problem in U.S. industry from early in the history of the factory.[68] Underlying the practice were (and are) beliefs about what constituted a fair day's work, the fear that exceeding a certain rate or "stint" would result in the elimination of jobs, and the worry that any increase in the pace of work in order to boost piece-work earnings would quickly lead to a reduction in rates. Japanese managers must have been aware of these problems, since a Japanese translation of Frederick W. Taylor's *Principles of Scientific Management* (1911) was published in 1913,[69] and since western views on management generally were widely discussed. Yet I have never encountered a mention of the problem specifically with reference to Japanese industry in the period before 1920 (which I know best and in which such a reference would most likely be found); nor have I discovered an indigenous word for "stint". Managers often complained about the slow pace of Japanese workers, but they attributed this pace to bad work habits, individual laziness, even overwork – never, that I know of, to a collective effort of workers to control time against the employer.[70]

Employers did adopt U.S. pay schemes that based individual pay rates on output per unit of time, with workers who produced more getting a higher hourly rate. In the United States such plans represented an effort by employers to overcome group restrictions on output by appealing to the individual worker's wish for higher earnings. These plans appealed to the same desire in Japan but were evidently not inspired by the problem of output restriction. On the contrary, when production processes permitted, management frequently adopted incentive plans that used the group rather than the individual as the unit of account. The earnings of small work groups were calculated as a whole: groups who produced more in a given time earned more, and individuals shared according to some prearranged allocation.[71] Somewhat similar schemes had been tried in the United States, and were poison to Taylor. In his view, they were bound to fail because they gave the individual no significant incentive: group members would share any group gain whether they worked hard or not.[72] Japanese managers were apparently not anxious about this possibility and relied on the wish of individual workers to be seen by their workmates as doing their utmost to increase the earnings of the group.

From personal experience, managers were sensitive to the effect of hierarchic relations on the control of time. Autobiographies of businessmen are full of passages about youthful periods of heroic sacrifice and hard work for a company or patron. Satō Kiichirō, who went from Tokyo university to the Mitsui bank in 1917, explains why he worked day and night without holidays after joining the bank: "To tell the truth, I did not work hard because I liked to, but if I did not my superior would be embarassed. So I worked with the idea of helping my superior achieve his objectives: if I must give an explanation, that would be it".[73]

. . .

VII. CONCLUSION

To return to Thompson, he was surely right that the values attached to time by pre-industrial people profoundly affect the nature of worker adaptation to factory time-discipline. He would appear to be mistaken in predicting (in so far as he did) that the pre-industrial time-sense is necessarily a source of resistance to the factory.

For Thompson these features seem to be at or near the heart of worker resistance to early capitalist industry since he speaks of time-measurement "as a means of labour exploitation". The idea sounds Marxian: the employer pays the worker for only part of his working time, taking the remainder without compensation. That would indeed be exploitive, and would sufficiently explain worker resistance. But that is not what Thompson means by exploitation.[74] The issue, instead, is the loss of human values and a way of life associated with task-orientation: presumably the blurring of the distinction between life and work, the capacity for play, the sense of necessity in the round of tasks appointed by nature's rhythms. These values were obliterated by the enforcement of factory time with the aid of puritanism. "Puritanism, in its marriage of convenience with industrial capitalism, was the agent which converted men to the new valuations of time; which taught children in their infancy to improve each shining hour; and which saturated men's minds with the equation, time is money". This conversion entailed "the most far-reaching conflict" and was marked by "exploitation and . . . resistance to exploitation".[75] Exploitation then appears to consist in the loss of vital inner freedoms, submission to machine time and acceptance of a crabbed time-is-money view of life. None of these things could have happened without task-orientation; without this prior state of grace, there could not have been this fall. Moreover this is an experience which "the developing world must live through and grow through".[76]

The Japanese do not seem to have had such a fall. Tokugawa peasants had a time-sense strikingly different from task-orientation. They cannot have had a fine sense of clock time, of course, and the resulting initial awkwardness with the factory regime might have developed into a serious issue. But it did not, and the prolonged period of conflict with management was mainly over other matters. One of the reasons it did not would seem to be that workers also had significant views on the ownership of time – an aspect of time-sense that Thompson does not treat directly. Time for workers *and* managers was enmeshed in social structure: an aspect of social relations that could only in marginal cases be disregarded so that time could be bought and sold like rice-cakes. The simultaneously high economic and social evaluations of time seem to have been crucial in facilitating the establishment of time-discipline in Japanese factories. The real struggle in Japanese industry was over the moral implications of the employer-employee relationship. As these became clearer, time-discipline, to all appearances, steadily tightened without crisis over the process.

Tokugawa peasants seem so far removed from the attitudes attributed to pre-industrial English working people by Thompson that I cannot help wondering if he has not exaggerated the strength and prevalence of task-orientation in eighteenth-century England. The most convincing instances of task-orientation cited come from ethnographic accounts of pre-market societies. Contemporary criticisms of the work habits of English common people, though bearing heavily on time, do not on the whole point specifically to task-orientation. They do indeed suggest a strong resistance to work on terms satisfactory to employers and moralists, but do not necessarily reveal the reasons for resistance. Thompson quotes the complaint of a writer in an agricultural magazine in 1800 that "When a labourer becomes possessed of more land than he and his family can cultivate in the evenings . . . the farmer can no longer depend on him for constant work".[77] This sounds like a wish for independence on the worker's part rather than necessarily a casual attitude towards time. He also quotes Francis Place who, speaking from experience, wrote in 1829 that working men ran from twelve- to eighteen-hour working days when they could no longer stand them, and that "in proportion as a man's case is hopeless will such fits more frequently occur and be of longer duration".[78] This may show a lack of time-discipline from an employer's viewpoint, but it is difficult to see what it necessarily has to do with task-orientation.

Thompson himself seems to be of two minds about the prevalence and strength of task-orientation. On the one hand, it was so deeply seated that the first generation of factory workers had to be taught by their masters the value of time. On the other:

> The entire economy of the small farmer may be task-oriented; but within it there may be a division of labour, and allocation of roles, and the discipline of an employer-employed relationship between the farmer and his children. Even here time is beginning to become money, the employer's money. As soon as actual hands are employed the shift from task-orientation to timed labour is marked. It is true that the timing of work can be done independently of any time-piece – and indeed precedes the diffusion of the clock.[79]

This is a telling passage not only because it seems to place the beginning of timed labour rather far back in English history, but also for the individualism it sees within the family of the small farmer in England.

Perhaps the conflict over time between employers and workers in eighteenth-century England was not over the value of time, but over who owned it and on what terms. In the first half of the nineteenth century in the United States work was regarded as ennobling only when it was independent, self-directed and self-profiting, or was undertaken in preparation for that state. The man who, as a more or less permanent arrangement, sold his time did so, according to Lincoln, "because of either a dependent nature . . . or improvidence, folly, or singular misfortune". According to a nineteenth-century treatise on wages in the United States, the man who worked for hire "not only will not, but cannot, being a man, labor as he would for himself'.[80] The Boston carpenters, masons and stonecutters in 1835 proclaimed that the "God of the Universe has given us time, health and strength. We utterly deny the right of any man to dictate to us how much of it we shall sell".[81]

Many English working people in the late eighteenth century would have understood and sympathized with this statement. No Japanese in 1835 could possibly have understood the statement[82] or taken a favourable view of it if they did. The consequence of this difference for the pre-industrial meaning of time in the two cultures may account in part for the greater struggle over time in English factories, and possibly also the slacker time-discipline in English and American industry today. If so, the source of the divergence would seem to have less to do with time-sense (as Thompson uses the term) than with different conceptions of the individual in society.

NOTES

1. E. P. Thompson, "Time, Work-Discipline and Industrial Capitalism", *Past and Present*, no. 38 (Dec. 1967), p. 86.
2. *Ibid.*, p. 60.
3. *Ibid.*, p. 58.
4. Pierre Bourdieu, "The Attitude of the Algerian Peasant toward Time", in Julian Pitt-Rivers (ed.), *Mediterranean Countrymen* (Paris, 1969), p. 57. Jacques Le Goff describes a similar attitude in fourteenth-century Europe: "On the whole, labor time was still the time of an economy dominated by agrarian rhythms, free of haste, careless of exactitude, unconcerned by productivity – and of a society created in the image of the economy, *sober and modest*, without enormous appetites, undemanding, and incapable of quantitative efforts": Jacques Le Goff, *Time, Work and Culture in the Middle Ages* (Chicago, 1980), p. 44. David Landes holds that, before the railway, task-orientation was characteristic of rural societies everywhere: David Landes, *Revolution in Time: Clocks and the Making of the Modern World* (Cambridge, Mass., 1983), pp. 25, 72.
5. Thompson, "Time, Work-Discipline and Industrial Capitalism", pp. 83, 85, 90.
6. *Ibid.*, p. 57.
7. *Ibid.*, p. 80.
8. *Ibid.*, pp. 91, 93.
9. Thompson attributes great importance to the development of wage labour in farming bringing a shift from task-orientation to timed labour (*ibid.*, p. 61). In the latter half of the Tokugawa period, Japanese farming was carried on almost exclusively with family and family exchange labour.
10. "It is characteristic of cotton that if fertilization is late the branches and leaves grow luxuriantly but the blossoms are sparse . . . After midsummer a fast-acting fertilizer [*ashi-hayaki koe*] may be used. Although all plants require fertilizer, in the case of cotton the timing of the application is particularly important in determining profit and loss for the farmer". The author also states that in Bingo province dried sardines were used as fertilizer because they were "fast-acting", helping to bring the plant to maturity before the typhoon season: Ōkura Nagatsune, *Menpo yōmu* [Essentials of Cotton Farming] (1833), in *Nihon kagaku koten zenshū* [Classics of Japanese Science], ed. Saigusa Hiroto (Tokyo, 1942–6), xi, pp. 270, 286.
11. Itō Masanari of Kozuki province, *Nōgyō mōkun* [Lessons on Farming] (1840), in *Nihon nōsho zenshū*. [Collection of Books on Japanese Farming], 31 vols. (Tokyo, 1977–81), v.

12. Thompson, "Time, Work-Discipline and Industrial Capitalism", p. 59. Landes also makes the point: "We have already noted the contrast between the 'natural' day of the peasant, marked and punctuated by the *given sequence* of agricultural tasks, and the man-made day of the townsman. The former is defined by the sun. The latter is bounded by artificial time signals and the technology of illumination and is devoted to the same task or an array of tasks *in no given sequence*": Landes, *Revolution in Time*, p. 72 (my italics).

13. *Hyakushō denki* [Farmers' Tales] (Tokyo, 1977), i, p. 46.

14. For representative statements explicitly or implicitly advocating planning, see Miyanaga Shōun, *Shika. nōgyō dan* [Farm Family Talks] (1789), in *Nikon nōsho zenshū*, vi, pp. 43, 238; Fuchizawa En'emon, *Keiyū kōsaku shō* [Farming in Keiyu] (1847), *ibid.*, ii, p. 12; Takamine Yoshitada, *Nōmin no kinkōsaku no shidai oboegaki* [Methods of Cultivation for Peasants] (1789), *ibid.*, ii, p. 291; Onuki Man'emon, *Nōka shōkei skō* [Short-Cuts for Farm Families] (1822), *ibid.*, xxii, p. 20; Ōzeki Masunari, *Kashoku kō* [Thoughts on Farming] (1821), *ibid.*, xxii, p. 113. The books cited above come from the provinces of Etchū, Rikchū, Iwashiro and Shimotsuke; all except Shimotsuke were relatively backward economically.

15. Miyanaga Shōun, *Shika nōgyō dan*, p. 208.

16. Ōhata Saizō of Kii province, *Saizōki* [Saizō's Record] (c. 1700), in *Hōken chihō keizai shiryō* [Regional Materials on the Feudal Economy], ed. Ono Takeo (Tokyo, 1932), ii, p. 410.

17. Sunakawa Yasui of Awa province, *Nōjuku kanseiki* [A True Account of Farming Technique] (1723), *in Nihon nōsho zenshū*, x, p. 333; Miyaoi Yasuo of Shimōsa province, *Nōgyō yōshū* [Essentials of Farming] (1812), *ibid.*, iii, p. 17; Miyanaga Shōun, *Shika nōgyō dan*, pp. 166, 201, 270. Here again was proverbial advice: "In drought, keep the boats repaired; in summer, make winter clothing".

18. Yoshida Tomonao of Kōzuke province, *Kaikō suchi* [Handbook on Cultivating New Land] (1795), in *Nihon nōsho zenshū*, iii, pp. 99–215.

19. Itō Masanari, *Nōgyō mōkun*, p. 253.

20. The author of *Yōsan kinuburui* [Secrets of Sericulture] (1813) tells how since the 1760s the development of sericulture and weaving had transformed the economy of his home district in Ōmi. As a result, tens of thousands of people now made their living from weaving and "the wilderness around these mean villages has been developed". He believed that in this way whole provinces could be enriched: "It is urgent to open up unused areas of river bottom . . . planting them with mulberry as a basis for sericulture. When silk products of a *kuni* [province] are sold to other provinces, the country and people are enriched. This is called profit to the province [*kokueki*]". Sansō koten kankōkai (ed.), *Sansō koten shūsei* [Classics on Sericulture and Mulberry] (Tokyo, 1930), ii, pp. 221, 322.

21. Ta Tomonao, *Yōsan suchi* [Handbook of Sericulture] (1794), National Diet Library, Tokyo, 1:5.

22. Shōji Kichinosuke, *Kinsei yōsan hattatsu shi* [Development of Sericulture in the Tokugawa Period] (Tokyo, 1964), p. 29.

23. Miyanaga Shōun, *Shika nōgyō dan*, p. 216. Elsewhere the author explains the connection between the gods, farming and the family. Heaven decreed all occupations, including the back-breaking work of farming. Persons who did this work "sincerely" would accumulate "hidden virtue" [*intoku*] and would some day receive the "rewards" [*yōhō*] of the gods, which "reach even to descendants" (pp. 61–2).

24. Miyaoi Yasuo, *Nōgyō yōshū*, pp. 15–16.
25. *Nihon nōsho zenshū*, xxii, p. 335.
26. Fukushima Teiyū of Musashi province, *Kōsaku shiyō sho* [Methods of Cultivation] (1839–42), *ibid.*, xxii, pp. 203–80, discusses over thirty crops grown in his village, in most cases listing several varieties of each: twenty-five for rice, twelve for potatoes, six for wheat, fourteen for buckwheat.
27. Frederick Barth describes a somewhat similar need to plan cropping among the Fur-speaking agriculturalists in central Africa: "Every individual needs to obtain plots of several kinds, suitable for different crops and uses. A configuration of sizes and types of farm implies an allocation of labour to alternative products: millet, and some onions, for basic subsistence, and readily marketable crops such as tomatoes, wheat, garlic, onions for cash needs . . . In the course of the year, every person will need to cultivate at least one farm [plot] in each category. One may choose to distribute the labour more equally between summer and winter crops. Individual skills and preferences, and established usufruct rights to irrigated land, will influence these allocations": Frederick Barth, "Economic Spheres in Darfur", in Raymond Firth (ed.), *Themes in Economic Anthropology* (London, 1978), p. 189.
28. "From the spring ploughing through planting, transplanting and weeding to the autumn, every task has its proper time. Even a single day's delay of a task may result in "top failure in a bumper year": Miyanaga Shōun, *Shika nōgyō dan*, pp. 208–9.
29. The diary of the Noguchi family in modern Fukuoka prefecture provides concrete illustrations of how one operation's getting off schedule affected others: *Noguchi ke nikki* [Diary of the Noguchi Family] (1847–65), in *Nihon nōsho zenshū*, xi, p. 225.
30. [Unknown author from Hizen province], *Sato kagami* [Village Mirror] (*c.* 1830–40), *ibid.*, xi, p. 105; Fukushima Teiyū, *Kōsaku shiyō sho*, p. 206.
31. The importance of varieties is suggested in Miyanaga Shōun, *Shika nōgyō dan*, pp. 79–81. The author listed only those varieties used in his and neighbouring villages: nine early, twenty-four middle and thirty-three late varieties.
32. Deciding the optimum proportions of different varieties was a complicated matter. Varieties often had particular soil preferences and so were not perfectly interchangeable. Also, although early varieties relieved pressure on the autumn planting, they yielded poorly and tended to interfere with the spring wheat harvest; late varieties yielded well but required more labour to protect them from birds and animals, encroached on the autumn planting, and were subject to damage from early winter weather. Although middle varieties alleviated these strains and yielded well, they concentrated labour at the busiest time of year for other crops.
33. For examples, see Nakamura Satoru, "Kinsei senshin chiiki no nōgyō kōzō" [The Structure of Agriculture in Advanced Regions in the Tokugawa Period], *Kyōto daigaku jimbun kagaku kenkyūsho chōsa hōkoku* [Survey Report of the Kyoto Univ. Humanistic Sciences Inst.], no. 12 (Mar. 1965), p. 83; Yokoseni Mitsuaki, "Kinsei kōki minami Kantō no nōgyō gijutsu" [Farming Technique in Southern Kantō in the Late Tokugawa Period], *Nihon Rekishi* [Japanese History], no. 96 (June 1956), pp. 56–7. The farm family studied by Yokoseni used from eight to thirteen varieties of rice each year between 1849 and 1868, with frequent changes of mix, some varieties being tried for a few years and then dropped in favour of others.

34. *Nihon nōsho zenshū*, xxii, p. 331.

35. *Noguchi ke mikki*, pp. 211–84.

36. Ōkura Nagatsune, *Menpo yōmu*, p. 281.

37. The diary, covering the period 1720–1942, was discovered in 1942 by Toya Toshiyuki, a young scholar of agrarian history who later died as a soldier in the Philippines. The Ishikawa were owner-cultivators with approximately one *chō* of land in the late Tokugawa period and therefore may be thought well-off but not rich, though they had in addition a modest income as low-ranking samurai. Toya Toshiyuki, *Kinsei nōgyō keiei ran* [On Farm Management in the Tokugawa Period] (Tokyo, 1949), pp. 157–68. The diary for four years – 1728, 1804, 1840 and 1867 – is printed *ibid.*, pp. 169–228.

38. There were 354 days in the ordinary year in the lunar calendar, making it eleven days short of the solar year. To compensate, an additional month was inserted every thirty-three or thirty-four months.

39. Compiled in response to questions concerning agriculture by Doi Seiryō (1546–1626), the lord of a small domain in Iyo province, in *Nihon nōsho zenshū*, x.

40. *Ibid.*, pp. 109–20. Also included are estimates of labour for a great variety of ancillary tasks: twenty days a year for house repair, twenty for cleaning wells and ditches, three for cutting and shaping wood for the handles of farm tools, and so on.

41. Takamine Yoshitada, *Nōmin no kinkōsaku no shidai oboegaki*, pp. 293–308. To the best of my knowledge, farmers generally had no way of measuring these values precisely. Few western-style clocks can have been present in peasant villages, though it is possible that fire-clocks and sand-clocks were used.

42. For example, Fukushima Teiyū, *Kōsaku shiyō sho*, gives (a) the cost of each item of expense for a married couple without children cultivating six *tan* of paddy and six *tan* of dry fields, and (b) the value of the crops produced. Each item of expense and production is given in both physical and monetary values. These figures therefore yield the return on an unknown number of man-days of work; and a reasonable estimate of the number of man-days can be derived from the number of man-days for various operations required on three *tan* of paddy and four *tan* of dry fields given elsewhere in the book, making possible the calculation of return per man-day. For the data, see pp. 286–94.

43. Ōhata Saizō, *Saizōki*, p. 401; Furushima Toshio and Nagahara Keiji, *Shōhin seisan to kisei jinushisei* [Commercial Production and Parasitic Landlordism] (Tokyo, 1954), pp. 23, 32, 36; Ōkura, *Nōgu benri ron*, p. 212.

44. Miyanaga Shōun, *Shika nōgyō dan*, p. 218.

45. *Nihon shomin seikatsu shiryō shūsei* [Materials on the Life of the Japanese Common People] (Tokyo, 1979), xxi, pp. 757, 760, 762–8; Oka Mitsuo, *Hōken sonraku no kenkyū* [Study of the Feudal Village] (Tokyo, 1962).

46. Andō Seiichi, "Kinsei zaikata shōgyō no tenkai" [The Development of Rural Commerce in the Tokugawa Period], *Kishū keizai shi kenkyū sōsho* [Studies in the Economic History of Kishū], v (July 1956), pp. 4–5.

47. Maeda Masaharu, *Nihon kinsei sonpō no kenkyū* [Study of Village Law in the Tokugawa Period] (Tokyo, 1952), p. 44.

48. *Nihon shomin seikatsu shiryō shūsei*, xxi, p. 782.

49. *Ibid.*, pp. 769–73, 777–8, 781–2.

50. Yasumaru Yoshio, *Nihon no kindaika to minshū shisō* [Japanese Modernization and Popular Thought] (Tokyo, 1974), pp. 20–1, 63–5.

51. Shiozawa Kimio, "Iwate ken Kemuyama mura no ichi nōka keiei" [One Farm Family's Management in Kemuyama Village, Iwate Prefecture], *Keizaigaku* [Economics], no. 28 (July 1953), pp. 92–133.

52. David Landes makes a persuasive case that western city people developed an acute appreciation of the value of time before mechanical clocks became available. Hence, "The clock did not create an interest in time measurement; the interest in time measurement led to the invention of the clock". Landes, *Revolution in Time*, pp. 51, 58, 71–2.

53. Nakanishi Yō, "Daiichi taisen zengo no rōshi kankei" [Labour-Capital Relations at the Time of the First World War], in Sumiya Mikio (ed.), *Nihon rōshi kankei shiron* [Historical Essays in Labour-Capital Relations in Japan] (Tokyo, 1977), p. 86; Kōgakkai (ed.), *Meiji kōgyō shi* [Meiji Industrial History], 2nd edn. (Tokyo, 1929), iii, pp. 190–2.

54. Ministry of agriculture and commerce figures show 234 strikes in the period 1897–1907; in a total of six (2.56 per cent) of these, "shortening working hours and so on" was an issue. There are no relevant data for 1908–13. Home ministry figures for the period 1914–30 give two slightly different totals for the number of "strikes and factory closures" resulting from labour disputes (5,471 and 5,965). Working hours and holidays were an issue in 4.45 per cent and 4.14 per cent of these, respectively. Even these low figures exaggerate somewhat the importance of time as an issue, owing to the exceptionally large number of strikes involving workers' hours in the single year 1921. This was a year of unusual labour turbulence, and workers tended in the course of labour disputes originating over other issues to exploit the International Labour Organization's recent endorsement of the eight-hour day. For the period 1922–30 there were 8,829 labour disputes of all kinds, and for each dispute the ministry assigned one issue as primary and others as secondary. Working hours and holidays were classified as the primary issue in 2.3 per cent of all disputes. Nihon rōdō undō shiryō iinkai (ed.), *Nihon rōdō undō shiryō* [Materials on the Labour Movement in Japan] (Tokyo, 1959), x, pp. 424–534.

55. *Rōdō sekai* [The World of Work], 15 Sept. 1899; Yokoyama Gennosuke, *Naichi zakkyogo no Nihon* [Japan after Mixed Residence] (Tokyo, 1959), pp. 32–3; Masumoto Uhei, *Kōjō yori mitaru Nihon rōdō seikatsu* [Working Life in Japan Seen from the Factory] (Tokyo, 1919), p. 128; *Kurogane* [Black Metal], 1 Sept. 1920–15 Mar. 1924, especially the letters of 1 Mar., 1 Sept. 1921, pp. 1, 3, respectively.

56. Thomas C. Smith, "The Right to Benevolence: Dignity and Japanese Workers, 1890–1920", *Comp. Studies in Society and Hist.*, xxvi (1984), pp. 587–613.

57. Strikes pertaining to time often seem to have resulted less from the enforcement of precise schedules than from changes in the margin of latitude allowable. For examples, see *Rōdō oyobi-sangyō* [Labour and Industry], Sept. 1916, pp. 57–8, Mar. 1917, pp. 26–7.

58. At Yokosuka, workers reporting on time but leaving work early received half a day's pay if they had worked half of the normal hours. Considerably more severe was the provision that workers who were fifteen minutes or less late, but thereafter worked the full day, received only 70 per cent pay: *Yokosuka kaigun kōshō Shi* [History of the Yokosuka Naval Arsenal] (Tokyo, 1935), i, pp. 99, 141.

59. Workers, who were paid by the day, were not paid for holidays and therefore viewed them as a mixed blessing. In 1923 the Yawata steel mill instituted four paid national holidays a

year, so that workers' patriotic appreciation of these festivals would not be dampened by
the cost to them in lost earnings.

60. *Kōjō oyobi shokkō* [Factories and Workers] (Tokyo, 1900), pp. 24–6; *Kōjō chōsa yōryō*
    [Factory Survey Summary] (Tokyo, 1897), pp. 75–6; Yokoyama Gennosuke, *Naichi
    zakkyogo no Nihon*, pp. 32–3; Yokoyama Gennosuke, *Nihon kasō shakai* [Lower-Class
    Society in Japan], in *Yokoyama Gennosuke zenshū* [Collected Writings of Yokoyama
    Gennosuke], ed. Sumiya Mikio (Tokyo, 1972), i, pp. 221–33; *Yokosuka kaigun kōshō
    shi*, i, pp. 139, 141, 144–5.

61. *Rōdō sekai*, 15 Dec. 1898, p. 256.

62. *Yūai shinpō* [Friendly Society News], 15 May 1914, p. 215.

63. For an early expression of this view, see the Mitsubishi personnel handbook for the
    Nagasaki shipyard, *Rōdōsha toriatsukaikata ni kansuru chōsa hōkokusho* [Report on
    the Handling of Workers] (n.p., Nagasaki?, 1914), i, pp. 51–3. Even among intellectuals
    extraordinarily sympathetic to workers the discussion of working hours emphasized
    the productivity effect of the shortened hours. See the answers to the questionnaire on
    working hours in *Rōdō oyobi sangyō*, July 1917, pp. 14–25.

64. *Rōdō oyobi sangyō*, Jan. 1919, p. 35.

65. *Ibid.*, Mar. 1918, pp. 176–7.

66. This is suggested by workers' letters to *Rōdō oyobi sangyō*, but it is perhaps most clearly
    illustrated by the statement in October 1919 of the Yūaikai, Japan's leading labour
    organization, endorsing the nine principles concerning labour adopted by the Paris peace
    conference. The Yūaikai statement strongly emphasized those principles dealing with
    the dignity of workers – that workers were not articles of commerce, not appendages
    (*fuzokuhin*) of the machine, not to be treated as mere things (*busshitsuka*) – but said
    nothing about the eight-hour day, the forty-eight-hour week, or the one-day-off-a-week
    principle (*ibid.*, Oct. 1919, p. 1).

67. Japanese returning from study or work in western factories typically extolled the time-
    discipline found there and made comparisons disparaging Japanese workers, who were
    said to work at an unhurried pace, loaf when not directly supervised, and generally take
    several times the number of persons to perform a given task than in "advanced western
    countries". One cliché had it that "unlike western workers, Japanese sell time, not
    labour". These comparisons were perhaps exaggerated with the intention of shaming and
    exhorting Japanese workers, but they also contained a substantial element of truth. At the
    same time, however, critics of Japanese workers increasingly recognized that long hours
    and infrequent holidays had much to do with poor performance. Men and women who
    day after day worked twelve to fourteen hours, barely managing to feed their families
    and under constant threat of lay-off, could not reasonably, it was argued, be expected
    to work with élan. Employers acknowledged this, but were loath to risk reducing hours
    in the expectation that increased productivity would offset higher labour costs. Little
    therefore was done to reduce hours until the depression following the Second World
    War, when the government, the public and employers began to feel international pressure
    for the eight-hour day at the Paris peace conference and subsequent I.L.O. conferences.
    The *Nihon rōdō nenkan* [Japan Labour Yearbook] for 1920 described the reaction of
    employers to these pressures: "If we examine the so-called eight-hour system, we discover
    that it is eight hours only nominally and in fact eight-hours-plus-overtime. Overtime is

normally two hours a day but sometimes as many as four. Japanese workers generally want only to maximize their earnings and are not concerned with the eight-hour day, and employers have taken advantage of their attitude to contrive a stop-gap policy. Since the depression began in February, however, industry has been forced to curtail operations and shorten working hours. Some companies with eight-hours-plus-overtime systems have so shortened overtime as to establish a true eight-hour system". *Nihon rōdō nenkan* [Japan Labour Yearbook] (Osaka, 1921), ii, p. 104.

68. Daniel Nelson, *Managers and Workers: Origins of the New Factory System in the United States* (Madison, 1975), ch. 4; Frederick W. Taylor, *The Principles of Scientific Management* (New York, 1967), pp. 9–29.

69. Hazama Hiroshi, *Nihon rōmu kanri shi kenkyū* [Study of the History of Japanese Labour Management] (Tokyo, 1964), p. 18.

70. From an early date, it was a common worker tactic, called *taigyō* or go-slow, to come to work but do little or nothing during labour disputes. This, however, was an undisguised dispute tactic, not an everyday and more or less covert work rule.

71. For an early example of such a scheme at the Mitsubishi Nagasaki shipyard, see *Rōdōsha toriatsukaikata no kansura chōsa hōkokusho*, pp. 41–2. A more detailed example and remarks on the currency of group incentive plans can be found in Andrew Gordon, "Workers, Managers and Bureaucrats in Japan: Labor Relations in Heavy Industry, 1853–1945" (University Microfilms, Ann Arbor, 1981), pp. 321–6 (soon to be published by Harvard University Press).

72. Taylor, *Principles of Scientific Management*, pp. 70–7.

73. Yamada Katsundo, *Watakushi no shūgyō jidai* [My Apprenticeship] (Tokyo, 1957), p. 125.

74. Thompson, "Time, Work-Discipline and Industrial Capitalism", pp. 80, 93–4.

75. *Ibid.*, pp. 91, 93–5.

76. *Ibid.*, p. 95.

77. *Ibid.*, p. 77.

78. *Ibid.*, p. 76

79. *Ibid.*, pp. 86, 61.

80. Daniel I. Rodgers, *The Work Ethic in Industrial America, 1850–1920* (Chicago, 1979), pp. 34–5.

81. John R. Commons (ed.), *A Documentary History of American Industrial Society* (New York, 1958), vi, p. 98. Quoted in David Brody, "Time and Work during Early American Industrialism" (paper for the German-American Symposium, April 1984).

82. The word *kenri*, which came to be the equivalent of the English word "right", was used in Chinese texts studied in the Tokugawa period to combine the words "power" (*kenryoku*) and "interest" (*rieki*). It was first used in Japan in the modern sense of legal or human rights in the mid-nineteenth century in translations of western works on political theory and law. *Kenri* was an extraordinarily bad choice for the purpose, since the Chinese characters carried a strong suggestion of power and interest.

CHAPTER THREE

Satanic Fields, Pleasant Mills: Work in an Indian Steel Plant[1]

JONATHAN PARRY

INTRODUCTION

According to the argument of one of E.P. Thompson's best-known essays (1991 [1964]), modern machine production requires and promotes a new concept of time and a new kind of work discipline. In the pre-industrial world, work is task-oriented and governed by the rhythms of nature. The working day expands or contracts according to the task in hand; and bouts of intense labour alternate with long periods of idleness. But this 'more humanly comprehensible' world in which 'social intercourse and labour are intermingled' gives way to the (by implication, inhumane) world of modern industry, which is governed by abstract clock-time that imposes a new kind work discipline and which effects a new kind of differentiation between 'work' and 'life'. The main catalyst behind this revolutionary transformation is large-scale machine production, which requires an elaborate synchronization of tasks (and demands that the plant be kept in constant operation in order to repay the capital invested in it).

Consistent with Thompson's thesis is a whole library portraying the 'human actuality' of modern factory production. Despite himself, Burawoy (1988) is co-opted through the game of 'making out' into cooperating with management in the production of greater surplus value by the pressure to fulfil or exceed his target quota ('to make out'). Success in the game is a mark of a man's worth amongst his peers; it becomes an obsession, is the main topic of conversation on the shop floor, and is a sharp spur to frenetic productive endeavour. In a plant near Paris, Linhart (1985) solders the chassis of Citroen 2CVs, one every four or five minutes:

' ... as soon as a car enters a man's territory, he ... gets to work. A few knocks, a few sparks, then the soldering's done and the car is already on its way ... and the worker starts again. Sometimes, if he has been working fast, he has a few seconds respite ... either he takes advantage of it to breathe for a moment, or else he intensifies his effort and 'goes up the line' so that he can gain a little time ... After an hour or two he has amassed the incredible capital of two or three minutes in hand, that he'll use up smoking a cigarette, looking on like some comfortable man of means as his car moves past already soldered, keeping his hands in his pockets while the others are working. Short-live[d] happiness: the next car's already there ... and the race begins again... If, on the other hand, the worker's too slow, he 'slips back' ... And (now) the slow gliding of the cars ... looks as relentless as a rushing torrent which you can't manage to dam up: eighteen inches, three feet, thirty seconds certainly behind time ... the next one ... coming forward with its mindless regularity and inert mass ... sometimes it's as ghastly as drowning ...' (p. 118-9)

Though several historians have sought to qualify Thompson's picture of a sharp break between the two types of productive regime,[2] much anthropological writing has appropriated Thompson uncritically. An exemplary instance is Ong's much-cited study of spirit possession amongst Malaysian factory women (1987). Her story begins with the easy-going rhythms of 'traditional' kampong life where a young woman's work was supervised, if at all, by her female kin; where work was task-oriented and 'slow stretches of dull routine were lightened by songs and jokes ...' (p. 111). But this pastoral idyll is shattered by factory discipline, by the reduction of work to 'time-motion manipulations', and by the constant surveillance of male supervisors. What this dislocating experience provokes is a series of minor acts of resistance, of which seizure by ghosts is the most dramatic. And what these represent is a kind of ritual of rebellion 'against a loss of autonomy/humanity in work' (p. 7), and 'a mode of un-conscious retaliation against male authority in human relations' (p. 207).

Little in any of the foregoing rings true to my data. If I am to believe my informants, the old world of peasant production is far less benign than Thompson and Ong suggest; while much factory work cannot really be represented as the all-day everyday grind so vividly captured by the authors I've cited. Indeed, a good deal of it is better described as consisting in long fallow periods of comparative idleness punctuated by bouts of intense activity; the very terms which Thompson used to characterize task-oriented pre-industrial production. Nor do I see any clear evidence of a sharpening division between 'work' and 'life'. Significant numbers of industrial workers in certain niches of the labour market appear to be no less leisured than Sahlins' proverbially leisured hunter-gatherers (1972: chapter 1), and it is not obvious that the shift from 'production for use' to 'production for exchange' has, as he supposes (chapters 2 and 3), been accompanied by a marked intensification of labour.

My ethnographic focus is on a notoriously leisured segment of the Indian labour force, workers in a large-scale public sector enterprise. In drawing attention to the staccato character of their productive activities it is not, however, my intention to swell the chorus which calls for their privatization. In this respect, matters are not really so different in private sector factories operating under similar production constraints.

In another respect, however, they are. Though this is not an issue I can elaborate here (but see Parry 1999a and b), the 'primordial' bonds of caste, religion and regional ethnicity have far greater salience on private than on public sector shop floors.

THE SETTING

Until the mid-1950s, Bhilai was a small village in the Durg district of Chhattisgarh, central India. That village now gives its name to a large 'company town', the site of one of the largest steel plants in Asia. The Bhilai Steel Plant (BSP), a public sector undertaking built with Soviet cooperation and technology, began production in 1959. It was one of a handful of mega-projects that were designed to kick start India's post-Independence 'modernization' and that epitomized the Nehruvian project. Profits being secondary to employment in the planning priorities of the time, the new plant was deliberately located in what was then regarded as a remote and 'backward' rural area. At the start of my fieldwork in 1993, BSP, along with its subsidiary mines and quarries, had nearly 55,000 workers on its direct pay-roll. But despite this massive workforce it ran at a profit; and had a record of considerably more harmonious industrial relations than the other state-run steel plants and the vast majority of private sector factories, which now surrounded it and for which it served as a magnet. Today these include around 200 factories, some now quite sizeable, housed on an industrial estate a little removed from the plant.

The plant itself covers an area of nearly seventeen square kilometres. Immediately fringing its perimeter walls is its spacious and orderly township. Elsewhere the perimeter fence abuts onto what still look like rural villages; while at other points the plant and the township are surrounded by a sea of unregulated urban sprawl that envelops old villages like Girvi and Patripar in which much of my fieldwork was done, and into which many migrant workers from other corners of the country have now moved. Most of the original villagers stayed on, and the lucky ones have jobs in the steel plant. Lucky because the BSP workforce is the local aristocracy of labour, enjoying pay, perks and benefits that make them the envy of every other working class family in the area. Initially, however, the local villagers were reluctant recruits to its labour force,[3] and lacked the industrial experience and skills it required. As a result it was largely migrant labour from outside the region who built BSP. They came from every corner of the country; and many stayed on, bringing their families to join them.

IN THE HAPPY WORLD OF THE FIELDS

As far as work is concerned, and despite its discontents, my local Chhattisgarhi informants do not generally compare the new industrial 'civilization' unfavourably with the old world of task-oriented peasant agriculture. Before I knew better, I went to some pains to prod them into telling me how oppressive a life ruled by the clock and the factory siren is, and into indulging their nostalgia for the happy world of the fields. My enquiries were met with incomprehension or amused incredulity. "Highest is agriculture, business is middling, lowest is employment," they would quote; only to ruefully reflect on how today the relative valuation contained in that old adage has been reversed.

The fact is that agricultural work is now regarded with deep distaste, especially by the young. Though many local households in the neighbourhoods I studied still own some land in the surrounding countryside, even unemployed youngsters re-solutely refuse to so much as supervise the work of day-labourers in the fields, let alone work in them themselves. They are *suvidhabhogi* ('privileged', literally 'enjoyers of amenities'), their fathers complain, and unwilling to toil up to their knees in mud in all weathers, or to spend broken nights guarding the crops. For their part, the young see agriculture as emblematic of the rustic world of their 'thumb-impression' (*angutha-chhap*) elders. "How, with my education, will I work on the land?", they rhetorically ask.

Certainly most young men prefer cash in hand from casual labour on a construc-tion site to grains in the household's storage bins. The returns are more immediate, more predictable and more individualized. For the fruits of an uncertain harvest one has to wait, but contract labour provides the wherewithal for *sharab* (liquor) and *satta* (a numbers racket) that evening. And, if there is no family land and one is forced to work for daily wages, then contract labour pays better. Unsupervised by senior kin, it also holds out the promise of flirtation, romance and even sexual adventure; a significant proportion of illicit love affairs and secondary unions being initiated be-tween members of mixed gangs of contract workers in such apparently unpromising settings as the BSP slag dump (Parry 2001). But above all, many agricultural tasks are regarded as harder and more unpleasant than those required in most forms of contract labour. For the majority of my informants, whose conditions of existence are considerably less harsh than those described by Breman (1996) and for whom no work that day is much less likely to mean going hungry, there is also perhaps some sense that cultivation imposes greater compulsion. When the weather conditions are right, it is *now* that the fields need ploughing or the seed to be sown. But if one's body aches, one may well decide that one's presence on the building site can wait until next week. Task-orientation imposes its own time-discipline which may be at least as coercive as that of the contractor.

Though fathers deplore their sons' lack of stoicism, foot-dragging and even out-right refusal to go to the fields, their own attitude to working the land is generally ambivalent. One of the ex-villages I studied still has fields of its own, but the real preoccupation is with rocketing real estate values rather than paddy production. But many long-serving BSP workers of local origin invest the substantial sums that they receive on retirement in land further out which they farm with hired labour. Land ownership is still a source of prestige and an asset reckoned in marriage. Such investments also have the important advantage not only of growing in value, but also of lacking liquidity. They are therefore relatively immune to being whittled away by the importunate demands of kin – most likely, of unemployed sons with hare-brained schemes for making a fortune or with problems involving the police.

But while land is certainly valued, the endless complaint is that today there is no profit in cultivation. So insistently is this repeated that it took me some time to realize that crop yields are in fact very much higher than they were in pre-BSP days, by a factor of perhaps four or five times. In any event, the complaint is, on my calculations, considerably exaggerated, and is premised on non-family labour doing most of the work. What is certainly the case, however, is that agricultural production in much of this region is marked by its insecurity; that, within living memory, Chhattisgarh has in several years experienced famine conditions, and that quite a high proportion of the least privileged segments of the Chhattisgarhi industrial labour force who now live in these Bhilai neighbourhoods were driven out of their villages of origin by dearth, drought and hunger. Their lack of nostalgia for the lost world of peasant production should not occasion surprise.

However, there is possibly also an ideological element to it. In the ex-villages studied, well over half of the land was, in pre-BSP days, controlled by the *malguzar* (a landlord-cum-revenue official), to whom most other households were beholden, whose autocratic ways are legendary, and in whose fields they were required to work. Cultivation is thus associated with subordination, particularly perhaps by the Satnamis, the largest Untouchable caste in the region. They suffered most from these exactions, and it is their young men who are today (or so their fathers complain) particularly averse to the fields. Meanwhile, competition from industry has driven up agricultural wages, while the fortunes of the old *daus*, the erstwhile landed elite, have generally declined. While in the past a *daus*'s womenfolk would not have toiled in the fields, now they are forced to do so. So while there are some who disdain agricultural labour for its association with past servitude, there are others who resent it as the signifier of their present fall from grace.

Whether fathers or sons, *daus* or Satnamis, all agree that for back-breaking toil, ploughing and levelling the fields and transplanting the paddy in the monsoon rain, are hard to beat. It is true that new labour arrangements, in the form of work-teams hired on a contract basis to perform a specific task, e.g. so much per acre, have intensified the effort required. These arrangements have introduced a new element of self-exploitation and a new equation between time and money. Consistent with Thompson, it is a variant on industrial piece-work rates that keep the workers at it from dawn to dusk. Though what is less consistent with Thompson is that, even in its traditional forms, agricultural production is certainly not understood as a more humane and desirable way of making a living than work in a factory, whether public or private. In some BSP departments, working conditions seem extremely exacting; but when I asked workers how they managed to tolerate them, I was several times told that, as the son of a farmer, they had no problem.

Whether industrial workers in Bhilai feel alienated from factory work is a difficult question. Even within the regular BSP workforce I was struck by the variation between workers in different departments, between workers with different tasks within the same department, and above all between relatively recent recruits and the older men who joined in the pioneer days. Some take an obvious pride in their jobs, enthusiastically describing improvements they had initiated, for example, a better door-opening mechanism for the coke oven batteries or a new fitting which allows the rollers in the Rail Mill to be changed in half the time. Others, it was obvious, lacked any commitment, regarded work as nothing but drudgery and were interested only in doing as little of it as possible. But the one generalization which does seem safe is that, while industrial workers are conventionally supposed to be alienated from the factory, factory work has most conspicuously alienated these neophyte proletarians from agriculture, in which they are increasingly de-skilled and of which they are increasingly disdainful.

IN DARK SATANIC MILLS

My experience of the BSP shop floor has mainly been in the coke oven department, supplemented by short periods in the older of the two steel-melting shops (SMS 1) and the plate mill. The coke ovens and SMS 1 rate as 'hard' shops where real men work. Though conditions today are considerably less harsh than they were in the past, and, though the bonuses are better here than elsewhere, new recruits go to great lengths to avoid being posted to either shop.

Across the rail tracks, a monumental fountain – 'The Fountain of Love' – marks the start of coke oven territory. Just behind it stretches a massive rectangular phalanx of batteries, approximately 800 meters long, twenty meters broad and fifteen high. Their function is to convert coal into coke for the blast furnaces. Located to one side are two modern batteries with a larger capacity, but this phalanx consists of the eight older ones, four blocks of two laid end-to-end. Each battery has sixty-five vertically arranged ovens separated from each other by a heating chamber. eighteen tons of coal are charged into each oven from a charging car which runs along the top of the battery, and eighteen or so hours later, twelve tons of coke are pushed out of the oven by a kind of giant ram-rod attached to the pusher car on one side of the battery ('pusher side') into a quenching car positioned on the other side ('coke side').

From the batteries seeps a dense, acrid fog of fumes and smoke, flames whooshing high into the air at unpredictable intervals from vents on top of the ovens. To the right of the road that runs beside them is a tangle of massive overhead pipes mounted on concrete pillars, snaking in and out of each other in all directions and angrily spitting steam and boiling liquids. A fenced-off patch of hard rust-coloured ground below bears, like a bitter reproach, a now faded sign saying "Site for Garden". Behind it are the administrative buildings and then the by-products plants; and further on still are the coal handling yards with their seventeen kilometres of conveyor belt running through galleries of corrugated iron constructed on stilts above the ground. Obscured from view, on the 'coke side,' where the quenching car waits to drive the red-hot coke into a tower where it is doused with phenol water, are the coke sorting plants and the galleries through which the coke is conveyed to the blast furnaces. Between the cooling towers and the steaming grey phenol-water soak-pits, into which one could disappear without a trace save for one's plastic identity card and wrist-watch, are public relations department hoardings bearing the injunction to "Have a Nice Day".

Even when you are on the ground, the coke oven department might present itself as a plausible model for a latter-day industrial version of Signorelli's frescoes of hell. But when you are on top of the batteries you could really believe that you have arrived in the master's imagination. Even at mid-day, visibility seems to demand landing lights; the ambient air temperature reaches fifty degrees Celsius; and the surface of the deck is so hot that on the first occasion I went up there with the rod group, I had to spend the shift hopping from foot to foot as layers from the thick rubber soles on my shoes were left sizzling on the deck behind me. Here, and on the platform down below that runs beside the ovens, men move around like ambulant mummies, so thoroughly swathed against the heat that even their mothers might not recognize them. The older workers chew tobacco compulsively to take the taste of the dust from their mouths and it is widely held that those who work on the batteries must drink liquor to clean the gas from their guts. But, though the coke ovens are more insalubrious, they are less immediately dangerous than SMS 1, where huge ladles of molten steel, 'thimbles' of red hot slag and just-cast ingots are shifted around by crane or train in a space which is much more confined.

Some tasks which are done in such shops are extraordinarily taxing. Take Dukalu, a mason in SMS 1, who works in incredible temperatures in the cramped area right behind the furnaces preparing the brick-lined channels through which the molten metal is tapped. Or in the coke ovens, take Itvari's rod group. They mainly work on the oven-tops where they clear obstructions and adjust the bricks which regulate the in-take of air at the bottom of the heating chambers. This they do with long metal rods which they insert through the vertical flues on the oven deck. So intense is the heat that I found it difficult to even look into the heating chamber to see the brick and the burner, let alone stand over the flue long enough to adjust it some thirty feet below with a rod that's red hot within seconds. But other work-teams from the refractory group have even tougher tasks: the spray groups who work in front of the open doors plugging gaps and cracks in the brickwork with a mortar and acid slurry which they direct at the walls through a compressed-air spray; or the hot repair group, who patch the brickwork inside the oven doors while they are charged, building a partition wall with a heat-resistant lining a few feet in to separate off the burning coal from the area of wall on which they will work, the mason laying the bricks with his body half in and half out of the oven.

What is striking about such work teams, however, is that the distribution of work within them is often conspicuously unequal; the chargeman, notionally in charge, often being the most obvious, if not the only, passenger. More striking still is that although such jobs are extremely demanding, the amount of the working day spent on them is not. On the first occasion I accompanied the rod group, we were through in an hour and a half; on the second, in just over two. For the rest of the shift we sat about chatting, drinking tea and going for a stroll.

Even in the hard shops, not all jobs are that hard. Much of the work requires neither a good deal of skill nor physical stamina. Jagdish is 'helper' to a technician whose job is to change the nozzle valves on the giant ladles that pour the molten steel into the ingot moulds in SMS 1. I joined him there one day at the beginning of the second shift at 2.00 p.m.. By 2.30 p.m. he was ready to start work. By 3.00 p.m. the first task was done and we spent the next hour and a half chatting, drinking tea in the canteen and reading the newspaper. At 4.30 p.m. there was another job to be done. That took twenty minutes, and by then he was ready to leave. Though the second shift ends at 10.00 p.m., Jagdish boasts that in the four years he has been in the shop he is yet to stay beyond five. Or take Ganesh, a Satnami from the same neighbourhood who is a welder working in a team which services the evaporation cooling system on the SMS 1 furnace doors. The job he was assigned during the shift I spent with him took nearly three hours. But for the previous two days he had nothing to do at all. Or, more extreme, take Prakash, another welder and another neighbour, who works in the Bloom and Billet mill where his job is to cut free the blockage when one of the red hot slabs of steel gets jammed on the rollers, which he does from behind an asbestos screen with an oxyacetylene torch. When the mill shuts down for maintenance, he works consistently at repairing the guides which direct the blooms. But otherwise the hours are unpredictable, maybe one in a week, maybe one in a month. In his spare time in the plant, Jagdish normally reads a romance and plays *satta*, Ganesh strolls about and smokes *ganja* (hemp), while Prakash plays *pasa* (a dice game) or reads. What really concerns the officers is that they can find their workers when they are needed, and those who sleep or play cards in their locker-room are much less likely to attract their displeasure than those who wander off on their own. But managerial surveillance is only minimally constraining, and, by contrast with Bhilai's larger private sector factories, there is no clandestine network of informers and stool-pigeons.

In many operations jobs, for example, the teeming crane drivers in SMS 1 or the pushing car operators in the coke ovens, the worker is expected to remain at or near his post for four hours at a stretch, though he is unlikely to be working throughout that time. The unwritten convention is that he can then go home. But even those without such semi-official license can generally get away in good time if they keep on the right side of their superiors, and can square or evade Security at the gates. Certainly, it is not unusual to find somebody who went on the first shift at 6.00 a.m. and is back by 9.00 a.m.. When, an hour after his shift had started, I went to find Madanlal in the SMS 1 stripping yard where the steel ingots are removed from the moulds, he and one of the other five crane operators on duty had already left for some 'important work' (fixing his motor-bike, I discovered). But even so the three that remained were not overstretched, and I sat and chatted with them for seventy-five minutes before the first wagon arrived. The maximum number that might come in a shift would be ten or twelve, which they reckon they could clear in roughly three hours. Their delivery, however, is sporadic, so the shift consists of short periods of intense activity interspersed with longish intervals of leisure. As this example suggests, manning levels are sufficiently generous to allow groups of workers to organize their own in-formal duty rosters; one worker might sometimes substitute for a mate in a different shift. And if all else fails, a worker can always take casual leave or get a friend to deposit your token. Here, at any rate, the constraints of industrial time discipline are not really oppressive.

The coke oven batteries are manned by various teams: the heating group who monitor and regulate the temperatures in the heating chambers and clean and main-tain the gas lines; the refractory group who repair the brickwork; mechanical and electrical maintenance, and operations, who charge and push the ovens. For each pair of batteries there are around fifty operations workers in each of three shifts. On any one shift, maybe seven would be on their weekly holiday and on average six or seven more might be eligible for leave. What remains is a notional comple-ment of 36 to 37, while conventional wisdom is that 30 to 31 workers are required to run the shift efficiently. In other words, a 15 to 20 percent surplus is built into the manning levels required, so that, from the point of view of productive efficiency, it really does not matter if these extra hands report for duty or not. But even if more than that absent themselves, as regularly happens on the night shift and at festival times, production continues more or less normally. Extra hands might be borrowed from other batteries, a shortage in one category of operative is filled by upgrading a worker from a lower one, and various routine cleaning tasks will remain undone. On the larger canvas of the plant as a whole, it is therefore not surprising that there is no simple correlation between peaks in the graph for absenteeism and troughs in the graph for production.

The heating group is subdivided into various sections, of which the group which cleans and maintains the hydraulic main pipe that runs along the oven tops has the nastiest job. They begin at 6.00 a.m. but on most days the majority of the unit will have left the plant by 9.00 a.m., when the general shift members of the heating group are just starting their day. With the latter I once spent a week on batteries A and B. A typical day might begin with Tamrakar, the unusually dynamic chargeman on bat-tery B, inspecting the burners in the heating chambers through the vertical flues at the top. By eye he could instantly tell which were giving off less heat than they should, and which pipes and valves in the basement would therefore need cleaning. Tamrakar, Senior Gas Man Motilal and the team of six workers under them would then go down to the cellars below the ovens to start work. The atmosphere down there is suffocating, but the group would work steadily for an hour and a half. We would then go out for some air before congregating at 11.00 a.m. for tea in the 'Gas Man Room', a dark and dirty cellar with a few lockers which the general shift heating men from the two batteries use as a common-room-cum-dormitory. After tea it would be time for lunch and a nap; another short cleaning job (taking may be thirty minutes), tea-time again, and then it would be time to pack up.

However, all this needs to be put into perspective. That week the group would be coming into the plant on their day off to do an extra job necessitated by the temporary closure of the main gas line for repairs. Whilst sometimes there are real emergencies to cope with. At 7.30 a.m. on December 11th 1995, there was a complete failure of the electricity board's power supply to the plant. BSP has its own generating capacity which is supposed to provide emergency cover which can keep essential operations ticking over, but the sudden load-shedding placed an intolerable strain on the system, which also failed. For some time there was not an amp of electricity throughout the plant. In the coke ovens the immediate consequences were catastrophic. Without a functioning extractor system, there was a massive build-up of combustible gases in the batteries. By 8.00 a.m., when the senior manager in charge of the heating group reached the plant, the place was ablaze, flames pouring out of the oven doors and lapping all over the tops. At ground level you could hardly see five paces ahead, while the batteries were "just like a scene from *The Towering Inferno*". The one area which was not on fire was the basements and walkways under the batteries, where the heating group does much of its work; while the rest of the plant stood helplessly by for a week, the gas men worked like Trojans rigging up ways of preventing dangerous concentrations of gas, and restoring each battery in turn. Not all could be relied on, but the senior manager picked his best and had them working round the clock in relays, some hardly going home throughout the week. The moral of the tale, of course, is that some types of industrial work might also be described as consisting of long fallow periods of idleness interspersed with bouts of intense activity.

But there is also another; during that week of chaos, work ground to a virtual halt in much of the rest of the plant. Without coke for the blast furnaces there was no pig iron, without pig iron, no steel could be made or rolled. An electricity sub-station was flooded by heavy monsoon rain in July 1994, putting three blast furnaces out of action. The steel melting shops cut production because they were short of pig iron; the coke ovens because they were not getting enough blast furnace gas and because, anyway, they could not store so much output when blast furnace demand was so low. On the first occasion that I visited one of the coal handling plants, there were four hundred wagons waiting to be unloaded, about four shift's work. However, on the previous day there had been not a single wagon to process. Moreover, productive intensity is by no means constant throughout the year. In the last quarter up to April, shop managements desperately struggled to fulfil their targets, but in the next three months much machinery was shut down for maintenance and workers in operations had relatively little to do. In short, as in peasant agriculture, production has seasonal highs and lows. A good deal of what might seem to be shirking is simply a consequence of an idleness enforced by breakdowns, failures in supply and essential maintenance.

A good deal, but not, I think, everything. Barring major, but exceptional, convulsions like the *'Towering Inferno'* incident, and despite frequent hiccups on one battery or other (e.g. a spillage of coal from the overhead bunker blocking the path of the charging car or the "mis-pushing" of coke when the quenching car is not in place which melts its track and brings down the trolley-wire), production continues in most parts of the shop, and the daily output of the major shops is in fact quite constant. In the coke ovens, for example, the range of variation in the number of ovens pushed per day in January 1998 was between 348 and 401; whilst in November 1997, which was typical, the blast furnaces produced between 11, 000 and 13,000 tons of hot metal a day. Plainly, not every sleeping worker sleeps only while production is temporarily suspended.

Shirking is a social fact, explicitly acknowledged (and sometimes exaggerated) by workers themselves. "*BSP men bhagne ka 'culture' hai*" ("BSP has a 'bunking off' culture"); *Biharis*, *Chhattisgarhis* or others are *kamchor* (shirkers, literally 'work-thieves'), who 'think of the plant as their father's factory, that they can come and go as they like'. The problem, as one worker explained, as we sat over a third cup of tea in the canteen, is the lack of incentives. "Good worker, no prize; bad worker, no punishment", as he pithily put it in English, going on in Hindi to contrast the private sector where "a worker works only after folding his hands" [in supplication] and for at least seven hours a shift. "But here, if an officer orders him to do some job, [he lifts one buttock off the bench and contorts his face a pantomime of desperation] he says that he needs the latrine. When he is told to be quick, he will ask, 'What, will you stop my shit?' "

What the old-timers of peasant origin say, of course, is that these youngsters *can't* work because they were not raised on the pure milk and ghee that they enjoyed; or *won't* work because their fathers had to pay such a large bribe to get them a job in the plant that they regard it as their property. Largely absent from workers' accounts is any hint that *kamchori* (shirking) is seen, in the manner of Scott (1985), as a weapon of the weak against managerial oppression. So far as I could discern, there was no disapproval of 'rate-busters' as class collaborators; little sense that avoiding work was a way of denying or mitigating the claims of a superordinate class; and only rarely the plea that avoiding work is justifiable because the demands made on the worker were unjust. For the most part, it is not, I think, plausible to see skiving as *Svejk-ian* – a form of class resistance.

A more compelling consideration is the relatively high level of manning which allows labour to be used with relatively low intensity. Indeed, I sometimes had the impression that if the full complement were to report for duty, they might actually impair productive efficiency. One afternoon spent 'coke side' with the hot repair group (a spray group was working alongside), I counted sixteen of us (including three officers and two chargemen) on the two meter wide platform which was strewn with equipment and fragments of brick. Laden with red hot coke, the quenching car shunted up and down within a few feet and, as the door-extractor car advanced menacingly towards us, we would scamper for cover at the end of the battery. The masons worked rapidly in relays, but the only contribution which half the group made, apart from increasing the risk of a fatal fall, was to go on some desultory errand for another tool, or to echo an instruction which had already been given.

Not surprisingly, many bright young recruits develop a sense of futility and alienation, frustrated that their talents and training (often in a trade which is totally irrelevant to the job they are actually assigned in the plant) are squandered. The feeling that there is not enough to do turns into a feeling that it is not worth doing anyway. When the heating group now tell the tale of their heroic hour at the time of the '*Towering Inferno*', their eyes light up as they recall the sense of togetherness and their 'relish' (*maja*) for 'real' work. What is also relevant here is the way in which recruitment happens. A young man will register at the employment exchange for a plant attendant's post as soon as he has passed his tenth class exams. But the queue of applicants is so long that in 1994 BSP were still only interviewing those who had registered in 1983. In the interim, many will have spent their days loafing about, drinking, gambling and getting into fights. Others will have continued their education, and may well have an MA or a BSc by the time they are called for interview. The first category are often demoralized, sometimes even semi-criminalized, and without any habit of labour; while the second aspire to work with computers in a comfortable office and disdain the 'nut-bolt' work to which they are actually assigned as fit only for some *unparh gvar* (illiterate yokel).

Additionally, there is the fact that slacking is possible because managerial power to prevent it is quite circumscribed. It must be emphasized, however, that both the possibility and propensity for it is rather unevenly distributed. In battery operations, for example, a dereliction of duty is immediately obvious in a way that it is not in amongst General Shift workers doing routine maintenance tasks. But just as striking as this variation between work groups is that variance within them. I was often surprised by the absence of effective informal sanctions against their most manifestly indolent members (a product perhaps of the fact that in many routine non-operations jobs, work which is shirked is likely to remain undone rather than falling to somebody else's lot).

The notified absenteeism rates seem high, though the relationship that these bear to reality is unclear. On the one hand, the way in which the figures are calculated exaggerates its extent, but, on the other, it takes no account of the number of workers, often with exemplary attendance records, who lodge their tokens at the beginning of the shift and then turn round and go home. The pattern the rates show is largely predictable: highest in the hardest shops, during the summer months, in the week after pay-day, on the night shift and at festival or harvest times. Also predictable is that Chhattisgarhis are more likely to be sporadically absent throughout the year, whereas the attendance of outsiders tends to be more regular until they go back to their place of origin and fail to reappear for some weeks after their leave has expired. As for its causes, boredom and frustration is certainly one. The money-lending businesses of some workers is said to be another – the debtors staying away from the plant in order to avoid their creditors. More certain is that alcohol is a major cause; some workers in the neighbourhoods I studied regularly went on long binges and did not report for duty for weeks on end.

Incidences of absenteeism are very uneven; some workers being absent with true dedication and some who are rarely absent at all. 336 workers in the coke oven department (11.1 percent of its workforce) were officially notified as absent for fifty days or more during 1997, and of these 217 (7.2 percent) were absent for more than 100 days. Of the 105 workers in the heating group who were reported absent in the eleven month period between April 1991 and February 1992, 75 were away for ten days or less. Again, out of 96 (notoriously susceptible) operations workers on batteries A and B for whom I have information, 13 had no absences at all during 1997, 37 had less than 10 days, 21 had between 11 and 50 days, 13 had between 50 and 100, and 12 had more than 100.[4]

It is only in the case of this last category that BSP's disciplinary procedures are likely to grind into action. The process is extremely protracted, many officers judging that it is more trouble than it is worth. And, if a worker comes from a well-known criminal family and his brother is legendary for having walked down a crowded street with the severed head of a supposed police informer held aloft, one may well conclude that inertia is the best policy. Nor is it obvious what other sanctions a middle-ranking officer has to buttress his authority. The present promotion system makes a worker's advancement quasi-automatic and overtime was abolished in 1987. With a workforce that enjoys considerable security of employment, officers who have rather limited power, work conditions that are often unpleasant, the real issue perhaps is not why absenteeism rates are high, time-keeping lax and workers less industrious than they might be. Given that most of them could almost certainly get away with less, the puzzle is rather why so many of them attend pretty regularly and work as hard as is necessary to run the plant at its rated capacity.

The most obvious answer is pecuniary. A day's absence is a day's pay foregone; whilst bonuses are forfeited at an escalating rate below twenty-three days attendance per month. Given BSP wage levels compared to those of the private sector, an average of twenty days (involving the sacrifice of one-fifth to one-quarter of possible gross earnings) might seem quite sustainable, until one realizes that for many workers this represents a much more significant proportion of net pay, since they have taken substantial loans from the plant which are repaid in fixed monthly instalments.

Monetary considerations are not the only ones. Worker compliance is 'bought' by management acquiescence in their informal duty rosters and by the system of 'see-offs'. Who should do which jobs, and for how long, is governed by union agreements. But, when manning is short, the shift-manager must ask the oventopman to put in an extra couple of hours or to drive the charging car when that job is normally done by somebody of a superior grade. Whilst the worker might in theory refuse, he is in practice unlikely to do so. Though getting past the gates is his own concern, the tacit *quid pro quo* is a blind eye to him leaving the plant whenever he is not actually needed; with the explicit (though unofficial) understanding that when he is asked to work beyond customary norms he is given a 'see-off' – a day's compensatory leave where he will be marked present when in fact he is not. Crudely, then, the workers work in exchange for their liberty to leave (or perhaps never appear) when their labour is not required.

A third answer lies in the camaraderie of the work-group and the fast friendships which develop within it. Take Tarlok, a plant attendant in the plate mill, who had occupied his time between registering at the employment exchange and getting a BSP job by doing a BLLB. At first, he explained, his life in the plant felt utterly useless (*"bahut bekar lagta tha"*), and it seemed "absurd" (*"atpata"*) that after finishing a degree he should be doing a job of this kind. He felt trapped, thought it would be better to be unemployed, and spent his working day waiting to meet his friends in the evening. But now his closest friends are work mates in the plant, where he is "set" and where "time passes well" (*"ab achcha time pass hota hai"*), so that a day away seems "worthless" (*"faltu"*).

Enemies, as one worker put it, are a luxury one cannot afford in the plant. Many jobs in the 'hard' shops are dangerous and, even when they are not, the production of steel demands close collaboration. The pitside worker in SMS 1 is daily at the mercy of the teeming crane driver who shifts 270 ton ladles of molten steel across the shop floor; the finishing stand operator in the plate mill counts on his colleagues on the roughing and vertical stands to send down the plates at the right intervals and temperature if he is to manage his job properly. In operations, even quite senior managers will often lend a hand when it is needed. The coke from oven 23 must be pushed at 3.35pm; the pushing car operator needs a break and the officer in charge might take over while he goes for tea. But things tend to be different in the General Shift, where the majority of workers are doing unskilled routine tasks which do not have the same immediacy and where relations between officers and workers tend to be more distant and hierarchical.

It is, of course, not only work which requires cooperation but also escaping it. At the principal gates to the plant there are regular checks on departing workers at certain times of the day. Unless one leaves immediately after lodging one's token, it is difficult to get out during the night shift without proper authorization. The second shift (2.00 p.m. until 10.00 p.m.) is easiest, while on the first (6.00 a.m. to 2.00 p.m.) there is checking after 10.00 a.m. Most shift-workers have a partner (*joridar*). On the first shift, the standard division of labour between, say, oventopmen partners is that one works the first three hours (allowing him to get away before the checking starts), the other does the remaining five and next day they swop. Here, admittedly, we find echoes of Thompson's rule of the clock, though what it really rules are arrangements for leaving the job rather than performing it. It is with your *joridar* that you cooperate over when you work, but it is with others that you must cooperate while working, which again involves personal negotiation within a framework laid down by the customary practices of the work-group. Amongst the oventopmen, there is a division of labour between the 'hatchman' and the 'valveman'. The latter has lighter duties and it has to be decided who will act in which role for how many ovens in that shift.

The solidarity of the BSP work group and their sense of 'togetherness' (*apanapan*) is reinforced by a rather robust institutional sub-culture which has roots in the Nehruvian vision of modernity for which BSP was always intended to serve as a beacon, and in which the divisions of caste, region and religion were to be transcended for the greater good of the nation. It is true that there are some workers who say that they prefer to keep work and home quite separate and that there is a conspicuous absence of any attempt to domesticate plant space. Nobody even puts a calendar picture in the 'Gas Man Room', and nobody brings a pillow from home so that they can sleep more comfortably. But despite what this seems to suggest, the friendships which many workers form in the plant often acquire considerable significance outside it and 'work' and 'life' are by no means compartmentalized. Entire work groups are almost invariably invited, and at least some of their members will invariably come, to life-cycle rituals in the household and the group as a whole can be expected to rally round in times of trouble.

THE PRIVATE SECTOR COMPARISON

What I hope this discussion has demonstrated is that, as far as those who have permanent jobs in a public sector industry are concerned, large-scale machine production does not necessarily impose a new and more exacting work discipline, or require new attitudes towards time. But it would be rash to assume that things must be radically different in the private sector, however much that contrast is stressed in local discourse: on the industrial estate "not even a moment to straighten one's back" and "while there is work there is a hand on your back, and when there is none there's a kick up your bum".[5] It would be just as rash, though, to attribute to that sector a homogeneity which it does not have. My observations here relate to the larger-scale 'organized' sector factories.

Take the one I know best, an engineering company with around 500 employees. Though management strives to impose a regime of incessant productive activity, and though it has done what it can to curtail malingering (workers cannot leave before the end of their shift and the canteen has been re-located outside the factory gates to prevent them sloping off for tea without passing the security guards), its success is unspectacular and for many the working day is still punctuated by long fallow periods. As Chandavarkar (1994: 337) suggests, management's problem has less to do with the work culture of the Indian proletariat still habituated to the rhythms of peasant agriculture than it has to do with the fact that a great deal of industrial production inevitably proceeds in a staccato fashion and continuous work flows are difficult to sustain. In all shops the intensity of labour visibly depends on the state of the order books. But even when they are full, work in the foundry shop alternates between bursts of frenetic activity and extended lulls. In the machine shop, by contrast, the continuous vigilance of the operator is indeed required when there is work in hand, though he can often leave his lathe to run itself while he briefly chats with a neighbour before the next adjustment is required. But in the fettling shop, work really is a ceaseless grind and there is scarcely a moment "to straighten one's back".

At one extreme would be work by the furnaces in one of the re-rolling mills where those who do the toughest jobs might put in a maximum of two hours (extremely hard) labour per shift in bursts of thirty minutes each. At the other is assembly-line production run on Taylorist principles. It was on the line in a cigarette-making company that I encountered a factory regime which most perfectly exemplified the picture of a working day governed by the remorselessly repetitive demands of the machine. Two and a half hours 'overtime' (sometimes four) is routinely required, and on six days a week the operator is rooted to his position for two stretches of five hours repeating the same movements every few seconds. In short, different types of industrial process are associated with different intensities of labour and impose work disciplines of different degrees of rigour. Not only does Thompson's stark contrast between work in the fields and the factory romanticize the former but it also ignores the very variable nature of the latter.

I was sitting one day in the house of Gajraj Singh, an employee in the engineering firm previously mentioned, while he was working at his sewing machine. It was his day off and he makes a supplementary income as a tailor. But before he joined the company he had done it full-time, and was telling me that his income from tailoring was nearly as good as it is in the factory. Why, then, did he not continue with tailoring? To make a reasonable living at it, he explained, requires long hours of consistent application and, as soon as you think you are through for the day, some importunate customer shows up demanding the suit for his son's wedding. By contrast a job in the factory is "restful". They give you a task, you do it and then you take a break. You work for four hours and wander for four. Eight hours belong to the factory, but after that your time is your own and nobody comes to harass you at home.

The discipline of the clock also has its advantages, especially perhaps in a country like India where landless labourers and share-croppers are at the beck and call of their masters at all times of day and night.

NOTES

1. This paper is a radically abbreviated version of (Parry 1999a) and focuses on one part of its argument.
2. See, for example, Smith 1986; Roberts 1992; Gutman 1988; Cooper 1992; and Whipp 1987.
3. The reasons for this are discussed in Parry 1999a and 2008.

4. These figures should be read in the context of the fact that, in addition to his weekly day-off, a worker is entitled to fifty-one days of paid leave in the year (though twenty of these are on half-pay). In theory, he is therefore required to work only 262 days, and must work at least 240 to be entitled to the full-quota of holiday. In practice many exchange some of their leave for cash.

5. *Jab tak kam hai pith men hath hai, kam nehin hai to gand men lat hai.*

REFERENCES

Breman, J. 1996. *Footloose Labour: Working in India's informal economy*, Cambridge: Cambridge University Press.

Burawoy, M. 1988. Thirty Years of Making Out. In R. Pahl (ed.), *On Work: Historical, comparative and theoretical approaches*, pp. 190–209, Oxford: Basil Blackwell Ltd.

Chandavarkar, R. 1994. *The Origins of Industrial Capitalism in India: Business strategies and the working classes in Bombay, 1900 – 1940*, Cambridge: Cambridge University Press.

Cooper, F. 1992. 'Colonizing Time: Work rhythms and labour conflict in colonial Mombasa'. In N. Dirks (ed.), *Colonialism and Culture*, Ann Arbor, MN: University of Michigan Press.

Gutman, H.G. 1988. 'Work, Culture and Society in Industrializing America, 1815–1919'. In R. Pahl (ed.), *On Work: Historical, Comparative and Theoretical Approaches*, pp. 125–37, Oxford: Basil Blackwell Ltd.

Linhart, R. 1985. 'The Assembly Line', In C.R. Littler (ed.), *The Experience of Work*, pp. 117–31, Aldershot: Gower.

Ong, A. 1987. *Spirits of Resistance and Capitalist Discipline: Factory in Malaysia*, Albany, NY: State University of New York Press.

Parry, J.P. 1999a. 'Lords of Labour: Working and shirking in Bhilai', *Contributions to Indian Sociology*, 3(1-2): 107–40.

Parry, J.P. 1999b. 'Two Cheers for Reservation: The Satnamis and the steel plant'. In R. Guha and J. Parry (eds), *Institutions and Inequality: Essays in honour of André Béteille*, pp. 168–69, Delhi: Oxford University Press.

Parry, J.P. 2001. 'Ankalu's Errant Wife: Sex, marriage and industry in contemporary Chhattisgarh', *Modern Asian Studies*, 35(4): 783–820.

Parry, J. P. 2008. 'The Sacrifices of Modernity in a Soviet-built Steel Town in Central India'. In F. Pine and J. de Pina, *Cabral, on the margins of religion*, pp. 233–62. Oxford: Berghahn Books.

Roberts, J.S. 1992. 'Drink and Industrial Discipline in Nineteenth-century Germany', In L. R. Berlanstein (ed.), *The Industrial Revolution and Work in Nineteenth-century Europe*, pp. 102–24. London: Routledge.

Sahlins, M. 1972. *Stone Age Economics*, Chicago: Aldine.

Scott, J. 1985. *Weapons of the Weak: Everyday forms of peasant resistance*. New Haven, CT: Yale University Press.

Smith, T.C. 1986. 'Peasant Time and Factory Time in Japan', *Past and Present*, 111: 165–97.

Thompson, E.P. 1991 (1964). Time, Work Discipline and Industrial Capitalism, In E.P. Thompson, *Customs in Common*, pp. 352– 403, Harmondsworth: Penguin.

Whipp, R. 1987. 'A time to every purpose: an essay on time and work', In P. Joyce (ed.), *The Historical Meanings of Work*, pp. 210–36, Cambridge: Cambridge University Press.

CHAPTER FOUR

The Production of Possession: Spirits and the Multinational Corporation in Malaysia

AIHWA ONG

The sanitized environments maintained by multinational corporations in Malaysian "free trade zones"[1] are not immune to sudden spirit attacks on young female workers. Ordinarily quiescent, Malay factory women who are seized by vengeful spirits explode into demonic screaming and rage on the shop floor. Management responses to such unnerving episodes include isolating the possessed workers, pumping them with Valium, and sending them home. Yet a Singapore[2] doctor notes that "a local medicine man can do more good than tranquilizers" (Chew 1978:51). Whatever healing technique used, the cure is never certain, for the Malays consider spirit possession an illness that afflicts the soul *(jiwa)*. This paper will explore how the reconstitution of illness, bodies, and consciousness is involved in the deployment of healing practices in multinational factories.

Anthropologists studying spirit possession phenomena have generally linked them to culturally specific forms of conflict management that disguise and yet resolve social tensions within indigenous societies (Firth 1967; Lewis 1971; Crapanzano and Garrison 1977). In contrast, policymakers and professionals see spirit possession episodes as an intrusion of archaic beliefs into the modern setting (Teoh, Soewondo, and Sidharta 1975; Chew 1978; Phoon 1982). These views will be evaluated in the light of spirit possession incidents and the reactions of factory managers and policymakers in Malaysia.

Different forms of spirit possession have been reported in Malay society, and their cultural significance varies with the regional and historical circumstances in which they occurred (see Maxwell 1977; Skeat 1965[1900]; Winstedt 1961; Firth 1967;

Endicott 1970; Kessler 1977). In the current changing political economy, new social conditions have brought about spirit possession incidents in modern institutional settings. I believe that the most appropriate way to deal with spirit visitations in multinational factories is to consider them as part of a "complex negotiation of reality" (Crapanzano 1977:16) by an emergent female industrial workforce. Hailing from peasant villages, these workers can be viewed as neophytes in a double sense: as young female adults and as members of a nascent proletariat. Mary Douglas' ideas about the breaking of taboos and social boundaries (1966) are useful for interpreting spirit possession in terms of what it reveals about the workers' profound sense of status ambiguity and dislocation. Second, their spirit idiom will be contrasted with the biomedical model to reveal alternative constructions of illness and of social reality in the corporate world. I will then consider the implications of the scientific medical model that converts workers into patients, and the consequences this therapeutic approach holds for mending the souls of the afflicted.

ECONOMIC DEVELOPMENT AND A MEDICAL MONOLOGUE ON MADNESS

As recently as the 1960s, most Malays in Peninsular Malaysia[3] lived in rural *kampung* (villages), engaged in cash cropping or fishing. In 1969, spontaneous outbreaks of racial rioting gave expression to deep-seated resentment over the distribution of power and wealth in this multiethnic society. The Malay-dominated government responded to this crisis by introducing a New Economic Policy intended to "restructure" the political economy. From the early 1970s onward, agricultural and industrialization programs induced the large-scale influx of young rural Malay men and women to enter urban schools and manufacturing plants set up by multinational corporations.

   Before the current wave of industrial employment for young single women, spirit possession was mainly manifested by married women, given the particular stresses of being wives, mothers, widows, and divorcées (see, for example, Maxwell 1977, and Kessler 1977). With urbanization and industrialization, spirit possession became overnight the affliction of young, unmarried women placed in modern organizations, drawing the attention of the press and the scholarly community (see Teoh, Soewondo, and Sidharta 1975; Chew 1978; Lim 1978; Jamilah Ariffin 1980; Ackerman and Lee 1981; Phoon 1982; Ong 1987).

   In 1971, 17 cases of "epidemic hysteria" among schoolgirls were reported, coinciding with the implementation of government policy (Teoh, Soewondo, and Sidharta 1975:259). This dramatic increase, from 12 cases reported for the entire decade of the 1960s, required an official response. Teoh, a professor of psychology, declared that "epidemic hysteria was not caused by offended spirits but by interpersonal tensions within the school or hostel" (1975:260). Teoh and his colleagues investigated a series of spirit incidents in a rural Selangor school, which they attributed to conflicts between the headmaster and female students. The investigators charged that in interpreting the events as "spirit possession" rather than the symptoms of local conflict, the *bomoh* (spirit healer) by "this devious path . . . avoided infringing on the taboos and sensitivities of the local community" (p. 267). Teoh had found it necessary to intervene by giving the headmaster psychotherapeutic counseling. Thus, spirit incidents in schools occasioned the introduction of a cosmopolitan therapeutic approach whereby rural Malays were "told to accept the . . . change from their old superstitious beliefs to contemporary scientific knowledge" (p. 268).

This dismissal of Malay interpretation of spirit events by Western-trained professionals became routine with the large-scale participation of Malays in capitalist industries. Throughout the 1970s, free-trade zones were established to encourage investments by Japanese, American, and European corporations for setting up plants for offshore production. In seeking to cut costs further, these corporations sought young, unmarried women[4] as a source of cheap and easily controlled labor. This selective labor demand, largely met by *kampung* society, produced in a single decade a Malay female industrial labor force of over 47,000 (Jamilah Ariffin 1980:47). Malay female migrants also crossed the Causeway in the thousands to work in multinational factories based in Singapore.

In a 1978 paper entitled "How to Handle Hysterical Factory Workers" in Singapore, Dr. P. K. Chew complained that "this psychological aberration interrupts production, and can create hazards due to inattention to machinery and careless behaviour" (1978:50). He classified "mass hysteria" incidents according to "frightened" and "seizure" categories, and recommended that incidents of either type should be handled "like an epidemic disease of bacteriological origin" (pp. 50, 53). In a Ministry of Labour survey of "epidemic hysteria" incidents in Singapore-based factories between 1973 and 1978, W. H. Phoon also focused on symptoms ranging from "hysterical seizures" and "trance states" to "frightened spells" (1982:22–23). The biomedical approach called for the use of sedatives, "isolation" of "infectious" cases, "immunization" of those susceptible to the "disease," and keeping the public informed about the measures taken (Chew 1978:53). Both writers, in looking for an explanation for the outbreak of "epidemic/mass hysteria" among Malay women workers, maintained that "the preference of belief in spirits and low educational level of the workers are obviously key factors" (Chew 1978:53; Phoon 1982:30). An anthropological study of spirit incidents in a Malacca shoe factory revealed that managers perceived the "real" causes of possession outbreaks to be physical (undernourishment) and psychological (superstitious beliefs) (Ackerman and Lee 1981:796).

These papers on spirit possession episodes in modern organizations adopt the assumptions of medical science which describe illnesses independent of their local meanings and values. "Mass hysteria" is attributed to the personal failings of the afflicted, and native explanations are denigrated as "superstitious beliefs" from a worldview out of keeping with the modern setting and pace of social change. "A monologue of reason about madness" (Foucault 1965:xi) was thereby introduced into Malaysian society, coinciding with a shift of focus from the afflicted to their chaotic

effects on modern institutions. We will need to recover the Malays' worldview in order
to understand their responses to social situations produced by industrialization.

SPIRIT BELIEFS AND WOMEN IN MALAY CULTURE

Spirit beliefs in rural Malay society, overlaid but existing within Islam, are part of the
indigenous worldview woven from strands of animistic cosmology and Javanese,
Hindu, and Muslim cultures (Mohd. Taib bin Osman 1972). In Peninsular Malaysia,
the supernatural belief system varies according to the historical and local interactions
between folk beliefs and Islamic teachings. Local traditions provide conceptual coherence about causation and well-being to village Malays. Through the centuries,
the office of the *bomoh*, or practitioner of folk medicine, has been the major means
by which these old traditions of causation, illness, and health have been transmitted.
In fulfilling the pragmatic and immediate needs of everyday life, the beliefs and
practices are often recast in "Islamic" terms (Mohd. Taib bin Osman 1972:221–222;
Endicott 1970).

I am mainly concerned here with the folk model in Sungai Jawa (a pseudonym), a
village based in Kuala Langat district, rural Selangor, where I conducted fieldwork
in 1979–80. Since the 1960s, the widespread introduction of Western medical practices and an intensified revitalization of Islam have made spirit beliefs publicly in-
admissable. Nevertheless, spirit beliefs and practices are still very much in evidence.
Villagers believe that all beings have spiritual essence (*semangat*) but, unlike humans,
spirits *(hantu)* are disembodied beings capable of violating the boundaries between
the material and supernatural worlds: invisible beings unbounded by human rules,
spirits come to represent transgressions of moral boundaries, which are socially
defined in the concentric spaces of homestead, village, and jungle. This scheme
roughly coincides with Malay concepts of emotional proximity and distance, and the
related dimensions of reduced moral responsibility as one moves from the interior
space of household, to the intermediate zone of relatives, and on to the external
world of strangers (Banks 1983:170–174).

The two main classes of spirits recognized by Malays reflect this interior-exterior
social/spatial divide: spirits associated with human beings, and the "free" disembodied forms. In Sungai Jawa, *toyol* are the most common familiar spirits, who steal
in order to enrich their masters. Accusations of breeding *toyol* provide the occasion
for expressing resentment against economically successful villagers. Birth demons
are former human females who died in childbirth and, as *pontianak*, threaten newly
born infants and their mothers. Thus, spirit beliefs reflect everyday anxieties about
the management of social relations in village society.

It is free spirits that are responsible for attacking people who unknowingly
step out of the Malay social order. Free spirits are usually associated with special
objects or sites *(keramat)* marking the boundary between human and natural spaces.

These include (1) the burial grounds of aboriginal and animal spirits, (2) strangely shaped rocks, hills, or trees associated with highly revered ancestral figures *(datuk)*, and (3) animals like were-tigers (Endicott 1970:90–91). As the gatekeepers of social boundaries, spirits guard against human transgressions into amoral spaces. Such accidents require the mystical qualities of the *bomoh* to readjust spirit relations with the human world.

From Islam, Malays have inherited the belief that men are more endowed with *akal* (reason) than women, who are overly influenced by *hawa nafsu* (human lust). A susceptibility to imbalances in the four humoral elements renders women spiritually weaker than men. Women's *hawa nafsu* nature is believed to make them especially vulnerable to *latah* (episodes during which the victim breaks out into obscene language and compulsive, imitative behavior) and to spirit attacks (spontaneous episodes in which the afflicted one screams, hyperventilates, or falls down in a trance or a raging fit). However, it is Malay spirit beliefs that explain the transgressions whereby women (more likely than men) become possessed by spirits *(kena hantu)*. Their spiritual frailty, polluting bodies, and erotic nature make them especially likely to transgress moral space, and therefore permeable by spirits.

Mary Douglas (1966) has noted that taboos operate to control threats to social boundaries. In Malay society, women are hedged in by conventions that keep them out of social roles and spaces dominated by men. Although men are also vulnerable to spirit attacks, women's spiritual, bodily, and social selves are especially offensive to sacred spaces, which they trespass at the risk of inviting spirit attacks.

Spirit victims have traditionally been married women who sometimes become possessed after giving birth for the first time. Childbirth is a dangerous occasion, when rituals are performed in order to keep off evil spirits (see Laderman 1983:125–126). As a rite of passage, childbirth is the first traumatic event in the ordinary village woman's life. I visited a young mother who had been possessed by a *hantu*, which the ministrations of two *bomoh* failed to dislodge. She lay on her mat for two months after delivering her first child, uninterested in nursing the baby. Her mother-in-law whispered that she had been "penetrated by the devil." Perhaps, through some unintended action, she had attracted spirit attack and been rendered ritually and sexually impure.

The next critical phase in a woman's life cycle comes at middle age. Kessler (1977) observes that among Kelantanese fisherfolk, possessed women were often those threatened with widowhood, divorce, or their husbands' plan to take a second wife. Laderman (1983:127) claims that Trengganu village women who resist their assigned roles as mothers and wives are said to become vulnerable to spirit attacks and may be transformed into demons. These ethnographic observations from different Malay communities demonstrate that in village life, spirit attacks are most likely to occur when women are in transition from one phase of life to another. On such occasions, they are perceived to be the greatest threat to social norms, and taboos enforce some degree of self-control in order to contain that threat.

In everday life, village women are also bound by customs regarding bodily comportment and spatial movements, which operate to keep them within the Malay social order. When they blur the bodily boundaries through the careless disposal of bodily-exuviae and effluvia, they put themselves in an ambiguous situation, becoming most vulnerable to spirit penetration.

Until recently, unmarried daughters, most hedged in by village conventions, seem to have been well protected from spirit attack. Nubile girls take special care over the disposal of their cut nails, fallen hair, and menstrual rags, since such materials may fall into ill-wishers' hands and be used for black magic. Menstrual blood is considered dirty and polluting (cf. Laderman 1983:74), and the substance most likely to offend *keramat* spirits. This concern over bodily boundaries is linked to notions about the vulnerable identity and status of young unmarried women. It also operates to keep pubescent girls close to the homestead and on well-marked village paths. In Sungai Jawa, a schoolgirl who urinated on an ant-hill off the beaten track became possessed by a "male" spirit. Scheper-Hughes and Lock remark that when the social norms of small, conservative peasant communities are breached, we would expect to see a "concern with the penetration and violation of bodily exits, entrances and boundaries" (1987:19). Thus, one suspects that when young Malay women break with village traditions, they may come under increased spirit attacks as well as experience an intensified social and bodily vigilance.

Since the early 1970s, when young peasant women began to leave the *kampung* and enter the unknown worlds of urban boarding schools and foreign factories, the incidence of spirit possession seems to have become more common among them than among married women. I maintain that like other cultural forms, spirit possession incidents may acquire new meanings and speak to new experiences in changing arenas of social relations and boundary definitions. In *kampung* society, spirit attacks on married women seem to be associated with their containment in prescribed domestic roles, whereas in modern organizations, spirit victims are young, unmarried women engaged in hitherto alien and male activities. This transition from *kampung* to urban-industrial contexts has cast village girls into an intermediate status that they find unsettling and fraught with danger to themselves and to Malay culture.

SPIRIT VISITATIONS IN MODERN FACTORIES

In the 1970s, newspaper reports on the sudden spate of "mass hysteria" among young Malay women in schools and factories interpreted the causes in terms of "superstitious beliefs," "examination tension," "the stresses of urban living," and less frequently, "mounting pressures" which induced "worries" among female operators in multinational factories.

Multinational factories based in free-trade zones were the favored sites of spirit visitations. An American factory in Sungai Way experienced a large-scale incident in 1978, which involved some 120 operators engaged in assembly work requiring the use of microscopes. The factory had to be shut down for three days, and a *bomoh* was hired to slaughter a goat on the premises. The American director wondered how he was to explain to corporate headquarters that "8,000 hours of production were lost because someone saw a ghost" (Lim 1978:33). A Japanese factory based in Pontian, Kelantan, also experienced a spirit attack on 21 workers in; 1980. As they were being taken to ambulances, some victims screamed, "I will kill you! Let me go!" *(New Straits Times*, 26 September, 1980). In Penang, another American factory was disrupted for three consecutive days after 15 women became afflicted by spirit possession. The victims screamed in fury and put up a terrific struggle against restraining male supervisors, shouting "Go away!" *(Sunday Echo*, 27 November, 1978). The afflicted were snatched off the shop floor and given injections of sedatives. Hundreds of frightened female workers were also sent home. A factory personnel officer told reporters:

> "Some girls started sobbing and screaming hysterically and when it seemed like spreading, the other workers in the production line were immediately ushered out. . . . It is a common belief among workers that the factory is "dirty" and supposed to be haunted by a *datuk"* [*Sunday Echo*].

Though brief, these reports reveal that spirit possession, believed to be caused by defilement, held the victims in a grip of rage against factory supervisors. Furthermore, the disruptions caused by spirit incidents seem a form of retaliation against the factory supervisors. In what follows, I will draw upon my field research to discuss the complex issues involved in possession imagery and management discourse on spirit incidents in Japanese-owned factories based in Kuala Langat.

The Cryptic Language of Possession

The political economy of Islam is set up and orchestrated around the silence of inferiors.
Fatna A. Sabbah, *Woman in the Muslim Unconscious*

Young, unmarried women in Malay society are expected to be shy, obedient, and deferential, to be observed and not heard. In spirit possession episodes, they speak in other voices that refuse to be silenced. Since the afflicted claim amnesia once they have recovered, we are presented with the task of deciphering covert messages embedded in possession incidents.

Spirit visitations in modern factories with sizable numbers of young Malay female workers engender devil images, which dramatically reveal the contradictions between Malay and scientific ways of apprehending the human condition. I. M. Lewis has suggested that in traditionally gender-stratified societies, women's spirit possession episodes are a "thinly disguised protest against the dominant sex" (1971:31). In Malay society, what is being negotiated in possession incidents and their aftermath are complex issues dealing with the violation of different moral boundaries, of which gender oppression is but one dimension. What seems clear is that spirit possession provides a traditional way of rebelling against authority without punishment, since victims are not blamed for their predicament. However, the imagery of spirit possession in modern settings is a rebellion against transgressions of indigenous boundaries governing proper human relations and moral justice.

For Malays, the places occupied by evil spirits are nonhuman territories like swamps, jungles, and bodies of water. These amoral domains were kept distant from women's bodies by ideological and physical spatial regulations. The construction of modern buildings, often without regard for Malay concern about moral space, displaces spirits, which take up residence in the toilet tank. Thus, most village women express a horror of the Western-style toilet, which they would avoid if they could. It is the place where their usually discreet disposal of bodily waste is disturbed. Besides their fear of spirits residing in the water tank, an unaccustomed body posture is required to use the toilet. In their hurry to depart, unflushed toilets and soiled sanitary napkins, thrown helter-skelter, offend spirits who may attack them.

A few days after the spirit attacks in the Penang-based American factory, I interviewed some of the workers. Without prompting, factory women pointed out that the production floor and canteen areas were "very clean" but factory toilets were "filthy" (kotor). A datuk haunted the toilet, and workers, in their haste to leave, dropped their soiled pads anywhere. In Ackerman and Lee's case study, Malay factory workers believed that they had disturbed the spirits dwelling in a water tank and on factory grounds. Furthermore, the spirits were believed to possess women who had violated moral codes, thereby becoming "unclean" (1981:794, 796–797). This connection between disturbing spirits and lack of sexual purity is also hinted at in Teoh and his colleagues' account of the school incidents mentioned above. The headmaster had given students instructions in how to wear sanitary napkins (1978:262),[5] an incident which helped precipitate a series of spirit attacks said to be caused by the "filthy" school toilets and the girls' disposal of soiled pads in a swamp adjacent to the school grounds (1978:264).

In the Penang factory incident, a worker remembered that a piercing scream from one corner of the shop floor was quickly followed by cries from other benches as women fought against spirits trying to possess them. The incidents had been sparked by datuk visions, sometimes headless, gesticulating angrily at the operators. Even after the bomoh had been sent for, workers had to be accompanied to the toilet by foremen for fear of being attacked by spirits in the stalls.

In Kuala Langat, my fieldwork elicited similar imagery from the workers[6] in two Japanese factories (code-named ENI and EJI) based in the local free-trade zone. In their drive for attaining high production targets, foremen (both Malay and non-Malay) were very zealous in enforcing regulations that confined workers to the work bench. Operators had to ask for permission to go to the toilet, and were sometimes questioned intrusively about their "female problems." Menstruation was seen by management as deserving no consideration even in a workplace where 85–90 percent of the work force was female.[7] In the EJI plant, foremen sometimes followed workers to the locker room, terrorizing them with their spying. One operator became possessed after screaming that she saw a "hairy leg" when she went to the toilet. A worker from another factory reported:

> Workers saw "things" appear when they went to the toilet. Once, when a woman entered the toilet she saw a tall figure licking sanitary napkins ["Modess" supplied in the cabinet]. It had a long tongue, and those sanitary pads . . . cannot be used anymore.

As Taussig remarks, the "language" emanating from our bodies expresses the significance of social disease (1980). The above lurid imagery speaks of the women's loss of control over their bodies as well as their lack of control over social relations in the factory. Furthermore, the image of body alienation also reveals intense guilt (and repressed desire), and the felt need to be on guard against violation by the male management staff who, in the form of fearsome predators, may suddenly materialize anywhere in the factory.

Even the prayer room *(surau)*, provided on factory premises for the Muslim work force, was not safe from spirit harassment. A woman told me of her aunt's fright in the *surau* at the EJI factory.

> "She was in the middle of praying when she fainted because she said . . . her head suddenly spun and something pounced on her from behind."

As mentioned above, spirit attacks also occurred when women were at the work bench, usually during the "graveyard" shift. An ENI factory opertor described one incident which took place in May 1979.

> "It was the afternoon shift, at about nine o'clock. All was quiet. Suddenly, [the victim] started sobbing, laughed and then shrieked. She flailed at the machine . . . she was violent, she fought as the foreman and technician pulled her away. Altogether, three operators were afflicted. . . . The supervisor and foremen took them to the clinic and told the driver to take them home. . . .
>
> She did not know what had happened . . . she saw a *hantu*, a were-tiger. Only she saw it, and she started screaming. . . . The foremen would not let us talk with her for fear of recurrence. . . . People say that the workplace is haunted by the *hantu* who dwells below. . . . Well, this used to be all jungle, it was a burial ground before the factory was built. The devil disturbs those who have a weak constitution."

Spirit possession episodes then were triggered by black apparitions, which materialized in "liminal" spaces such as toilets (see also Teoh, Soewondo, and Sidharta 1975:259, 262, and Chew 1978:52), the locker room and the prayer room, places where workers sought refuge from harsh work discipline. These were also rooms periodically checked by male supervisors determined to bring workers back to the work bench. The microscope, which after hours of use becomes an instrument of torture, sometimes disclosed spirits lurking within. Other workers pointed to the effect of the steady hum and the factory pollutants, which permanently disturbed graveyard spirits. Unleashed, these vengeful beings were seen to threaten women for transgressing into the zone between the human and nonhuman world, as well as modern spaces formerly the domain of men. By intruding into hitherto forbidden spaces, Malay women workers experienced anxieties about inviting punishment.

Fatna Sabbah observes that "(t)he invasion by women of economic spaces such as factories and offices . . . is often experienced as erotic aggression in the Muslim context" (1984:17). In Malay culture, men and women in public contact must define the situation in nonsexual terms (cf. Banks 1983:88). It is particularly incumbent upon young women to conduct themselves with circumspection and to diffuse sexual tension. However, the modern factory is an arena constituted by a sexual division of labor and constant male surveillance of nubile women in a close, daily context. In Kuala Langat, young factory women felt themselves placed in a situation in which they unintentionally violated taboos defining social and bodily boundaries. The shop floor culture was also charged with the dangers of sexual harassment by male management staff as part of workaday relations.[8] To combat spirit attacks, the Malay factory women felt a greater need for spiritual vigilance in the factory surroundings. Thus the victim in the ENI factory incident was said to be:

> possessed, maybe because she was spiritually weak. She was not spiritually vigilant, so that when she saw the *hantu* she was instantly afraid and screamed. Usually, the *hantu* likes people who are spiritually weak, yes. . . . one should guard against being easily startled, afraid.

As Foucault observes, people subjected to the "micro-techniques" of power are induced to regulate themselves (1979). The fear of spirit possession thus created self-regulation on the part of workers, thereby contributing to the intensification of corporate and self-control on the shop floor. Thus, as factory workers, Malay women became alienated not only from the products of their labor but also experienced new forms of psychic alienation. Their intrusion into economic spaces outside the home and village was experienced as moral disorder, symbolized by filth and dangerous sexuality. Some workers called for increased "discipline," others for Islamic classes on factory premises to regulate interactions (including dating) between male and female workers. Thus, spirit imagery gave symbolic configuration to the workers' fear and protest over social conditions in the factories. However, these inchoate signs of moral and social chaos were routinely recast by management into an idiom of sickness.

The Worker as Patient

Studies of work experiences in modern industrial systems have tended to focus on the ways time and motion techniques (Taylorism) have facilitated the progressive adaptation of the human body to machines, bringing about the divorce of mental and manual labor (Braverman 1974). Others have maintained that control over the exact movements of the workers allowed by Taylorism has banished fantasy and thoroughly depersonalized work relations in the modern factory (Gramsci 1971:303; Ellul 1964:387–410). Indeed, Taylorist forms of work discipline are taken to an extreme in the computer-chip manufacturing industries set up by multinational corporations in Malaysia (see Ong 1987). However, contrary to the above claims, I would argue that the recoding of the human body-work relation is a critical and contested dimension of daily conduct in the modern factory.

I have elsewhere described the everyday effects of the sexual division of labor and Taylorist techniques on Malay factory women (1987). Here, I wish to discuss how struggles over the meanings of health are part of workers' social critique of work discipline, and of managers' attempts to extend control over the work force. The management use of workers as "instruments of labor" is paralleled by another set of ideologies, which regards women's bodies as the site of control where gender politics, health, and educational practices intersect (cf. Foucault 1980).

In the Japanese factories based in Malaysia, management ideology constructs the female body in terms of its biological functionality for, and its anarchic disruption of, production. These ideologies operate to fix women workers in subordinate positions in systems of domination that proliferate in high-tech industries. A Malaysian investment brochure advertises "the oriental girl," for example, as "qualified *by nature and inheritance* to contribute to the efficiency of a bench assembly production line" (FIDA 1975, emphasis added). This biological rationale for the commodification of women's bodies is a part of a pervasive discourse reconceptualizing women for high-tech production requirements. Japanese managers in the free-trade zone talk about the "eyesight," "manual dexterity," and "patience" of young women to perform tedious micro-assembly jobs. An engineer put the female nature-technology relationship in a new light: "Our work is designed for females." Within international capitalism,[9] this notion of women's bodies renders them analogous to the status of the computer chips they make. Computer chips, like "oriental girls," are identical, whether produced in Malaysia, Taiwan, or Sri Lanka. For multinational corporations, women are units of much cheap labor power repackaged under the "nimble fingers" label.

The abstract mode of scientific discourse also separates "normal" from "abnormal" workers, that is, those who do not perform according to factory requirements. In the EJI factory, the Malay personnel manager using the biomedical model to locate the sources of spirit possession among workers noted that the first spirit attack occurred five months after the factory began operation in 1976. Thereafter,

> "we had our counter-measure. I think this is a method of how you give initial education
> to the workers, how you take care of the medical welfare of the workers. The worker
> who is weak, comes in without breakfast, lacking sleep, then she will see ghosts!"

In the factory environment, "spirit attacks" *(kena hantu)* was often used interchangeably with "mass hysteria," a term adopted from English language press reports on such incidents. In the manager's view, "hysteria" was a symptom of physical adjustment as the women workers "move from home idleness to factory discipline." This explanation also found favor with some members of the work force. Scientific terms like *"penyakit histeria"* (hysteria sickness), and physiological preconditions formulated by the management, became more acceptable to some workers. One woman remarked,

> "They say they saw *hantu*, but I don't know. . . . I believe that maybe they . . . when they come to work, they did not fill their stomachs, they were not full so that they felt hungry. But they were not brave enough to say so."

A male technician used more complex concepts, but remained doubtful.

> "I think that this [is caused by] a feeling of 'complex' – that maybe 'inferiority complex' is pressing them down – their spirit, so that this can be called an illness of the spirit, 'conflict *jiwa*,' 'emotional conflict.' Sometimes they see an old man, in black shrouds, they say, in their microscopes, they say. . . . I myself don't know how. They see *hantu* in different places. . . . Some time ago an 'emergency' incident like this occurred in a boarding school. The victim fainted. Then she became very strong. . . . It required ten or twenty persons to handle her."

In corporate discourse, physical "facts" that contributed to spirit possession were isolated, while psychological notions were used as explanation and as a technique of manipulation. In ENI factory, a *bomoh* was hired to produce the illusion of exorcism, lulling the workers into a false sense of security. The personnel manager claimed that unlike managers in other Japanese firms who operated on the "basis of feelings," his "psychological approach" helped to prevent recurrent spirit visitations.

> "You cannot dispel *kampung* beliefs. Now and then we call the *bomoh* to come, every six months or so, to pray, walk around. Then we take pictures of the *bomoh* in the factory and hang up the pictures. Somehow, the workers seeing these pictures feel safe, [seeing] that the place has been exorcised."

Similarly, whenever a new section of the factory was constructed, the *bomoh* was sent for to sprinkle holy water, thereby assuring workers that the place was rid of ghosts. Regular *bomoh* visits and their photographic images were different ways of defining a social reality, which simultaneously acknowledged and manipulated the workers' fear of spirits.

Medical personnel were also involved in the narrow definition of the causes of spirit incidents on the shop floor. A factory nurse periodically toured the shop floor to offer coffee to tired or drowsy workers. Workers had to work eight-hour shifts six days a week – morning, 6:30 A.M. to 2:30 P.M.; afternoon, 2:30 P.M. to 10:30 P.M.; or night, 10:30 P.M. to 6:30 A.M. – which divided up the 24-hour daily operation of the factories. They were permitted two ten-minute breaks and a half-hour for a meal.

Most workers had to change to a different shift every two weeks. This regime allowed little time for workers to recover from their exhaustion between shifts. In addition, overtime was frequently imposed. The shifts also worked against the human, and especially female cycle; many freshly recruited workers regularly missed their sleep, meals, and menstrual cycles.

Thus, although management pointed to physiological problems as causing spirit attacks, they seldom acknowledged deeper scientific evidence of health hazards in microchip assembly plants. These include the rapid deterioration of eyesight caused by the prolonged use of microscopes in bonding processes. General exposure to strong solvents, acids, and fumes induced headaches, nausea, dizziness, and skin irritation in workers. More toxic substances used for cleaning purposes exposed workers to lead poisoning, kidney failure, and breast cancer (Federation of Women Lawyers 1983:16). Other materials used in the fabrication of computer chips have been linked to female workers' painful menstruation, their inability to conceive, and repeated miscarriages *(Business Times [Asia]*, 9 October 1982:19; *San Francisco Chronicle*, 14 January 1987:23,27). Within the plants, unhappy-looking workers were urged to talk over their problems with the "industrial relations assistant." Complaints of "pain in the chest" were interpreted to mean emotional distress, and the worker was ushered into the clinic for medication in order to maintain discipline and a relentless work schedule.

In the EJI factory, the shop floor supervisor admitted, "I think that hysteria is related to the job in some cases." He explained that workers in the microscope sections were usually the ones to *kena hantu*, and thought that perhaps they should not begin work doing those tasks. However, he quickly offered other interpretations that had little to do with work conditions: There was one victim whose broken engagement had incurred her mother's wrath; at work she cried and talked to herself, saying, "I am not to be blamed, not me!" Another worker, seized by possession, screamed, "Send me home, send me home!" Apparently, she indicated, her mother had taken all her earnings. Again, through such psychological readings, the causes of spirit attacks produced in the factories were displaced onto workers and their families.

In corporate discourse, both the biomedical and psychological interpretations of spirit possession defined the affliction as an attribute of individuals rather than stemming from the general social situation. Scientific concepts, pharmaceutical treatment, and behavioral intervention all identified and separated recalcitrant workers from "normal" ones; disruptive workers became patients. According to Parsons, the cosmopolitan medical approach tolerates illness as sanctioned social deviance; however, patients have the duty to get well (1985:146, 149). This attitude implies that those who do not get well cannot be rewarded with "the privileges of being sick" (1985:149). In the ENI factory, the playing out of this logic provided the rationale for dismissing workers who had had two previous experiences of spirit attacks, on the grounds of "security." This policy drew protests from village elders, for whom spirits in the factory were the cause of their daughters' insecurity. The manager agreed verbally with them, but pointed out that these "hysterical, mental types" might hurt themselves when they flailed against the machines, risking electrocution. By appearing to agree with native theory, the management reinterpreted spirit possession as a symbol of flawed character and culture.[10] The sick role was reconceptualized as internally produced by outmoded thought and behavior not adequately adjusted to the demands of factory discipline. The worker-patient could have no claim on management sympathy but would have to bear responsibility for her own cultural deficiency. A woman in ENI talked sadly about her friend, the victim of spirits and corporate policy.

> "At the time the management wanted to throw her out, to end her work, she cried. She did ask to be reinstated, but she has had three [episodes] already. . . . I think that whether it was right or not [to expel her] depends [on the circumstances], because she has already worked here for a long time; now that she has been thrown out she does not know what she can do, you know."

The nonrecognition of social obligations to workers lies at the center of differences in world-view between Malay workers and the foreign management. By treating the signs and symptoms of disease as "things-in-themselves" (Taussig 1980:1), the biomedical model freed managers from any moral debt owed the workers. Furthermore, corporate adoption of spirit idiom stigmatized spirit victims, thereby ruling out any serious consideration of their needs. Afflicted and "normal" workers alike were made to see that spirit possession was nothing but confusion and delusion, which should be abandoned in a rational worldview.

The Work of Culture: Hygiene and Dispossession

Modern factories transplanted to the Third World are involved in the work of producing exchange as well as symbolic values. Medicine, as a branch of cosmopolitan science, has attained a place in schemes for effecting desired social change in indigenous cultures. While native statements about bizarre events are rejected as irrational, the conceptions of positivist science acquire a quasi-religious flavor (Karnoouh 1984). In the process, the native "work of culture," which transforms motives and affects into "publicly accepted sets of meanings and symbols" (Obeyesekere 1985:147), is being undermined by an authoritative discourse that suppresses lived experiences apprehended through the worldview of indigenous peoples.

To what extent can the *bomoh's* work of culture convert the rage and distress of possessed women in Malaysia into socially shared meanings? As discussed above, the spirit imagery speaks of danger and violation as young Malay women intrude into hitherto forbidden spirit or male domains. Their participation as an industrial force is subconsciously perceived by themselves and their families as a threat to the ordering of Malay culture. Second, their employment as production workers places them directly in the control of male strangers who monitor their every move. These social relations, brought about in the process of industrial capitalism, are experienced as a moral disorder in which workers are alienated from their bodies, the products of their work, and their own culture. The spirit idiom is therefore a language of protest against these changing social circumstances. A male technician evaluated the stresses they were under.

> "There is a lot of discipline. . . . but when there is too much discipline . . . it is not good. Because of this the operators, with their small wages, will always contest. They often break the machines in ways that are not apparent. . . . Sometimes, they damage the products."

Such Luddite actions in stalling production reverse momentarily the arrangement whereby work regimentation controls the human body. However, the workers' resistance[11] is not limited to the technical problem of work organization, but addresses the violation of moral codes. A young woman explained her sense of having been "tricked" into an intolerable work arrangement.

> "For instance, . . . sometimes . . . they want us to raise production. This is what we sometimes challenge. The workers want fair treatment, as for instance, in relation to wages and other matters. We feel that in this situation there are many [issues] to dispute over with the management. . . . with our wages so low we feel as though we have been tricked or forced."

She demands "justice, because sometimes they exhaust us very much as if they do not think that we too are human beings!"

Spirit possession episodes may be taken as expressions both of fear and of resistance against the multiple violations of moral boundaries in the modern factory. They are acts of rebellion, symbolizing what cannot be spoken directly, calling for a renegotiation of obligations between the management and workers. However, technocrats have turned a deaf ear to such protests, to this moral indictment of their woeful cultural judgments about the dispossessed. By choosing to view possession episodes narrowly as sickness caused by physiological and psychological maladjustment, the management also manipulates the *bomoh* to serve the interests of the factory rather than express the needs of the workers.

Both Japanese factories in Kuala Langat have commenced operations in a spate of spirit possession incidents. A year after operations began in the EJI factory, as well-known *bomoh* and his retinue were invited to the factory *surau*, where they read prayers over a basin of "pure water." Those who had been visited by the devil drank from it and washed their faces, a ritual which made them immune to future spirit attacks. The *bomoh* pronounced the *hantu* controlling the factory site "very kind"; he merely showed himself but did not disturb people. A month after the ritual, the spirit attacks resumed, but involving smaller numbers of women (one or two) in each incident. The manager claimed that after the exorcist rites, spirit attacks occurred only once a month.

In an interview, an eye witness reported what happened after a spirit incident erupted.

> "The work section was not shut down, we had to continue working. Whenever it happened, the other workers felt frightened. They were not allowed to look because [the management] feared contagion. They would not permit us to leave. When an incident broke out, we had to move away. . . . At ten o'clock they called the *bomoh* to come . . . because he knew that the *hantu* had already entered the woman's body. He came in and scattered rice flour water all over the area where the incident broke out. He recited prayers over holy water. He sprinkled rice flour water on places touched by the *hantu*. . . . The *bomoh* chanted incantations *[jampi jampi]* chasing the *hantu* away. He then gave some medicine to the afflicted. . . . He also entered the clinic [to pronounce] *jampi jampi*."

The primary role of the *bomoh* hired by corporate management was to ritually cleanse the prayer room, shop floor, and even the factory clinic. After appeasing the spirits, he ritually healed the victims, who were viewed as not responsible for their affliction. However, his work did not extend to curing them after they had been given sedatives and sent home. Instead, through his exorcism and incantations, the *bomoh* expressed the Malay understanding of these disturbing events, perhaps impressing the other workers that the factory had been purged of spirits. However, he failed to convince the management about the need to create a moral space, in Malay terms, on factory premises. Management did not respond to spirit incidents by reconsidering social relationships on the shop floor; instead, they sought to eliminate the afflicted from the work scene. As the ENI factory nurse, an Indian woman, remarked, "It is an experience working with the Japanese. They do not consult women. To tell you the truth, they don't care about the problem except that it goes away."

This avoidance of the moral challenge was noted by workers in the way management handled the *kenduri*, the ritual feast that resolved a dispute by bringing the opposing sides together in an agreement over future cooperation. In the American factory incident in Penang, a *bomoh* was sent for, but worker demands for a feast were ignored. At the EJI factory, cleansing rituals were brought to a close by a feast of saffron rice and chicken curry. This was served to factory managers and officers, but not a single worker (or victim) was invited. This distortion of the Malay rite of commensality did not fail to impress on workers the management rejection of moral responsibility to personal needs – *muafakat* (see Banks 1983:123–124). Women workers remained haunted by their fear of negotiating the liminal spaces between female and male worlds, old and new morality, when mutual obligations between the afflicted and the *bomoh*, workers and the management, had not been fulfilled.

The work of the *bomoh* was further thwarted by the medicalization of the afflicted. Spirit possession incidents in factories made visible the conflicted women who did not fit the corporate image of "normal" workers. By standing apart from the workaday routine, possessed workers inadvertently exposed themselves to the cold ministrations of modern medicine, rather than the increased social support they sought. Other workers, terrified of being attacked and by the threat of expulsion, kept up a watchful vigilance. This induced self-regulation was reinforced by the scientific gaze of supervisors and nurses, which further enervated the recalcitrant and frustrated those who resisted. A worker observed,

> "[The possessed] don't remember their experiences. Maybe the *hantu* is still working on their madness, maybe because their experiences have not been stilled, or maybe their souls are not really disturbed. They say there are evil spirits in that place [that is, factory]."

In fact, spirit victims maintained a disturbed silence after their "recovery." Neither their families, friends, the *bomoh*, nor I could get them to talk about their experiences.

Spirit possession episodes in different societies have been labeled "mass psychogenic illness" or "epidemic hysteria" in psychological discourse (Colligan, Pennebaker, and Murphy 1982). Different altered states of consciousness, which variously spring from indigenous understanding of social situations, are reinterpreted in cosmopolitan terms considered universally applicable. In multinational factories located overseas, this ethnotherapeutic model (Lutz 1985) is widely applied and made to seem objective and rational. However, we have seen that such scientific knowledge and practices can display a definite prejudice against the people they are intended to restore to well-being in particular cultural contexts. The reinterpretation of spirit possession may therefore be seen as a shift of locus of patriarchal authority from the *bomoh*, sanctioned by indigenous religious beliefs, toward professionals sanctioned by scientific training.

In Third World contexts, cosmopolitan medical concepts and drugs often have an anesthetizing effect, which erases the authentic experiences of the sick. More frequently, the proliferation of positivist scientific meanings also produces a fragmentation of the body, a shattering of social obligations, and a separation of individuals from their own culture. Gramsci (1971) has defined hegemony as a form of ideological domination based on the consent of the dominated, a consent that is secured through the diffusion of the worldview of the dominant class. In Malaysia, medicine has become part of hegemonic discourse, constructing a "modern" outlook by clearing away the nightmarish visions of Malay workers. However, as a technique of both concealment and control, it operates in a more sinister way than native beliefs in demons. Malay factory women may gradually become dispossessed of spirits and their own culture, but they remain profoundly diseased in the "brave new workplace."[12]

NOTES

Acknowledgments. I am grateful to the National Science Foundation (grant no. BNS-787639), and the International Development Research Centre, Ottawa, for funding the fieldwork and writing of the project. Some of the material contained in this paper has been published in my book, *Spirits of Resistance and Capitalist Discipline: Factory Women in Malaysia* (1987).

1. "Free trade zones" are fenced-off areas in which multinational corporations are permitted to locate export-processing industries in the host country. These zones are exempt from many taxation and labor regulations that may apply elsewhere in the economy.

2. "Singapore is an island state situated south of Peninsular Malaysia. Although separate countries, they share historical roots and many cultural similarities and interests.

3. That is, West Malaysia. East Malaysia is constituted by the states of Sabah and Sarawak in northern Borneo. In Peninsular Malaysia, more than half the population (approximately 13 million) is made up of Malays. Ethnic Chinese form the main minority group, followed by Indians.

4. Mainly between the ages of 16 and 26 years. Many dropped out after six or seven years because they saw no improvement in their jobs as production workers and because of marriage. In the cities, the women lived in rooming houses or dormitories or with relatives.

5. Most village girls began buying and wearing sanitary pads after they enrolled in secular schools or began work in factories. In some cases, schools and factories supplied these market items to encourage the girls to wear them, often against their will. Village girls had previously worn homemade girdles lined with kapok.

6. Most of the factory women in the Kuala Langat free-trade zone lived with their families in the nearby villages, commuting to work every day. Although parents were eager for their daughters to earn wages, they were also anxious about the social effects of their participation in the wider, culturally alien world (see Ong 1987:Parts II and III).

7. Government regulations required multinational factories to provide female workers with maternity leave of 60 consecutive days. This right has had the unintended effect of discouraging multinational factories from recruiting married women. Those who got married on the job were offered family planning classes and free contraceptives.

8. In a survey, the Malaysian Federation of Women Lawyers found that some managerial staff in multinational factories were guilty of demanding sexual favors in return for promises of work benefits, bonuses, and promotion. However, their victims "ignorant of their rights [had] nobody to turn to to voice their woes" (Federation of Women Lawyers 1983:18).

9. Such talk is not confined to Japanese corporations. In the world of semiconductor production, American and European firms also perpetuate such views.

10. I therefore see a more complex process at work than Ackerman and Lee who note that by reifying spirit possession as the cause of these bizarre incidents, the management of a shoe factory served "to reinforce the belief in the reality of spirit possession" (1981:797).

11. The vast majority of electronics workers in Malaysian free-trade zones are not unionized, even though government policy does not formally forbid union organization. However, the Ministry of Labour has repeatedly frustrated the efforts of electronics workers to unionize.

12. This phrase is borrowed from Howard's (1985) study of changing work relations occasioned by the introduction of computer technology into offices and industries.

REFERENCES CITED

Ackerman, Susan, and Raymond Lee 1981 Communication and Cognitive Pluralism in a Spirit Possession Event in Malaysia. *American Ethnologist* 8(4):789–799.

Banks, David J. 1983 *Malay Kinship*. Philadelphia, PA: ISHI.

Braverman, Harry 1974 *Labor and Monopoly Capital: The Degradation of Work in the Twentieth Century*. New York: Monthly Review Press.

Chew, P. K. 1978 How to Handle Hysterical Factory Workers. *Occupational Health and Safety* 47(2):50–53.

Colligan, Michael, James Pennebaker, and Lawrence Murphy, eds. 1982 *Mass Psychogenic Illness: A Social Psychological Analysis*. Hillsdale, NJ: Lawrence Erlbaum Associates.

Crapanzano, Vincent 1977 Introduction. In *Case Studies in Spirit Possession*. Vincent Crapanzano and Vivian Garrison, eds. pp. 1–40. New York: John Wiley.

Crapanzano, Vincent, and Vivian Garrison, eds. 1977 *Case Studies in Spirit Possession*. New York: John Wiley.

Douglas, Mary 1966 *Purity and Danger: An Analysis of Pollution and Taboo*. Harmondsworth, England: Penguin.

Ellul, Jacques 1964 *The Technological Society*. John Wilkinson, trans. New York: Vintage.

Endicott, Kirk M. 1970 *Analysis of Malay Magic*. Oxford, England: Clarendon Press.

Federation of Women Lawyers (Malaysia) 1983 *Women and Employment in Malaysia*. Presented at the Seminar on Women and the Law, 29 April–1 May, 1983. Kuala Lumpur. Unpublished manuscript.

FIDA (Federal Industrial Development Authority), Malaysia 1975 *Malaysia: The Solid State for Electronics*. Kuala Lumpur.

Firth, Raymond 1967 Ritual and Drama in Malay Spirit Mediumship. *Comparative Studies in Society and History* 9:190–207.

Foucault, Michel 1965 *Madness and Civilization: A History of Insanity in the Age of Reason*. R. Howard, trans. New York: Pantheon.

1979 *Discipline and Punish: The Birth of the Prison*. Alan Sheridan, trans. New York: Vintage.

1980 *An Introduction. History of Sexuality*, Vol. 1. Robert Hurley, trans. New York: Vintage.

Gramsci, Antonio 1971 *Selections from the Prison Notebooks*. Quentin Hoare and Geoffrey Nowell Smith, trans. New York: International Publishing.

Howard, Robert 1985 *Brave New Workplace*. New York: Viking Books.

Jamilah Ariffin 1980 Industrial Development in Peninsular Malaysia and Rural-Urban Migration of Women Workers: Impact and Implications. *Jurnal Ekonomi Malaysia* 1:41–59.

Karnoouh, Claude 1984 Culture and Development. *Telos* 61:71–82.

Kessler, Clive S. 1977 Conflict and Sovereignty in Kelantan Malay Spirit Seances. In *Case Studies in Spirit Possession*. Vincent Crapanzano and Vivian Garrison, eds. pp. 295–331. New York: John Wiley.

Laderman, Carol 1983 *Wives and Midwives: Childbirth and Nutrition in Rural Malaysia*. Berkeley: University of California Press.

Lewis, Ioan M. 1971 *Ecstatic Religion: An Anthropological Study of Spirit Possession and Shamanism*. Harmondsworth, England: Penguin.

Lim, Linda 1978 *Women Workers in Multinational Corporations: The Case of the Electronics Industry in Malaysia and Singapore*. Ann Arbor: Michigan Occasional Papers in Women's Studies, No. 9.

Lutz, Catherine 1985 Depression and the Translation of Emotional Worlds. In *Culture and Depression*. Arthur Kleinman and Byron Good, eds. pp. 63–100. Berkeley: University of California Press.

Maxwell, W. E. 1977 Shamanism in Perak. In *The Centenary Volume, 1877–1977*. pp. 222–232. Singapore: The Council, Malaysian Branch of the Royal Asiatic Society, 1977/1978. [Originally published 1883]

Mohd. Taib bin Osman 1972 Patterns of Supernatural Premises Underlying the Institution of the *Bomoh* in Malay Culture. *Bijdragen tot de Taal-Land-en Volkekunde* 128:219–234.

Obeyesekere, Gananath 1985 Depression, Buddhism, and the Work of Culture in Sri Lanka. In *Culture and Depression*. Arthur Kleinman and Byron Good, eds. pp. 134–152. Berkeley: University of California Press.

Ong, Aihwa 1987 *Spirits of Resistance and Capitalist Discipline: Factory Women in Malaysia*. Albany: State University of New York Press.

Parsons, Talcott 1985 Illness and the Role of the Physician: A Sociological Perspective. In *Readings from Talcott Parsons*. Peter Hamilton, ed. pp. 145–155. New York: Tavistock.

Phoon, W. H. 1982 Outbreaks of Mass Hysteria at Workplaces in Singapore: Some Patterns and Modes of Presentation. In *Mass Psychogenic Illness: A Social Psychological Analysis*. Michael Colligan, James Pennebaker, and Lawrence Murphy, eds. pp. 21–31. Hillsdale, NJ: Lawrence Erlbaum Associates.

Sabbah, Fatna A. 1984 *Woman in the Muslim Unconscious*. Mary Jo Lakeland, trans. New York: Pergamon Press.

Scheper-Hughes, Nancy, and Margaret Lock 1987 The Mindful Body: A Prolegomenon to Future Work in Medical Anthropology. *Medical Anthropology Quarterly* 1(1):1–36.

Skeat, Walter W. 1965[1900] *Malay Magic*. London: Frank Cass.

Taussig, Michael 1980 Reification and the Consciousness of the Patient. *Social Science and Medicine* 14B:3–13.

Teoh, Jin-Inn, Saesmalijah Soewondo, and Myra Sidharta 1975 Epidemic Hysteria in Malaysian Schools: An Illustrative Episode. *Psychiatry* 38:258–268.

Winstedt, Richard O. 1961 *The Malays: A Cultural History*. London: Routledge and Kegan Paul.

Part 2:
Industrial Work: Skill, Control and Consent

SECTIONAL INTRODUCTION

The readings in Part 2 focus on the shop floor and raise issues about skill, control and consent. Under capitalism, workers characteristically lack their own means of production and rely exclusively on wages to live. The problem for capital is generally less one of persuading workers to come to work than of persuading them to work when they have come. The obvious solution is enhanced control. In early capitalism, as Marx put it, labour was only *formally* subsumed by capital. Work organization remained largely in the hands of workers. The historical trend was towards its *real* subsumption. Work was ever more strictly supervised, centralised and controlled. Braverman's *Labor and Monopoly Capital* (1974), from which the first chapter is an excerpt, updates that story as capitalism evolved into its twentieth century avatars and employers sought to direct labour in new and more far-reaching ways.

Most crucial were methods pioneered by F.W. Taylor's 'scientific management' movement. The main difficulty for management, as Taylor identified it, is that workers know more about the job than they do: how long it takes to perform a task, the short-cuts and how to simulate work while actually 'soldiering' (marking time). Taylor's principal prescription was to break production down into smaller and smaller tasks with standardised stopwatch times. That also had the advantage that cheap unskilled workers could now do most operations; that the so-called 'Babbage principle' could be applied whereby only the skilled parts of a complex operation needed to be carried out by skilled workers at skilled rates of pay. The overall effect was to cheapen and de-skill labour; to separate 'conception' (a function of management) from 'execution' (the mindless task of workers) and to thereby dehumanize their productive activity; for, as Marx said, 'what distinguishes the worst of architects from the best of bees is this, that the architect raises his structure in imagination before he creates it in reality'. This separation destroys what is distinctively human about human work, that it is governed by conceptual thought. De-skilling, Braverman argues later in the book, has subsequently degraded other forms of work, including domestic labour, leading to a 'general atrophy of competence'. It has, in particular, affected clerical work, blurring the distinction (increasingly one of gender) between white- and blue-collar workers. Marx had predicted the polarization of society between owners and non-owners of the means of production (see Part 5), and the increasing homogenization of the latter. Braverman's agenda is seemingly to show that he was right.

That he was right is highly debateable, as some of the readings in Part 5 will suggest. There are, however, other qualifications to Braverman's thesis that are more immediately relevant here. One is that 'Taylorism' may be self-limiting because it provokes resistance. As Braverman himself shows, Taylor's own 'experiments' produced plenty of that; and Beynon's chapter about assembly line workers in Ford's (Liverpool) Halewood plant evokes it vividly. Ford workers did not identify with the industry or with the cars they turned out; and Beynon's picture is of a workforce continually on the brink of a walk-out, and continually engaged in defiant turpitude, disobedience, and minor acts of sabotage. Sometimes, through sheer bloody-mindedness, workers did succeed in preventing speed-ups and in taking back some control of the line, but these victories were limited and temporary. The workforce had no influence on demand in the car market or on company investment decisions, which were what ultimately determined the conditions under which they worked. What also crucially limited their leverage was that hardly any were skilled, which meant they were easily replaced. Though management authority was never absolute and always disputed, Taylorist methods did promote control by requiring only an overwhelmingly unskilled workforce. In that respect, Braverman's analysis applies.

While Beynon compares the bargaining position of assembly-line workers unfavourably with that of skilled labour, other shop floor ethnographies suggest that assembly-line work may be more skilled than he accepts. Consider, for example, Linhart's (1985) compelling account of his difficulties in mastering his task on the line in a Citroën plant near Paris (also Cavendish 1985). The categorization of jobs according to the level of skill they demand is notoriously malleable to extraneous influence, and Linhart reports that though the hierarchy of grades within the workforce was supposedly a hierarchy of skills, it was in reality a reflection of the racial hierarchy of the factory. Though Braverman sometimes writes as though skill were easy to measure, it is frequently both contested and contextual.

In opposition to Braverman, critics have pointed to considerable unevenness between industries in the extent to which de-skilling has occurred and questioned his picture of a progressive homogenization of work (e.g. Elger 1979). In the San Francisco's ship repair yards, workers have, over the past twenty-five years, lost much of their control over conditions. Blum (2000), however, claims this degradation has occurred *without* de-skilling, though he perhaps passes rather too lightly over the recent creation of a category of cheap, unskilled 'utility workers'. His point is that Braverman did not properly recognise the limited ability of capital to de-skill jobs. For technical reasons, some are simply not amenable to the kind of rationalization he envisaged; and the wider context is written out of his account. It is not the loss of skill that explains the present plight of this workforce, but rather the subversion of its bargaining position brought about by the shifting geopolitical priorities of the U.S. government, U.S. Navy requirements and global competition.

For Braverman (as for Marx), de-skilling is literally dehumanizing. There may, however, be *some* circumstances in which it has a more benign aspect, as is suggested by Vialles' study (1994) of French abattoirs where animal slaughter is carried out on an industrial scale, and carcases are processed on a (dis-)assembly line. The fragmentation of tasks, the de-skilling of labour and the separation between conception and execution, Vialles suggests, allow workers to largely evade the distinctly uncomfortable meaning of their work. It may be no accident that the very first industrial production lines were in the Chicago slaughterhouses.

In some rapidly industrializing countries, such as India, labour is cheap and capital scarce, and the incentive to replace skilled workers with machines is consequently muted. In others, for example many parts of sub-Saharan Africa, a predominantly rural short-term migrant labour force has few craft (let alone industrial) skills to lose. In such circumstances, as Crisp (1983) has shown with the West African gold mining industry, Taylorist management methods may be associated with efforts to skill, rather than de-skill, the workforce. Here, however, they were also clearly responsible for sparking numerous strikes, leading Crisp, following Burawoy (1979), to suggest that Taylorism is not just self-limiting, but that it contains within itself the seeds of its own destruction.

In any event, many management regimes have developed less blatant and constraining systems of control that allow workers a degree of (sometimes perhaps illusory) autonomy. In the third reading in this section, Burawoy shows how workers were able to subvert the intentions of senior management and exercise surreptitious discretion over the intensity of their labour, and how in the process consent to the factory regime was 'manufactured' and how they drove themselves on to higher output. Key to this was the shop floor culture of 'making out', producing something over the target quota for the shift and earning a proportionate bonus. 'Making out' was a shop floor obsession, a constant topic of conversation during breaks, and a measure of self-worth and of the worth of others. But it wasn't merely the extra money that lured operators into the game. It was rather that the game itself was a way of reducing fatigue, passing time, relieving boredom and demonstrating competence to oneself and to others. The result was that operators intensified their efforts and colluded with management in the production of surplus value.

To play the game successfully, operators needed the cooperation of auxiliary workers to supply materials and check calibrations. Since the latter are not direct producers, management was reluctant to employ enough of them. Operators consequently faced delays that made the difference between 'making out' or not, leading to friction between them and auxiliaries, and between operators themselves (who had to vie for the auxiliaries' attention). What was essentially a conflict between workers and management was transformed into one between workers. Hierarchical domination translated into lateral antagonism as a result of the way in which work was organised. This is an illustration of one of Burawoy's main theoretical claims, that 'consent is produced at the point of production-independent of schooling, family life, mass media, the state and so forth' (1979: xi). 'Variations in the character and consciousness that workers bring with them to the workplace explain little about the variations in the activities that take place on the shop floor' (p. 202). It is a claim that few anthropologists, trained in a discipline that emphasizes the interconnections between different aspects of social life, would easily accept, and that other chapters in this volume invite us to question (e.g. the contributions by Ong, Ching Kwan Lee, De Neve and Nash). Sometimes, as Fernandes (1997: 4, 119f) reports for a Calcutta jute mill, neighbourhood disputes find their way onto the shop floor, where, reversing the process Burawoy describes, lateral conflicts between workers get transformed into conflicts between unions and management. Sometimes social bonds extraneous to the factory mitigate conflicts, labour and management, as Engelshoven (1999) has shown with the diamond ateliers of Surat, in the Indian state of Gujarat. Living and working conditions are extremely harsh, and the owners have a reputation for violence. Owners and workers share, however, a common identity as members of a single upwardly-mobile caste; workers credit the owners with that rise, and dream of one day being like them. That is what secures their consent (cf. De Neve 2008).

Burawoy's point about work as a measure of self-worth comes out in numerous other industrial studies, though perhaps nowhere more strikingly than in Kotkin's (1994) account of steelworkers in Soviet Russia, where industrial labour and the historical mission of the industrial working class were highly valorised by official ideology, and where work defined who people were, both morally and socially.

Even workers in a single plant may, however, evaluate their jobs in very different ways, as our final selection in this section illustrates. This deals with the way in which those who work at the La Hague nuclear processing plant on the Cotentin peninsula in Normandy manage to deny the very considerable dangers that confront them and that 'eat at them silently'. This denial forms the basis of their consent and in Zonabend's analysis is made to seem compelling by the way in which both management and workers deploy language and metaphor. In this chapter we have one of her most striking examples of the way in which these workers talk about risk. Discourse divides the workforce into two polarised 'personality types': *kamikazes*, bold warrior types who scorn danger, are prepared to work beyond normal limits, and take risks and short-cuts; and *rentiers*, cautious family men who avoid risk and manage their 'dose capital' carefully. What emerges, however, is that the distribution of these 'personality types' is closely correlated with the division of labour. The *kamikazes* tend to work in mechanical jobs, *rentiers* tend to work in chemical parts of the plant, and their contrasting attitudes to risk have much to do with the way in which the dangers of the two types of job are symbolically constructed. In mechanical jobs the chief danger is *irradiation*. The 'dose' consists of rays. Rays suggest warmth and radiance. The image is one of cleanliness, strength and light. The rays are like the burn of strong alcohol with which real men fortify themselves. As the true soldiers of nuclear energy, the *kamikaze* takes his dose like a man and is prepared to do so because language and metaphor have transformed radioactivity into male energy and sexual potency. The risks he takes prove his masculinity and are a way of saying that he isn't scared. The first dose is even a kind of initiation, something to get done with, like losing one's virginity. By contrast, the danger which faces the chemical worker is that of *contamination* from radioactive dust particles, which are a far less heroic foe. Contamination conjures up the image of filth, pollution and decay, it is something that spreads. The wife of the worker who has caught a dose refuses to sleep with him. The husband responds by concealing his pollution and the result is a mistrustful repression and silence at home. We end here, then, at the point that the next section starts – with the relationship between 'work' and 'life'.

RECOMMENDED FURTHER READING

Blum, J. 2000. 'Degradation without De-skilling: Twenty-five years in the San Francisco shipyards', in M. Burawoy et al., *Global Ethhnography: Forces, Connections, and Imaginations in a Postmodern World*, pp. 106–36, Berkeley, CA: University of California Press.

Cavendish, R. 1985. 'Women on the line', in C.R. Littler (ed.), *The Experience of Work*, pp. 105–16, Aldershot: Gower.

Crisp, J. 1983. 'Productivity and Protest: Scientific management in the Ghanaian gold mines, 1947–1956', in F. Cooper (ed.), *Struggle for the City: Migrant labor, capital, and the state in urban Africa'*, pp. 91–130, London: Sage Publications.

De Neve, G. 2008. ' "We are all *sondukarar* (relatives)!": Kinship and its morality in an urban industry of Tamilnadu, South India,' *Modern Asian Studies*, 42(1): 211–46.

Engelshoven, M. 1999. 'Diamonds and Patels: A Report on the Diamond Industry of Surat', *Contributions to Indian Sociology* (new series), 33(1): 353–77.

Linhart, R. 1985. 'The Assembly Line', in C. L. Littler (ed.), *The Experience of Work*, pp. 117–31, Aldershot: Gower.

OTHER WORKS CITED

Elger, T. 1979. 'Valorisation and De-skilling: A Critique of Braverman', *Capital and Class*, 7: 58–99.

Kotkin, S. 1994. 'Coercion and identity: Workers' Lives in Stalin's Showcase City', in L.H. Siegelbaun and R. G. Suny (eds), *Making Workers Soviet: Power, class and identity*, pp. 274–310, Ithaca, NY: Cornell University Press.

Fernandes, Leela. 1997. *Producing Workers: The politics of gender, class and culture in the Calcutta jute mills*, Philadelphia: University of Pennsylvania Press.

Vialles, N. 1994. *Animal to Edible*, Cambridge: Cambridge University Press.

CHAPTER FIVE

Scientific Management

HARRY BRAVERMAN

The classical economists were the first to approach the problems of the organization of labor within capitalist relations of production from a theoretical point of view. They may thus be called the first management experts, and their work was continued in the latter part of the Industrial Revolution by such men as Andrew Ure and Charles Babbage. Between these men and the next step, the comprehensive formulation of management theory in the late nineteenth and early twentieth centuries, there lies a gap of more than half a century during which there was an enormous growth in the size of enterprises, the beginnings of the monopolistic organization of industry, and the purposive and systematic application of science to production. The scientific management movement initiated by Frederick Winslow Taylor in the last decades of the nineteenth century was brought into being by these forces. Logically, Taylorism belongs to the chain of development of management methods and the organization of labor, and not to the development of technology, in which its role was minor.

Scientific management, so-called, is an attempt to apply the methods of science to the increasingly complex problems of the control of labor in rapidly growing capitalist enterprises. It lacks the characteristics of a true science because its assumptions reflect nothing more than the outlook of the capitalist with regard to the conditions of production. It starts, despite occasional protestations to the contrary, not from the human point of view but from the capitalist point of view, from the point of view of the management of a refractory work force in a setting of antagonistic social relations. It does not attempt to discover and confront the cause of this condition, but accepts it as an inexorable given, a "natural" condition. It investigates not labor in general, but the adaptation of labor to the needs of capital. It enters the workplace not as the representative of science, but as the representative of management masquerading in the trappings of science.

A comprehensive and detailed outline of the principles of Taylorism is essential to our narrative, not because of the things for which it is popularly known – stopwatch, speed-up, etc. – but because behind these commonplaces there lies a theory which is nothing less than the explicit verbalization of the capitalist mode of production. But before I begin this presentation, a number of introductory remarks are required to clarify the role of the Taylor school in the development of management theory.

It is impossible to overestimate the importance of the scientific management movement in the shaping of the modern corporation and indeed all institutions of capitalist society which carry on labor processes. The popular notion that Taylorism has been "superseded" by later schools of industrial psychology or "human relations," that it "failed" – because of Taylor's amateurish and naive views of human motivation or because it brought about a storm of labor opposition or because Taylor and various successors antagonized workers and sometimes management as well – or that it is "outmoded" because certain Taylorian specifics like functional foremanship or his incentive-pay schemes have been discarded for more sophisticated methods: all these represent a woeful misreading of the actual dynamics of the development of management.

Taylor dealt with the fundamentals of the organization of the labor process and of control over it. The later schools of Hugo Münsterberg, Elton Mayo, and others of this type dealt primarily with the adjustment of the worker to the ongoing production process as that process was designed by the industrial engineer. The successors to Taylor are to be found in engineering and work design, and in top management; the successors to Münsterberg and Mayo are to be found in personnel departments and schools of industrial psychology and sociology. Work itself is organized according to Taylorian principles, while personnel departments and academics have busied themselves with the selection, training, manipulation, pacification, and adjustment of "manpower" to suit the work processes so organized. Taylorism dominates the world of production; the practitioners of "human relations" and "industrial psychology" are the maintenance crew for the human machinery. If Taylorism does not exist as a separate school today, that is because, apart from the bad odor of the name, it is no longer the property of a faction, since its fundamental teachings have become the bedrock of all Work design. Peter F. Drucker, who has the advantage of considerable direct experience as a management consultant, is emphatic on this score:

> Personnel Administration and Human Relations are the things talked about and written about whenever the management of worker and work is being discussed. They are the things the Personnel Department concerns itself with. But they are not the concepts that underlie the actual management of worker and work in American industry. This concept is Scientific Management. Scientific Management focuses on the work. Its core is the organized study of work, the analysis of work into its simplest elements and the systematic improvement of the worker's performance of each of these elements. Scientific Management has both basic concepts and easily applicable tools and techniques. And it has no difficulty proving the contribution it makes; its results in the form of higher output are visible and readily measurable.

Indeed, Scientific Management is all but a systematic philosophy of worker and work. Altogether it may well be the most powerful as well as the most lasting contribution America has made to Western thought since the Federalist Papers.[1]

The use of experimental methods in the study of work did not begin with Taylor; in fact, the self-use of such methods by the craftsman is part of the very practice of a craft. But the study of work by or on behalf of those who manage it rather than those who perform it seems to have come to the fore only with the capitalist epoch; indeed, very little basis for it could have existed before. The earliest references to the study of work correspond to the beginnings of the capitalist era: such a reference, for example, is found in the *History of the Royal Society of London*, and dates from the middle of the seventeenth century. We have already mentioned the classical economists. Charles Babbage, who not only wrote penetrating discussions of the organization of the labor process in his day, but applied the same concept to the division of mental labor, and who devised an early calculating "engine," was probably the most direct forerunner of Taylor, who must have been familiar with Babbage's work even though he never referred to it. France had a long tradition of attempting the scientific study of work, starting with Louis XIV's minister Colbert; including military engineers like Vauban and Belidor and especially Coulomb, whose physiological studies of exertion in labor are famous, through Marey, who used smoked paper cylinders to make a graphic record of work phenomena; and culminating in Henri Fayol, a contemporary of Taylor, who in his *General and Industrial Management* attempted a set of principles aimed at securing total enterprise control by way of a systematic approach to administration.[2] The publication of management manuals, the discussions of the problems of management, and the increasingly sophisticated approach taken in practice in the second half of the nineteenth century lend support to the conclusion of the historians of the scientific management movement that Taylor was the culmination of a pre-existing trend: "What Taylor did was not to invent something quite new, but to synthesize and present as a reasonably coherent whole ideas which had been germinating and gathering force in Great Britain and the United States throughout the nineteenth century. He gave to a disconnected series of initiatives and experiments a philosophy and a title."[3]

Taylor has little in common with those physiologists or psychologists who have attempted, before or after him, to gather information about human capacities in a spirit of scientific interest. Such records and estimates as he did produce are crude in the extreme, and this has made it easy for such critics as Georges Friedmann to poke holes in his various "experiments" (most of which were not intended as experiments at all, but as forcible and hyperbolic demonstrations). Friedmann treats Taylorism as though it were a "science of work," where in reality it is intended to be a *science of the management of others' work* under capitalist conditions.[4] It is not the "best way" to do work "in general" that Taylor was seeking, as Friedmann seems to assume, but an answer to the specific problem of how best to control alienated labor – that is to say, labor power that is bought and sold.

The second distinctive feature of Taylor's thought was his concept of control. Control has been the essential feature of management throughout its history, but with Taylor it assumed unprecedented dimensions. The stages of management control over labor before Taylor had included, progressively: the gathering together of the workers in a workshop and the dictation of the length of the working day; the supervision of workers to ensure diligent, intense, or uninterrupted application; the enforcement of rules against distractions (talking, smoking, leaving the workplace, etc.) that were thought to interfere with application; the setting of production minimums; etc. A worker is under management control when subjected to these rules, or to any of their extensions and variations. But Taylor raised the concept of control to an entirely new plane when he asserted as an *absolute necessity for adequate management the dictation to the worker of the precise manner in which work is to be performed*. That management had the right to "control" labor was generally assumed before Taylor, but in practice this right usually meant only the general setting of tasks, with little direct interference in the worker's mode of performing them. Taylor's contribution was to overturn this practice and replace it by its opposite. Management, he insisted, could be only a limited and frustrated undertaking so long as it left to the worker any decision about the work. His "system" was simply a means for management to achieve control of the actual mode of performance of every labor activity, from the simplest to the most complicated. To this end, he pioneered a far greater revolution in the division of labor than any that had gone before.

Taylor created a simple line of reasoning and advanced it with a logic and clarity, a naive openness, and an evangelical zeal which soon won him a strong following among capitalists and managers. His work began in the 1880s but it was not until the 1890s that he began to lecture, read papers, and publish results. His own engineering training was limited, but his grasp of shop practice was superior, since he had served a four-year combination apprenticeship in two trades, those of patternmaker and machinist. The spread of the Taylor approach was not limited to the United States and Britain; within a short time it became popular in all industrial countries. In France it was called, in the absence of a suitable word for management, "l'organisation scientifique du travail" (later changed, when the reaction against Taylorism set in, to "l'organisation rationnelle du travail"). In Germany it was known simply as *rationalization*; the German corporations were probably ahead of everyone else in the practice of this technique, even before World War I.[5]

Taylor was the scion of a well-to-do Philadelphia family. After preparing for Harvard at Exeter he suddenly dropped out, apparently in rebellion against his father, who was directing Taylor toward his own profession, the law. He then took the step, extraordinary for anyone of his class, of starting a craft apprenticeship in a firm whose owners were social acquaintances of his parents. When he had completed his apprenticeship, he took a job at common labor in the Midvale Steel Works, also owned by friends of his family and technologically one of the most advanced companies in the steel industry. Within a few months he had passed through jobs as clerk and journeyman machinist, and was appointed gang boss in charge of the lathe department.

In his psychic makeup, Taylor was an exaggerated example of the obsessive-compulsive personality: from his youth he had counted his steps, measured the time for his various activities, and analyzed his motions in a search for "efficiency." Even when he had risen to importance and fame, he was still something of a figure of fun, and his appearance on the shop floor produced smiles. The picture of his personality that emerges from a study recently done by Sudhir Kakar justifies calling him, at the very least, a neurotic crank[6]. These traits fitted him perfectly for his role as the prophet of modern capitalist management, since that which is neurotic in the individual is, in capitalism, normal and socially desirable for the functioning of society.

Shortly after Taylor became gang boss, he entered upon a struggle with the machinists under him. . . . The following account, one of several he gave of the battle, is taken from his testimony, a quarter-century later, before a Special Committee of the U.S. House of Representatives:

> Now, the machine shop of the Midvale Steel Works was a piecework shop. All the work practically was done on piecework, and it ran night and day – five nights in the week and six days. Two sets of men came on, one to run the machines at night and the other to run them in the daytime.
>
> We who were the workmen of that shop had the quantity output carefully agreed upon for everything that was turned out in the shop. We limited the output to about, I should think, one-third of what we could very well have done. We felt justified in doing this, owing to the piecework system – that is, owing to the necessity for soldiering under the piecework system – which I pointed out yesterday:
>
> As soon as I became gang boss the men who were working under me and who, of course, knew that I was onto the whole game of soldiering or deliberately restricting output, came to me at once and said, "Now, Fred, you are not going to be a damn piecework hog, are you?"
>
> I said, "If you fellows mean you are afraid I am going to try to get a larger output from these lathes," I said, "Yes; I do propose to get more work out." I said, "You must remember I have been square with you fellows up to now and worked with you. I have not broken a single rate. I have been on your side of the fence. But now I have accepted a job under the management of this company and I am on the other side of the fence, and I will tell you perfectly frankly that I am going to try to get a bigger output from those lathes." They answered, "Then, you are going to be a damned hog."
>
> I said, "Well, if you fellows put it that way, all right." They said, "We warn you, Fred, if you try to bust any of these rates, we will have you over the fence in six weeks." I said, "That is all right; I will tell you fellows again frankly that I propose to try to get a bigger output off these machines."
>
> Now, that was the beginning of a piecework fight that lasted for nearly three years, as I remember it – two or three years – in which I was doing everything in my power to increase the output of the shop, while the men were absolutely determined that the output should not be increased. Anyone who has been through such a fight knows and dreads the meanness of it and the bitterness of it.
>
> . . .

I began, of course, by directing some one man to do more work than he had done before, and then I got on the lathe myself and showed him that it could be done. In spite of this, he went ahead and turned out exactly the same old output and refused to adopt better methods or to work quicker until finally I laid him off and got another man in his place. This new man – I could not blame him in the least under the circumstances – turned right around and joined the other fellows and refused to do any more work than the rest.

. . .

I hunted up some especially intelligent laborers who were competent men but who had not had the opportunity of learning a trade, and I deliberately taught these men how to run a lathe and how to work right and fast. Every one of these laborers promised me, "Now, if you will teach me the machinist's trade, when I learn to run a lathe I will do a fair day's work," and every solitary man, when I had taught them their trade, one after another turned right around and joined the rest of the fellows and refused to work one bit faster.

. . .

I said, "I know that very heavy social pressure has been put upon you outside the works to keep you from carrying out your agreement with me, and it is very difficult for you to stand out against this pressure, but you ought not to have made your bargain with me if you did not intend to keep your end of it. Now, I am going to cut your rate in two tomorrow and you are going to work for half price from now on. But all you will have to do is to turn out a fair day's work and you can earn better wages than you have been earning."

These men, of course, went to the management, and protested that I was a tyrant, and a nigger driver, and for a long time they stood right by the rest of the men in the shop and refused to increase their output a particle. Finally, they all of a sudden gave right in and did a fair day's work.

. . .

Every time I broke a rate or forced one of the new men whom I had trained to work at a reasonable and proper speed, some one of the machinists would deliberately break some part of his machine as an object lesson to demonstrate to the management that a fool foreman was driving the men to overload their machines until they broke.

. . .

I said to the men, "All right; from this time on, any accident that happens in this shop, every time you break any part of a machine you will have to pay part of the cost of repairing it or else quit. I don't care if the roof falls in and breaks your machine, you will pay all the same."[7]

. . .

The issue here turned on the work content of a day's labor power, which Taylor defines in the phrase "a fair day's work." To this term he gave a crude physiological interpretation: all the work a worker can do without injury to his health, at a pace that can be sustained throughout a working lifetime. (In practice, he tended to define this level of activity at an extreme limit, choosing a pace that only a few could maintain, and then only under strain.) Why a "fair day's work" should be defined as a physiological maximum is never made clear. In attempting to give concrete meaning to the abstraction "fairness," it would make just as much if not more sense to express a fair day's work as the amount of labor necessary to add to the product a value equal to the worker's pay; under such conditions, of course, profit would be impossible. The phrase "a fair day's work" must therefore be regarded as inherently meaningless, and filled with such content as the adversaries in the purchase-sale relationship try to give it.

Taylor set as his objective the maximum or "optimum" that can be obtained from a day's labor power. "On the part of the men," he said in his first book, "the greatest obstacle to the attainment of this standard is the slow pace which they adopt, or the loafing or 'soldiering,' marking time, as it is called." In each of his later expositions of his system, he begins with this same point, underscoring it heavily.[8] The causes of this soldiering he breaks into two parts: "This loafing or soldiering proceeds from two causes. First, from the natural instinct and tendency of men to take it easy, which may be called *natural soldiering*. Second, from more intricate second thought and reasoning caused by their relations with other men, which may be called *systematic soldiering*." The first of these he quickly puts aside, to concentrate on the second: "The natural laziness of men is serious, but by far the greatest evil from which both workmen and employers are suffering is the *systematic soldiering* which is almost universal under all the ordinary schemes of management and which results from a careful study on the part of the workmen of what they think will promote their best interests."

> The greater part of systematic soldiering . . . is done by the men with the deliberate object of keeping their employers ignorant of how fast work can be done.
>
> So universal is soldiering for this purpose, that hardly a competent workman can be found in a large establishment, whether he works by the day or on piece work, contract work or under any of the ordinary systems of compensating labor, who does not devote a considerable part of his time to studying just how slowly he can work and still convince his employer that he is going at a good pace.
>
> The causes for this are, briefly, that practically all employers determine upon a maximum sum which they feel it is right for each of their classes of employes to earn per day, whether their men work by the day or piece.[9]

That the pay of labor is a socially determined figure, relatively independent of productivity, among employers of similar types of labor power in any given period was thus known to Taylor. Workers who produce twice or three times as much as they did the day before do not thereby double or triple their pay, but may be given a small incremental advantage over their fellows, an advantage which disappears as their level of production becomes generalized. The contest over the size of the portion of the day's labor power to be embodied in each product is thus relatively independent of the level of pay, which responds chiefly to market, social, and historical factors.

The worker learns this from repeated experiences, whether working under day or piece rates: "It is, however," says Taylor, "under piece work that the art of systematic soldiering is thoroughly developed. After a workman has had the price per piece of the work he is doing lowered two or three times as a result of his having worked harder and increased his output, he is likely to entirely lose sight of his employer's side of the case and to become imbued with a grim determination to have no more cuts if soldiering can prevent it."[10] To this it should be added that even where a piecework or "incentive" system allows the worker to increase his pay, the contest is not thereby ended but only exacerbated, because the output records now determine the setting and revision of pay rates.

Taylor always took the view that workers, by acting in this fashion, were behaving rationally and with an adequate view of their own best interests.

. . .

The conclusions which Taylor drew from the baptism by fire he received in the Midvale struggle may be summarized as follows: Workers who are controlled only by general orders and discipline are not adequately controlled, because they retain their grip on the actual processes of labor. So long as they control the labor process itself, they will thwart efforts to realize to the full the potential inherent in their labor power. To change this situation, control over the labor process must pass into the hands of management, not only in a formal sense but by the control and dictation of each step of the process, including its mode of performance. In pursuit of this end, no pains are too great, no efforts excessive, because the results will repay all efforts and expenses lavished on this demanding and costly endeavor.

The forms of management that existed prior to Taylorism, which Taylor called "ordinary management," he deemed altogether inadequate to meet these demands. His descriptions of ordinary management bear the marks of the propagandist and proselytizer: exaggeration, simplification, and schematization. But his point is clear:

> Now, in the best of the ordinary types of management, the managers recognize frankly that the . . . workmen, included in the twenty or thirty trades, who are under them, possess this mass of traditional knowledge, a large part of which is not in the possession of management. The management, of course, includes foremen and superintendents, who themselves have been first-class workers at their trades. And yet these foremen and superintendents know, better than any one else, that, their own knowledge and personal skill falls far short of the combined knowledge and dexterity of all the workmen under them. The most experienced managers frankly place before their workmen the problem of doing the work in the best and most economical way. They recognize the task before them as that of inducing each workman to use his best endeavors, his hardest work, all his traditional knowledge, his skill, his ingenuity, and his goodwill – in a word, his "initiative," so as to yield the largest possible return to his employer.[11]

As we have already seen from Taylor's belief in the universal prevalence and in fact inevitability of "soldiering," he did not recommend reliance upon the "initiative" of workers. Such a course, he felt, leads to the surrender of control: "As was usual then, and in fact as is still usual in most of the shops in this country, the shop was really run by the workmen and not by the bosses. The workmen together had carefully planned just how fast each job should be done." In his Midvale battle, Taylor pointed out, he had located the source of the trouble in the "ignorance of the management as to what really constitutes a proper day's work for a workman." He had "fully realized that, although he was foreman of the shop, the combined knowledge and skill of the workmen who were under him was certainly ten times as great as his own."[12] This, then, was the source of the trouble and the starting point of scientific management.

[Editor's Note: Here Braverman includes a long story, as told by Taylor himself in *The principles of scientific management*, about handling pig iron at the Bethlehem Steel Company. The plant had a gang of 75 handlers. Taylor and his assistants calculated that each worker ought to be able to load 47 long tons per shift into rail wagons, whereas the established norm was 12.5 tons. A worker called 'Schmidt' – 'a little Pennsylvania Dutchman who had been observed to trot home for a mile after his work in the evening', who was known to place 'a high value on the dollar' and was of a 'mentally sluggish type' – was singled out, and cajoled into working at the new rate. For that he was paid $1.85 per day in place of the $1.15 that the others received. Gradually other workers were 'trained' to work at that rate, until after some time the entire gang was doing so.]

. . .

The merit of this tale is its clarity in illustrating the pivot upon which all modern management turns: the control over work through the control over the *decisions that are made in the course of work*. Since, in the case of pig-iron handling, the only decisions to be made were those having to do with a time sequence, Taylor simply dictated that timing and the results at the end of the day added up to his planned day-task. As to the use of money as motivation, while this element has a usefulness in the first stages of a new mode of work, employers do not, when they have once found a way to compel a more rapid pace of work, continue to pay a 60 percent differential for common labor, or for any other job. Taylor was to discover (and to complain) that management treated his "scientific incentives" like any other piece rate, cutting them mercilessly so long as the labor market permitted, so that workers pushed to the Taylorian intensity found themselves getting little, or nothing, more than the going rate for the area, while other employers – under pressure of this competitive threat – forced their own workers to the higher intensities of labor.

Taylor liked to pretend that his work standards were not beyond human capabilities exercised without undue strain, but as he himself made clear, this pretense could be maintained only on the understanding that unusual physical specimens were selected for each of his jobs:

> As to the scientific selection of the men, it is a fact that in this gang of 75 pig-iron handlers only about one man in eight was physically capable of handling 47½ tons per day. With the very best of intentions, the other seven out of eight men were physic-ally unable to work at this pace.[13]

. . .

Taylor spent his lifetime in expounding the principles of control enunciated here, and in applying them directly to many other tasks: shoveling loose materials, lumbering, inspecting ball bearings, etc., but particularly to the machinist's trade. He believed that the forms of control he advocated could be applied not only to simple labor, but to labor in its most complex forms, without exception, and in fact it was in machine shops, bricklaying, and other such sites for the practice of well-developed crafts that he and his immediate successors achieved their most striking results.

From earliest times to the Industrial Revolution the craft or skilled trade was the basic unit, the elementary cell of the labor process. In each craft, the worker was presumed to be the master of a body of traditional knowledge, and methods and procedures were left to his or her discretion. In each such worker reposed the accumulated knowledge of materials and processes by which production was ac-complished in the craft. The potter, tanner, smith, weaver, carpenter, baker, miller, glassmaker, cobbler, etc., each representing a branch of the social division of labor, was a repository of human technique for the labor processes of that branch. The worker combined, in mind and body, the concepts and physical dexterities of the specialty: technique, understood in this way, is, as has often been observed, the predecessor and progenitor of science. The most important and widespread of all crafts was, and throughout the world remains to this day, that of farmer. The farm-ing family combines its craft with the rude practice of a number of others, including those of the smith, mason, carpenter, butcher, miller, and baker, etc. The apprentice-ships required in traditional crafts ranged from three to seven years, and for the farmer of course extends beyond this to include most of childhood, adolescence, and young adulthood. In view of the knowledge to be assimilated, the dexterities to be gained, and the fact that the craftsman, like the professional, was required to master a specialty and become the best judge of the manner of its application to specific production problems, the years of apprenticeship were generally needed and were employed in a learning process that extended well into the journeyman decades. Of these trades, that of the machinist was in Taylor's day among the most recent, and certainly the most important to modern industry.

As I have already pointed out, Taylor was not primarily concerned with the ad-vance of technology (which, as we shall see, offers other means for direct control over the labor process). He did make significant contributions to the technical know-ledge of machine-shop practice (high-speed tool steel, in particular), but these were chiefly by-products of his effort to study this practice with an eye to systematizing and classifying it. His concern was with the control of labor at any given level of technology, and he tackled his own trade with a boldness and energy which astonished his contemporaries and set the pattern for industrial engineers, work designers, and office managers from that day on. And in tackling machineshop work, he had set himself a prodigious task.

The machinist of Taylor's day started with the shop drawing, and turned, milled, bored, drilled, planed, shaped, ground, filed, and otherwise machine- and hand-processed the proper stock to the desired shape as specified in the drawing. The range of decisions to be made in the course of the process is – unlike the case of a simple job, such as the handling of pig iron – by its very nature enormous. Even for the lathe alone, disregarding all collateral tasks such as the choice of stock, handling, centering and chucking the work, layout and measuring, order of cuts, and considering only the operation of turning itself, the range of possibilities is huge. Taylor himself worked with twelve variables, including the hardness of the metal, the material of the cutting tool, the thickness of the shaving, the shape of the cutting tool, the use of a coolant during cutting, the depth of the cut, the frequency of regrinding cutting tools as they became dulled, the lip and clearance angles of the tool, the smoothness of cutting or absence of chatter, the diameter of the stock being turned, the pressure of the chip or shaving on the cutting surface of the tool, and the speeds, feeds, and pulling power of the machine.[14] Each of these variables is subject to broad choice, ranging from a few possibilities in the selection and use of a coolant, to a very great number of effective choices in all matters having to do with thickness, shape, depth, duration, speed, etc. Twelve variables, each subject to a large number of choices, will yield in their possible combinations and permutations astronomical figures, as Taylor soon realized. But upon these decisions of the machinist depended not just the accuracy and finish of the product, but also the pace of production. Nothing daunted, Taylor set out to gather into management's hands all the basic information bearing on these processes. He began a series of experiments at the Midvale Steel Company, in the fall of 1880, which lasted twenty-six years, recording the results of between 30,000 and 50,000 tests, and cutting up more than 800,000 pounds of iron and steel on ten different machine tools reserved for his experimental use. His greatest difficulty, he reported, was not testing the many variations, but holding eleven variables constant while altering the conditions of the twelfth. The data were systematized, correlated, and reduced to practical form in the shape of what he called a "slide rule" which would determine the optimum combination of choices for each step in the machining process.[15] His machinists thenceforth were required to work in accordance with instructions derived from these experimental data, rather than from their own knowledge, experience, or tradition. This was the Taylor approach in its first systematic application to a complex labor process. Since the principles upon which it is based are fundamental to all advanced work design or industrial engineering today, it is important to examine them in detail. And since Taylor has been virtually alone in giving clear expression to principles which are seldom now publicly acknowledged, it is best to examine them with the aid of Taylor's own forthright formulations.

FIRST PRINCIPLE

"The managers assume . . . the burden of gathering together all of the traditional knowledge which in the past has been possessed by the workmen and then of classifying, tabulating, and reducing this knowledge to rules, laws, and formulae. . . ."[16] We have seen the illustrations of this in the cases of the lathe machinist and the pig-iron handler. The great disparity between these activities, and the different orders of knowledge that may be collected about them, illustrate that for Taylor – as for managers today – no task is either so simple or so complex that it may not be studied with the object of collecting in the hands of management at least as much information as is known by the worker who performs it regularly, and very likely more. This brings to an end the situation in which "Employers derive their knowledge of how much of a given class of work can be done in a day from either their own experience, which has frequently grown hazy with age, from casual and unsystematic observation of their men, or at best from records which are kept, showing the quickest time in which each job has been done."[17] It enables management to discover and enforce those speedier methods and shortcuts which workers themselves, in the practice of their trades or tasks, learn or improvise, and use at their own discretion only. Such an experimental approach also brings into being new methods such as can be devised only through the means of systematic study.

This first principle we may call the *dissociation of the labor process from the skills of the workers.* The labor process is to be rendered independent of craft, tradition, and the workers' knowledge. Henceforth it is to depend not at all upon the abilities of workers, but entirely upon the practices of management.

SECOND PRINCIPLE

"All possible brain work should be removed from the shop and centered in the planning or laying-out department. . . ."[18] Since this is the key to scientific management, as Taylor well understood, he was especially emphatic on this point and it is important to examine the principle thoroughly.

In the human, as we have seen[a], the essential feature that makes for a labor capacity superior to that of the animal is the combination of execution with a conception of the thing to be done. But as human labor becomes a social rather than an individual phenomenon, it is possible – unlike in the instance of animals where the motive force, instinct, is inseparable from action – to divorce conception from execution. This dehumanization of the labor process, in which workers are reduced almost to the level of labor in its animal form, while purposeless and unthinkable in the case of the self-organized and self-motivated social labor of a community of producers, becomes crucial for the management of purchased labor. For if the workers' execution is guided by their own conception, it is not possible, as we have seen, to enforce upon them either the methodological efficiency or the working pace desired by capital. The capitalist therefore learns from the start to take advantage of this aspect of human labor power, and to break the unity of the labor process.

This should be called the principle of the *separation of conception from execution*, rather than by its more common name of the separation of mental and manual labor (even though it is similar to the latter, and in practice often identical). This is because mental labor, labor done primarily in the brain, is also subjected to the same principle of separation of conception from execution: mental labor is first separated from manual labor and, as we shall see, is then itself subdivided rigorously according to the same rule.[b]

The first implication of this principle is that Taylor's "science of work" is never to be developed by the worker, always by management. This notion, apparently so "natural" and undebatable today, was in fact vigorously discussed in Taylor's day, a fact which shows how far we have traveled along the road of transforming all ideas about the labor process in less than a century, and how completely Taylor's hotly contested assumptions have entered into the conventional outlook within a short space of time. Taylor confronted this question – why must work be studied by the management and not by the worker himself; why not *scientific workmanship* rather than *scientific management?* – repeatedly, and employed all his ingenuity in devising answers to it, though not always with his customary frankness. In *The Principles of Scientific Management*, he pointed out that the "older system" of management

> makes it necessary for each workman to bear almost the entire responsibility for the general plan as well as for each detail of his work, and in many cases for his implements as well. In addition to this he must do all of the actual physical labor. The development of a science, on the other hand, involves the establishment of many rules, laws, and formulae which replace the judgment of the individual workman and which can be effectively used only after having been systematically recorded, indexed, etc. The practical use of scientific data also calls for a room in which to keep the books, records, etc., and a desk for the planner to work at. Thus all of the planning which under the old system was done by the workman, as a result of his personal experience, must of necessity under the new system be done by the management in accordance with the laws of the science; because even if the workman was well suited to the development and use of scientific data, it would be physically impossible for him to work at his machine and at a desk at the same time. It is also clear that in most cases one type of man is needed to plan ahead and an entirely different type to execute the work.[19]

The objections having to do with physical arrangements in the workplace are clearly of little importance, and represent the deliberate exaggeration of obstacles which, while they may exist as inconveniences, are hardly insuperable. To refer to the "different type" of worker needed for each job is worse than disingenuous, since these "different types" hardly existed until the division of labor created them. As Taylor well understood, the possession of craft knowledge made the worker the best starting point for the development of the science of work; systematization often means, at least at the outset, the gathering of knowledge which *workers already possess*. But Taylor, secure in his obsession with the immense reasonableness of his proposed arrangement, did not stop at this point. In his testimony before the Special

Committee of the House of Representatives, pressed and on the defensive, he brought forth still other arguments:

> I want to make it clear, Mr. Chairman, that work of this kind undertaken by the management leads to the development of a science, while it is next to impossible for the workman to develop a science. There are many workmen who are intellectually just as capable of developing a science, who have plenty of brains, and are just as capable of developing a science as those on the managing side. But the science of doing work of any kind cannot be developed by the workman. Why? Because he has neither the time nor the money to do it. The development of the science of doing any kind of work always required the work of two men, one man who actually does the work which is to be studied and another man who observes closely the first man while he works and studies the time problems and the motion problems connected with this work. No workman has either the time or the money to burn in making experiments of this sort. If he is working for himself no one will pay him while he studies the motions of some one else. The management must and ought to pay for all such work.[20]

. . .

Taylor here argues that the systematic study of work and the fruits of this study belong to management for the very same reason that machines, factory buildings, etc., belong to them; that is, because it costs labor time to conduct such a study, and only the possessors of capital can afford labor time. The possessors of labor time cannot themselves afford to do anything with it but sell it for their means of subsistence. It is true that this is the rule in capitalist relations of production, and Taylor's use of the argument in this case shows with great clarity where the sway of capital leads: Not only is capital the property of the capitalist, but *labor itself has become part of capital*. Not only do the workers lose control over their instruments of production, but they must now lose control over their own labor and the manner of its performance. This control now falls to those who can "afford" to study it in order to know it better than the workers themselves know their own life activity.

But Taylor has not yet completed his argument: "Furthermore," he told the Committee, "if any workman were to find a new and quicker way of doing work, or if he were to develop a new method, you can see at once it becomes to his interest to keep that development to himself, not to teach the other workmen the quicker method. It is to his interest to do what workmen have done in all times, to keep their trade secrets for themselves and their friends. That is the old idea of trade secrets. The workman kept his knowledge to himself instead of developing a science and teaching it to others and making it public property."[21] Behind this hearkening back to old ideas of "guild secrets" is Taylor's persistent and fundamental notion that the improvement of work methods by workers brings few benefits to management. Elsewhere in his testimony, in discussing the work of his associate, Frank Gilbreth, who spent many years studying bricklaying methods, he candidly admits that not only *could* the "science of bricklaying" be developed by workers, but that it undoubtedly *had been:* "Now, I have not the slightest doubt that during the last 4,000 years all the methods that Mr. Gilbreth developed have many, many times suggested themselves to the minds of bricklayers." But because knowledge possessed by workers is not useful to capital, Taylor begins his list of the desiderata of scientific management: "First. The development – by the management, not the workmen – of the science of bricklaying."[22] Workers, he explains, are not going to put into execution any system or any method which harms them and their workmates: "Would they be likely," he says, referring to the pig-iron job, "to get rid of seven men out of eight from their own gang and retain only the eighth man? No!"[23]

Finally, Taylor understood the Babbage principle[c] better than anyone of his time, and it was always uppermost in his calculations. The purpose of work study was never, in his mind, to enhance the ability of the worker, to concentrate in the worker a greater share of scientific knowledge, to ensure that as technique rose, the worker would rise with it. Rather, the purpose was to cheapen the worker by decreasing his training and enlarging his output. In his early book, *Shop Management*, he said frankly that the "full possibilities" of his system "will not have been realized until almost all of the machines in the shop are run by men who are of smaller calibre and attainments, and who are therefore cheaper than those required under the old system."[24]

Therefore, both in order to ensure management control and to cheapen the worker, conception and execution must be rendered separate spheres of work, and for this purpose the study of work processes must be reserved to management and kept from the workers, to whom its results are communicated only in the form of simplified job tasks governed by simplified instructions which it is thenceforth their duty to follow unthinkingly and without comprehension of the underlying technical reasoning or data.

THIRD PRINCIPLE

The essential idea of "the ordinary types of management," Taylor said, "is that each workman has become more skilled in his own trade than it is possible for any one in the management to be, and that, therefore, the details of how the work shall best be done must be left to him." But, by contrast: "Perhaps the most prominent single element in modern scientific management is the task idea. The work of every workman is fully planned out by the management at least one day in advance, and each man receives in most cases complete written instructions, describing in detail the task which he is to accomplish, as well as the means to be used in doing the work. . . . This task specifies not only what is to be done, but how it is to be done and the exact time allowed for doing it. . . . Scientific management consists very largely in preparing for and carrying out these tasks."[25]

In this principle it is not the written instruction card that is important. Taylor had no need for such a card with Schmidt, nor did he use one in many other instances. Rather, the essential element is the systematic pre-planning and pre-calculation of all elements of the labor process, which now no longer exists as a process in the imagination of the worker but only as a process in the imagination of a special management staff. Thus, if the first principle is the gathering and development of knowledge of labor processes, and the second is the concentration of this knowledge as the exclusive province of management – together with its essential converse, the absence of such knowledge among the workers – then the third is the *use of this monopoly over knowledge to control each step of the labor process and its mode of execution.*

As capitalist industrial, office, and market practices developed in accordance with this principle, it eventually became part of accepted routine and custom, all the more so as the increasingly scientific character of most processes, which grew in complexity while the worker was not allowed to partake of this growth, made it ever more difficult for the workers to understand the processes in which they functioned. But in the beginning, as Taylor well understood, an abrupt psychological wrench was required. We have seen in the simple Schmidt case the means employed, both in the selection of a single worker as a starting point and in the way in which he was reoriented to the new conditions of work. In the more complex conditions of the machine shop, Taylor gave this part of the responsibility to the foremen. It is essential, he said of the gang bosses, to "nerve and brace them up to the point of insisting that the workmen shall carry out the orders exactly as specified on the instruction cards. This is a difficult task at first, as the workmen have been accustomed for years to do the details of the work to suit themselves, and many of them are intimate friends of the bosses and believe they know quite as much about their business as the latter."[26]

Modern management came into being on the basis of these principles. It arose as theoretical construct and as systematic practice, moreover, in the very period during which the transformation of labor from processes based on skill to processes based upon science was attaining its most rapid tempo. Its role was to render conscious and systematic, the formerly unconscious tendency of capitalist production. It was to ensure that as craft declined, the worker would sink to the level of general and un-differentiated labor power, adaptable to a large range of simple tasks, while as science grew, it would be concentrated in the hands of management.

EDITOR'S NOTES

[a] Here Braverman refers to Marx's discussion of the difference between the architect and the bee referred to in the Introduction to Part 2.

[b] Braverman is alluding here to his subsequent discussion of the de-skilling of office work, referred to in the Introduction to Part 2.

[c] From the name of its inventor Charles Babbage (1791–1871), see Introduction to Part 2.

NOTES

1. Peter F. Drucker, *The Practice of Management* (New York, 1954), p. 280.
2. See Sudhir Kakar, *Frederick Taylor: A Study in Personality and Innovation* (Cambridge, Mass., 1970), pp. 115–17; and Henri Fayol, *General and Industrial Management* (1916; trans., London, 1949).
3. Lyndall Urwick and E. F. L. Brech, *The Making of Scientific Management*, 3 vols. (London, 1945, 1946, 1948), vol. I, p. 17.
4. See Georges Friedmann, *Industrial Society* (Glencoe, Ill., 1964), esp. pp. 51–65.
5. Lyndall Urwick, *The Meaning of Rationalisation* (London, 1929), pp. 13–16.
6. Kakar, *Frederick Taylor*, pp. 17–27, 52–54.
7. *Taylor's Testimony before the Special House Committee*, in Frederick W. Taylor, *Scientific Management* (New York and London, 1947), pp. 79–85.
8. Frederick W. Taylor, *Shop Management, in Scientific Management*, p. 30. See also Taylor's *The Principles of Scientific Management* (New York, 1967), pp. 13–14; and *Taylor's Testimony in Scientific Management*, p. 8.
9. *Shop Management*, pp. 32–33.
10. Ibid., pp. 34–35.
11. *The Principles of Scientific Management*, p. 32.
12. Ibid., pp. 48–49, 53.
13. *The Principles of Scientific Management*, pp. 61–62.
14. *The Principles of Scientific Management*, pp. 107–109.
15. *The Principles of Scientific Management*, p. 111.
16. Ibid., p. 36.
17. Ibid., p. 22.
18. *Shop Management*, pp. 98–99.
19. *The Principles of Scientific Management*, pp. 37–38.
20. *Taylor's Testimony before the Special House Committee*, pp. 235–236.
21. Loc. cit.
22. Ibid., pp. 75, 77.
23. *The Principles of Scientific Management*, p. 62.
24. *Shop Management*, p. 105.
25. *The Principles of Scientific Management*, pp. 63, 39.
26. *Shop Management*, p. 108.

CHAPTER SIX

Controlling the Line

Huw Beynon

Most workers endure supervision while they are at work. Many of them resent it and have built up defences against the supervisor. Coal mining perhaps provides the most well-known examples of the sort of controls that workers have developed at work. Writing in the 1920s Carter Goodrich describes a court case which arose out of the Minimum Wages Act. An overman was asked whether a particular miner did his job properly: 'I never saw him work,' he replied. 'But isn't it your duty to visit each working place twice a day?' asked the magistrate. 'Yes,' replied the overman, but 'they always stop work when they see an overman coming, and sit down till he's gone . . . they won't let anybody watch them' (Goodrich, 1920, p. 137). Particular features of mining, not least the danger involved in the work, have contributed to the proliferation of quite extensive job control by the miners. While such controls are not highly developed in every work situation there is every reason to expect that, in a society where most people have only their labour to sell, a conflict over control will be a feature of work situations. Although the syndicalist call of 1911 – 'the mines for the miners' – has died away, the idea of worker control still exists within the British working class. On the shop floor of many factories the division between the supervisor and the men can be characterized as a 'frontier of control' – management's rights on the one side and those of the workers on the other. It is in this way, in disputes over control at work, that the class struggle has been fought out by the British working class during this century. At the lowest, and most fundamental level, it has involved a conflict over how much work the men do and how much they get paid for it. At its most developed level it has produced an ideological conflict over who runs the factory and why, to a questioning of the essential nature and purpose of production within a capitalist society.

The unionization period at Halewood was marked by very severe conflicts along the frontier of control. It involved the workers in a major struggle for a degree of job control within the factory, and this struggle was based upon the relationship between the worker and his supervisor. Victories in these struggles were far from hollow ones, for in their defeat of the supervisor the workers and their stewards laid down the essential basis for a say in the way their lives were to be regulated while they were in the plant. These struggles were of crucial importance for the development of the shop stewards' committee and in examining them it will be useful to begin by drawing upon the experiences of the small-parts section of the paint shop.

Eddie Roberts was the shop steward for the section, George was his stand-in and Kenny was their close friend. All three of them had been on the section from the early days. Kenny was a militant.

> I don't know what I am, or what I want to do. I hate Ford's. I'd give up a wage increase to have Henry Ford on this section and give him a good kick up the arse. I'd thought of going to Australia. Of opening a shop. Can you be a socialist and own a shop?

Kenny hated Ford's and loved a fight. He hated having to get up early in the morning. He hated being told what to do. He hated having to work his balls off for nothing. He arrived on the section from the wet deck. Bert (the wet deck steward) couldn't handle him. 'I spotted him so I thought I'd unload him on to Roberts . . . It worked out good.' Kenny was amazed by the small-parts section.

> I came there and I was put on the front of the line. There was all these hooks and they *all* had to be filled with bits and pieces. I tell you Huwie it was murder. I'd get home and I'd go straight to bed. I couldn't stand it. So I decided that I'd had enough. I started to fill every other hook – to leave big gaps. The foreman went mad. Berserk he went. He started jumping on and off the line, running down the shop filling up the hooks. I ask you. He was shit-scared. 'You *must* fill them all' he kept screaming. Well the lads caught on and they started leaving empty hooks. He was going crazy. Then we got hold of Eddie to complain that the foreman was working. We did that every day.
>
> The situation is a lot better now. In fact we've got one of the easiest sections in the plant. It can be done see. You can control it if you have a go.

The paint shop is the earliest process that the car shell passes through in the PTA [Paint and Trim Assembly Plant]. Stoppages of work there will stop production and lay off the rest of the workers in the PTA within a matter of hours. The paint shop workers were aware of this and during periods of market boom when they were working high schedules they pressed their advantage. Certain sections were able to establish and maintain control over line speeds and the allocation of work. In the small-parts section the advantages of their position in the production process had been exploited to the full by a high level of solidarity and cohesion amongst the men on the section and an audacious, gifted leadership. As a result of this, and the decline in through-put of the section which accompanied the new fascia panels, the manning of the section in 1968 was almost twice as high as management considered reasonable. Eddie explains:

We've just had to destroy the foremen. When we were here first the foremen really threw their weight around and it took a bit of time to sort things out. Kenny was up at the end of the line. He did a great job. Since then they've tended to send weak foremen down to us. They leave us alone and we leave them alone. One or two of them have tried to get on top but they're easy to beat. There are lots of things you can do to make it bad for them. The lads would do half the job, and play around with them. I'd set him up for cases and destroy him in the office. Every time I was in the office I'd say something about him. That's what we *had* to do. We *had* to destroy the foremen.

We've got it pretty easy now. The blokes are told what has to be done at the beginning of the shift and they work out the speeds, and the times when they're going to take their breaks for tea and cards. Occasionally the foreman will come on to the section during the shift and tell me or George that they want some more parts done quickly – so will the lads do it, as a favour? He goes on about how appreciative he is and that, and the lads do it for him. They just take longer breaks.

I don't know what it is. Some sections like this one are good sections with all good jobs. It's because you've had blokes like myself and Kenny and George who've come to stay I suppose. We've decided not to be beaten down by Ford's or to leave. On other sections the jobs are really bad. I can't understand it. I've been down to talk to the lads on one of those sections, to try to persuade them to do something. They just say they'll be leaving soon. At the other extreme you get the daft buggers in the boiler house who've been here since the start-up and still haven't done anything. For all we say though, there's no easy job in this plant. We're going to have to give way on manning on this section soon. We've just been fortunate with the change in the fascia panels. Most jobs in this plant, even the easy ones, are pretty bad really. There's no joy in putting things on hooks.

In the small-parts section of the paint shop the method of work, along with the strategic position of the section in the plant, assisted the organized attempts of the workers to obtain strong areas of job control. The fact that they were able to maintain these controls during a period of declining work schedules was largely due to the influence that Eddie – the steward and deputy convenor – was able to exert over the supervisor and plant manager. It has already been suggested that bluff plays an important part in negotiations between shop stewards and representatives of management. Periods of months can go by without either side calling the other's bluff. In some factories the bluff is never called. In a period of expanding output it would not be worth it for management to challenge the areas of job control in the small-parts section because this carried the risk of a stoppage. In the long-term, however, the bluff would be called and Eddie knew this; he also knew that when that happened they would have to settle for a reduction in manning.

The extent and durability of job controls are subject to the market. Fluctuations in the sales of cars, in the rate of capital investment, soon reveal themselves in the social relations on the shop floor. It is in this sense that unionism and workplace organization can be seen as a direct consequence of economic forces. Workers who restrict their output, who 'malinger' at work, frequently justify themselves by their need to regulate the supply of labour. 'If we all worked flat out it would be dead simple what would happen. Half of us would be outside on the stones with our cards in our hands.' The Labour government's notion of 'shake out' in the 1960s was but a euphemism for the fact that by maximizing the return on capital working men are put out of a job. The idea of maximizing returns and cutting labour costs is instilled into the minds of modern managers, particularly those who have attended courses in business economics in our universities. Yet a similar understanding is denied to workers because they are in a position to see beyond it. Maximizing returns makes sense only if you're not going to be maximized into the dole queue. Workers who understand this are called 'bloody-minded' because they have come to understand something important about how the economic system operates.

We are left with arguments about 'fairness'. 'A fair day's work for a fair day's pay.' But what is fair? Fair for whom? What sort of fairness commits some men to a life on the line while others write books about them. It's not a fair world and there is no way of deciding what is a fair day's work from these men. The very act of asking them to work there *at all* is manifestly unfair. People who sit in offices, ride in lifts and Company cars have no right to demand that the lads on the line work harder, because to ask the same thing from themselves would be unthinkable.

It's got nothing to do with fairness. What it has to do with is economics and power. In these terms it is important to examine the strengths and vulnerabilities of the job controls established by the Halewood workers, and in doing so I shall now concentrate upon the experiences of the workers in the trim and final assembly departments. The situations in these departments differed in a number of important respects from the paint shop. In these departments the assembly line exerted an even greater pressure upon the nature of work and work relationships. In these departments the operator, the steward and the foreman were under a greater, and more continuous, pressure than that experienced by their counterparts in the paint shop. Here thousands of components are assembled around the painted body shell, which moves upon a line that never stops. To miss a job means the threat of chaos because someone further down the line has a job which depends upon your job. In the small-parts section an empty hook was an important act of defiance which laid the ground for a movement toward job control, but it did not involve the *sabotage* of the job. On the assembly line a missed job could mean precisely this. Although this means that the individual operator has a greater amount of power at his disposal, in the early days of the plant this power was essentially superficial and illusory. Unless you were sure of the support of your steward and workmates, to miss a job on the line at this time meant that you took on the whole world.

One of the most firmly held policies of the Ford Motor Company has been its opposition both to piece rates and to negotiations over job manning and individual workloads. The Company has held consistently to its right to manage its factories as it thinks fit – to employ whom it likes and to use those in its employ as it likes. In 1969 I had a conversation with a senior Labour Relations executive of the Company, who made clear to me his objections to 'mutuality agreements' with the trade unions over such things as the timing of jobs and the allocation of work. Such an agreement would make the management and the trade unions jointly responsible for ascertaining the time for a particular job, the organization of work, speed of the line and so on.

> No. We cannot accept mutuality at this time. Where the trade union movement fails to see these areas of common interest we are inhibited from going down the mutuality road. The first duty we have to our employees is the business. We're not going to be a loss maker. People can look at Ford's, look at its assets and think that the company is safe. Ford's can go to the wall like any other company. If we're not competitive, we make losses and we go to the wall. It's in their interests – share-holders, customers and workers – for us to stay competitive.

Clearly, therefore, any move toward 'mutuality' or the establishment of extensive job control by the workers through their union is seen to involve a direct threat to the competitive position and profitability of the company. It was not felt that this insistence upon the manager's right to manage and pursue efficiency should of necessity give rise to conflict. To quote from the same conversation:

> No: I may be naive over this but I can't see that at all. Management don't set difficult work standards. All we want is maximum use of the plant; we can do this in a number of ways – overtime, shift working. All we want then is the plant to produce *the number of cars that we know it can produce* – we're simply asking for *good continuous effort*. And it's here that we need a good working relationship between the foreman and the shop steward in order to achieve these standards. On the track, for example, there may be a work allocation on the basis of three two-doors followed by one four-door followed by three two-door and then a mistake occurs and three four-doors come down together. Now it's in these sort of situations that a good working relationship with the steward is vital. If the relationship is good they can work out whether to put men in on the line or to let the bodies go down the line and gradually move them back again. In these sort of cases cooperation becomes so important.
>
> The unions have taken the wrong turning over this. They seem to think that increased efficiency means that we are asking the men to sweat blood. We're not doing this at all. We aim to set standards that can reasonably be met.

In spite of this, however, it would be true to say that there was no common agreement in the Halewood plants over what constituted 'good continuous effort' or a 'reasonable' workload. The management's insistence that it was its right to make the vital decision on these issues, in itself produced mistrust. The question of job timings and job control was the source of very severe conflict in the Halewood assembly plant throughout the 1960s.

On the assembly line each worker is termed an operator, he works at a particular station and work is allocated to him at that station. He is surrounded by stacks of components and maybe a man is sub-assembling these for him. His job is to attach his components to the body shells as they come to him. Obviously the faster the line runs, the less time he has on any particular body shell, and consequently the smaller the range of tasks that he is able to do. If the line is running, for example, at thirty cars an hour, he is allocated two minutes' work on each car that passes him. The allocation of the two minutes' work is done on the basis of the times recorded for each operation by the Works-study Department of the Ford Motor Company. Most of the assembly-line workers I talked to were suspicious of the timings. It wasn't so much that they thought that the times were rigged but more that they thought the whole idea of timing jobs to be a questionable one – both ethically and scientifically. As two of them put it:

> They say that their timings are based upon what an 'average man' can do at an 'average time of the day'. That's a load of nonsense that. At the beginning of the shift its all right but later on it gets harder. And what if a man feels a bit under the weather? On night shift see, I'm bloody hopeless. I just can't get going on nights. Yet you've always got the same times: Ford's times. It's this numbering again. They think that if they number us and number the job everything is fine.
>
> *They* decide on *their* measured day how fast *we* will work. They seem to forget that we're not machines y'know. The standards they work to are excessive anyway. They expect you to work the 480 minutes of the eight hours you're on the clock. They've agreed to have a built-in allowance of *six minutes* for going to the toilet, blowing your nose and that. It takes you six minutes to get your trousers down.

The 'science' of the stopwatch was conceived in America at the beginning of the century. Much of it emerged from the factories of men like Ford, but the chief publicist of 'scientific management' was Frederick 'Speedy' Taylor. Like Ford he was an eccentric. As a boy he insisted when he played with his friends that their games conform to detailed, rigid rules. The longer he lived the less he slept, for he had perfected a device that woke him if he dozed in his chair. His mission was to make labour scientific; to calculate the most efficient means of working, through detailed timings of physical movements, and by related incentive payment schemes. His schemes met with considerable opposition and eventually in 1912 a Congressional Committee was set up to investigate his methods.

Men still claim scientific status for work-study methods. Usually, however, such claims come from those who are not on the receiving end of the stopwatch. (The extent to which the 'professional classes' support increased rationalization and productivity on the shop floor yet deny the applicability of such criteria to their own work is one of the more interesting phenomena of modern society.) Unbiased opinion rarely disagrees with Professor Baldamus's contention that the whole work-study operation hinges upon 'intuitive guesses as to what is in fact a normal, reasonable, fair, average or right degree of effort for any particular task'. Even writers closer in their identification with the aims of management are reluctant to make sweeping claims for science and objectivity in work study. One of the books written for students of management on methods of payment makes it clear that 'the allocation of points encourages one of the major fallacies about job evaluation' that it is 'a scientific or at the very least an objective technique which introduces definitive criteria into the emotive and subjective matter of determining levels of remuneration'. It goes on to conclude that 'the measurement is spurious', and overwhelmingly laden with subjective evaluation 'as any examination of the way factors and their weightings are determined will reveal' (North and Buckingham, 1969, p. 197).

The works-study engineer, the man with the clock, bore the brunt of much of the antagonism engendered by job timings in the PTA plant. . . . Their dads were workers and they'd been to grammar school, got a few O levels and jacked it in. They didn't believe in the Ford Motor Company either. It was just their job.

Some of them were attending evening classes, for a qualification in works management, or personnel management. A bit of work study and a bit of industrial sociology and psychology. They didn't like it much. 'It's all a load of baloney tha'. As far as I can see it's all about manipulation. And the lecturer's only there for the cash. I don't blame him, like, but it's a bit difficult to take it seriously. I'm going to pack it in and go to India.' The few that I spoke to were sympathetic towards the workers, one of them in particular being even more dubious about the science of job timings than the lads themselves.

. . .

Apart from the timings themselves, the main problems faced by the operatives on the assembly line related to *speed-up*. The history of the assembly line is a history of conflict over speed-up – the process whereby the pace of work demanded of the operator is systematically increased. This can be obtained in a number of ways, the most simple involving a gradual increase in the speed of the line *during* a shift. In other words a man may start a shift with a work allocation of two minutes to coincide with a line speed of thirty cars an hour and then find that he is working on a line that is moving at thirty-five cars an hour. He gets suspicious after a bit because he finds that he can't make time on the job. He can't get those few stations up the line which allow him a break and half a ciggie now and then. We have already seen that this practice was common in the pre-union era of the American motor industry and also at Dagenham. The long-service stewards and workers at Halewood insist that plant management made frequent use of this type of speed-up in the early days of the plant. Production managers out to make a name for themselves can only do it through figures – through their production and their costs. They abuse their supervision to this end. To serve the god of production is also to serve yourself and in this climate a few dodges are all part of the game. These dodges could be controlled though. They provoked a number of unofficial walkouts on the trim lines. 'The lads said "Sod you. We're not doing it, we're just not doing it." It worked as good as anything else y'know. We just said "no" and if they pushed it we went home.' No procedure could sort out issues like these. This was naked aggression being met with violent defiance. Management was trying to force the lads to do the unthinkable and they weren't having it. An agreement had to be reached and management conceded to the stewards the right to hold the key that locked the assembly line. Little Bob Costello had the key on the A shift, and the line speeds were changed with great ceremony, watched and cheered by the workers on the line. This wasn't enough for some sections. Some stewards had been able to obtain an additional safeguard. The first man on these sections was given an extra time allowance for counting the cars that entered the section. If the number of cars in any hour exceeded the stipulated line speed he was able to stop the line.

Some control then was obtained by a straightforward refusal to obey – by rebellion. Instances such as this one were commonplace in the plant before negotiated agreements had been made over the control of the work. Individual acts of sabotage were also common at this time. Men pulled the safety wire and stopped the line. These acts were part of a general movement toward job control and in substance differed only slightly from the formally articulated acts of defiance just mentioned. In an organized plant, however, sabotage takes on a different significance.

In the late 1960s the management at Halewood was forced to lower the minimum age of recruitment to eighteen, letting in a flood of lads who couldn't believe their eyes. What a place this was. These lads wanted the money. They dressed well, lived it up, with girls and music. The PTA plant at Halewood had nothing to offer them but money. They wanted to take their Fridays off and have a good time. They didn't want to put petrol tanks in motors. A gang of these lads worked together on the high-line. They started by peeling the foreman's orange, carefully, removing the fruit and filling the skin with Bostic. The new remoulded orange was returned to the supervisor's bag. And they watched him trying to peel it. Bostic is a marvellous substance. It sticks and it burns. Bostic bombs were manufactured and hurled into the steel dumper rubbish containers. Explosions . . . flames twenty feet high. Someone could have been killed. On the trim lines they started pulling the safety wire. On one shift after the 1970 strike the line was stopped on thirty-six occasions. Foremen were restarting the line without checking.

In one respect incidents like these involve a fundamental challenging of the whole thing because these lads just didn't want to produce motors. This denial is so fundamental that it has nothing whatsoever to do with trade unionism. In the summer of 1969, for example, the convenor met the works manager who asked him if there was any dispute outstanding that they could sort out. There wasn't, but the weather was beautiful – hot and sunny. The lads kept coming in late from their dinner breaks. 'If they can play football they can work. They're just a lazy bunch of bastards.' It got hotter and hotter, it was too hot to work. 'But they played football . . .' They weren't going to work – take the roof off. Senior plant management went into the paint shop to check the complaint. One of them was streaming with sweat. 'What did the lads want?' They wanted iced lime juice. This unfortunately couldn't be supplied but would orange be all right? Yes, orange would do fine. They drank it and went home.

Trade unionism is about work and sometimes the lads just don't want to work. All talk of procedures and negotiations tends to break down here. The lime juice incident illustrates this well. It could be coped with, it was good fun but it had little to do with conventional union–management relations. There comes a point, however, where certain sorts of individual action come into direct conflict with the very nature of trade union collectivism. The steward organization was developed to protect the members against management and, as such, an important part of its function was to obtain a degree of internal discipline within the workforce. Bostic bombs could kill someone. The lads *had* to stop. They had to be sorted out and the convenor had to do it. Once more that was all. Just one more Bostic bomb and they'd be outside the gate.

> All right Eddie. We'll take it from you Eddie. We'll not take it from him [the supervisor] though. We'll not take it from him. Treating us like little kids. We're not at school y'know.
> They're not bad lads. It's just working in this fucking place.

Controlling the membership is part of the steward's job. The nature of the relationship between the union and the employer can mean that the steward rather than the manager disciplines individual workers for not working properly. This is one side of the picture. In an organized shop individual acts of defiance or 'laziness' can threaten the unity and organization achieved by the mass in collective action. But although individual acts of sabotage *can* be antipathetic to unionism, not all sabotage need be.

In the paint shop the car, after an early coat of paint, passes through the wet deck where a team of men armed with electric sanders – 'whirlies' – sand the body while it is being heavily sprayed with water. From the wet deck the car shell goes right through the painting system and emerges finished some three hours later. In 1967 Bert Owen was the steward for the wet deck. The lads on the deck played in a football team, went away on coach trips, drank together in the pub. They had their own nicknames for each other. A lad called John Dillon worked there. So they all took *Magic Roundabout* names: Dougal, Florence, Zebedee. 'Did you see it yesterday?' 'It's clever mind – how they do it.' There was also Mumbles, Big Ears and Uncle Fester. And Bert. They sang songs. Played about.

If there was a problem on the wet deck, a manning problem, speed-up, if the foreman had stepped out of line, they always had a comeback. They could sand the paint off the style lines – the fine edges of the body that give it its distinctive shape. And nobody could know. The water streaming down, the whirlies flailing about, the lads on either side of the car, some of them moving off to change their soaking clothes. The foreman could stand over them and he couldn't spot it happening. Three hours later the finished body shell would emerge with bare metal along the style lines. They *knew* it was happening.

'The bastards . . . now look here, Bert, this has gone far enough. I've taken as much as I'm going to from them fuckers. You tell them to stop.' Stop what? Bert was al-ways prepared to urge them to improve their work but really it was the equipment, or the paint, or the metal. 'All right, Bert, they can have what they want.' They'd sing then. After a victory. They'd stand there with their whirlies – singing. In the wet. 'Walk on through the wind, walk on through the storm, and you'll n – e – ver walk a – lone . . .' For the rest of the shift.

Few sections had this degree of cohesion or such assistance from the means of production. Things were quite different on the trim lines where the car assembly workers at Halewood met speed-up in its most developed form. While little Bob's key foiled the more flagrant excesses of management, other, more sophisticated, means of increasing the work content were more difficult to combat. These derive from the fact that fluctuations in the market demand for cars result in the speed of the line, and the mixture of models (and therefore jobs) coming on to the line, varying from week to week and even from day to day. As a consequence of this both the allocation of jobs and the number of men employed on a particular section has to be altered and renegotiated with each change of speed or model mix. In this situation speed-up can be obtained by an increased rationalization of work allocation at the higher speeds, i.e. a less than proportionate increase takes place in the number of men employed on a section and this manning ratio is maintained when lower speeds are returned to. For example, a hundred men might work on a section with a line speed of thirty cars an hour; with an increase in the speed of the line to forty cars an hour (by 33 per cent) the manning might be increased to 125 (or only 25 per cent) and then when the speed is dropped again to thirty the manning might be cut to ninety-five. Again the stewards maintain that such practice was commonplace in the early days of the plant.

The establishment of controls over speed-up achieved through variations in the manning ratios was obviously difficult to obtain given the company's principle of refusing to negotiate the allocation of work – a principle formally recognized in the agreement signed by the company and the trade unions. In spite of this, however, several sections had established unwritten agreements as to the manning ratios that would operate at the various speeds. By 1968 most of the sections in the trim and final assembly departments had established a code of custom and practice which governed the allocation of work and it is important to look at some of the ways in which these controls were established.

By 1968 the shop stewards' committee was in a position to establish a level of consistency in the job control exercised by each of its stewards on their section. Its ability to secure this consistency derived from the actual controls over job regulation that had been built up unevenly throughout the plant. Within the trim department areas of strongly developed job control coexisted with sections where such control was quite rudimentary. These strong areas of control were invariably associated with the fact that sometime in the past, the steward, or another operative on the section, had stuck his neck out and opposed the supervisor. One steward describes what happened on his section:

> I've told you that it was pretty bad when we came here first. The supervisors used to treat you like dirt. I've always been able to stick up for myself like, they knew that if they messed me about they'd have some trouble on their hands, so it wasn't too bad

for me. You see I don't think any man, any supervisor, should consider himself above another man. I don't think he should ask another man to do what he wouldn't do himself. A lot of the lads who came here first were given a really bad time. I've never been able to sit back and watch another man take a beating. To see a man struggling with a job. So I started telling the supervisor that he was out of line. Then the lads asked me to represent them – to be the steward – and I've done that ever since.

Such opposition frequently produced situations of severe conflict and sometimes this conflict developed into a personal battle between the steward and the supervisor. In order to establish controls over the supervisor's decisions, the stewards resorted to a number of different tactics. One of the most successful stewards on the trim sections obtained his autonomy by restricting his negotiations with the supervisor to a torrent of abuse and a recorded 'failure to agree'. Les explains:

I expect everyone has told you how bad it was down there in the beginning have they? It was murder. We had no representation. We were just supposed to do exactly as we were told. Well I started shouting my mouth off and the lads asked me to be the steward. That started it. I was working on the line. A member would have a dispute with the foreman and ask for me, but the foreman wouldn't get me a relief. I'd have to wait he said. So we stopped the job. Yes it was really bad then. You had no say in anything – in who did what or how much work or nothing.

Anyway we stopped the job a few times and things got a bit better but not much. They still thought that we hadn't to be listened to. So I thought sod this, we won't listen to you. I used to swear blind at them all the time – I still do a bit, it's the only way sometimes – swear blind and 'fail to agree'. Then we'd go up the office and I'd abuse him again. Call him a stupid bastard in front of management. It was the only way on my section. I had forty 'failure to agree's going at one time.

The bitterness in this situation exploded when one of the supervisors attempted to plant a component in Les's haversack which was subsequently searched by a security guard. Les, however, had been forewarned.

. . .

While this incident is obviously an extreme example, it should not be readily dismissed as an entirely misleading and atypical one. Many of the stewards experienced periods of perpetual confrontation with their supervisors. During the autumn of 1967, for example, the issue of job control became important within the material handling sections of the plant. These sections had previously been relatively unorganized, but had by this time produced two active shop stewards. The material handling department receives and stores components, and then distributes them to the stations on the lines. The workers in these departments were part storeman, part clerk and part fork-lift driver. They were split up all over the plant, and organization was difficult. Jack Jones was another of the young stewards on the A shift. He was smart and a bit cheeky. Like so many others he'd come to Ford's for the cash and with some idea that he might 'get on a bit'. He had been a long-distance lorry driver and then a storeman at English Electric. Ford's made him into a unionist. 'It was so obvious when I came here. It was obvious that you had to have an organization. Everyone was getting screwed. This place without an organization would be last.' Bill Brodrick who was a mate of his encouraged him to take on the steward's job. Jack became a steward in 1964. He had a lot of trouble organizing the section. His job made him isolated. It was impossible for him to be on the spot with a grievance. He had to be told of the problem and relieved from his job. Frequently he had up and downers with the foreman and the superintendent. In 1967 one of these culminated in Jack being sued for libel. In building up an organization on the section the steward enforces unwritten agreements from his supervisor. When the supervisor is placed under pressure by his superiors he often breaks these secret understandings. Jack committed his feelings to print. He filled in a procedure report calling the supervisor a 'perpetual liar' and a 'deceitful bastard'. The supervisor went to law, but he wasn't allowed to push it too far. Higher management persuaded him that the case was better dropped and Jack Jones escaped his chance to testify in the dock.

The right of the shop steward to have freedom of access to his members on a section, and his right to negotiate with the supervisor over allocation of work and the like were therefore established in the main by way of periods of severe conflict between the stewards and supervision. These rights were minimal requirements for a degree of job control by the men on the assembly line, and they had to be fought for. Once they were obtained the steward and the shop stewards' committee were able to build upon them.

This conflict over 'rights' is a fundamental one and permeates union–management relationships. It is not restricted to the shop floor. During a meeting of the Ford NJNC [National Joint Negotiating Committee] in 1970, the Company's director of labour relations, Bob Ramsey, clashed with the committee's secretary, Reg Birch, of the AUEW [Amalgamated Union of Engineering Workers]. The basis of the clash appeared trivial. They were arguing about the men who worked in the Ford plants; Ramsey claimed that they were Ford workers who happened to be members of the AUEW, the TGWU [Transport and General Workers' Union] or whatever, Birch that they were first and foremost union members who happened to be working for the Ford Motor Company. There is no doubt that Birch and Ramsey were touching the nerve end of quite fundamental differences in principle. This clash of principles reveals itself on the shop floor in the conflict along the frontier of control. It is these principles that are at stake when the foreman starts to allocate work and the steward retorts 'Hang on a minute. *You* tell us what's to be done and *we'll* decide who does it.' It is a direct clash over management's right to manage. A clash of power and ideology.

The position of the steward in the car plant is rooted in this clash. In the early years at Halewood the day-to-day life of the plant was virtually one endless battle over control. The establishment of a steward in a particular section was clearly related to the attempt by the workers to establish job control in that section. If the steward wasn't up to the job he was replaced, or he stood down leaving the section without a steward for a while. Where a steward stuck with the job, he and the men on his section were involved in a perpetual battle with foremen and management. Even in 1967 the stewards felt that the overwhelming majority of the problems that they had to deal with on their section were related either to speed-up or 'the blue-eye system', the favouritism practised by foremen in allocating work and overtime or in moving men from one section to another.

The problem of overtime is an important one. Initially it can be seen as a point of tension between the steward and his members. The stewards didn't like overtime.

. . .

This tension between the steward and his members over overtime is part of a general ideological struggle. At the moment it is important to recognize issues of overtime allocation as part of the conflict over control which the workers are involved in on the shop floor. Assembly-line workers work for money and they want overtime because it gives them more money to pay off hire-purchase debts, mortgages and the like. The foreman allocates overtime. He says who works when. This is part of his prerogative. His right to manage. The individual operator can exercise no control over the supervisor's decisions – apart, that is, from buying him pints in the local. On the assembly line one man is as good as the next man. The operator can stake no claims on the basis of ability or expertise. He is in the supervisor's pocket. If he doesn't behave, or if the supervisor just doesn't happen to 'like' him, he can lose his overtime for a week or forever. In a skilled work situation things are slightly different. At the Rolls Royce factory in Bristol, for example, men can control their right to overtime on certain jobs by virtue of the fact that they control the tools, or the knowledge, vital to the completion of the job. The foreman *has* to ask *them*. The assembly-line foreman can ask *anyone*. The emergent shop stewards' committee was a response to this situation. On many sections, the allocation of overtime was taken out of the hands of the supervisor and replaced by an overtime rota, administered by the steward.

Men became stewards in their battles with supervisors over injustices, over the workers' rights as opposed to management's indiscriminate right to manage. Frequently their response was crude. The vulnerability of their situation defied subtlety.

. . .

As part of the logic of management's 'right to manage', the supervisor can expect his instructions to be obeyed. In case the operator objects to the order a procedure exists whereby he can object personally and then through his steward. Where no agreement can be obtained it is assumed that the man will obey the order until a decision has been reached at a higher level in the procedure. The procedure, therefore, assumes that the supervisor has authority. It exists to safeguard the worker from a wrong decision. It makes no sense for the supervisor to put a complaint in procedure for such an act negates management's authority and the very nature of the procedure. In a climate where the 'right to manage' was being perpetually challenged by the 'rights' of the workers it is not surprising, and certainly revealing, that many supervisors became confused about what was theirs 'by right'.

As the organization developed the stewards presented more subtle challenges to management and supervision. In order to deal with disputes over work allocation most of the stewards (thirty-four) had had some training in the techniques of work study. Twelve of them had in fact decided to become work-study experts and had attended an advanced course on the subject that had been organized by the WEA [Workers' Educational Association]. By virtue of the expertise gained on such courses, and also by their length of service in the plant, a number of the stewards had developed a far greater understanding of these techniques than had their supervisors. This had a number of consequences. For example, it meant that if an operator complained that he was being asked to do too much work, the steward was able to base a case upon the efficacy of the job timings which often served to drive a wedge between the supervisor and the works-study department. In these arguments the steward usually had to rely upon intuition, but one steward who had been bought a stopwatch by the men on his section was able to make more accurate checks upon the timings. It was through negotiations of this sort being carried out by individual stewards on their sections that the shop stewards' committee was able to establish an agreement for the whole PTA plant which prevented management re-timing any job without the prior agreement of the steward involved. Controls that were established within certain sections could therefore be extended through the committee to other sections which previously had not achieved such controls. Certain sections, however, still demonstrated greater worker control over job allocation than others, and the expertise and experience of the steward was one of the factors which explained this uneven development. Given the timings of the jobs that had to be manned on a particular section, there were any number of ways in which these jobs could be allocated to the men who worked on the section. As with most things there is an easy way and a hard way, and on several sections of the trim and final assembly departments the steward was more likely to know the easy way than the supervisor. A combination of this expertise and support from the men on their sections resulted in the steward's allocating work on at least six of the eighteen sections of the trim and final assembly departments in 1967. Given the speed of the line and the model mix, these sections functioned almost autonomously, with all the coordinating tasks being performed by the shop steward.

. . .

These controls over the job gained the operative a degree of autonomy from both supervision and higher management. Through their steward they were able to regulate the distribution of overtime, achieve a degree of job rotation within the section, and occasionally sub-assembly workers, in particular, were able to obtain 'slack' work schedules. But there were quite precise limits to the way in which workers can run the section. An example of these limits was revealed on the wet deck. The lads didn't like working in the plant. They looked forward to the weekends. The Friday shift was the worst. Particularly on nights, because it messed up your Saturday as well. So the *Magic Roundabout* lads decided to have a rota. Eight of them contributed to a pool. Every eighth week one of them took the Friday shift off, and got paid a shift's money from the pool. It became too regular, too open and was noticed by management. Friday absenteeism is a problem in a car plant. Perpetual absenteeism, like lateness, is a sacking offence. So management intervened with threats and the pool was abandoned. Not a few managers found examples of working-class collectivism such as this one emotionally attractive. A member of the Central Industrial Relations staff at Warley, for example, explained the militancy of the Halewood plant in terms of Liverpool's working-class tradition:

> They say that there are a different type of people in the North. They're not as materialistic as the people in the South. They've not got their own houses or their own cars. They're much more easy going altogether. They don't take life so seriously. Apparently if they go in for a claim that is just not on, they prefer to be told to 'fuck off out of it'. That's how labour relations are conducted up there. Now in Dagenham they'll come in with a claim that you know and they know is hopeless and you'll argue round and round it all day. In Halewood you'd just say 'fuck off' and that would be the end of it. They're much more easygoing there; the men are much more independent of their wives; they drink more; go and watch the football . . . I suppose they'll change. When they get into debt with buying a house they'll have to go to work I suppose.

Do you think that that would be a good thing?

> Ah, now that's a *philosophical* question not a *business* question. It's like those questions on class we were discussing earlier; they make life very complicated if you think too much about them. I can see that it wouldn't be a good thing. I can see that there's something attractive about that way of life; but it's not much good for business. And business is what counts I suppose.

And business *is* what counts. However things *should* be, that certainly is how things are. The need for capital to produce a surplus, a profit, is an inexorable need. It is this which structures the world of the shop steward in an assembly plant. The stewards may be able to prise away some of management's controlling rights but they can hang on to these for only as long as the needs of business dictate. Essentially the controls obtained over the job by shop floor union activities involved little more than a different form of accommodation to the more general controls imposed by management. Johnny saw this very clearly:

> As I've said, I don't like Ford's. I don't like what they do, what they stand for, or what they've done in the past – in this country and America. I can see the time when the bomb goes up, you know. I can see myself leading the lads off my section and just destroying

this place. I can see that happening. But you've got to cope with this plant as it is now, you've got to come in every day and represent the lads. That means you've got to set up some relationship with the supervision and with management. Sometimes I think 'what the hell are you doing? you're just doing management's job.' But I think its better for the lads if I do it. It *is* better for the lads if I allocate the jobs and the overtime because if I do it it will at least be done fairly.

While the controls established within the sections may not have involved a very radical challenge to management's organization of the plant, they were radical enough to reveal conflict between a worker rationality and a management rationality, and it was at times when this conflict became manifest that the vulnerability of worker control over work was cruelly exposed. While the stewards were able to exert a degree of influence over the way in which jobs were timed, and a strong degree of control over work allocation, they had not established any control over the market, and its expression in the variations in the speed of the assembly line.

A district secretary of the GMWU, an ex-convenor of the MSB plant at Halewood, explained how the absence of piece rates increased the vulnerability of the steward's position when alterations took place in line speeds.

> They're killing themselves up there in that plant. A steward on that estate is on a hiding to nothing. They just won't be able to last. It's different with piece rates. A steward's job is a lot easier then. He can negotiate the rate and then let the lad make his time. If management wants to change anything the steward can start talking about the rate. Now up there the rate is fixed so the steward's got nothing to bargain with. He spends all his time arguing about workloads. They set a line speed and they get things sorted out and then they change the speed and he's back where he started. It's heart-breaking and back-breaking. They're killing themselves up there in that plant.

With severe variations in the speed of the line, even the most well organized sections had difficulty in maintaining and re-establishing 'traditional' areas of job control. One of the senior stewards concurred with the union officer. 'We're mad,' he said, 'we're crazy I think, sometimes I don't know why we do it. We're running flat out all the time and just to stay in the same place.'

. . .

CHAPTER SEVEN

Thirty Years of Making Out

Michael Burawoy

The study of changes in the labor process is one of the more neglected areas of industrial sociology. There are global theories, which speak generally of tendencies toward rationalization, bureaucratization, the movement from coercive to normative compliance, and so forth. There are the prescriptive theories of human relations, of job enrichment, job enlargement, worker participation, and so on, which do express underlying changes but in a form that conceals them. There are attempts to examine the implications of technological change for worker attitudes and behavior, but these do not examine the forces leading to technological change itself. There are also theories of organizational persistence, which stress the capacity of enterprises to resist change. The few attempts at concrete analysis of changes in the labor process have usually emerged from comparisons among different firms. Such causal analysis, based on cross-sectional data, is notoriously unsatisfactory under the best of conditions, but when samples are small and firms diverse, the conclusions drawn are at best suggestive. As far as I know, there have been no attempts to undertake a detailed study of the labor process of a single firm over an extended period of time. Thus, my revisit to Geer, thirty years after Roy, provides a unique opportunity to examine the forces leading to changes on the shop floor.

. . .

TECHNOLOGY

Whenever technology changes its character, it has a transformative impact on the organization of work. However, the study of technological innovation and adoption is still in its primitive stages. Apart from the conventional models of neoclassical economics, which stress the cumulative role of science in the pursuit of ever greater efficiency, there have been few attempts to examine the political and social forces leading to technological change in advanced capitalism. A notable exception is the recent work by David Noble, which suggests that capitalists choose among available technologies not only to increase productivity but, in addition, to gain control over the labor process and push smaller capitalists out of business.[1] A recent study of the mechanization of harvesting shows that growers develop new technologies but that adoption is contingent on the level of class struggle.[2]

Undoubtedly the examination of the forces leading to technological change is important. However, if we are to understand the changes in the labor process that are brought about by social imperatives other than those introduced by new machines, we must keep technology constant, since it would be impossible to isolate its impact. Fortunately, machine-tool technology, in its principles at least, has remained relatively constant over the past century, with the exception of the recent development of computer-controlled machines. It therefore provides a useful basis for studying "non-technical" sources of change in the organization of work. Thus, the machine shops described in the writings of Frederick Winslow Taylor bear a remarkable resemblance to those of Geer and Allied.[3] The agglomeration of speed drills, radial drills, vertical and horizontal mills, chuck and turret lathes, grinders, etc., could be found in essentially the same forms in machine shops at the end of the nineteenth century as they are today. Even in the layout of its machines, the Jack Shop, where Roy worked, closely resembled the small-parts department where I worked. The organization of work and the incentive schemes, as well as the various forms of output restriction and the informal worker alliances, all described by Roy, are to be found today and can be traced back to the turn of the century.

However, outside the small-parts department there have been major changes in technology, in the direction of increased automation. The most impressive change at Allied came in the machining of rough cylinder-block castings. First introduced at a Ford plant in 1935, these monstrous integrated machine tools are programmed to perform several operations simultaneously (milling, tapping, boring, drilling, grinding, etc.) at each work station before the cylinder block is automatically transported to the next work station. Despite, or perhaps because of, its sophistication, this elaborate technology was out of order much of the time. In some departments one or two computer-controlled machines had been installed, but they, too, seemed to experience considerable downtime. Generally, the wide variety and relatively small volume of engines produced at Allied made it uneconomic to transform the technology of the entire plant, and, when new automated equipment was introduced, it frequently created more problems than it solved. As I shall suggest toward the end of this chapter, piecemeal technological innovation can easily become the focus of struggles on the shop floor.

Even in the small-parts department, by no means the most technologically sophisticated of the departments of the engine division, machines are now more reliable, flexible, precise, and so forth than they were in 1945. A very noticeable change from Geer is the absence of the huge belt lines that used to power the machine tools. Now each machine has its own source of power. In the remaining sections of this chapter

I shall indicate how these small changes in technology have become part of, have facilitated, and have sometimes stimulated changes in productive activities and production relations.

THE PIECE-RATE SYSTEM

In a machine shop, operators are defined by the machine they "run" and are remunerated according to an individual piece-rate incentive scheme. While machine operators comprise the majority of workers on the shop floor, there are also auxiliary workers, whose function it is to provide facilities and equipment as well as assistance for the "production" workers (operators). For each production operation the methods department establishes a level of effort, expressed in so many pieces per hour, which represents the "100 percent" benchmark. Below this benchmark, operators receive a base rate for the job, irrespective of the actual number of pieces they produce. Above this standard, workers receive not only the base rate for the job but, in addition, a bonus or incentive, corresponding to the number of pieces in excess of "100 percent." Thus, output at a rate of 125 percent is defined as the "anticipated rate," which – according to the contract – is the amount "a normal experienced operator working at incentive gait" is expected to produce and represents 25 percent more pieces than the base rate. Producing at "125 percent," an operator will earn himself or herself an incentive bonus that adds around 15 percent to the amount earned when producing at 100 percent or less. Earned income per hour is computed as follows:

> Base earnings (determined by job's labor grade)
> + Base earnings × (% Rate – 100%) (if rate is greater than 100%)
> + Override (determined by job's labor grade)
> + Shift differential (25 cents for second and third shifts)
> + Cost-of-living allowance

In 1945 the computation of earnings was simpler. The system of remuneration was a straight piece-rate system with a guaranteed minimum. There were no extra benefits. Each operation had a *price* rather than a *rate*. Earnings were calculated by simply multiplying the number of pieces produced in an hour by the price. If the result was less than the guaranteed minimum, the operator received that guaranteed minimum, known as the day rate. If output was greater than that corresponding to the day rate, an increase of 25 percent in the number of pieces led to a 25 percent increase in earnings. How the day rate was determined was not always clear. It reflected not only the job but also the operator's skill. Thus Roy received a day rate of 85 cents per hour, but Al McCann, also working on a radial drill on second shift but a more experienced operator, received a day rate of $1.10. The day rate on first shift was 5 cents lower than on second shift, so that, to make 85 cents an hour, Joe Mucha, Roy's day man, had to work harder than Roy. The price for a given operation, however, was the same for all operators.

The two systems thus encourage different strategies for achieving increased earn-ings. In 1945 Geer operators might fight for higher day rates by bargaining indi-vidually with management, but this did not guarantee them increased earnings if they were regularly turning out more pieces than corresponded to the day rate. Further-more, the very operators who might be eligible for higher day rates would also be the ones for whom a guaranteed minimum was not so important. So the way to drive up income was to increase prices, and this could be accomplished either by fighting for across-the-board-increases on all prices or by fighting with the time-study man for improved prices on particular jobs. Operators did in fact spend a great deal of time haggling with time-study men over prices. These ways of increasing earnings are now relatively insignificant compared to two alternative methods. The first is via increases in the base earnings for the job and the fringes that go along with each labor grade. These are all negotiated at three-year intervals between management and union. Under the present system, the methods department is not necessarily involved in changes in the *price* of an operation, since this varies with base earnings. Increases in fringes, such as override, are also independent of the piece-rate system. The second method is to transfer to another job with higher base earnings – that is, of higher labor grade – or with easier rates. Frequently, the higher the labor grade, the easier the rates; for to encourage workers to remain on the more skilled jobs, of the higher labor grades, and thereby avoid the cost of training new workers, the rates on those jobs tend to be looser. In 1945, when earnings were closely tied to experience and less as-sociated with particular types of jobs, transfer to another job was frequently used as a disciplinary measure, since it was likely to lead to reduced earnings.[4]

The implications are not hard to foresee. Whereas in 1945 bargaining between management and worker over the distribution of the rewards of labor took place on the shop floor, in 1975 such bargaining had been largely transferred out of the shop and into the conference room and worker-management conflict on the shop floor had found a safety valve in the organization of job transfers on a plant-wide basis. As a consequence of changes in the system of remuneration, management-worker conflict has abated and individualism has increased.

MAKING OUT – A GAME WORKERS PLAY

In this section I propose to treat the activities on the shop floor as a series of games in which operators attempt to achieve levels of production that earn incentive pay, in other words, anything over 100 percent. The precise target that each operator aims at is established on an individual basis, varying with job, machine, experience, and so on. Some are satisfied with 125 percent, while others are in a foul mood unless they achieve 140 percent – the ceiling imposed and recognized by all participants. This game of making out provides a framework for evaluating the productive activities and the social relations that arise out of the organization of work. We can look upon making out, therefore, as comprising a sequence of stages – of encounters between machine operators and the social or nonsocial objects that regulate the conditions of work. The rules of the game are experienced as a set of externally imposed relationships. The art of making out is to manipulate those relationships with the purpose of advancing as quickly as possible from one stage to the next.

At the beginning of the shift, operators assemble outside the time office on the shop floor to collect their production cards and punch in on the "setup" of their first task. If it has already been set up on the previous shift, the operator simply punches in on production. Usually operators know from talking to their counterpart, before the beginning of the shift, which task they are likely to receive. Knowing what is available on the floor for their machine, an operator is sometimes in a position to bargain with the scheduling man, who is responsible for distributing the tasks.

In 1945 the scheduling man's duties appeared to end with the distribution of work, but in 1975 he also assumed some responsibility for ensuring that the department turned out the requisite parts on time. Therefore, he is often found stalking the floor, checking up on progress and urging workers to get a move on. Because he has no formal authority over the operators, the scheduling man's only recourse is to his bargaining strength, based on the discretion he can exert in distributing jobs and fixing up an operator's time. Operators who hold strategic jobs, requiring a particular skill, for example, or who are frequently called upon to do "hot jobs" are in a strong bargaining position vis-à-vis the scheduling man. He knows this and is careful not to upset them.

By contrast, Roy complained that the scheduling man was never to be found when he needed him and, when he was around, showed little interest in his work.[5] This caused great annoyance when the time clerks were not sure which job Roy had to punch in on next. Equally significant was the relative absence of hot jobs in 1945.[6] In sum, the department takes its responsibility to get jobs finished on time more seriously, but, so long as operators are making out, this responsibility falls on the shoulders of the scheduling man rather than on the foreman or superintendent.[7] The change is possibly a result of heightened departmental autonomy and responsibility, reflected in departmental profit-and-loss statements and in the penalties incurred by the company when engines are delivered late to the customer.[8]

After receiving their first task, operators have to find the blueprint and tooling for the operation. These are usually in the crib, although they may be already out on the floor. The crib attendant is therefore a strategic person whose cooperation an operator must secure. If the crib attendant chooses to be uncooperative in dispensing towels, blueprints, fixtures, etc., and, particularly, in the grinding of tools, operators can be held up for considerable lengths of time. Occasionally, operators who have managed to gain the confidence of the crib attendant will enter the crib themselves and expedite the process. Since, unlike the scheduling man, the crib attendant has no real interest in whether the operator makes out, his cooperation has to be elicited by other means. For the first five months of my employment my relations with the crib attendant on second shift were very poor, but at Christmas things changed dramatically. Every year the local union distributes a Christmas ham to all its members. I told

Harry that I couldn't be bothered picking mine up from the union hall and that he could have it for himself. He was delighted, and after that I received good service in the crib.

Many of Roy's troubles also originated in the crib. As in 1975, so in 1945: there were not enough crib attendants. Roy dramatically shows how the attendant who tries to serve operators conscientiously becomes a nervous wreck and soon transfers off the job. Problems may have been more acute under Geer, in Roy's time, since tools and fixtures were then located in the crib according to size and type rather than assembled in pans according to job, as in 1975. On the other hand, there were always at least two crib attendants when Roy was working at Geer, whereas in 1975 there was never more than one on second shift.

While I was able to secure the cooperation of the crib attendant, I was not so fortunate with the truck drivers. When I was being broken in on the miscellaneous job, I was told repeatedly that the first thing I must do was to befriend the truck driver. He or she was responsible for bringing the stock from the aisles, where it was kept in tubs, to the machine. Particularly at the beginning of the shift, when everyone is seeking their assistance, truck drivers can hold you up for a considerable period. While some treated everyone alike, others discriminated among operators, frustrating those without power, assisting those who were powerful. Working on the miscellaneous job meant that I was continually requiring the truck driver's services, and, when Morris was in the seat, he used to delight in frustrating me by making me wait. There was nothing I could do about it unless I was on a hot job; then the foreman or scheduling man might intervene. To complain to the foreman on any other occasion would only have brought me more travail, since Morris could easily retaliate later on. It was better just to sit tight and wait. Like the crib attendants, truckers have no stake in the operator's making out, and they are, at the same time, acutely conscious of their power in the shop. All they want is for you to get off their backs so that they can rest, light up, chat with their friends, or have a cup of coffee – in other words, enjoy the marginal freedoms of the machine operator. As one of the graffiti in the men's toilet put it, "Fuck the company, fuck the union, but most of all fuck the truckers because they fuck us all." Operators who become impatient may, if they know how, hop into an idle truck and move their own stock. But this may have unfortunate consequences, for other operators may ask them to get their stock too.

While it is difficult to generalize, it does appear that under Geer the service of the truck drivers – or stock chasers, as they were called – was more efficient. For one thing, there were two truckers in 1945 but only one in 1975 to serve roughly the same number of operators. For another, as the setup man told me from his own experience,

> "In the old days everyone knew everyone else. It was a big family, and so truck drivers would always try and help, bringing up stock early and so on. In those days operators might not even have to tell the truck driver to get the next load. Now everyone moves around from job to job. People don't get to know each other so well, and so there's less cooperation."

As they wait for the stock to arrive, each operator sets up his machine, if it is not already set up. This can take anything from a few minutes to two shifts, but normally it takes less than an hour. Since every setup has a standard time for completion, operators try to make out here, too. When a setup is unusually rapid, an operator may even be able to make time so that, when he punches in on production, he has already turned out a few pieces. A setup man is available for assistance. Particularly for the inexperienced, his help is crucial, but, as with the other auxiliary personnel, his cooperation must be sought and possibly bargained for. He, too, has no obvious stake in your making out, though the quicker he is through with you, the freer he is. Once the machine is set up and the stock has arrived, the operator can begin the first piece, and the setup man is no longer required unless the setup turns out to be unsatisfactory.

The quality and concern of setup men vary enormously. For example, on day shift the setup man was not known for his cooperative spirit. When I asked Bill, my day man, who the setup man was on day shift, he replied, "Oh, he died some years ago." This was a reference to the fact that the present one was useless as far as he was concerned. On second shift, by contrast, the setup man went about his job with enthusiasm and friendliness. When he was in a position to help, he most certainly did his best, and everyone liked and respected him. Yet even he did not know all the jobs in the shop. Indeed, he knew hardly any of my machines and so was of little use to me. Roy experienced similar differences among setup men. Johnny, for example, was not a great deal of help, but when Al McCann came along, Roy's life on the shop floor was transformed.[9] Al McCann had been a radial-drill operator of long experience and showed Roy all the angles on making out.

In 1945 there were more setup men than in 1975; this was due in part to wartime manpower policies but also to a greater need for setup men. Fixtures and machines have improved and become more standardized over the past thirty years, and the skill required in setting up has therefore declined. Moreover, under Geer, there was greater diversity in the operations that any one machine could perform, and it therefore took operators much longer to master all the jobs that they would have to run. On the other hand, it appears that mobility between different machines is now greater and average experience therefore less than at the end of the war. Roy also reports that, according to his fellow workers, the setup function was itself relatively new; this suggests again how recent was the specialization of the functions that earlier were performed by a single person – the foreman.

The assigned task may be to drill a set of holes in a plate, pipe, casting, or whatever; to mill the surface of some elbow; to turn an internal diameter on a lathe; to shave the teeth on a gear; and so on. The first piece completed has to be checked by the inspector against the blueprint. Between inspector and operator there is an irrevocable conflict of interest because the former is concerned with quality while the operator is concerned with quantity. Time spent when an operation just won't come right – when piece after piece fails, according to the inspector, to meet the specifications of the blueprint – represents lost time to the operator. Yet the inspector wants to OK the piece as quickly as possible and doesn't want to be bothered with checking further pieces until the required tolerances are met.

When a piece is on the margin, some inspectors will let it go, but others will enforce the specifications of the blueprint to the *n*th degree. In any event, inspectors are in practice, if not in theory, held partly responsible if an operator runs scrap. Though formally accountable only for the first piece that is tagged as OK, an inspector will be bawled out if subsequent pieces fall outside the tolerance limits. Thus, inspectors are to some extent at the mercy of the operators, who, after successfully getting the first piece OK'd, may turn up the speed of their machine and turn out scrap. An operator who does this can always blame the inspector by shifting the tag from the first piece to one that is scrap. Of course, an inspector has ample opportunity to take revenge on an operator who tries to shaft him. Moreover, operators also bear the responsibility for quality. During my term of employment, charts were distributed and hung up on each machine, defining the frequency with which operators were expected to check their pieces for any given machine at any particular tolerance level. Moreover, in the period immediately prior to the investigation of the plant's quality-assurance organization by an outside certifying body, operators were expected to indicate on the back of the inspection card the number of times they checked their pieces.

The shift since the war is clear. Under Geer, as Roy describes it, the inspector was expected to check not only the first piece but also, from time to time, some of the subsequent pieces. When the operation was completed on all the pieces, operators had to get the inspector to sign them off the old job before they could punch in on a new one. The responsibility has now shifted toward the operators, who are expected to inspect their own pieces at regular intervals.[10] Furthermore, improved machining, tooling, fixtures, etc., permit greater worker control over quality. It is now also argued that problems with quality result, not from poor workmanship, but from poor design of the product. For all these reasons, we now find fewer inspectors, and the trend is toward decreasing their numbers even further.[11]

When an inspector holds up an operator who is working on an important job but is unable to satisfy the specifications on the blueprint, a foreman may intervene to persuade the inspector to OK the piece. When this conflict cannot be resolved at the lowest level, it is taken to the next rung in the management hierarchy, and the superintendent fights it out with the chief inspector. According to Roy's observations, production management generally defeated quality control in such bargaining.[12] I found the same pattern in 1975, which reflects an organizational structure in which quality control is directly subordinated to production. Not surprisingly, the function of quality control has become a sensitive issue and the focus of much conflict among the higher levels of Allied's engine division. Quality control is continually trying to fight itself clear of subordination to production management so as to monitor quality on the shop floor. This, of course, would have deleterious effects on levels of production, and so it is opposed by the production management. Particularly sensitive in this regard is control of the engine test department, which in 1975 resided with production management. The production manager naturally claimed that he was capable of assessing quality impartially. Furthermore, he justified this arrangement by shifting the locus of quality problems from the shop floor to the design of the engine, which brought the engineers into the fray. Engineering management, not surprisingly, opposes the trend toward increasing their responsibility for quality. Therefore, the manager of engineering supported greater autonomy for quality control as a reflection of his interest in returning responsibility for quality to the shop floor. To what extent this situation has been preserved by the vesting of interests since Allied took over from Geer is not clear.[13]

After the first piece has been OK'd, the operator engages in a battle with the clock and the machine. Unless the task is a familiar one – in which case the answer is known, within limits – the question is: Can I make out? It may be necessary to figure some angles, some short cuts, to speed up the machine, make a special tool, etc. In these undertakings there is always an element of risk – for example, the possibility of turning out scrap or of breaking tools. If it becomes apparent that making out is impossible or quite unlikely, operators slacken off and take it easy. Since they are guaranteed their base earnings, there is little point in wearing themselves out unless they can make more than the base earnings – that is, more than 100 percent. That is what Roy refers to as goldbricking. The other form of "output restriction" to which he refers – quota restriction – entails putting a ceiling on how much an operator may turn in – that is, on how much he may record on the production card. In 1945 the ceiling was $10.00 a day or $1.25 an hour, though this did vary somewhat between machines. In 1975 the ceiling was defined as 140 percent for all operations on all machines. It was presumed that turning in more than 140 percent led to "price cuts" (rate increases), and, as we shall see in chapter 10, this was indeed the case.

In 1975 quota restriction was not necessarily a form of restriction of *output*, because operators *regularly* turned *out* more than 140 percent, but turned *in* only 140 percent, keeping the remainder as a "kitty" for those operations on which they could not make out. Indeed, operators would "bust their ass" for entire shifts, when they had a gravy job, so as to build up a kitty for the following day(s). Experienced operators on the more sophisticated machines could easily build up a kitty of a week's work. There was always some discrepancy, therefore, between what was registered in the books as completed and what was actually completed on the shop floor. Shop management was more concerned with the latter and let the books take care of themselves. Both the 140 percent ceiling and the practice of banking (keeping a kitty) were recognized and accepted by everyone on the shop floor, even if they didn't meet with the approval of higher management.

Management outside the shop also regarded the practice of "chiseling" as illicit, while management within the shop either assisted or connived in it. Chiseling (Roy's expression, which did not have currency on the shop floor in 1975) involves redistributing time from one operation to another so that operators can maximize the period turned in as over 100 percent. Either the time clerk cooperates by punching the cards in and out at the appropriate time or the operators are allowed to punch their own cards. In part, because of the diversity of jobs, some of them very short, I managed to avoid punching any of my cards. At the end of the shift I would sit down with an account of the pieces completed in each job and fiddle around with the eight hours available, so as to maximize my earnings. I would pencil in the calculated times of starting and finishing each operation. No one ever complained, but it is unlikely that such consistent juggling would have been allowed on first shift.[14]

How does the present situation compare with Geer? As Roy describes it, the transfer of time from one operation or job to another was possible only if they were consecutive or else were part of the same job though separated in time. Thus Roy could finish one job and begin another without punching out on the first. When he did punch out on the first and in on the second, he would already have made a start toward making out. Second, if Roy saved up some pieces from one shift, he could turn those pieces in during his next shift only if the job had not been finished by his day man. Accordingly, it was important, when Roy had accumulated some kitty on a particular job, that he inform Joe Mucha. If Mucha could, he would try to avoid finishing the job before Roy came to work. Shifting time between consecutive jobs on a single shift was frequently fixed up by the foreman, who would pencil in the appropriate changes. Nonetheless, stealing time from a gravy job was in fact formally illicit in 1945.

> Gus told me that Eddie, the young time study man, was just as bad, if not worse, than the old fellow who gave him the price of one cent the other day. He said that Eddie caught the day man holding back on punching off a time study job while he got ahead on a piecework job. He turned the day man in, and the day man and the time cage man were bawled out.
>
> "That's none of his damn business. He shouldn't have turned in the day man," exclaimed Gus angrily.
>
> Gus went on to say that a girl hand-mill operator had been fired a year ago when a time study man caught her running one job while being "punched in" on another. The time study man came over to the girl's machine to time a job, to find the job completed and the girl running another.
>
> Stella has no use for time study men. She told me of the time Eddie caught Maggie running one job while being punched in on another. Maggie was fired.[15]

I shall have much more to say about time-study men in chapter 10, but these examples do suggest that, while chiseling went on, it was regarded as illegitimate at some levels of management.

What can we say about overall changes in rates over the past thirty years? Old-timers were forever telling me how "easy we've got it now," though that in itself would hardly constitute evidence of change. To be sure, machines, tooling, etc., have improved, and this makes production less subject to arbitrary holdups, but the rates could nonetheless be tighter. However, an interesting change in the shop vernacular does suggest easier rates. Roy describes two types of jobs, "gravy" and "stinkers," the former having particularly loose and the latter particularly tight rates. While I worked in the small-parts department, I frequently heard the word "gravy" but never the word "stinker." Its dropping out of fashion probably reflects the declining number of jobs with very tight rates and the availability of kitties to compensate for low levels of output. How do Roy's own data on output compare with 1975 data? Recomputing Roy's output on piecework in terms of rates rather than dollars and cents, I find that during the initial period, from November to February, his average was 85 percent and that during the second period, from March to August, it was 120 percent.[16] During the first six months of 1975, the average for the entire plant was around 133.5 percent. For the different departments this average varied from 142 percent among the automatic screw machines and automatic lathes to 121 percent in the small-parts department, where I worked. The small-parts department functions as a labor reservoir for the rest of the plant because turnover there is high, rates are notoriously tight, and it is the place where newcomers normally begin. Nonetheless, of all the departments, this one probably most closely resembles Roy's Jack Shop in terms of machines and type of work. Thus, overall rates are indeed easier to make now, but my experiences in my own department, where most of my observations were made, bore a close resemblance to Roy's experiences.[17]

What is the foreman's role in all these operations? He is seen by everyone but senior plant management as expediting and refereeing the game of making out. As long as operators are making out and auxiliary workers are not obstructing their progress, neither group is likely to invite authoritarian interventions from the foreman. For their part, foremen defend themselves from their own bosses' complaints that certain tasks have not been completed by pointing out that the operators concerned have been working hard and have successfully made out. We therefore find foremen actively assisting operators to make out by showing them tricks they had learned when they were operators, pointing out more efficient setups, helping them make special tools, persuading the inspector to OK a piece that did not exactly meet the requirements of the blueprint, and so on. Foremen, like everyone else on the shop floor, recognize the two forms of output restriction as integral parts of making out. When operators have made out for the night and decide to take it easy for the last two or three hours, a foreman may urge more work by saying, "Don't you want to build up a kitty?" However, foremen do not act in collusion with the methods department and use the information they have about the various jobs and their rates against the operators, because rate increases would excite animosity, encourage goldbricking, increase turnover, and generally make the foreman's job more difficult.

However, the operator's defense, "What more do you want? I'm making out," does have its problems, particularly when there is a hot job on the agenda. Under such circumstances, operators are expected to drop what they are doing and punch in on the new job, "throwing everything they've got" into it and, above all, ignoring production ceilings – though of course they are not expected to turn *in* more than 140 percent. On occasions like this, unless the foreman can bring some sanctions to bear, he is at the mercy of the operator who may decide to take it easy. For this reason, foremen may try to establish an exchange relationship with each individual operator: "You look after me, I'll look after you." Operators may agree to cooperate with their foreman, but in return they may expect him to dispense favors, such as the granting of casual days, permission to attend union meetings during working hours, permission to go home early on a special occasion, etc. One of the most important resources at the disposal of the foreman is the "double red card," which covers time lost by operators through no fault of their own at a rate of 125 percent. Red cards may be awarded for excessive time lost while waiting for materials because a machine is down or some other adventitious event occurs that prevents an operator from making out. Bargaining usually precedes the signing of a red card; the operator has to persuade the foreman that he has made an earnest attempt to make out and therefore deserves compensation. Finally, one may note, as Roy did, that rules promulgated by high levels of plant management are circumvented, ignored, or subverted on the shop floor, with the tacit and sometimes active support of the foreman, in the interests of making out.

In 1945 foremen and superintendent played a similar role in facilitating making out, although they seemed to view many of these activities as illicit. The ambivalence of Steve, Roy's superintendent on second shift, is revealed in the following conversation.

> I told Steve privately that I was made out for the evening with $10.00.
> "That's all I'm allowed to make isn't it?" I asked.
> Steve hesitated at answering that one. "You can make more," he said, lowering his eyes.
> "But I'd better not," I insisted.
> "Well, you don't want to spoil it for yourself," he answered.[18]

Shop management frequently sided with operators in their hostility to the methods department when rates were tight and making out was impossible. Yet operators were always on the lookout and suspicious of foremen as potential collaborators with the methods department. The primary criterion by which foremen were evaluated was their relationship with time-study men.

> As already indicated, the second shift operators felt, in general, that the "better" supervisors were on their shift. They cited the connivance of Brickers, Squeaky and Johnson [day-shift supervisors] with the enemy, the methods department, pointing out that they were "company men," would do nothing for the workers, would not permit loafing when quotas were attained, and "drove" the operators on piecework jobs that were regarded as "stinkers." On the other hand, the night shift supervisors were known to have "fought for their men" against the "big shots," sought to aid operators in getting better prices from time study, winked at quota restriction and its hours of loafing, did

not collaborate with methods in the drive to lower "gravy" prices, and exhibited a pleasing insouciance when operators puttered away on day work.[19]

Another possible change revolves around the attitude of the foreman to goldbricking. Certainly, in 1945, foremen were not well disposed toward operators' taking it easy when rates were impossible, whereas in 1975 they tended to accept this as a legitimate practice. In general, Allied operators appeared to be less hostile and suspicious of shop supervision and exhibited greater independence in the face of authoritative foremen. As suggested earlier, foremen are now also relieved of some of the responsibility for the completion of particular jobs on their shift, this function being assumed by the assertive presence of the scheduling man. In all these respects my account of changes are similar to those described by Reinhard Bendix, Frederick Taylor, Richard Edwards, and others, namely, the diminution of the authority of the foreman and the parceling-out of his functions to more specialized personnel.[20]

THE ORGANIZATION OF A SHOP-FLOOR CULTURE

So far we have considered the stages through which any operation must go for its completion and the roles of different employees in advancing the operation from stage to stage. In practice the stages themselves are subject to considerable manipulation, and there were occasions when I would complete an operation without ever having been given it by the scheduling man, without having a blueprint, or without having it checked by the inspector. It is not necessary to discuss these manipulations further, since by now it must be apparent that relations emanating directly from the organization of work are understood and attain meaning primarily in terms of making out. Even social interaction not occasioned by the structure of work is dominated by and couched in the idiom of making out. When someone comes over to talk, his first question is, "Are you making out?" followed by "What's the rate?" If you are not making out, your conversation is likely to consist of explanations of why you are not: "The rate's impossible," "I had to wait an hour for the inspector to check the first piece," "These mother-fucking drills keep on burning up." When you are sweating it out on the machine, "knocking the pieces out," a passerby may call out "Gravy!" – suggesting that the job is not as difficult as you are making it appear. Or, when you are "goofing off" – visiting other workers or gossiping at the coffee machine – as likely as not someone will yell out, "You've got it made, man!" When faced with an operation that is obviously impossible, some comedian may bawl out, "Best job in the house!" Calling out to a passerby, "You got nothing to do?" will frequently elicit a protest of the nature, "I'm making out. What more do you want?" At lunchtime, operators of similar machines tend to sit together, and each undertakes a postmortem of the first half of the shift. Why they failed to make out, who "screwed them up," what they expect to accomplish in the second half of the shift, can they make up lost time, advice for others who are having some difficulty, and so on – such topics tend to dominate lunchtime conversations. As regards the domination of shop-floor interaction by the culture of making out, I can detect no changes over the thirty years. Some of the details of making out may have changed, but the idiom, status, tempo, etc., of interaction at work continue to be governed by and to rise out of the relations in production that constitute the rules of making out.

In summary, we have seen how the shop-floor culture revolves around making out. Each worker sooner or later is sucked into this distinctive set of activities and language, which then proceed to take on a meaning of their own. Like Roy, when I first entered the shop I was somewhat contemptuous of this game of making out, which appeared to advance Allied's profit margins more than the operators' interests. But I experienced the same shift of opinion that Roy reported:

> . . . attitudes changed from mere indifference to the piecework incentive to a determi-
> nation not to be forced to respond, when failure to get a price increase on one of the
> lowest paying operations of his job repertoire convinced him that the company was
> unfair. Light scorn for the incentive scheme turned to bitterness. Several months later,
> however, after fellow operator McCann had instructed him in the "angles on making
> out," the writer was finding values in the piecework system other than economic ones.
> He struggled to attain quota "for the hell of it," because it was a "little game" and
> "keeps me from being bored."[21]

Such a pattern of insertion and seduction is common. In my own case, it took me some time to understand the shop language, let alone the intricacies of making out. It was a matter of three or four months before I began to make out by using a number of angles and by transferring time from one operation to another. Once I knew I had a chance to make out, the rewards of participating in a game in which the outcomes were uncertain absorbed my attention, and I found myself spontaneously cooperating with management in the production of greater surplus value. Moreover, it was only in this way that I could establish relationships with others on the shop floor. Until I was able to strut around the floor like an experienced operator, as if I had all the time in the world and could still make out, few but the greenest would condescend to engage me in conversation. Thus, it was in terms of the culture of making out that individuals evaluated one another and themselves. It provided the basis of status hierarchies on the shop floor, and it was reinforced by the fact that the more sophisticated machines requiring greater skill also had the easier rates. Auxiliary personnel developed characters in accordance with their willingness to cooperate in making out: Morris was a lousy guy because he'd always delay in bringing stock; Harry was basically a decent crib attendant (after he took my ham), tried to help the guys, but was overworked; Charley was an OK scheduling man because he'd try to give me the gravy jobs; Bill, my day man, was "all right" because he'd show me the angles on making out, give me some kitty if I needed it, and sometimes cover up for me when I made a mess of things. In the next chapter I will consider the implications of being bound into such a coercive cultural system and of constituting the labor process as a game.

THE DISPERSION OF CONFLICT

I have shown how the organization of a piecework machine shop gives rise to making out and how this in turn becomes the basis of shop-floor culture. Making out also shapes distinctive patterns of conflict. Workers are inserted into the labor process as individuals who directly dictate the speed, feed, depth, etc., of their machines. The piece wage, as Marx observed, "tends to develop on the one hand that individuality, and with it the sense of liberty, independence, and self-control of the labourers, on the other, their competition one with another."[22] At the same time, the labor process of a machine shop embodies an opposed principle, the operator's dependence on auxiliary workers – themselves operating with a certain individual autonomy. This tension between control over machinery and subordination to others, between productive activities and production relations, leads to particular forms of conflict on the shop floor.

I have already suggested that pressures to make out frequently result in conflict between production and auxiliary workers when the latter are unable to provide some service promptly. The reason for this is only rarely found in the deliberate obstructionism of the crib attendant, inspector, trucker, and so on. More often it is the consequence of a managerial allocation of resources. Thus, during the period I worked on the shop floor, the number of operators on second shift expanded to almost the number on first shift, yet there was only one truck driver instead of two; there were, for most of the time, only two inspectors instead of four; there were only two foremen instead of four; and there was only one crib attendant instead of two or three. This merely accentuated a lateral conflict that was endemic to the organization of work. The only way such lateral conflict could be reduced was to allow second-shift operators to provide their own services by jumping into an idle truck, by entering the crib to get their own fixtures, by filling out their own cards, by looking through the books for rates or to see whether an order had been finished, and so on. However, these activities were all regarded as illegitimate by management outside the shop.[23] When middle management clamped down on operators by enforcing rules, there was chaos.

In the eyes of senior management, auxiliary workers are regarded as overhead, and so there are continual attempts to reduce their numbers. Thus, as already recounted, the objective of the quality-control manager was to reduce the number of inspectors. Changes in the philosophy of quality control, he argued, place increasing responsibility on the worker, and problems of quality are more effectively combatted by "systems control," design, and careful check on suppliers, particularly suppliers of castings. But, so long as every operation had to have its first piece checked, the decline in the number of inspectors merely led to greater frustration on the shop floor.

A single example will illustrate the type of conflict that is common. Tom, an inspector, was suspended for three days for absenteeism. This meant that there was only one inspector for the entire department, and work was piling up outside the window of Larry (another inspector). I had to wait two hours before my piece was inspected and I could get on with the task. It was sufficiently annoying to find only one inspector around, but my fury was compounded by the ostentatious manner in which Larry himself was slowing down. When I mentioned this to him, jokingly, he burst forth with "Why should I work my ass off? Tom's got his three days off, and the company thinks they are punishing him, but it's me who's got to break my back." In this instance, conflict between Tom and the company was transmuted into a resentment between Tom and Larry, which in turn provoked a hostile exchange between Larry and me. "Going slow," aimed at the company, rebounds to the disadvantage of fellow workers. The redistribution of conflict in such ways was a constant feature of social relations on the shop floor. It was particularly pronounced on second shift because of the shortage of auxiliary workers and the fact that the more inexperienced operators, and therefore the ones most needing assistance, were also on that shift.

Common sense might lead one to believe that conflict between workers and managers would lead to cohesiveness among workers, but such an inference misses the fact that all conflict is mediated on an ideological terrain, in this case the terrain of making out. Thus, management-worker conflict is turned into competitiveness and intragroup struggles as a result of the organization of work. The translation of hierarchical domination into lateral antagonisms is in fact a common phenomenon throughout industry, as was shown in a study conducted on a sample of 3,604 blue-collar workers from 172 production departments in six plants scattered across the United States:

> . . . work pressure in general is negatively correlated to social-supportive behavior, which we have called cohesive behavior, and positively related to competitive and intra-group conflict behavior. Cohesive behavior is generally untenable under high pressure conditions because the reward structure imposed by management directs employees to work as fast as they can individually.[24]

The dominant pattern of conflict dispersion in a piecework machine shop is undoubtedly the reconstitution of hierarchical conflict as lateral conflict and competition. However, it is by no means the only redistribution of conflict. A reverse tendency is often found when new machinery is introduced that is badly coordinated with existing technology. Here lateral conflict may be transformed into an antagonism between workers and management or between different levels of management.

To illustrate this point, I will draw upon my own experience with a machine that is designed to balance pulleys so that they don't break any shafts when they are running in an engine. The balancing machine, introduced within the past five years, is very sensitive to any faults in the pulley – faults that other machining operations may inadvertently introduce or that may have been embedded in the original casting when it came from the foundry.

The pulley is seated on a fixture attached to a rotating circular steel plate. The balancing plate and pulley can be automatically spun, and this indicates two things:

first, the place where excess stock should be removed to compensate for imperfections in the pulley and, second, the degree of imbalance in the pulley. When an area of excess weight is located, holes are drilled in the pulley to remove stock; the pulley is then spun again and more holes are drilled as needed. This process is repeated until the pulley balances to within one or two ounces, according to the specifications on the blueprint. The most difficult part of the job is getting the balance set up. Before any pulley can be balanced, it is necessary first to balance the fixture and plate by placing clay on the plate. This complicated procedure for setting up is designed to ensure that the pulley is indeed balanced when the dial registers it as being balanced – that is, when the pulley is turned through 180 degrees on the fixture, the recording is still within one or two ounces, or whatever the specification happens to be.

The small pulleys were easy. Often they didn't even need balancing. Just a touch from the drill to indicate they had been attended to was all that was necessary. That was gravy. But the big seventy-five pounders presented a very different picture. They were the most difficult to balance and naturally the most critical. It was tough enough hauling them up onto the balance and then taking them off, let alone balancing them to within an ounce. Both Bill and I tried to pretend they weren't there, although there were always a good number sitting by the balance, four or five layers of sixteen, piled on top of one another. We balanced them only when we had to, and then with extreme reluctance. They often posed insuperable problems, due to defects in the castings or in the taper, which meant that they would not fit properly on their fixture. On one or two occasions I came on second shift to discover the unusual sight of Bill cursing and sweating over the mess the pulleys were in and hearing him say how, after ten years on the miscellaneous job, he was getting too old to face it any more. "It's all yours, Englishman. Perhaps they'll give you a little bonus to keep you on," he laughed. It wasn't so much that the pulleys were not offering him enough money, since Bill would have his time covered with a double red card. It was more that he had been defeated; his job had taken over; he had lost control. No amount of energy or ingenuity seemed sufficient to get those pulleys to balance, yet they still had to be delivered to the line. "They expect me to make pulleys on this machine. Well, I only balance pulleys, and if they won't balance, they won't balance. They don't understand that if they've got blowholes in them they just won't come down."

I came in one day at 3 P.M., and Bill warned me that the big shots would be breathing down my neck for the seventy-five pounders. "Those pulleys are hot, man!" Sure enough, no sooner had he left than I found myself encircled by the foreman, the night-shift superintendent, the foreman of inspectors, the scheduling man, the setup man, and, from time to time, a manager from some other department. Such royal attention had me flustered from the start. I couldn't even set up the balance properly. The superintendent became impatient and started ordering me to do this, that, and the other, all of which I knew to be wrong. It was futile to point that out. After all, who was I to contradict the superintendent? The most powerful thought to lodge in my head was to lift the pulley off the balance and hurl it at their feet. As the clay piled up on the plate, way beyond what was necessary to balance it, the superintendent began to panic. He obviously thought his neck was on the line, but he had little idea as to how the machine worked. He was an old-timer, unaccustomed to this new-fangled equipment. And so he followed the directions on the chart hanging from the machine – directions that Bill had instructed me to ignore because they were wrong. When the superintendent thought the plate was balanced, we started drilling holes in the pulley – more and more holes, until the surface was covered with them. Clearly something was wrong. I'd never seen such a mess of holes. But the superintendent was more concerned with getting the pulleys out of the department and onto the engines. He didn't dare ask me to turn the pulleys through 180 degrees to see if they were really balanced – the acid test. I knew they wouldn't balance out, and probably so did he. By the end of the shift I had managed to ruin twenty-three pulleys.

The saga continued the following day. When I arrived at the balance, the superintendent was already there, remonstrating with Bill, who was trying to explain how to balance the plate. He was surrounded by yellow-painted pulleys – the pulleys I had "balanced" the night before – which had been pulled off the engines just before they were due to be shipped out. Amazingly, no one was after my neck. The superintendent was fussing around, trying to vindicate himself, saying that the chart was misleading. It wasn't his fault, he complained, and how much better it was in the old days before we had these fancy machines that didn't work properly. Bill was not upset at all, even though he'd been on the pulleys all day. It didn't take much imagination to see why, since he was now a hero, having retrieved the situation. Management had come round to him in the morning demanding to know what incompetent had balanced the pulleys. Since he alone knew how to work the balance, Bill sensed his newly won power and importance. The superintendent, however, was in hot water, and his prestige, already at a low ebb, had taken a further dive. No one was particularly surprised at my ineptitude, since I had never demonstrated any mechanical skill or understanding.

I have just described two types of conflict that can result from the introduction of a new piece of technology. In my first example, the new machine was out of tune with the surrounding technology and as a result turned what was potentially a lateral conflict into one between management and worker. In my second example, the new machine allowed an operator to monopolize some knowledge (and this is quite likely when the machine is unique to the shop); this enhanced his power and led to a severe conflict between shop management and middle management when the operator was not around.[25] There is no space here to explore other patterns of conflict crystallization, dispersion, and displacement. All I wish to stress is the way in which the specific organization of work structures conflict and how direct confrontation between management and worker is by no means its most common form.

Indeed, over the past thirty years conflict between management and worker has diminished, while that among workers has increased. This was how Donald Roy reacted to my observations at Allied:

> Your point in regard to the big switch of hierarchical conflict to the side of inter-worker competition pleases me immensely. . . . But in retrospect I see that in my time the main line of cleavage was the worker management one. With the exception of the mutual irritations between machine "partners" of different shifts operator relations were mainly cooperative, and most of the auxiliaries (stock chasers, tool crib men, etc.) were helpful. There were employees in the Jack Shop then who recalled the "whistle and whip" days before the local union was organized.[26]

There are a number of suggestions in his dissertation as to why there should have been greater antagonism between management and worker and less competition and conflict among workers. First, because of wartime conditions, there were more auxiliary workers for the same number of operators. Second, there was a generalized hostility to the company as being cheap, unconcerned about its labor force, penny-pinching, and so on,[27] whereas the attitudes of workers at the engine division of Allied were much more favorable to the company. This was exemplified by the large number of father-son pairs working in the plant. If your son had to work in a factory, many felt that Allied was not a bad place. Third, Allied treated its employees more fairly than Geer. Part of this may be attributed to the greater effectiveness of the union grievance machinery in 1975 than in 1945. Furthermore, as part of Allied, a large corporation, the engine division was less vulnerable to the kinds of market exigencies that had plagued Geer Company. It could therefore afford to treat its employees more fairly. Also, Allied did not appear to be out to cut rates with the militant enthusiasm that Roy had encountered. Fourth, as Roy himself notes above, the period of CIO organizing was still close at hand, and many Geer employees remembered the days of sweatshops and arbitrary discipline. Among the workers I talked to, only the older ones could recall the days of the "whistle and whip," and, when they did, it was mainly in reference to the tribulations of their fathers.

CONCLUSION

Between Geer Company of 1945 and Allied Corporation, thirty years later, the labor process underwent two sets of changes. The first is seen in the greater individualism promoted by the organization of work. Operators in 1975 had more autonomy as a result of the following: relaxed enforcement of certain managerial controls, such as inspection of pieces and rate-fixing; increased shop-floor bargaining between workers and foremen; and changes in the system of piece rates – changes that laid greater stress on individual performance, effort, and mobility and allowed more manipulations. The second type of change, related to the first, concerns the diminution of hierarchical conflict and its redistribution in a number of different directions. As regards the relaxation of conflict between worker and management, one notes the decline in the authority of the foreman and the reduction of tensions between those concerned with enforcement of quality in production and those primarily interested in quantity. The greater permissiveness toward chiseling, the improvement of tooling and machines, as well as easier rates, have all facilitated making out and in this way have reduced antagonism between worker and shop management.[28] The employment of fewer auxiliary workers, on the other hand, has exacerbated lateral conflict among different groups of workers.[29]

These changes do not seem to support theories of intensification of the labor process or increase of managerial control through separation of conception and execution. What we have observed is the expansion of the area of the "self-organization" of workers as they pursue their daily activities. We have seen how operators, in order to make out at all, subvert rules promulgated from on high, create informal alliances with auxiliary workers, make their own tools, and so on. In order to produce surplus value, workers have had to organize their relations and activities in opposition to management, particularly middle and senior management.

. . .

NOTES

1. David Noble, "Before the Fact: Social Choice in Machine Design," paper presented at the National Convention of the Organization of American Historians, April 1978. For a more general history of the role of science in the development of capitalism, see his *America by Design: Science, Technology, and the Rise of Corporate Capitalism* (New York: Alfred A. Knopf, 1977).
2. William Friedland, Amy Barton, and Robert Thomas, "Manufacturing Green Gold: The Conditions and Social Consequences of Lettuce Harvest Mechanization" (unpublished ms., University of California, Santa Cruz, 1978), and William Friedland and Amy Barton, *Destalking the Wily Tomato* (Davis, Calif.: Department of Applied Behavioral Sciences, College of Agriculture and Environmental Sciences, University of California, 1975).
3. See, for example, Taylor's *Shop Management* (New York: American Society of Mechanical Engineers, 1903).
4. Donald Roy, "Restriction of Output in a Piecework Machine Shop," (Ph.D. diss., University of Chicago, 1952), p. 76.
5. Ibid., pp. 419–23.
6. Roy refers to hot jobs on two occasions (ibid., pp. 405, 504).
7. When a job was really "hot," the scheduling man might appeal to the foreman or even to the superintendent for support if the operator appeared recalcitrant.
8. I have not been able to discover the nature or existence of equivalent penalties during the war.
9. Roy, "Restriction of Output," p. 307.
10. The change is one of degree, since Roy was also expected to check his pieces from time to time (ibid., pp. 267, 338).
11. Indeed, the general manager expected managers of quality control to make consistent efforts to cut the numbers of inspectors.
12. Roy, "Restriction of Output," p. 388.
13. From conversations with various management officials and reading between the lines of Roy's dissertation, I am left with the impression that Geer Company tended to be more

concerned with shipping the goods out than with quality control, particularly in view of the demand. (Managers of Geer have, of course, tended to deny this.) The problem of quality control has been endemic in the engine division since Allied took over. As long as quality control is subordinated to production, it is impossible to find good quality-control managers. What conscientious quality-control manager could possibly countenance subjugation to the imperatives of shipping? It is not surprising, therefore, to learn that there is a considerable turnover of quality-control managers.

14. My day man, Bill, never penciled in the time but always got his cards punched in on the clock at the time office. This restricted his room for manipulation; but since he was very experienced on the miscellaneous job, this did not reduce his earnings by very much. When I filled in for him on first shift, I did in fact pencil in the times, and no one complained. This may have been a reflection of my power, since, with Bill away, hardly anyone knew how to do the various jobs or where the fixtures were. By penciling in the times, I reckoned I could earn the same amount of money as Bill but with less effort.

15. Roy, "Restriction of Output," p. 240.

16. Ibid., table 4, p. 94.

17. During the week 17 November 1975 to 23 November 1975, there were sixteen radial-drill operators in the small-parts department. Their average "measured performances" for the entire year (or for the period of the year since they had begun to operate a radial drill) were as follows (all figures are percentages): 92, 108, 109, 110, 110, 111, 112, 115, 116, 119, 125, 133, 137, 139, 141, 142. The average was 120 percent, which turns out to be precisely Roy's average in his second period. Moreover, the average period spent on a radial drill in the *first eleven months of 1975* among these sixteen operators was of the order of six months, though a number of these operators had probably been operating radial drills for years. The data do not suggest significant differences between the rates on radial drills in Geer's Jack Shop and on radial drills in Allied's small-parts department.

18. Roy, "Restriction of Output," p. 102.

19. Ibid., p. 290.

20. Reinhard Bendix, *Work and Authority in Industry: Ideologies of Management in the Course of Industrialization* (New York: John Wiley, 1956); Frederick Taylor, *Shop Management;* Richard Edwards, "The Social Relations of Production in the Firm and Labor Market Structure," *Politics and Society* 5 (1975): 83–108.

21. Donald Roy, "Work Satisfaction and Social Reward in Quota Achievement," *American Journal of Sociology* 57 (1953): 509–10.

22. Karl Marx, *Capital*, 1:555.

23. I vividly recall being bawled out by a manager who came into the time office long after he should have gone home. He found me going through the books to see how many pieces had been handed in on a particular operation. Second-shift shop-floor management allowed and even encouraged operators to look these sorts of things up for themselves rather than bother the time clerks, but senior management regarded this as a criminal act.

24. Stuart Klein, *Workers under Stress: The Impact of Work Pressure on Group Cohesion* (Lexington, Ky.: University of Kentucky Press, 1971), p. 100.

25. This enhanced power was one of the attractions of the miscellaneous job, which no one wanted because it was rough, dirty, and dangerous as well as low-paying. Since the other operators on second shift knew virtually nothing about the jobs I did, I was able to develop a certain bargaining power, although by no means as great as Bill's.

26. Personal communication, July 1975.
27. Roy, "Restriction of Output," chap. 11.
28. A similar argument, made by Lupton, is worth citing in full:

> In Jay's, I would also say that the "fiddle" [chiseling] was an effective form of worker
> control over the job environment. The strength and solidarity of the workers, and
> the flexibility of the management system of control, made a form of adjustment
> possible in which different values about fair day's work, and about "proper" worker
> behaviour, could exist side by side. I have no doubt that, if management controls
> had been made less flexible, and management planning more effective, the "fiddle"
> would have been made more difficult to operate and probably output could have
> been slightly increased. But this might have destroyed the balance of social adjust-
> ment between management and the workers, and the outcome might have been
> loss in work satisfaction. The shop would no longer have been a "comfortable," may
> be not even a "happy," shop. And, in turn, this might have produced higher labor
> turnover, absenteeism and the like. One can only guess about these things, since there
> are so many other considerations involved: the existence of alternative employ-
> ment, the ability of existing management-worker relationships to withstand the
> impact of radical change, for example, but it seems to be that when relationships
> are adjusted in a way similar to that I have described, which resembles the indul-
> gency pattern noted by Gouldner, then any attempt to "tighten up" might lead to
> resentment and resistance. In the circumstances, management might prefer to live
> with the "fiddle" at the cost of what they believe to be some slight loss of output,
> and regard this as the price they pay for a good relationship. [Tom Lupton, *On the
> Shop Floor* (Oxford: Pergamon Press, 1963), pp. 182–83]

Though Lupton fails to see the organization of work as the consequence and object of
struggles between workers and managers, among workers and among managers, his characterization of *the functions* of the "fiddle" are illuminating.

29. In interpreting these changes we will repeatedly come up against a difficult problem,
namely, the degree to which Roy's observations reflect the exigencies of wartime conditions. For example, during the war, government contracts encouraged the overmanning
of industry, since profits were fixed as a percentage of costs. Boosting costs did not change
the rate of profit. As a consequence, we should not be surprised to discover cutbacks in
personnel after the war. Thus, Roy informs us that after V-J Day, just before he left Geer,
there was a reorganization in which foremen were demoted and the setup function was
eliminated (Roy, "Restriction of Output," pp. 60, 219). Hostility of workers to the company must have been, at least in part, engendered by wartime restraints on union militancy and by the choking-off of the grievance machinery.

CHAPTER EIGHT

The Nuclear Everyday

Françoise Zonabend

Imagine the state of mind in which most of the technicians taken on at the la Hague plant found themselves:

> I'm from Lorraine originally, started off in the iron and steel industry, but we soon real-ised that was on its last legs. Then in 1977 COGEMA put an ad in one of the eastern newspapers . . . I've worked my way up. Getting in here was like getting into NASA, you were headed for the realms of high-tech.

> La Hague, COGEMA . . . meant nothing at all to me to begin with, what I mainly thought was that working in nuclear energy was like working at the sharp end of industry . . .

> I didn't know much about nuclear energy, but for me it represented the future . . .

Things are different now. Young people entering the plant today know where they stand as regards the risks to which they will be exposed. Yet they all banish their anxiety with the same refrain: 'There's less risk in working here than there is in taking your car out each morning.'

That leaves them with the avowed satisfaction of having a steady job and pride at having access to the latest equipment: 'What's good here is that COGEMA has a huge budget and if there's any new machinery they buy it straight away. We're up at the forefront of technology. The engineers are always going on trips to look at and find out about new equipment.'

But ex-employees and new recruits agree in stating that high technology is no sub-stitute for an interesting job. Some recall nostalgically: 'In the old days we did things because it was "our" plant, we were involved and we were also all mates, so we got organised to make a go of it.' Others acknowledge that; 'It's interesting to start with, working at the plant, afterwards it becomes a bore!' And they all say: 'When you've seen the way they work on-limits . . . not specially effective, sometimes plain stupid . . . It makes you think . . . The very latest technology soon proves inadequate when it comes down to the reality of the job.' The work's 90 per cent routine with no say of your own.'

One source of tedium is the sheer size of the establishment: 'Before there were two rest rooms, now there are maybe fifteen . . . People are scattered about and no longer know one another.' Another source is the complexity of the reprocessing operation, which leads to a compartmentalisation of the various shops, laboratories, and other treatment stations. All these units are involved in the same process, but they take no notice of one another. Each one acts on its own account.

One young female lab technician complained of the lack of professional relations and exchange of ideas between shops:

> We do routine checks on the concentration of radioactive products in the water in the ponds. Occasionally, when the plant is having problems, we do special analyses of precipitates that form where they ought not to. That's more interesting, except we're not told anything about the operation, we have no idea where the stuff comes from, at what point it formed . . . And afterwards we don't know what they do with our findings!

In other words, the purpose of an experiment, the significance of a particular activity, may elude those charged with carrying it out.

Boredom further arises out of the repetitive nature of the jobs (chopping up uranium rods with the aid of remote handling gear, using a press to compact drums of waste one after another) or their monotony (watching control panels or computer screens). Moreover, these features are tending to become more marked as technology progresses. With the object of improving safety, the trend is towards more and more automation of production tasks and a greater and greater degree of computerisation of control functions. Man, regarded as the weak link in the man/machine partnership, is gradually being eliminated. In the new UP_3 plant, all the technical solutions have been worked out with this in mind, giving rise to a fresh problem, namely the possible psychological consequences of this kind of marginalisation of man at work.

> Working in UP_3 will be very different, the plant is almost entirely computer-controlled, which means the work will be of a more abstract nature. The operator will have screens in front of him, showing the network of rooms, and he will have to imagine what is actually going on in there, not just in two but also in three dimensions. It'll be a watching and waiting job, monotonous and sedentary, and he'll have to be able to put up with such working conditions, on top of which there will be essential safety instructions and physical checks. These are the job criteria by which we select technicians.

The speaker was the psychologist in charge of recruiting technical staff. His statement echoes those of trade unionists who are also concerned with these problems:

> We're getting rather worried about the future of relations between man and machine . . . What the man does with his machine . . . Sitting in front of a television screen with centralised control, if he's not really familiar with his equipment he's not necessarily

going to be able to follow what's going on or be properly aware of when an incident or
an accident occurs. If a person is bored or feels he's over-qualified for the job he's being
asked to do, there's a risk he'll lose his motivation, in which case he's not going to keep up
with his equipment, he's not going to try and improve his tool, he's not going to be
trying to do anything . . .

Lack of interest leads to a loss of vigilance, and the thing that makes this all the
more serious and causes it to set in the more swiftly is this tendency to represent
the machine or the tool as being wholly reliable, so much so, in fact, that those who
design or use them will sometimes refuse to believe that their instruments might be
faulty in any way.[1] The other side of this reliability on the part of the equipment is
that the people who operate it are required to comply with a growing number of
safety directives that add to the burden of the regulations to be observed and the repetitive nature of the checks that need to be carried out. 'It's more and more a matter
of following orders and filling in forms. You spend the whole night filling notebooks,
doing the rounds, doing your rules of three . . . That's what an operator's job is now.
You don't need to be a technician to press buttons!'

Asking skilled technicians to perform such simple, relatively lowly tasks does not
enable them to express the full range of their abilities or expertise. Too much safety is
boring, and boredom spawns the *desire for risk*. 'You sometimes find yourself hoping
for a problem, be it mechanical or chemical, even nuclear, involving contamination,
even if that's not what you really want . . . You're watching for the snag, the little
hiccup, you know . . . Because the job's an awful bore apart from incidents!'

On top of the monotony, the wearisome uniformity of movement, and the pleth-
ora of orders and checks to be carried out, there is the effect of a certain kind of
language, namely the somewhat belittling language used by the training-course instructor and by others in positions of responsibility to describe the tasks involved in
the reprocessing of spent nuclear fuel. Think of the words borrowed from the vocabulary of cooking and housekeeping that were used during the course. Described in
such terms, the tasks that these men are required to perform in irradiated or contaminated areas appear to bathe in a world where everything is safe, imbued with an
almost domestic bliss. They can bring little satisfaction, either real or symbolic. The
feminine guise in which those tasks are represented, emphasising their benign if not
innocuous aspect, renders virtually intolerable work that is in fact performed under
extremely arduous physical conditions (in vinyl suits, amid heat and noise, at great
speed) and carries incalculable biological consequences. These men are working in
the most modern nuclear installation in the world, doing jobs that may be dull but
are none the less dangerous, and people speak to them in the kind of language that is
normally reserved for women.

In the circumstances, what satisfaction is to be gained from carrying out operations on-limits and fulfilling functions that, because of the danger involved, will
always engender a certain amount of anxiety, even if it is denied and suppressed?

What motivation is a man to find day after day to help him perform tasks that may be jeopardising his physical integrity?

To adapt to this system of constraints and controls, to push aside anxiety, triumph over fear, and render boredom tolerable, workers in the nuclear industry use certain tricks of language and exploit certain flights of fancy. Taking the language that is used to describe their jobs, these men proceed to make it their own. In doing so, however, they transform it. They subvert it by adding words, employing metaphors, and adopting peculiar turns of phrase to such effect that they contrive to shatter it from within and recover an image of themselves that is more rewarding than the one that takes such a beating from the hierarchy.

In place of the official scientific presentation of work in a nuclear environment they substitute their own language, their own interpretation, their own way of seeing it and 'having their being' within it. In short, they refashion an industrial world to suit themselves.

THE KAMIKAZE AND THE *RENTIER*

When talking about themselves, people who work in the French nuclear industry divide themselves into two categories. On the one hand there are the *rentiers* ('person living on dividends from property, investments, etc.' (*COD*), i.e., a byword for caution; Tr.), who before venturing 'on-limits' will make sure that every precaution has been taken, even going to the lengths of working out other types of precaution that they feel might be more reliable. On the other hand there are the *kamikazes*, men who are always prepared to work 'on-limits' without bothering too much about the safety regulations, men for whom speed and efficiency (getting the job done in the shortest possible time) will always take precedence over safety.

Both labels relate to the notion of risk: calculated risk in the case of the first group, risk courted in the case of the second. *Rentiers* invent procedures that they believe will enable them to manage their 'dose' capital in their best interests, which in this context means they try to keep their levels as low as possible. Kamikazes, on the other hand, approach radioactivity quite fearlessly (or perhaps unwittingly), regardless of any 'doses' they may accumulate. The *rentier* manages risk 'like a good family man'. The kamikaze approaches it in the manner of a 'warrior' who scorns danger but who may, of course, be going to his death . . . We all know the fate that awaited the kamikaze.

The people in charge of recruitment are well aware of these two types of behaviour, these two attitudes towards danger. Indeed, they seek to identify them among candidates in order to steer them towards the jobs best suited to their individual temperament and to the exigencies of production.

Kamikazes are found mainly in the mechanical part of the plant because there you have to get stuck in. In the chemical part there's a different mentality, there you get mainly *rentiers*. Maybe it has something to do with the history of the plant and the fact that there were more militant trade-unionists in the chemical section who took a very firm line on safety. I don't know. But it's true, there are two ways of dealing with poor working conditions: either you demand more money in compensation, or you demand greater safety. On the mechanical side the operators will ask for an extra allowance. The chemists will plunge into months of talks before coming up with a programme for reorganising the workplace and providing rest periods. It's a case of two different ways of seeing things.

Be they kamikazes or *rentiers*, however, all nuclear workers agree in the way in which they talk about the risks they run, the doses they find themselves receiving, and the many perils they face when working 'on-limits'.

For instance, you will hear people who have 'copped a dose' exclaim:

We got ourselves a fix.

We got our balls loaded [*On a pris plein les couilles*].

We got lit up.

We took a bellyful.

We were pumped full of lead.

We got our whiskers stiffened [*On a pris plein les moustaches*].

Words that speak of maleness and sexuality, expressions redolent of virility, of potency, a vocabulary for men who look danger in the face. So many verbal attempts, in short, to counteract the rumours that circulate incessantly, alleging that workers in the nuclear industry are not 'real' men.

And when talking of radioactive matter, technicians will exclaim: That's farting like a good'un . . .' (*ça pète pas mal*) or 'It's spitting like hell . . .' – metaphors that evoke the clash of arms and the din of battle, turns of speech that transform the culinary language normally offered to them (with its 'soups' and 'juices' and 'gravies') into a war chant. Yet another way, in fact, of modulating feminine into masculine and taking a verbal stand against the encroachments of women upon a world made for men.

Actually, not all workers talk about radioactivity in this way, especially not women.

The engineers, as members of management, prefer to speak of *fifrelins*,[2] a term that carries a note of contempt, indicating how little importance they attach to any doses of radioactivity they may receive. The attitude of scornful indifference affected by certain engineers with regard to radioactive pollution is in fact notorious. As a member of the Radioprotection Department recalled:

I saw an engineer who had become contaminated through visiting a building. He was in street clothes, an ordinary suit, you know, because they don't wear overalls, not those fellows! When they noticed at the exit control they tried to stop him . . . But there was nothing they could do, they had to let him go. 'Do you realise who you're talking to?' he said, and off he went home in that state.

The higher up people are in the hierarchy, the less heed they pay to these 'trifles' that irradiate everything around them!

> The physicists, the research people, they're the worst of all! They think they're above the rules. You know those target-holders, little discs that have become irradiated, they wrap them in a newspaper, pop them in the briefcase, and it's off home to Paris . . . The doses aren't large, but it gives you some idea of the way they think!

I was told this by a radioprotection officer attached to one of the research laboratories.

As for the female technicians who work on-limits, they avoid putting a name to radioactivity. They will speak of 'something' or simply 'it', as in 'I said to myself, I've got something on me' or 'It spreads everywhere.'

Do they believe they are warding off the danger by refusing to name it, or are they, through the pronoun, alluding to the hidden, invisible aspect of radioactivity? Women (the ones I met, at least) manifest a very different attitude towards radioactivity than do men. They admit to being scared of it. They acknowledge their anxiety regarding its potential biological effects.

> I don't feel as easy in my mind working here as I would somewhere else. When an analysis arrives and I know it's radioactive, I try to stay calm, but it's easier said than done . . . And then every month when the film results come back and I find I've been contaminated, that really gets me! Especially if I've taken a bit more than I expected.

And they will confess anxiously: 'I always have the feeling I'm taking something home on me!'

'It' sticks to their skin! The skin being an organ that, for a woman, constitutes the membrane within which life is born and sustained. Hence their understandable anxiety in the face of this nuclear world inhabited by invisible powers. What is more, they know they are subject to a special regulation banning them from any ionising environment as soon as they exhibit the first signs of pregnancy. Is that sufficient? Might they not have unsuspected long-term effects, those impalpable, deadly emanations? It is a huge question and a never-ending torment, for no one can give them the answer. As wives and mothers, these female technicians are afraid of jeopardising their own power to give life. The fantasies that have always hovered around the phenomenon of gestation and that the march of scientific knowledge was beginning to dispel have undoubtedly found fresh strength in this world haunted by invisible but intensely noxious waves. This makes it easier to understand certain admissions from women that seem to adumbrate a fear of giving birth to 'freaks'. Such fears and anxieties do in fact find more or less explicit expression among the women who live in the vicinity of the reprocessing plant and whose husbands and sons work there.

So what is at issue psychologically in one and the same reality will differ according to the sex, occupation, and social status of the subject. Women talk about radioactivity in allusive terms. Management engineers pretend nonchalance. Technicians translate it into male energy. However, these various semantic strategies are not, in themselves, sufficient to banish fear and refashion a world in which a person may live and work without too much anguish. To achieve that sort of mastery over the dangers incurred, other forms of conjuration are required, other ways of representing the industrial world.

STRENGTH AND DECAY

Listening to these people talk about the dangers of radioactivity, you very soon become aware that they draw a subtle distinction between irradiation and contamination. In their eyes, the two dangers are not of the same order. Irradiation, caused by the rays emitted by a nuclear substance, is seen in a positive light. Here images of 'cleanness' come high on the list; ideas of 'strength' and 'power' loom large. By contrast, the contamination that arises from contact with radioactive dust particles is thought of in negative terms and associated with an impression of 'filth', allied to the notion of 'decay'.

'You cop doses, you get irradiated . . . It's true you may be putting your life at risk . . . But you're tough, for heaven's sake . . .' 'Contamination's not the same, it's disgusting . . . shitty . . . you're messed up [daubé[3]] . . . you're rotten.'

Simplifying somewhat, we get the following sequences:

IRRADIATION	CONTAMINATION
RAY	DUST
CLEAN	DIRTY
STRENGTH	DECAY
'you're tough'	'you're rotten'

Why should the apparently heterogeneous notions introduced into each sequence be grouped together in a single category? What properties do they have in common? What system of explanation underlies the coherence suggested by the words?

It is worth noting that each of these terms, irradiation and contamination, possesses a double meaning, a fact that will surely not have escaped those who use them on a daily basis. Both of them play on a literal sense and a figurative sense that carries obvious moral overtones. *Irradiation*, in everyday parlance, is 'an emission of light rays'. In the figurative sense, the word takes on the idea of a benign influx of warmth or radiance. The French word *contamination* has since the fourteenth century had the meaning 'blemish resulting from some unclean contact' in both the physical and moral senses of 'unclean'. Granted, the medical vocabulary from which use of the term in a nuclear setting is derived relates back to the Latin connotation of the word, which contains no more than the idea of 'communication by contact'. However, it looks very much as if the French folk memory has retained only the former acceptance, which spread under the influence of the Catholic church.

Irradiation: a word that evokes bright light, bedazzlement, and invokes myths of the regeneration of man through light (the phoenix, for example, being reborn from its ashes in a great burst of flame). It is a word to which people may also, more prosaically, attach images drawn from those television programmes featuring a 'superman' who, having been subjected to the influence of nuclear radiation, exhibits prodigious strength in everything he does. It is a bit like the 'burn' you get from alcohol, the *eau-de-vie* that is supposed to give men strength, indeed life! More powerfully, more radically still, the films shown during training courses relate how in the dawn of our world it was radioactive radiation that enabled life to emerge. Men have never had much difficulty in finding reasons to glorify irradiation.

Contamination plays in a different register entirely. This term, with its connotations of 'blemish' and 'corruption', is invariably, in the nuclear context, associated with 'dust', a word that in turn relates to such concepts as 'filth' and 'rubbish' and, in our Christian societies, beyond that to death. 'You are dust, and to dust you shall return'.[4]

These nuclear dust particles, these invisible dejecta, taint and corrupt a person, making him 'rotten'. It is a rottenness, a decay that leads to biological and social disorders. The contaminated person is regarded as sick (and does indeed receive prompt and elaborate medical attention). Above all, he may spread the contagion around him, upsetting the whole social order.

Wives do in fact refuse to have sex with husbands who have been contaminated. Anne, twenty-three, married to a temporary decontaminator, told journalists who came to interview her: 'When I saw him come home with his bottles I was scared to touch him. I had to control myself. It was daft because there was no risk to me . . . but I was pregnant.[5]

Insidiously, contamination comes between couples, breaching the social order. It is understandable, in the circumstances, that men should choose to say nothing, inventing other excuses to account for the shaming bottles. 'My husband says nothing about what goes on up there. He never tells me anything. Sometimes I see him come home with his hands all red and swollen as if they'd had a good scrubbing. Once or twice I asked what had happened. He told me: "It's nothing." So I don't ask any more.'

Around the contaminated man, nothing is said. It is a way of marginalising him, of holding him at a distance. No doubt these women have realised that their silence helps 'their' menfolk to bear this feeling of gradual decomposition, this burden of risk, but it is at the cost of something being repressed on both sides.

Contamination may occur through the medium of objects or tools that are perhaps not tainted in themselves but that simply by virtue of belonging to the world of *le nucléaire* have no place outside it. Otherwise there is a danger of their spreading confusion by effecting an overlap between what as a rule are mutually exclusive worlds. I hate him bringing anything from the plant back to the house!' exclaimed Isabelle, a thirty-five-year-old schoolteacher, when her husband, a technical operator, took from his pocket the film-badge that he had forgotten to leave in its proper place. In the village of Flamanville there was once a rumour that a woman had fallen ill after her husband, who worked at the nuclear power station, had installed central heating in his house with tubing 'borrowed' from work!

From sexual ostracism to defiling the family home, contamination leads to all kinds of social disturbance. Understandably, people try to steer clear of it.

Incidentally, the work of linguists and ethnologists has shown that 'order' and 'disorder' constitute the foundation of all social organisation. In his *Vocabulary of Indo-European Institutions*,[6] Emile Benveniste writes as follows:

> Order. This is one of the key notions of the legal as well as of the religious and moral worlds of Indo-Europeans: it is 'Order' that governs the disposition of the universe, the movements of the stars, and the periodicity of the seasons and the years as it governs the relations between men and gods and ultimately among men themselves. Nothing that has to do with man and the world escapes the dominion of 'Order'. It is thus the foundation, both religious and moral, of all society; without this principle, everything would revert to chaos.

Investigating the definition of what is 'dirty' in the eyes of primitive societies, Mary Douglas has shown that it is in fact a relative idea, part of a symbol system through which a culture organises the sensible world, with the result that 'thinking about dirt implies thinking about the relationship of order to disorder, being to non-being, form to formlessness, and life to death'.[7]

These remarks may be transferred to the nuclear domain. In this invisible, impalpable, inaudible world the human imagination does its usual job of restoring to that world the kind of materiality and humanity that will enable man to comprehend and move within it. Through the medium of symbolic thought, the perils of nuclear energy are slotted into what societies know and have always known.

The nuclear industry does not only furnish words for conceptualising its dangers; it also supplies technical properties on which a system of representations can be hung.

The training course, whether through the instructor, through the nurse, or through the films shown, dealt mainly with 'contamination'. 'Irradiation' was scarcely mentioned, probably because it is harder to detect with monitoring instruments. As one radioprotection expert explained to me:

> A person can become irradiated, go through all the controls, and leave the building without anything happening, without setting off a single alarm. Once you've left the source of irradiation, it stops. Actually, it goes on irradiating inside the fellow and the damage done by that irradiation remains, but it can't be measured because here all the measuring instruments at the exits of the buildings are for contamination. To find out if there are any particles left in the hair, on the hands . . . But if you've just

spent an hour in front of a source of irradiation that has destroyed a few cells, it doesn't show up on such monitoring devices. That will be detected during a medical inspection or when the film-badge results come back . . . But it's very unusual for an immediate connection to be drawn between cause and effect . . . A person is told: 'You're tired!' It happens, no one asks too many questions. From there to thinking that irradiation is something you always get away with . . . well, it's not a big step! That's how people are able to say they're tough.

On the one hand, then, there is irradiation, which is not detected immediately, which can be concealed from oneself and others, and which a person may try to ignore or forget about, even though he knows that it goes on lurking, like some invisible yet voracious beast, deep inside him. On the other hand there is contamination, which triggers the alarms, alerting one and all to the fact that an incident has occurred. As a result, the eyes of the group are inevitably turned on the person who has caused the rumpus, and the general reaction is to give that person a wide berth. As witness what happened to this visitor to the plant when her watch set off the dreaded sound signal during the exit controls. In the coach back to town everyone kept well away from her, leaving her sitting on her own in a corner like someone with the plague!

Irradiation is seen as something superficial, fleeting, momentary. In talking about it, people will say casually: 'I copped a dose' or 'I got a dose.' With irradiation a person is still on the side of order. In this plant devoted to reprocessing waste (*déchets*), he symbolically escapes the world of filth (*ordure*).

Contamination, however, is experienced as penetrating flesh and blood. It may be inhaled or ingested, whence this definition that workers give of it: 'Contamination is when you've eaten a dose.' And men speak of it as 'shit' (*merde*), while women talk of 'poo' (*caca*). The contamination produced by the 'waste' reprocessed in this plant is regarded as particularly fearsome because it spreads through the medium of excremental dust particles. Decomposition then sets in, and the result is disorder.

Playing on these notions of clean and dirty, strength and decay, and order and disorder, workers at the plant have recreated a world of coherence, a world of their own on which they can then seek to get a purchase in order to prove their power and their ability to brave and surmount the perils of *le nucléaire*.

It is not a game that can be taken very far, because the players know full well that too much exposure to sources of irradiation or contamination will eventually lead to death. There is, however, a small area of freedom, a gap (perhaps the one left by managing the doses a person is 'permitted') in which it is possible to play with fire. The game (or rather, the tricks, the word 'game' (*jeu*, which also denotes 'gambling'; Tr.) being probably excessive in this context) may take two directions: either these men confront radioactivity directly, or they endeavour to make themselves masters of it by avoiding it. Both approaches in fact amount to the same thing, namely denying the danger that threatens. Both tactics have the same objective: being able to bear the burden of fear that is implicit in the job.

THE MAGIC OF NUCLEAR POWER

Men will employ these tactics in accordance with their temperament (whether kamikaze or *rentier*) but above all in accordance with the system of representations that they have worked out (order or disorder, strength or decay).

Kamikazes, as true soldiers of nuclear energy, prefer a clean, manly war fought in terms of direct confrontations with irradiation, a danger that threatens particularly in the mechanical section of the plant, where not surprisingly a large number of kamikaze technicians are to be found. To wage his war, the kamikaze will employ various tactics. He may, for instance, exceed orders as regards exposure times. Alternatively, he may (deliberately or unwittingly) neglect to take all the usual precautions before embarking on a job. Examples are the operators who will actually manhandle the drums filled with radioactive waste or the ones who work in the shearing shop and by-pass the elaborate safety measures that slow down the rhythm of production.

> You find the kamikazes in the shops where things don't always go according to plan. At the top of the plant the spent fuel comes in, is removed from its packing, and is then cut up and dissolved . . . But the spent-fuel containers have to be emptied out . . . and that's not funny. The stuff gets jammed and needs to be unblocked. I've known crackpots who have gone in with a crowbar to unjam stuff in what we call a duck's beak, that's a sort of pipe with a bend in it. Afterwards it's not difficult to shunt this or by-pass that,[8] but these are safety factors we're taking about! Shifts may not pass on the orders, people forget, but it's gambling with safety. Each shift gets by as best it can, but hiccups can occur . . .

It is mainly among the kamikazes that, under the influence of words, radioactivity becomes transformed into male energy, into sexual potency. 'In the engineering shops people take risks to prove that they're men . . . It's a way of saying, "I'm not scared"!'

For them the irradiation incident becomes something to talk about, breaking the monotony of the job: 'I wonder if they aren't quite happy to have copped a little dose . . . Now they have a story to tell . . . At last, something happened to them one day . . . They can talk about it . . . The comment was made by an operator with reference to two technicians who had suffered slight irradiation while repairing pipework in an '800' zone. He added: 'And after all, they'd got a dose, they hadn't caught AIDS . . . I think a person's more annoyed about becoming contaminated than about copping a dose.'

Here again we have the contamination-blemish idea as something a person must seek to guard against or keep under control. Since contamination is particularly to be feared in the chemical part of the establishment, that was predictably where the greatest concentration of *rentier* technicians was to be found. Such people are all the more cautious about managing their 'dose capital' for the fact that they are dealing with contamination. Control, for them, consists firstly in ensuring that this danger does not arise and secondly in seeking to understand any incident that does occur so as to evolve certain knacks, certain ways of doing things, 'tricks of the trade' that the old hands then try to pass on to the younger generation.

> When there's a puncture in a sleeve or a glove box, the person shields it with his body, calls his mates to come and help, maybe one of them will then slip a face-mask on the one in a bad position and another bring a sleeve, ask him to move out of the way very carefully, and quickly slip the sleeve on . . . With two old hands it works a treat. Whereas the normal tendency when a sleeve gives is to panic . . . You've had it when that happens . . . it means months of decontamination, you must wear a mask to work in the place for months before it's all cleaned up. Basically, the key to protection is ventilation and the way you take your hand out. When there's a break in the seal, the draught has to be going in the same direction, so if you make a sudden movement you risk stopping the draught and catching it yourself. That's something you have to know . . . It's no good saying you only have to wear gloves and everything'll be all right.

To control contamination more effectively a person may in fact choose to confront it with his bare hands.

> I personally work without gloves, because with gloves you take them off and you don't check yourself. If a glove's punctured you don't notice. Whereas working bare-handed you check yourself more often. If you come out of a glove box you don't automatically think of checking yourself, but bare-handed it's a different matter That way you don't spread contamination all over the place . . .

These tricks and tactics, by giving a man the feeling that he can get the better of adversity (in this case contamination or irradiation), introduce little cracks into the monolithic complex of rules, orders, and obligatory systems by which he is usually bound. In an environment dominated by danger, man has contrived a chink of freedom. Through rediscovering the pleasure of playing a game, making up his own rules, working out his 'ploys', he turns the situation round, controlling the risk rather than being in perpetual thrall to it. These tiny, everyday procedures constitute so many defensive strategies to combat anxiety.

But there is more than just the pleasure of mastering a technological mechanism. With this concept of the 'knack', the nuclear worker has found a way of avoiding blame. Play is known to have a disjunctive role. In play it is 'every man for himself', or at least a person has his special partners – in this case, the shift he works with. But if they forget to inform the next shift, if they omit (which can happen, because in any game the 'ploys' remain secret) to explain what they have done to get round a particular safety measure, an incident may subsequently occur as a result of the ignorance in which the relieving shift has been kept. That shift may then quite rightly place the blame for the incident on the previous shift. 'Incidents are invariably caused by people not obeying orders.'

And if a worker, be he kamikaze or *rentier*, should chance to fall victim to an incident involving radioactivity, those who do not themselves subscribe to the belligerent kamikaze approach or to the wiles of the *rentiers*, as the case may be, are able to think: 'He had it coming to him.' Once again there is a human occasion at the origin of the mishap. Above all, it becomes easy to believe that if you make your own behaviour conform to the regulations you may escape the dangers that threaten you:

> In the nuclear industry there is a risk, but you have every means of protecting yourself, everything you need to deal with it, to keep a check on yourself. Plus the Radioprotection Department is there to keep an eye on things, to monitor whether or not you've received any doses. So in the normal course of events you're not in any danger!

One can see the symbolic effectiveness of these defensive strategies that locate the opening of hostilities elsewhere, off-loading the responsibility onto someone else, even if in the event the victim is self-confessedly consenting or even innocent. The important thing is that the original error can be pinned on a person, thus exculpating the technology on which the worker's safety depends. Given this kind of explanation, a person feels reassured. He knows what methods to employ in order to steer clear of danger, and if an incident occurs none the less, it is easy for him to say he is not to blame.

The only way to limit the risk of these dangerous 'games' is to tighten up the orders, create automatic responses, eliminate all desire for initiative.

> In theory you're not supposed to think about the orders. For instance, in the plutonium shop there are orders about critical mass. No one's ever going to disregard those because the stakes are too high, even if they know they're well below the norms and the risk is only potential. There no one is going to disobey orders, at least I should hope not. Otherwise the orders consist in following procedures. When there's a problem, if it's during the day you go up the hierarchy, if it's at night the duty supervisor deals with it himself, either falling back on discipline or now he calls in a duty engineer who looks after coordination in the plant. There's very little initiative. Or what there is is minimal. Problems are caused by people taking the initiative in some way, hence the difficulty of keeping in full touch with what has been done before you, that's an enormous potential risk . . . That's the danger, people are bound together . . . There's a half-hour changeover period between shifts, each person at his work station briefs the one who's going to take his place.

Rules and regulations exert a stranglehold on the worker. So let it not be thought that these language games in which the technicians indulge, the system of representations with which they view the world of nuclear energy, have anything to do with fecklessness or immaturity. This is a deliberate mode of behaviour, an indispensable way of helping to render psychologically tolerable the boredom, the monotony, and (it would appear) the burden of anxiety arising out of their daily activities.

Without this way of thinking, without these organising exercises, and without these responses of denial or defiance, it would be impossible for them to go on working in such perilous realms, where man is in some sense an intruder. In failing to acknowledge this and ignoring the complexity of the man/workplace/technology equation, the nuclear-technology experts are in turn at risk of finding themselves facing some unexpected situations.

Apparently tamed or circumvented in this way, the dangers of nuclear energy become malleable, manageable. A person may then play with that energy in a positive way and on his own account, as we have just seen, like a sort of white magic that will ward off the perils surrounding him. He may, however, use it in the form of black magic, which is what happened in 1978 when a shiftworker, wanting to 'get back' at a foreman with whom he was not seeing eye to eye, placed some discs of irradiated metal under the seat of the man's car.[9] Radioactivity may, if the need arises, be harnessed in the service of revenge.

THE MEDALLIONS OF THE NUCLEAR INDUSTRY

Understandably, this idea of bracing oneself for danger and the daily employment of this virile, bellicose vocabulary can lead some people to wish to undergo a kind of nuclear 'baptism of fire' and hence unconsciously to provoke an incident (the 'snag' (le pépin) they all talk about, playing things down as usual). Indeed, it seems that until a person has received 'a dose', 'his dose', not only does he not have a story to tell; he remains in a condition of suspense, waiting for the incident that, statistically, is bound to occur. So it is plausible to see these provocative schemes as processes aimed at freeing the person who initiates them from an intolerable wait. Indeed, until a person has been the victim of an incident it is just as if he had not yet received his initiation and triumphed over the traumatism that that initiation brings, as it were changing the individual psychologically and biologically, causing him to advance from the state of novice to that of initiate, from man to superman.

This initiatory process is made all the more striking by the fact that each occasion when a person goes 'on-limits', each *passage* from one place to another, is accompanied by a series of rituals that act as so many processes of transformation. 'You have dressing and undressing every day. You change completely. There's a stage you go through, a sort of threshold you cross at the point where you change colour . . . I'm not saying your personality changes . . . But almost!'

A man is daily made ready to accomplish his initiation. Dressing, the time spent 'on-limits', and undressing constitute so many rituals of integration, aggregation, and then separation, marking the passage from one world to the other. Each day, whether a man doggedly avoids being soiled by contamination or deliberately brushes with manly irradiation, he duly performs the rites indispensable to his purification. The outfits that he dons and then throws away are the tangible objects of the proper unfolding of the rite. That gives them a special status: those vinyl membranes become true protective skins.

> In my laboratory I insist on no one using gloves to work. If they mess up their hands, too bad . . . But if they're wearing gloves that can't happen . . . They feel protected, don't even check themselves any more, and spread contamination everywhere, on the

keyboards, on the telephone, without realising . . . You get secondary contamination all over the place!

However, it is impossible to say in advance how serious the incident will be and consequently how severe the traumatism. In this dangerous environment, where man is attempting to play tricks with the invisible, chance plays a not inconsiderable role. It would appear advisable, therefore, to kit oneself out with a few extra protections in order more effectively to keep it at bay. But where, in an industry that forbids the wearing of any personal objects and thus rules out recourse to the traditional fetishes of our Christian societies, are such things to be found?

I mentioned the way in which the training-course instructor presented the organisation of worker-protection in an ionising environment, how everything was said and demonstrated (with film back-up) in such a way as to persuade trainees that, so long as an operator follows the safety directives to the letter, no incident can occur. In other words, if you stick to the radioprotection technicians' instructions, if you dress properly, and if you are careful to carry the instruments that will measure the ambient radioactivity, you will be fully protected. No one will receive more than his permitted dose, as allotted to him in line with the official norms. Nothing is ever said (during the training course, at least) about the incidents that may occur (a punctured glove, a torn garment, a leaking pipe, a spillage) or about the elaborate procedures that are so essential if large-scale contamination or irradiation is to be avoided.

The training cycle does not include instruction in the 'tricks of the trade', the knacks acquired by old hands. A person may gain access to that sort of knowledge later, on the job, when doing shift work. In the absence of any direct transfer of such information, which might have provided trainees with skills enabling them to face danger and get on top of it without experiencing too much anxiety, a substitution occurs in the way in which the various measuring instruments are perceived. What happens is that they become actual means of protection. In other words, people no longer see these objects with which they equip themselves when going 'on-limits' for what they are, namely tools to measure ambient radioactivity; they see them as objects capable of affording protection.

Some technicians who had been working at the plant for more than ten years and were taking the course on a refresher basis voiced the same thought:

> The way in which worker safety is approached on the course is dramatic. You get the impression that the dosemeters and work suits are not just means of control and measurement but means of protection in their own right. If I'm wearing my dosemeter I'm protected . . . Which is totally absurd . . . A dosemeter isn't a charm for warding off bad luck!

A perfect illustration of this in concrete terms was contained in the laconic reply given by one technician when I asked him whether he experienced any apprehension at going on-limits: 'None at all . . . Anyway, I'm protected, I have a chest film badge, a wrist film badge, even a pen-dosemeter.'

No need here of crosses or of effigies of the Virgin or one's patron saint. No need to commend oneself to God or his saints before starting on a job. The firm supplies its own protective medallions.

The symbolic transformation undergone by these objects explains or at least renders comprehensible certain modes of behaviour that I was told about but never managed to observe or verify (it was always 'other people' who acted in this way, never the speaker). I was told, for instance, that there was a 'traffic in films' on the site! Unexposed film badges were stolen from the shops and replaced by used ones. Why? Presumably, for these 'medallions' to be effective they must be without blemish. Hence these substitutions in which some people allegedly indulge. How is one to know? Whom is one to believe?

GUILT AND PUNISHMENT

You do not play with fire or try to outsmart radioactivity with impunity. Sooner or later you will have to pay. Had not the nurse stated on the training course: 'We all get the same punishment'?

Everything to do with the manipulation of the atom, whether it be releasing its energy for conversion into electricity or, as at la Hague, recycling nuclear substances, is unconsciously experienced in the public mind as a transgression ineluctably inviting chastisement. And the first to be punished, of course, are those who come closest to radioactive matter, namely the men and women who work in the nuclear industry.

Their punishment may take many forms. It may affect them directly, or it may strike at their families. It may manifest itself immediately or at a later date, long after they have ceased to work at the plant. For some the punishment may never come. For others it lies in the future. For one or two it is there already, taking the form of cancer, an illness that is often seen in terms of punishment undermining a person's physical integrity.

If people are able to speak of punishment in connection with cancer, it is because, for the sufferer, the disease is accompanied by a feeling of blame, as evinced by the fact that they will conceal it from themselves or refuse to talk about it. 'I know one man who died of leukemia. He wouldn't say anything, didn't even want to talk about it in case it was classified as an occupational disease. It's like that with lots of people. When they have cancer they don't want to talk about it!'

Sick people will generally refuse to sign the papers that would get them recognised as suffering from an occupational disease. Granted, the administrative procedures tend to be lengthy and meticulous and the legislation concerning occupational disease not easy for workers to exploit.

It's up to the attending physician to make a declaration of presumption of occupational disease, which leads to an inquiry and a whole process of very complicated
investigations . . . So the initial step is never taken, the local doctors don't even mention
the possibility to their patients . . . We've tried, as a trade-union, to get doctors into

good habits, but we've not succeeded . . . Ever. So people don't say anything. You can also wait until the fellow's dead and go and see his widow, but you need an expert opinion, the body has to be exhumed . . . You get the picture, it never works . . . Not surprising, really. So there's no note on the file. It doesn't find its way into COGEMA's epidemiological statistics. Whenever you try to do a study of cancer at the plant, it never works.

The silence that tends to surround this particular illness at every level confirms those afflicted by it in their feeling of culpability. Why is it never mentioned anywhere?

Yet a person need not be directly affected in physical terms for the idea of guilt to crop up, the notion of a price to be paid. You only have to listen to these men and women talking about the biological misfortune that will inevitably befall them one day. There are those, for instance, who believe that illness will eventually strike them down, and at the least physiological irregularity uncovered during their twice-yearly examinations they will panic and start to question the veracity of the diagnoses proposed by the establishment's Medical Department. 'I don't believe that "ghost of Chernobyl" story! They gloss over any abnormality in the blood formula by saying "it's because of Chernobyl", but what's to say it's true? Chernobyl suits them fine! They're doing it to cover up the illness . . .'

The wives are no less suspicious. One whose husband left the plant some years ago admitted: 'It haunts me even now! Because he did get contaminated . . . He took some big doses . . . and cancers can take twenty years to show . . . So it's still on my mind!' Another said anxiously:

> Deep down I ask myself: 'Can you be sure? Aren't the analyses rigged? Isn't there always a tendency to play things down? I know perfectly well that the analyses aren't rigged, but can one ever be certain . . .?' And then it's all done according to norms. But a norm can be set anywhere, at any level. Are they reliable, those norms? Your norm won't be the same as mine. Oh, I don't talk to him about it, what's the use? I talk to him about his cigarettes instead . . . he smokes like a chimney, and that worries me more than his job. It's more concrete, too, more immediate, you can put your finger on it. . .

Smoking undoubtedly channels many fears relating to cancer. But because it is 'concrete', because 'you can put your finger on it', in this case it is probably also acting as the symbolic medium of a more muted and in any case incommunicable distress arising out of fear of *le nucléaire*.

Other workers seek to fend off this fear by making themselves less vulnerable, though they realise there is no escaping one's destiny:

> I've had mates who've had cancer. One had cancer of the oesophagus, but he used to smoke two or three packets of cigarettes a day, another one drank and smoked – letting off both barrels, if you like! So is it a question of dose? Yes, there are cases of cancer up there, but you try to account for them by excesses of that sort . . . I don't smoke myself, and I don't drink . . .

Above all there is a swirl of expiatory rumour that surrounds those who work at the plant and that delivers its verdict whenever misfortune strikes a person's family. If a child is born with a deformity of some kind, even a hare-lip, or if a woman miscarries or suffers any prolonged illness, immediately word goes round: 'What do you expect – he works at the plant!'

Other rumours whisper that these men will be punished 'unto their children's children'. The saying goes that by working in the nuclear industry men lose their virility. They go bald. They cannot have children, or they have only daughters. It is even alleged that there was a fashion at the plant a few years ago for vasectomy. Was it for fear of engendering freaks? Rumour does not say. It is in the nature of rumour, of course, to speak in truncated images. You have to 'take my word for it'. An anonymous word that quotes no sources and names no names.

AN ANCESTRY DISCOVERED

To sustain this feeling of guilt, shatter this solitude, and adjust more easily to the rigours of anxiety, the men of la Hague have fashioned a collective memory, forged a certain self-awareness, and put together a destiny for themselves by latching on to an illustrious line of forebears: the miners.

Every account of work at the plant and of the risks incurred there is accompanied by a refrain on the subject of the miners of old: 'Our fathers went down the mine . . . We work in the nuclear industry. They sacrificed their lives . . . We put our lives at risk too.'

It is as if, by situating themselves in relation to a past where there was danger, they are reducing the very modern, very special sort of danger they face every day. 'Did silicosis ever stop miners' sons from going down the mine? Yet they knew what they were in for!'

The fact of having hit upon this line of descent (for that is indeed what they are claiming), of having forged this link with valiant ancestors, helps the nuclear worker of today to resign himself to a fate that has always existed, a destiny that none can escape. Since time immemorial men have laid down their lives that others might live in greater comfort. Workers in the nuclear industry are perpetuating the line of the great heroes of the modern age.

NOTES

1. The story goes that, before the fast-breeder was started up, certain technicians had expressed doubts about the soundness of certain welds in the tank into which the sodium was to flow. The engineers who had designed the tank simply did not want to know.
2. The (French) Le Robert dictionary defines *fifrelin* as 'small mushroom' or 'trifle, valueless small change'.

3. According to my informant, this expression was imported by workers from the Marcoule reprocessing plant (near Avignon) when they transferred to la Hague.

   Among the many meanings of the verb *dauber* are 'to roughcast', 'to insult', 'to strike', and 'to cook meat in a casserole'. Of these the last two may seem apt metaphors for the damage done by radioactivity. I have the impression that, so far as contamination is concerned, the image people have is primarily that of stewed meat. The meaning 'to strike' would fit better with irradiation in the pattern I am describing. However, *daubé* is always used with reference to contamination. In his structural analysis of cooking, Claude Lévi-Strauss of course placed 'boiled' (*le bouilli*) alongside 'rotten' (*le pourri*) (see 'Le triangle culinaire', in *L'Arc* 26, p. 28).

4. Genesis 3:19.

5. See Jean Darriulat, 'La Hague, une usine nucléaire qui vieillit mal' ('a nuclear plant that is ageing badly'), in *Le Matin*, 1979.

6. Emile Benveniste, *Vocabulaire des institutions indo-européennes*, Paris, Minuit, 1969, p. 100.

7. Mary Douglas, *Purity and Disorder*, London, Routledge & Kegan Paul, 1967.

8. The speaker actually used the words *shunter* and *bi-passer*, derived from English (Tr.).

9. This incident gave rise to judicial proceedings in 1978.

Part 3:
'Work', 'Life' and Gender

SECTIONAL INTRODUCTION

On the eve of the English Industrial Revolution (as the conventional story unfolds) most households were units of production as well as consumption, and characteristically *all* household members were productively engaged, regardless of age and gender. With factory employment, the workplace was separated from the home, and the sphere of 'work' was increasingly identified with the egoistic values of the market, as against the values of mutuality, reciprocity and community that supposedly governed relations outside it. The worker was not only alienated from the means of production, and from control of the labour process and the product, but also, as Marx saw it, from his fellow men and his own humanity. He was only 'at home' when at home. As its productive base was eroded, the household was reduced to a site of consumption. Though women initially entered the industrial workforce in numbers, they were progressively eased out of it as the nineteenth century went on. Households became dependent on the wage of a single male breadwinner, and the domestic sphere came to be seen as the sphere of women and consumption, as opposed to the male sphere of 'work' and production. 'Work' was increasingly separated from 'life', and their separation was increasingly gendered.

How general has this trajectory been? The readings in Part 3 review that question from a comparative angle. Though it downplays the gender dimension, the opening chapter by Carrier provides a synthetic account of these historical developments in the West. Carrier takes his lead from Mauss (1966 [1925]) rather than Marx, specifically from Mauss's account of primitive and archaic exchange, in which persons and things are inseparable, and the gift is imbued with the personality of the donor. Carrier's concern is with how things have become progressively alienated from the persons who produce and exchange them, and how these producers have been progressively alienated from each other. The latter have gradually lost control of the production process, which increasingly takes place in a context divorced from social relationships (like kinship) that are not solely economic. Step by step they cease to control, shape and be embodied in the production process and in what they produce, and share less with those they work alongside. Carrier traces this trend through an evolutionary sequence of four productive stages: cottage industry, putting out, the early factory and the modern factory. Parts of his analysis are familiar from Braverman (1974), though not his more Maussian focus on personhood. Work becomes separated from other aspects of life and is seemingly divorced from the 'true' self. Persons are split between, on the one hand, a 'relational self' that engages in durable relationships with friends and family, and that has an inalienable identity (as a member of a family, nation, race and gender), and, on the other, a 'peripheral self' engaged in the world of work, where people experience each other as independent individuals. By implication, the ideology of individualism is created in alienated production, but is only one of the discourses about the person that characterise Western industrial societies. Elsewhere, Carrier (1994; 1995) shows how the same process of progressive alienation is played out in the sphere of circulation (or exchange), and how retail trade has in parallel been de-skilled and de-personalized.

As to the gender part of the story, a shelf of historical writings on Europe deal with the growing exclusion of women from the industrial workforce, often prompted by the preoccupation of middle class public opinion with the sexual perils of the workplace, and its concern for their 'true' vocation as mothers (e.g. Humphries 1988; McBride 1992; Scott 1987). The same trend, and even the same reasoning, is reported elsewhere, from the Indian mines (Simeon 1999) and the Calcutta jute mills (Fernandes 1997; Sen 1999), for example. In India, manual labour is not highly esteemed (especially when performed for others), and the household's ability to withdraw its womenfolk from such employment is an important marker of its status and respectability and, of course, of its material capacity. Most women denied jobs in increasingly masculinized industries cannot, however, afford to retreat into domesticity but must seek out some less desirable source of livelihood. In the case of migrant labour, the gender division is often one between the urban industrial employment of men and the agricultural labour of women in the village fields (e.g. Fernandes 1997; De Haan 1994). It should not be forgotten, however, that, as in Southeast Asia, a great deal of industrial expansion in the late-twentieth century relied on a largely female workforce (e.g. Ong 1987; Wolf 1992).

Male and female workers may not, of course, think about the home/work division, about their work groups, or about the proper tenor of shop floor relations, in quite the same way (e.g. Ashwin 1999: chapter 7 on a post-*perestroika* Russian mine; Yelvington 1995, for a Caribbean case). What ethnography also brings out is how gender identities are sometimes made (or at least 'finished') in factory employment, as is documented, for example, by Salzinger's chapter in this volume on 'Anarchomex', a middle-sized, U.S. managed Mexican factory that produced electrical systems for the motor industry. The pseudonym is apt because of the striking absence of management on the shop floor and its 'chaotic' lack of discipline, one manifestation of which was constant flirting and 'macho' displays. Management had only itself to blame, not only because of its bureaucratic, impersonal and ineffectual labour regime, but also because of its insistence that 'maquila jobs are women's jobs'. In practice, however, the company was forced to employ a large proportion of men who, not unpredictably, felt a continual need to prove their masculinity. True, there was some continuity with what went on outside the factory, but within it 'macho-ness' took a hypertrophic form as young men responded to their 'embattled situation at work'. Gendered identities are not set in stone when workers come onto the shop floor, but 'are made on the job'.

Similarly, Westwood (1984) had earlier shown how jobs at a hosiery factory in the English Midlands encouraged acceptance of conventional gender roles amongst its largely female workforce. Home and workplace interpenetrate, Westwood stresses, and are part of a single world. But the situation she describes is ambivalent. On the one hand, the home/workplace divide is subverted through the domestication of shop floor space (*see also* Dunn 2004, on women workers in a Polish baby food factory). On the other, shop floor culture idealises marriage, motherhood and domesticity, which are seen as an escape from the all day, everyday grind of the factory. By anti-thesis, the capitalist labour process entrenches a repressive ideology of gender relations. The grass is always greener on the other side and, when you are stuck at your factory workbench, the other side is domestic bliss. Though the ideological separation between home and workplace is in some ways subverted, in the end shop floor culture seems to reinforce it.

In other instances, however, the disciplinary regime of the factory clearly depends on counteracting the work/life distinction, as many managements consciously recognise. In the case of the electronics factory in southern China described in Lee's contribution to this volume, this is because kinship obligations and 'localist' loyalties are crucial to the way in which the predominantly female labour force is controlled. It is through such identities that workers are recruited, tasks assigned, wages set, skills transmitted, promotions granted and dormitory life organised. Young women workers are under the surveillance of brothers, male cousins, senior kinswomen, or, at least, others from their 'native place', who may feel themselves responsible to the management for their compliance since it was their intercession that got them the job. A similar picture emerges from Pun's (2005) account of a similar factory in the same urban agglomeration (Shenzen). It's a far cry from Carrier's characterization of the 'modern' Western factory (where workers work together only because they have a commodity relationship with the company and not because they are related to each other) and from Burawoy's claim (1979; *see also* the Introduction to Part 2) that the attitudes and values that workers bring from outside are largely irrelevant to the way that relations in production operate; a claim that again postulates a marked disjunction between 'work' and 'life'. What both Shenzen studies also show is that consumption for these women workers is a key signifier of the modernity to which they aspire, and that it is as would-be consumers that they reconcile themselves to the hardships of their factory jobs, dreaming of consumption even as they produce (Pun 2003).

Consumption, pivotal in the articulation between labour and capital, and to workers' perceptions of the relationship between 'work' and 'life', is also central to the chapter by Freeman that follows, and that deals with women workers in data-processing companies in the Caribbean. These jobs are repetitive, alienating, poorly paid and subject to a high degree of surveillance. But though they are materially no better off, and though their jobs are unskilled, these women work with computers in relatively salubrious office-like conditions, and are anxious to differentiate themselves from blue-collar workers and be seen as 'professionals', which is one important reason why they want no truck with unions. They occupy a 'space of invention', constituting themselves (with the active collusion of management) as a 'pink-collar' workforce through their fashionable dress styles and participation in global consumption patterns. On their paltry pay, however, they are constrained to supplement their incomes, not only by working plots of land and raising pigs and poultry, but also by working as seamstresses and by trading fashion items purchased in places like Miami, to which they can travel only because the company gives 'air miles' as bonuses. 'Production' and consumption, their work for the company and their activities outside it, are inextricably intertwined. It is the pseudo-professional aura that surrounds their work, and the *savoire-faire* about style that the company encourages them to cultivate, that make them value their jobs in it and feel that they are a cut above ordinary workers. There are interesting parallels with Mills' (1997) discussion of the appropriation of urban fashions by rural Thai women working in Bangkok garment factories.

Had Henry Ford believed Burawoy's proposition about the autonomy of relations in production he would hardly have gone to such lengths to violate his workers' privacy. Investigators from the company's 'Sociology Department' watched over and sanctioned their financial and sexual prudence, their hygiene and habits, and, of course, their interest in unions. But it was not only Ford who felt obliged to go *outside* the factory to instil a working class culture conducive to industrial discipline and efficiency. That has also been a major impetus behind the construction of company towns, where workers not only work for the company but live in its housing (so joblessness means homelessness); join the clubs and use the recreational facilities it provides; are treated in the company hospital; send their children to a company school; and may receive wages in scrip exchangeable only at the company store. 'A job in the company town,' says Carlson (2003:98), 'was more than employment; it was a way of life – the boss's way'. Sometimes the motivations for building such towns included philanthropic ones, though more frequently the main impetus was a desire to reduce labour turnover and to provide a bulwark against unions. For the U.S. after 1900, Crawford (1995:7) notes 'a startling correlation between strikes and other labour struggles and the subsequent appearance of new company towns'. Even private sector enterprises, driven by market imperatives, may have reasons for not taking the work/life distinction too seriously.

Public sector ones routinely ride roughshod over the work/life distinction. Parry (2001) shows how the management of a large-scale state-run steel plant in central India intervenes to buttress the stability of the marriages of its workers, prompted partly by a paternalistic sense of its 'civilising' mission and by its *Brahmanical* view of what modern India should be like, and partly by the need to economise on the welfare provisions it makes for their families. In the USSR during the 1920s and '30s there was a systematic attack on the 'bourgeois' family and on 'private life', and an attempt to collapse the distinction between public and private, work and home. The work sphere was to take over the whole of existence (Kotkin 1995: 218; Figes 2008). At least up until the mid-1980s, nearly all welfare available to Chinese industrial workers was administered through the workplace (Walder 1986). Rofel (1999: 234f) has vividly described how thereafter the enterprise continued to intervene in the domestic arrangements of workers, and to monitor and control their sex lives.

Although this erosion of the division between 'work' and 'life' has been carried furthest in communist-bloc command economies, it is, as we have seen, scarcely unknown to the world of large capitalist corporations. A blurring of the boundaries seems most likely to take place when what companies want is a skilled and stable workforce with a long-term commitment to the job. When what is required is a flexible one that can be hired and fired as the demand for labour fluctuates, the company is unlikely to show much interest in the lives of workers outside the factory. The extract from Dore that appears as chapter 13 is drawn from his classic study of two British and two Japanese factories (belonging respectively to English Electric and Hitachi). The contrast here is between the far sharper separation of work and home in the British than in the Japanese case, where much 'leisure' consists of obligatory socializing with workmates, and where the company saturates the lives of workers to a far greater extent and accepts a significant degree of responsibility towards their families (who are expected to accept that the worker's obligations to it take precedence). The contrast, Dore shows, is of a piece with others that reflect a crucial difference between a Japanese system based on lifetime employment where what the enterprise buys is a generalised capacity to perform a range of tasks, as against a more market-oriented British system which is premised on much higher rates of labour turn-over, and where workers are recruited to specific roles (like electrician or foundryman). And what ultimately explains this, he argues, is the very different historical contexts in which the two industrial systems developed.

Dore was dealing with a big and successful corporation at a time when the Japanese economy was booming. But such large-scale enterprises account for only a minute fraction of the total number of manufacturing companies in Japan, and (in the mid-1990s) for only about one-quarter of their workforce. In smaller factories wages are considerably lower, there is no expectation of a job for life, identification with the firm is much weaker, workers are more liable to put family before firm and leisure activities are more likely to be kept separate from work (Roberson 1998). In short, they are more like Dore's 'British system' than his 'Japanese' one. But the two kinds of Japanese factory are symbiotically related; and it seems plausible to suppose that Hitachi are only able to provide their workers with lifetime employment at enviable rates of pay so long as they can 'put out' work to smaller companies with cheap flexible labour.

The day labourers that Gill describes in the final chapter of Part 3 perform much the same role; Dore's 'Japanese system' requires Gill's 'men of uncertainty' to meet the demand for labour when it is there, and to be dumped when it is not. For the most part these workers are rootless and ageing single men, cut off from their kin and employed on very short term contracts. They are the antithesis of the 'salary man' depicted in Dore's study, workers who live apart from the two defining institutions of Japanese society, the company and the family (Gill 1999; 2001). Gill contrasts two systems of employment and recruitment amongst construction site labour during the recessionary period of the 1990s. The *yoseba* is a day labour market in which much of the labour is unionised. Most workers who find employment through it live in *doya* doss houses and manage to maintain a considerable degree of independence and autonomy. Increasingly, however, the only way to find employment is through now increasingly prevalent *ninpudashi*, boarding houses that not only supply them with food and accommodation, but also act as labour recruiters and control their access to jobs. Unsurprisingly, those who frequent them are not unionised and are liable to become the virtual wage slaves of their owners. Domestic life is inseparable from the world of work, and labour protests are virtually impossible. At the bottom of the proletarian hierarchy, and under modern recessionary conditions, 'home' and 'work' are again inseparably fused.

The broad conclusion that seems to emerge is that although there may be forces of a general nature that affect the way and extent to which 'work' and 'life' are differentiated (for example, the employers' need for a stable workforce and their fear of labour militancy), there is no simple, let alone unilinear, trajectory that results in their increasing separation as industrialisation proceeds. The problematic nature of teleological narratives of that sort will be the central focus of Part 4.

RECOMMENDED FURTHER READING

Carrier, J.G. 1994. 'Alienating objects: the emergence of alienation in retail trade', *Man*, 29(2): 359–80.

Gill, Tom. 2001. *Men of uncertainty: The social organization of day laborers in contemnporary Japan*, Albany: SUNY.

Humphries, Jane. 1988. 'Protective legislation, the capitalist state and working-class men: the case of the 1842 Mines Regulation Act', in R. Pahl (ed.), *On work: Historical, Comparative and Theoretical Approaches*, Oxford: Basil Blackwell Ltd, pp. 95–124.

Mills, Mary-Beth. 1997. 'Contesting the Margins of Modernity: Women, migration and consumption in Thailand', *American Ethnologist*, 24: 37–61.

Parry, J.P. 2001. 'Ankalu's Errant Wife: Sex, marriage and industry in contemporary Chhattisgarh', *Modern Asian Studies*, 35(4): 783–820.

Pun, Nagai. 2005. *Made in China: Women factory workers in a global workplace*, Durham, NC: Duke University Press.

Rofel, Lisa. 1999. *Other Modernities: Gendered yearnings in China after socialism*, Berkeley, CA: University of California Press.

Westwood, Sally. 1984. *All day, Everyday: Factory and family in the making of women's lives*, London: Pluto Press.

OTHER WORKS CITED

Ashwin, Sarah. 1999. *Russian Workers: The anatomy of patience*, Manchester: Manchester University Press.

Braverman, H. 1974. *Labor and Monopoly Capital: The degradation of work in the twentieth century*, New York: Monthly Review Press.

Burawoy, M. 1979. *Manufacturing Consent: Changes in the labour process under monopoly capitalism*, Chicago: Chicago University Press.

Carlson, Linda. 2003. *Company Towns of the Pacific Northwest*, Seattle: University of Washington Press.

Carrier, J.G. 1995. *Gifts and Commodities: Exchange and Western Capitalism since 1700*, London: Routledge.

Crawford, Margaret. 1995. *Building the Workingman's Paradise: The design of American company towns*, New York: Verso.

De Haan, A. 1994. *Unsettled Settlers: Migrant workers and industrial capitalism in Calcutta*, Hilversum: Veloren.

Dunn, Elizabeth. 2004. *Privatizing Poland, Baby Food, Big Business and the Remaking of Labor*, Ithaca, NY: Cornell University Press.

Fernandes, Leela. 1997. *Producing workers: The politics of gender, class and culture in the Calcutta jute mills*, Philadelphia: University of Pennsylvania Press.

Figes, Orlando. 2008. *The Whisperers: Private life in Stalin's Russia*, London: Penguin Books.

Gill, Tom. 1999. 'Wage Hunting at the Margins of Urban Japan', in S. Day, E. Papataxiarchis and M. Stewart (eds), *Lilies of the Field: Marginal people who live for the moment*, pp. 119–36, Boulder, CO: Westview Press.

Kotkin, S. 1995. *Magnetic Mountain: Stalinism as civilization*, Berkeley, CA: University of California Press.

Mauss, M. 1966 (1925). *The Gift: Forms and functions of exchange in archaic societies*, (trans I. Cunnison), London: Cohen & West.

McBride, T. 1992. 'Women's Work and Industrialization', in L.R. Berlanstein (ed.), *The Industrial Revolution and work in nineteenth-century Europe*, pp. 63–80, London: Routledge.

Ong, A. 1987. *Spirits of Resistance and Capitalist Discipline: Factory women in Malaysia*, Albany, NY: State University of New York Press.

Pun, Ngai. 2003. 'Subsumption or Consumption? The Phantom of Consumer Revolution in "Globalizing China"', *Cultural Anthropology*, 18(4): 469–92.

Roberson, J.E. 1998. *Japanese Working Class Lives: An ethnographic study of factory workers*, London: Routledge.

Scott, Joan W. 1987. '"L'ouvrière! Mot impie, sordide. . . .": Women workers in the political discourses of French political economy, 1840–60', in P. Joyce (ed.), *The historical meanings of work*, pp. 119–42, Cambridge: Cambridge University Press.

Sen, Samita. 1999. *Women and Labour in Late Colonial India: The Bengal Jute Industry, 1890–1940*, Cambridge: Cambridge University Press.

Simeon, Dilip. 'Work and Resistance in the Jharia coalfield', *Contributions to Indian Sociology* (new series), 33(1–2): 43–76.

Walder, Andrew. 1986. *Communist Neo-Traditionalism: Work and authority in Chinese industry*, Berkeley, CA: University of California Press.

Wolf, Diane. 1992. *Factory Daughters: Gender, household dynamics and rural industrialization in Java*, Berkeley, CA: University of California Press.

Yelvington, Kevin. 1995. *Producing Power. Ethnicity, Gender and Class in a Caribbean Workplace*, Philadelphia: Temple University Press.

CHAPTER NINE

Emerging Alienation in Production: A Maussian History

JAMES G. CARRIER

. . .

Anthropologists drawing inspiration from Marcel Mauss's *The gift* (1990) have generally focused on the ways people transact objects in small-scale non-industrial societies. My purpose is to apply Mauss's insights to the ways people produce objects in industrial societies. In such societies production is important in its own right. Moreover, the realm of production is an important aspect of people's experiences of objects and social interactions. Consequently, understanding it is important for understanding how people experience and think about social relations, identities and objects in industrial societies.

I use a Maussian model (Carrier 1991) that derives particularly from Gregory's (1980; 1982) application of *The gift* to Melanesian societies and from Parry's (1986) analysis of *The gift* and the debates surrounding it. The core of this model is a distinction (here idealised) between two forms of social life. In one form, people are bound to each other and to the things that surround them by durable links that provide a personal identity for the individual (see Mauss 1985) and that define people's obligations towards one another. These links are so strong that people and things cannot be said to exist independently of each other. In the other form, people are not so linked to each other and to the things around them, in which circumstances people and things can be said to exist as entities with their own independent sources of being and with no enduring obligations to each other. For Mauss and for many who have used his ideas, these two different forms of social life describe, if only in iconic form, pre-capitalist and capitalist societies.

My simplified rendering suggests a degree of overlap with Marxian analyses of modern capitalist society. These two approaches differ, however, in the ways that they have developed and the uses to which they are put.[1] Broadly speaking, scholars have used the Marxian model, especially that deriving from his more mature work, to analyse the nature and consequences of the social organisation of production in capitalist societies, particularly with regard to the formation of classes and the appropriation of surplus value. While some have used the model to analyse earlier and precapitalist societies (e.g. Godelier 1977; Hindess & Hirst 1975; Kahn 1980; Kahn & Llobera 1981; Wolpe 1980), that use has been secondary within the stream of Marxist scholarship. Conversely, scholars have used the Maussian model to analyse the nature and consequences of the cultural understanding of circulation in pre-capitalist societies, especially with regard to relations among people and between people and objects. Even though Mauss developed his model in terms of his understanding of industrial capitalist societies, there has been but little application of the model to such societies (e.g. Titmuss 1971).

My purpose is not only to provide a synchronic picture of industrial production in Maussian terms. In addition, I want to pursue a point of Parry's (1986: 466), that Mauss was concerned with how the development of the West has meant that 'economy becomes progressively disembedded from society . . . [and] economic relations become increasingly differentiated from other types of social relationship'. I will present an idealised description of changes in production over the past few centuries to help show what this differentiation means and what some of its consequences are.

In other words, I will trace the growth of alienation in production that accompanied the rise of industrial capitalism. 'Alienation' has many meanings, and I need to specify how I use it.[2] The core of 'alienation' as I use it here is a sense of separation. A thing is alienated from a person when it is seen as separate from that person; a person is alienated when seen as separate from surrounding people or things. Thus, alienation refers to how people perceive and understand themselves and their environs (Parry 1986: 455).[3] However, it has correlates that are more social and material. People who have little control over a thing or activity are likely to be more alienated from it than are people with more control; people obliged to co-operate with strangers are likely to be more alienated from their activities than are people who interact with family and friends.

I use this model of alienation to give shape to a historical sketch of commercial production relations[4] in the two leading and innovating economic powers of the modern era, Britain and the United States. However, the issues and changes that concern me apply more generally to Western industrial capitalist societies (see for example Bauman 1982; Medick & Sabean 1984; Polanyi 1957). I cast this history in terms of four kinds of production, focusing especially on the last two. The first kind I call cottage industry – production by households as independent economic units. The second is putting out – production by the household under contract with a merchant capitalist who provides raw materials and purchases the finished product. Third is early factory production – production in a central place but with much of the labour recruited and organised using family relationships. The last is modern factory production – production in a central place with all labour recruited and organised by the capitalist treating labour as a commodity.

Both the kinds and their sequence are constructs that simplify and essentialise a more complex and fluid history. Actual production conforms to these kinds only approximately and their sequence is really only a general drift towards increasing alienation. Equally, although I point to some local variations and counter-movements, especially in modern factory production, I do not deal with these systematically. Neither do I deal with the historical processes by which these forms of production emerged.

These limitations are appropriate to my purposes here, which are as much provocative and polemical as they are analytical. Anthropologists are broadening the scope of their approaches to include Western societies. They can make a fruitful contribution to the study of the West if they apply the models that they have developed in the study of non-Western societies.[5] In particular, the Maussian approach suggests that growing alienation in production is part of the broader differentiation of life into more 'purely' economic and more 'purely' social aspects. As a result of this differentiation, people come to conceive of themselves and their environs in two distinct ways. In one way, objects as well as other persons are separated from the self and are conceptualised in terms of abstract and impersonal frameworks and forces (such as utility, unit cost, sign value and 'the market'). In the other conception, objects and other persons are not so separated, and are conceptualised in terms of their relationships to the self and to personal forces (such as kinship, affection and obligation). (Schneider [1980] illustrates the contrast between these two conceptions.) This differentiation is manifest as an increasing distinction in the ways that people experience and think about their lives at work (i.e., as producers) and their lives at home. Work, and its associated objects and relations, are alienated from the individual, while home is not.[6]

This differentiation is also a tension, for people seem to want to colonise the alienated realm with more durable, less alienated relationships. Beaglehole (1932: 132) argues that there is a general tendency for people to form 'an enduring and intimate relation' with the objects in their lives. He argues that this appears even in the face of modern factory production, as when

> the workers and machine tenders ... speak of the instrument of labour and the products thereof as their 'own'. In many cases the worker will rationalise ... this identification of himself with the objects with which or upon which he works. But since he usually speaks of his 'love' for his machine or his tools, he shows that other than utilitarian considerations are influencing his relations with the machine he calls his own.

Similarly, Granovetter (1985: 490) argues that economic relations between people in different firms are not in fact alienated and impersonal, each rationally calculating how to use the other to best advantage. Instead, over the course of time these relations frequently 'become overlaid with social content that carries strong expectations of trust and abstention from opportunism'. Equally, Mars (1982) describes how many groups of co-workers form social relationships that reduce their alienation from one another just as he shows how workers frequently manipulate their work to gain greater control over it. These colonisations of the realm of production and of economic life more generally show that workers respond actively to the growing alienation that has characterised industrial capitalist production. It is important to recognise, however, that in many cases these colonisations are only partial. They may stress or strengthen links between employees and their colleagues, their equipment or their work, but often they do so by stressing the separation of these things from the firm itself (see for example Harris 1987).

COTTAGE INDUSTRY

Cottage industry is production, within the household, of things intended for sale, using household labour and social relations (see for example Medick 1976). I will describe it in terms of cloth production in England. This was one of the first areas of manufacture to become intensified and industrialised, and at the beginning of the rise of industrial capitalism cottage industry was the most common form of cloth production. This form of production has been portrayed in Neil Smelser's *Social change in the Industrial Revolution* (1959), on which this discussion draws.[7]

In its basic form, production occurred within the household using its own tools and equipment and working on its own raw materials, and was undertaken by household members: 'the father wove and apprenticed his sons into weaving. The mother was responsible for preparatory processes; in general she spun, taught the daughters how to spin, and allocated the … [subsidiary tasks] among the children' (Smelser 1959: 54–5).[8] The cloth was then sold to a merchant. This basic pattern was widespread and durable. It is the cottage-craftsman system that Esther Goody (1982: 12) describes in Yorkshire woollen manufacture in the eighteenth century, and it was still being practised in Europe long after the bulk of textile production had been mechanised, as is illustrated by Louise Tilly's (1984) description of linen weaving in northern France around 1900.

For two reasons, producers were not alienated from production. First, they controlled production in a number of ways. As I have just noted, they used their own tools, equipment and raw materials. Likewise, producers controlled the pace and timing of production, which was subordinated to their needs rather than to the dmands of some outside agent, whether an employer or the market (though obviously producers were likely to be sensitive to price and demand, as well as to their own needs). Weaving families routinely had farm holdings as well, and produced cloth as a subsidiary employment (Thirsk 1978), as one of a number of occupations, some for money and some not, that together provided for their subsistence (e.g. Kumar 1988; Thompson 1967). This was a durable practice. Many of the northern French linen weavers in the early twentieth century that Tilly (1984) describes produced cloth in the winter and worked in agriculture in the summer.

Secondly, the organisation of production was embedded in the household structure, and the cloth that resulted embodied the identities of the household members that structure defined and linked. The obligation to labour and the discipline used to coordinate and regulate production were based on the durable relationships between people in the household. The son who helped his father weave was helping the man who had produced much of the food the child ate, who oversaw his up-bringing and who was training him in his craft, who would have a say in his marriage, who would bequeath property to the boy in his old age and who, in time, the boy would help bury (e.g. Tilly 1984). Whether the son loved his father or resented him, he was bound to him in enduring ways.

This co-operation reflected that mixture of affective and utilitarian motives that characterises systems in which economic and social relations are intertwined. Co-operation reflected the cultural value placed on mutual ties and obligations among family in the household, and so had a moral dimension. Equally, subsistence was sufficiently tenuous that need drove family members to each other. Segalen's (1983: 78) point about French rural households is apt: 'The household had to produce in order to live, and often only lived in order to produce, production guaranteeing the perpetuation of the human grouping.' In addition, common labour practices obliged parents and children to look to each other for support. Training in most occupations occurred only within the household, even in crafts with formal apprenticeship (Rule 1987: 100–1). Thus, children who wanted to acquire skills had to look to their parents; parents who wanted to secure their children's futures had to train them themselves. Similarly, when adults sought labour to assist the household, generally they looked to their own children. It is true that prosperous households frequently employed workers to assist in production, but such a household was unlikely to treat them as impersonal labourers. Instead, they lived with the family. And aside from family members, workers who lived with their employers 'were probably the largest element in the labour force' in the sixteenth and early seventeenth centuries (Beier 1987: 23). This is how Mervyn James (1974: 23; see also Beier 1987: 24–5) describes the relationship between employee and household among middling farming families in the Durham area in the sixteenth and seventeenth centuries:

> Servants were incorporated in the family, being housed, fed and clothed, as well as paid wages, in return for their 'fidelity' and 'service'; and the developed Puritan (and Catholic) morality of the post-Reformation period required the householder to treat them as he would his children, and be responsible for their moral and spiritual, as well as material, welfare.

Thus, while need and desire drove family members to look to each other in producing their livelihoods, the general form and content of their relations applied to the household as a whole, not just to the family members within it. The things the household produced bore the mark of those relations.

PUTTING OUT

In the simplest form of putting out, a merchant capitalist would supply a weaver, for instance, with yarn and specify the size and quality of the desired cloth as well as when the work was to be completed. The merchant might also provide yarn fixed to a frame and ready for weaving, and in extreme cases even the loom (Smelser 1959: 59). In any event, the cloth was woven by the weaver in his own household with the assistance of his family. The merchant would collect it, inspect it, pay the weaver and perhaps supply yarn for another cloth. Putting out emerged in part because merchants sought greater control over production in order to assure a more regular and uniform supply of cloths than independent producers supplied. In cotton production putting out began to appear late in the seventeenth century and was common by the middle of the eighteenth (Smelser 1959: 58). A similar system was developing among London craft workers from the middle of the sixteenth century (Davis 1966: 61). In the more crowded guilds prosperous members who owned retail shops began to provide materials to poorer artisans without shops to be made up into goods, which they would then buy back for sale in their shops.

The technical operations of cloth production in the putting-out system were comparable to those of cottage industry, but the social relations were different. Putting out entailed a differentiation of production and control that reduced the autonomy of the producer, and hence led to a greater alienation from the process and product than had existed under cottage industry.[9] For instance, the producer did not own the yarn being woven and had to surrender the cloth to the merchant. Perhaps more important, the coordination exercised by the merchant tended to fragment production and reduce workers' influence on the product: the people who carded and spun were not likely to weave, those who wove sometimes did not put the yarn to the frame but received it already made into warps. Similarly, producers were less able to subordinate production to their needs and desires. This was because the merchant began to control the timing of production, that being one of the attractions putting out had for merchants. It was also because the merchant indicated the nature and quality of the cloth to be produced and could penalise producers if they did not conform. And, of course, the weaver did not control the disposition of the finished cloth. Once producers agreed to take work put out by a merchant, they lost their influence over the social and market relations with the consumer.[10]

Even though putting-out workers were more alienated from process and product than were independent household producers, this alienation was only partial. Although raw materials belonged to the merchant, most weavers continued to own the tools and equipment used to transform the yarn into cloth. And although weavers had to produce within the time specified, they were able to exercise some discretion about the pace of the work. This partial loss of control over production meant the product was less of an embodiment of the producers than it was in cottage industry. However, the relationships the product embodied remained the web of household relationships in which production took place.

The putting-out system was not simply a passing stage in the evolution of industrial capitalism, but has continued up to the present. It is important to the making of objects that carry an aura of hand-craft production, such as Harris Tweed cloth (cf. Ennew 1982). Equally, it is important in many ordinary branches of industry (Allen & Wolkowitz 1987; Boris & Daniels 1989; Pennington & Westover 1989), though modern forms do not make use of household labour and household relations in the way that earlier forms did. In most branches of industry, however, its heyday is over, as it was superseded by forms of factory production, to which I now turn.

EARLY FACTORY PRODUCTION

Factory production emerged because it allowed the capitalist greater supervision, and so greater control over the quality and pace of production (see Marglin 1974; for a more detailed discussion of the emergence of factory production, see Robinson & Briggs 1991). With its emergence, production moved out of the household to a separate place under the control of the capitalist rather than the producer, and it took place within commodity relations rather than household relations, though the degree of these changes varied over the history of factory production, the subject of this and the next section.

Much early factory production was 'patriarchal' (see Staples 1987). Like household production, it incorporated household relationships and identities. Like modern factory production, it entailed production outside of the household. Briefly, in typical patriarchal production capitalists employed adult male contractors who agreed to produce a specified number of items within a specified time and were paid according to an established price structure. These contractors then hired their own assistants, 'mostly – though not exclusively – family members or relatives' (Staples 1987: 68). Thus, two sets of relations co-existed. First was a commodity relationship between capitalist and contractor; second was a familial relationship, tinged with monetary interest, between contractor and assistant.

This system appeared in the cotton-spinning factories that were established towards the end of the eighteenth century. Factory owners hired spinners, who in turn employed their own assistants, and usually 'the spinners chose their wives, children, near relatives'. This practice was regularised in the craft rules of the time, which 'explicitly prohibited members from recruiting assistants outside the narrowly defined classes of children, brothers, orphan nephews, etc.' (Smelser 1959: 189).

This pattern existed in coal mining long before textile factories were built. Mine owners employed miners at a piece rate, and miners drew on their own families for assistance. In her discussion of mine labour in the early part of the nineteenth century, Humphries explains the attraction of family members, an attraction that shows the mixture of personal and utilitarian motivation to which I have already referred. A prime attraction was that the wage paid to such an assistant did not go outside the family. In addition, such assistants were easier than strangers to supervise and control

(Humphries 1988: 106). Moreover, miners felt safer with their own families, who were more likely to come to their aid in an emergency (1988: 107). But just as miners desired assistants who were family members, so they were also compelled to look to their families, for often family labour 'was the *only* source of labour. Other helpers were simply not available' (1988: 106). Desire and need drove the family together.

Moving production to a central place allowed the capitalist to take advantage of changes in productive technology, especially early powered equipment, more readily than was possible for household producers. This led to an increasing fragmentation of the production process, so that individual producers were ceasing to shape what they made by the exercise of their skill, and became instead routine operatives. Smelser (1959: 128) writes, for instance, that the introduction of the self-acting spinning mule in the 1820s 'substituted the role of a "minder" for that of a highly skilled spinner'. And as the machines belonged to the factory owner, workers were less likely to own their tools and equipment. Moreover, mechanisation meant that workers 'became more subordinated to a work discipline, because the power-source lay in steam, not in their own muscles; they could no longer pace their industry in the cottage or even work sixteen hours a day during the last days of the week in a hand-mule shed to make up for a leisurely Monday and Tuesday' (Smelser 1959: 118).

As this indicates, alienation of the product from the producers was greater than it had been. To begin with, the patriarchal factory system brought about important changes in the social relationships in which production took place. The addition of the relationship between owner and contractor added a further layer of authority and control, and a clear commodity relation, to the familial relation that usually bound contractor and assistants. In addition, there were changes in the relationship between workers and production. With the moving of production to a central place, the factory-owning capitalist could oversee the production process more closely than the putting-out merchant.[11] And in at least some industries capitalists used rates of pay in a way that reduced workers' ability to set their own pace. Capitalists did so by setting rates at a level that would allow workers 'their customary subsistence *if* they worked hard and *drove their assistants to similar heroic efforts*' (Humphries 1988: 106).

At the same time, attacks on the system whereby apprenticeship was regulated by craft associations undercut the control by skilled workers over their production. In 1814 Parliament repealed sections of the Statute of Artificers of 1564 and thereby allowed 'free' apprenticeships, unregulated by craft associations and therefore freely manipulable by employers (see Bauman 1982: 56–9). Rule (1987) shows that this was a conscious attack on the idea that skill and the use of it for gain was a possession of workers that was regulated by associations of workers, rather than subordinated to the impersonal market.

Artisan groups claimed that skilled workers possessed the right to exercise their trade to earn a reasonable living, and that collectively they had the right to regulate themselves and the exercise of their skills. Craft custom was taken as the guide to work practices and the employer was not expected to interfere with the production process 'so long as properly made goods were produced to the quantum regarded as normal by the trade' (Rule 1987: 109). Artisans resisted the interference by employers with their right to regulate their skills just as they disciplined fellow artisans who violated craft custom (1987: 112). Thus, while artisans' rights were exercised by individuals, they were maintained by the craft as a group, based on a common artisanal identity that cut across the links between specific workers, their assistants and their employers.[12]

The right of individual workers to earn from their trade was acquired by serving an apprenticeship. This provided training in the skills of the craft and regulated entry to the trade, and so protected the property of skill of those who possessed it.[13] Just as important, the apprentice acquired special language, habits and clothing, the knowledge of artisanal custom and ritual and of the obligations of artisans to each other, and a sense of the honour and dignity of the craft (Rule 1987: 108–10). In short, the apprentice acquired a durable identity and set of relationships in a craft group, which marked those who were to be admitted to the body of people recognised as regular artisans (those with the right to live by their trade).

The legal abolition of formal craft control, then, meant that workers as a group, collectively possessing and being possessed by their productive skills, were being replaced by individual workers negotiating the sale of their labouring time. As Bauman (1982: 8) notes, the repeal of the Statute of Artificers changed 'beyond recognition' the 'very character of apprenticeship as an initiation into a totality of patterned existence of the closely-knit trade community: the craftsmen's resistance ... was a struggle for the restoration of such a community'.

Thompson's discussion of the change in the ways that people thought about time brings out many of the respects in which the shift to early factory production increased the alienation of workers from their work. He argues that under the older, pre-factory regime time was frequently defined by the task at hand and its inherent rhythms, so that the work-day 'lengthens or contracts according to the task' (1967: 60). However, the spread of centralised manufacturing increased the capitalist's desire to coordinate diverse production tasks; the spread of powered machinery reduced the producers' ability to regulate the intensity of their work; the breakdown of craft control meant that workers were selling their labour power rather than their product. The result was a novel understanding of work time. No longer a reflection of the task at hand, it came to be a factor, beyond the control of workers, that governed and coordinated the pace and processes of production, and so came to be the governor of the worker.[14]

MODERN FACTORY PRODUCTION

The patriarchal system gradually gave way to modern factory production, often through a set of intermediate stages (e.g. Edwards 1979: ch. 6; Hareven 1982; Staples 1987). This entailed replacing the capitalist's supervision of production with direct control, and subordinating the worker to production (see Stone 1975). Modern factory production eliminated the older familial and craft-community relations between workers and their assistants, as it eliminated much of the need for skilled work. With the emergence of the modern factory system, workers were less likely to experience themselves as part of a durable web of relations that defined them in terms of their links with their co-workers and their tasks. Instead, they were more likely to experience themselves and their co-workers as independent entities. Increasingly, workers were alienated from production and its products.[15]

The rise of the modern factory extended the fragmentation of the production process that had begun in the patriarchal system, in spite of recurrent efforts by workers to circumvent the factory regime and maintain some control over their work (see for example Penn 1985). Spurred by Braverman's *Labor and monopoly capital* (1974), greatest attention has been paid to the fragmentation of planning and execution. Changes in mechanisation and the organisation of the production process generally reflected the interests of the capitalist in producing a certain kind of object in a certain way. The result was that the modern factory became a purpose-built tool that embodied the interests of its owners and designers. This removed control from workers and vested it in management and in the physical setting and paraphernalia of production that management controls. This is most pronounced in production using assembly lines to make objects from interchangeable parts, and it produces what Edwards calls the 'technical control' of labour. This sort of control 'is embedded in the physical and technological aspects of production and is built into the design of machines and the industrial architecture of the plant' (Edwards 1979: 131).

The classic examples of this were the early Ford Motor Company plants on Bellevue Avenue in Detroit and, after 1910, at Highland Park (this discussion draws on Hounshell 1984: ch. 6). In conventional mass manufacture all operations of a particular sort, such as milling, had been carried out in a single department to which parts were brought for the job. As a result, the factory was organised spatially around the different sorts of operations, and hence the different skills, tools and sets of workers used in them. In the Ford factories, however, machinery was located according to its place in the production process. Equally, much production conventionally used machinery that could perform a range of operations, determined by the operator. Ford, however, used machinery designed to perform only one job, extremely efficiently (cf. Braverman 1974: 110–12). Thus, both the design of the machinery and the spatial arrangement of production embodied as rigorously as possible, and furthered as much as possible, the production goals of Ford management. Work discipline was built into the very factory itself.

Likewise, in conventional mass assembly workers performed a range of operations to assemble one unit at a time from parts provided for them at their work station. However, the development of the moving assembly line eliminated the co-operation and interaction that static assembly entailed, and limited each worker to a single task. It also forced workers to work at a uniform and more efficient pace. The result was an extraordinary increase in output per worker (Hounshell 1984: 248). These various innovations mechanised production and radically changed the workers' tasks. The result was that 'the machine ultimately set the pace of work... . This was the essence of the assembly line and all the machinery that fed it' (1984: 252–3).

I have focused on the assembly line because it makes especially clear some of the distinguishing features of modern factory production. These were the breaking down of production into more and simpler steps and the increasing subordination of the worker to the production process. These changes further decreased workers' control over production and decreased the likelihood that people would be linked in durable ways to their co-workers.

Regarding the first of these, the skill needed to guide production that had buttressed the independent authority of the producer under the patriarchal system became built into the material work environment. Concern with the making of things became the province of managers and engineers, while workers became sources of labour power for specific lengths of time spent on specific operations. The modern factory also altered the social relationships among workers. Under the patriarchal system workers needed to interact with each other if production was to proceed smoothly. Under the new system, the plant was designed as much as possible to eliminate that need. Workers had to interact only with the machines they tended or the parts they assembled. This facilitated the disappearance of the family teams that existed under patriarchal capitalism. Employees who worked next to each other at Ford did so because each had a commodity relationship with the company, not because each had a kinship relationship with co-workers. Production could be, as indeed it was, carried out with strangers.

Not all production under the modern factory regime is as mechanical as the moving assembly line, and in fact many companies abandoned rigid production systems. Even Ford abandoned single-purpose production for a more flexible system in the 1920s (Hounshell 1984: ch. 7). However, replacement systems tend to enmesh workers in a set of bureaucratic rules and procedures and pay incentive systems that structure the work situation in a way that is less concrete but no less effective than the physical structuring of the Ford line (see Edwards 1979: ch. 8). Such systems may give individual workers somewhat more control than did the moving assembly line, but they further weaken the bonds between workers. They often replace the indifference of the Ford line with hostility, encouraging 'workers to pursue their self-interests in a narrow way as individuals' (Edwards 1979: 145) and so replacing 'antagonism between worker and shop management' with 'lateral conflict' (Burawoy 1982: 72).[16]

In the 1980s many were arguing that it was necessary to reduce the alienation of workers from their work. For example, in *Vanguard management*, an influential book of the time, James O'Toole urged executives to see workers as 'stakeholders', with a legitimate interest in and claim on the company that employs them. He reported favourably on companies that subsidised ownership of stock by their employees, that involved workers in corporate decisions, that gave them freedom and responsibility to determine their own work practices, that encouraged them to see the way that their work related to the overall goals and operations of the company, and so forth (1985: esp. ch. 4).[17] Many of these policies could make going to work more pleasurable and interesting, but only a handful of companies have instituted them, even though they have been advocated since the beginning of this century (Edwards 1979: 91–7). But these policies would not reduce alienation to the levels of the pre-modern regime, for workers would remain confronted with the extensive division of labour that reduces their impact on production, and they would continue to produce with others in social relationships derived from the workplace itself rather than pre-existing structures.

IMPERIUM

To flesh out and qualify my schematic discussion of modern production, it is useful to look at one company in some detail, 'Imperium', David Halle's pseudonymous chemical plant in northern New Jersey in the late 1970s.[18] Halle's study is useful because the plant he describes is very different from the Ford line that I have used to exemplify modern factory production. Further, Halle (1984: 145–9) challenges Braverman's assertions about the loss of worker control, attending closely to the ways in which workers seek to evade management control and its attendant impersonality, and so exercise their own control over production and introduce personal relations into the plant. (Harris's [1987] study of an English chemical works includes many of the points I make here.)

The Imperium plant was designed to incorporate the most modern production equipment. Although management issued detailed instructions on how work was to be done, workers exercised significant control because of their collective knowledge of how the plant worked. Two sorts of this knowledge were especially important (Halle 1984: 119–25). First, workers knew the quirks of their equipment better than did management, especially the effects of the many, minor and often unrecorded modifications that had been made. Secondly, and more importantly, workers learned shortcuts, operating practices that were easier and quicker than the formal production instructions, but that produced a product that satisfied the laboratory technicians who assessed the output.

> In many cases workers come across such devices by accident. A chief [of a production team] forgets to do something the formula card [that is supposed to dictate procedure] says he should do – cooling slowly or adding an ingredient – and the laboratory does not comment, so the 'accident' becomes a technical discovery, a useful component of the men's practical knowledge (1984: 121).

In a tacit agreement with management, which left them alone so long as output was regular and met specifications, workers used this knowledge to organise production to increase the amount of free time they could spend on social activities within the plant (1984:139). To a degree, workers could control production. This was a furtive and restricted influence, however, compared to the overtly recognised and extensive control exercised by the artisans that Rule (1987) describes, or by household weavers taking jobs put out by merchant capitalists.

Equally, the relationships of Imperium workers with each other were not merely reflections of their common commodity relationship with their employer. Instead, many workers were linked through kinship, for membership in family and friendship networks was important for being hired in the first place. Thus, Halle found (1984: 5) that of 121 blue-collar workers, 37 per cent, were closely related: 'there are twenty-three brothers and seven brothers-in-law. Ten men are cousins, twelve fathers or sons, and six uncles or nephews.' Not only were personal relationships often important for getting a job, workers also engaged in intense social interaction with their fellows. They spent much of the work day talking to one another, about 'work, sports, fishing, hunting, food, politics, sex, and local gossip', they played cards and they cooked and ate together (1984: 141; cf. Roy [1960] for clothing workers).

These relationships, however, are of a different order from those among workers in older regimes. First, the relationships developed in the workplace frequently did not extend outside the plant. This was particularly so for married workers, who 'spend more and more time with their families. They tend not to stop at the tavern after work or to spend much of their leisure time with male friends from work' (1984: 44). This tendency to restrict work-based friendships to the workplace is illustrated by Goldthorpe and his colleagues in their study of households in the industrial new town of Luton, Bedfordshire. They found (1969: 88) that less than a fifth of the people that couples identified as friends were also work-mates. They note (1969: 90), however, that 'white-collar couples draw more heavily on friends made through work' than do blue-collar couples (see also Hunt & Satterlee 1986). Allan (1979: 70) suggests that members of the working class tend to 'limit their sociable relations [to] particular social contexts and structures', so that work-mates remain work-mates and tend not to become friends.[19] It appears, however, that when groups of workers seek to challenge existing working practices and relations, they may very well increase the inter-personality of work relationships and even extend them into time spent away from work (e.g. Sacks 1984).

Likewise, pre-existing relations among Imperium workers had a different meaning from those among workers in older systems of production. Though many at Imperium were related and perhaps even beholden to relatives who helped them get jobs at the plant, kin ties did not determine the actual relationships within which production took place. Production relations did not reflect interpersonal relations. The fathers who got jobs for their sons did so as a favour, not because they had to draw on close kin in order to produce; the sons whose fathers worked at Imperium did not work for their fathers, they worked for Imperium; they were not paid by their fathers, they were paid by Imperium. Here, then, sociality was added on (somewhat furtively) to the more purely economic relations that existed at Imperium; it did not permeate economic relations in the way that occurred in older production regimes.

Halle himself makes this point when he suggests a reason for the reduced importance of family relations at work and the greater alienation of work relations from
other interpersonal relations. People had less need for each other, a situation whose
origin often lies outside the organisation of production itself. He writes:

> The development of government welfare and insurance programs ... and company-
> financed fringe benefits such as medical insurance and pensions, together with a steady
> income from a stable job, have removed much of the economic rationale for those old
> relations of cooperation and solidarity. People help each other less, mostly because
> there is less need to do so (Halle 1984: 47).

In other words, as basic economic survival comes to depend more and more on transactions with impersonal and bureaucratic structures, economy becomes disembedded
from society and relationships at work become more and more alienated from interpersonal relations (see also Hareven 1982).

ALIENATION IN PRODUCTION

I have described how production and the things produced gradually became more
alienated from producers. With the passage of time workers had less control over production and were less likely to be linked to each other in durable relationships. As a
part of this process, people's involvement in a key area of life took a new form. In the
early system of cottage industry, people were involved in production according to
their identity within the durable relationships that sprang from their membership
in the family. However, with time people's involvement in production was increasingly likely to be based on attributes seen as alienable from the individual. This is
most clearly evident in the emergence of the idea that the worker is only a provider of
labour power that can be bought and sold like any other commodity, and that, like any
other commodity, is deployed at the discretion of the firm. Like the field of economy
more generally, production became an area of life independent of people's social identities and obligations, with a distinct rationale, economic gain (Crowley [1974] and
Silver [1990] describe the emergence of this attitude in the eighteenth century).

What people were experiencing, then, was the emergence of a new understanding of persons and their work (e.g. Calhoun 1982: esp. 65), one that sees persons as
having two distinct aspects, a core and a periphery. The core is made up of 'things
which people believe to be real things, which are in an important sense thought to
be internal to the individual or continuous with the individual as a concrete being'
(Barnett & Silverman 1979: 51). This inalienable self is engaged in durable, inalienable identities and relationships – most notably those of the family but also such
identities as nationality, race and gender. Further, because of the importance of these
relations, people are likely to experience this core in a relational way – at least in comparison to the peripheral self. That is, although the core is internal to the individual,
it springs in part from the relationships that help constitute it.

The periphery, on the other hand, is made up of a set of less integral attributes that relate to one's performance at specific transient tasks. This self is pertinent in relationships among 'individuals (more or less) freely entering into agreements to do certain things in accordance with certain standards and rules' (Barnett & Silverman 1979: 51), such as at work. And in the context of these relations, people experience each other not relationally but autonomously, as independent individuals. This self is evaluated, commodity-like, in terms of its utility to the employer. Because their involvement in production came to be based on their suitability for the job, people therefore became substitutable one for another. Describing their research at ChemCo, their pseudonym for an agricultural chemicals factory in East Anglia, Nichols and Beynon (1977: 193) report that 'the men we talked to … knew that they, as individuals, weren't really needed by ChemCo – that others could come in "off the street" and do their job. They were told this day after day'. This is just another way of saying that in employment relations people are but fungible suppliers of labour power, assessed on the quality of what they have to sell.

As might be expected, workers frequently resisted these changes.[20] Textile workers responded with outbursts of violence against their employers and the machinery they were expected to use, most spectacularly in the Luddite movement in the early 1800s. Skilled artisans agitated against the repeal of the apprenticeship statutes and disrupted the work of those who violated customary practices. When modern factories emerged workers responded with growing unionisation and strikes, and less spectacularly by simply quitting.[21] Less spectacularly still, workers frequently found informal ways to assert their control over production and to introduce sociality into the impersonality of the firm.

CONCLUSION

As I said at the outset, my goal here has been to show that we can produce an anthropological understanding of Western societies by applying models developed in the study of non-Western societies. In this article I have used a Maussian model to organise an idealised sketch of changes in the organisation of production over the past few centuries. This model is particularly suited to my goal because it has been shaped by the study of people involved in both non-capitalist, village-based social relations and capitalist social relations.[22] Such studies are provocative, for they raise questions and point to problems that are much less apparent to those who study only the organisation of economic life in the modern West.

In particular, they highlight Mauss's point that the rise of industrial capitalism has not resulted in the wholesale transformation of society to conform with a commodity logic. Instead, that rise has resulted in a greater differentiation of life into more personal and more impersonal spheres. It is likely that this sort of differentiation has always existed (see for example Bloch & Parry 1989). However, with the rise of industrial capitalism it seems to have become more pronounced both in fact and in people's perceptions. This is particularly clear in the case of the core economic activities of production and exchange. What I have described for early forms of production held generally for early forms of exchange: people dealt with each other in ways that reflected their positions within an encompassing set of durable personal relations and obligations. With the passage of time, however, circulation became more clearly differentiated into separate spheres of market exchange and gift transactions, just as (though I have not pursued this point) production became more clearly differentiated into the spheres of mass production and artistic or craft production. To recall a point made earlier, the first of each of these pairs is seen to be impersonal and regulated by abstract forces such as 'the market', while the second is seen to be personal and regulated by personal forces like 'affection', 'creativity' or bonds between people. And as I have also argued, this has been accompanied by a differentiation of the self. On the one hand is the impersonal self, an autonomous entity linked by external necessity to impersonal institutions like the state and the firm; while on the other is the inner self, a relational entity linked to and defined by personal others.

I will close by suggesting that the progressive, linked differentiations that I have described pose an important problem for members of society, a problem in which the growing impersonality of production plays a key part. The value that we place on personal identities and relations (indeed, the very notion that these are distinctive) is in an important way a consequence of the growth of impersonal economic relations. However, the same impersonal practises and beliefs that lead us to value these personal aspects of our lives also threaten them and make them problematic. This is most apparent when people transact objects with each other as part of personal relationships, transactions that are most visible in formal gift-giving but that also include more mundane sharings and givings, such as those involved in keeping house (see for example Barker 1972; Corrigan 1989; Ellis 1983; Murcott 1983).

These transactions are important for generating and sustaining personal relations. However, the objects available to us are overwhelmingly things that we construe as impersonal commodities, produced in impersonal firms and acquired in impersonal retail transactions. It is necessary, then, for people to transform the objects materially or symbolically so that they lose their impersonality and become endowed with the social identities and relations that they will affect (see for example Carrier 1990; Miller 1988). The need to undertake this sort of transformation is not unique to industrial capitalist societies (Carsten 1989). However, the greater and more insistent differentiation of life that I have described, together with the growing perception that purchased objects are impersonal commodities, means that this transformation is more urgent than it has been in the past.

In effect, I am using the Maussian model not only to suggest that there is greater differentiation of social life, but also to suggest that this differentiation means that people are increasingly likely to be confronted with the task of negotiating the boundary between the two realms, respectively personal and impersonal. To identify, as I have, the processes that lead to a growing alienation of people from each other, from their activities and the products of those activities in an important area of their lives, is only one part of the task of generating a Maussian account of modern society. The other part is to identify the complementary processes that allow people to appropriate the impersonal things that surround them, so that they can use those things to build and maintain their personal selves and social relationships.

NOTES

This article has benefited from comments by and conversations with Achsah Carrier, Colin Campbell, Burke Grandjean, Rosemary Harris, Tim Ingold, Paul Kingston, Jonathan Parry and Gianfranco Poggi.

1. Distinguishing them necessarilly simplifies complex bodies of work and ignores some intellectual developments at the expense of others. For instance, I ignore the recent Marxian interest in consumer culture. Miller (1987) is a nice statement of the ambiguity of the links between consumer culture studies and Marxist thought.
2. I could use a term other than alienation. The reader, however, probably would translate it mentally into 'alienation', so there would be no point.
3. 'Separation' has the corollary that the thing or person alienated from oneself is perceived as having an independent basis of existence. Broader aspects of this are described in Taussig (1977).
4. I ignore private, household production, for while it remains important (e.g. Cowan 1983; Martin 1984; Pahl 1984), its relative significance has decreased in the modern West.
5. This will not only enrich the study of Western societies. In addition, it will benefit anthropology by strengthening these models and consequently the discipline's understanding of non-Western societies (see Carrier in press).
6. As should be obvious, I dissent from the influential view that people in capitalist societies see themselves only or even overwhelmingly as independent individuals fully distinct from surrounding people and things (e.g. Strathem 1988).
7. The book has attracted criticism, but generally on theoretical and interpretative, rather than empirical, grounds (e.g. Anderson 1976; Calhoun 1982: 191–6). Anderson (1976: 325) does raise doubts about the ubiquity of the family-based production units that Smelser describes for early spinning factories, which I discuss in the section 'Early factory production', but he asserts equally that such a pattern was common in a range of industries (1976: 320, 325).
8. For a technical description of production, see Smelser (1959: 51–2); Carus-Wilson (1966 [1941]) describes historical changes in fulling, an aspect of cloth production that had moved out of the household by this time.
9. Some of the more prosperous cottage textile producers had themselves put out work to other households, particularly carding and spinning (Smelser 1959: 55–6; for other industries see Rule 1987: 102–4).
10. Thirsk (1978) suggests the existence of regional, and possibly national, markets in England in the seventeenth century, and doubtless some producers preferred a more standardised and predictable market for their wares. However, much cottage production was for local consumption, bought and sold in regulated local markets in a Web of long-standing

personal relationships (see for example Davis 1966: 4–6). This personal framework for the disposition of goods disappeared with the rise of putting out.

11. This was a part of the general concern with observation, supervision and control that accompanted the emergence of industrial capitalism. Key aspects of this in English industrialisation are described by Thompson (1967); the broader topic is described by Foucault (1979).

12. This collective control of work did not disappear in the first quarter of the nineteenth century, as Stone's (1975) description of the organisation of American steel production before the 1890s shows. More strikingly, Salaman's (1986: 45–54) description of the organisation of fire stations in the London Fire Brigade prior to 1981 echoes Rule's description of craft workers. Firemen at a station had a strong common identity: they were self-recruited, they came from a narrow cultural and social background, they spent extended periods of time in each other's company, they were relatively free of external supervision. In 1981, this cohesive body of autonomous skilled workers came under attack in the pursuit of equity by the Greater London Council, their governing body. The fire service was almost totally white and male, and the Greater London Council, issued an Equal Opportunity directive that led to the increased supervision of local stations and the centralised recruitment of new fire fighters.

13. Apprenticeships also provided some craft masters with a cheap supply of assistants, as well as the premium that many were able to charge for taking on apprentices. However, masters had to pay the costs of looking after their apprentices, which may have more than outweighed the income from their labour and premium. Certainly textile factories found them more expensive than hiring free labour (Smelser 1959: 187). However, when obligations to apprentices were reduced, employers could find apprenticeship financially attractive.

14. The subordination of workers to abstract clock time remains problematic. Roy (1960) describes how workers under a modern, repetitive production regime try to impose their own structure on their undifferentiated work time in order to give it meaning and make it tolerable. See more generally Mars's (1982) description of modern 'donkey' workers.

15. These changes were commonly associated with the development of more efficient production machinery (see for example Hounshell 1984: ch. 6). However, the changes in pottery production that Josiah Wedgwood introduced late in the eighteenth century (see Forty 1986: 30–4; McKendrick et al. 1982: ch. 3) show that important elements of the modern factory regime can emerge without significant development in mechanisation or machine technology. Further evidence that the relationship between mechanisation and alienation is complex is in Stone (1975) and Calhoun (1982: esp. 65). They note that workers were not opposed to machinery per se, but to machinery used to reduce their control over their work.

16. Obviously, work in different areas of the economy is organised in different ways (e.g. Baron & Bielby 1984; Baron et al, 1986; Baron et al, 1988). Equally, the success of this change depended to a degree on the organisation and orientation of workers themselves (e.g. Stepan-Norris & Zeitlin 1991: esp. 1178–81).

17. Braverman (1974: 445n) raises theoretical questions about the significance of reforms such as these; Blanchflower & Oswald (1988) and Kelley & Harrison (1991) raise empirical questions; Grentier (1988) describes how one such programme is used to subordinate labour and attack unions.

18. As Blauner (1964: esp. 6–7) has noted, there are important differences between continuous-process production, as in a chemical works like Imperium, and assembly production, as in plants like Highland Park. He also notes, however, that such standardised production differs fundamentally from unique-product manufacturing, such as long existed in the printing industry (1964: ch. 3).

19. Allan's observation (1979: 70) that working-class people are more likely to see their friends as 'situation-specific' approaches an important point, that the middle-class notion of friendship entails the idea that people exist independently of specific contexts, that there is a core being or personality that exists in all situations. Mauss (1985) argues that this belief in the existence of a relatively consistent and unique self is characteristic of modern industrial society. Bernstein (1971) describes the nature of such a belief and speculates on its uneven social distribution.

20. This passage only alludes to the issue of labour response to management attempts to control production. The complexities of this response are described in Brecher *et al.* (1978), Harris (1987), Penn (1985) and Price (1983).

21. At Ford's Highland Park plant in 1913, labour turnover associated with the installation of the moving assembly lines was so high that in order to achieve a net increase in the work force of 100, it was necessary to hire more than 950 workers. The other 850 refused to stay at their jobs. At the end of 1913, less man 5 per cent, of the company's 15,000 workers had been at Ford for three years or more (Hounshell 1984: 257–9; note, however, that labour turnover generally was quite high in manufacturing firms in the early twentieth century [see Jacoby 1985: 115–17]).

22. The most notable anthropologist in this regard is Gregory (1980; 1982). Of course, such studies present difficulties. For instance, they tend to exaggerate and reify differences between types of social relations by turning them into differences between kinds of societies (see Carrier in press). Bloch & Parry's (1989) and Thomas's (1991) discussions of forms of circulation in village societies show that the differences between types of society are not so profound as some Maussians seem to think.

REFERENCES

Allan, G.A. 1979. *A sociology of friendship and kinship*. London: Allen & Unwin.

Allen, S. & C. Wolkowitz 1987. *Homeworking: myth and realities*. London: Macmillan.

Anderson, M. 1976. Sociological history and the working-class family: Smelser revisited. *Social Hist.* **1**, 317–34.

Barker, D.L. 1972. Young people and their homes: spoiling and 'keeping close' in a South Wales town. *Sociol. Rev.* **20**, 569–90.

Barnett, S. & M. Silverman 1979. Separations in capitalist societies: persons, things, units and relations. In *Ideology and everyday life (eds)* S. Bamett & M. Silverman. Ann Arbor. Univ. of Michigan Press.

Baron, J.N. & W.T. Bielby 1984. The organization of work in a segmented economy. *Am. Sociol. Rev.* **49**, 454–73.

———, F.R. Dobbin & P. Devereaux Jennings 1986. War and peace: the evolution of modern personnel administration in U.S. industry. *Am. J. Sociol.* **92**, 350–83.

———, P. Devereaux Jennings & F.R. Dobbin 1988. Mission control? The development of personnel systems in U.S. industry. *Am. Sociol. Rev.* **53**, 497–514.

Bauman, Z. 1982. *Memories of class*. London: Routledge & Kegan Paul.

Beaglehole, E. 1932. *Property: a study in social psychology*. London: George Allen & Unwin.

Beier, A.L. 1987. *Masterless men: the vagrancy problem in England 1560–1640*. London: Routledge & Kegan Paul.

Bernstein, B. 1971. A sociolinguistic approach to socialization. In *Class, codes and control*, vol. 1 (ed.) B. Bernstein. London: Routledge & Kegan Paul.

Blanchflower, D.G. & A.J. Oswald 1988. Profit-related pay: prose rediscovered? *Econ. J.* **98**, 720–30.

Blauner, R. 1964. *Alienation and freedom: the factory worker and his industry*. Chicago: Univ. of Chicago Press.

Bloch, M. & J. Parry 1989. Introduction: Money and the morality of exchange. In *Money and the morality of exchange* (eds) J. Parry & M. Bloch. Cambridge: Univ. Press.

Boris, E. & C.R. Daniels (eds) 1989. *Homework: historical and contemporary perspectives on paid labor at home*. Urbana: Univ. of Illinois Press.

Braverman, H. 1974. *Labor and monopoly capital: the degradation of work in the twentieth century*. New York: Monthly Review Press.

Brecher, J. *et al.* 1978. Uncovering the hidden history of the American workplace. *Rev. radic. polit. Econ.* **10**, 4 (Winter), 1–23.

Burawoy, M. 1982. *Manufacturing consent: changes in the labor process under monopoly capitalism*. Chicago Univ. of Chicago Press.

Calhoun, C. 1982. *The question of class struggle*. Chicago: Univ. of Chicago Press.

Carrier, J.G. 1990. Reconciling commodities and personal relations in industrial society. *Theory & Soc.* **19**, 579–98.

—— 1991. Gifts, commodities and social relations: a Maussian view of exchange. *Social. Forum* **6**, 119–36.

—— in press. Occidentalism: the world turned upside-down. *Am. Ethnol.*

Carsten, J. 1989. Cooking money: gender and the symbolic transformation of means of exchange in a Malay fishing community. In *Money and the morality of exchange* (eds) J. Parry & M. Bloch. Cambridge: Univ. Press.

Carus-Wilson, E.M. 1966 (1941). An industrial revolution of the thirteenth century. In *Essays in economic history* (ed.) E.M. Carus-Wilson. New York: St Martins Press.

Corrigan, P. 1989. Gender and the gift: the case of the family clothing economy. *Sociology* **23**, 513–34.

Cowan, R.S. 1983. *More work for mother*. New York: Basic Books.

Crowley, J.E. 1974. *This Sheba, self: the conceptualization of economic life in eighteenth century America*. Baltimore: Johns Hopkins Univ. Press.

Davis, D. 1966. A *history of shopping*. London: Routledge & Kegan Paul.

Edwards, R. 1979. *Contested terrain: the transformation of the workplace in the twentieth century*. New York: Basic Books.

Ellis, R. 1983. The way to a man's heart: food in the violent home. In *The sociology of food and eating* (ed.) A. Murcott. Aldershot: Gower.

Ennew, J. 1982. Harris tweed: construction, retention and representation of a cottage industry. In *From craft to industry: the ethnography of proto-industrial cloth production* (ed.) E. Goody. Cambridge: Univ. Press.

Forty, A. 1986. *Objects of desire*. London: Thames & Hudson.

Foucault, M. 1979. *Discipline and punish: the birth of the prison*. New York: Random House.

Godelier, M. 1977. *Perspectives in Marxist anthropology*. Cambridge: Unvi. Press.

Goldthorpe, J.H., D. Lockwood, F. Bechhofer & J. Platt 1969. *The affluent worker in the class structure*. Cambridge: Univ. Press.

Goody, E. 1982. Introduction. In *From craft to industry: the ethnography of proto-industrial cloth production* (ed.) E. Goody. Cambridge: Univ. Press.

Granovetter, M. 1985. Economic action and social structure: the problem of embeddedness. *Am.J. Sociol.* **91**, 481–510.

Gregory, C.A. 1980. Gifts to men and gifts to God: gift exchange and capital accumulation in contemporary Papua. *Man* (N.S.) **15**, 626–52.

———— 1982. *Gifts and commodities*. London: Academic Press.

Grenier, G.J. 1988. *Inhuman relations: quality circles and anti-unionism in American industry*. Philadelphia: Temple Univ. Press.

Halle, D. 1984. *America's working man: work, home, and politics among blue-collar property owners*. Chicago: Univ. of Chicago Press.

Hareven, T.K. 1982. *Family time and industrial time: the relationship between the family and work in a New England industrial community*. New York: Cambridge Univ. Press.

Harris, R. 1987. *Power and powerlessness in industry: an analysis of the social relations of production*. London: Tavistock.

Hindess, B. & P.Q. Hirst 1975. *Pre-capitalist modes of production*. London: Routledge & Kegan Paul.

Hounshell, D.A. 1984. *From the American system to mass production, 1800–1932*. Baltimore: Johns Hopkins Univ. Press.

Humphries, J. 1988. Protective legislation, the capitalist state and working-class men: the case of the 1842 Mines Regulation Act. In *On work* (ed.) R.E. Pahl. Oxford: Basil Blackwell.

Hunt, G. & S. Satterlee 1986. Cohesion and division: drinking in an English village. *Man* (N.S.) **21**, 521–37.

Jacoby, S.M. 1985. *Employing bureaucracy: managers, unions and the transformation of work in American industry, 1900–1945*. New York: Columbia Univ. Press.

James, M. 1974. *Family, lineage and civil society*. Oxford: Clarendon Press.

Kahn, J.S. 1980. *Minangkabau social formations: Indonesian peasants and the world-economy*. Cambridge: Univ. Press.

———— & J.R. Llobera (eds) 1981. *The anthropology of pre-capitalist societies*. London: Macmillan.

Kelley, M.R. & B. Harrison 1991. Unions, technology, and labor-management cooperation. In *Unions and economic competitiveness* (eds) L. Mishel & P. Voos. New York: M.E. Sharpe.

Kumar, K. 1988. From work to employment and unemployment: the English experience. In *On work* (ed.) R.E. Pahl. Oxford: Basil Blackwell.

McKendrick, N., J. Brewer & J.H. Plumb 1982. *The birth of a consumer society*. Bloomington: Indiana Univ. Press.

Marglin, S.A. 1974. What do bosses do? The origins and functions of hierarchy in capitalist production. *Rev. radic. polit. Econ.* **6**, 33–60.

Mars, G. 1982. *Cheats at work: an anthropology of workplace crime*. London: George Allen & Unwin.

Martin, B. 1984. 'Mother wouldn't like it'; housework as magic. *Theory, Cult. Soc.* **2**, 2, 19–36.

Mauss, M. 1985 (1938). A category of the human mind: the notion of person; the notion of self (trans.) W.D. Halls. In *The category of the person* (eds) M. Carrithers, S. Collins & S. Lukes. Cambridge: Univ. Press.

—— 1990. *The gift: the form and reason for exchange in archaic societies (trans.) W.D. Halls*. London: Routledge.

Medick, H. 1976. The proto-industrial family economy: the structural function of household and family during the transition from peasant society to industrial capitalism. *Social Hist.* **1**, 291–315.

—— & D.W. Sabean (eds) 1984. *Interest and emotion: essays in the study of family and kinship*. Cambridge: Univ. Press.

Miller, D. 1987. *Material culture and mass consumption*. Oxford: Basil Blackwell.

—— 1988. Appropriating the state on the council estate. *Man* (N.S.) **23**, 353–72.

Murcott, A. 1983. Cooking and the cooked. In *The sociology of food and eating* (ed.) A. Murcott. Aldershot: Gower.

Nichols, T. & H. Beynon 1977. *Living with capitalism: class relations in the modern factory*. London: Routledge & Kegan Paul.

O'Toole, J. 1985. *Vanguard management: redesigning the corporate future*. Garden City: Doubleday & Company.

Pahl, R.E. 1984. *Divisions of labour*. Oxford: Basil Blackwell.

Parry, J. 1986. *The gift*, the Indian gift and the 'Indian gift'. *Man* (N.S.) **21**, 453–73.

Penn, R. 1985. *Skilled workers in the class structure*. Cambridge: Univ. Press.

Pennington, S. & B. Westover 1989. *A hidden workforce: homeworkers in England, 1850–1985*. Basingstoke: Macmillan.

Polanyi, K. 1957. *The great transformation: the political and economic origins of our time*. Boston: Beacon Press.

Price, R. 1983. The labour process and labour history. *Social hist.* **8**, 57–75.

Robinson, R.V. & C.M. Briggs 1991. The rise of factories in ninetenth-century Indianapolis. *Am. J. Socio.* **97**, 622–56.

Roy, D.F. 1960. Banana time: job satisfaction and informal interaction. *Hum. Org.* **18**, 158–68.

Rule, J. 1987. The property of skill in the period of manufacture. In *The historical meanings of work* (ed.) P. Joyce. Cambridge: Univ. Press.

Sacks, K. 1984. Kinship and class consciousness: family values and work experience among hospital workers in an American Southern town. In *Interest and emotion: essays in the study of family and kinship* (eds) H. Medick & D.W. Sabean. Cambridge: Univ. Press.

Salaman, G. 1986. *Working*. London: Tavistock.

Schneider, D. 1980. *American kinship: a cultural account* (2nd edn). Chicago: Univ. of Chicago Press.

Segalen, M. 1983. *Love and power in the peasant family*. Oxford: Basil Blackwell.

Silver, A. 1990. Friendship in commercial society: eighteenth-century social theory and modern sociology. *Am. J. of Sociol.* **95**, 1474–1504.

Smelser, N. 1959. *Social change in the industrial revolution*. Chicago: Univ. of Chicago Press.

Staples, W.G. 1987. Technology, control, and the social organization of work at a British hardware firm, 1791–1891. *Am. J. Sociol.* **93**, 62–88.

Stepan-Norris, J. & M. Zeitlin 1991. 'Red' unions and 'bourgeois' contracts? *Am. J. Sociol.* **96**, 1151–200.

Stone, K. 1975. The origins of job structures in the steel industry. In *Labor market segmentation* (eds) R.C. Edwards, M. Reich & D. Gordon. Lexington, MA: D.C. Heath.

Strathern, M. 1988. *The gender of the gift: problems with women and problems with society in Melanesia*. Berkeley: Univ. of California Press.

Taussig, M. 1977. The genesis of capitalism amongst a South American peasantry: Devil's labor and the baptism of money. *Comp. Stud. Soc. Hist.* **19**, 130–55.

Thirsk, J. 1978. *Economic policy and projects: the development of a consumer society in early modern England*. Oxford: Clarendon Press.

Thomas, N. 1991. *Entangled objects: exchange, material culture and colonialism in the Pacific*. Cambridge, MA: Harvard Univ. Press.

Thompson, E.P. 1967. Time, work discipline and industrial capitalism. *Past and Present* **38**, 56–98.

Tilly, L.A. 1984. Linen was their life: family survival strategies and parent-child relations in nineteenth-century France. In *Interest and emotion: essays on the study of family and kinship* (eds) H. Medick & D.W. Sabean. Cambridge: Univ. Press.

Titmuss, R.M. 1971. *The gift relationship: from human blood to social policy*. London: Allen & Unwin.

Wolpe, H. (ed.) 1980. *The articulation of modes of production*. London: Routledge & Kegan Paul.

CHAPTER TEN

Gendered Meanings in Contention: Anarchomex

LESLIE SALZINGER

The phrase "women on the global assembly line" is so resonant because it implies some of the most salient aspects of transnational production – the disproportionate number of women workers on the line and management's equally disproportionate level of shop-floor control. However, it misses a set of less obvious, but equally important, dynamics. In particular, the phrase obscures the flexibility and local specificity of gendered meanings at work. In the process, it makes it impossible to imagine that gendered meanings might themselves become an object of struggle, and thus that gendered meanings on the shop floor might work against, rather than in the service of, managerial control. Yet this is precisely the situation in Anarchomex.

Anarchomex is one of Autoworld's oldest outposts in Ciudad Juárez. Like Particimex, it produces harnesses – auto electrical systems – that will later be assembled into the company's cars and trucks elsewhere on the continent. In early 1992, after a decade of operation, managers idled half the plant, choosing to cut their losses rather than to continue to deal with the shop-floor chaos that emerged every time they ran the plant full-throttle. In order to make up for the lost production, they built another, smaller, factory nearby and moved the rest of the production there. By the time I entered the plant in February, first shift had fallen from its maximum of 1,300 to 996 workers, and when I left in April it was down to 770. The back half of the plant was ghostly, with sheeted lines gathering dust beneath the fluorescent lights – shadows of grander days.

Anarchomex is a failure. Yet plant managers are knowledgeable and experienced. What went wrong? Trips from the cacophonous shop floor up to distant managerial offices suggest an answer. Anarchomex managers do not know too little; on the contrary, their failure arises from investment in rigidly gendered frameworks which keep them from addressing their workers in recognizable terms. In Anarchomex, men make up 60 percent of the workforce. However, managers remain convinced that maquila work is feminine by definition. Thus, they implicitly impugn the masculinity of the men at work on the line and, in the process, inadvertently constitute gendered meanings as a terrain of contention. In response, male workers spend their days contesting such aspersions. They claim the work as masculine territory, both in language and practice, and they address their female counterparts as potential sexual partners rather than co-workers, implicitly negating managers' claims about the work's inherently feminine nature. These ongoing struggles over the gendering of maquila work and the meaning of masculinity absorb worker energy and attention during the workday and make it impossible for managers to incorporate workers in productive terms. As a result, the struggle over gendered meanings disrupts managerial control, and the operation of gender as a discursive structure is laid bare. Who workers are at the outset is not the problem. It is the content of legitimate masculinity, and who gets to decide just what that is, which is at issue in production. Here, gender is clearly operating on the shop floor, but the assumed feminine character of global assembly undermines production itself.

DISTANT MANAGERS

. . .

The preference for women workers is reflected in all the plant's job advertisements, which continue to ask for "*operadoras*" – female line workers – even though the woman who places the ads acknowledges, with gentle understatement, "We still get men applying, because now they know we can make exceptions." This reality is reflected in the assistant personnel manager's sarcastic comment that hiring criteria begin with being female, single, eighteen to thirty years old, and having lived in the city for at least a year, but end with "having at least ten fingers."

As this comment indicates, despite managerial preferences, the exigencies of offshore production within a tight labor market for women workers ensure that the actual workforce is consistently quite far from its model. Autoworld decisions are made far away, and its Mexican outposts are often asked to crank up production on short notice. Managers in Anarchomex and Particimex alike complain about the problems caused by headquarters' sudden demands for new shipments of a particular model, after the boards set up for its production have long since been dismantled in response to prior corporate plans. Combined with the plant's large size, these production patterns frequently force Anarchomex managers to hire large numbers of workers within short time periods. This makes it impossible for those hiring to hold out for the wished-for 80 percent female workers.

In addition, although maquila jobs are understood by workers, as by managers, to be women's jobs in the aggregate, within this aggregate, workers distinguish jobs as more or less masculine or feminine. Jobs in electronics are marked as feminine,[1] whereas those which are performed standing are understood to be relatively masculine.

A manager in Auto-world's central Juárez office expresses this clearly: "Harnesses has more movement, it's done standing, the work is more aggressive. Electronics is more manual labor. Women like that work more." Local women workers, equally embedded in these narratives, tend to look elsewhere, for instance Panoptimex, before considering Anarchomex. The combination of these two processes ensures that, whether they're hiring under the pressure of full capacity or not, 60 to 65 percent of Anarchomex workers are male and 30 to 40 percent are under twenty. This predominance of available male workers does not lead Anarchomex managers to modify their notion of an ideal workforce; in fact, the situation only reinforces managers' sense that the right worker mix would fix all their shop-floor control problems.

The tenacity with which Anarchomex managers hold to this gendered model of the ideal worker is due in part to their assumption that the "right" workers can be found but not formed, but it has other roots as well. The most obvious of these is their participation, along with their colleagues in other Juárez maquilas, in transnational managerial conversations where the status of young women as paradigmatic export-processing workers remains unquestioned. Nonetheless, we have seen that maquila managers in fact do very different things with this "common sense." In the context of their glaring inability to actually fulfill the image, one might have expected that managers in Anarchomex would shift strategies. This has not been the case.

One of the central dynamics operating here is that these men define masculinity in paradigmatically patriarchal terms, and patriarchs are not who they imagine working in their plant. To the contrary, only a young woman would appropriately subject herself to the routinized, boring, low-wage work conditions they see as intrinsic to maquila production. They strongly believe that men should be "breadwinners," with all the familial authority that such a situation implies. What's more, they themselves, Mexican and American alike, enact masculinity as a position of command and responsibility, and they expect other men to behave similarly. For their workers, however, performance of this sort of masculinity is virtually impossible. The jobs at Anarchomex provide no space to exercise such qualities on the shop floor and do not pay enough to support such behavior at home. This is not something that these managers are comfortable thinking through, however, particularly the Mexicans, who see themselves as part of a responsible local elite, legitimately concerned about working-class masculinity. Thus, they frame the problem this way: Line jobs are women's jobs. If men take the jobs anyway, well, that is their responsibility, isn't it? In accepting the job, they accept women's work, and in so doing, they become exemplars of the problem of the decline of working-class masculinity. There's nothing Anarchomex managers can do about that.

This set of beliefs has different logics for Mexican and U.S. managers. Smith takes maquila wages at face value. Raising salaries is always a mistake; it only creates "bidding wars" among maquilas over workers. The Mexican personnel manager, typically, is more ambivalent about wages. "We sacrifice a lot for peanuts," he says, discussing the decision to save money on worker salaries. Despite these differences in the evaluation of the situation, they both take low maquila wages for granted, and their assessments follow upon this fact of life.

Given the unshakable fact of non-breadwinner wages, men who engage in such work are evidently impaired.[2] Marcos, the top quality manager, articulates this most clearly when he comments, "I'm twenty years old. I know that with this job I can't support a family. *Obviously*, I'm going to look for something better." He is not alone. The production manager argues that women make better maquila workers, because (real) men have "more ideas about self-improvement. It's the culture here of Mexico." In one way or another, every high-level manager in the plant I interviewed, when asked why the factory still advertised only for women, made clear his view that a man who appropriately understood his familial responsibilities wouldn't choose maquila work.

The consequence of these beliefs comes through clearly in the disparaging terms in which managers discuss male workers. As usual, the Mexicans' analysis closely tracks the unease among Juárez elites. Thus, the assistant personnel manager implies that men and women are increasingly similar among the working class. "Young men don't need much money, they live with their families. And now the man tells the woman that she needs to work." The personnel manager comments sympathetically that (working-class) "women here don't want husbands anymore." Working-class men in Juárez have lost their rightful familial place; hence they are willing to accept, and it is reasonable to offer them, emasculating jobs such as those in Anarchomex.

Smith, as usual, sees workers from a greater distance. He is less concerned with explaining this inappropriate willingness than with describing it. "I'm not sure about the Mexican male anymore. In the early days, maquilas, that was women's work. Now it's just a part of survival." Clarifying his sense that men become feminized in accepting Anarchomex jobs, he returns to his focus on workers as bodies: "Maybe part of the explanation is that the Mexican man is smaller in features, smaller in stature and fingers, so maybe here it doesn't make much difference."

Smith and his staff's basic gendered assumptions make them unwilling to accept the fact that they employ a primarily male workforce at non-breadwinner wages.[3] Thus, their shop-floor rhetorics and practices ignore the presence and belittle the experience of the men who in fact make up the greater part of their labor force. This keeps them from speaking effectively to the majority of those on the shop floor and thus ultimately undermines their control in production. These are not "mistakes" on their part. They are highly structured decisions – decisions based on what they are capable of seeing, given their own sense of masculinity, national identity, and corporate location. Thus, gender intervenes here not through the fixed selves of those hired, but through the fixed ideas of those who hire them.

IN PRODUCTION: MEANINGLESS LABORS

Against the background of these managerial frameworks, production in Anarchomex is a chaotic affair. The factory itself is an enormous barn-like structure – dingy, old, and confusing. Exposed fluorescent lights hang from cavernous, unfinished ceilings.

Walls and floors are a regulation dark gray. On the right side of the building, huge boards circulate on raised platforms. Workers stand on the platforms, following the boards as they go. On the left, smaller boards revolve at a brisker pace, interspersed with splicing stations draped with wires of every imaginable color and length. At each splicing station, a single worker stands hunched over mysterious chemicals, soldering the wires to be used in the rest of the process. Throughout the building, apparently unoccupied workers can be seen wandering the factory floor – often chatting casually with those at work. A popular local radio station blares from speakers in the ceiling, silenced only when managerial visitors appear.

Despite concerns about hiring women workers for assembly jobs, once a mixed workforce arrives, managers make no effort to ensure the allocation of particular jobs to women. On the contrary, on the line, gender distinctions are downplayed. Direct production workers – men and women both – are all located indistinguishably at the bottom. Offline jobs are another story. Only men are hired as material handlers, ensuring that the sole entry-level jobs requiring or even permitting mobility are entirely male. Supervisors and their assistants ("technicians") are also men, although there were reports in the plant of a woman supervisor who had been hounded out by male workers who wouldn't listen to her. Support workers, chosen by supervisors, are generally male as well, although this is complicated by the fact that women asked by supervisors to be supports tend to refuse. Thus, although women are much sought after in hiring, on the shop floor, supervisory practices on the line do not recognize gender, and outside direct production, managerial practices reserve positions of mobility and authority for men.

As in Particimex, the great majority of workers are on the assembly lines – more experienced on the larger lines, less so on the smaller ones. They stand, following the moving boards through their stations, then returning to their initial location to catch the next one in its rounds. Behind them hang long colored wires and baskets of small plastic components. They turn to grasp their particular set of wires, perhaps a red, two oranges, and a yellow, then turn to plug them into the appropriate slot on the revolving board, bending and reaching to rout the wires as they walk alongside the moving board. At the end of each "station" the last insertion beeps and a number lights above the board, telling them their job is completed. On the smaller lines, workers often reverse the order of insertions, plugging in the final cable first, as this means that every insertion elicits a satisfying beep.

During the first days, weeks, even months of work, the process is challenging and mesmerizing. José describes this period: "At first I said, this is *hard*, but I've got to do it. But then after like a week, man, I was so happy there! . . . At first I said to my brother and my sister, 'Yes, I've put myself in hell there!' But afterward, nahhh, what the hell?" During the month I spend on the line I am alternately exhilarated and traumatized by my daily ability or inability to keep up. Throughout the entire period I have nightmares in which, just as I hear the "click" that means that the wire is now engaged and can only be removed by a support person, I realize it is the orange not the green wire that belongs in this spot. Nine hours of push, click, pull, *damn!* repeating throughout the night.

The obsessive quality of the work diminishes quickly, however. Whether it's the five-minute cycle time of the big lines or the one- to two-minute cycles of the smaller lines, the work eventually becomes unbearably predictable. By the time I meet José, a mere six months after he and the rest of his line were hired, the entire group is busy switching stations to stave off the overwhelming boredom, and he is threatening to quit because no one is willing to move to his particular location. When Miguel, a support worker who's been in the factory eight years, tells me he is planning to leave, he explains his decision in a lengthy digression about those aspects of factory structure that ensure that he will see the same people, day after day, thus continually foreclosing the possibility of novelty in his social life. The obstacles to using the work itself to generate interest are too self-evident to merit discussion.

Like most of the other Juárez maquilas, the uninspiring nature of the work is significant because the work pays poorly even in local terms, so the money itself is not sufficient to instill loyalty to the job. Wages – not coincidentally like those in Panoptimex[4] – are close to $40 a week, raised to $50 by various benefits. This is low enough that it provides no real possibility of maintaining a family.[5] The few workers who support families independently work several jobs, and Anarchomex matters in large part for the access it provides to state health and housing systems. Most workers live with their parents, siblings, and/or members of their extended families. Thus, many use the money for personal expenses above and beyond food and shelter or understand it principally as a ticket to some level of symbolic independence from, and a way of expressing appreciation to, their parents. Thus Susana says she works "to dress myself," and Margo, "so as not to be asking [for money]." The money matters, of course, but in many cases it is not crucial to daily survival. Combined with the fact that similar jobs are available elsewhere, in most cases losing the job would not set off a severe financial crisis.

At the same time, there are no incentives for the quality of production, and only the most minor rewards for seniority (about $3 monthly for every year worked). Promotions – rare in any period – have been halted for economic reasons during my stay in the factory. Even a cursory look around the factory reveals few workers over twenty-five, even fewer over thirty. In line with the salary and hiring structures, most workers assume that once they have children they will need to seek either better paying (for the men) or more flexible (for the women) jobs. The few workers who nurse illusions of advancement within the plant either leave quickly, disappointed, or are the subject of ongoing teasing by their co-workers. Thus, neither pay nor expectations of promotion are viable inducements at work.

The problems caused by the combined absence of intrinsic interest and material incentives in the work are not helped by the half-hearted efforts at generating factory loyalty and reforming personal habits that take place during the week-long induction period. The "training program" is full of motivational films about quality and gifts of knick-knacks emblazoned with the company name. The obvious skepticism of new workers is reflected in the unconvinced attitude of the trainer himself, however, who seems embarrassed in the face of the exercises he asks the group to do. Mostly the week passes in presentations of rules directed at making us better people: the plant nurse discusses "personal hygiene"; the head of safety shows gory pictures intended to convince us not to wear jewelry or run on the shop floor; the "social worker" advises against betting and playing and selling and cursing on the shop floor. The capstone of the experience is a full day organized around a video designed to foster "excellence" both at home and at work. Upon hearing that we are scheduled to do this training, the "social worker" laughs, "Bring your pillows!" she advises. During lunch at the end of the week, one of my new co-workers comments matter-of-factly, "Excellence is important for the bosses, not for one of us."

The distance workers feel from management is enhanced by the physical layout of the factory. There is no location from which a supervisor can see his entire line at once, still less an omniscient vantage point from which the entire workforce is visible. Everything on the shop floor obstructs the view of everything else. Supervisors are not around anyhow. They are notable for their absence on the shop floor, spending much of their day doing paper work, keeping track of a half-dozen indices. Even "technicians," the promoted workers who do the bulk of hands-on supervision, are ultimately judged by the numbers. No one is there by the production line, hanging over workers' shoulders and watching them work. It is numbers that supervisors pore over, not bodies.

The impersonal nature of supervisor/worker relationships is echoed in the realm of sexuality, removing another arena where personal, supervisory power might have been exercised. Autoworld has strict policies regarding sexual harassment throughout its Mexican operations. Supervisors are actually fired if they are discovered having affairs with their workers and refuse to call them off.[6] Portes boasts, "We're more advanced here," and later elaborates, "I have only little girls here, I have to protect them." Even more muted instances of these sorts of interactions are frowned upon. For instance, quality checker is a relatively cushy job, and supervisors often allocate it to the prettiest girl on the line. However, Smith makes clear that he disapproves of this practice, and workers explicitly objected when an attractive young woman was chosen for this job on my line, noting acerbically that several women with higher educational levels had been passed over.

The few labor control mechanisms that do exist are of a punitive nature. There is no union, and the personnel office plays little part in workers' daily experience. As in most maquilas, absenteeism is highly penalized by the pay structure, and workers lose a third of the week's salary for missing a single day of work. Technicians are constantly coming by and scolding people for producing defects, for sitting down, for disappearing from their posts. However, as their title indicates, technicians' primary focus is on technical and not personnel issues. Thus, their labor control method of last (if frequent) resort is to call meetings in which they bring workers into a small room and tell them about their line's numbers in mind-numbing detail – numbers of defects, of harnesses unmade, of extra workers per line – and angrily exhort them to improve. The factory has made a perfunctory effort to remedy this situation through appointing quality checkers, whose job is to get workers to sign acknowledgments of their mistakes. However, most workers have a deal with the checker that she can sign off for them, and when she tells them they simply nod brusquely and keep working.

In this context, it is workers who keep each other in check on a daily basis. Assembly is done standing by a moving line. Workers are mobile, following the boards as they go. If experienced workers want to take a break, they can work ahead, intruding on the previous workstation and reappearing just in time to finish a subsequent board, by now already moving through an adjacent worker's territory. However, in most workstations, part of the assigned task is contingent upon the completion of previous jobs and is difficult to do once later stages have been finished. As a result, this work rhythm – or even a real inability to keep up – disrupts the work of those nearby. Those who are often behind, for whatever reason, soon feel the wrath of their co-workers. Thus, the limits on work pace are social and lateral, depending on the tolerance of co-workers and the thick-skinnedness of the worker in question. This peer monitoring constitutes co-workers as the central arbiters of success at work. Ultimately, this not only enforces speed but undermines production quality, as defects are a problem for absent supervisors, but not for aggressively present co-workers.

This process goes beyond undermining efficiency. Workers' shop-floor autonomy occasionally generates active, (minimally) collective resistance as well. When workers are called in and told about enforced vacations, a technician queries, "Is that legal?" His comment is immediately followed by disgusted snorting noises, emerging from around the room. Despite the prompt public silence that greets the supervisor's "I don't want backtalk," disgruntled discussion continues on the line for the rest of the day. Several young women go so far as to have me drive them to another maquila which they had heard was hiring. On the small harness line where I train, Sergio repeatedly turns the line's speed down. He is openly supported in this by his co-workers. The technician lets the situation continue, unremarked, quietly recalibrating the line on a regular basis. The most effective instance of this sort of intermittent resistance occurs shortly before my arrival on the same line in response to a particularly nasty supervisor. José tells me the story. "So, we finally got tired of it. We wanted to unite, all of us, no? To talk to the manager. In fact, the line was walking and yes we came together and yes we were going to go. And no, lots cracked and returned to their places again. We tried three times. The ones who didn't turn back, who stayed ahead, were two *güeras* (blond women). But when they saw everyone else . . ." He shrugs. Eventually, despite the line's inability to stick together for long enough to reach the door, their ongoing disquiet became obvious and the supervisor was moved. None of these incidents change the conditions of work in any fundamental way. Most have no discernible impact at all. So I do not by any means intend to exaggerate their importance. Nonetheless, they indicate the potential for resistance that lies latent in the autonomous social world of the shop floor. Once workers sideline managers to become each others' shop-floor interlocutors, the conditions of control shift and new forms of resistance become possible, although they are by no means assured.[7]

On the Anarchomex shop floor, co-workers are the central authorities for each other, both in the labor process and outside it. Managers and supervisors, convinced that they have the wrong workers at the outset, spend little time in production. In those infrequent moments when they are actually on hand, they are more likely to yell than to persuade.[8] These practices leave workers' sense of self – whether gendered or otherwise – relatively untouched. In periods of heavy production, when supervisory yelling-resources are stretched thin, workers have little internal motivation to produce quality harnesses. At the same time, by relying on social pressure between workers around the assembly line to enforce speed, labor control practices effectively locate the essential social dynamics in production between workers and not between workers and management. As a result, shop-floor subjectivities are evoked among workers, effectively foreclosing managerial ability to set their terms at the outset, or to be in a position to legitimate them as a means of control later on.

GENDER IN PLAY

. . .

In this fraught context, both male and female workers respond to the absence of direct supervision by constituting shop-floor subjectivities which are beyond the reach of managerial legitimation. They enter this process from quite different vantage points, however. Male workers enter on the defensive – their masculinity questioned outside the plant by popular images of feminine maquila workers and inside by the very managers who hired them. Female workers encounter no such challenges to their femininity from their bosses, but their status as workers is under siege by their male co-workers, who address them as sexual rather than productive subjects. In this context, male workers defiantly assert the manliness of the work – representing it as inherently masculine and themselves as paradigmatic harness workers. At the same time, female workers choose the pleasures of their male co-workers' flirtatious if constraining address over managers' more distant and unrewarding naming. In Anarchomex, gendered meanings emerge as a shop-floor battleground, and male workers unequivocally control the field.[9]

Making Work Manly

Male workers' definition of harness work as masculine is a literally never-ending struggle, and in waging it, they employ a variety of tactics: feigning ignorance that others define harness assembly as feminine; describing the work and factory through masculine tropes; portraying female sexuality as inherently disruptive on the shop floor. Managers are the most problematic opponents in this symbolic struggle, so male workers are particularly disturbed by my suggestions that management prefers female workers. In every interview I do with a man, my allusion to the managerial preference for women is met with an incredulous, "They say they prefer women?" even though each one of them has, in fact, responded to an ad or sign that specifically requested women workers. Miguel says off-handedly, "There in the factories they hire all women, but then they hire all men," and then quickly changes the subject. Roberto responds by offering an alternate explanation for women's presence. Blithely ignoring the fact that half those on his own line are women, he explains that the reason there are so many women here is because here there are easy splicing jobs, so women can do *them*. At the end of a long interview, José admits, "The ad did say only women over eighteen years old," but then goes on emphatically, "Then I went, and it's that *no*, that is they said only women, but it wasn't true. *Look, Leslie, that wasn't meant seriously.*"

In these interviews, male workers frequently redescribe the work or the factory through highly symbolic, masculine images. They define the work as easy when emphasizing the other, gruelingly masculine jobs they have done, but as challenging when affirming the truly masculine nature of *this* work. Thus, as we sit down for an interview, Sergio, the fastest worker on the small harness line where I work, launches into a long unprompted speech. He elaborates on the unique challenges of his station, claims having learned to do it on his own, and insists to an invisible audience that therefore, "nobody can tell me anything about it." On the big line, Mario and Güero tell me every time I come by that they could work twice as fast as the line's current pace if they so desired. On the shop floor, male workers often and conspicuously employ the term "*jale*" – an expression otherwise used for masculinized manual labor – or even more assertively, "*estoy jalando*" – I am laboring – to describe harness assembly or work in the plant.

The sheer size of the factory and the harnesses produced are also repeatedly and symbolically emphasized. José describes his emotions upon first applying for the job after a long period working at another maquila that he labels "easy women's work." "They told me, Christ, you can't keep up. I mean they really drive you. And I believed them, because it was Anarchomex, those were the *biggest* harnesses, everyone said, in all of Juárez." Sergio previously worked at TVA, like Anarchomex one of the oldest and largest maquilas in Juárez, but one that has continued to employ a predominantly female workforce. He comments, "It does have a rep, because TVA is big, but it's not big, I would call Anarchomex *really* big."

Many of these comments assert the essential masculinity of the work through explicit distinctions between *their* relationship to the work and the relationship they claim to be typical of their female co-workers. Thus Sergio, trying to decide if he is willing to take on the challenge of a support position, tries to explain why his reluctance suggests that a woman certainly wouldn't or shouldn't take on such a task: "I say and think they're slower. That is they do work fast, but . . . They put you there to be a support, and *there* you can't fool anybody, *there* you're going to be put to the test. . . . I, for my part, *still* don't want to be a support. Although I knew they wanted me to be. . . . Women aren't slow, but it seems to me they can't do it." On the big line, Mario and Güero work side by side. All day long they carp about the inefficiency of the women nearby. "Guys are faster than girls," Mario asserts. Lupe is a repeated target, accused of laziness for her tendency to work fast and then sit down between boards. "I'd never sit down," says Mario disdainfully, typically noting her sitting, but not the speed that makes it possible. On my last day at Anarchomex, Lupe asks me to take over for a couple of boards as we chat. "Put *that* in your book," says Miguel. "Lupe got you to work so that she could just goof off." In fact, Mario and Güero work in a rhythm similar to Lupe's, although for different reasons. In order to go off and chat with women on other lines, they consistently work ahead of their stations, crowding Margo, who works in the station just before theirs. This allows them to disappear for five minutes and return in time to catch the next board. "They keep doing it," she complains in frustration, "even though I ask them politely." They take no notice. Working faster than their nearby female co-workers in order to go flirt with women elsewhere in the factory – this is what it is all about.

The men's critiques are most vigorous when they describe how their female co-workers' sexuality wreaks havoc in production. Commenting critically on two female co-workers whose flirting is unacceptably assertive, José speaks in the voice of a supervisor, "If the line were faster and there was more pressure, I can assure you they wouldn't have time to go around grabbing like that." Similarly, when I express my surprise to several workers at management's sending a woman home for wearing a mini-skirt, Miguel comments, "Girls shouldn't wear minis, it's distracting." And Roberto offers, "They shouldn't wear minis. The point at work is to be on the ball, it's impossible that way."

Women workers assert a distinct relationship to the work. They make meanings that sidestep and even ignore the actual experience of labor – focusing instead on the social experience of the shop floor. When a group of workers on the small line are promoted to utilities, only the men turn in their old blue smocks for the yellow ones symbolizing their new position. The women prefer not to call attention to the change. They would rather affirm their similarities with their friends than their productive capacities. For similar reasons, Ingrid, whose years of seniority make her a natural choice for a support person, lasts a matter of months in the position. "I'm one of those people who is very hysterical sometimes," she explains. "A support person who offended everyone. That is, I have a very strong character." The fact is that support people always end up offending people, it is part of the job. In a man, this seems normal. For a woman, experiencing and seeing herself experienced in this role is untenable.

Despite women's lack of interest in claiming the work, they respond to men's suggestions that they really aren't serious workers through a stubborn dismissiveness. They don't create identity around the work, but wages are something else again. This insistence on the right to work in the face of male denials can be seen most clearly in the perspectives of Susana and Raúl, a couple who has recently moved in together.

Raúl comments: "It isn't necessary for the woman to work. It's not her obligation. . . . Some women are working just to buy nice clothes. . . . In my case, I would have to work because I have to work, in order to depend on myself, I like to depend on myself." However, Susana responds to the idea that she quit work and allow Raúl to support her by saying: "I don't like to just be sitting around. You feel like an idiot, useless, that you can't . . . It's not for me. As soon as he's supporting you, you feel bad." Women make little effort to claim a privileged relationship to the physical work of the factory, but neither are they willing to cede their status as legitimate wage earners to their male co-workers.

In the face of managerial denial, the masculinization of harness assembly is an ongoing project for male workers, and it compels the bulk of their attention and energy on the shop floor. The strategies through which they make their claims are varied and creative, but their tactics share an implicit interlocutor – managers – and an explicit other – women workers. Managers generally dismiss and ignore these claims, but women workers deal with them on an ongoing basis. With little at stake, women in Anarchomex cede any claims to the work itself, insisting only that work in general is a legitimate occupation. As a result, gendered meanings interfere with production for everyone on the Anarchomex shop floor. Only managers think harness assembly is important, but they have long since ceased to address their actual shop-floor audience.

Sexing the Self

In the context of managerial disrespect, male workers go beyond marking harness assembly as masculine. They also use their interactions with female co-workers as an arena in which to perform an alternate, legitimate masculinity. Thus, they constantly proposition, hassle, and court women workers, articulating terms for shop-floor femininities that are both highly sexualized and narrowly constrained. Women workers, who experience no such managerial depreciation of themselves as women, turn to this social context for meaning and pleasure, rather than as an opportunity to rebut an aspersion on their character. In this context, the shop floor emerges not as an arena of harness production, but of male-dominated sexual play. The interactions prescribed here by male workers are as clear-cut as managers would have hoped production norms to be: men initiate; women respond. For women, stepping outside these bounds is aggressively sanctioned. Nonetheless, within these ritualized limits, gendered performances are pleasurable, compelling, and primary for men and women alike, distracting them from production and undermining managerial ability to address those aspects of worker subjectivity of most immediate concern on the plant floor.

These processes have given daily life in Anarchomex a distinctively playful, sexualized social texture. An applicant tells me that he wants to work in harnesses because it has a reputation for being "less serious." Ernesto says he came because his brothers told him that "there it's cool, with a lot of teasing and fooling around." Susana explains that, before applying for a job at the plant, she borrowed her sister's uniform to slip onto the shop floor undetected and see if she'd have fun working there. "I came with the intention to work, and, yes, no? Enjoy myself." Other workers commented that they'd come to the plant after being told it had a lot of *ambiente* (atmosphere). And indeed workers do spend the day at play as well as at work. The shop floor is full of catcalls. It is impossible to walk from one line to another without a whistle, a tease, a kiss, "Eh, *güerita*!" At any given moment on the line someone is always visiting – chatting, occasionally "helping," sometimes with disastrous results for the quality of the work. On the small line I trained on, adjacent workers often combine their two stations and work on the same board so they can talk more easily. In the bathrooms, there are always a couple of women sitting in the shower stalls gossiping or grouped around the mirrors comparing lipstick shades and the durability of the arches in their bangs. Before moving in with her boyfriend, Susana used to get to work at 5:20 every morning, a full forty minutes early, in order to chat and gossip with her friends. She is not unusual. Many workers arrive early, frequently leaving their homes by 4:30 A.M. in order to socialize before work. They are tired all day on the line, but it's worth it.

Workers see no conflict between the idea of the factory as a center of social life and as a place of work. Susana tells me: "Having a boyfriend looks worse at school. There you're studying, you go there to study, not to have a boyfriend. Here in the factory it's different. You go to work, but at the same time you go to find friends or to find a boyfriend. It's different at school." Bathroom graffiti tells a similar story – covering the stalls, it focuses entirely upon sexual and romantic attachments and rivalries between workers. Complaints about pay or speed-ups or generic supervisory hassling, even personal insults directed at technicians and supervisors, are notable for their absence. By the same token, workers discussing whether they like the work focus almost entirely on their ability to make friends on a particular line, to "*cotorrear*" (to banter/flirt), to find or create the companionship that forestalls the otherwise corrosive boredom and depression that the work evokes. In the absence of a managerially generated framework, workers must create their own meanings at work.

Within this context, male voices assert their presence, setting the tone for new workers as soon as they enter the factory – marking it as a masculine space. New workers don orange "training" smocks, in contrast to the navy blue smocks required for ordinary workers. As they walk down the long aisles between the lines, the low-pitched catcalls resonate around them, "Carrots, carrots!" But soon the women among the newcomers notice a different call. "Carrot, come! Come here! Here's your bunny rabbit!" Whistles and kissing sounds follow the new worker as she walks past line after line to her station. Within a couple of days she is angling for the navy smock used by other workers, an escape from the heightened visibility of the brilliant newcomers' uniform.

The new smock only changes the intensity of the erotic hazing, however. Although the whispers and calls diminish, soften and personalize with the new uniform, the male voices never stop. Sexuality – for both young men and young women in the plant – is a primary entertainment, occupation, preoccupation; and in the game of flirtation, men act and women respond. Male workers leave their posts to go flirt with prospective girlfriends. Women workers turn their backs on harness boards to chat with suitors. Men call out or visit, women smile and chat in response, either enthusiastically or with polite distance. But women ignore advances at their peril. The specter of teasing or ostracism is far more alarming than that of an irate supervisor yelling as the mistakes roll in.

On my line, a young woman in the adjoining station has a steady stream of suitors. They stand near her on the platform, obstructing everyone and everything. There are grumbles, but they are muted, it's all in the day's work. One day after one of her usual giggling conversations, she reports that a particularly serious young man has asked her to marry him. "I told him not to be silly," she says calmly, working away. When some young men from engineering are sent to check me out during my training period, my irritated response at their disingenuousness earns me a gentle reproof from my trainer José. "Don't be so angry. You'll offend them." My station partner Lupe keeps count of our suitors, and when a young man comes and stands hang-dog, she offers to cover for me so that I can talk to him. When I neglect to take the opportunity, she is more explicit. "If you act like that, no matter how pretty you are, sooner than you know, no one will pay any attention to you." In fact, being labeled "stuck up" is a constant threat for young women in the plant, and it is often a source of worried self-examination by shyer young women on the line.

There is broad agreement in the factory on the appropriate roles for men and women in these games of flirtation. In response to my comment that supervisors in other factories catcall women, Sergio responds, "I think that's how we [men] *all* are. I mean, I find myself among them, because all of a sudden there's 'Hey babe' and 'Hey beautiful.'" Susana echoes his comments from the other side, "Just imagine if I called out to a guy, 'Carrot, here's your bunny rabbit!' How bad I'd feel! It makes me ashamed. But it doesn't make men ashamed. For them, it feels natural." Men's catcalling within the factory is repeatedly described as a "normal" attribute of maleness – so normal that men who do not participate are forced into convoluted-sounding explanations of what they attempt to cast as their more gentlemanly be-havior. Nonetheless, both men and women agree that catcalls from women to men, or even a woman seeking out a man to talk, are not appropriate. In uncomfortable conversation with me, Miguel comments, "A girl, she has her rights too, but the fact is, it looks bad."[10] Marisela elaborates, "It's always the man who talks to a woman. You cheapen yourself, no? Here, what we think is that one cheapens oneself talking to a guy." These opposing sets of rules for men and women are once again particu-larly evident in Susana's and Raúl's differing reflections on the subject. When I com-ment in an interview that having an established partner in the factory must take away the freedom to flirt, Raúl objects: "Yes I can, yes we *can* flirt. You get bored if you don't flirt. And let's say that you're married and there's your wife. Pretty unlikely, you're not going to do anything because there's your wife. No way!" On the other hand, in response to a similar comment, Susana agrees: "It's better that you get a boyfriend outside the plant, who isn't always there, because you have problems. Let's say you're talking with a [male] friend, and they go tell him and . . . Better that you work in one place and have your boyfriend in another."

The consensus on flirting norms within the plant is all the more striking against the backdrop of the actual diversity of sexual practices among these women outside it. Lupe says that she'd never had sexual relations with a man until she married. However, when I ask Marisela how she feels as a single mother in the plant, she comments dryly, "There are no more virgins in the maquilas." What is striking is that despite Lupe and Marisela's disagreement about private sexual behavior, their prescriptions for appropriate public behavior for women in the plant are identical. *Cotorreo* is fine, even required, but it must be in response to a man, not initiated by a woman.

Male workers are particularly assertive in noting women's transgressions of these rules on the shop floor. On the smaller line where I trained, men and women have far more egalitarian relationships on a daily basis than those on the larger line, where workers have more varied seniority and experiences in the factory. The group entered together, six months ago, and worked together through the tenure of an unusually nasty and abusive supervisor. Women here are markedly more assertive in teasing and flirting games than on the larger lines. Despite – or perhaps because of – the relative similarity of men and women's shop-floor behavior on the line, in private interviews men from this line are particularly insistent in their critiques of the sexualized play of their female co-workers. Thus Ernesto comments when I ask about men's catcalling, "Some women do it too, they're brazen. It's 'Hey *papacito*!'" Several others comment on two women on the line who are married but "act like they're single." José elaborates: "There are girls that are beyond the limit, they're too much. There on the line there are at least two who say things." He pauses. "Let's just say it, they almost seem like women from outside, from the street, let's say. . . . Sometimes it's *cotorreo*, but lots of times it goes beyond that."

Public breaches are quickly sanctioned by women as well as by men. The women's bathroom is full of graffiti accusing particular women – identified by name and line number – of seeking out men sexually or of stealing others' boyfriends within the factory. Reports of men's graffiti are similar. The few notes on the bathroom walls expressing less acceptable desires and attitudes are left unsigned: "Beto, the one in quality, is like a mango," comments an anonymous writer. "I'm a whore, what of it?" writes another, similarly unidentified.

It would be all too easy to see gender relations on the Anarchomex shop floor as a simple reflection of those outside, for in many ways, Anarchomex's gendered practices feel like those of a Juárez street corner. The catcalls and expectations of willing acceptance, the rule-bound, unequal, and mutual flirting, are relentlessly familiar – if somewhat more intense than the external norm. This "natural" appearance – the texture of an unreconstructed locale – is an illusion, however. Whatever the logic outside, the gender dynamics internally both implicitly and explicitly respond to internal conditions. There is nothing casual about male workers' attitude toward their female counterparts in the plant. On the contrary, their determined sabotage of women workers in production and their intense insistence that women's sexuality is a liability at work are both ultimately directed toward rectifying their embattled situation at work. Heterosexuality in Anarchomex is an arena where men can reclaim a piece of what they have lost elsewhere.

GENDERED MEANINGS AS A FULCRUM OF STRUGGLE

In Anarchomex, gender itself becomes an object of shop-floor contention. Patriarchal managers define maquila work as inappropriate for real men, thus ignoring or insulting male workers. In response, these workers struggle to redefine the work, as well as the social space of production, as masculine. In making claims to the shop floor, they define their female co-workers as potential girlfriends, thus directly contesting managerial definitions of women as iconic maquila workers. This process undermines managerial control. Male workers are too involved in fighting over masculinity and female workers in responding to their male counterparts to attend to supervisors' criticisms or praises. Managers thus lose all purchase on shop-floor selves.

One might interpret Anarchomex as evidence that men simply cannot be incorporated into transnational production. However, the success of Andromex suggests that this is not the case. In Andromex, managers successfully fill feminized jobs with men by making small but symbolically significant changes in shop-floor practices and rhetorics, thus making it possible for them to address men as "men" in maquila work. In Anarchomex, managers make no effort to address men as "men" at all. Hence, they insult and alienate male workers, thereby failing to integrate men into production and ultimately enacting a classic self-fulfilling prophecy. Despite managerial convictions that men – their accumulated habits of being – are the problem, the problem is actually closer at hand. The issue is not who men "are," but who they become on the shop floor.

Workers, whether female or male, do not enter the shop floor with their gendered selves set in stone. To the contrary, gendered subjectivities are made on the job. In Anarchomex, managers' conviction that men are always-already inappropriate harness workers brings gendered meanings into contention, thus creating the recalcitrant workers they fear they acquired at the outset. Despite the belief, shared by both transnational managers and their critics, that fixed gendered subjectivities are at work in global production, it is gendered tropes and meanings that are in operation, and the subjects who emerge in that process are not imported, they are made in place.

NOTES

1. Fernández-Kelly (1983), Iglesias (1985), Tiano (1994).

2. Karen Hossfeld (1990, p. 163) came across a similar ideological framework in her interviews with employers in high-tech Silicon Valley factories. "Employers repeatedly asserted that they believed the low-level jobs were filled only by women because men could not afford to or would not work for such low wages."

3. Milkman (1987) uses the term "idioms" to describe the gendered language through which managers describe decisions around job gendering. This formulation implies that categories such as the trope of productive femininity are merely post hoc rationalizations, and thus that they always fit by definition. I am arguing here that such descriptions are constitutive as well as opportunistic, and therefore can misportray as well as justify job gendering.

4. Although the plants don't formally coordinate wages, big corporations make an effort to be in a top range. Hence, despite differences in the way in which various aspects of the wage packet are calculated, plants like Panoptimex and Anarchomex pay almost identically in total.

5. See Chapter 4, note 11.

6. Gianini explains this policy: "Personnel wants to hire bombshells, gorgeous women. You get a supervisor with a concubine, three to four girls on the line and they find out about each other . . . it could shut down the whole line."

7. Farnsworth-Alvear (1997, p. 171) describes another factory where worker interaction is ultimately about each other and not about production. She suggests that this is not "resistance," but that it nonetheless "combated the very basis of industrial discipline." I am trying to capture a similar situation here.

8. See Foucault (1979) for a discussion of the differential efficacy of "punitive" versus "disciplinary" modes of control.

9. Gottfried and Graham (1993) describe a Japanese transplant in which managerial attempts to refashion production inadvertently undercut the work's masculine texture. The language used by male workers to respond to this situation is remarkably similar to that which I report here.

10. This is one of the many conversations where I play as the symbolic "feminist." This is due not only to my own comments, but to the general linkage made along the Mexican side of the border between American women and dogmatic claims about gender equality.

CHAPTER ELEVEN

Localistic Despotism

CHING KWAN LEE

. . .

Dagongzai, a generic term for "workers laboring for the bosses," had become the new collective identity claimed by millions of workers in south China since the mid-1980s. In everyday language, this term designated a newly formed social group whose presence could hardly be missed by observers of any city or town in south China. "Worker" was, of course, no new social category in a socialist society whose official ideology extolled workers as "masters" of the country. Yet, whereas "workers" referred largely to the masses laboring in state or collective enterprises, depending on these *danwei* (state units) for standardized wages and welfare, *dagongzai* worked in "bosses' factories." This latter type of enterprise was brought about by economic reforms and the term conjured up a contradictory image: it had an aura of modernity and prosperity on the one hand, and the reality of unrestrained and ruthless exploitation on the other. A woman worker from Sichuan told me laughingly that when she first heard people saying "dagong," she did not understand. Then, after working in Shenzhen for several years, she took that to mean "could be fired by the boss."

Along newly constructed, dusty highways, young women workers were easily seen waiting for minibuses or long-distance coaches to make their "factory-hopping" trips. They brought with them all their possessions: a neatly folded mosquito net, a bamboo sheet of bedroll, and two large aluminum bowls, all packed into a red plastic bucket. On the other side of the worker was a plastic carry-on luggage bag, with a folded blanket tied onto it by a rope. The scene left not much to the imagination: she had just removed everything from her bunk in a factory dormitory, en route to a new one. Every day, some of Liton's women workers packed and waited on the main highway just outside the factory for buses that would take them away while dropping off others who would replace them.

INSIDE BOSSES' FACTORIES

Liton (China) Electronics Limited was located in one of the many "industrial villages" in Xixiang, a town in the Baoan District in the City of Shenzhen, bordering Hong Kong. "Just two years ago, one could still see rice fields and fish ponds from the factory windows," one manager told me on my first visit to the plant. Now, block after block of gray, concrete, multistory factory buildings lined the two sides of the main street that extended seemingly endlessly into the distance. When container trucks passed by, creating a white swirl of dust, sand, and litter trailing behind them, there was a surrealist wilderness to this "industrializing" area. Along with a Japanese garment factory and a Hong Kong–owned plastic mold factory, Liton, with an 800-person work-force in mid-1992, was among the largest establishments in the village. The factory premises consisted of three buildings, each having five stories, and occupied a total area of about 200,000 square feet for production, dormitory, and canteen facilities. In the same neighborhood, there were the notorious, jerry-built "sweat shops" each employing just a dozen garment or handbag workers; new but shabby restaurants whose paint-chipped tables and chairs were set on the road; and convenient stores selling cigarettes, snacks, cold drinks, and daily necessities to workers. Further away from the factory complexes were service establishments: beauty salons, *karaoke* lounges, boutiques, and large restaurants. This was downtown Xixiang, frequented by workers on Sundays and in the evenings of the slack production season.

Wages and Despotic Punishment

Like other large factories in Shenzhen, Liton was fenced on four sides by high concrete walls and a main entrance gate guarded twenty-four hours a day. Equipped with batons hung on their belts, security guards checked the bags that workers brought along when leaving the factory premises. Since visitors were not allowed in, security guards paged workers to come down from the dormitory to meet their visitors outside the main entrance. On each shop floor, a security guard held an electronic detector bat to be randomly applied to workers at the end of every shift. He also made sure that workers did not punch in the time cards for other workers, and that every time a worker went to the bathroom, she had gotten a "leave seat permit" from her line leader. Mottoes were painted in large red Chinese characters, saying "Ask Your Superiors when You Have Problems," "Quality Comes First," "Raise Productivity," "No Spitting," "No Littering," and so on. Some of the factory regulations were written on large sheets of papers, framed and hung on the wall. Notice boards at the entrance of each shop floor detailed the hourly production target and the actual hourly output; the score of each line worker's production performance assessed by her line leader; the names of the "best" and the "worst" worker of the week; and the daily score of the cleanliness of each production line evaluated by the floor supervisor. These visible inscriptions of rules in the physical factory setting showed only the tip of the regimental iceberg. New recruits were asked to read a ten-page handbook of elaborate factory regulations governing everyday demeanor at work and in the dormitory. These despotic rules were strikingly similar to those Karl Marx described for the prototypical factory of his time: "In the factory code, the capitalist formulates his autocratic power over his workers like a private legislator, and purely as an emanation of his own will. . . . The overseer's book of penalties replaces the slave-driver's lash. All punishments naturally resolve themselves into fines and deductions from wages."[1]

Liton's rule book stipulated fines for violations related to all details of workers' attire, demeanor, and behavior:

3. Workers must put on their factory identity cards. Violation is fined RMB 5.
4. At work, workers are strictly prohibited from wearing slippers, spitting, and littering. Violation is fined RMB 10. Stepping on the grass or parking bicycles by the flower pots will be fined RMB 5. . . .
5. About other kinds of deductions: . . . punching time cards for others is fined three days' wages; not lining up, not wearing head scarves, not putting lock on the locker, not wearing factory shoes and uniforms, going to bathroom without a "leave seat permit," folding up uniform sleeves, and having long nails are all fined RMB 1 each. . . . Leave of absence without prior permission of supervisor is fined RMB 30 for the first day and RMB 15 for the second. Leave of absence with prior permission is fined RMB 15 and deduction of all monthly bonus. . . . Refusal to do overtime shift is fined RMB 2 for the first time, RMB 4 for the second, RMB 8 for the third, and deduction of all wages for the fourth.

Among these rules, workers considered most despotic and "unfair" those that stipulated the docking of wages even when workers had doctor's certifications of their illnesses. On the assembly lines, it was not unusual to find workers sobbing, looking pale, or leaning on their chairs while trying hard to catch up with the pace of the line. Line leaders or supervisors who pitched in, out of fear of failing to achieve the output target, would not hesitate to insult them in front of other workers. A line leader said, "Once, I was sick and I asked my supervisor to sign my sick leave application. He looked at my time card and he counted that I only did forty hours of overtime that month, while others had 120 hours. He got very angry and suggested that there must be something terribly wrong with me for doing so little overtime and still getting sick. I felt very hurt. He refused to sign that paper to let me out." Other workers made the point that what was "unfair" about working for the bosses was not that there was unequal pay or unequal work positions. Inequality per se was a fact of life even in their "socialist" home villages: "There is inequality in the villages too. Some families have larger houses and larger pieces of land, and earn more in their sideline trades and production. We who come out to work knew that Hong Kong managers get higher pay than us workers, because they have more knowledge about production. What is really unfair is that the supervisors will not believe you when you are really sick. They treat us as though we are all liars even when some of us nearly fainted at work. The company still docks RMB 15 for sick leave with a doctor's letter."

Space, Time, and Body

Workers' physical movements during work hours were strictly limited to the floor where they worked. The most sacrosanct area in the entire plant was the office on the second floor of the main building. The coolness of the air-conditioned office made it a world apart from the hot and humid shop floors and especially from the suffocating warehouse in the basement. Whenever workers were summoned by the personnel manager into the glass-partitioned, brightly lit office, they showed an unself-conscious stiffness and alertness, envious of the office women who were better groomed and whose uniforms were not soaked with sweat sticking to their backs. Making or receiving phone calls in the office was a privilege reserved for senior line leaders or above. Canteens and dormitories were all ranked into A, B, and C categories. Canteen A was for all general, nonmanagerial, nontechnical workers, who brought along their own aluminum bowls for rice and soup. Canteen B served better food in larger quantities for senior line leaders and above, while Canteen C was the air-conditioned dining room for all the Hong Kong managers and staff, visitors, and department heads. The meals in Canteen C were prepared by a different cook, who served fish and fresh fruit exclusively for senior staff. Dormitories were distinguished by whether they had an electric fan and by the number of bunks in each room. There were twelve bunks in each worker dormitory room and six bunks in those for line leaders and above. The Hong Kong staff dormitory was air-conditioned and was located about fifteen minutes' walk from the factory premises.

The temporal dimension of factory life was both rigid and flexible. Working hours were paced by shop-floor bells and punch-card clocks. Every day, breakfast started at 7:10 and production lasted from 7:30 until the forty-five-minute lunch break that started at 12:15. The normal workday ended at 4:30 PM. Production imperatives defined the length and the frequency of overtime shifts. In a normal workday, two hours of overtime work were mandatory. Flexibility of total working hours served employers most obviously during the "peak season," usually the summer months, when order contracts were signed for overseas Christmas inventory, and when five hours of daily overtime on weekdays and full-day Sunday overtime were very common. Worker dormitories were locked during work hours. Although labor laws in the Shenzhen Special Economic Zone specified that no more than two hours of overtime shift were allowed daily, production in Xixiang (outside the Zone) went on around the clock. Clusters of fluorescent lights and the hustling noise of machines were commonplace elements of the nighttime scenery.

That the arrival of industrial capitalism brought with it new apprehension and a politics of time has been noted in studies on the first generation of the English working class, the Kabyle peasants, and Malaysian women workers.[2] The transformation involved was from a task-oriented notion of time, which followed the "logic of need" and in which work mingled with social intercourse, to a notion of time as "timed labor." The latter was one in which "the employer must use the time of his labor, and see it is not wasted: not the task but the value of time when reduced to money is dominant. Time is now currency: it is not passed but spent."[3] At Liton, women workers new to the factory environment also found managerial control over their physical and temporal freedom, rather than the length of the work day or the high temperature of the shop floor, a most painful bodily experience. One woman said, "It's actually more exhausting at home, with the blazing sun. Here, at least we have a shelter above our head. Although tending the field is very busy and hard work, we have a lot of free time. You can play with village friends. Here, you have to hold your urine until they give you permission to go to the bathroom."

Mui-ying, a twenty-year-old Guangdong woman, recalled how work at home was more fun than factory work, because of the former's embeddedness in socializing and its freedom from discipline, all that factory work was not: "We Chaozhou girls have a tradition of doing embroidery work at home. Our mothers taught us and we got subcontracted work to do after school. Usually there were ten to fifteen girls sitting together, joking while working. . . . Working is different from *dagong*. When you work you can arrange your time freely, but when you *dagong*, there are rules from your boss. You'll be scolded if you refuse to work or do something wrong in the factory. . . . In the beginning, everyone here cried a lot."

Managerial power and the practice of moving workers around to do different kinds of tasks was as much detested by the workers as the spatial confinement. Both amounted to workers' loss of control over their bodily movements. Among new recruits, especially those straight from their peasant homes, tears were shed and explicit resistance was staged against line leaders' or foremen's transfer instructions. In the workers' interpretation, job transfer was an affront to personal dignity, which was buttressed by specific tasks assigned to specific individuals, and therefore workers should not be replaced and interchanged arbitrarily, like cogs in a machine. One woman explained to me why she resented and even openly resisted a transfer: "Management did not treat us as human beings. They show no respect for workers. If I work in that position, then I should not be kicked around like a football. When my work is done, I am entitled to my rest. But when the line leaders move you around, they give you work to make you exhausted." I had seen several women workers simply sit still and look elsewhere when their line leaders wanted them to fill other slots. It usually took some threats of disciplinary measures by the foreman and the floor supervisor to effect a transfer of these new recruits.

All these hardships of laboring in bosses' factories found objective inscriptions on women's bodies, according to women workers. Objective indicators of workers' suffering from despotic disciplines included weight loss, deterioration of "face color," and skin conditions, all indicators of worsening health in Chinese folk medicine. One woman described to me how her body suffered after becoming a factory worker: "You see how terrible my face color is now. I have lost my appetite. They fix the time we have to eat, even though you are not hungry. When you are hungry, they don't allow you to eat. At home, I ate whenever I wanted to, a little at a time. When I was hungry, I could eat up to three big bowls of rice. Now, all I get is a stomachache. The water in Shenzhen is bad. Many of us get rashes on our skin because of the water."

Related to issues of bodily health, food was an area that workers saw as evidence of employers' exploitation and disregard of their well-being. Complaint letters deposited in the "Opinion Box" and opened only by two senior Hong Kong managers had conveyed persistent complaints about the quality of food in Canteens A and B. Workers told me that they detested the poor "pig" food so much that many would rather pour the food down the drain outside the canteen and came to work with empty stomachs. A worker wrote a cynical, rhyming verse (in Chinese) to criticize Canteens A and B:

> The meals of the canteens are really terrible.
> Mixing rice water with dry bread.
> Where is the improvement when more is paid to you?
> In our meals, there is always sand in the vegetables.
> The rice is either half-cooked or half-burnt.
> And we always have cheap cucumbers.
> We are hungry but we cannot summon our appetite.
> So we work with feeble minds and foggy eyes.

ORGANIZING LOCALISM

The despotic labor regime was organized through localistic networks. At Liton, with a workforce coming from fourteen different provinces in the country, "localism" was the dominant idiom both workers and managers invoked to interpret events and social relations in the factory. Localism was the a priori assumption, the quintessential conceptual tool that workers and management deployed with varying degree of consciousness and moral conviction. On numerous occasions, workers manipulated localistic ties to achieve concrete goals, while at other times they just found it a natural course of action needing no instrumental or moral justification. Localism at Liton implied more than preferential treatment given to people of the same localistic origins. It also implied the reconstitution within the factory of communal gender hierarchies embedded in localistic networks. Male (about 20 percent of total employees) locals were put in positions of authority in the production hierarchy and their roles as brothers, uncles, and cousins became an integral part of managerial control over their sisters, nieces, and younger cousins who occupied inferior production positions as workers or line leaders.

The organizational chart of Liton's Shenzhen production departments (see Figure 1) unmistakably bore the imprints of localism and genderism. Under the two Hong Kong production managers, there were four production supervisors, all of whom were Hakka men from the county of Longchuan in Guangdong. Three of them shared the same surname, Yeh, while the other one was a Lui. Both surname groups were cousins originating from villages close to each other. Of the nine production forepersons, six were men and three were women, and five out of the nine forepersons were locals of the supervisors' Hakka clique. Ninety percent of the line leaders were women from different counties of Guangdong. All assembly workers were women, and they had different kinds of kin and localistic relationships among themselves and with those in junior management. All technicians and repair workers in production were young men from Guangdong.

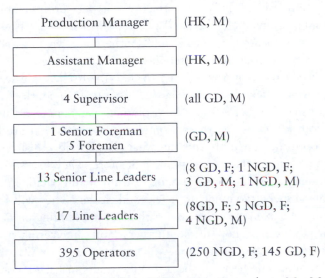

Key: HK – Hong Kong; GD – Guangdong; NGD – Non-Guangdong; M – Male; F – Female

FIGURE 1: Localistic and gender distribution in the Shenzhen production department of Liton, July 1992

Constructing Localistic "Otherness"

On the shop floor, workers identified each other more by province or county of origin and by the patron who brought them in than by name. When I first appeared on the shop floor, my name interested them less than that of my "patron." The first thing women workers asked me was "Who introduces you here?" Somehow rumor had it that I was the sister of the boss. During my first month at Liton, this hearsay apparently held more sway than my own introduction as a student writing a paper about Shenzhen workers.

Different dialects could be heard on the line and marked the exclusive boundaries of localistic communities. Even for people of the same province, there were diverse subdialects for different counties and villages. Workers would talk in Mandarin, the national language, only when they chose to communicate with people other than their locals. Workers also underscored localistic connections by extending small favors to locals sitting near them: when they obtained a "leave seat permit," they took with them the mugs of one or two other locals to refill with hot water. Or whenever they had a chance to move around the shop floor, they exchanged greetings by pulling locals' ponytails, punching them on the back, or dropping them a note.

The boundary of "locals" was flexible and to a certain degree relative, depending on whether one found closer locals in particular situations. The range of one's locals included the closest ones from the same kin group in the same village, to those from the nearby villages, the same county, nearby counties, the same province, or just "northerners" versus "southerners." This last distinction was very prominent in the popular imagination of south China. "Northerners" referred to those migrants whose province of origin was north of the Yangtze River and "southerners" were those born south of the Yangtze River. Each group constructed the "other" in derogatory terms, in binary opposition to those each group would use to describe itself. Qing-wah came from the northern province of Hubei, and her view about north-south distinctions was representative of many of her natives: "Northerners wear more fitting clothes and have unpretentious outlooks. Southern women wear clothes that are big and long. The colors are confusing and loud. And they wear all this gold and silver. Northerners are easily satisfied, but southerners always want more. They look down on people and use foul language. Northerners are more restrained and pacific in temperament. Guangdong women spend too much on snacks and clothes. They will spend RMB 60 for a pair of pants. We from the north always think about sending money home every time we get our paychecks. They [the southerners] don't like eating rice, saying that it will make them fat. So they spend money on snacks every day. We are careful with money. We buy peanuts and beer only occasionally when our friends come to visit."

A Guangdong woman sitting next to Qing-wah, on hearing these comments, immediately rebutted: "But you northerners are very fierce. You see in the dormitory, you people never line up one by one for hot water. You just pass your slot in the queue to your locals. Southerners get water for themselves one by one. . . . From our perspective, your women have no sense of beauty. Those bright red and bright green colors, we find them very outdated and exaggerated. You see those two women there, with the red flower hairpins? They are definitely from the north, we don't wear these anymore. I don't know how to describe it, but they have a special way of walking, too."

Constitution of Workers' Interests

Consciousness of localistic differences easily transformed into antagonism when shop-floor behavior carried consequences for workers' interests. Localistic nepotism colored the enforcement of despotic rules, the assignment of tasks, the opportunities for promotion, and the transmission of skills. Approval of applications for long leave was among the most sought-after scarce commodities at Liton. Even though workers on leave would be deducted RMB 15 for the first day, RMB 10 for the second, and so on, management had the discretion to approve or reject applications, which always caused complaints about favoritism. A Guangdong line leader talked to me for almost an hour about her bitterness against her foreman: "A few days ago I asked Deng to allow me a fortnight's leave to go home. I have not had any visit home since 1990 and my mom is already seventy years old. He insisted that I could only get eight days. I was very angry. I knew he granted thirteen days to a repair worker, and another worker got more than eight. Deng said I could look up the factory regulations or ask the personnel manager whether that was the rule. . . . Of course, I could not blame him. I can only blame myself for having been born with the wrong family name. If I could have been a Yeh or a Deng. . . . The new worker in my line has just come for three days and she has already been promoted to be the tester. I just found out that she's a local of Deng. . . . I know he is trying to make me quit by making things difficult for me. If I quit, he can promote his local folks to replace me."

On the line, the time allowed for leaving one's seat varied with workers' localistic connections to the foreman or supervisor. The brother of one of the Yehs was notorious for the physical freedom he enjoyed on the line where he was a repair worker. His seat was always empty, and he was seen joking, laughing, and hanging around his locals' seats. Both the line leader and other repair workers pointed to this example as an illustration of extreme nepotism. In more subtle ways, localistic affiliation affected the allocation of difficult and easy tasks. For the same pay rate, some women workers were made to do the most detested type of assembly work: soft soldering. The smell and the smoke of melting iron was so irritating that many workers complained about having sore eyes and nausea at the end of the workday. Women workers could not help noticing the pattern that workers who did not have the right connections got all those soft soldering tasks. Moreover, because front line positions set the pace for the entire line and were often blamed by management for falling behind the daily output target, those positions were without exception assigned to northerners without important connections with management. More than a few workers remarked that "you never see line leaders' locals in those positions."

Good work, like the opportunity to do overtime shifts during slack seasons, was assigned by management, who, it was widely believed, reserved those opportunities for their own acquaintances. Overtime work was remunerated at 1.5 times the normal hourly rate and therefore constituted a significant portion of a worker's paycheck. A complaint letter written to senior management was representative of stories I gathered while chatting with workers. The letter, undersigned by "ten D-Line workers," read: "A few days ago, a new line leader, Tsang Yu-ling, was assigned to manage our line. Eighty percent of the line workers did not want to work with her. Why? From the beginning, she used two kinds of attitudes in dealing with workers. With northerners, the only thing she knew was to yell and scold. On June 8, in the afternoon, the foreman asked Ma Kin-fa and Tong Hu to stay for four hours of overtime shift.

When the foreman was gone, she asked the two workers to leave and asked her cousins to replace them. They were from other lines and did not even know how to use the numeric screwdriver."

Promotion from worker to line leader or material handler, or from the shop floor to the office, again relied on the patronage of locals. None of the twenty to thirty Yehs was a general worker. All were line leaders, material handlers, repair workers, or above. On the other hand, a group of Jiangxi workers had no locals high in the management hierarchy, and they found it difficult to change work positions, to apply for leave, or to introduce relatives or locals into the factory, not to mention having a chance to get a promotion. They had to "bribe," that is, pay money, to those "friendly" line leaders and foremen to curry favors that were free to the latter's acquaintances.

Finally, even when one was given the chance to be promoted, the transmission of skill seldom crossed localistic lines. One day, when Yee-mi, a Hubei worker, was promoted from worker to line leader of the printed circuit line, she started to learn to distinguish the different lands of integrated circuits (ICs). The line leader of the printed circuit line was standing there, staring into the distance, while Yee-mi was studying the individual ICs with the help of one of her Hubei locals from a different section. I went toward them and asked why it was this local who was teaching her. She sourly remarked that the line leader avoided her every time she asked her about the ICs.

Even when nepotism did not display itself so explicitly, it was so much an entrenched idiom workers used to interpret factory life that instances of nepotism were always talked about, believed in, and acted on. There was widespread disbelief about the fairness of promotion tests. Rumors were circulated on the shop floors and in the dormitories that workers who scored highest were passed over in favor of foremen's or supervisors' acquaintances who did not perform as well. Although the truthfulness of stories like these was never confirmed, similar perception and logic were applied to everyday work relations. Lei-wah was complaining about her foreman and the latter's cousin, who was a new worker in the line: "My foreman does not need me anymore. His cousin has picked up the technique of organizing the line. He stays after work to teach her so that she can be a line leader. She knew nothing when he brought her in a couple of weeks ago. We other line leaders dare not confront her, even though she always makes mistakes. We just remain silent and watch. See those defective pieces? They're all from her section of the line. But what can you say, they are relatives and she does not have to worry about any blockage on the line. She *cannot* be blamed. He [the foreman] will ask why we don't help her and ask us to clear that piled-up work for her, because she's new.'" When this cousin of the foreman was eventually promoted to become line leader, Lei-wah took a resigned attitude toward a déjà vu incident, and expressed her discontent by spreading her criticism of this localistic promotion. The constitution of worker interests was therefore strongly associated with localistic affiliation.

Although localism was a powerful, almost tyrannical, fault line fracturing the female work force into localistic subgroups, the logic of practice on the shop floors compelled workers to traverse localistic lines. Through these everyday practices, localism was subject to transformation: trusting friendships could be built among nonlocals, as women worked alongside each other and helped each other to survive the hostile environment that their class position condemned them to share. The story of Wang Wah-chun was interesting in this regard. Born in the province of Guangxi, Wang told me that her best friend at Liton was Liang Ying, a Guangdong woman line leader on the third floor. I challenged her as to why she could be such good friends with a nonlocal. She told me how she initially pretended to be a Guangdong woman from Gaozhou so that Liang Ying would treat her as a local:

> It's funny. When I first met Liang Ying, she asked me where I was from. I lied and said I was from Gaozhou, the same county as hers. My sister was married to a man in a village in Gaozhou, and I learned from her about things and places in Gaozhou. So, Liang really believed that I was her local and we became very good friends. We helped each other a lot. When she had to do overtime shifts, I'd take her bucket to save her water for bathing. She always saves good food from Canteen B for me. You know, we workers can only eat in Canteen A. When I am sick, she'll also buy me medicine. Later, I felt I had to tell her the truth and she was shocked and laughed for a long time. I said if I had not pretended to be her local, she might not have been so good to me, at least not at the beginning. There are very few people here from Gaozhou. Many have left. We always talked until midnight in the dorm, about everything, our families, boys, and anything unhappy at work. She also teaches me the basic skills to be a line leader.

Wang's case indicated that localism mediated the establishment of expressive relationships among women workers. Yet such localism was not an unbreakable social rule. It operated more as an assumption that was susceptible to change in the light of concrete experience. Common concerns among teenage women drew them together in emergent communities on the shop floor, transcending their localistic sentiments. Sitting close to each other on the line gave rise to opportunities for developing casual conversation groups, especially when work flow was slack and management's grip on workers' behavior was looser. They gossiped about coworkers' dating activities, discussed incidents of favoritism that did not involve bad feelings toward anyone within the group, exchanged news, and compared traditions in each other's home villages. When I was working on the printed circuit line, my neighbors were three women from three different provinces – Guangdong, Hubei, and Jiangxi. We sat next to each other and chatted in an atmosphere of friendliness and gaiety. One day, the three other women were having a bet among themselves. The one who lost would buy the others peanuts and beer after work. The bet was about whether the welfare manager could deliver the movie screening he had promised. The manager failed thrice to put up the show. Workers had become so cynical about everything he promised that they were determined to get some fun out of the event anyway. In the end, he failed again and we went out to the small outdoor grocery store next to the factory for peanuts and beer.

GENDER AND LOCALISTIC CONTROL

For the majority of young, single women, this localistic, despotic factory regime embodied an additional dimension of control, founded on gendered organizational hierarchy and the managerial construction of women as "maiden workers." The organizational chart of the production department (Figure 1), for instance, shows a typical gendered structure of opportunity within the factory; women, especially northerners, occupied the lowest ranks of general workers while technical and managerial positions were reserved almost exclusively for men, especially those from Guangdong. Yet to comprehend how managerial authority was reinforced or how gender authority rooted in workers' localistic communities was transposed onto work relations, the following anecdotes were illustrative. Because male locals were usually higher up in the organizational hierarchy, management could make use of their familial authority over female kin/workers. Mei-fun told me an incident regarding her application for long leave to go home. Her brother was a technician at Liton. "I told Mr. Lui [one of the managers from Hong Kong] that I needed to go home because my mother was sick. She's not sick, but I needed an excuse to apply for leave. Mr. Lui went away without saying whether he approved or not. Later, I realized that he had asked my brother if our mother was sick. My brother did not know I was applying for leave, and he told Mr. Lui that he did not get any letter from home about that. Mr. Lui then told my brother about my application, and asked my brother whether, if he were the manager, he would approve it. My brother said no. I was so embarrassed."

Locals, particularly those with kinship ties, also functioned unwittingly to tie women workers to the one employer who recruited them as a group. Deng Su-ying, a nineteen-year-old woman from Jiangxi, was subjected to the "parental" surveillance of her uncle and aunts, both working at Liton. Her uncle was the first among their ten locals to work at Liton. After he came, his wife, two sons and daughters-in-law, and nieces came one by one. Deng's uncle worked in the canteen while his wife and other female relatives worked on the assembly line on the same shop floor as Su-ying. Su-ying said that because her parents had entrusted her to her uncle, he and his wife kept very close tabs on her: "In the dorm, my aunt, my cousins, and I live in the same room. My aunt's bunk is just below mine. Every time I go out, she asks where and with whom I am going. Some of my friends left Liton for a higher-paying factory. My uncle and aunt did not allow me to go. They are afraid that I may learn bad things in other factories. Here, they can watch me every minute of the day."

Male locals, although fewer in number than female locals, were considered more resourceful and more daring in making requests of senior management. After the Lunar New Year holiday, when many workers brought their locals to Shenzhen to find jobs, workers were busy seeking the assistance of supervisors and foremen through their male locals who worked as security guards, canteen workers, technicians, or janitors. "It's easier for men to talk to men. They played basketball together in the playground." Successfully recommending women's locals into the factory affirmed the higher status of male locals. The chain of assistance might involve several indirect connections not strictly of a localistic nature. Usually the middlemen would persuade foremen and supervisors by citing locals of these recruits as examples of reliable workers, or passing on good comments about potential recruits. It was common practice to send gifts or invite middlemen to dinner after a successful "introduction." During the recruitment period, line leaders and workers alike made use of their bathroom visits to sneak to the reception corner of each shop floor to give hints to their locals who were taking simple recruitment tests there. These tests would require candidates to write the English alphabet and solve simple mathematical problems. No one cared to stop these "mutual help" practices.

. . .

"Maiden Workers" as Identity

Single women themselves also subscribed to the notion of "maiden workers," giving it meanings different from those given it in managerial ideology. First, women considered dating a legitimate focal concern because of their maiden status, which entitled them to enjoy a higher degree of freedom in exploring romantic relationships. Through localistic networks, women came in touch with male locals who worked in other factories and in other businesses. When I was invited by some Jiangxi women at Liton to a birthday party for a nineteen-year-old Jiangxi woman in a nearby electronics factory, a young man among them bought a birthday cake that cost RMB 40, five times his daily wage. Other women in the party told me that he was pursuing the birthday girl, after failing to win the hand of another local who had gone home to get married.

One taboo circumscribed this new-found freedom. Romantic relationships with nonlocals were widely believed to be futile. Women whose boyfriends came from localistic origins different from theirs were despised as "fooling around." Zhang Shen-kui did not see much future in the interprovincial romance of her Guangxi forewoman with a Hubei man: "If she was serious about getting married, she would not go out with a northern man. He will dump her, I'm sure. Northern men don't want southern women. [If they get married] she will not get used to eating noodles every day, and their parents won't agree. It's too far from their natal homes, and if anything bad happened to the woman, her parents and relatives are too far away to be of any help. . . . It's too lonely working in Shenzhen, so people just find anyone to go out with, to make life bearable."

Despite this commonly heard taboo, women workers held tolerant attitudes toward others' dating and sexual behavior. Romantic relationships were considered personal matters in which even locals and acquaintances had no right to interfere. Chan Sau-chu told me that she did not feel offended when her roommate, another Guangdong woman, had her boyfriend, a repair worker at Liton, come over and stay until 3 AM. They pulled the curtain of the woman's bunk and slept together while other roommates did their usual routines in the dorm. Chan found that inconvenient and inconsiderate for the other women, but she also said, "It's not my business." Moreover, the exigencies in Shenzhen allowed women to renegotiate gender identity through experimenting with new dating practices. Even Deng Su-ying, the Jiangxi woman whose aunt shared the same room with her and kept a close watch on her social life, was able to contest the taboo against interprovincial romance. She had just met a Guangdong young man who was a line leader in the wire room. "My uncle and aunt said nothing, although I know they don't like him because he's from Guangdong. After all, my parents are so far away. And even if my parents were here, these days they leave it to us to decide. They always say, if they make the marriage choice and if bad things happen, we will blame them."

The second meaning that young women attached to their status of maiden workers was that they should prepare themselves for a future beyond factory work. Instead of the attitude of resignation about gainful employment that male workers and management assumed, young women saw future marriage as the beginning of adulthood and enduring responsibilities, both emotionally and financially. Their vision of marriage was not of dependent housewifery, but of a partnership in an endeavor more important and meaningful than being a laborer in the bosses' factory. Frustrated by the bleak opportunity of moving up the factory hierarchy, given the sexist, discriminatory managerial ideology, a number of women took evening courses in accounting, English, typing, and even computers so as to equip themselves to change to jobs with better prospects. Northern women's language barrier did not allow them to take evening courses, yet they, too, thought about getting beyond factory work when they eventually returned home. Many had entrepreneurial ambitions. Opening a small retail business, such as a grocery or snack store, or a small neighborhood restaurant were the most commonly cited plans. In a typical home village in the north, women reported that initial capital of five to seven thousand RMB would suffice. That amount was well within the reach of workers who made an effort to save up part of their paychecks.

. . .

BEYOND THE SHOP FLOORS: DORMITORIES
AND SHOPPING MALLS

The plant in Shenzhen encapsulated the bulk of workers' life because dormitories were in many ways extensions of shop floors. Life in the dormitories and in leisure hours saw the same patterns of gendered localism among women workers. Room assignments were deliberately made to allow locals to stay together, a policy that was intended to show the humane, considerate side of the company. Each room had six to twelve bunks, and roommates usually came from no more than two different provinces. Among these scattered enclaves of localistic groups, subtle everyday processes marked their boundaries and reinforced their localistic identities. Dormitory routines, such as getting hot water in thermos bottles or tap water in buckets, were occasions for building bonds within localistic groups, and therefore creating conflicts between groups. Verbal and physical fights took place when workers accused each other of reserving places in the line for locals. One woman would fill up not one bucket but several so that her locals would not need to wait in the long line. In the rooms of women from northern provinces such as Sichuan and Hubei, there was bottle after bottle of chili sauce they shared to make the southern cooking provided at the canteen more edible. Southern women made fun of the northern women's taste for hot foods and inferred that their hot temper came from the chili sauce they ate in such large quantities. Poker games were a common pastime that women played only with locals, chatting loudly in their local dialects. When I went to visit a group of Jiangxi women in their room, there was much emphasis on the uniqueness of "Jiangxi poker," whose rules were different from poker in other provinces. While they engaged attentively in the game and the conversation in their own dialect, I had to watch quietly because nobody ever suggested teaching an outsider their "local game."

Besides the flourishing of different dialects, another kind of sound bore the mark of different localistic clustering in the dormitory. Although not every worker owned a radio – cassette player to be put next to her pillow in her bunk, it was usual to find one radio set shared among several roommates. Guangdong women tuned loudly, and somewhat proudly, to Hong Kong radio stations or Cantonese-speaking mainland stations, while northerners tuned to Mandarin-speaking ones. More electrical and electronics appliances, such as lamps, fans, cameras, and pots for boiling water, were lined up by the beds of Guangdong women, while northern women's rooms looked more meagerly furnished. In winter months, a popular pastime among northern women was knitting sweaters and scarves for their families. "We knitted every year at home. In the villages, there was nothing much to do in the winter and the weather was cold. So every woman knitted." However, Guangdong women proudly told me that they did not know how to knit, and there was a general attitude that only rural, rustic women knitted. Yet one thing seemed to transcend localistic boundaries: posters of popular singers and movie stars from Hong Kong were common decorative items in all the bunks I visited, irrespective of women's place of origin.

Excursions into downtown Xixiang were made with women locals in the evenings, but mostly on Sundays and the days immediately after the delivery of their paychecks, the twenty-third of each month. Two or three women went together, both for companionship and for safety. Xixiang was notorious for its migrant population and for the "chaos" that was supposedly caused by these migrant workers. "It's chaotic outside" was how many workers warned me about downtown Xixiang. They were well informed about recent murders, rapes, and thefts on the street. On the main street of Xixiang, small groups of women joined hands as they passed by boutiques, restaurants, theaters, *karaoke* lounges, and numerous beauty parlors. Deng Su-ying explained gender differences in leisure activities to me: "Men go to these places. We heard them talking about the girls in the massage parlors and that it cost RMB 30 for an hour-long massage. Some of them go for a haircut every two weeks. Women don't spend their hardearned money that way." Indeed, in restaurants and coffee shops, young men were frequently seen drinking several bottles of beer and depositing piles of peanut shells on the floor all around them. Even when women strolled along the street in small groups, young men sitting on the fences along the road frequently made passes at the women by uttering flirtatious words or whistling.

For women workers, the dubious moral status of lounges, restaurants, and beauty parlors left them not many niches in the public area. Window-shopping in the malls and small boutiques allowed them free entertainment that was at once morally appropriate and eye-opening. Moreover, they purchased essentials regularly: shampoo, soap, skin care items, towels, snacks, and clothes. These shopping trips were occasions when the local Shenzhen society intersected with a newly arrived social group whose labor undergirded its prosperity. Localistic identities were actively constructed and contested in these everyday contacts.

One day, after they got their paychecks, I went shopping with Hon-ling and Kwai-un, both from the northern province of Hubei. We were looking at some hairpins in a newly opened store in a shopping mall. The storekeeper heard that they spoke Mandarin and was reluctant to quote the prices of the hairpins Hon-ling was interested in. It was a common practice that prices were not marked and the final transaction price depended on how the customer bargained with the storekeeper. This storekeeper was murmuring to herself in Cantonese, "Buk-mui," a contemptuous term for "women from the north." Because I kept silent and Hon-ling and Kwai-un spoke to me in Mandarin, the storekeeper must have thought that I too was a *buk-mui*. I was getting a bit angry about the treatment my friends were getting from this woman, and I started to ask her the prices in Cantonese, making sure that she realized I was from Hong Kong. Her facial expression changed instantaneously and she politely told me the price of every item in sight. "You, 'Miss Hong Kong,' of course can see that we are selling the best-quality items," she said, smiling. "I'll offer you a discount." Hon-ling and Kwai-un smiled to each other and when our eyes met, we all decided that we should be leaving. They were happy that I was able to embarrass the storekeeper, but they confessed that they had gotten used to southerners' contemptuous attitude toward *buk-mui*. What happened downtown was just a continuation of what took place inside the factory.

Later, we went into a boutique selling blouses and overcoats. Honling was interested in a rust-red overcoat that looked very much like mine, the Timberland jacket I had bought in the United States. This storekeeper was more enthusiastic about

Mandarin-speaking customers than the last one, and after some bargaining, we managed to cut two-thirds off the original price. Hon-ling was happy to get the jacket for
RMB 50, especially after she knew how much I had paid for mine. A disposable cash
income brought more than consumer items. It was a resource with which women
workers from the north asserted their dignity in the face of society's imposition of an
image of migrant peasant daughters as poverty-stricken and miserable.

CONCLUDING REMARKS

The world of labor in Shenzhen was marked by a double juxtaposition: of despotism
and localism, and of class and gender domination. The absence of proactive state regulation and union intervention might have provided a conducive environment for the
formation of a regime of explicit, punishment-oriented, coercive control. But this is
not an adequate explanation because it cannot account for the pivotal and constitutive
roles of gender and localism in production politics. Localism and genderism not only
organize the labor market and channel the supply of labor from all over China to
Shenzhen (see Chapter Four), they are also incorporated into the factory to facilitate
and legitimate managerial control. Class domination, now in the guise of gendered
localistic authority exercised by male locals over female locals, becomes more effective and less overt.

Along the way of unraveling the intersection of these three kinds of power in
structuring shop-floor politics, I have also called attention to an enlarged terrain of
contest in production. The politics of production is of course inscribed in the spatial,
technological, organizational, and wage structures as well as in managerial ideology.
Yet in addition to this conventional understanding, I agree with Michael Burawoy
that there is a need to restore a politics of subjectivity or identity as a critical political
moment in production. Yet my analysis diverges from his "class first" or "class only"
one in that I have found that workers' identities were crafted by their simultaneous
locations in the three interlocked hierarchies of gender, localism, and class. Colloquial
expressions, such as "maiden workers" and its corollaries, "northern maidens" and
"southern maidens," encapsulate this more subtle, contest of collective identities at
the point of production. Management practices construct and reproduce a dominant
conception of maidens as docile, short-term, ignorant, but quiescent laborers. Nevertheless, in the interstices of everyday life, I found women workers pursuing fragm-
entary and opportunistic clever tricks, maneuvers, and joyful discoveries with which
they reappropriate, to a certain extent, the system to their own ends, deflecting and
escaping its power without leaving it.[4] "Maiden workers" to them means a relatively
independent, modern, and romantic lifestyle in anticipation of marriage and adulthood. Hence the forged telegram, the recommendations of locals as new recruits,
and the hiding of boyfriends in the dormitory.

NOTES

1. Michael Burawoy, *The Politics of Production* (London: Verso, 1985), p. 88.
2. E. P. Thompson, "Time, Work-Discipline, and Industrial Capitalism," *Past and Present* 38 (1967): 56–97; Pierre Bourdieu, "The Attitude of the Algerian Peasant towards Time," in *Mediterranean Countrymen: Essays in Social Anthropology of the Mediterranean*, ed. Julian Pitt-Rivers (Paris: Mouton, 1963), quoted in Aihwa Ong, *Spirits of Resistance and Capitalist Discipline: Factory Women in Malaysia* (Albany: State University of New York Press, 1987), p. 8.
3. E. P. Thompson, "Time."
4. Michel de Certeau, *The Practice of Everyday Life* (Berkeley and Los Angeles: Univeristy of California Press, 1984), p. xiii.

CHAPTER TWELVE

Femininity and Flexible Labor: Fashioning Class Through Gender on the Global Assembly Line

Carla Freeman

Inside Data Air, one of Barbados's largest and long-standing informatics companies (started in 1983), hundreds of women sit in clustered computer stations, entering diagnostic codes and coverage rates for by-pass surgery and appendectomies for one of America's largest insurance companies now performing its claims adjusting 'off-shore'. In another of the company's divisions, data from over 300,000 ticket stubs from a single American airline's 2000 daily flights are entered by another hundred operators. One of roughly a dozen companies performing information processing in Barbados, Data Air employs close to 1000 workers, almost all of whom are women. It is the glamorous adornment of the office-like setting and of the well dressed operators more than the predominance of women alone, however, that sets this workplace apart from other offshore industries (e.g. garments, textiles and electronics assembly plants). The data processing companies are the newest members of a tightly concentrated circle of economic enterprises which encompass the entire 300-year history of this legendary sugar isle. Just west of the data processing firms are aging factory shells dating from the 1960s and 1970s when enclave manufacturing was thought to be the cornerstone of economic diversification. Beyond them is a new cruise ship terminal, the latest enhancement to the tourism industry which has driven the island's economy since independence in 1966. And at the water's edge, looming large and unbowed is the sugar terminal, a steel rhomboid with a capacity for over 200,000 tonnes of sugar – but under foreign management today, and lucky to see the fruits of a once unimaginably small 50,000 tonne crop.

In the last 15 years, the Caribbean, and Barbados in particular, has become the locus of a new high-tech service industry called 'offshore informatics'. Clerical services are increasingly moving from North American offices to the Caribbean, where women process and edit texts (from Shakespeare to pornography, academic journals to airline tickets and health insurance claims) via satellite hook-ups and sophisticated computer technologies. In many ways, the industry bears unmistakable marks of factory-like production, based on the export processing model of development widely adopted in the Caribbean following Puerto Rico's Operation Bootstrap in the 1950s. Much along the lines spelled out by Braverman (1974), as well as his feminist critics (Carter, 1987; Davies, 1982; McNeil, 1987; Pringle, 1988), work is increasingly fragmented, deskilled and feminized in the race by multinational capital to increase its profits.

In the 'post-industrial' US we are by now well aware of the movement of labor-intensive manufacturing industries. We have watched the flight of factories first from northeastern metropolitan centers to southern, mid-western or simply suburban parts of the country, and ultimately to developing countries 'offshore' in Asia, Central and South America and the Caribbean. While the labels on our clothes have for decades announced the global loci of production, the recent NAFTA debates brought this intensifying phenomenon to the consciousness of Americans, Mexicans and Canadians across class and regional divides. What has seldom been mentioned, however, is that computer-based service work – frequently presented as the panacea to economic restructuring, is also amenable to offshore flight. Information-centered office work that was once skilled or semi-skilled and involved the performance of varied tasks from book-keeping to filing, typing to receiving, now faces increasing rationalization and deskilling in what some have hailed as the 'paperless office'. Today, 'pools' of data entry operators, word processors, and other information workers perform their jobs on anonymous 'typing floors'. Businesses facing exponential increases in the production and management of information have been experimenting with a number of alternative strategies for 'streamlining' data flows, and reducing their costs. Some companies, for example, have centralized secretarial work into large and impersonal data processing floors; others have moved labor-intensive information work out of the workplace altogether and into the arena of suburban homes, paying operators to process insurance claims and credit card applications at 'piece rates'.

At the core of these transformations are women workers – on *both* 'sides' of the international division of labor. Those in the US face job losses or restructuring. 'Homeworkers' or 'temporary workers' are offered low pay with no benefits under the banner of flexibility, which purportedly allows women to juggle wage work with childcare and other domestic obligations. Those 'offshore' in the 'developing world' are promised a clean, cool, comfortable job – and, most importantly, access to the linchpin of modernity – computers. Indeed, critics have described informatics as an electronic sweatshop, where once-skilled white-collar workers have been reduced to production-line automatons, demoted and proletarianized. Supporters of the industry, on the other hand, emphasize its clean and clerical, 'professional' white-collar setting, and take pains to disassociate it from traditional factory work.

However, with different ends in mind, women, local officials and the transnational management all sustain a veil of ambiguity around the informatics industry and its job categories. Each group points to its office-like nature including fashionable and professional-looking workers to hail different measures of local/transnational success: from the transfer of technology to the developing world, to the promotion of a new growth industry and foreign exchange for the ailing sugar and tourism-based economy, and the creation of avenues for the advancement of women in Barbados.

Herein lies a clue to the unique stature of the industry and its offshore workers that sets it/them apart from their manufacturing counterparts, and, to a great extent, ensure that these unorganized working women will remain so. Informatics' novelty and its widely touted links to the 'information revolution' have created a rhetorical space of invention outside the conventional occupational categories. This space is filled with ambiguous but powerful notions of a computer age where new kinds of literacy and practice represent the promise of modernity, and, in effect, where those associated with informatics have been able to define a workplace identity almost from scratch.

By choosing to work in the large 'open offices' of the offshore informatics zone, Barbadian women can break with socially constructed constraints in several (perhaps ironic) ways. In such workplaces, they sever the symbolic 'over-lordship' of the white 'massa', for their remote (sometimes overseas) foreign white employers, who are not seen as carrying the burden of an association with slavery and racial hierarchy. Second, in the cool, clean realm of informatics, production supersedes all else, and lit-tle in the way of family connections, village origin, political affiliation let alone seniority affects pay scales or promotions. Generally, informatics workers have little direct contact with managers. Supervisors hand out work but even they rely on computers to calibrate operators' absences, performance and biweekly progress – a process largely immune to personal animus. While women clearly express resentment and stress associated with electronic monitoring, they *also* prefer it to the capriciousness and favoritism of the traditional supervisor.

On the other hand, some of the advantages of local paternalism are not missed by workers even in this super-high-tech arena, and by lobbying energetically, data entry operators have succeeded in forcing transnational firms, much against their will, to bend and 'harmonize' with the local scene. For example, workers on the night shift of Data Air convinced management of the need for a privately operated transportation system to supplement the local bus service in the evenings, to ensure their safe journeys home. This costs Data Air $100,000 a year, and through intraindustry pressure has become a standard perk within the informatics sector at large.

Strong pressure from female employees has also forced foreign companies locating in the West Indies to rethink their standard worker profile (typically defined as young, single, well educated and childless females) abandoning, for example, the usual pregnancy tests which elsewhere in the world have been a commonplace in recruitment policy. Instead, in Barbados, one can now find foreign managers extolling the commitment and superior labor of self-sacrificing mothers, as opposed to mercenary and ‘consumer-obsessed’ young girls reflecting the simple reality of child bearing in young women’s lives, and the fact that motherhood has never precluded wage work for West Indian women. Within this dialectic between local and global forces, other foreign transnational management practices have also been resisted. When ‘Total Quality Management’ (or TQM) was introduced, the inter-hierarchical ‘teams’ and attempts at Japanese styled participatory ‘work circles’ were met with suspicion and unease. Some women complained that meeting together with managers ‘just wasn’t right’, and that the mandatory use of first-names, designed to enhance familiarity and a ‘corporate family’ ethic, was ‘awkward’ and even ‘disrespectful’. At the other extreme, workers’ attempts to preserve some familiar aspects of local capitalist paternalism, such as company health coverage, have been uniformly resisted – along with any pressure toward unionization – by foreign transnationals.

While much of the literature about transnationals and women’s labor has portrayed internationally consistent hegemonic measures to ‘tap into’ and ‘use up’ global female workforces, the Barbadian informatics zone reveals striking examples in which women workers have been deeply involved in the establishment of unique images and practices integral to the formation of the informatics industry. As such, they counter the assumption that multinational corporations simply scour the globe availing them-selves of systematically cheap and docile pools of female labor, and demonstrate that these are active processes in which corporations, state administrators, local elites *and local women workers all* participate in the process of defining – indeed, creating – these female labor forces and the work they perform in particular, locally specific ways.

Because of its new and highly valued status within the rubric of ‘offshore industries’ informatics has opened up the possibility for new definitions, new associations and, indeed, new identities. It is this space of invention that helps to explain one of the most striking phenomena surrounding the informatics sector in the Barbadian economy – the simultaneous lack of interest in unionization, and the degree to which women are willing to work long hours performing demanding and tedious work for a lower wage than that offered in a number of other sectors.

Informatics has introduced a workplace discipline wholly unprecedented in the Barbadian context. Operators working on rotating shifts undergo constant surveillance by supervisors in their glass-enclosed offices and even more persistently, by the electronic panopticon of the computer itself. Their pay is determined by their ability to meet production quotas measured by keystrokes per hour, and demands of 99 percent accuracy. Lateness, absences and bathroom breaks are recorded and calibrated along with speed, accuracy and longitudinal progress. High unemployment (24 percent in general and estimated at 30 percent for women) is undeniably an important factor in the appeal of these jobs, but it is not the only one. In many cases data processors pass up better-paying jobs in other sectors of the economy. Among these are not only low-prestige jobs in agriculture and domestic work but also jobs in other service areas like retail sales, where the minimum wage rate is higher than data entry’s unregulated base pay, and where job demands are clearly less arduous.

Informatics remains a unique and elusive arena not only because of its slippery place between white- and blue-collar labor processes. 'Professionalism' and in particular 'professional looks' are noted by workers, management and state officials as distinguishing this industry from other sectors, particularly assembly-line manufacturing. High-tech modernity, as embodied most powerfully in the emblem of the computer and a distinct style of office-worker dress, lie at the heart of this image, and each of these three groups are distinctly invested with its importance – the corporate managers who count on a disciplined and flexible workforce, the government officials who anxiously hail informatics as a new cornerstone of national development and women workers, whose reasons are the most complex and interesting of all.

DISPUTING APPEARANCES: FASHIONING
THE GENDER OF CLASS

One hot afternoon at the crowded Lower Green bus stand in Bridgetown, Barbados, children in neat school uniforms and shoppers laden with heavy parcels hiding from the baking sun found their own hushed conversations punctuated by sudden shouting and defensive retorts. The morning shift at Global Informatics Ltd had been busy, and the women workers looked eager to leave when the clock struck 3:30. Five of the 60 young women workers on the shift emerged from the glass doors animated as they compared their daily work rates and resultant pay. At the shift's end, they changed from slippers to patent leather and well polished high heels and headed toward the bus stand. The commotion that erupted there centered around one of the data processors, boldly adorned in a floral skirt suit and donning an elaborately braided hair style with great aplomb. Suddenly she noticed her ex-boyfriend who had been waiting for her under a shady breadfruit tree. 'You see *she*? You *see* she?" he shouted to all around, motioning wildly for everyone to look closely. 'Don' mind she dress so, when Friday come, she only carryin' home $98!' What his outburst conveyed was, 'in case you people might mistake her for a middle-class woman with a good office job, let me tell you, she is really just a village girl with a factory wage'. Onlookers shifted on their feet, some showed signs of disdain for the public airing of a domestic dispute; a group of schoolgirls laughed. The taunts so disturbed another group of data processors at the bus stand that some beckoned a manager inside to come and 'stop the palava'.

The threat posed by mocking the image of prosperity and professionalism of the data processors is conveyed in a Barbadian adage that warns, 'Gold teet(h) don'(t) suit hog mout(h)', and implies that even extravagant adornments can't hide one's true station in life. What the adage and story together reveal is a deep tradition of propriety and expected conformity between class status and appearance. For 'Little England', the once prized sugar isle of the British empire, conformity and respectability lie at the heart of cultural tradition, and 'knowing one's place' is an admonition well known to Bajans of all generations. By exposing the realities of her meager wage in contradistinction to her impressive appearance, the disgruntled ex-boyfriend threatened to undermine a powerful set of images created and enforced by women workers and the informatics industry that employs them. His public outcry cautions against the dangers of masquerade. As Bourdieu so aptly put it, 'These calls to order ("Who does she think she is" or "not for the likes of us"), reaffirm the principle of conformity . . . They contain a warning against the ambition to distinguish oneself by identifying with other groups, that is, they are a reminder of the need for class solidarity' (1984: 380–1). While dress may seem a minor issue within a study of women workers in multinational industries, here amidst the high-tech glow of computer terminals within this new niche of the 'office-factory', dress and appearance become vital embodiments of the informatics sector and of new feminine identities for working women as members of a new pink-collar service class. As such, dress and appearance become central to the maintenance of ambiguous boundaries of class status, the diminution of class consciousness and to the frank absence of interest in unionization.

Despite a long history of trade unionism in Barbados and the well known strength of the Barbados Workers' Union (BWU), the largest industrial workers union representing a number of public and private sector trades and occupations, foreign-owned data entry companies are uniformly non-unionized. The Industrial Development Corporation claims that within the industrial relations context of the island, 'collective bargaining is the accepted practice for the agreement of employment terms and conditions, but union membership is not compulsory' (IDC, n.d.: 14). However, 'there is a sort of unwritten understanding that we [the unions] are not to go in there', as one labor unionist from the Barbados Workers Union described the relationship between labor and the offshore sector. While several union representatives expressed both annoyance at being kept out of these offshore industries, and keen interest in recruiting within this expanding new sector, during the Democratic Labour Party-led years of the fieldwork (1989–92) they avoided any strong efforts to unionize. The BWU stated matter of factly that in the face of rising unemployment, and the government's strong push to recruit foreign investment, there was little point in making waves within established offshore operations. And not surprisingly, from the management standpoint, the consensus was quietly but clearly against unionization. As one foreign general manager said:

> I'm not against unions; I used to be a union man. Unions have a role to play, but obviously as a manager of a company I would prefer to work without them. I can respond to problems without the interference of a middleman who is motivated by political ends.

His comment reflected a widely held sentiment toward the Barbados Workers' Union around whom frequent charges of 'conflict of interest' revolved. Three senior union officers were members of parliament for the governing DLP, including the General Secretary, Leroy Trotman. Another Deputy General Secretary actually served on the DLP cabinet. The quiet agreement by the unions to keep out of the offshore enterprises reflects, to a large degree, their compliance with the export-led economic development plan as articulated by the state and clearly espoused by the then-ruling

DLP. Interestingly, since 1993 when the Democratic Labour Party government lost office, the leadership of the Union, no longer serving simultaneously as members of govern-ment, turned the organizing of the offshore sector into a high-profile campaign. However, even now, with unemployment rates lower, the state of the economy more stable than in the previous period and greater activism on the part of the BWU, the informatics workers in both local and foreign owned companies are resistant to organizing.

Women are not drawn to labor organization not because they are naturally 'docile' and 'submissive' as multinational corporations have claimed for female workers across the global assembly line, but because their work in informatics offers them *symbolic* as well as economic capital that they are deeply interested in securing. The trade unions are seen as offering nothing that the human resources and employee relations departments of the firms do not already provide. The unions in Barbados, like other national institutions in the political–economic arena, have, according to an active female trade unionist, been a patriarchal stronghold not merely in allowing little participation of women within the movement itself, but also in its limited interest in predominantly female sectors of employment.

For the women workers in informatics, the emphasis on appearances and dress simultaneously comes to represent another medium of discipline (through corporate dress codes, peer pressure and pure expense) as well as an aperture of creative expression and a source of identification and pride. An identifiable *look* is both individually defined and collectively fostered. Both industry managers and operators themselves articulate standards for appropriate work attire – on one hand the official dress code specifies 'professional' appearance and deportment; on the other, operators and supervisors have honed and refined their own expectations that surpass those established by management. In one case, a group of employees started a campaign to introduce a company uniform in the colors of the company logo.

More generally, the level of surveillance and scrutiny operators and supervisors impose upon each other (more through gossip than formal reprimands) has introduced a self-awareness and self-discipline surrounding dress, hairstyles and general appearance that has reinforced this unmistakable image. The women's professional appearance is admired by industry affiliates as well as daily passers-by. New styles copied from foreign pattern books and boutiques, embellished with individualized details like a pocket handkerchief in matching fabric, a sash, belt or covered buttons to accent a bold color, carry enormous symbolic importance in the informatics scene in ways which defy socially prescribed identities linking class, job titles and appearances. The 'pink collar' then, with its ubiquitous 'skirt suit', represents a sort of feminine/professional disguise. The data entry operator essentially performs a repetitive, tedious, semi-skilled sort of 'blue-collar' work but in place of the dust and fumes of garment and electronics houses, she is situated within a cleaner, cooler 'white-collar' setting. As part of the trade, she is expected to appear distinctly feminine and 'professional'.

As the earlier vignette implies, preoccupation with appearances, deportment and 'respectability' is a well known and much discussed phenomenon in the West Indies, associated particularly with women aspirating to the norms of white European society. However, the lines between respectability and 'show-offiness' or 'dibby dibby styles' (whorish or sexually 'loose' appearances) are crucial. Admonishments in the employee-written newsletter echo the old Bajan adage 'a pick fowl en' got nuh pedigree. . .' or, 'since one's feathers speak loudly of one's station in life, one should take care to dress in an appropriate manner'. One manager noted to me:

> Women are expected to dress professionally here. This is not a production mentality like jeans and tee shirts. When you see a group of the young ladies like the ones from Data Air, you see that they're much better dressed than the ones from the assembly plants . . . They're probably not getting paid much better but their work environment is a cleaner one, a purer one, and they in fact live out that environment. The Data Air office is very plush so the young ladies working in there perceive that they are working in an office and they dress like it and they live like it . . . it only got started when the data entry business got started – this new breed of office-type workers. They equate themselves with . . . clerical staff in an office and they carry themselves in that way.

Like multinationals in other parts of the world, these high-tech service enterprises have shrewdly tapped into a strong Barbadian concern with appearance and have turned this set of cultural values to the advantage of international capital, by encouraging workers to identify with a well defined corporate image. By setting standards for appearance that give workers pride, the companies enhance the operators' commitment and sense of obligation to their employer. And, by creating a professional-looking working environment through decor and office ergonomics ($200 swivel chairs and custom designed work spaces), corporate managers expect in return, not only professional-*looking* workers but ones who are also willing to put in overtime on demand, as this is what professionals are expected to do. Corporate imperatives such as meeting deadlines, accommodating rush orders, or processing heavy batches of tickets or encyclopedia chapters on tight schedules, demand a great deal of overtime and flexible scheduling on the part of the workforce (e.g. staying late, coming in on weekends and working double shifts). One way of encouraging a willingness to put in 'the extra mile' is to make employees feel that it is to their benefit as well to see these goals met.

What we are witnessing in Barbados is the emergence of a new West Indian woman who moves within a transnational arena, both as a producer, through the data she processes, and even more literally as a consumer, as she increasingly seeks out imported goods and invents new styles to mark her status. In light of the low wages of informatics workers, maintenance of this requisite 'professional' appearance is only made possible through additional economic activities – some of which closely resemble traditional market exchanges or home-based services, and others which are much more radically transformative transnational movements involving air travel.

As an incentive scheme to promote high levels of production and reliability at work, highly productive informatics operators are rewarded with bonus pay and special 'thank you cards', redeemable for airline travel (compliments of Data Air's parent company). With such vouchers, women fly between Barbados, San Juan, Miami and New York on weekend or week-long shopping sprees, sometimes specifically orchestrated by local travel agents, and including inexpensive motels and ground transport to convenient shopping malls. In their travel, they are both generating income through the re-sale of goods, and 'checking styles' as they scour department stores and fashion books. Through the purchase and informal marketing of imported clothes, accessories and household goods, these new 'suitcase traders' add another dimension to their position and identity as workers in the transnational economy.

Traditionally Barbadians have always supplemented their wages in the formal economy with income from informal trade and production. This practice is common among all classes. Doctors and members of parliament, white and black, will keep chickens, pigs or Barbadian black-belly sheep for occasional sale. Working-class men might cut hair or fish in their free time to earn extra money, and since the days of slavery, female country higglers have been the primary actors in vibrant produce markets across the West Indies. In addition to sewing clothes and school uniforms, women typically bake cakes, prepare traditional foods or braid hair for friends and acquaintances. What is different about the informatics sector is the degree to which it intensifies this cultural tradition by increasing both the demand for and the supply of new goods. By cultivating workers' identity in terms of a professional style, the informatics sector has become a site of display – a showcase of not only new age technology but also of new age femininity, and the latter has become entwined with fashion and 'accessorizing' in ways that deliberately distinguish them as a group from women workers in similar income brackets (hence the demand side of the equation). Informatics workers, therefore, not only subsidize low wages through their extra informal labor, but also sustain the mirage of professional prosperity and upward mobility for women that the Barbadian government and the international corporate sector so anxiously assert. At the same time the travel vouchers help to stimulate the supply of new and imported fashions and styles. Recently, among the data processors, fashion design and sewing courses have become popular after-work 'improvement' activities, and the installment purchase of sewing machines is a frequent expenditure. Home-based needle working (seamstressing), and the new 'suitcase trading' have become central arenas through which data processors not only supplement their formal income, but also refine their own 'professional look'.

The informal sector is important not simply for supplementing women's formal wage and increasing their purchasing power, but also in terms of the enjoyment and satisfaction women derive from creating and supplying new consumer goods and styles for their friends, family, fellow workers and themselves. The role played by the informal needleworker and suitcase trader is significant, therefore, not simply in providing a cheaper alternative to the machine-made clothes in the boutiques mushrooming around the island, and enabling fashion to play such a large role in the lives of working-class women, but they appear as well to be bound up in a growing globalization of consumption and aesthetics.

The links between women's practices as producers and consumers challenges what has for the past decade seemed to be a useful way of formulating the gendered contours of the international division of labor. Mies (1986) argued that the international division of labor 'worked' only when the following two conditions were fulfilled: production costs were dramatically lowered by export-oriented enterprises which depended on the cheap labor of docile and malleable Third World women; and consumer-housewives in rich industrialized countries were mobilized to purchase goods produced in the Third World. Both of these strategies, she argued, depended largely on women – Third World women as producers, First World women as consumers. Her analysis of the silent relationship between women on 'both sides' of the international division of labor was ground-breaking. However, Mies's model misses the complexities of transnationalism as these young Bajan data processors now experience it. What Mies could not have expected was the increasing rate at which Third World women too become consumers. Specifically, what the informatics workers demonstrate is the integral relationship between their experience as producers and the form and context in which they increasingly consume transnational goods, styles and culture. What makes mass consumption possible among these Barbadian women, however, is not simply their employment in the transnational arena, but their involvement in newly expanded practices of informal marketing and trade. Women's wage-earning employment as data processors becomes closely intertwined with informal economic activities that simultaneously place them within an international sphere where they are both the producers and consumers of services, commodities and styles. Women in developing countries who just a short while ago may have provided only the labor behind these consumer goods that Mies depicts as the very life-blood of suburban housewives of the industrialized West, now *themselves* demand many such items of adornment and convenience.

A number of recent writings about consumption, and fashion in particular (e.g. Craik, 1994; de Certeau, 1984; Miller, 1987; Pringle, 1988; Willis, 1991; E. Wilson, 1985), have challenged the notion that consumption essentially implies extravagance, waste and false consciousness. Others (e.g. Lee, 1993; Rutz and Orlove, 1989; Wilk, 1990, etc.) have reminded us that consumption is as central to exchange as production. I take up these arguments in order to suggest that we explore the ways in which production and consumption are integrally connected – not simply as economic activities but in creating feminine identities – in this case, among a new category of workers. This entails a view of consumption not simply as a passive act – or worse, of consumers as uncritical dupes of multinational advertising. Rather, consumption becomes a process with creative possibilities and multiple meanings. For the data processors, consumption provides a means for social differentiation – for *making oneself* through the expression of taste, where taste is a signifier of class (Bourdieu, 1984). New forms of consumption do not, in and of themselves, transform people into different sorts of human beings. However, as Mintz recently remarked about the working classes in late 18th-century Britain, 'consuming exotic products purchased with their own labor – which allowed them to see themselves as *being* different because they were able to choose to consume differently – surely helped to *make* them different' (1996: 78). The suggestive power of consumption that allows people to *imagine themselves otherwise* by participating in such practices embodies both creative as well as potentially transformative qualities.

Elements of danger (as exhibited by the bus stand episode) and pleasure, embodied in the professional image-making of the informatics zone, lie in the blurring between this symbolic work and its economic underpinnings, indeed, in the delineation of class itself. The informatics operators in Barbados cannot concoct their jobs per se – they earn factory wages and have no *organized* effect on the use or structure of either the economic capital or the political order in the society in which they live. These companies may, as many others have done, suddenly decide to leave Barbados in search of more profitable conditions elsewhere in the developing world. However, the status women derive from their work (even if more 'symbolic' than economic-ally 'real') has enabled them to contribute to the definition of a new occupational category whose mystery allows them some power of invention, and this in turn, extends beyond the realm of informatics.

At the same time, the concern about appearance and the desire to look profes-sional has as much to do with demarcating a line which separates them from factory workers as it does with identifying with their foreign bosses. It has little or nothing in fact to do with the actual service aspect of their job, as their clients are by definition overseas and invisible. But it has everything to do with the public persona they and their employer wish to cultivate in their own communities.

Part of the intriguing nature of this emphasis on professional demeanor and de-portment is precisely related to the hidden nature of the work. Others (Hochschild, 1983; Leidner, 1993; Paules, 1991) have noted the importance of emotional labor and the gendered dimensions of service work in other occupations (e.g. restaurant waitresses, airline flight attendants). For a job performed not only in the 'back office' but thousands of miles away from its clients' gaze, the importance of appearances is notably ironic. In fact, professional dress is as important for the workers' *commute* as for the workplace itself. While most informatics companies are located in a central-ized information processing zone in the capital city of Bridgetown, one company recently set up an operation in the countryside to save women the commute, and save themselves transportation costs demanded by women on the night shift. The experiment failed miserably, however, as the lackluster building, surrounding cane fields and view of the plantation yard held little appeal. Despite the early hours and often long bus rides demanded by shift work, women prefer to go to town. Indeed, unlike their urban American counterparts who don smart suits with running shoes en route to the office, the Bajan data operators display shiny patent leather or well polished shoes and bags on their commute to work or fast food lunch break. In the chilly recesses *inside,* however, high heels are often kicked under desks, in favor of stocking feet, plastic slippers or 'software' as sneakers are commonly called.

By escaping the paternalism of the traditional Barbadian workplace for a comparatively meritocratic, impersonal informatics company, and simultaneously challenging foreign management to localize their practices and workplaces with selected components of that same paternalism, Barbadian women have created a hybrid space between the transnational and the local. In this space, they are freer than at any time in Barbadians' living memory to construct a gendered occupational identity that marks itself with valued emblems of middle-class status, and through their patterns of consumption and their unique 'pink-collar' production, they are engaged in blurring class distinctions themselves. On the other hand, with the emphasis on distinguishing themselves from the ranks of their factory-working neighbors, class solidarity is clearly de-emphasized.

Of course, the mystery is not only liberating but burdensome as well, and both the freedom and the weight falls heaviest upon the shoulders of the women themselves – as they are pushed into a double or even triple day to make ends meet, *and* sustain the 'professionalism' mirage. Their efforts to achieve middle-class status converge but are not identical with corporate and government efforts to convince them of the 'professional' nature of their work, and it bears repeating that at every turn the informatics workers are confronted with surveillance, discipline and their structurally subordinate status. By trying on fashions, adopting a new look and publicly obscuring the labor process of informatics in favor of its office appearance, I am not arguing that women are convinced that they are indeed 'professionals'. However, they are adamant that they are not factory workers, and, as such, become less interested and even hostile to movements towards class solidarity through unionization, since this would require an identification with occupational categories they precisely wish to deny. Their self-concepts (as revealed in taste, style and practices) have changed along with the distinct fashioning of informatics in ways that mark new identities along the transnational continuum of gender and class. At the heart of this lies disjuncture and contestation between material realities and symbolic appearances, between local paternalism and transnational anonymity, between compliance and resistance, and between alienation and pleasure.

REFERENCES

Bourdieu, Pierre (1984) *Distinction: A Social Critique of Judgement and Taste.* Cambridge, MA: Harvard University Press. (Orig. 1979.)

Braverman, Harry (1974) *Labor and Monopoly Capitalism.* New York: Monthly Review Press.

Carter, Valerie J. (1987) 'Office Technology and Relations of Control in Clerical Work Organ-
    izations', in Barbara D. Wright (ed.) *Women, Work and Technology: Transformations*.
    Ann Arbor: University of Michigan Press.

Craik, Jennifer (1994) *The Face of Fashion: Cultural Studies in Fashion*. New York: Routledge.,

Davies, Margery W. (1982) *Woman's Place is at the Typewriter: Office Work and Office
    Workers 1870–1930*. Philadelphia: Temple University Press.

de Certeau, Michel (1984) *The Practice of Everyday Life*. Berkeley: University of California
    Press.

Hochschild, Arlie R. (1983) *The Managed Heart: Commercialization of Human Feeling*.
    Berkeley: University of California Press.

Lee, Martyn J. (1993) *Consumer Culture Reborn: The Cultural Politics of Consumption*.
    New York: Routledge.

Leidner, Robin (1993) *Fast Food, Fast Talk: Service Work and the Routinization of Everyday
    Life*, Berkeley: University of California Press.

McNeil, Maureen (1987) *Gender and Expertise*. London: Free Association Books.

Mies, Maria (1986) *Patriarchy and Accumulation on a World Scale: Women in the Inter-
    national Division of Labor*. London: Zed Books.

Miller, Daniel (1987) *Material Culture and Mass Consumption*. Oxford: Basil Blackwell.

Mintz, Sidney (1996) *Tasting Food, Tasting Freedom*. Boston, MA: Beacon Press.

Paules, Greta Foff (1991) *Dishing it Out: Power and Resistance among Waitresses in a
    New Jersey Restaurant*, Philadelphia, PA: Temple University Press.

Pringle, Rosemary (1988) *Secretaries Talk: Sexuality, Power and Work*. London: Verso.

Rutz, Henry J. and Benjamin S. Orlove (1989) *The Social Economy of Consumption: Mono-
    graphs in Economic Anthropology*. Lanham, MD: University Press of America.

Wilk, Richard (1990) 'Consumer Goods as Dialogue about Development', *Culture and History*
    7: 79–100.

Willis, Susan (1991) *A Primer for Daily Life*. New York: Routledge.

Wilson, Elizabeth (1985) *Adorned in Dreams: Fashion and Modernity*. Berkeley: University of
    California Press.

CHAPTER THIRTEEN

The Enterprise as Community

RONALD DORE

The corporation buses come thick and fast outside the gates of the English Electric factories at closing time, though not always for the destinations that people most often want to go to. 'Improving the service on the No. 69 route' is a common item on the works committee agenda, and sometimes a welfare officer will actually remonstrate with the bus company. But by and large, once one is outside of the factory gates, one is a citizen. One rides on the corporation buses *que* rate-payer, not *qua* English Electric employee.

From the Furusato factory, some of those who are not on bicycles walk out to bus queues, some to the train station. In the queue for each major route, in the group of workers decanted at each suburban station down the line, one is likely to see one man wearing a rather formal blue serge uniform. He is the communications committee member for the station. If he takes his job seriously he may make it his business to board the train last in the mornings, making sure that everyone is aboard before he nods to the porter who nods to the guard to blow his whistle. He it is, at any rate, who represents his fellow-commuters in any negotiations with the railways over changes of timetable. In strikes or breakdowns he really comes into his own, marshalling his patient team while he telephones to the factory to check on alternative transport.

In neither firm, of course, does one entirely cease to be an employee as soon as one walks through the factory gate. Both firms recognize in a multiplicity of ways that the employment relationship entails obligations and considerations beyond the mere exchange of labour service and cash. In Hitachi they go a good deal *further* than in English Electric.

This is certainly so, for *manual* workers, in the matter of fringe benefits of a conventional kind. . . . At English Electric these are supplemented by a contributory pension scheme, intended to be self-financing, which provides a supplement for staff and for skilled craftsmen, though the latter become eligible to join only from their *eleventh* year of service. There are no pension provisions for manual workers other than craftsmen who must rely on pensions from the state. In Japan, where a state scheme for contributory old-age pensions for employees began only during the war, and where universal non-contributory pensions began – and then on a very small scale – only a decade ago, firms have traditionally paid all permanent workers a lump-sum retirement gratuity based on grade, length of service and final salary. Recently, foreseeing the enormous cost of such a scheme when the big post-war intakes of workers begin to reach retirement age, the policy has been to hold constant the gratuity provisions and supplement them with a contributory scheme for which the firm contributes half the cost.

The big difference in retirement provisions, however, is that the working life at Hitachi is shorter. Retirement is at 56 (except for directors) compared with English Electric's 65. Increasingly, however, Hitachi 're-employs' the retired for an extra four or five years – but at a lower salary. A man may be cut back to the wage of a 30- or 35-year-old, but if his retirement gratuity pays off any remaining house mortgage and provides a little extra to launch his children into the world, he may be able to manage well enough. Others may be found jobs with the smaller sub-contractors of Hitachi where retirement comes later. Of the 79 men who retired from the Furusato factory in 1966, 10 stayed on and 45 were found other jobs.

These monetary provisions apart, in neither company need a long-serving member entirely sever his links with the firm when he retires. Both firms provide a certain amount of sociability for the retired – membership in clubs, annual dinners and outings for veterans. English Electric, through a fund set up in memory of the first chairman, provides a small number of old people's homes.

But the differences in other types of welfare provisions are greater than in the matter of pensions. Some of these differences, and the assumptions underlying them, are worth looking at in more detail.

THE SCOPE OF ENTERPRISE WELFARE

First, Hitachi's provisions are much wider in scope and more costly. Housing is the outstanding example. The Bradford factory has some twenty-seven company-owned flats and houses available, at more or less economic rents, for employees moving into the district. The welfare department also tries on occasion to help its workers to get into corporation housing. But this represents a supplementary reserve of assistance in a situation where the basic principle is that a man's housing is his own affair. Hitachi, by contrast, operates on the principle that the company must take the prime responsibility. At the Furusato factory, there are hostels enough to accommodate all the unmarried men and women high school and university graduates. (Middle school graduates are recruited locally and so are expected to live at home, though they can, if necessary, be accommodated too.) Then there are large company estates with rented accommodation which cater for some 40% of the married men employees.

. . .

VOLUNTARY CHOICE

A second difference is that more of English Electric's schemes are on a voluntary contractual basis.

. . .

At Hitachi factories, both the sports and social association (president, the works manager; vice-president, the union chairman) and the Mutual Aid Fund, are in theory independent organizations – and have been since the first embryo organization on these lines was created in 1919 – but even if there is, buried somewhere in the rules, a stipulation that membership is voluntary, no one knows of it. In practice every-one belongs. The degree of company subsidization is greater, too. For the Mutual Aid Fund, for example, the company pays 100 and the individual 30 yen a month.

THE FUNCTION OF WELFARE SERVICES

A third difference is that English Electric, unlike Hitachi, attaches no very great posi-tive value to its welfare and fringe benefits. The firm is prepared, as part of its civic duty (in much the same way as it has co-operated since the war with government savings campaigns, arranges for mass X-rays and blood donations, trains apprentices who will leave the firm and permits deductions to be made from wages for charities) to provide facilities for its workers, provided that it is not too costly in money or man-agerial time. But the costs and benefits have to be nicely calculated.

. . .

There is, to be sure, some recognition of the advantages of being a 'good employer'; at the most basic level, pensions and sick pay schemes have to be competitive with those of other employers; beyond that there is a feeling that some of the traditions of the more paternalistic past – the annual Gala Day with flower show, the annual dance, the foreman's dinner – are worth keeping up because thet do, after all, help marginally to create good will towards the company amongst its employees. But if it turns out that the support for the sports club football team or for the male voice choir is so thin that both need reinforcement by outside 'associate members' no one is greatly disturbed

At Hitachi, by contrast, the section of the general affairs department which deals with these matters is positively entrepreneurial. They are happy to offer interviewers an account of their philosophy – solemn little homilies about all work and no play making Jack a dull boy. In the mid-sixties, to increase participation in sports activities, they started nominating a *rekkuriidaa* (*recreation leader*, of course) in each section and giving them a special weekend training camp. In other fields, too, their activity is impressive. The auditorium of the Hitachi factory, built to celebrate the firm's fiftieth anniversary, seats 1,200. It has been slightly overshadowed by the union's bigger audi-torium built a few years later, but it fights back with some promotional skill. For every concert put on at the union auditorium by the Workers' Musical Society (a militant left-wing body, very keen on togetherness and audience participation) the company auditorium arranges a concert (albeit, to the welfare section's chagrin, a somewhat more sedate and unexciting concert) under the auspices of the capitalist-sponsored Industrial Musical Society. There is an athletics stadium, one large and one smaller baseball stadium, a gymnasium, a swimming pool and various tennis and volley-ball courts. To celebrate the firm's sixtieth anniversary in 1970 several thousands of pounds were spent on a spectacular fireworks display. The annual sports day is a grand affair, and the fact that preparations for the fancy dress parade which is one of its central features cause some loss of production in the previous weeks is thought to be an unfortunate but necessary cost.

TIMES OF TROUBLE

Fourthly, there is a difference in the handling of less formal welfare matters – personal contingencies not catered for in explicit rules. In Hitachi these are matters for the line supervisors. One's foreman or superintendent is the man one goes to if in trouble. If a man dies, the foreman tells a couple of the work team to take two or three days off to help the widow with the funeral arrangements, and the whole team would norm-ally go to the funeral. The foreman has the responsibility for sick visiting, though he may delegate a workmate to do the job. In an English Electric factory, by contrast, these matters are taken care of not through the authority structure of the small work team, but in the first place by customs of spontaneous *collateral* assistance among workmates. If a man dies, his mates will make a collection for the widow; the fore-man may or may not take the lead in organizing it; it is more likely to be the shop steward, though the welfare office may see to ordering a wreath, from money col-lected on the shop floor, and some paid time might be allowed to attend the funeral. To that extent the event is officially recognized.

. . .

UNIONS AND WELFARE

A fifth difference lies in the union's role in welfare matters. At English Electric, by and large, the unions are completely uninvolved. A chief shop steward at the Bradford factory was also, as chairman of the works committee, responsible for making grants from the hardship fund mentioned above, but this was in his personal capacity. The combine committee has shown some concern with pensions and sick pay, but by and large unions have been concerned with matters of wages and work in their dealings with employers – though most unions, of course, also act as friendly societies and pro-vide sick pay for their members, another form of collateral mutual aid entirely inde-pendent of the employment relationship.

The situation is different at Hitachi. In the 'soft' side of welfare the union is some-what ambiguously involved. On the one hand the union chairman is vice-president of the sports and social association and *exofficio* member of the organizing committee for the annual sports day. On the other, the union is in competition with the company offering its own auditorium, its own hiking clubs and its own loan schemes. On the 'hard' side of welfare involving monetary benefits, however, the union is actively con-cerned to make sure that the firm improves its provisions, pressing for better benefits as well as higher wages. One of the elected full-time officials is fully occupied with welfare matters. His job is partly to run the union's rival welfare services, partly to make sure that the company does not skimp its obligations in such matters as housing repairs, partly to prepare negotiating positions for demands for higher retirement gratuities. Company welfare is counted as part of the rights of employees to be guarded and extended.

VIRTUE

Another aspect of Hitachi's closer approach to being a 'total community' lies in its concern with its employees' morals. . . . One English Electric factory did send some of its apprentices to Outward Bound for character training, but the scale of Hitachi's concern for moulding the values and attitudes of its employees is made much more openly evident – and for all grades of employees. Nor is the concern limited to the brief period of training. Under the influence of the former president of the com-pany a number of Hitachi factories have branches of the Ethical Society, a body supported from the expense accounts of a number of Japanese companies, whose primary function is to publish a monthly magazine entitled *Kōjō*, which is best translated, perhaps, as *Aiming High*. The magazine's short stories and its articles on health in middle age, on gardening (the cultivation of flowers and the cultivation of the spirit), on the life struggle of a blind architect, on the persistence and intel-lectual enthusiasm of night-school students, its reminiscences of their youth by retired business men (including 'how I went to secret Marxist study groups but was held back by instinctive patriotism from total commitment – and didn't care if people called me a coward'), its advice to mothers on how to react when their 8-year-old sons get an erection and on how to get the most out of PTA meetings, its straight-forward little homilies on kindliness in little things by the society's leader, promote virtues not dissimilar from those of Outward Bound – enthusiasm for work and vigorous play, healthy extraverted camaraderie, serious-mindedness, patriotism, honesty, clean living and high thinking. The society also arranges weekend outings to put clean living and high thinking into practice – getting up before dawn to stand naked under a waterfall intoning uplifting poetry, for example, or visiting the Ise shrine. The slogan which decorated more than one office wall in the Hitachi factory – 'a world without kindness is grim: a world without sweat is decadent' – is a part of the Ethical Society's initiation pledge.

THE FIRM AND THE FAMILY

A final and related difference: an English Electric man's family is his own concern and responsibility. Wives and girl-friends may be brought to the annual dance or to the Gala Day for the ambiguous pleasure of seeing the dim-witted or dastardly colleagues and superiors who figure in their husband's reports of his factory life. There is a widow's pension scheme for the very highest categories of staff, but even at that managerial level, hardly any obvious penetration of American organization man's belief that a wife's qualities intimately affect a man's performance. Welfare officers will, if necessary, help sort out serious family problems. But by and large the family of employees is of concern to the company as such only in so far as his work efficiency is manifestly affected by family problems, to his workmates only in so far as association breeds personal friendship.

In Hitachi the long arm of the company's concern reaches further. A man's family are peripheral members of the company family. The company, for instance, offers a system, of educational loans for employees' children, and maintains a dormitory in Tokyo for the children of employees attending universities or cram schools preparing for university entrance. Perhaps the best indication of the scope of the company's concern is to be found in a list of the various uses of the Mutual Aid Fund. Each member of the firm receives, automatically and according to a standard tariff, varied only according to length of service (not, for instance, rank), gifts of money for a variety of occasions – his own wedding (with an additional present of the firm's electrical appliances for girls leaving the firm to marry), on the birth of a child, or when that child first enters primary school or when it gets married. Condolence gifts are made on his own death, or the death of a member of his family, or for flood or fire disaster. Gifts ranged in 1966 from £35 as condolence 'incense money' on an employee's death and £10 as an average wedding gift, to a standard £2.50 for a child's starting school. It does not matter that the fund is 20% contributory, 80% financed from the company's general funds; the principle is that the joys and sorrows of one are the joys and sorrows of all.

The family is involved at another level too. A foreman's wife may call on the sick wife of her husband's subordinates; and a man might send his wife round to a superior's house with a 'thank you' present when he has been shown some special consideration. . . . This sense of family involvement is, of course, facilitated by and much heightened by the fact that a large proportion of families live cheek by jowl in the company housing estates.

The firm's recognition of the fact that their workers are not just individual sellers of labour, but also family men, is two-edged. The British system sharply separates the man's role as employee from his role as husband and father, and the firm disclaims responsibility for, or jurisdiction over, the latter. The Japanese firm, by contrast, admits a concern for both, but where there is possibility of conflict requires – to some degree at least – the subordination of the family role. The fact that a man had planned to take his children for an outing would be seen as a rather 'selfish' reason for trying to avoid overtime work on a Sunday if an order had to be finished. For a manager, a good wife is one who accepts that her husband's work must come first, and resigns herself to seeing little of him during the week – or even, should the need to sweeten the firm's clients or to express solidarity with his colleagues take him to the golf course on Sundays, at the weekends either. If the firm requires a man to go to a distant works he will accept the 'posting' and may, for the sake of the children's schooling or for some other reason, leave his family behind. (One young English Electric manager, by contrast, chose his firm because he wanted to live close to his Liverpool family and the Aintree racing ambience, then left it for another firm largely because he decided he would rather live in London.)

This is not *just* a matter of the demands of the organization. It is partly a reflection of the fact that for all the Japanese concern with 'the family' as a corporate group – its ancestry, its honour and its property – less value has been placed in Japan than in England on the actual quality of personal relations within the family, except on the relation of a mother with her children. There is in this something similar to the man's world/woman's world division found in some traditional British working-class areas.

But this is not quite the whole story; ethical traditions at a different level are also involved. One historical ancestor of the modern Japanese corporation (see Chapter 14) is the samurai band of the semi-autonomous fiefs into which Japan was divided during the Tokugawa period. This was more a hierarchical network of *family* groups than of individuals. The death of one family head and his replacement by his heir did not in theory alter the network of loyalties and obligations between families. The whole family was subordinated to the lord's family – from which it followed, for any particular individual, that the interests of his own family should be subordinated to the interests of the fief. That was the path of true virtue, true fief patriotism, true loyalty to one's feudal lord.

. . .

Hitachi workers and English Electric workers differ markedly in the degree of their involvement in the firm; in the etent to which their work roles take precedence over other roles. Most Hitachi men of the rank of foreman or above – and, indeed, a good number of ordinary workers – have calling cards on which they are identified by their firm, department and title. A Hitachi man often wears his Hitachi badge when he goes off for a holiday. An English Electric manager, by contrast, may show where his primary identification lies by wearing his Round Table or his Young Conservative ties to the works (though some foremen can be seen, at work, wearing a Foreman's Association tie).

. . .

THE FIRM AND THE INDIVIDUAL

Once again we come back to the lifetime employment pattern *v.* the market-oriented pattern as a precondition for the differences outlined above. Time builds up identification; not just time past, the familarity of long association, but also the prospect of time to come. And this is not just a matter of individual experiences. English Electric also has 50-year-old workers with a quarter of a century of service who expect to finish out their time with the firm. They too have *some* feeling for the firm. They are likely to tell you, with a tinge of sardonic pride, how English Electric never makes money because of its tradition of workmanship. ('Customer'll ring up and say he's got a generator we made in 1923 and still working but just needs a little spare part – and we'll waste hours digging out the blueprint and making it for him.') But still they feel themselves less totally and definitively English Electric men than their counterparts would feel themselves Hitachi men because personal experience is translated into sentiment and attachments only by refraction through the norms of the work community – the *shared* norms of their fellow-workers. It is overstating the case to say that one feels only what one is supposed to feel, but it is safe to say that one is more easily disposed to feel what one is supposed to feel – the more so the more oversocialized and conformist the society is. And in English Electric the relevant norms faithfully reflect the organizational assumptions underlying them – the limited commitment, the basic market orientation.

It is not just that the Japanese system enhances enterprise consciousness; it also – the other side of the coin – does less to develop individualism. Man-imbedded-in-organization has no great need to make personal moral choices; the organization's norms set guidelines; the organization's sanctions keep him to the path of virtue. It is the man between organizations, the man of limited commitment, who has the greater responsibility of choosing. 'When you buy a man over from a rival firm, you don't buy all that firm's secrets', said one English Electric manager. 'Of course, you couldn't help but be influenced by what you know about your old firm's plans and so on. But you don't give away confidences. Your people in your *new* firm wouldn't trust you if you did.' This kind of deliberate autonomous reserve, the acceptance of universal rules which is at the core of the integrity of man-in-the-market (whether it be in practice an operational norm or merely an ideal norm in the British business world) is something that the Hitachi worker has little need for, little chance to develop.

CHAPTER FOURTEEN

Yoseba and *Ninpudashi:* Changing Patterns of Employment on the Fringes of the Japanese Economy

TOM GILL

. . .

DAY LABORERS AT THE *YOSEBA*

Yoseba are open-air casual labor markets. Most major Japanese cities have a *yoseba*, and the biggest ones, in descending order of size, are Kamagasaki in Osaka, San'ya in Tokyo, Kotobuki in Yokohama, and Sasashima in Nagoya. Among minor *yoseba* are Takadanobaba in Tokyo, Chikkō in Fukuoka, Shinkaichi in Kobe, Uchihama in Kyoto, Don in Hiroshima, Tenmonkan in Kagoshima and Shūri in Naha, Okinawa. There is a massive Japanese-language literature on *yoseba* and an academic society devoted to their study.[1] There is also a fast-growing *yoseba* literature in English, including de Barry (1985) and Fowler (1996) on San'ya, and Ventura (1992) and Stevens (1997) on Kotobuki, while Matsuzawa (1988) provides a useful brief overview of the institution. The *yoseba* at Kotobuki is the main source of casual labor for the construction industry in Yokohama. It also supplies warehouse and longshoring labor to the docks at Yokohama and other ports, but containerization has greatly reduced this sector of the market for casual labor. Other once-significant employers, such as transportation and manufacturing, have all but disappeared.

    Yoseba have a long and complex history, which I discuss elsewhere (Gill forthcoming 2001). The word literally means a 'gathering place,' and denotes an open-air labor market, where men gather early in the morning to negotiate employment for the day with street-corner labor recruiters known as *tehaishi* ('arrangers'). There are many kinds of *tehaishi*: some are independent small businessmen, while others are employees of the companies that use the labor, or have a special association with one or several of those companies. Some are themselves *yakuza*; those who are not will generally be paying off the *yakuza* in some form for the right to operate unmolested in the *yoseba*. These protection payoffs are called *shobadai*.[2] *Tehaishi* tend to have specialties: some will specialize in dock-work, others in construction. In Kotobuki, which has far more foreign workers than most other *yoseba*,[3] some, *tehaishi* specialize in recruiting Korean Chinese, or Filipino laborers. The day wage varies with degree of skill and the balance of supply and demand, but by the time the *tehaishi* has taken his cut, popularly estimated at 25 to 30 percent, the unskilled laborer will likely have roughly ¥10,000, or $90, in hand. Men who do skilled or dangerous work may get up to twice that amount.

Day laborers tend to be single men. Some are lifelong bachelors, others are divorced or separated. Many of them live in cheap lodging houses called *doya* – a slang reversal of the word *yado*, standard Japanese for an inn. *Doya* charge anything from ¥1,000 to ¥3,000 a night for rent of a tiny room just big enough to lie down in. This makes them very cheap compared with most other kinds of hotel, but surprisingly expensive compared with small apartments rented by the month. Their appeal to day laborers stems from the fact that unlike apartments, they do not require a major non-returnable down payment or letter of guarantee from a responsible citizen, or even proof of identity. In Kamagasaki, San'ya and Kotobuki, there are concentrations of a hundred or more *doya*: hence these places are sometimes referred to as *doya-gai* (lodginghouse towns) as well as *yoseba*. These locations are associated with gambling and heavy drinking, and are sometimes compared with the American skid row (Caldarola 1968; Giamo 1994; Marr 1997).

Government attempts to regulate the day labor market date back to the mid-seventeenth century (Leupp 1992: 160–4), and still persist today, in the form of public casual labor exchanges that have been set up in each of the four main *yoseba*. Kamagasaki, San'ya, and Kotobuki actually have two casual labor exchanges each, one run by the Ministry of Labor and the other by the local authorities. The Ministry of Labor also runs a system of unemployment insurance tailor-made for day laborers. The worker carries a handbook, in which revenue stamps are affixed and franked by employers for each day worked. So long as a man has the stamps to demonstrate 26 days' work done in the previous two calendar months, he is entitled to a payment of ¥7,500 (roughly $65) per day of weekday unemployment in the following month. As well as the *tehaishi* and the labor exchanges, the modern day laborer can also seek work through personal connections or by responding to job advertisements carried in sports newspapers. A few of the most efficient men even have mobile telephones with which they can swiftly ascertain demand for labor at several different building sites on any given morning.

Although *yoseba* workers are often referred to as 'day laborers' (*hiyatoi rōdōsha*), they do not necessarily work only on one-day contracts. Some *tehaishi* come looking for men to work for periods ranging from a week to several months, often on large-scale rural construction projects. Among these men are some who have been exposed to radiation while being employed to do dangerous work at nuclear power stations. The topic of the 'nuclear gypsies' (*genpatsu jipushii*) is one where fact and street-myth mingle, but there certainly have been some cases of this. Tanaka (1988) has a valuable account of subcontracting and day laboring in the nuclear power industry. Another *yoseba* myth is of sick men being allowed to die by hospitals because they lack health insurance, or even being given lethal doses of medicine and then being sold as cadavers to medical schools or for illegal organ transplants. Once again it is impossible to guess how much truth there may be in these rumors, but enough cases have surfaced to suggest that the answer is not zero.

But besides these extreme cases, there are plenty of other everyday threats to the lives of the day laborers. *Bentō to kega wa jibun mochi* ('Your lunch-box and your injuries are your own affair') is a popular *yoseba* saying. It can be very difficult to make construction companies take responsibility for worksite accidents, especially where the end employer is separated from the worker by a chain of subcontractors such as I described above. A further serious issue is the safety of the on-site dormitories where men are housed during major construction projects. In eastern Japan these dormitories are referred to as *hanba*, a term which confusingly enough is used synonymously with *ninpudashi* in western Japan. They tend to be thrown up with scant regard for safety, and cases of fires at them are regular minor news items. Several occurred during my own *yoseba* fieldwork (1993–5). One was at a very dangerously designed worker's dormitory in Ebina, 20 miles from Yokohama, where eight men died in a nocturnal fire on July 6, 1994. Most of the 53 men staying there were migrant workers from Hokkaido and Tohoku. Press reports said the dormitory belonged to a small construction company called Komuro-gumi.[4] In fact it belonged to Tōkyū Construction, the same company that was in charge of the tunnel project described above. Tōkyū was using Komuro-gumi as a subcontractor. Komuro took the blame; Tōkyū may have had to make a quiet payoff to its subcontractor, but the firm escaped negative publicity. Life is indeed unfair.

DAY LABORERS AT THE *NINPUDASHI*

In sharp contrast to the very extensive literature on *yoseba*, relatively little attention has been paid by academics and journalists to the *ninpudashi*.[5] Yet this is an institution which is arguably every bit as important as the *yoseba* in contemporary Japan, if not more so.

The word *ninpu* is a fairly coarse Japanese term for a navvy or manual laborer. *Dashi* derives from the verb *dasu*, to produce, give, or supply something. Hence *ninpudashi* are navvy-suppliers, businesses that specialize in supplying casual laborers. It is a crude term, considered downright insulting by the people who run these businesses.

They prefer the term *rōdō geshuku*, or 'workers' boarding house,' or better still *jinzai hakengyō*, or 'personnel supply business.' I use the term '*ninpudashi*' here because it is the standard term used by the day laborers who patronize them.

I first came across the word in the summer of 1994, on a fieldtrip to northern Kyushu. In retrospect it is amazing, not to say shameful, that I had not become aware of the institution during over a year of fieldwork with day laborers before then. But in Fukuoka and Kitakyushu, even the most insensitive fieldworker cannot miss the *ninpudashi*, for they dominate the casual labor market in these two neighboring industrial cities on the north coast of Japan's southernmost main island. The *ninpudashi* combine the roles of the *yoseba* (casual labor introductions) and the *doya* (cheap, low-grade accommodation). The owner of the *ninpudashi* supplies the worker with a room, either a small *doya*-like individual room, or a larger room shared with several other workers. Meals will generally be provided, though probably at extra cost. He also supplies the worker with employment, activating a network of contacts to find casual work around the city or neighboring cities. Very often he will also supply transportation, having his own minibus, or even a fleet of minibuses, to get the men to the worksites.

The attractions for the worker are manifest: a roof over his head, two or three square meals a day, and no need to get out of bed at half past four to look for a *tehaishi* and negotiate a contract with him. But at the same time, the *ninpudashi* is potentially a powerful tool of exploitation. Wages are generally paid to the *ninpudashi*, not directly to the worker. At the end of the month, the *ninpudashi* will calculate how much the man has earned, then subtract the cost of room rent, meals, and sundries. Some will charge extra for TV-watching and showers, for example, or will supply alcohol and tobacco on credit at higher prices than in the shops. Nor will the wages necessarily be paid immediately at the end of the month. Payment may be delayed, typically until the 15th or 20th of the following month, sometimes even later. Since day laborers are often short of money, they may be unable to wait that long for payment – in which case the *ninpudashi* may lend him an advance against wages, often with high rates of interest attached. Combining the roles of landlord and recruiter gives the *ninpudashi* decisive advantages over both these *yoseba* figures. In the *yoseba*, the *doya* manager must always calculate how likely a man is to get enough work to pay the room rent, and how many days he should allow arrears to mount up before cutting his losses and throwing the man out. In contrast, the *ninpudashi* owner determines the man's level of employment himself and gets the money directly, passing it on only after he has taken off what he determines the man to owe him. And whereas the *tehaishi* must compete against other *tehaishi*, offering higher wages or better terms at times when labor is scarce, the *ninpudashi* owner can monopolize the labor of the men working for him through the hold he has over them as their landlord.

Perhaps most significantly, *ninpudashi* do not guarantee to find employment for their tenants every day. There may be 40 men staying at the boarding house, but only enough work available for 20. In that case men will be 'rested,' on average, every other day. But not all men will necessarily conform to the average. Troublemakers who complain about conditions may find themselves 'resting' considerably more often than their more docile brothers. Hence the *ninpudashi* is in a strong position to erode solidarity between workers and stimulate mutual competition among them in its place. Rent is payable every day, whether a job is supplied or not. Hence it is all too possible that after a prolonged lean spell, some of the men may find that far from earning money for their own use, they are grappling with a steadily mounting debt owed to the *ninpudashi*. Many men voiced suspicions that *ninpudashi* would deliberately take on more men than they could find work for, because filling the rooms and keeping many of the men idle was more economically advantageous to the *ninpudashi* than having their men fully employed and some of their rooms empty. In the worst cases, day laborers can get so deeply into debt that they are effectively stripped of their human rights and reduced to the status of rather literal wage slaves. In such a situation the worker's one recourse may be to do a runner – or a *tonkō* as it is known. Unions of *ninpudashi* owners maintain blacklists designed to avoid employing men who have absconded from other *ninpudashi*, however, and in some cases the ultimate sanction against abscondence may be the threat of violence, by *yojinbō* – hired bully-boys.

Shortly after World War II, *ninpudashi* were made illegal under article 44 of the Employment Security Law, a piece of legislation inspired by the leaders of the allied Occupation. This article outlawed the practice of taking money for job introductions in any form, and hence criminalized the *tehaishi* at the *yoseba* as well as the *ninpudashi*, and indeed more conventional temporary employment agencies as well (as discussed by Bishop in Chapter 6). Kamata (1971) contends that illegality just made the boarding house business more brutal, while the police usually turned a blind eye. In 1986 the government of Nakasone Yasuhiro passed the Labor Dispatch Business Law (*Jinzai Hakengyō-hō*), which legalized the practice of agencies taking money from an employer and paying their own, lower wage to the worker. This, I believe, was a major factor favoring the renaissance of the *ninpudashi* business, which had been going through some lean times with the decline of the coal and steel industries that spawned it in northern Kyushu.

During the mid-1990s I gained the impression that there was a pattern to casual employment practices in Japan, with *yoseba* tending to predominate to the east of Osaka and *ninpudashi* to the west, especially in Kyushu. Osaka itself has Japan's biggest *yoseba*, in Kamagasaki, but also a concentration of boardinghouses at the nearby district of Taishō, estimated by day-laboring activists to be home to some 7,000 workers.

The dominance of *ninpudashi* in Kitakyushu was explained to me by local labor activists as being related to the district's traditional association with the iron and steel industry. Kitakyushu is an artificially constructed city, formed by the union of five formerly independent cities – Kokura, Tobata, Wakamatsu, Yahata, and Moji. Moji was a port city, while Yahata and Tobata were both dominated by a single employer – Nippon Steel, formerly known as Yahata Steel. The area was naturally suited to steel production, having a plentiful water supply and coal from the nearby Chikuhō coalfield. During the 1970s and 1980s, however, Japan's steel industry was steadily supplanted by rivals in South Korea and elsewhere. Today the once mighty plant at Yahata is long closed, and Nippon Steel has built an amusement park, Space World, on part of the disused site. The Tobata plant continues to operate at a reduced scale, while the closure of the Chikuhō coalmines in the 1970s left Chikuhō as one of the most economically depressed areas in all Japan (Allen 1994).

Nippon Steel used to employ something like the subcontracting system that I described above for the construction industry. Like construction, iron and steel is an industry highly sensitive to changing economic trends, and the advantages of a flexible workforce are obvious. So rather than relying entirely on its own directly-employed workforce, the company would delegate parts of the smelting operation to bosses (*oyakata*), who would be entrusted with supplying the required amount of labor on each day. The *oyakata* would run their own boarding houses, where they would provide board and lodging for men who were effectively their own private workforce. Their wages would be paid by the *oyakata* rather than by Nippon Steel, and hence the company had no responsibility to provide them with 'lifetime employment' or anything like it. Meanwhile, there was a constant struggle for control of the casual workforce among rival labor racketeers – a struggle that was bloody and sometimes murderous.[6]

The boarding houses peaked in 1960, when there were nearly 200 of them. When the steel industry went into decline, the owners of the boarding houses gradually shifted their attention to construction, and today they are the prime suppliers of casual labor to building sites in the Kitakyushu area. Meanwhile, the notorious pre-war *yoseba* at Harunomachi ('Spring-town'), a slum district in the lee of the Yahata steelworks, is long gone. The main post-war *yoseba* was at Senbō, just next to the Tobata steelworks. However, when I got to Senbō in the mid–1990s I found that the *yoseba* had virtually withered away, with no more than a couple of dozen men standing in the street. In the neighboring city of Fukuoka, there is a small *yoseba* located at Chikkō, very close to the Hakata docks, reflecting the fact that like Kotobuki in Yokohama, it used to supply labor principally to the longshoring industry. Even today some 40 percent of work is at the docks, the remainder in construction. In the mid-1990s there were only about 200 day laborers looking for work at Chikkō on the average morning, whereas a day laborer union activist estimated that there were some 10,000 day laborers in the city as a whole. The rest were mostly staying at *ninpudashi*, which for all their drawbacks still represented a surer way of keeping oneself housed and fed than the uncertain prospects of the daily hunt for work on the street corner. Several day laborers said that they would use the *yoseba* when employment prospects were good, retreating to a *ninpudashi* when they were bad. During the 1990s they were usually bad. The small *doya-gai* in Fukuoka was located some way from the *yoseba*, and the casual labor exchange was in yet a third part of the city. Hence there was no concentration of facilities for day laborers to compare to the *yoseba/doya-gai*/labor exchange package at Kamagasaki, San'ya, and Kotobuki. Life is less convenient, and the potential for solidarity far lower, than in cities with major *yoseba*. As for the boarding houses, they varied greatly in style. Some were shabby little buildings resembling *doya*; others were smart new multi-story buildings, with covered forecourts where fleets of minibuses stood ready to take the men to work. In Fukuoka and Kitakyushu, the going rate for unskilled casual labor in the late 1990s was in the region of ¥8–9,000 a day, compared with Y12 13,000 in the major *yoseba* cities of Osaka, Tokyo, and Yokohama. Regional variation in standard of living accounted for some of this differential, but the relative weakness of labor *vis-á-vis* capital was undoubtedly a factor too. All the big *yoseba* have day laborer unions; there are none active in *ninpudashi* districts.

. . .

THE CHANGING PATTERNS

The bursting of the speculative bubble at the start of the 1990s sent the Japanese construction industry into a drastic decline. Real estate prices collapsed, housing starts plummeted and heavily indebted companies cut back on investment in new plant. The bloated construction industry, which a 1998 OECD report found to account for a portion of the economy roughly double the figure for most industrialized countries, was forced into a contraction which saw layoffs even at the big general contractors, while thousands of smaller companies were forced into bankruptcy.

Naturally, the first workers to feel the pinch were day laborers. Employment at all the big *yoseba* collapsed. For example, the number of person-days transacted at the Kotobuki Labor Center, which accounts for over 90 percent of formal labor contracts transacted in Kotobuki, fell from 154,574 in 1986 to 38,348 in 1999. This was a crippling 75 percent fall, which had all but killed off the system of state-mediated casual labor by the end of the century. The *tehaishi* do not supply statistics for the informal labor market, but by the end of the 1990s a lot of familiar faces had disappeared from the morning streets of Kotobuki, as many *tehaishi* simply withdrew from the market. With the market so weak, freelance manual work out of a *yoseba* ceased to be an option for the young working-class men that had once formed a large part of the population. Consequently the *yoseba* population aged dramatically – far faster than the rate for the general population. The mean age of workers using the Kotobuki Labor Center rose from 39 in 1975 to 45 in 1985 and then to 52 in 1997.

Growing numbers of day laborers were forced into homelessness, and throughout the later 1990s Yokohama City Hall (located a ten-minute walk from Kotobuki) was surrounded by over a hundred cardboard boxes in which homeless people would spend the night. Shanty towns and tent cities spread out in every major city – at the west exit of Shinjuku station and along the left bank of the Arakawa river, to name but two famous Tokyo locations, and around Tennōji Park in Osaka[7] and in Wakamiya

Park in Nagoya, among many others. The great majority of these homeless people were unaffiliated men of middle age and above – the kind of people who used to be able to make a living as day laborers. The fast-rising numbers of homeless bore testimony to the important role that the day-laboring system had played as the employer of last resort in the Japanese economy, and the degree to which the system was being eroded.

The inescapable fact of rising homelessness, coupled with vigorous campaigning by day laborer unions and homeless support groups, has led to a gradual softening of attitudes toward *yoseba* on the part of city governments. For many years it was virtually impossible for men based in the *yoseba* to acquire welfare payments, largely because of an unwritten rule made up by bureaucrats, to the effect that one had to have a fixed address to apply for welfare, and that a *doya* room did not constitute a fixed address. In Yokohama that rule has been relaxed to the point where some 80 percent of the region's 6,500 *doya* rooms are now occupied by welfare recipients, a figure that has doubled in the last five years or so. Kotobuki is now well on its way to completing the transition from 'workers' town' to 'welfare town' discussed by Stevens (1997), and it has in fact become very difficult for the traditional wandering day laborer to get a room in Kotobuki. Other city governments have been slower to move, and consequently there are far more empty *doya* rooms in San'ya and Kamagasaki than in Kotobuki, and far more homeless men in Tokyo and Osaka than in Yokohama.[8]

Right at the end of the 1990s, the Tokyo government finally started to show signs of relaxing its hard line on welfare for *doya* occupants, and started to approve a number of applications. Some *doya* owners responded by making slight cuts in room rents to meet the ¥2,300 maximum that the metropolitan government had set for nightly accommodation expenses for welfare recipients. Even so, the *doya* population of San'ya is a fraction of what it used to be, and the place has something of the atmosphere of a ghost town. Rising numbers of homeless and of welfare recipients, and a high mortality rate, account for some of the disappearances, but not all of them.

According to activists with a day-laborer union called the San'ya Dispute League (San'ya *Sōgidan*), quite a large part of the day-laboring population of San'ya has disappeared into *ninpudashi*. The word has been much less common in the Kanto region around Tokyo and Yokohama, and has tended to be used in a different sense to that understood in the Kansai: as a straightforward job introduction agency, without the residential component. However, *Sōgidan* activists say they have clear and mounting evidence of a new wave of residential *ninpudashi* cropping up in Tokyo's four main satellite prefectures: Kanagawa, Saitama, Chiba, and Ibaragi. Rather than looking for workers in the *yoseba* – which are invariably located in fairly central urban places – employers keep them in boarding houses in quiet, out-of-the-way places, where land is cheap and few prying government officials or journalists are likely to show their faces. They are bussed into construction sites in the Tokyo-Yokohama region and bussed out again at the end of the day.

It would appear, then, that a sea change is coming over the unobserved outer margins of the Japanese economy. The old way of life associated with day laboring out of the *yoseba* is crumbling away, and the *yoseba* working population is draining away in three directions: toward welfare, toward homelessness and early death, and toward the *ninpudashi*. *Ninpudashi* are far more resilient than *yoseba* to changing economic forces, because of the system described above, of rotating under-employed workers while deducting their board and lodging from their pay packet at source. They have remained viable at levels of economic activity so low that the *yoseba* have steadily lost their function as labor markets, metamorphosing into slum districts for single men like the U.S. skid row, or in Kotobuki's case, into a vast economy-class welfare institution.

One reason why *ninpudashi* have attracted far less attention than *yoseba* from academics and journalists is because they are far less noticeable, and also far harder to study. A *yoseba*, by definition, is a gathering place: a concentration of largely un-attached men with little to lose in terms of possessions or social status. As such they have always had a certain rebellious potential. While the *yoseba* have never ful-filled the quixotic hopes of utopian Japanese Marxists, that they might be catalysts for the revolution, they do have a history of street-rioting[9] and far higher rates of alcoholism and crime than other urban districts. They can be studied by anyone who chooses to walk into them. By contrast, *ninpudashi* are closed environments that are very difficult for researchers to penetrate, especially foreign researchers. They are also strictly controlled environments, in which much smaller groups of men are con-centrated, and where the balance of power is far more decisively on the side of the recruiter/landlord. The gradual shift from *yoseba* to *ninpudashi* represents a small, barely noticed, yet decisive defeat for labor in its never-ending struggle with capital on the fringes of the Japanese economy.

NOTES

1. The Japan Association for *Yoseba* (JASY; *Yoseba Gakkai*). JASY publishes an annual journal, *Yoseba*, which reached its 13th edition in 2000. Volume 3 of *Yoseba* (1990) in-cludes an annotated bibliography of 100 *yoseba*-related books and papers in the Japanese language. During 2000 JASY was making preparations to publish a new bibliography, this time of 300 books and papers in Japanese. I myself contributed an appendix listing some 40 English-language *yoseba* books and papers, annotated in Japanese. Anyone wishing to delve into this goldmine of proletarian sociology, economics, history and literature, can contact JASY at the following address: C/o Matsuzawa Tessei, Tokyo Women's University, 2–6–1 Zenpukuji, Suginami-ku, Tokyo, Japan. E-mail: tessei@ twcu.ac.jp. My own address is tpgill@iss.u-tokyo.ac.jp (English or Japanese) or tpgill@yahoo.com (English only).
2. Like *doya*, this term is a slang reversal: *basho*, standard Japanese for 'place,' is reversed to give *shoba*, and *dai* (money, fee) is added. Some *tehaishi* will park their minibuses just out-side the *yoseba*, to avoid paying *shobadai*. Others, who specialize in long-term contracts, will come to the *yoseba* in their minibuses at weekends, when the yakuza patrols are off duty, again to avoid paying *shobadai*.

3. Foreign manual workers in Japan are mostly illegal, and tend to avoid the *yoseba* districts because of the higher risk of arrest and deportation in these places with concentrations of casual workers. Kotobuki is something of an exception, because of its ethnic Korean land-lord class and the continuing demand for strong young men to work at the Yokohama docks. Out of a general population of about 7,000, the foreign population peaked at just over 1,000 in the mid-1990s and was down to about 500 by the end of the decade, as the recession ate into job opportunities. In recent years the great majority of foreigners in Kotobuki have been Korean. There was a thriving Filipino community there in the late 1980s and early 1990s, described by Ventura (1992), but nowadays there are fewer than 100 Filipinos living in Kotobuki. The size and make-up of the foreign population changes very fast.

4. See for example *Asahi Shinbun*, July 6 1994, evening edition, p.17.

5. As far as I know, *ninpudashi* merit little more than a few fleeting references in the English-language literature on Japanese casual labor. JASY is of course fully aware of the institution and does discuss it in its Japanese-language publications, but not to anything like the same degree as the *yoseba*.

6. I know of no English-language account of this dramatic phase in Japanese labor history. There is a vividly-written Japanese-language account by Kamata Satoshi, which I whole-heartedly recommend (Kamata 1994 [1971]).

7. I say *around* Tennōji Park, because in 1990 the Osaka city government tried to put an end to this large park's traditional role as a center for homeless people by erecting a high fence around it, instituting an admission fee of ¥150 and closing the park down after dark. A lawsuit by pro-homeless activists demanding that these moves be rescinded was defeated in court in 1993 (see Dohi 1999). Ever since then there have been rows of makeshift dwel-lings around the outside of the park.

8. One side effect of this has been a growing trend for homeless men in Tokyo to move to the neighboring city of Yokohama and try their luck with the more liberal regime there. With city finances coming under increasing strain, it is surely only a matter of time before this creates a diplomatic problem between the two huge cities.

9. The 1960s and 1970s saw numerous riots in all the major *yoseba*. Things quietened down after the economic recession following the oil crises in the mid-1970s, but there were major riots in Kamagasaki in 1990 and 1993. I have further detail in Gill (forthcoming 2001).

REFERENCES

Allen, M. 1994. *Undermining the Japanese Miracle: Work and Conflict in a Coalmining Com-munity*. Cambridge: Cambridge University Press.

Bishop, B. 2000. 'The Diversification of Employment and Women's Work in Contemporary Japan,' in J.S. Eades, T. Gill & H. Befu (eds), *Globalization and Social Change in Contem-porary Japan*. Melbourne: Trans Pacific Press.

Caldorola, C. 1968. 'The *doya-gai*: a Japanese version of skid row.' *Pacific Affairs* 41: 511–25.

de Barry, B. 1985. 'San'ya: Japan's internal colony,' in E.P. Tsurumi (ed), *The Other Japan: Postwar Realities*, pp 112–18. Armonk: M.E. Sharpe.

Dohi, M. 1999. 'The community design process at Kamagasaki. Osaka, Japan,' in *Democratic Design in the Pacific Rim*, pp 228–40. Michigan: Ridge Times Press.

Fowler, E. 1996. *San'ya Blues: Laboring life in Contemporary Japan*. Ithaca: Cornell University Press.

Giamo, B. 1994. 'Order, disorder and the homeless in the United States and Japan,' *Doshisha American Research* 31: 1–19.

Gill, T. (forthcoming 2001). *Men of Uncertainty: The Social; Organization of Day Laborers in Contemporary Japan*. Albany: State University of New York Press.

Kamata, S. 1971 (1994). *Shinitaeta fukei* (The extinct landscape). Tokyo: Diamond-sha.

Leupp, G.P. 1992. *Servants, Shophands and Laborers in the Cities of Tokugawa Japan*. Princeton: Princeton University Press.

Marr, M.D. 1997. 'Maintaining autonomy: the plight of the American skid row and Japanese *yoseba*,' *Journal of Social Distress and the Homeless*, 6(3): 229–50.

Matsuzawa, T. 1988. 'Street labor markets, day laborers, and the structure of oppression,' in G. McCormack and Y. Sugimoto (eds), *The Japanese Trajectory: Modernization and Beyond*, pp 147–64. Cambridge: Cambridge University Press.

Stevens, C. 1997. *On the Margins of Japanese Society: Volunteers and the Welfare of the Urban Underclass*. London: Routledge.

Tanaka, Y. 1988. 'Nuclear power and the labor movement,' in G. McCormack and Y. Sugimoto (eds), *The Japanese Trajectory: Modernization and Beyond*, pp 129–46. Cambridge: Cambridge University Press.

Ventura, R. 1992. *Underground in Japan*. London: Jonathan Cape.

Part 4:
The Road(s) to Industrial 'Modernity'

SECTIONAL INTRODUCTION

'The country that is more developed industrially only shows, to the less developed, the image of its own future', wrote Marx (1961 [1867]), neatly encapsulating the teleological assumptions that continued to inform much subsequent thinking about industrialization. Many Marxist and non-Marxist writers went on supposing that history moves in a preordained direction, whether that is towards the overthrow of capitalism or its apotheosis in a globalized version of industrial modernity. Whichever, industrial societies converge on broadly the same design. The implication once unblushingly drawn was that the African (for which read Indian or Indonesian) Industrial Revolution would lead these late-starters along a trail already blazed by the West. Manchester had lessons for Mexican 'development'. With the move from field to factory, peasants would become proletarians. Though contemporary anthropology is deeply suspicious of teleological narratives of this kind, it is not clear that we can do without them entirely if we suppose that urban industrial societies constitute a specific type. There is a real tension between anthropological relativism and, for example, the not implausible proposition that mining communities the world over (or at least those based on modern mechanized systems of extraction) resemble each other in non-trivial ways.[1]

The lead chapter in Part 4, Gluckman's position paper of 1961 on 'Anthropological problems arising from the African Industrial Revolution,' is still valuable because it poses these issues so sharply. In particular, it takes up two Copperbelt ethnographies (from what is now Zambia) by Mitchell (1956) and by Epstein (1958), colleagues of Gluckman at the Rhodes-Livingstone Institute. These discuss the problem of 'why tribalism persists, both in tribal areas and in towns, in spite of the industrial revolution which has produced such great social changes.' In fact, the apparent continuity is largely illusory since tribalism means something different in the two different settings. In the rural areas, being a tribesman means being part of a specific social and political system. In the towns it does not, and 'tribe' is above all the way in which the migrant worker identifies, pigeon-holes, and decides on the behaviour appropriate towards an otherwise amorphous mass of strangers with whom he has contact. This 'tribalism' is a specifically urban phenomenon, and in town Africans act 'primarily within a field whose social structure is determined by the urban,

industrial setting. An African townsman is a townsman, an African miner is a miner'
who 'possibly resembles miners everywhere' (Gluckman). Industrial modernity prevails with the result that 'Central African towns differ only in degree from any town,
anywhere in the world probably', and '…common interests arising from indus-trial
and urban association seem steadily to overcome tribal ties and divisions'. Being
African (as opposed to European), being a trade unionist or a white-collar worker is
in many situations a more salient identity than being a Bemba. In negotiations with
employers 'trades unions transcend tribes' (Mayer 1962: 581). Hence, 'the starting
point for an analysis of urbanization must be an urban system of relations, in which
the tribal origins of the population may even be regarded as of secondary interest.
The comparative background for all these analyses is urban sociology in general.'

Moodie (1983) adds a qualification for the South African Gold mines, where new
recruits have their old identities stripped away when they are initiated into the workforce, and where those who work together underground on jobs that are dangerous
develop a strong ethos of cooperation and solidarity that is carried over into social
relations in the compounds in which they live. Miners, says Moodie, 'associate ultimately on the basis of common interests, not common tribe', though this is more true
of, for example, Sotho and Xhosa workers than of Mozambiquan Shangaan, who
come with the single-minded aim of making money and stubbornly resist socialization into mine culture. While the Xhosa miner is (as Gluckman claimed) a miner, the
Shangaan miner remains a Shangaan.

More than a qualification, Ferguson's (1999) powerful monograph, of which the
article reprinted as Chapter 16 provides a useful digest, is a sustained assault on
what he characterizes (some say caricatures [Grillo 2000]) as the linear assumptions
of the Rhodes-Livingstone scholars, and of their mentor, Gluckman, taking them to
task on their home Copperbelt territory where Ferguson himself worked in the
1980s. By then, the collapse of mine profitability had led to a dramatic increase in
urban poverty, a reduction in life expectancy and a desperately demoralizing loss
of faith in old teleological certainties. Zambians themselves were quite as deluded
by these as the social scientists who had dreamt them, though the Zambian's rude
awakening has cost them more dearly. History, they found, had gone into reverse:
de-urbanization (out-migration from the Copperbelt now exceeds in-migration),
de-industrialization and the return of nationalized mines to foreign ownership. The
evolutionary trajectory has not proved linear; the Rhodes-Livingstone ethnographers
could only imagine that it was by focusing on one particular segment of the working
class at one particular point in time, and rather than try to put them in a sequence
we should focus on the simultaneous co-existence of social forms and try to understand how their prominence varies with politico-economic circumstance. What
Zambians now experience 'is modernization through the looking glass, where modernity is the object of nostalgic reverie, and "backwardness" the anticipated (or
dreaded) future.' It's not only an economic crisis, but a crisis of meaning. Since they
were themselves just as wrapped up in the modernization narrative as their ethnographers, they now experience their plight as 'abjection', as being cast aside by history

and expelled from the modern world. In the past, Zambian copper, in the form of power and telephone cables, connected the world. But in the new globalized order, Zambia has been disconnected by new technologies and a slump in demand for its principal product.

In the chapter that follows, Joshi tells a similar story about the demoralized state of the dwindling workforce in the textile mills of the north Indian city of Kanpur. Those that remain are on the brink of closure, and workers now vilify their public sector managements (by comparison with which the earlier European-dominated private sector regime has begun to seem benign), and recall their former militancy with indifference. Unlike Fergusons' miners, who in land-plentiful Zambia can petition their chief for an area to cultivate, and who at least have the option of returning to the countryside, here only the more fortunate ex-millhands who have viable smallholdings can consider going back to their ancestral villages. Others eke out a precarious living (as rickshaw-pullers and the like) in the informal urban economy or establish some household-based enterprise. The reel runs backwards, from factory to field and from 'modern' manufacture to cottage industry. Most mill workers were men and households now increasingly depend on the earnings of women at home. While women feel empowered, men feel emasculated. Forced back into the realm of women and children, for whom they can no longer provide and over whom their authority seems increasingly tenuous, they experience a 'crisis of masculinity'.

Breman (2004) discusses the comparable case of the Ahmedabad textile mills (in western India). As a result of economic liberalization, market competition and the demand for flexibility, a workforce that had come to be regarded as an Indian 'aristocracy of labour' lost, almost overnight, its protection and privilege, with many forced to find jobs in the informal economy. For rural south India, Kapadia (1999) records how skilled male gem cutters have been driven into itinerant labour. What it all seems to show is the fragility of modernity, the unreliability of its promises, the sometimes transitory nature of its benefits, and the ways in which the demands of flexibility can almost instantaneously turn inclusion into exclusion.

Many workers, moreover, have always moved back and forth between the rural and urban economies. De Haan (1999), for example, has documented a pattern of rotating migration from the Bhojpur region to the Bengal jute mills that has persisted for more than a century. It is therefore dubiously described as a transitional phenomenon. Generation after generation, workers have moved from field to factory, and finally back again. The trajectory was never unilinear. For the central Indian steel town of Bhilai, Parry (2004) argues, the extent to which migrant rural labour makes a one-way transition to urbanism significantly varies between the workforces of public and private sector factories, and between different levels of the industrial hierarchy. This is not only a consequence of material possibilities and pragmatic considerations, but also of a vision of modernity that privileged state-employed steel plant workers have deeply internalized and that antithetically constructs the village as an area of darkness and ignorance. As with Stalin's Magnitogorsk (brilliantly evoked by Kotkin 1995), the steel plant had been rhetorically represented as a 'beacon' for the future, and a 'temple' to progress, that would enable India to 'catch and overtake' the world's most 'advanced' nations (*see also* Parry 2008).

Subjective perceptions of modernity are taken up again in Rofel's chapter in this section. Her ethnography relates to women workers in a large state-run silk factory in the southern Chinese city of Hangzhou. The monograph from which this extract is taken demonstrates how much of their behaviour and attitudes, specifically their ideas of 'modernity', depends on when they entered the workforce. Rofel distinguishes three cohorts. For the first, those recruited at around the time that the Communists came to power, factory employment was not only a liberation from patriarchal control at home but also an opportunity to become heroines of socialist labour and to participate in building a brave new communist order. For the Cultural Revolution generation, political awareness, rather than labour, was central to their sense of self and their vision of China as a modern nation. For the post-Mao cohort, who have developed a kind of 'hyper-feminity', 'modernity' means something different again. In popular discourse, state enterprises and their workers are now identified with the problem to be overcome, with what holds China's modernity back, and with *female* labour; while market entrepreneurialism is glamorized as competitive and efficient, and associated with male initiative and dynamism. 'Modernity' is neither unilinear nor irreversible; it is certainly not singular, and it is significantly gendered.

The final reading in Part 4 makes a different kind of point about the standard teleological narrative in that it challenges the widely assumed association between industrial capitalism and 'free labour'. Ideal-type capitalist labour is 'free' in a double sense: workers are legally free to sell their labour to whoever they like, and are free from ownership of the means of production. That is, 'free' labour is labour that is coerced, not by institutions like slavery, but by the imperative that it sells itself on the market for a wage in order to live. As Marx, Weber and Polanyi all saw it, such labour was a precondition for the development of industrial capitalism; and a large part of Polanyi's masterwork, *The Great Transformation*, was concerned with the institutional revolution that set workers 'free' and turned their labour into a ('fictitious') commodity. In his analysis (1957 [1944]: 40f), the requirements of modern machine manufacture were a major impetus to that. In many parts of the world, however, 'capitalistic' industries have utilized workers who are far from free. In fact, Mintz (1985: 47f) argued that, well before England's Industrial Revolution, Caribbean sugar plantations developed a system of industrial production worked by slave labour. Equally, much migrant labour owns some of the means of production; many have peasant holdings to fall back on. This is an advantage to capital that allows it to escape the costs of reproducing its own labour, and a disadvantage in that it supposedly creates problems of 'commitment' and allows workers to sustain themselves during strikes. Such a safety net partly explains why employers in small-scale Indian industries sometimes attempt to reduce the freedom of their workers through debt bondage (Breman 1999; Engelshoven 1999; Gooptu 2001: chapter 2; Kapadia 1999), though this, as De Neve's chapter shows, can backfire.

In the 1970s, the power loom weaving industry in the south Indian town of Kumarapalayam was booming. Experienced labour was short and the employers started to offer advances (*baki*) intended to bind the workers to them until the debt was discharged. By the time of De Neve's fieldwork in the mid-1990s, a substantial advance, sometimes equivalent to more than six months' wages, was standard. But the strategy failed dismally. In bonding their workers, the owners bonded themselves. If they sacked an unsatisfactory worker they were liable to lose their advance, and they had little sanction against malingering. As a palliative they introduced piece-rates, subsequently supplemented by increased surveillance and physical intimidation. But bonded workers would nevertheless routinely abandon their employers for jobs in other workshops whose owners were prepared to advance a sum sufficient to pay off the worker's former boss and leave something over for the worker himself. Some would abscond to another town without discharging their debts. But despite the employers' disillusionment with the system, the size of the advance required to attract new workers continued to rise. For that, however, the employers themselves appear to be largely responsible. The whole strategy was doomed to fail as long as they were prepared to 'poach' each other's labour, and their inability to resist that temptation seems to be at least partly explained by caste. The employers' associations are caste-based, and caste divisions fracture the unity of capital. As De Neve shows more explicitly, however, the solidarity of labour is no stronger. Worker resistance is atomized and individualistic as each tries to get the largest advance. Workers can escape from one employer to another, but not from their overall situation; and high labour turnover and a system of *baki* payments that are extremely variable in amount fragment the workforce and ensure that the level of labour activism is low. In the handloom industry of Bhavani, just across the river, *baki* is by contrast never paid and there is a strong tradition of union militancy. It is to such issues of class-consciousness and class conflict that the final part of this reader will turn.

NOTES

1. Compare Dore 1973 for a distinctive variant on the convergence thesis. Though Japan industrialized later, its industry did not develop systems of work organization similar to those of England, as would be expected on the commonsense proposition that, if anywhere, it is in the domain of work that the same technology is likely to produce the same institutions. But though the two countries had trodden different paths to their industrial present, and had created what were in many ways different industrial systems, Dore believed that these differences were now being muted as the first in the field tried to 'catch up' with the comparatively late starters. In fact, it was its late start that gave Japanese industry certain advantages.

RECOMMENDED FURTHER READING

Breman, Jan. 2004. *The Making and Unmaking of an Industrial Working Class: Sliding down the labour hierarchy in Ahmedabad, India*, Amsterdam: Amsterdam University Press.

Dore, R. 1973. *British Factory - Japanese Factory: The origins of national diversity in industrial relations*, Berkeley, CA: University of California Press.

Ferguson, J. 1999. *Expectations of Modernity: Myths and meanings of urban life on the Zambian Copperbelt*, Berkeley, CA: University of California Press.

Moodie, T. Dunbar. 1983. 'Mine Culture and Miners Identity of the South African Gold Mines.' In Bellinda Bozzoli (ed.), *Town and countryside in the Transvaal*, pp. 176–97, Johannesburg: Ravan Press.

Parry, J.P. 2004. 'Nehru's Dream and the Village "Waiting Room": Long-distance labour migrants to a central Indian steel town,' *Contributions to Indian Sociology*, 37(1–2): 217–49.

Parry, J.P. 2008. 'The Sacrifices of Modernity in a Soviet-built Steel Town in central India.' In F. Pine and J. de Pina-Cabral, *On the margins of religion*, pp. 233–62, Oxford: Berghahn Books.

OTHER WORKS CITED

Breman, Jan. 1999. 'The study of Industrial Labour in post-colonial India– the informal sector: a concluding review', *Contributions to Indian Sociology*, 33(1-2): 407–31.

De Haan, Arjan. 1999. 'The *badli* System in Industrial Labour Recruitment: Managers' and workers' strategies in Calcutta's jute industry', *Contributions to Indian Sociology*, 33(1-2): 271–301.

Engelshoven, M. 1999. 'Diamonds and Patels: A report on the diamond industry of Surat', *Contributions to Indian Sociology* (new series), 33(1): 353–77.

Epstein, A.L. 1958. *Politics in an Urban African Community*, Manchester: Manchester University Press.

Gooptu, N. 2001. *The Politics of the Urban Poor in Early Twentieth-century India*, Cambridge: Cambridge University Press.

Grillo, Ralph. 2000. Review of J. Ferguson, Expectations of modernity: Myths and Meanings of Urban Life on the Zambian Copperbelt, *Journal of the Royal Anthropological Institute*, 6(3): 554–55.

Kapadia, K. 1999. 'Gender Ideologies and the Formation of Rural Industrial Classes in South India Today'. *Contributions to Indian Sociology*, 33(1-2): 329–52.

Kotkin, S. 1995. *Magnetic Mountain: Stalinism as civilization*. Berkeley, CA: University of California Press.

Marx, Karl. 1961 [1867]. Preface to the first German edition. *Das Capital*, vol. 1, Moscow: Foreign Languages Publishing House.

Mayer, Philip. 1962. 'Migrancy and the Study of Africans in Towns', *American Anthropologist*, 64: 576–92.

Mintz, S. 1985. *Sweetness and Power: The place of sugar in modern history*, Harmondsworth: Penguin.

Mitchell, J. Clyde. 1956. *The Kalela dance*. Rhodes-Livingstone Papers, no. 27. Manchester: Manchester University Press.

Polanyi, K. 1957 [1944]. *The Great Transformation: The political and economic origins of our time*, Boston: Beacon Press.

CHAPTER FIFTEEN

Anthropological Problems Arising from the African Industrial Revolution

Max Gluckman

In this paper I summarize some of the results which have emerged from the work of the Rhodes-Livingstone Institute staff of anthropologists through the last twenty years. This work has covered both urban and tribal situations. I limit my discussion to our own researches in Northern Rhodesia and Nyasaland, but I want to pay tribute to the stimulus and help we have received from the analyses of our colleagues in other regions. Inevitably, we have depended mainly on scholars working in South Africa, and here I acknowledge particularly the studies of Professor Schapera in Bechuanaland and Dr. Hellmann in Johannesburg.

Perhaps out of the tradition of anthropology, we have been interested largely in the problem of why tribalism persists, both in tribal areas and in towns, in spite of the industrial revolution which has produced such great social changes. Our main argument is that in the rural areas membership of a tribe involves participation in a working political system, and sharing of domestic life with kinsfolk; and that this continued participation is based on present economic and social demands, and not merely on conservatism. On the other hand, tribalism in towns is a different phenomenon entirely. It is primarily here a means of classifying the multitude of Africans of heterogeneous origin who live together in the towns, and this classification is the basis on which a number of new African groupings, such as burial and mutual help societies, are formed to meet the demands of urban life. In both rural and urban areas, these affiliations to fellow-tribesmen have to be analysed as they operate alongside new forms of association, such as Christian sects, political pressure groups, and economic groups. These new associations are clearly more important in the towns than in the rural areas. Persisting loyalty to a tribe therefore operates for a man in two quite distinct situations, and to a large extent he can keep these spheres of activity separate.

Two important, and to some extent opposed, methodological principles have influenced our approach. The first is the standard rule of anthropological research that one must collect data by direct observation of a restricted field of social life, and that these data primarily determine the lines of one's analysis. This entails an emphasis in analysis on actual social situations which have been observed – law cases, the boycott of a butcher's shop, a trade union meeting, a tribal dance in the town, the activities of married couples in the urban setting, and so forth; and it requires that we cast away any preconceptions deriving from our knowledge that most of the urban dwellers come from a tribal home, until we have analysed these social situations as the precipitates of a particular type of social field. The second principle arises from a general orientation in sociological analysis. This is the assumption, which is confirmed by empirical observation, that in the new Central African towns we are dealing with a system, though not of course a perfect system with a closed, repetitive pattern. Urban life exhibits sufficient regularities for us to extract systematic inter-connexions which we can arrange to exhibit a structure, and we can study how this structure changes. Since we are examining a structure of social relations, we know that it has to be analysed in terms of roles; and that these roles will themselves influence the behaviour of the occupants of the roles, whatever their origin and their personal differences of temperament. In terms of this orientation, we should expect the fact that tribal Africans live in a town and participate in the activities of industry, commerce, and general urbanism, to exert dominant pressure on their behaviour. Hence the starting-point of our analysis of tribalism in the towns is not that it is manifested by tribesmen, but that it is manifested by townsmen. The African newly arrived from his rural home to work in a mine, is first of all a miner (and possibly resembles miners everywhere). Secondarily he is a tribesman; and his adherence to tribalism has to be interpreted in an urban setting.[1] Here the general orientation of an analysis based on our view of social system is supported by the field data which dominate our field notebooks.

All this seems obvious to me, and I know the approach is well validated in socio-logical literature. But it has to be stressed again and again, for it is fundamentally important and it has been overlooked in past researches which have thus been viti-ated. Even much present research is vitiated thus. We can understand easily that practical men, dealing with the Africans who flock into the new towns, and who know that these Africans have just left tribal homes, should think of them as the same individuals who a few days ago were tribesmen. What is more surprising is that this approach dominated the thinking of a generation of anthropologists who first tackled the study of urban Africans, and that it still influences present-day students of the urban situation. The tradition of anthropology is still 'tribalistic', and with it goes a tendency to make the tribe and the tribesman the starting-point of analysis.

Hence anthropologists have tended – if I put it over-succinctly – to think in terms of 'detribalization', as if this were a slow, long-time process.[2] On the contrary, it seems to me apparent that the moment an African crosses his tribal boundary to go to the town, he is 'detribalized', out of the political control of the tribe. And in the town, the basic materials by which he lives are different: he walks on different ground, eats food at different hours and maybe different food at that. He comes under different political authorities, and associates with different fellows. He works with different tools in a different system of organization.

In short, this patent set of observations, as well as our theoretical orientation, should lead us to view the Africans in urban areas as acting primarily within a field whose structure is determined by the urban, industrial setting. An African townsman is a townsman, an African miner is a miner. We may anticipate that as soon as Africans assemble in towns and engage in industrial work, they will begin to form social relationships appropriate to their new situation: they will try to combine to better their conditions in trade unions, and associations of law-breakers will emerge as well as friendly and burial societies, and so forth. Of course, these Africans continue to be influenced by many factors arising outside of the urban situation: the rapid growth of the towns and their own inexperience of towns, the constant movement of African labourers between tribe and town and between towns and the tribal culture and life from which they come, as well as customary linkages and hostilities between different tribes. But even these tribal influences operate now in an urban milieu, and not in a rural milieu. The urbanized African is outside the tribe, but not beyond the influence of the tribe. Correspondingly, when a man returns from the towns into the political area of his tribe he is tribalized again – de-urbanized – though not beyond the influence of the towns.

I have given this introduction to emphasize the methodological principles which underlie the researches of my colleagues in urban areas. Now I shall examine shortly some of these researches, before passing to some corresponding points in research in the tribal areas. I deal with two recent books, Professor J. C. Mitchell's study of *The Kalela Dance* which is performed on the Northern Rhodesian Copperbelt[3] and Dr. A. L. Epstein's book on the Copperbelt town of Luanshya, *Politics in an Urban African Community*[4].

One of Epstein's main themes is how, during the growth of a copper-mining town, typical urban associations and industrial groupings ousted European attempts to work with authorities based on tribal affiliations. When the copper-mine at Luanshya was established in the early 1930's, Europeans provided managerial staff and skilled working force: the heavy labour was performed by thousands of Africans from tribes spread over British, Belgian, and Portuguese territories. The mine, like many industrial enterprises in Europe's industrial revolution, had to provide both order and some social services for this heterogeneous population. Government's resources were not adequate for these tasks, and in any case European and African mineworkers dwelt on the private property of the mine. The Africans were housed in a compound under a

Compound Manager. He was responsible for the housing, part of the feeding, and some welfare work for the Africans, for dealing with their working conditions and complaints, and for maintaining order among them and settling their quarrels. Faced with thousands of Africans of different tribes, the mine officials, reasonably enough, thought that it would be wise to deal with them through representatives of the tribes as groups. Therefore the Compound Manager instituted a system of Tribal Elders, who were elected, and given special robes and special houses. He planned that the mine management could communicate with its African labourers through the Elders, while the Elders in turn would inform the management of the wishes and complaints of their tribesmen. In addition, the Elders would look after the welfare of newcomers, involved in the ceaseless drift of men within a system of migrant labour. Finally, the Elders came to judge the small disputes that arose between men, and between men and their wives. The people themselves welcomed this institution; and a similar system was established in Luanshya Municipal Location, which had grown up distinct from the mine's compound.

Most of the Elders, chosen by the Africans themselves, were fairly closely related to the royal families of the tribes concerned. The authority system of the tribes was projected into the urban, industrial sphere.

This system of administration worked fairly well until, in 1935, there were major disturbances throughout the copper-mining towns. These disturbances arose out of African demands for better pay and working conditions. A strike began on two other mines, and the Compound Manager at Luanshya asked his Tribal Elders what would happen there. They assured him that there would be no disturbances. The Manager asked the Elders to go among the miners and calm them, but one of the Elders, a senior man, was driven away from a meeting, and accused of being in league with the Europeans. A mob stormed the Compound Office, and the Elders had to seek sanctuary within it. Clearly they had neither influence nor power within the strike situation. Yet after the disturbances, the Elders resumed their previous role. By 1937 there were some forty accredited Elders on the mine, and Epstein says (p. 36) that 'the system of Tribal Elders operated satisfactorily in the main, and was appreciated by the mass of the people'.

I have time only to touch on Epstein's analysis of the background to this development. He stresses the tribal background of the Elders – their frequent affiliation with the families of chiefs, their knowledge of tribal customs and values, their skill in adjudicating in disputes, and so forth. Yet, in a way paradoxically, they came simultaneously to be associated with the European mine management. During the strike they were driven away as in league with the Europeans. Two important elements in their position have therefore to be stressed. First, as tribal representatives, whose authority was based on the political system of the tribe, they had no connexion with the situations in which African miners worked in the mine itself. Here the workers were organized in departments and gangs within which tribal affiliation was irrelevant; and it was in this situation that common interests had brought the miners to joint action in the strike. This was industrial action, in which tribal allegiances, and hence the Elders, lacked all influence. But, secondly, in the administrative system the Elders had become representatives of the mine itself, in dealing with its workers, and hence when those workers came into dispute with the mine, they regarded the Elders as enemies. When the strike had ended, the Elders could resume their former role.

This position changed slowly until a second series of strikes broke out on the Copperbelt in 1940. There were disturbances, with shooting of miners, at Nkana mine, but none at Luanshya. At Mufulira, a strike committee of seventeen men was set up to negotiate with the management. At all mines, the authority of the Elders was rejected, and the strike committee at Mufulira was the beginnings of a new regime which was to oust tribal affiliation as a basis for handling industrial matters among African miners. For after the war, the British Government (now a Labour Government) sent out trained trade unionists to help Africans form trade unions. The development of trade unionism was present among the Africans themselves, but it was now encouraged by Government policy. Eventually, the African Mineworkers Union emerged as a powerful, organized, industrial union throughout the mining towns of Northern Rhodesia, negotiating with management. As its last step on the way to power, the Union insisted that the Tribal Elders system be abolished, for the trade union leaders saw the Elders as a threat to their own authority, and as a means which the mine might use to oppose them. An overwhelming vote of the miners approved of this abolition. The trade union had finally ousted the formal organized power of tribal representatives from the industrial field, though later I will describe how tribal affiliation continued to influence trade union politics.

In the Municipal Compound developments were not so clear-cut. Epstein suggests that the monolithic structure of the mine with its centralized power over the working, residential, etc., lives of the workers, provoked the response of a monolithic African trade union, also catering for many aspects of the miners' lives. The Municipal Compound, on the other hand, is inhabited by Africans employed in many trades and by many employers. But there similar developments have occurred, in that Government's attempt to work with institutions based on tribal affiliations has been opposed by the emergence of associations from life in the town.

Epstein goes on to point out that the dominance of the trade union did not eliminate tribal allegiances within the industrial field. To some extent, these allegiances have ceased to be so significant in industrial matters where the Africans are opposed in their interests to the European mine officials. But tribal affiliation is still important in matters between Africans. Thus elections within the union for official posts in the union have to some extent been fought on tribal lines: for example, other tribes complained that the leadership was dominated by the Bemba tribes; and tribalism entered into other activities.

Nevertheless even here it is not straight tribal hostility and loyalty that are operating. During the early years of the mine, the posts open for educated and semi-skilled Africans were largely taken by Nyasalanders and Barotse. Bemba, who are the most powerful tribe near the mine, filled many minor authoritative posts. Hence while many Africans see the struggle for leadership on the mine in tribal terms, this covers a struggle between groups of different skill.[5] After the firm consolidation of the trade union's power, a dispute began with the mines and the European trade union not only for better pay for Africans, but also for the opening to Africans of better-paid posts demanding higher skill. Hence the issue emerged, whether the union was to press for a few highly paid openings for a few well-educated Africans, or for much better all-round opportunities for the mass of relatively unskilled labourers. Out of this struggle, a new and militant leadership, more representative of the labourers, won many union elections. The struggle reached its climax when the mine management opened new skills to Africans and put them on a monthly salary, instead of payment by ticket of work done. It also insisted that they join a new and separate union, formed by salaried Africans and led by a Barotse. The old union came out on strike against this move; and eventually the Government, holding that this was a political strike, arrested 62 trade union leaders and deported them to their tribal areas.

The significance for us of this strike is that it brought into the open the emergence within the African urban population of affiliations based on what we can call 'class principles'. The African union, after its victory, has been split by a division of interests between component categories with independent interests. This division on 'class' lines has what Epstein calls a 'pervasive' effect spreading into many institutions. Professor Mitchell has examined the effect of this situation on the activities of a popular dance-team on the Copperbelt, in his analysis of *The Kalela Dance*. It is danced by teams of Africans who come from single tribes. During their dances they mock other tribes, by alleging that these have, among many unpleasant habits, loose, and even perverted, sexual lives. Thus on the surface the dance proclaims proudly the virtues of the team's own tribe, and derides other tribes. Yet the members of the derided tribes attend the performance and laugh as loudly as any at the salacious wit against themselves. Mitchell was struck by the fact that, despite this surface of tribal competitiveness, the dancers had named their hierarchy of officials after the hierarchies of British or civil dignity. Moreover, the dancers did not wear tribal dress: instead they were dressed in smart and clean European clothes, and they had to maintain their tidiness and smartness throughout the dancing. This was insisted on, although the dancers themselves were mostly unskilled, and poorly educated, labourers. He interprets the dance as reflecting the aspirations of all Africans for a European way of life, or civilization, and he shows from other data how the values implicit here form a prestige scale for all Africans. But, he argues, these unskilled labourers are not striving through the dance to participate in the European part of Central African society: this is cut off from them by the colour-bar. They are striving in the dance to associate themselves with the new African élite. While in political activity the Africans may combine against the Europeans, internally they are differentiated on a class scale, which people are striving to ascend.

Yet the dancing-team is a tribal team, deriding other tribes. Its actions have therefore also to be related to a persisting significance of tribal allegiances in the towns.

Here Mitchell works out that tribalism in the town operates as a primary mode of classifying the heterogeneous masses of people, whom a man meets, into manageable categories. With his fellow-tribesmen he can converse, and he shares their customs and way of life. In practice, Mitchell discovered that there was far less tribal inter-marriage in the towns than is usually assumed, so that a man marries the sisters and daughters of his fellow-tribesmen. More than this, by the use of social distance scales, Mitchell found that all the many tribes in the towns were grouped into several limited categories by other Africans, and that specific institutionalized modes of behaviour had developed between various tribal categories. Thus he discovered that joking relationships between tribes in this region had developed in modern times, and were not, as previously thought, traditional. Mitchell thus stresses that tribes in towns form categories by which people group one another, and this categorization determines a lot of action in casual as well as intimate relationships. Both he and Epstein stress that in domestic situations, where as we have seen most marriages occur within tribes, tribal custom and practice are effective, though much modified by the demands of the urban situation.

In some towns in Central and South Africa, but not on the Copperbelt, member-ship of a tribe has become the basis for forming various kinds of associations.

These studies show that we can find plenty of systematic regularities in the new African towns. These regularities are obvious in that people live and go about their business within the towns in relative security and absence of fear. Hence clearly there is some kind of working, integrated social system in these towns. But the social system must not be thought of as rigid, tight, closed, or self-consistent. The social field of the towns consists of many semi-independent areas of life, where people associate for specific purposes: to run a home and raise children, to be entertained with friends, to work and improve status, to achieve political objectives, etc. Different principles of organization may be effective in the various areas of relations. Hence a trade union can oust Tribal Elders, and with them tribal authority from the town, without affecting tribalism as a category or even loyalty to a tribal chief in other situations. I would stress, too, that this situation is not confined to Africans. Tribalism acts, though not as strongly, in British towns: for in these Scots and Welsh and Irish, French, Jews, Lebanese, Africans, have their own associations, and their domestic life is ruled by their own national customs. But all may unite in political parties and in trade unions or employers' federations. Tribalism in the Central African towns is, in sharper form, the tribalism of all towns.

These urban studies emphasize that tribal association in these towns does not dominate political life. Tribalism is not an organized set of political relations. Here modern urban tribalism differs radically from tribalism in the rural areas. In the rural areas, under British rule, each tribe is an organized political unit, with a complex internal structure. At its head, in Central Africa at least, there is usually a traditional chief, with a traditional council of elders, and a system of villages and other political units. For here it has been Government policy to rule-through the tribal organization. Government has thus lent its powerful support to the continued working of the African political systems, as systems. We may also say that continuing, and in the sociological sense conservative, loyalty to chiefs has been important here. Moreover, since the new industrial and urban political associations develop in the towns, they only affect tribal allegiances indirectly. But we also consider that the tribal system in the rural areas serves new needs of tremendous importance to the modern African.

In order to earn the money we all know them to require, Africans in Northern Rhodesia mostly go out to work, for longer or shorter periods, in mines and other labour centres. (I have not space to deal with events in tribes which have gone in for cash-cropping or -fishing.) But they consider they have little security in their life in the towns. It is difficult for them to rear their children as they would like there; till recently they could not own houses, and few now can do so; there is no provision for unemployment; sickness and accident compensation may not exist and are always low; there is little provision for the old. The insecurity of town employment for each personally is great, and they remember the years of great depression when mines closed down, and thousands of African workers (indeed like American workers) had to return to the land. In this situation, they look for security to their tribal homes: ever-present needs in the modern total field where they make their living, as well as sentiment, tie them to the rural areas.[6]

These tribesmen are therefore earning their living in two widely separated areas, and ultimately they feel that their main security lies in the tribal land – and objectively this seems to be true. Hence Watson says of the Mambwe that they raid the towns for money from their rural base. The success of tribes in achieving the required deployment of their men on two labour fronts varies according to a complex of variables I cannot here examine. But all tribes do turn in the end to their right to land, for ultimate support.

Land here is not an individual item of land which a man owns for himself and by himself. For he secures his rights to land in two ways. First, as a citizen of the tribe he is entitled to some arable and building land, and to the use of public pasturage, fishing waters, and wild products. Secondly, in all tribes except those who shift their gardens widely and have an abundance of land, he gets rights to land from membership of a village and a group of kinsfolk. That is, a man's right to land in the tribal home depends on his accepting membership of a tribe, with all its obligations. This right of every subject, while he is a subject, to land, is jealously safeguarded. I examined the development of land-holding in all the Central and Southern African tribes, and found that in no case, as land got scarcer and more valuable, had chiefs expropriated to themselves an unreasonable quantity of land. Instead, they had in various tribes, as pressure on land increased, steadily legislated to safeguard the fundamental right of every tribesman to some land. The first step by the chief was to take power to commandeer land allocated to a subject which he was not using, for distribution to the landless. Then – in a developmental series – the chief took power to take over for the landless, land which had lain fallow for a certain period: the cycle of soil degradation has here begun. The final step was to restrict each family to a limited area of garden land. People get around these laws by various devices, but the trend of development in the view of both the leaders and the mass of the tribesmen is clear. Every man who is a member of the tribe has a right to live and support his family on the tribal land.

I am sure that honest fellow-feeling and sympathy and justice have contributed to this legislation. But in addition those who remain behind have an interest in the work of those who go away to the towns, for these bring home the money which the people require. In a way, those who stay at home hold the land as security for support in money from those who go out to work. And those who go out to work pass money to those who remain, in payment for this security. So that they get security by their continued allegiance to the tribe, for they hold land from the chief in return for loyalty and support. Hence they adhere to their chiefs; and as they adhere to their chiefs, they accept with the chiefs, for the rural areas, the organized system of tribal political relations. Very few tribesmen wish to overturn the tribal political system as such, though new interest groups, and new élites, in the tribes may struggle for power in tribal councils. With acceptance of the tribal political system goes acceptance of many customs and observances built into that system.

In tribes where land is worked in co-operating groups of kindred, or where kin organize their departures to town so that some remain at home to work the land and care for dependants, security in holding of land also involves acceptance of kinship obligations, and with these of many parts of the tribal culture. I cannot elaborate this theme, for lack of space.

We see, in short, that tribalism persists in the rural areas because of Government support, and because the tie to tribal land is of the utmost importance to a man. With this tie goes acceptance of the tribal political system with its culture, and of its smaller constituent units with their culture. In short, tribalism in the rural areas consists of participation in a highly organized system of social relations, based strongly on the chief's rights as trustee for his people over the tribal land. Tribalism in the towns is not such an organized system of political and other social relations. It is an important basis for grouping people in categories, and it is most important in social life. Associations form between fellow-tribesmen, and tribal loyalties and hostilities may influence the working of urban-type groups. But here specific urban and industrial groups have developed, and ousted attempts by Europeans to transplant African tribal authority systems to deal with urban-industrial problems. Class linkages are also beginning to pervade the life and culture of the new towns. In all these respects, Central African towns differ only in degree from any town, anywhere in the world probably. In crisis, common interests arising from industrial and urban association seem steadily to overcome tribal ties and divisions.

I want to stress that I am here summarizing studies in British Central Africa. In other territories, British, South African, Belgian, French, or Portuguese, developments may have been very different. And we must assume in our analysis the presence of a powerful body of European settlers. In West Africa, again, things have been different;

and once independence from colonial rule is established, the position of chiefs in the total political situation varies radically.

I hope my description and analysis are clear enough within the space allowed me, and you will accept that I have not had a chance to qualify my argument or to state some of the complications. Perhaps I can then briefly summarize the main methodological problems which I think arise:

1. The starting-point for analysis of urbanization must be an urban system of relations, in which the tribal origins of the population may even be regarded as of secondary interest. The comparative background for these analyses is urban sociology in general. We have to start with a theory about urban social systems; but these social systems are to be seen as made up of loose, semi-independent, to some extent isolated, sub-systems. Field data have to be collected with this view in mind, and over-concentration on the ethnic origins of the people may sidetrack observation of the critically important events. Because towns are occupied by members of many tribes, the role of tribal affiliation is prominent in inter-tribal contexts. I believe that the specifically anthropological contribution to our understanding of this process of urbanization is the interpretation of detailed records of complex social situations, such as Mitchell made of the Kalela dance, and Epstein of a butcher-shop boycott. Anthropologists may be able to assume the existence of certain important urban sub-systems; transport, management of enterprises, police, administration, sewage collection, etc. The validation of facts and generalizations in the urban areas requires complex quantitative research, of the kind done by Mitchell for our region. But the interpretation of what is measured depends on having the correct systematic view of the area of urban life.

2. If the developments in an urban area are to be examined, a good method is the analysis of the system at certain critical points, where disturbances and struggles provide social situations which exhibit the arrangement of alignments, and which show trends of development. This requires an analysis through time, which I consider far more satisfactory than an analysis of 'functional' aspects. Both Mitchell and Epstein have adopted this method.

3. Our examination of town and rural areas shows that it is possible for men to dichotomize their actions in separate spheres, and this may be an important contribution to the working of the embracing social field. But knowledge of the total field may be necessary to analyse the areas within it, as we have seen in examining the continued adherence of men to their tribal chiefs. Here long-term developments may have to be surveyed over a whole region: it is important to be aware that all Central and Southern African tribes have stressed the rights of all subjects to some land.

4. Within the working of the total field, it is possible to close areas for analysis, and neglect the complexity of important events and institutions which effect social life in the selected area. Thus Epstein did not have to analyse the internal working of mine management to make sense of political developments in the African population of Luanshya; the tribal systems can be analysed without examining in detail the urban areas, though their presence must be taken into account throughout the analysis.

NOTES

1. See Gluckman, 1945.
2. See essays in Mair, 1938 (here only I. Schapera and M. Fortes took the point of view I am representing). The view I am criticizing emerged clearly in Malinowski, 1946; cf. my critical essay, *An Analysis of the Sociological Theories of Bronislaw Malinowski* (1948).
3. 1956.
4. 1958. See also his publications on the work of African Urban Courts, cited in his bibliography.
5. See also McCulloch, 1956.
6. The two works which stress this problem most for the region are: Watson, 1958 and Gluckman, 1943.

REFERENCES

Epstein, A. L. 1958. *Politics in an Urban African Community.* Manchester University Press for the Rhodes-Livingstone Institute.

Gluckman, M. 1943. *Essays on Lozi Land and Royal Property.* Rhodes-Livingstone Paper, No. 10.

———. 1945. 'Seven-Year Research Plan of the Rhodes-Living-stone Institute'. *Human Problems in British Central Africa: The Rhodes-Livingstone Journal,* No. 4, December.

———. 1948. *An Analysis of the Sociological Theories of Bronislaw Malinowski.* Rhodes-Livingstone Paper, No. 16.

Mair, L. P. (ed.) 1938. *Methods of Study of Culture Contact in Africa.* International African Institute, Memorandum XV.

Malinowski, B. 1946. *The Dynamics of Culture Change.* Yale University Press.

McCulloch, M. 1956. *A Social Survey of the African Population of Livingstone.* Rhodes-Livingstone Paper, No. 26.

Mitchell, J. C. 1956. *The Kalela Dance.* Rhodes-Livingstone Paper, No. 27.

Watson, W. 1958. *Tribal Cohesion in a Money Economy.* Manchester University Press for the Rhodes-Livingstone Institute.

CHAPTER SIXTEEN

Global Disconnect: Abjection and the Aftermath of Modernism

James Ferguson

INTRODUCTION

In a recently completed book, *Expectations of Modernity* (1999), I explore how mineworkers in the town of Kitwe on the Zambian Copperbelt have dealt with a long period of economic adversity. The book deals with a range of ethnographic questions: changing forms of labor migration; new patterns of urban-to-rural mobility; the dynamics of household formation and dissolution; the relation of urban cultural forms to the micro-political-economic relations linking urban workers to their rural kin and allies. In all of these domains, I have been less interested in constructing a developmental sequence of social and cultural forms than in exploring their temporal coexistence; less interested in a succession of "typical" forms over time than in an understanding of the whole spread (what Stephen Jay Gould (1996) calls the "full house") of diverse modes of getting by that may exist at any one moment, and how that spread is affected by political-economic shifts over time.

In arguing for nonlinear, variation-centered models of social transformation (aiming to reconstruct what Gould (1996) calls the "bush" of actual variation rather than an ideal tree or ladder of succeeding "typical forms"), I have been concerned to demonstrate the inadequacy of what I call the modernist metanarratives through which urban life in Africa has so often been understood. Here, my target is not only the explicit Eurocentrism that allowed the Rhodes-Livingstone Institute anthropologists to see the Copperbelt as the new Birmingham of an African Industrial Revolution, but equally the still-ubiquitous use of a set of linear, directional concepts to frame scholarly understandings of urban Africa – what I call the "-izations": urbanization, modernization, proletarianization, commoditization, etc.

The period since the mid-1970s or so in Zambia poses a formidable challenge to such habitual ways of understanding the meaning of urban Africa. With declining terms of trade, increasingly worked-out mines, and the crushing burden of a debt crisis, Zambia's copper-based, urban industrial economy has seen a sustained and profound contraction. This has brought with it not only impoverishment and hardship, but also a strange flood of new "-izations." The "Industrial Revolution in Africa" seems to have been called off: industrialization has been replaced by "de-industrialization". The long-documented flow of migrants to the Copperbelt cities, too, is now running backwards, with urban-to-rural migration now outpacing rural-to-urban – a phenomenon for which the term "counterurbanization" has been coined. The apparently inevitable process of proletarianization, meanwhile, is now replaced by mass layoffs and "back to the land" exercises: the "unmaking," rather than the making, of a working class. And now, with the privatization of the state-held mining company, it seems that even "Zambianization" (the nationalist policy of replacing white management with qualified black Zambians) is being replaced by what is now being called "de-Zambianization," the rehiring of white, expatriate management.

A new generation of Zambians, then, has come of age in a world where the modernist certainties their parents grew up with have been turned upside down, a world where life expectancies and incomes shrink instead of grow, where children become less educated than their parents instead of more, where migrants move from urban centers to remote villages instead of vice versa. It is the modernization story through the looking glass, where modernity is the object of nostalgic reverie, and "backwardness" the anticipated (or dreaded) future.

In reflecting on this extraordinary turn of events, this paper will move between two levels. The first level is the lived experience of actual Zambian workers, who have seen the modernist story-line transformed, in their own lifetimes, from a marvelous promise to a cruel hoax. The second level is a set of global transformations that allow us to see the Zambian case as part of a much more general phenomenon, which I argue is nothing less than the collapse of the global modernist project that once seemed to define the future of what we used to call "the developing world." I have in mind here not only the collapse of the developmentalist vision of the world that saw the "new nations" of the Third World as western nation-states in embryo, and spoke breathlessly of the "coming of age" of "emerging" African nations that would one day soon – through the miracle of political and economic development – somehow resemble England and France. That was one side of the story. But the other was a vision of historical progress through a process of hooking citizens up into a national – and ultimately universal – grid of modernity. This paper will discuss specifically the "grid" of electrical service, and the idea of a universal participation in modernity via copper connectivity as a metaphor for this. But we might think as well here of health care, where the postwar modernist ideal of a universal grid (epitomized in such things as the campaigns for universal vaccination against polio or smallpox) can be contrasted against today's tendency to fragmentation and privatization (which gives us not the polio vaccine, but AIDS combo therapy: managing the disease for those who can pay, while the poor are bluntly notified that it is economically more rational for them to die). Or schooling, where the universal grid of public education is today under siege all over the world. Or public space and the rule of law, where walled communities and fortified private spaces increasingly undermine the social and political promise of a universalistic "public." (I note that recent figures show that private police in "the new South Africa" now outnumber public police by a factor of three to one.)

By reflecting on Zambia's recent experience of decline and – in modernist terms – "failure," I do not mean to suggest that this experience forms a template for an inevitable African future (or even an inevitable Zambian future). On the contrary, my analysis of recent Zambian history leads to an emphasis on non-linear trajectories and multiplicities of pathways; to say that Africa is going "down" today is as false and misleading as it was to say that it was going "up" in the 1960s. But there is no disputing that the social experience of "decline" (notwithstanding the variety of causes and contexts) is today of quite wide relevance across many areas of the African continent (and, indeed, in many other regions – e.g. Russia or Indonesia – where recent political-economic restructuring has had comparable effects). For that reason, an analysis of the political and theoretical significance of that social experience may perhaps be of some wider relevance.

As an ethnographic point of entry into the social experience of decline on the Copperbelt, consider the following brief anecdote. One afternoon in 1989, I was chatting with a young officer of the mineworkers' union, who was expressing his dismay at how difficult it had become to find neckties of decent quality. Soon, we were talking about the two main retail shopping districts in Kitwe, one located in what had once been in colonial days the "European" town center, the other in the former "location" reserved for "Africans." What struck me was that these two shopping districts were still called (as they had been in colonial days) "first class" and "second class," respectively. Why, I wondered, did people continue this usage? Wasn't this an embarrassing holdover of colonial thinking, and of the idea of "second-class" status for Africans? Well, my companion replied, nobody really thought of it that way; it was just what the areas were called. Then he thought for a moment, and continued. "Anyway," he blurted with a bitter, convulsive laugh, "now it's all 'second-class', isn't it?" I take this very particular way of experiencing one's own social world as having become "second class" as a point of departure for what follows.

ABJECTION AND THE NEW WORLD SOCIETY

When Godfrey Wilson wrote his "Essay on the Economics of Detribalization in Northern Rhodesia" in 1941, he considered that the Africans of Northern Rhodesia had just entered into an economically and culturally interconnected "world society," a "huge world-wide community" within which they would soon find a place for themselves as something more than peasants and unskilled workers (Wilson 1941: 12–13). The "civilized" clothing and manners to which so many urban Africans attached such importance, he argued, amounted to a claim to full membership in that worldwide community. Indeed, Wilson suggested, it was for this very reason than many white settlers resented and feared the well-dressed African who politely doffed his hat in the street, preferring to see Africans in suitably humble rags. Fine formal evening wear, ballroom dancing, European-style handshaking – these, Wilson argued, were not inauthentic cultural mimicry but expressed "the Africans' claim to be respected by the Europeans and by one another as civilized, if humble, men, *members of the new world society*" (Wilson 1942: 19–20, emphasis added).[1]

That claim to a full membership in "the new world society," of course, was refused in a racist colonial society. The color bar explicitly distinguished between "first-class" whites, who held the privileges of such membership, and "second-class" natives, who did not (see Ferguson 1999, ch. 1). But nationalism promised to change all that, by overturning the colonial system and banishing forever the insulting idea that Zambians should be second-class citizens in their own land. The early years of Zambia's independence seemed on the verge of delivering on that promise. The color bar was indeed dismantled as educated black Zambians rose to unprecedented positions of power and responsibility; a booming economy and strong labor unions meanwhile helped even ordinary workers to enjoy a new level of comfort and prosperity. As an "emerging new nation," Zambia appeared poised to enter the world of the "first class." It would be like other modern nations right down to its state-of-the-art national airline. . . .With a rising standard of living, bustling urban centers, and such symbols of modern status as suits made in London and a national airline, membership in the "new world society" seemed finally to be at hand.

It was the faltering of the "Industrial Revolution" that changed all that. For no sooner had the "blitzkrieg" of industrialization turned the world upside down for millions of Central Africans than rapid industrial decline set in motion another, even more devastating blitz. The economic hardships this has entailed have been staggering (see Ferguson 1999, ch. 1). But equally important, if harder to measure, has been the sense of a loss of membership in that "world society" of which Wilson spoke. Zambia, in the good times, had been on the map, a country among others in the "modern world." It was, older mineworkers reminded me, a place regularly visited by internationally known musical acts conducting world tours. One man recalled an early 1960s concert by the American country-and-western star Jim Reeves, for instance, and asked me with great feeling why such American acts no longer came to Zambia. But it is not just country-and-western acts that have stopped coming to Zambia. In the 1970s, international airlines such as British Caledonian, UTA, Lufthansa, and Alitalia connected Lusaka via direct flights to Frankfurt, Rome, London, and other European centers; British Caledonian even offered a flight to Manchester. Zambia's own national airline, Zambia Airways, also flew an impressive fleet of planes, proudly piloted by black Zambian pilots, to international destinations both expected (London, Frankfurt, New York) and surprising (Belgrade, Bombay, Larnaca). But as the economic situation deteriorated, the European carriers one by one dropped Zambia from their routes. Finally, in 1996, it was announced that Zambia Airways itself would be liquidated. Like the "Industrial Revolution," it had all apparently been a big mistake. Efficiency required that it be shut down. Today, a thrice-weekly British Airways plane to London is the only flight leaving Zambia for a non-African destination.

For many Zambians, then, as these details suggest, recent history has been experienced not – as the modernization plot led one to expect – as a process of moving forward or joining up with the world but as a process that has pushed them out of the place in the world that they once occupied. The only term I have found to capture this sense of humiliating expulsion is abjection (which I adapt from Kristeva (1982); see also Borneman (1996)). *Abjection* refers to a process of being thrown aside, expelled, or discarded. But its literal meaning also implies not just being thrown out but being thrown *down* – thus expulsion, but also debasement and humiliation. This complex of meanings, sad to report, captures quite precisely the sense I found among the Copperbelt mineworkers – a sense that the promises of modernization had been betrayed, and that they were being thrown out of the circle of full humanity, thrown back into the ranks of the "second class," cast outward and downward into the world of rags and huts where the color bar had always told "Africans" they belonged.

With much talk today of globalization, of new forms of worldwide interconnection, and of yet another "emerging" "new world society," it is useful to consider briefly where Zambia fits in all of this, and what the story I have told here of decline and abjection might have to say about the nature of this "new world order." The meaning of the Zambian case, I suggest, is not simply that it illustrates a gloomy process of decline and disconnection that has had no place in many of the rosier accounts of the new global economy. Beyond simply illustrating the downside of global capitalism, what has happened in Zambia reveals something more fundamental about the mechanisms of membership, exclusion, and abjection upon which the contemporary system of spatialized global inequality depends.

When the color bar cut across colonial Africa, it fell with a special force upon the "westernized Africans": those polished, well-dressed, educated urbanites who blurred the lines between a "civilized," first-class white world, and a supposedly "primitive," second-class black one. It was they – the "not quite/not white" (Bhabha 1997) – whose uncanny presence destabilized and menaced the racial hierarchy of the colonial social order. And it was they who felt the sting not just of exclusion but of abjection: of being pushed back across a boundary that they had been led to believe they might successfully cross. In a similar way, when the juncture between Africa and the industrialized world that had been presented as a global stairway (leading from the "developing" world to the "developed") revealed itself instead as a wall (separating the "first world" from the "third"), it was the Copperbelt and places like it – proud examples of just how modern, urban, and prosperous an emerging Africa could be – that experienced this boundary-fixing process most acutely, as a kind of abjection. The experience of abjection here was not a matter of being merely *excluded* from a status to which one had never had a claim but of being *expelled*, cast out-and-down from that status by the formation of a new (or newly impermeable) boundary. It is an experience that has left in its wake both a profound feeling of loss as well as the gnawing sense of a continuing affective attachment to that which lies on the other side of the boundary. When Copperbelt workers of an older generation spoke to me with such feeling of having once, long ago, owned a fine tuxedo or attended a concert by the Ink Spots or eaten T-bone steak at a restaurant, they were registering a connection to the "first class" that they had lost many years before but still felt, like the phantom pains from a limb long ago amputated.

When the Copperbelt mineworkers expressed their sense of abjection from an imagined modern world "out there," then, they were not simply lamenting a lack of connection but articulating a specific experience of *disconnection*, just as they inevitably described their material poverty not simply as a lack but as a loss. When we think about the fact that Zambia is today disconnected and excluded in so many ways from the mainstream of the global economy, it is useful to remember that disconnection, like connection, implies a relation and not the absence of a relation. Dependency theorists once usefully distinguished between a state of being undeveloped (an original condition) and a state of being underdeveloped (the historical result of an active process of underdevelopment). In a parallel fashion, we might usefully distinguish between being unconnected (an original condition) and being disconnected (the historical result of an active process of disconnection). Just as being hung up on is not the same thing as never having had a phone, the economic and social disconnection that Zambians experience today is quite distinct from a simple lack of connection. Disconnection, like abjection, implies an active relation, and the state of having been disconnected requires to be understood as the product of specific *structures and processes of disconnection*. What the Zambian case shows about globalization, I will suggest, is just how important disconnection is to a "new world order" that insistently presents itself as a phenomenon of pure connection.

GLOBAL REDLINING AND THE NEOLIBERAL NEW WORLD ORDER: ZAMBIA IS NO EXCEPTION?

As Neil Smith has recently argued, in spite of aggressive "structural adjustment" and a rhetorical celebration of "free-market capitalism," "what is remarkable about the last two decades [in Africa] is its virtual systematic expulsion from capitalism" (1997: 180). Indeed, a recent 35-page feature in *The Economist* on "The Global Economy," made almost no reference to Africa at all, making only a passing note of the "threat" to rich countries that may be posed by "the 500m or so people, most of them in Africa, who risk being left out of the global boom." With private ventures in the continent falling by 25 percent in the 1980s, and even further in the 1990s,

Africa "has been treated to a crash course in the most vicious aspects of free-market capitalism while being largely denied any of the benefits" (pp. 180, 181). Effectively "redlined" in global financial markets, and increasingly cut off from governmental aid flows as well, most of sub-Saharan Africa today functions as "a veritable ghetto of global capital" (p. 179) – a zone of economic abjection that also makes a convenient object lesson for Third-World governments in other regions that might, without the specter of "Africanization" hanging over them, be tempted to challenge capital's regime of "economic correctness" (Smith 1997; Ferguson 1995).

The very possibility of "redlining" on such a massive scale reveals that the much-vaunted "flexibility" of the new forms of global economy involves not simply new forms of connection but new forms of disconnection as well. With increasing international wage competition and pressure on state welfare provisions, as Smith (1997: 187) notes, "the global economy is ever more efficient at writing off redundant spaces of accumulation: the flexibility of investment and market options is matched by a wholly new flexibility in disinvestment and abandonment." It is precisely this "flexibility" that makes global "redlining" possible, and that makes Zambia's recent deindustrialization just as integral a part of globalization as the appearance of Mexican car factories or Shanghai skyscrapers.

To speak of expulsion and abandonment here is not to suggest that Zambia is today somehow outside of the world capitalist system (and thus needs to be brought back into it). The mining industry, though shrunken, continues to dominate the Zambian economy, and may even (if the current plan for full privatization brings the new capital for exploration and development that its boosters promise) expand again in years to come; capitalists continue to profit from Zambia's copper. Other forms of capitalist production of course remain important as well. But the more fundamental point here is that the abjected, "redlined" spaces of decline and disinvestment in the contemporary global economy are as much a part of the geography of capitalism as the booming zones of enterprise and prosperity; they reveal less the outside of the system than its underbelly. Expulsion and abandonment (in Smith's terms), disconnection and abjection (in my own), occur within capitalism, not outside of it. They refer to processes through which global capitalism constitutes its categories of social and geographical membership and privilege by constructing and maintaining a category of absolute non-membership: a holding tank for those turned away at the "development" door; a residuum of the economically discarded, disallowed, and disconnected – to put it plainly, a global "second class."

In its "Industrial Revolution" era, it was copper that connected Zambia to the world. The world needed Zambia's copper, and it was copper that put the new nation on the economic world map, while bringing in the export earnings that financed everything from cars for urban workers to state prestige projects like Zambia Airways. But copper not only connected Zambia economically, it also provided a vivid symbol of a specifically modern form of world connection. The copper wire bars produced by Zambian refineries literally did connect the world, via telephone and power cables that were forming a rapidly ramifying net across the globe. From the Soviet rural electrification program, to the United States' model Tennessee Valley Authority project, to the new South Africa's township electricity programs, electrification has provided the twentieth century with perhaps its most vivid symbol of modernization and development. Fusing a powerful image of universal connection in a national grid with the classical Enlightenment motif of illumination of the darkness, electrification has been an irresistible piece of symbolism for the modernist state (expressed perhaps most vividly in Lenin's suggestion that the "backward" Soviet peasantry be uplifted by melting enough church bells into copper wire to permit the placing of a light bulb in every village (Coopersmith 1992: 154–5)).[2] It was no different in Zambia, where the electrification of the townships was a compelling symbol of inclusion, a sign that Africans, too, were to be hooked up with the "new world society."

Today, the Copperbelt mine townships are still wired for electricity. But the service is intermittent, as equipment often breaks down, and the copper power cables are from time to time stolen for sale as scrap. What is more, few township residents can afford to pay the monthly charges for the use of electricity, so electric appliances go unused as women huddle around charcoal fires preparing the daily meals and the townships' skies fill with gray smoke each morning.

Nowadays, global interconnection does not depend so much on copper. The development of fiber optics and satellite communications technology, for instance, means that there is today much less need for copper-wired telephone cables. This "advance" in global connectivity is actually one of the causes of Zambia's drastic economic marginalization; the world "out there" can increasingly connect itself without relying on Zambia's copper (Mikesell 1988: 40).[3] Ironically, then, the communication revolution that is generally thought of as "connecting the globe" is playing a small but significant part in disconnecting Zambia.

There is a fundamental point suggested in this small detail. That is that what we have come to call globalization is not simply a process that links together the world but also one that differentiates it. It creates new inequalities even as it brings into being new commonalities and lines of communication. And it creates new, up-to-date ways not only of connecting places but of bypassing and ignoring them.

Most Zambians, let us remember, have never made a telephone call in their lives. Indeed, two out of three human beings alive today can say the same, according to one estimate.[4] With new technologies, will telecommunications now become more equally distributed, or even truly universal? One wonders. According to one recent report, at least, cellular telephone technology promises not to "hook up" the African masses but rather to make obsolete the very idea that they need to be "hooked up": many of the poorest parts of the world, the article claims, may now *never* be wired for phone service (*The Economist* 1993). For cellular technology allows businesses and elites to ignore their limited and often malfunctioning national telephone systems and do their business via state-of-the-art satellite connectivity, bypassing altogether the idea of a universal copper grid providing service to all.

Wilson's "new world society," for all its faults, implied a promise of universality and even ultimate equality that is strikingly absent from the current visions of the "new world order." In the plotline of modernization, some countries were "behind," it is true, but they were all supposed to have the means to "catch up" in the end. And Zambia was no exception. "Second-class" countries could and (the story promised) surely would eventually rise to the ranks of the "first class." Today, this promise is still mouthed by the ideologists of development here and there. But it is without much conviction. More characteristic is *The Economist's* casual casting aside of that troublesome 500 million "or so" who have inexplicably missed the bandwagon of global growth. In the neo-liberal "new world order," apparently, Zambia (along with most of the rest of Africa) *is* to be an exception.

Many of the people I spoke with on the Copperbelt understood this very well – understood that "Africa," in the new global dispensation, was becoming a category of abjection. I noticed that whenever people were trying to convey their problems – to describe their suffering, to appeal for help, to explain the humiliation of their circumstances – they described themselves not as Zambians but as Africans. On the one hand, the term evoked all the images associated with Africa in contemporary international media discourse: pictures of poverty, starvation, and war; refugees, chaos, and charity. On the other, of course, it evoked the old colonial usage of African as a stigmatized race category. Putting the two connotations together suggested (tragically, if accurately) a reimposition of the old, despised "second-class" status but within a new macro-political order. As one old man put it, at the end of a wrenching narration of his country's downward slide: "We are just poor Africans, now" (see also Ferguson 1997).

THE END OF DEVELOPMENT

A number of recent critical analysts have heralded the end of the "age of development."[5] For Wolfgang Sachs, editor of the influential critical work *The Development Dictionary* (1992), the whole project of development today "stands like a ruin in the intellectual landscape," a disastrous failure now made "obsolete," "outdated by history" (1992: 1, 2). It is not only that development has failed to deliver the economic growth and sociocultural modernization that it promised; more fundamentally, the whole ideal of development can no longer carry any conviction. Economically, Sachs argues, the very idea of the whole planet consuming at First-World levels presents an ecological disaster if not an impossibility, while socially and culturally, development offers only a thinly veiled westernization, a colonizing global monoculture that must choke out the "traditional" world's wealth of diverse local modes of life. To the extent that Third-World people have themselves sought development, in this view, they have been misguided; the schemas of development have provided only "the cognitive base for [a] pathetic self-pity" (1992: 2), which has been self-defeating, and which must continue no longer.

Esteva argues in similar fashion that development has led Third-World peoples "to be enslaved to others' experience and dreams" (Esteva 1992: 7). When United States President Harry Truman labeled two billion people as "underdeveloped" in 1949,

> they ceased being what they were, in all their diversity, and were transmogrified into an inverted mirror of others' reality: a mirror that belittles them and sends them off to the end of the queue, a mirror that defines their identity, which is really that of a heterogeneous and diverse majority, simply in the terms of a homogenizing and narrow minority. (Esteva 1992: 7)

According to Esteva, the world would be well advised to do without such a concept (which is in any case "doomed to extinction" (1992: 7)), and proceed to emulate the "marginals" at the fringes of the capitalist economy who are rejecting the "needs" imposed by the economic worldview of development and reinventing a world without scarcity (much like Sahlins' "original affluent society" of hunters and gatherers) (1992: 19–22).[6]

There is reason to be doubtful of such sweeping claims for the end of development. Most obviously, it is clear that ideas of development – often remarkably unreconstructed ones at that – hold great sway in many parts of the world today, perhaps especially in areas (notably, many parts of East and Southeast Asia) that have enjoyed recent rapid economic expansion (though the recent "crash" that has stricken many countries in the region may yet shake that developmentalist faith). More theoretically, one might well be suspicious of criticisms of inevitable linear teleologies and progressive successions of epochs that proceed by constructing their own inevitable linear teleologies and progressive successions of epochs, as so many contemporary "post-" and "end of . . ." narratives seem to do.[7] But it remains true that something has happened in recent years to the taken-for-granted faith in development as a universal prescription for poverty and inequality. For Africa, at least, as for some other parts of the world, there is a real break with the certainties and expectations that made a development era possible. The "rolling back" of the state, the abandonment of the goal of industrialization, the commitment to what are euphemistically called "market forces" and "private enterprise," and the shattering of expectations for economic convergence with the West, all come together to create a very real end, at least at the level of perceptions and expectations, of at least the grander versions of the development project in Africa.

Is this something to be celebrated? Critics like Sachs and Esteva give to this question an unequivocally affirmative answer. Development, they point out, has distorted people's understandings of their own histories, imposed Eurocentric values and ideals, and crowded out innumerable local ways of doing things. The sooner it disappears, they suggest, the better. There is much to recommend this view. Certainly, there is no reason why the people of former colonial territories should accept economic and cultural convergence with the West (whether it is owning a car, wearing suits made in London, or having a "modern family") as the ultimate measure of achievement or

progress; the critics are quite right to attack the ethnocentrism of such an assumption, and to point out its historical contingency (see Escobar's excellent critique
(1995)). Moreover, the ecological and human degradation created by what have been
termed "overdeveloped" societies is only too evident; it is not obvious that such
societies constitute a model to be emulated. It is also possible to show, as I have attempted to do in my own previous work (Ferguson 1994), that the conceptual problematic of development has served, in concrete instances and through specifiable
mechanisms, aswhat I have termed an "anti-politics machine," systematically mis-
recognizing and depoliticizing understandings of the lives and problems of people
living in what has long since come to be known as the Third World.

But critics such as Sachs and Esteva sometimes seem to forget that the post-World
War II conceptual apparatus of development did not create global inequality at a
stroke but only provided a new means of organizing and legitimating an only-too-real
inequality that was already very well established. It was not Truman's speech in 1949
that sent Africa and other colonial territories to the "back of the queue," as Esteva
implies; conquest, colonial rule, and centuries of predatory violence and economic
exploitation saw to it that they were already there. "Development" was laid on top
of already-existing geopolitical hierarchies; it neither created north-south inequality nor undid it but instead provided a set of conceptual and organizational devices
for managing it, legitimating it, and sometimes contesting and negotiating its terms
(see Bose 1997; Cooper 1997; Cooper and Packard 1997; Gupta 1997, 1998). The
subordinate position ascribed to the Third World in development discourse was
therefore not a figment of the imagination or a mere Eurocentric illusion but reflected an intractable political-economic reality that could not, and cannot, be wished
or relabeled away. Third-World people who have sometimes viewed themselves as
located "at the end of the queue" are therefore not victims of a self-destructive mys-
tification, and they hardly require to be scolded for "pathetic self-pity."

Nor is there any reason to link the forecast end of development with any general
liberation or new autonomy, as many critics have tended to do. For if development
did not inaugurate the inequalities it organized, neither can its demise be expected to
make them suddenly disappear. Just as the end of one mode of organizing and legitimating a global hierarchy (colonialism) did not end inequality but reconfigured it,
so does the (very partial) disintegration of another ("development") inaugurate not
a new reign of freedom from scarcity and global hierarchy but a new modality of
global inequality.

It is here, too, that we might register the ethnographic fact that the end of "the
age of development" for Copperbelt workers (and, I suspect, for many others on
the continent) has been experienced not as a liberation but as a betrayal. The "world
society" that Godfrey Wilson anticipated has been taken out of play, and Zambians
have been bluntly told that they are, and for the foreseeable future will remain, just so
many "poor Africans." That the development story was a myth, and in some respects
a trap, does not make the abrupt withdrawal of its promises any easier to take, or

any less of a tragedy for those whose hopes and legitimate expectations have been shattered. If nothing else, "development" put the problem of global inequality on the table and named it as a problem; with the development story now declared "out of date," global inequality increasingly comes to appear not as a problem at all but simply as a naturalized fact.

In this context, simply celebrating the end of development is a response that is neither intellectually nor politically adequate. For without a continuing engagement with the problems of global inequality, there is a real danger that what Watts (1995) has termed "anti-development" critiques may aid and abet the current global abjection of Africa. The key questions in the present moment are less about the failures of Africa's developmentalist era than about what follows it. And here the celebration of social movements in a "postdevelopment era" has sometimes seemed to obscure the fact that the new political and economic institutions that govern the global political economy today are often even less democratic and more exploitative than those that preceded them. Not only international organizations such as the IMF, World Bank, and World Trade Organization, but also NGOs, social movements, and "civil society," today participate in new, transnational forms of governmentality that need to be subjected to the same sort of critical scrutiny that has been applied to "development" in the past (Ferguson 1995, forthcoming; cf. Watts 1995).

At a more conceptual level, if the modernist story of development has lost its credibility, the most pressing question would appear to be not whether we should lament or celebrate this fact but rather how we can reconfigure the intellectual field in such a way as to restore global inequality to its status as "problem" without reintroducing the teleologies and ethnocentrisms of the development metanarrative. What, in short, comes after "development" – both as an intellectual and cosmological framework for interpretation and explanation, and as a progressive political program for responding to its disastrous economic and social failures?

In seeking an answer to this question, we might do well to think seriously about the nonlinear loops and reversals that have characterized recent Zambian history. Much that was understood as backward and disappearing seems today to be most vital. Moore and Vaughan, for instance, have shown in their study of Zambia's Northern Province that the method of shifting cultivation known as *citemene*, long understood as the very essence of agricultural "backwardness," is alive and well in the 1990s, with most farmers continuing to incorporate it into their agricultural strategies – not as a way of trying to re-create the past but as a mode of coping with the overwhelming uncertainties of the present (Moore and Vaughan 1994: 234). Indeed, as a symbol of flexibility and diversification, they argue, the "old" *citemene* method appears especially well suited to the demands of both the present and the probable future.

I have made similar points in my book (Ferguson 1999). Urban/rural labor mobility, once seen as a sign of incomplete or stunted modernity and a failure to attain full proletarianization, today seems better adapted than ever to present and likely future conditions, while the supposed "main line" of permanent urbanization today appears as the anachronism (ch. 2). Likewise, in the domain of urban culture, it is a "old-fashioned" localism that prevails among today's Copperbelt mineworkers (ch. 3 and 4), while "up-to-date" cosmopolitanism is pressed to the wall (ch. 6). And the "modern" nuclear family that was supposed to represent the inevitable future of urban domesticity is, I have shown, a rare bird, too, surrounded as it is by a range of supposedly backward and pathological domestic strategies that appear better suited to contemporary conditions (ch. 7).

In the same spirit, we might wish to reappraise the place of the Copperbelt's long-denigrated "hangers-on": the unemployed, "useless" *lambwaza*. These are the heirs to the old Lamba "loafers":[8] originally, people of the Lamba ethnic group from the sparsely populated rural countryside surrounding the Copperbelt, ethnically stereo-typed as lazy and idle (Siegel 1989). The Lamba habit of hanging about the compounds "unproductively" in the early days apparently earned them disdainful descriptions like the following (cited in Rhodesia 1956: 7): "a degraded people on a degraded soil, a race of 'hangers on,' inhabiting the midden of the mines, hawkers of minor produce, vice, and the virtue of their women."

Yet the *lambwaza* of today – hawkers and hangers-on from every ethnic group – would seem to be as "up to date" in their adaptation to contemporary urban con-ditions as anyone. To say this is not to join in the tendency I have criticized elsewhere (Ferguson 1999: 157–8) of unreservedly celebrating the "coping" abilities of the urban poor and the vitality of the so-called informal sector; such a move can too easily end up whitewashing or romanticizing poverty and unemployment. But neither are we justified in assuming that that this often stigmatized group constitutes a failed, marginal class peripheral to the "main line" of a stable working class. For the urban people in this large and diverse category (who appear to have in common only their dependence upon one or another sort of social and economic improvisation) are not simply failures or victims; if anything, they seem to represent an especially viable and durable urban alternative in times like these (cf. MacGaffey 1991; White 1990). Some, at least, seemed to be managing the hard times of the late 1980s more successfully than many who had "real jobs."[9]

In all of this, what emerges is a new respect for what Stephen Jay Gould (1996) would call the "full house" of different urban strategies – that copiously branching "bush" of coexisting variation – and a corresponding revaluation of forms of life that a more linear, progressive narration might consign to the past (see the discussion of Gould's (1996) variation-centered alternative to teleological evolutionary narratives in Ferguson 1999: 42–3). For the "dead ends" of the past keep coming back, just as the "main lines" that are supposed to lead to the future continually seem to disappoint. It is this that gives the Copperbelt's recent history its "recursive" quality (as Moore and Vaughan (1994) have remarked for Zambia's Northern Province), the sense of a continual reiteration of familiar themes, as old and supposedly bygone practices, patterns, and even policies sprout up again when least expected.[10]

A new way of conceptualizing urban life may be emerging in all of this, one that values multiplicity, variation, improvisation, and opportunism and distrusts fixed, unitary modes of practice and linear sequences of phases. For urban Zambians seem to have come, by their own paths, to an understanding at which scholars have recently arrived as well: the realization that global modernity is characterized not by a simple, Eurocentric uniformity but by coexisting and complex sociocultural alternatives (Appadurai 1996), and that the successful negotiation of it may hinge less on mastering a unitary set of "modern" social and cultural forms than on managing to negotiate a dense bush of contemporary variants in the art and struggle of living.

It may also be possible, it has occurred to me, to detect a fundamental mutation in the way that people are coming to talk about historical and economic change in the region. When I have heard Zambians in recent years talk about different parts of Africa, for instance, it seems to me that they no longer speak about this or that place as being ahead or behind, progressing well or too slowly. Instead, people are more likely to speak in terms of nonlinear fluctuations of "up" and "down" (as in "Mozambique is very bad right now, but I hear that Tanzania is coming back up" or "Congo has been down so long, it is bound to come back up soon"), or in terms of particular niches and opportunities that might provide a bit of space here or there. Such usages evoke less the March of Progress than an up-to-date weather report: good times and bad times come and go, the trick is to keep abreast and make the best of it. Postmodernist in a literal sense, this new style of understanding is driven by a pragmatic logic, the need to come to terms with a social world that can no longer be grasped in terms of the old scripts.

Scholars might learn from this example. One might well resist the idea that economic processes are really just like the weather: completely unresponsive to human purposes and beyond the control of human agency. To put matters thus would be to naturalize economic phenomena and to obscure the fact that they are always the products of human activity, always linked to political practices, and always subject to change (Ferguson 1995).[11] But the attempts of ordinary people to map the changes they have been living through in nonlinear, non-teleological ways, and to take seriously the full range of multiplicity and variation in social life, might yet have much to teach us. In political terms, certainly, there would seem to be a compelling need to find new ways of approaching "progressive" politics in an era when the term itself requires to be put in quotation marks. The linear teleologies on which virtually all conventional liberal and leftist political programs have rested simply will not take us very far in dealing with the sorts of challenges raised by the contemporary politics of global inequality, on the Copperbelt or elsewhere.

But to say that received ideas of progress require to be critically interrogated is not to render the pursuit of equality or social improvement antique or laughable. Beyond the celebrations of the postmodern or the end of development lie profoundly challenging issues: how can democratic and egalitarian political movements address the transnational social and economic processes that bypass the control of nation-states as they connect and enrich some regions and social classes, even while they disconnect, impoverish, and abject others (Escobar and Alvarez 1992; Ferguson, forthcoming; Gupta 1998)? How can the responsibility of First-World citizens, organizations, and governments to impoverished and disaster-stricken regions and people be reformulated in a way that avoids the well-known limitations of developmental and humanitarian modalities of power (Malkki 1995)? How can we acknowledge the historical and ethical obligations of connectedness, responsibility, and, indeed, guilt that link western wealth and security with African poverty and insecurity in an era when the modernist grid of universal copper connectivity has begun to disintegrate?

These formidable conceptual and political problems must be faced at the end of this modernist era, as much by those who lament its passing as by those who celebrate it. As the people of the Copperbelt know only too well, the upending of the project of modernity is not a playful intellectual choice but a shattering, compulsory socioeconomic event. While the intellectual consequences are profound for all, such an event affects Copperbelt workers far more directly than it does First-World scholars;[12] and viewed from the vantage point of the Copperbelt, it is about as playful as a train wreck. That the view from the Copperbelt is so different from that available from the academy gives it no automatic privilege; certainly no magic solutions to the daunting questions and problems listed here emerge from the experience of the men and women who saw the "Industrial Revolution" come and go within the span of a single lifetime. But at a time when First-World academics are wont to speak perhaps a little too confidently of globalization or postmodernity, and a little too happily about "the demise of metanarratives" or "the end of development," there may be something to be gained from contemplating a place where the globalization of the economy has been experienced as disconnection and abjection, and where the much-celebrated end of the universalizing project of modernity has meant an end to the prospect of African equality, and the re-establishment of a global color bar blocking access from the "first-class" world.

A return to modernist teleology, a new grand narrative that would trace the hopeful signs of an Africa once more "emerging" out of the gloomy ashes of Africa's "development" disaster is neither plausible nor desirable. The modernization narrative was always a myth, an illusion, often even a lie. We should all learn to do without it. But if the academic rejection of modernization and development is not simply to reproduce at another level the global disconnects of capital, migration, and information flows, we must replace it with other ways of conceiving the relations of historical connectedness and ethical and political responsibility that link Africa and the rest of the world. If the people who have, in good faith, lived out the agonizing, failed plotline of development and modernization are not to be simply disconnected and abjected from the new world order, it will be necessary to find new ways of thinking about both progress and responsibility in the aftermath of modernism.

NOTES

This paper grew out of a talk that presented some of the major conclusions of a previously published book, *Expectations of Modernity: Myths and Meanings of Urban Life on the Zambian Copperbelt* (University of California Press, 1999). I hope that the reader will forgive the occasionally oral style, and the fact that the argument refers to ethnographic material presented in the body of the monograph and not in the paper itself.

1. Hannerz (1996) has made a similar suggestion regarding the pursuit of international popular culture by black artists and intellectuals in the Sophiatown district of Johannesburg in the 1950s.
2. After a 1920 meeting, H. G. Wells reported that "Lenin, who like a good orthodox Marxist denounces all 'Utopias', has succumbed at last to a Utopia, the Utopia of the electricians" (Coopersmith 1992: 154).
3. I do not suggest that the reduction in the amount of copper used in communication technology is the major factor here; it is clearly but one among a number of factors leading to the decline of the copper industry in Zambia. I mention the association only as a way of pointing out some of the ironies associated with the apparently universal process of globalization.
4. The figure (obviously to be taken with a grain of salt, given the absence of direct evidence) appeared in *Harper's* (1997).
5. In addition to the authors discussed here, see Escobar's important study (1995), which also heralds a "post-development era," as well as the recent *The Post-Development Reader* (Rahnema 1997); see also Marglin and Marglin 1990 and Nandy 1988.
6. For the "original affluent society" essay, see Sahlins 1972. For a telling critique, see Wilmsen 1989.
7. Through such ironic reinscriptions of modernist teleology, the contemporary necessity of having to come to terms with the breakdown of modernism (i.e., post-*modernism* (an aftermath of modernism)) is routinely transmuted into a new evolutionary epoch (post-modernity, the next rung on the ladder) with its own "up-to-date" worldview ("*Postmodernism*," a suitable "latest thing" for the final chapter of the social theory textbook), and, indeed, its own triumphalist metanarrative of emergence.
8. Debra Spitulnik has suggested (personal communication) that the word *lambwaza* probably derives from the stem *Lamba*, in combination with the French *ois*, which is both a normal French word ending (as in *chinois*, *bourgeois*, etc.) and a French morpheme connoting idleness and laziness (as in *oiseux* (idle, pointless, useless) and *oisif* (idle, unemployed)). If this is correct, *lambwaza* would have an original meaning linked both to a specific ethnic group (the Lamba) and to a trait stereotypically associated with that group ("laziness"). In my fieldwork, however, I did not note any special relation between the Lambas and the term *lambwaza*, which referred to any unemployed youth "hanging around" the city.
9. I cannot say more about this interesting group, as I did not study them in any systematic way (perhaps because I, too, carried in my head assumptions about main lines and incidental peripheries).
10. Compare the deliberately "recursive" exposition, particularly in dealing with the legacies of the RLI, in Ferguson 1999.
11. Such a naturalization of the logic of a "complex system" occurs in the uses of "complexity theory" by economists, as shown in Maurer's critical review (1995).

12. I speak of First-World scholars here, because Zambian scholars, unfortunately, have experienced the economic crisis I have described here only too directly. One of the most vivid illustrations (at least for an academic) of the abjection and disconnection that I have tried to describe can be seen by visiting the University of Zambia library. Once a fine university library that could adequately support serious research in a range of fields, it resembled (at least when I last saw it) a kind of sad museum, with virtually no recent books or current periodical subscriptions at all. Salaries for university lecturers in Zambia, meanwhile, had by 1989 dropped so low that only by taking second and third jobs, and/or resorting to subsistence farming, were lecturers able to sustain themselves.

REFERENCES

Appadurai, Arjun 1996 *Modernity at Large: Cultural Dimensions of Globalization*. Minneapolis: University of Minnesota Press.

Bhabha, Homi K. 1997 Of Mimicry and Man: The Ambivalence of Colonial Discourse. In *Tensions of Empire: Colonial Cultures in a Bourgeois World*. Frederick Cooper and Ann Laura Stoler, eds. Berkeley: University of California Press.

Borneman, John 1996 Until Death Do Us Part: Marriage/Death in Anthropological Discourse. *American Ethnologist* 23(2): 215–35.

Bose, Sugata 1997 Instruments and Idioms of Colonial and National Development: India's Historical Experience in Comparative Perspective. In *International Development and the Social Sciences: Essays on the History and Politics of Knowledge*. Frederick Cooper and Randall Packard, eds. Berkeley: University of California Press.

Cooper, Frederick 1997 Modernizing Bureaucrats, Backward Africans, and the Development Concept. In *International Development and the Social Sciences: Essays on the History and Politics of Knowledge*. Frederick Cooper and Randall Packard, eds. Berkeley: University of California Press.

Cooper, Frederick, and Randall Packard 1997 Introduction. In *International Development and the Social Sciences: Essays on the History and Politics of Knowledge*. Frederick Cooper and Randall Packard, eds. Berkeley: University of California Press.

Coopersmith, Jonathan 1992 *The Electrification of Russia, 1880–1926*. Ithaca, NY: Cornell University Press.

Economist, The 1993 Telecommunications Survey. *The Economist* 329 (7834): 68ff. (supplement).

Escobar, Arturo 1995 *Encountering Development: The Making and Unmaking of the Third World*. Princeton, NJ: Princeton University Press.

Escobar, Arturo, and Sonia Alvarez, eds. 1992 *The Making of Social Movements in Latin America: Identity, Strategy, and Democracy*. Boulder, CO: Westview Press.

Esteva, Gustavo 1992 Development. In *The Development Dictionary: A Guide to Knowledge as Power*. W. Sachs, ed. London: Zed Books.

Ferguson, James 1994 *The Anti-politics Machine: "Development," Depoliticization, and Bureaucratic Power in Lesotho*. Minneapolis: University of Minnesota Press.

——— 1995 From African Socialism to Scientific Capitalism: Reflections on the Legitimation Crisis in IMF-ruled Africa. In *Debating Development Discourse: Institutional and Popular Perspectives*. D. B. Moore and G. J. Schmitz, eds. New York: St. Martin's Press.

Ferguson, James 1997 The Country and the City on the Copperbelt. In *Culture, Power, Place: Explorations in Critical Anthropology*. Akhil Gupta and James Ferguson, eds. Durham, NC: Duke University Press.

———— 1999 *Expectations of Modernity: Myths and Meanings of Urban Life on the Zambian Copperbelt*. Berkeley: University of California Press.

Forthcoming. Transnational Topographies of Power: Beyond "the State" and "Civil Society" in the Study of African Politics.

Gould, Stephen Jay 1996 *Full House: The Spread of Excellence from Plato to Darwin*. New York: Harmony Books.

Gupta, Akhil 1997 Agrarian Populism in the Development of a Modern Nation (India). In *International Development and the Social Sciences: Essays on the History and Politics of Knowledge*. Frederick Cooper and Randall Packard, eds. Berkeley: University of California Press.

———— 1998 *Postcolonial Developments: Agriculture in the Making of Modern India*. Durham, NC: Duke University Press.

Hannerz, Ulf 1996 *Transnational Connections: Culture, People, Places*. New York: Routledge.

Harper's 1997 Harper's Index. *Harper's* 294 (1764): 15.

Kristeva, Julia 1982 *Powers of Horror: An Essay on Abjection*. New York: Columbia University Press.

MacGaffey, Janet 1991 *The Real Economy of Zaire: The Contribution of Smuggling and Other Unofficial Activities to National Wealth*. Philadelphia: University of Pennsylvania Press.

Malkki, Liisa H. 1995 Speechless Emissaries: Refugees, Humanitarianism, and Dehistoricization. *Cultural Anthropology* 11(3): 377–404.

Marglin, Frederique Apffel, and Stephen Marglin, eds. 1990 *Dominating Knowledge: Development, Culture, and Resistance*. New York: Oxford University Press.

Maurer, Bill 1995 Complex Subjects: Offshore Finance, Complexity Theory, and the Dispersion of the Modern. *Socialist Review* 25(3–4): 113–45.

Mikesell, Raymond F. 1988 *The Global Copper Industry: Problems and Prospects*. London: Croom Helm.

Moore, Henrietta L., and Megan Vaughan 1994 *Cutting Down Trees: Gender, Nutrition, and Agricultural Change in the Northern Province of Zambia, 1890–1990*. London: Heinemann.

Nandy, Ashis, ed. 1988 *Science, Hegemony, and Violence: A Requiem for Modernity*. Tokyo: United Nations University.

Rahnema, Majid, with Victoria Bawtree, eds. 1997 *The Post-Development Reader*. London: Zed Books.

Rhodesia, Government of Northern 1956 *Report of a Soil and Land-Use Survey: Copperbelt, Northern Rhodesia*. Lusaka: Department of Agriculture.

Sachs, Wolfgang, ed. 1992 *The Development Dictionary: A Guide to Knowledge as Power*. London: Zed Books.

Sahlins, Marshall 1972 *Stone Age Economics*. Chicago: Aldine Publishing Co.

Siegel, Brian V. 1989 The "Wild" and "Lazy" Lamba: Ethnic Stereotypes on the Central African Copperbelt. In *The Creation of Tribalism*. Leroy Vail, ed. Berkeley: University of California Press.

Smith, Neil 1997 The Satanic Geographies of Globalization: Uneven Development in the 1990s. *Public Culture* 10(1): 169–89.

Watts, Michael 1995 "A New Deal in Emotions": Theory and Practice and the Crisis of
    Development. In *Power of Development*. Jonathan Crush, ed. New York: Routledge.
White, Luise 1990 *The Comforts of Home: Prostitution in Colonial Nairobi*. Chicago:
    University of Chicago Press.
Wilmsen, Edwin N. 1989 *Land Filled with Flies: A Political Economy of the Kalahari*. Chicago:
    University of Chicago Press.
Wilson, Godfrey 1941 *An Essay on the Economics of Detribalization in Northern Rhodesia
    (part 1)*. Rhodes–Livingstone Paper no. 5. Livingstone, Northern Rhodesia: Rhodes–
    Livingstone Institute.
———— 1942 *An Essay on the Economics of Detribalization in Northern Rhodesia (part 2)*.
    Rhodes–Livingstone Paper no. 6. Livingstone, Northern Rhodesia: Rhodes–Livingstone
    Institute.

CHAPTER SEVENTEEN

Despair: The Decline of the Kanpur Textile Mills

Chitra Joshi

Since the late 1980s, the situation in Kanpur is much changed, with the cotton textile being an industry in a crisis. Most Kanpur mills have been closed, workers have been retrenched in large numbers. Some continue to be on the pay-rolls but there is no work. Salaries have been levelled to a flat minimum, pay is cut for all holidays. Workers have been forced to turn to other work: rickshaw-pulling, paan, vegetable and fruit vending, begging. The line of difference between the formal and informal sector, always thin and questionable, seems to have disappeared altogether. The decline of the factory industry has been accompanied by a mushrooming of cottage industries: the myth of a linear transition from the cottage/domestic sector to factory production, from proto-industrialisation to industrialisation, seems to have been reversed. In the pre-independence period a phase of stagnation was followed by a phase of growth and boom. But now there seems no hope of recovery. Economic experts have announced the end of cotton textile factory production in Kanpur, and the death of its working class.

After the growth of the 1950s, cotton textile production in India steadily declined. From 4.34 billion metres in 1972 it dropped to 3.4 billion metres in 1983, declining at an annual rate of around 1.5 per cent. The number of working looms reduced from 144,000 in 1971 to 133,000 in 1987. Since the 1960s the demand for coarse varieties of cloth has dipped. Per capita consumption of coarse varieties, which had gone up in the 1950s, fell after the 1960s due to increased durability of synthetic blends and decline of real income in rural areas.[1] Per capita consumption of cloth showed a continuous decline between 1970 and the 1990s from 13.5 metres in 1969–71 to nine metres in 1989–91. The market that cotton textiles lost, synthetics gained. Per capita purchase of synthetic textiles and blended fabrics increased at the rate of about 100 per cent per year in the period between 1973 and 1989.

Since the 1990s, changes in state policies have led to a rapid restructuring of the textile industry and a growth of the export market in cotton textiles. However, a major part of this demand is supplied by the informal sector, primarily by power-looms. The relative share of mills in cotton textile production declined rapidly since the mid-1980s, from 18 per cent in 1985–6 to 10 per cent by 1990–1 and 6 per cent by 1995–6, while that of powerlooms increased from 63 to 78 per cent over the same period. The figures for exports show similar trends. The share of mills in cotton tex-tile exports declined from 59 per cent in 1985–6 to 38 per cent by 1990–1, coming down to 23 per cent by 1995–6, while that of powerlooms went up from 34 per cent to 76 per cent in the same period.[2] The revival, limited to the powerloom sector, has meant no lease of life for textile mills.

While markets shrank, costs increased. The fixed costs of the National Textile Corporation (NTC) mills are astoundingly high and rapidly increasing. In 1993–4, fixed costs as a percentage of sales had mounted to 80 per cent in the NTC mills compared to a mere 21 per cent in other mills (in 1888–9 it was 56 per cent). All NTC mills, except the ones in Pondicherry and Tamil Nadu, are making losses. Their sales are insufficient to cover the variable costs and wage bills. In most NTC mills, losses are over four times their net worth. The accumulated losses of the British India Corporation (BIC) amount to 3.3 times its net worth, while Kanpur Textiles losses were twenty-five times its net worth.[3]

Composite mills which produced both yarn and cloth were the worst affected. The early phase of Kanpur industrialisation was based on the expansion of the com-posite mill sector. Not only were they cost efficient, but managerial control over the entire process of production of cloth was easier. Now powerlooms in India appear more cost efficient in terms of fixed costs, raw material use, and energy consumption. Economists consider most of the old composite mill units bankrupt and obsolete.

In this context of declining profits, private industrialists in Kanpur found it more profitable to invest in new expanding industries in centres outside Kanpur, where wage costs were lower and where such a long tradition of trade unionism was absent. . . . Disinvestmest in textile mills in Kanpur was accompanied by cost-cutting strategies directed primarily at workers. Wages were held back for months, provident fund, in-surance and other benefits were cut, workers were laid off and retrenched. Workers' anger against these policies led to a series of strikes in the 1970s.[4] Managements were inflexible, preferring their units to be declared 'sick' and taken over by the state.

. . .

How do workers confront this crisis? What are the strategies with which they negotiate their situation?

For working class families living in Kanpur for several decades, the closure of tex-tile mills means more than just a problem of survival. Their lives are so intertwined with work in the mills that a life without the mills seems unthinkable. Mill closure can mean death: a belief which underlines Niamat Rasul's fears: '*Agar mill band ho jai to hamari maut hai.*' (If the mills shut down, we will die). Niamat Rasul worked as a weaver in Elgin Mills 2 . . . like his father. Niamat's father came to Kanpur from a village in Barabanki district and they still have relatives there, but like many second-generation workers he identifies completely with the city and cannot conceive of an alternative.

Ties with their native villages are important for most rural migrants, but the possibilities of work and life in the village are not always open to those who move to the city with their families. Besides, it is not easy for rural migrants to reintegrate themselves with village life once they have lived in the city for several decades. Most rural migrants come from families with small holdings, income from which has to be supplemented with wage labour. Unemployed workers past their fifties saw themselves as too old for arduous toil in the fields. The loss of jobs was seen as a loss also for descendants. In working class families, skills in factory work were handed down through the generations. A mill job was almost like an inheritance which provided a sense of security. It was a way of ensuring a reproduction of skills, the basis of worker identity and pride.

. . .

The absence of work in the present imbues the past with a different significance. The drudgery and travails of work in the past have no space in these narratives. Mill work is glorified. The pain of work is represented in retrospect as pain which was fulfilling. Work on the machines wore them out, yet there was a bonding with the machine and a pride in their work. Niamat asserted that the mill authorities claimed that the workers were inefficient and lazy. This was not true. Workers in his mill produced around 120,000 metres of cloth. Another worker, Pramod Awasthi, boasted that the amount of cloth he had produced during his years of service could take a person holding one end of it to Delhi more than 2000 times. Muhammad Said was proud that the looms never stopped running in his mill: 'If we struck work for even a day the entire BIC management would try to negotiate.'

There is in these narratives a distancing from the oppressiveness of work discipline in the past. The long hours, the absence of work breaks, especially in the war years, are remembered now with a sense of male pride and achievement. Strict discipline is presented as an index of efficiency. Ramcharan, who started work in Muir Mills in 1946, talked of the times he worked four machines often on a meal of gur and chana alone: 'We have seen those days, those days when we were not allowed to go to the lavatory during work. To go to the lavatory was impossible for us.' He contrasts it with the present when there are no controls. Workers take frequent breaks for five–ten minutes, sometimes they stay away for half an hour at a stretch. This was read not as evidence of greater worker freedom, but of disinterested management.

Workers entering their fifties feel a sense of weariness about looking for alternative possibilities of work. Their bodies feel worn with age, with the daily wear and tear on the machines. In a context of worklessness, work was seen as physically empowering; non-work created a sense of physical disability. Images of decay and ageing are used alternately for the machine and the body of the worker. 'We are worn out like the machines. When I joined the mill there were no lines, no signs of age on my face, Today I am grey and old.' Besides, work elsewhere would not have the same meaning. Like the machines and the people who worked on them, the structure of the mills conveys a picture of dilapidation. The sprawling Lancashire-style mills in Kanpur are crumbling structures in a state of disrepair, with fallen roofs and broken walls.

The daily routine for most workers now consists in reporting at the mill gate for their attendance. Although most mills have been closed for eight-to ten years, workers crowd around mill gates at shift times, thrice a day in some mills like Kanpur Textiles, twice in others. Some move off to their gambling addas near the gate, others gather around union leaders for news, rumours, plans. The daily ritual is also a collective affirmation of anxieties, fears, hopes, and uncertainties. Although workers on the rolls in a state-controlled mill are paid wages, there is no certainty when they will be paid or how long this will continue.[5] The threat of total closure hangs like a noose. Dates are changed and extended. Even those hoping that the mills will reopen once again feel tormented by the uncertainty.

There was always a hope that millowners would pay arrears before festival time: 'We had pegged our hopes to Diwali. We got nothing. We waited for Eid there was nothing. We hoped Holi would bring something.' Descriptions of the city as *khandhar*, as an *ujra hua shahar* (a dilapidated, ruined town), carry in their narratives images of desolation and devastation. The magnitude of loss in their accounts is obviously greater than can be expressed in official estimates. Naresh Chauhan recounted the times when the mills employed around 70,000 workers. In addition, around 300,000 were employed in industries sustained by textiles. Official estimates show that textile mills in Kanpur never employed more than 50,000 workers, even at the best of times. This overestimation of numbers in worker accounts emphasises the meaning the city had in their lives. It was as if Kanpur was *of* the workers: workers constituted the city. And now the vanishing workforce signifies the destruction of the city, its death. The changed context of the present is apparent in the street life of areas like Gwaltoli, where a large number of mills are located. Thousands of workers had once walked in and out at shift time. Even the tea stalls and tobacco shops are connected with the running of the mills. Closure of mills means deserted streets.

Worker narratives move between articulations of despair and resignation to an assertion of their power. This sense of power expresses itself at times through threats of retribution, street violence, murder, looting and dacoity: 'If this mill is shut the revolt will spread to the streets, killings will begin, isn't that so? If we die of hunger we will throttle you and kill you. No car will be allowed to move, no bus, there will be looting and violence. There are no two views on this. When I am hungry I will snatch your spectacles from your eyes.' Yet there is an ambivalence in this voice of retribution. It slides easily into a despairing, helpless voice: I am forty years old . . . I am a substitute[a] . . . and I am old today. Where can I go? There is no respite. I cannot live or die. It is better to set myself on fire and die.

For women workers the despair runs deeper. Most women workers were employed on a contract basis and not treated as regular mill employees. Even the older workers, who were regular employees earlier, were turned into contract workers in the 1970s. Munni Devi, who was a regular employee at the Swadeshi Cotton Mills, remembers how the main gate through which all workers entered was suddenly closed to women workers. After a long dharna [picket]; women were allowed entry from a separate gate as thekedar's (contractor's) employees, not company employees. Most likely, this was before a major struggle in the Swadeshi Mills in 1978, when several workers were killed in the police firing, when the golikand (firing) happened and women were ordered out: 'We had access to only one gate, we could not use any other gate. We were turned out.'

For many workers today, stories about struggles in the past seem unreal and distant. In their narratives there is a constant return to the present, as though remembering the past might take them away from more pressing, immediate concerns. Younger-generation workers today have only heard stories about the great strikes of the 1930s or 1950s, not personally experienced them. This was equally true of many workers I met in the early 1980s. The most recent experience of collective struggle was the rail blockade of 1989, when workers stopped the movement of trains to and from Kanpur for over four days in protest against the proposed rationalisation and workload scheme. But the proximity in time of this event was not evident from their recollections: they were reluctant to recount details. What makes the remembering and retelling of these stories difficult in the 1990s and now is a sense of futility in relation to industrial struggles. Even those who personally participated in the strikes of the past gave a sketchy outline of them. For Ramcharan, who started work in Muir Mills in the 1940s, queries about the major eighty-day strike against rationalisation of work in 1955 initially evoked no response. His memory cued in only after a reference to tikadde vali hartal (strike for a three-loom system). For workers like him, moored within an oral tradition, such symbols and images – and not chronology – provide markers around which their past is organised. Ramcharan's focus was not so much on details of the strike, the militancy of the strikers, or the scale and spread of a strike which lasted eighty days. He talked only of his experience of the work and rigours of the four-loom system, opposition to which was one of the major demands of the strikers. Others like Niamat Rasul, who had heard about the 1955 strikes from his father, dwell on moments of repression. In his recounting, stories about the Kanpur Cotton Mill strikes of 1924 are woven in those of 1955: 'One day the English ordered a mounted police attack on workers. Many workers were thrown into boilers. My father told me that four workers were thrown into boilers. Two moments of state repression are here fused into one, and he rereads the events as moments of repression, not as heroic moments of worker solidarity. He fuses fantastical stories of repression in 1924 with memories of surveillance in working class neighbourhoods by mounted police in 1955.

Feelings of anger and retribution are tied up with workers' understanding of the crisis in the mill industry. The crisis appears as unreal in their narratives: a fabrication of corrupt managers. They repeatedly draw contrasts between present decline and past prosperity. Prosperity is attributed to efficient management, present decline to

managerial inefficiency. A series of contrasts between then and now are drawn: managerial efficiency versus inefficiency; incompetence versus competence; industrial discipline versus laxity; morality versus immorality. These contrasts are explained by two
other contrasts: private management and government control; European managers
and indigenous managers. At times the latter two oppositions fuse; private management appears as a distant past, it becomes a past when managers were European, the
decline begins with indigenous management. Managers in the past were technical
people, they knew their job; today, civil service officials on managerial chairs have no
clue about their work: 'Mill officials today do not know how to handle a wrench. They
have no knowledge about their job. They have to ask the mistri how a machine should
be fixed only then are they able to write the job on paper. Are these supervisors?'

When the mills were under private control, managers were upright and honest;
mill profits were *their* profits – a product of *their* capital, *their* efforts. With state
control, managers no longer identify with the mill. The company's loss is no longer
seen as their own loss. The capital belonging to the state exists to be embezzled and
appropriated. Now mill officials take fat commissions on orders to raw material suppliers, they trade in coal supplies coming in for use in the mills, they adulterate raw
material supplies with waste products, they fill up supervisory posts with incompetent relatives. In the past, managers were conscientious and factory discipline was
closely supervised: bobbins were never empty, looms never stopped.

Within the present scenario, different strategies have been put forward by economic experts, the state, and workers. The state has to negotiate between market
pressures from the new global order to close sick mills, and demands from labour representatives to keep the industry going. In the context of these pressures, decisions
are deferred and dates for final settlement postponed. The merger of unviable units
into healthy units, the modernisation of some mills, a freeze on retrenchment – these
restructuring plans were to be financed through the sale of surplus land in the mills.
But for pro-liberalisation economic experts, who now dominate, state-controlled textile mills are sick and beyond redemption. Plans to revive mills with a long history of
'low productivity', 'disinterested labour' and 'poor managerial supervision' are 'fairy
tale schemes'. The merger of two sick units, they point out, cannot produce a healthy
unit; and prohibitive costs make restructuring plans unviable.

For trade union activists the closure of mills spells their own demise. Workers
and trade union activists support alternative schemes for revival. Those working
with the BIC group of mills (Elgin 1, Elgin 2, Kanpur Textiles) felt that workers from
the three units could all be employed in one unit.[6] Voluntary retirement schemes
(VRS) are not seen as a real solution. Most trade union activists are emphatic in their
opposition to the VRS. Among ordinary workers, the opposition to VRS schemes is
not always unequivocal. Some seemed to feel that they could escape the uncertainties
of the present by opting for the VRS; others felt the compensation amount should be
increased. Many workers still on the rolls were wary of such schemes. Used to small
earnings, they fear lump-sum payments: such money is bound to disappear, leaving

them destitute. They recounted stories about workers who turned homeless after opting for the VRS: the money was grabbed by scheming relatives and wayward, unemployed sons.

So workers prefer the fiction of factory work. They go to the factory every day to report their attendance and collect their pay even when it comes after months of wait. Despite the irregularity of wage payments, being on the factory rolls appears to be important for the male sense of self. To accept the VRS was to be formally unemployed, a status male workers found difficult to accept. To be classed as a *berozgar* [unemployed] was particularly humiliating for males. In such a situation, regular subsistence for the family comes from women's waged work at home. In Muslim neighbourhoods, women are employed in sewing burqas. Many women, in both Muslim and Hindu neighbourhoods, work as out-workers with leather companies and make uppers for leather sandals.

Many labourers have now shifted from work in the mills to work in home-based industry. At one level, a shift from the factory to the home homogenises labour, erasing gender distinctions based on work at home and work outside: factory work, the source of male pride, is denied to working class men. Yet gender distinctions within the new work milieu continue. For instance, in hosiery units which have mushroomed in Kanpur mohallas [neighbourhoods], women do not work on the sewing machines. Men cut and sew vests and hosiery goods; women clean out the thread from the finished product, fix labels and do the ironing. Women's earnings are never more than a couple of rupees per day. Men in hosiery production earn up to Rs 100 per day. Other jobs like bidi making and wrapping toffees, are usually done at home by lower-caste women.

By the 1980s the characteristics of the workforce began to change radically. Up to the 1950s and 1960s, peasants moved from fields to factories; now there is a reverse movement – back to the villages for those who have land. If earlier the unemployed in the city – artisans and migrant peasants – fed the factory labour force, or moved between the 'informal' and 'formal' sector in a circular movement, now factories show no promise of reabsorbing labour. The factory, in fact, steadily feeds the labour market, dissolving boundaries between factory workers and others. Many ply rickshaws, adding to the scores of rickshaw-pullers in the city. The teleological notion that industrialisation is marked by a shift from the domestic to the factory sector has now been widely questioned: domestic industries, we know, continued to flourish through the period of industrialisation in the West.[7] What we see in Kanpur today is not a coexistence of different forms of production, but rather a reverse movement from factory to domestic industries.

At the turn of the twentieth century, when factory employment has shrunk and male workers are unemployed, the spaces through which working class men in the city derived their identity are under threat. If the factory was the sphere within which notions of masculinity were constructed, their dislocation in the present has unsettled these identities. Workless men at home appear an intrusion into spaces occupied earlier by women and children during a large part of the day. In women's stories, men idling at home all day disturb notions of time and domestic order. Even in domesticity, women had a different regime of time. For men, being berozgar means a double loss – a collapse of their worlds outside, and a diminished patriarchal presence in the household. For women, in contrast, the domesticisation of waged work in a context when men are unemployed is important in creating a sense of relative empowerment.

In a scenario where traditional large-scale industries are in retreat and crisis, the nature of the labour force is being rapidly transformed. If the phase of industrial expansion was accompanied by a masculinisation of the labour force, today a feminisation is possibly taking place at two levels. First, there is a shift from male to female labour with the displacement of men from factory work, and the employment of women in domestic industries. This female labour, however, remains invisible from public view. Not only is it engaged in invisible forms in home-based industries, it is unrecorded in official statistics. Second, there is a change in the social psychology of the workers – as we noted, a sense of loss of masculinity. Loss of work today implies more than economic hardship. It means also an emasculation of their selves and a destabilisation of their authority within the household.

Perhaps there is something to be said for this partial reversal of traditional gender roles. But not *that* much, in the end: at bottom, this is not the death of masculinity, which, as has often been shown, resurrects itself in new forms; it is, ultimately, the death of a world, a whole way of life, of a cultural form which was once seen as the backbone of urban, industrial India.

. . .

EDITOR'S NOTE

(a)   Many Indian factories maintain a regular pool of 'substitute' labour who remain on hand to fill in for regular workers who are absent.

NOTES

1.   C.P. Chandrashekar, 'Growth and Technical Change in Indian Cotton-Mill Industry', *EPW* [Economic and Political Weekly], 19:4 (1984), PE 22–PE 39.
2.   Tirthankar Roy, 'Economic Reforms and Textile Industry in India', *EPW*, 33:32 (1998).
3.   Omkar Goswami, 'State owned Enterprises in India', mimeo for OECD Paris. See also Goswami, 'Sickness and Growth of India's Textile Industry: Analysis and Policy Options', *EPW*, 25:44 and 25:45.
4.   See 'Report of the Citizen's Committee for Inquiry into the Kanpur Massacre', 23.2.1978. See leaflet issued by workers of JK Manufacturers Ltd. '*Kailash Mil Mein Sangarsh ka Elan: Sabhi Mazdur Bhaiyon ke Nam Ek Apil*' (Kanpur n.d.).
5.   On an average, most workers receive around Rs 2000 a month, paid at irregular intervals, usually once in three months.

6. The total strength of workers in all three units is now only 4000. Earlier each unit employed betwen 4000 and 5000 workers.
7. See, for instance, Ronald Aminzade, 'Reinterpreting Capitalist Industrialisation: A Study of Nineteenth-Century France', in Kaplan and Koepp, eds, *Work in France*, pp. 393–470; Maxine Berg, *The Age of Manufactures, 1700–1820* (London 1985); Pat Hudson, *Regions and Industries* (Cambridge 1981).

CHAPTER EIGHTEEN

The Poetics of Productivity

Lisa Rofel

Workers in post-Mao China live as what one might call an "absent presence." This is surprising, perhaps, since Maoist socialism rhetorically cast workers, along with peasants, as the central heroes of the nation. Maoism established their revolutionary consciousness as that which would bring China to a socialist modernity beyond western capitalism, and the current regime, though it has thoroughly repudiated the Maoist period, continues to identify itself as socialist. Yet in the discussions of how China can reach modernity encouraged by national political culture in the 1980s and 1990s, the most striking feature is how rarely workers figure at all. They are never portrayed as the kind of people deemed to be the appropriate subjects of a post-Mao – and for many, a postsocialist – modernity, who instead are those who know how to invigorate the economy and social life without the support of the state.

On the contrary, workers appear in official and elite commentary on the obstacles that might hinder China from ever reaching modernity. Those desiring broad social transformations represent workers as the quintessential embodiment of a Maoist past, marking a "historical lack" that China must overcome. They are depicted as both cause and consequence of the ills said to have befallen China as a result of the Cultural Revolution. Workers thus appear both outside of and as a hindrance to a reconstituted imaginary of modernity. Consequently, the state has subjected them to a novel disciplinary regime, whose epistemic violence is wedded to the coercions of rational initiatives for development. This postsocialist decentering of workers turns on China's own decentered relationship to those countries, especially the United States and Japan, that continue to produce modernity as a realm of unequal power. At the local level, these complex dynamics play themselves out in reconfiguring Hangzhou's world of silk production.

How have women workers negotiated this process of marginalization? How have they endured such a profound transformation in public representations of their place in a story of national progress? On the whole, it seems fair to say that workers reject the image of themselves as a "dilemma," accompanied as it is by negative valuations of their moral being and essential predilections. Yet the emergence of new gender meanings and relations have further complicated workers' engagement with this pervasive devaluation of themselves. The Maoist woman who heroically overcame her gender quickly became a parodic figure. She was roundly derided in comedy routines, soap operas, newspaper editorials, and even in some post-Mao feminist writings. It became nearly impossible to believe that anyone had ever taken her seriously. How could a modern nation support such nonsense, the jokes implied.

The ground of masculinity has also shifted. Official and popular discourses alike represent the gendered activity that will bring modernity not, as with Maoism, as a transgression of feminine identity in the state sector via labor, but rather as an assertion of a natural masculinity in the market via risk-taking exploits. As Lyn Jeffery (1995) has argued, the post-Mao imaginary of modernity feminizes the state sector as the realm of passive inactivity and loss, while the market economy signifies masculine prowess. Feminized subalterns – men and women who continue to work in the state sector – are marginalized as those who are dragging into the present the "socialist tradition" that hinders modernity.

This chapter traces how the post-Mao pursuit of modernity, known as "economic reform," constructs mobile discourses of dominance in which national priorities for development normalize workers even as they cast workers to the side of history. My descriptions rest on the assumption that the identity of subaltern selves is not intrinsic in the relations of production. Rather than accepting as transparent the identities of workers, one must ask how they are culturally produced, embraced, performed, challenged, and denied. As I argue throughout the book, changing parameters of meaning and power, in which gender, class, and the state intersect, produce a historically variable range of subaltern and other identities.

The first section of this chapter examines discourse on the recent socialist past and how it represents workers as embodying that past. The second section addresses new regimes of productivity that operate through the cool violence of statistics, turning on doubled practices of individuation and differentiation.

. . .

"EATING OUT OF ONE BIG POT"

When I arrived in China at the end of 1984, "economic reform" had just begun to seep cautiously and deliberately into the cities. One can easily describe the prosaic aims of this policy: to thoroughly readjust the role of the state in economic development. Reform has led to the introduction of a market economy, the appearance of privately owned companies, a reduction in the scope of mandatory state planning, the devolution of centralized planning to the local levels, the restriction of party cadres' interventions in the economic plans of their local work units, increased autonomy for technical managers of state-run enterprises, the establishment of "special economic zones" to attract foreign investment, and the introduction of new wage systems to increase productivity. Such radical change has brought China fully onto the playing field of transnational capitalism. It also has reinvigorated the deferred desires for modernity.

Yet economic reform is not a simple matter of economic policy. Nor does a view of political economy in which "materiality" and "culture" are structurally separable though linked sufficiently capture the process. As a means of radical disengagement from Maoist socialism, economic reform is also and most significantly a space of imagination. Dreams pile up, one upon another, in this space. The state and its hierarchically positioned citizens conjure up a future that can rid China of the haunting excesses of Maoism. Visions thrive of a wealthy and powerful nation that will finally disprove the predictions of colonial history. The party-state fantasizes about how it can re-create its moral authority. Factory managers creatively maneuver in the newly opened gaps of state power, finding, ways to bring their factories to life and make profits that are not exactly against state policies and not exactly within state policies, because their methods are dreamed up in the process of trying them out. At any moment, these activities are equally likely to land them in jail or make them new model citizens. And finally, the populace dreams of a life beyond any political culture – a fantasy, one might add, often nourished by the state. These imaginings reside in edicts from the state; projects of local bureaus of labor, textile, and foreign trade; meetings between party cadres and factory managers; new factory rules and regulations concerning worker discipline; television soap operas, erudite novels, and karaoke bars; endless newscasts of production statistics; social science surveys of "public opinion"; frenzied consumption; and quiet conversations between friends.

But these imaginings are not unified. For economic reform has given rein to the kinds of economic inequities and class stratification whose eradication once formed the basis of the moral authority of the Chinese Communist Party (CCP). At the same time, the post-Mao regime has officially abolished the class-status system under which party cadres, in dialogue with local communities, assigned each person a class label based on a combination of individual or family level of economic exploitation, status, and potential for revolutionary consciousness (Chan, Madsen, and Unger 1992; Hinton 1966). Good class labels included poor and middle peasant, proletariat, cadre, revolutionary martyr, and revolutionary intellectual (assigned to those who had joined Mao before the revolution). Bad class labels included landlord, rich peasant, bureaucratic capitalist, counterrevolutionary, rightist, and bad element. Class labels that wavered between good and bad included petty bourgeoisie and national capitalist (who were considered patriotic because they did not flee after the revolution). The purpose of the labels was manifold: to indicate how to redistribute wealth, to divide those who had revolutionary virtue from those who did not, to clarify the lines of class struggle, and to instill a "consciousness of class" so that individuals would re-orient their social identities and make revolution against those with whom they had formerly sought identification. The party cadres who instituted this system believed in language's creative role. To classify meant to create possibilities for action.

Both those in the party and those nearby used class labels as an index of each person's moral worth. Abstract classifications became lived representations as each person's entire social reality was defined in terms of her or his class label. Access to material wealth and power were inextricable from adjudications of socialist morality (Billeter 1985; Kraus 1981; J. Watson 1984).

Thought to be temporary when they were first assigned just after the socialist revolution, class labels became hereditary statuses through the paternal line. The creative moments of classification and its possibilities to incite transformations here gave place to naturalizing reification. Women and children were assigned the class label of their husband's family. As a result, marriage practices came to involve matching one's children with a partner who had a good class label. New forms of hierarchy arose, as those with "good" class labels became the arbiters of state power and cadres became a class status unto themselves (Billeter 1985; G. White 1976).

This classificatory system was always a process in which people interpreted "class" in specific local circumstances. Individuals' "material conditions" did not always fit objective measurement; other circumstances of local importance came into play, and the "subjective" matter of "revolutionary consciousness" created instabilities in indexing political virtue (Chan, Madsen, and Unger 1992; J. Watson 1984). In these respects, it might be more useful to think of class in China as analogous to race in the United States, overwhelmingly defining a person's social value and wavering, in politically explosive ways, between being understood as a social construction and being treated" commonsensically" as a natural inheritance. Taken together, the hereditary nature of the system, the unresolved tension between material conditions and consciousness, and the new forms of hierarchy that evolved out of the system eventually exploded into the Cultural Revolution (Billeter 1985; Kraus 1981; G. White 1976). Moreover, global cold war politics also contributed to the way these class identities continued to resonate in a national imaginary. With both the United States and, after 1960, the Soviet Union its superpower global enemies, the Chinese state was ever alert for enemies within and without. Cadres measured citizens' loyalties to the new regime by how closely they approximated "good" class consciousness.

With the repudiation of this class-status system, new roads to wealth and power through the accumulation of capital emerged to replace the accumulation of socialist moral wealth. New forms of knowledge also arose to explain social inequality and difference. One fundamental change was in the language of class. Most people I knew, including party cadres, studiously avoided the class labels of the previous era. They referred to someone's "social identity" (*shenfen*) rather than "class background" (*jieji chengfen*). They spoke of "workers" (*gongren*), but not the "proletariat" (*wuchan jieji*). They were likely to say "employee" (*gongzuo renyuan*) to refer not only to a vast array of people who worked in offices, department stores, or factories but also to engineers or designers. The term "city residents" (*shimin*) had replaced "the working class" (*gongren jieji*), and "the populace" or "the public" (*minzhong* or *dazhong*) was invoked rather than "the masses" (*laobaixing*). This shift in everyday terms of address displaces the figure of the subaltern as the subject of China's advance toward modernity.

Official language also made an ambiguous transition in the moral discourse on wealth (Anagnost 1997). Party pronouncements renounced the egalitarianism and collectivization of the Maoist era as decided hindrances to modernity. Many instead underscored the need to allow individuals to express their inherent talents in order to reinvigorate China's possibility of emerging into modernity. The idea of the pure individual mingled, however, with the sense that those social classes which had been the objects of attack under Maoism deserved recognition from the state.

Intellectuals, one of the major categories under attack during the Maoist period, especially emphasized their need to be recompensed. The Deng regime regarded intellectuals as essential to China's development. Official discourse both praised intellectuals and warned them about their proper place. Intellectuals I knew from the local university felt strongly hat they were the ones with the talents most important to further China's pursuit of modernity. Many hailed China's long imperial history of rule by the gentry-literati to remonstrate with the Deng regime, arguing that they still lacked their deserved social position and their rightful access to political and moral leadership. Not a few sported lapel stickers with Confucian aphorisms, as if to conjure up those lost glorious days.

As intellectuals negotiated the shifting meanings of their status within a system in which the state is still the main arbiter, market activity led to new forms of wealth and an incipient bourgeoisie emerged with the potential to usurp what many intellectuals viewed as their natural place as elites. The markets that flourished on the streets of Hangzhou were filled with peasants from the surrounding countryside and mainly young, unmarried men of working-class backgrounds. Less visible markets "behind" the street scenes – markets in foreign currency, illegally imported goods, and weapons – were run by high-level cadres and their children. Peasants sold produce directly from their household plots, while young men set up stands to sell the latest fashions from Hong Kong and America. Many of the latter were unemployed youth or those who had returned to Hangzhou after having been sent to the countryside during the Cultural Revolution and held no permanent position. There were also young male workers from the factories who refused to continue in their state-appointed jobs, preferring instead the lure of the market. Although markets appeared all over the country, the south of China – further away from the center of power – moved more quickly to experiment with them. People in Hangzhou prided themselves on being, as they put it, "quicker" than Chinese people to the north. The local government and party worked to stimulate rather than hinder this activity, sometimes sheltering the full knowledge of it from the central government.

A dangerous and exciting masculinity thrived in this arena. Popular discourse focused on the ability to take "risks" as necessary for success in market endeavors. Those who were most capable of taking risks were said to be young, unmarried men who could prove their worth as men in such exploits, showing their daring, savvy, strength, and ability to entice. They had to travel long distances to obtain goods from Canton, near Hong Kong, and avoid being taken advantage of along the way. They had to have an ever-widening network of social connections to lay their hands on these golden goods – the latest fashions. They had to appear publicly in the market, hawking their wares brazenly, though at any moment "the state" might shut them down in a campaign against spiritual pollution. Women who appeared as sellers in the market were, by contrast, viewed as too brazen, as bad women. They had, people hinted, an air of prostitution about them. How could women, especially unmarried women, do that kind of traveling and haggling with men, that kind of networking, without there being something unsavory about it? "Getting taken advantage of" had a wholly different meaning for them.

"I don't have the courage to do that," Xiao Bao, a young woman silk worker once commented to me. "Men can do that." The risk involved not merely the potential loss of money but engaging in moneymaking activities in the midst of a political culture in which the moral discourse on commercial wealth was ambivalent. Another risk was of abandoning the security of the state's social welfare system of lifetime job guarantees and benefits. Popular wisdom had it that these young men were hooligans or that they used unsavory means to gain wealth. Others remarked on the less visible markets in highly valued imports, nodding knowingly about the sons and daughters of high-level cadres who could take advantage of their family's power to conduct scams. Official discourse took pains to distinguish "selfish" means of garnering wealth from legitimate activity that contributed to the nation, but the line was difficult to draw with any certainty. Most people I knew, including workers, rejected the "radical egalitarianism" of the Maoist period, when wealth was supposed to be shared and only small differences in income were visible. Yet traces of the previous morality remained. In this turbulent moment, it wasn't clear which type of person should represent the nation, which group of people the state should favor in its post-Mao vision of modernity.

The Maoist past haunts these new regimes of truth, for post-Mao social differentiations are caught within the very social forms they are meant to overcome. Economic reform is meant to signal an abrupt break, an entirely new road to modernity that leaves the past far behind. But history paradoxically provides the very grounds on which people negotiate this new road. Invoking Walter Benjamin's image of the angel of history (Benjamin 1968: 257–58), one can imagine Maoism as that pile of debris whose wreckage continues to grow as the storm of progress blows China forward. One cannot understand the post-Mao moment's relationship to the Maoist past unless one pursues Benjamin's task of dispelling the myth of a single, unfolding history.

We must begin with Benedict Anderson's insight (1991) that national histories are often a matter of forgetting, or rather of remembering to forget. Even as official discourse in China exhorts people to forget what is often called "the ten years of chaos," it continuously revives the specter of Maoism and the need to overcome it in order to provide a source of moral authority for the post-Mao state. The differences that are so necessary to claims of modernity, differences often created between unequal nations to enable the colonizing of noncitizen others, can be reproduced equally within the nation to enable the disciplining of citizen-selves. The state needs to prove over and over again how it can vanquish Maoism. It would be easy enough, otherwise, to let the Cultural Revolution fade into the deep shadows of forgotten history. Instead, we find the Cultural Revolution is continually marked, remarked on, and used as a base point for all discussion of modernity, and tales of its meaninglessness and horrors are repeated and repeated. So long as the post-Mao regime is in power, the Cultural Revolution does not stand in danger of oblivion. History here offers a road to modernity strewn with national degradation and becomes, *pace* Nicholas Dirks (1990), not so much a sign of the modern as the uncertain site where the possibilities for modernity are construed.

The cultural reinscription of workers is intimately connected to this uneven and highly contested understanding of China's socialist history. More than any other group, workers became the most salient illustration of the socialist history that virtually everyone wished to overcome. Official and popular discourse represented them as literally embodying the past. This characterization was initially brought home to me, most startlingly, at a banquet my mentor instructed me to host not long after my arrival in China. I scarcely understood the import of the event at first. Under the aegis of Chen Li, president emeritus of the university, I invited the president of the provincial silk college, the chief engineer of the Hangzhou silk bureau, and a senior technical adviser to the provincial silk bureau. In addition, Chen Li and several professors from the university attended. Only gradually did I grasp that this banquet was not simply an occasion for a formal interview with my distinguished guests but a gesture critical to building a network of connections, or *guanxi*, that would smooth my way into the silk factories to speak with workers.

Chen Li advised me to submit written questions about the silk industry. Each of my illustrious guests – who, in turn, as a result of this banquet would become hosts of my research – had prepared formal written responses. They all had long years of experience in the silk industry, stretching back to the decade prior to the socialist revolution. That history had made them first targets of attack for engaging in capitalist exploitation and now objects of emulation for that same capitalist knowledge. Their comments were a mixture of facts, figures, and personal reminiscences. Having gone through the formalities, we launched into our meal. In the midst of awkward pleasantries, I asked a question about the problems workers now faced. Suddenly, everyone laughingly chimed in with an obviously clichéd and popular rhyme: "You work well, you work poorly, it's all the same; you work a lot, you work a little, it's all the same; you work or you don't work, it's all the same." They explained its meaning with much good humor: workers lacked the proper discipline for work. They had learned during the Cultural Revolution that they would be rewarded in the same way no matter what kind of effort they put into their work. They had learned laziness as a work ethic, my guests argued.

Workers had certainly challenged the discipline of the workplace during the Cultural Revolution. They had actively assaulted managerial authority, sometimes beating their managers as well. But the moral of that evening's verses, as I took it, was that workers had become flawed because of the failed promises of Maoism. Moreover, this flaw had settled into their natural disposition.

Thus we find the inscription of a new mythopoesis onto workers. No longer treating the subaltern as the hero of socialist progress, the state and nonparty elites have decentered and reconstituted her as one of the central obstacles that needs to be addressed if China is to move forward into modernity. Many, including some workers themselves, compel workers to signify internal lack, potentially hindering China from reaching modernity because they bring the past into the present in their very existence. In a conflicted process, the postsocialist construction of otherness fixes the subaltern worker in the position of historical otherness. The state tries to naturalize the historical difference that it has made workers represent. But as in relations between the colonizer and the colonized, there exists both a tacit acknowledgment and a disavowal of the relations of power that have made workers represent historical difference. On the one hand, it is recognized that Maoism produced a certain consciousness in workers; on the other hand, this historical variability is adamantly denied. The production of new forms of class and gender inequalities are at once tacitly admitted and vigorously disclaimed.

There thus exists a paradox, the simultaneous acknowledgment and disavowal of the conditions that are expressed in the stereotyping of workers. Desires, anxieties, and affirmations of China's postsocialist quest for modernity figure in the body of the worker. The official and popular representations of workers acknowledge the global conditions that force China to create new relations of exploitation but disavow that exploitation – and the dependency of China's modernity on workers – by displacing it onto the workers themselves. Attempts proliferate to fix and normalize workers so that their activity will support capitalist development. But these new forms of disciplining workers are displaced onto the history of socialism in China. And as with colonial discourses of difference, one detects a certain anxiety about the need to make a pure and clean historical break and perhaps the impossibility of doing so, as history bleeds into the present in the figure of the worker.

Workers embody history. They are said to live in what we might call, following Anne McClintock (1995), anachronistic space. According to this trope, workers do not inhabit history proper but exist in a permanently anterior time as anachronistic people. But in official representations, history is an ingestible substance that has been transformed into part of the essential nature of subalterns, replacing their mutable consciousness. Moreover, this process has led to a certain degeneracy. Newspaper editorials and casual comments alike implied that history had created an abnormality among workers, causing harm within the body politic and possibly inheritable tendencies that threatened the "quality" (*suzhi*) of the Chinese populace. This ambivalence about workers – viewing their behavior as the fallout of history yet naturalizing their collective character – pervaded the everyday commentary on them by others. My intellectual friends at the university took pains to explain that workers lacked a "high consciousness," that they were incapable of dreaming about the future, that they only cared about material goods and wages – as if workers' arguments about wages and material comfort were distinct in kind from those I heard from intellectuals rather than being very similar, that is, a richly symbolic dialogue about social worth and status.

One young professor, Wang Hangsheng, sympathetic to workers and from a worker background himself, invoked Confucius: "We have a saying from Confucius, '*Canglin shi er zhi lijie*' [when the granary is full, then one can know the proper manners; i.e., only the wealthy can have the leisure to learn proper etiquette]. Common workers, very few are motivated to have a high consciousness. How can they? They have to worry about just getting food to eat." Yet workers in state-run factories have a guaranteed lifetime income. Indeed, for all intents and purposes their granaries are full, if not exactly overflowing. Professor Wang's interpretation of the Confucian aphorism inverts their reality. He casts workers as those for whom "consciousness" of the future is the opposite of the materiality of the present, where they are thought to be rooted. One finds workers so treated in western scholarship as well, where measurement of workers' wages and productivity are assumed to offer a transparent means to perceive their behavior (see Walder 1987, 1991). Such use of quantitative measures contributes to the reification of workers, treating them as a commodity-form befitting capitalist relations of production and lending justification to the new disciplinary regime.

The essentialization of a disposition in workers toward laziness, disorderliness, and transient material desires – characteristics that establish them as hindering China's efforts to realize modernity – perhaps nowhere made itself more evident than in the accusation that the Cultural Revolution had taught workers to "eat out of one big pot" (*chi daguo fan*). Over the ensuing months I heard this cliché often enough; it had quickly turned into another hackneyed political phrase in the newspapers as well as a form of jesting – for example, mothers used it in teasing their children about their reluctance to do household chores. The expression refers to an extended family that shares both its food and living quarters. "Eating out of one big pot" happens – literally – only within the family. However, within the family it serves as a metaphor for the sharing of the family food and money "pot" without keeping close track of how much each individual has contributed. When I asked silk factory workers, both parents and children, about family finances, for example, they would insist no precise calculations existed among family members, even as they could easily tell me how much money children in their family handed over to their parents every month.

The linking of finances to food within the family makes this phrase a powerful representation of work relations in China. When used to refer to factory workers, "eating out of one big pot" means that no matter how much or how little workers produced, they all ate the same "food," that is, received the same wages.[1] Those who continued to work hard, so I was told, were not given their just "desserts." The metaphor has still deeper resonance for factories. The work unit in China, until recently, operated in a manner analogous to a family, with large work units, like Zhenfu, taking care of all its workers' needs. They had everything from a hair salon to a medical clinic within the factory grounds. The work unit dispensed all social benefits, from ration tickets to medical care to retirement pensions; it continues to give permission to marry and to help resolve a variety of personal conflicts, such as spousal conflict. In this manner, the state provided socialist support and also sought to pull citizens into an overarching loyalty to itself rather than to their familial relations. In the name of modernity, the post-Mao state castigates workers for having accustomed themselves to living as socialists in this way. Such criticism at once breaks with previous forms of knowledge about socialism and institutes new modes of discipline.

To cast workers as having fallen into an antimodern work ethic inverts and obscures the political history of workers' activities during the Cultural Revolution. That political history continues to be a highly emotional matter, for its evaluation necessarily reaches to the very foundations of socialism. Historical judgments of the causes and aftermath of the Cultural Revolution assign guilt and innocence from the highest levels of the state to the local struggles between people whose bonds had been thought to be inalienable – students and teachers, workers and managers, children and parents – as well as among peers, friends, and co-workers. An ambivalence thus pervades the new truth regime about workers, reflecting a larger paradox about how to unravel the past and thus how to morally evaluate the present. History provides the allegory of workers' fallen condition but it simultaneously is erased as their habits and competencies are naturalized. In this post-Mao story about workers, the socialist past becomes reified as a substantive force that appears to exist apart from human relations. It can do things to people and make people become what they originally were not. It resides in people as if it were a removable substance. One might call this reification a form of historical fetishism (see Taussig 1992). Like commodity fetishism, historical fetishism turns the Maoist past into an object whose effectiveness in the world appears to stand apart from specific social relations. The "Cultural Revolution," people now say, kept China from reaching modernity. This emotionally wrought ambivalence about Maoism underlies the equivocal acknowledgment and disavowal of workers' consciousness as agents in history.

This historical fetishism recalls Lukács's discussion of reification (1971). Lukács argued that with commodity fetishism, the human qualities of workers appear increasingly as "mere sources of error" (p. 89) when contrasted with the rationalization of abstract laws governing modern production. For Lukács, the structure of reification occurs not merely within the labor process; it becomes the dominant characteristic of modern society, sinking deeply into human consciousness and all modes of rational knowledge production. Thus every manifestation of life is treated as if it exhibited a necessity subject to strict, abstract laws and a totality ruled entirely by chance.

Although History decentered workers, they in turn decentered History by telling local stories of their specific pasts. None of the workers I knew ever characterized her- or himself as "eating out of one big pot." They all spoke instead of heroic exertions, volatile political struggles, and radically different forms of discipline than those of economic reform. While they sometimes spoke of the Maoist past as if it were a disembodied substance, they also destabilized this dominant discourse by recalling what it meant to be a worker during that time. Nor did they think of themselves as a natural collectivity. They distinguished themselves from one another in manifold ways, including by the different political campaigns that they felt had established their life trajectories, by specific experiences of the Cultural Revolution, by gender, by family history with silk production, and by class background prior to entering the factory. These diverse histories also led many workers to deny their difference from the rest of society, which has marginalized them and placed them on the other side of a vast gulf. For many, "worker," at least as it was re-created in an abject form, was not an obvious identification. Their challenges to the dominant meaning of their work identities were effected by the telling of different kinds of histories. This was one place where the radical transformations of the post-Mao period were exposed, where the very meanings, images, and subject positioning of workers were renegotiated. Official, elite, and popular commentary all rewrite Chinese history through the vision of a post-Mao modernity and, in so doing, bring that vision into existence and give it a universalizing force. Workers' local stories, however, cast doubt on the universal as they trace subtle differences in the phantasm of a singular modernity.

PRODUCING CULTURE

In the winter of 1985, still close to the beginnings of my fieldwork, the Central Textile Bureau instituted a new wage and bonus system, along with new disciplinary measures, for all textile-related industries. They called it, in a kind of fantasy of stationary permanence, the "position-wage system" (*gangwei gongzi zhi*). State cadres hoped these measures would be the heart of China's modernization program in state-run in dustries. They designed them to raise workers' productivity by joining punitive regulations to precise statistical measurements. The position-wage system, which applies to workers but not to cadres, replaces the old system based on seniority with one based entirely on the job position, or category. Jobs are divided into five main categories, in descending hierarchical order: (1) weaving, (2) warp preparation, (3) weft preparation and inspection, (4) transport, and (5) miscellaneous work – sweeping, machine cleaning, dining hall work. Weavers occupy the top category and receive the highest wages, with the other categories following in increments of five to ten yuan less at each step.[2] Workers just entering the factory for the first time are placed on this new wage scale, although they do not receive the official wages set for each category until they work for six and a half years. As for workers already at the factory, older workers whose seniority in the old system put their pay above the scale retain their original wages until retirement; those not yet receiving top wages are gradually given raises.

Bonuses for workers in this new system are based on individual piecework. After workers fulfill a predetermined quota, which represents their basic wage as set by job category, they earn the rest of their income through individual bonuses (though the range of the bonus is also differentiated by job category). The quotas are set such that workers must exceed them to make a living wage – in effect, the wages for each category include the bonus. The problematic nature of the bonus portion of the wage is reflected in the way that workers in the silk factory talk about it: most speak of their bonus being deducted if they fail to reach the maximum amount rather than of earning an extra amount. The wage thus actually has two components: one fixed and one variable.

Party cadres and technical managers in the silk industry explained to me that the position-wage system would rid workers of their tendency to "eat out of one big pot." They cast it as a way to liberate work relations from the constraining political categories of the Cultural Revolution and, indeed, of the entire Maoist era. In this way, the state displaces the issue of exploitation onto workers themselves. Party cadres and nonparty managers in the silk factories were unified on this matter, although much confusion and uncertainty remained: How was power to be divided between them? How autonomous would they be? How would they reconcile the factory's role in a centrally planned socialist economy, based on handing over their finished product to the state, with the novel demand – paradoxically by the state – that the factory begin to make a profit? Party cadres inside the factories seemed at once superfluous and still powerful in their ability to gain various advantages by invoking the name of the state.

Theoretically, a smooth, vertical chain of command exists from the central government's Textile Bureau to the Zhejiang provincial silk bureau to the Hangzhou municipal silk bureau to each of the thirty or so of Hangzhou's silk factories under its aegis. A parallel line exists from the Central Party Committee down to the branch party secretaries and party committees in each factory and in each workshop of each factory. Yet, while cleaving to this form of power, those at its center also wished to shake off its unwieldiness and thereby invigorate "the economy." They hoped that managers of state-run factories would turn a profit but not stray too far from the strictures of socialist control. The moral discourse on wealth reflected these dizzying extremes of anticipation and anxiety. All along the "descent lines" of socialist power, innovators developed active, creative means to maneuver in the postsocialist breaches that had opened. At any moment, they could be shut down and declared exemplars of spiritual pollution – or they could be declared models of the road to modernity. By whom? By any level of the government, anyone speaking in the name of the state.

THE POETICS OF PRODUCTIVITY

The central government devolved much of the responsibility for economic planning to the provincial and municipal levels. The Zhejiang provincial silk bureau now set production demands, ultimately answering to a higher level but with increasing independence, particularly in managing the lucrative export market. China's silk found eager buyers all over the world, but especially in Hong Kong, Taiwan (indirectly), Europe, and the United States. Hangzhou was one of the two or three major centers for this treasured trade. The windfall from silk exports gave rise to much dispute, as everyone, including the central government, desired a piece of it for their own ends. Factories had a certain amount of autonomy in expanding production, but they were not supposed to control directly any aspect of foreign trade. Still, factory managers quickly found ways to increase exports, even as their innovations could be declared dangerous or corrupt at any moment. These contentious, hope-filled maneuverings took on added urgency as everyone feared that the appropriate moment to seize the opportunity for wealth had just passed them by.

Thus newly created desires provided the impetus for the novel regime of truth and discipline embedded in the position-wage system. The state had never before permitted but also had never conceived of such closely refined statistical measurements. Managers viewed these statistics as a neutral and fair means to assess rewards for those who worked hard and punishments for those who did not, and they assumed that I would support their efforts and join in a discussion about the best ways to implement these modern forms of scientific management. After all, I was from the belly of the capitalist beast; I should know best. Their presumptions led me to realize that workers' interpretations of management's interpretations of "productivity" was one site where local histories were expressed.

Commentary on the new position-wage system among workers was open and heated. It eventually led to a tense confrontation with the top directors by one group of workers. Their range of engaged responses makes it impossible for me to treat the new system as an objective method of gathering statistical facts about a transparent reality. Rather, I understand statistical measures to be a means of establishing the authority of a certain vision of social order (Hacking 1991; Porter 1986; Joan Scott 1988b). In the case of China, that vision rests foremost with the state. At the same time, the statistical measures of third world workers like those in Hangzhou's silk factories are taken up and made into productive knowledge by the World Bank, western scholars, and transnational capitalist investors.

Individuation

The position-wage system pressures workers to labor more intensely by transforming the "collectivity" of Maoist production into individuated measurement. In the previous era, workers shared the responsibilities of production as well as its rewards in the form of small bonuses. They were collectively bound to one another in two ways: within each shift, small groups of workers, divided by job task, shared the burden of production; and within the shift rotation system, all workers who had operated the same machine shared the responsibility for production problems. Under the position-wage system, each worker is held responsible for her or his own position within the shift. At Zhenfu, each bolt of woven cloth, for example, carries the name of the worker who produced it. In the shops where the yarn is spun, matters are not as simple. In Zhenfu's weft preparation shop, the shop supervisor pulled one worker off the line and assigned her the task of counting how many broken threads each position had; each worker was docked accordingly.

This individuation of workers resonates with a broader national discourse on the need for individuals to distinguish themselves. The cultural production of individualism speaks at once across time and space: to the Maoist era of collective identification, now said to have hindered China from reaching modernity, and to western orientalism, which describes Asian cultures as lacking a modern concept of individual freedom. Thus a news article on the youth of Shenzhen, the export-oriented special economic zone (SEZ) created near Hong Kong, exemplifies official praise of the need for individual distinction. By lauding the Shenzhen youth, the statement instructs all Chinese citizens on the eight methods for individuating themselves:

> 1) [they have] the courage to assert themselves, to volunteer their services to become factory director; 2) they regard standing on their own feet, earning their own living, and striving to improve themselves as glorious; 3) [they realize that] time is money, time is efficiency; 4) they are particular about bearing and appearance, hoping to draw people's attention; 5) they strive to be a "bird whose head sticks out," to be in the limelight. They dare to compete to be first in their field. They dare to be first to wear a new style of clothing. Very few now believe that one should "know one's place" or that one should not seek to forge ahead. This is a quality youth should have. Jealousy now breeds not a feeling that the crowd should beat down him who "sticks out his head" but a competitive spirit to be better. 6) [They have] the daring to plan for themselves, be able to think it is always the other mountain that looks higher; 7) [they know that] social contact is for gaining information . . . ; 8) [they have] a feeling of responsibility that unites individual pursuits with the country's welfare. They have changed the view of the 1950s and 1960s that the pursuit of wealth is only for society's welfare. (*News Digest*, 13 September 1985, p. 3)

These new individuals need to be freed not simply from socialist moorings but from the stifling force of the crowd, from cultural strictures that hold them back. But since people do not live simply in "crowds," the article implicitly refers also to the particular social worlds in which people are enmeshed – families, networks of peers, and the hierarchical world of work. Modern subjects are those who have the strength to deny the power of the group. They place modern desires onto their very bodies – in the way their heads "stick out," in the clothes they wear, and in their display of emotions. As the final method discloses, this discursive production of individualism is part of the process of imagining a postsocialist modernity for China. It does not seek to liberate individuals so much as to constitute them as citizens of a post-Mao nation-state (L. Liu 1995).

Age

The individuation of workers leads to rewarding those who are most "productive." Yet this individuation operates through changing notions of cultural differentiation embedded in the very concept of productivity. These notions include "youthful energies," the "bitterness" of weaving, and gender difference. I first learned about the importance of youth from Yang Zhuren. Yang Zhuren, who held the modest post of secretary to the party office, had come forward to speak with me on my initial visits to Zhenfu. I had naively assumed at first that he must be a relatively unimportant figure with much time on his hands, the kind of time usefully spent receiving a relatively unimportant foreigner. Yang Zhuren himself downplayed his position to me. But as I later learned from others, Yang Zhuren's background in the army, his assignment to Zhenfu in 1970 to quell the Cultural Revolution, and his subsequent talent for amassing connections had enabled his gradual rise to become Zhenfu's most powerful party cadre. Yang Zhuren liked to regale me with stories about his simple peasant background and could enumerate with nostalgic pleasure the elaborate customs of his home village not far from Hangzhou. But he also was keenly aware of everything going on in the factory.

We spent long days discussing and disputing economic reform. As Yang Zhuren explained it,

> The previous system wasn't appropriate. With textile workers, when they are old, the quality of their work is not good. They say of textile workers, "They mature early, they contribute early, they deteriorate early." When someone has just entered the factory, after a few years, around twenty years old is when they produce the highest quality. But they were getting the lowest wages. It wasn't fair.

This representation of youths as the most productive workers stands in radical opposition to the former notion that older workers, as *shifu*, or masters in their trade, should be rewarded for their knowledge and experience. Such reverence for youth accords with the view, vigorously propagated in the 1990s, that people are their most creative and contribute most effectively to the advancement of society in the early years of their career. Indeed, this is a pervasive trope in many nations' discourses of modernity: the child or youth carries the promise of a new beginning in transcending a decayed and corrupted cultural tradition. It has certainly been thematized in China before but perhaps never with such concerted attention to the discipline of the laboring body.

Much talk in China circulates about the need to "juvenize" (*qingnianhua*), to encourage older people to step aside for the more capable youths now stuck in junior positions. This discursive elaboration of the positive qualities of youth represents a fundamental challenge to the kind of seniority still prevalent in the party, many workplaces, and the family. The assumption that the young have greater capacity also implies a direct relationship between biology and productivity. This notion owes much of its credibility to a milieu in which science has replaced Marxism as the ultimate arbiter of reality.

The new position-wage system privileges youths in that young people who enter the factory will, after only a few years, receive the same wages as those who have worked there for twenty or thirty years. Moreover, older workers who have reached the top of the scale will receive no further wage increases. Thus the wages at the senior end of the scale are effectively lowered. The system, based on changing interpretations of productivity, rewards a category of workers – youths – based on the hegemonic representation of their possessing greater potential capacity to produce. That youths do not always produce more is clear. They are often, as one assistant director of a collective silk-weaving factory put it, "the 'naughty' boys. After work they go out and play. They play late, so they have no energy to work the next day." These are the workers who have their pay docked most frequently. But the gap between youths' variable work performance and the current belief in their capacity has in no way diminished that belief or lessened its role in forming the position-wage system.

The disciplinary regime of post-Mao modernity thus depends on a fundamental transformation in notions of "productivity," a far from transparent process. Workers, as well as certain managers, provided outspoken commentary. Older workers offered me their perspective on the new system. Chen Shifu, only three years from retirement, was direct: she had begun silk work as a young child, had fought hard to become a weaver, and had worked diligently for thirty years. In the past, older workers could transfer to less strenuous jobs without losing any wages in their last few years before retiring, and Chen Shifu had looked forward to becoming a security gatekeeper. She felt she was entitled; she thought the "higher ups" – a common term for politically powerful superiors – should "look after" (*zhaogu*) her. But with the new position-wage system, transfer to another job category would mean a reduction in pay. Chen Shifu was angry. "These new changes," she said, "*xin bu-tong*" (won't go through my heart; i.e., my heart won't accept them).

Bitterness

Not only the cultural category of age but also various job categories were given new meaning by the position-wage system. Managers explained that weaving takes greater skill and labor intensity than the other tasks. Indeed, historically silk weaving was the most highly skilled craft in Hangzhou. But in the mid-1980s people in Hangzhou began to consider work in the silk industry to require virtually no skill relative to other, flashier industries like electronics or foreign tourism, then newly introduced into China. No young urban person wished to go into the silk industry. Hangzhou is now a center of light industry and tourism. Young people envied service employees in foreign hotels or tour guides; they fancied work in banks or computer chip factories. And, of course, young men who dared to do so worked in the emerging markets. Since 1982, when everyone but university students could "choose" to seek out their own job instead of receiving a mandatory job assignment from the state Labor Bureau, silk factories have desperately searched for labor, semi-illegally relying on migrant women from the countryside.

While all silk work is virtually indistinguishable in this wider perspective, within the silk industry weaving is recognized as taking more time to learn than prep work; more discrete tasks are involved. But as I quickly learned at Zhenfu, the "productivity" and skill of weaving are most closely tied to interpreting the job as "bitter" work. To "eat bitterness" – that is, to suffer hardship – was once the stuff of socialist pride. In the post-Mao period, however, the heroic glory of eating bitterness had faded. Postsocialist modernity requires not tales of loss but tales of gain.

The bitterness of weaving, as I learned during the time I spent at Zhenfu, comes from the fact that almost all the defects found in the finished cloth are blamed on the weaver. Everyone readily admits that such automatic condemnation is unjust – the fault is not always the weaver's. But the silk process makes it difficult to trace mistakes to any other source. I was in the weaving shop one day when an argument ensued between a weaver and several people representing other shops; the participants included Dai Hongyun, the prep shop's union leader and master worker. The vociferous dispute centered on a problem in the cloth still sitting in the weaver's loom. Yelling over the deafening noise of hundreds of looms, the weaver insisted that poor thread preparation in the prep shop led to the snag in the cloth. Dai Hongyun yelled back that the weaver's inattention when the thread got caught in his loom caused the problem. Qiu Shifu, the assistant shift supervisor, suspected the transport workers, who perhaps were too careless in carrying the bulky but delicate roll of warp over from the steam shop. The argument had to be settled before the weaver continued and the evidence disappeared, and its resolution rested in who could tell a more convincing story, who could talk the other person into giving way. They went back and forth for a long time; ultimately, the weaver yielded, but only because he could talk no one else into taking responsibility. The objective measures of productivity thus rest on local interpretations of work "experience." More than any other silk workers, weavers regularly have their pay docked for falling short of the new, more stringent quality standards. In this sense, their work is more bitter.

Gender

These cultural interpretations of status and skill that inform statistical measures of productivity are in turn shaped by changing conceptions of how gender relates to silk work. The understanding of productivity itself is clearly gendered, for the position-wage system applies only to what is increasingly considered women's work – weaving, prep, and inspection. Tasks such as machine repair and transport (including truck driving) are categorized as skilled technical labor and defined as men's work. The division between management and workers in the silk industry is also increasingly made along gender lines. Those who do the women's tasks (including those men who do so) are thereby produced as feminine subjects. Conversely, women and men who engaged in tasks designated as appropriate for men were seen as masculine. Many comments flowed freely among women workers, for example, about the masculinity of those women who prepared the warp or were shop supervisors.

Silk work in Hangzhou was not always women's work. Until well into the 1960s, local culture reserved silk weaving, as well as warp preparation, for men and for women who could demonstrate masculinity. Women prepared the weft thread and spun the thread out of the cocoons. With the 1958 Great Leap Forward campaigns to bring more women into the workforce, women in Hangzhou began to take on more of the weaving. By the mid-1960s, Hangzhou's silk industry was witnessing a decided feminization of its workforce. But this trend was halted during and just after the Cultural Revolution, when urban youth sent down to the countryside who wished to return were allowed to inherit their parents' factory jobs if their parents retired early. Young men entered the silk factories and took up jobs as weavers, machine repairmen, and transport workers. Even in the 1980s, nearly half of the silk weavers in Hangzhou were men. This gendered division of labor exists as a matter of historical contingency, dependent not on an inner structural logic or an inherent teleology in the relations of production but on political campaigns that construct specific meanings of gender.

With economic reform, an increasingly rigid distinction emerged between the production line jobs of weaving, prep, and inspection work, construed as manual labor, and those jobs more highly valued as skilled technical and mental labor – machine repair, transport, and managerial work. As part of this process, the manual labor tasks became women's work, while the technical and mental tasks were assigned to men and women thought to be masculine enough to handle them. This gendered division of labor has taken shape through gendered interpretations of work capabilities; women and men were and are said to have different capacities uniquely suited to these divergent tasks. Yang Zhuren, in a casual aside, once told me that the new system was created to categorize tasks considered boring, tasks requiring energy but little skill. Realizing the import of his remarks, he then quickly moved on to speak of other problems. Managers repeatedly told me that women are most suited to such tasks – they have the requisite patience, complain less about boring work, and have nimble fingers. Because gender capabilities are defined in opposition to one another, men are thought to be innately more capable of technical tasks. To the extent that particular women in the silk factories are viewed as able to do men's work, they are said to resemble men.

Representations of the appropriate managerial qualifications also operate through gender. Most important, people would comment that women lacked the necessary leadership qualities to be managers. In particular, women don't know how to talk people into doing things; they thus lack the skill needed to resolve disputes and make the social connections so necessary for getting anything done. Talking, or verbal persuasion, is at once a political, cultural, and social skill. The party operates most effectively and most powerfully when a party cadre can persuade someone verbally to do as the party wishes. To excel in this art means to lead the person who is the object of persuasion into embracing the party's wishes as her or his own; that is, to become the subject of these desires. Zhenfu was filled with such artful verbal maneuvers: supervisors talking workers into staying on the job rather than taking sick leave for the day; the youth league secretary attempting to talk young men back into the factory rather than skipping work to make money in the market. In honing this skill, leaders had to be authoritative but not authoritarian; compelling in their combination of moral, social, and emotional reasoning rather than blunt. Those who were most artful would remind a worker of her or his obligations to other workers – how much other workers would be unduly burdened if she or he refused to work. A worker might also be reminded of the importance of her contributions to the welfare of her factory, her family, and her country. Those few women acknowledged to have mastered the art of verbal persuasion were said to be just like men in their ability to talk.

The state certainly took the initiative in gendering work but, as in earlier eras, these differentiations took their power from diverse sources. That is, state cadres did not stand outside of culture, manipulating it from above. They and others naturalized and in the process materialized these gender relations. Educated women, for example, also insisted to me that women talked of petty things, that "they" lacked the ability to settle human affairs. It is possible, too, that the global conditions of textile labor, in which women predominate, have helped shape local changes in Hangzhou. Women workers themselves both accepted and recast these gendered work relations. While they never overtly challenged this mapping of gender onto work, neither were they patient, silent, or meek. Indeed, the major challenge that supervisors faced was keeping these women in their place – a subtle, never-ending contest that supervisors lost as often as they won. The more experienced *shifu* also had to teach new workers how to have "nimble fingers." Sometimes they complained of the migrant women from the countryside that their hands were too "stupid," that they weren't "quick" like city women. As the combination of global markets and diverse competing party and managerial interests within China continued to devalue the women's work of silk production, women workers in Hangzhou's silk factories tried desperately, and sometimes successfully, to leave their place in silk work altogether.[3] They fled to new work that was no less gendered. In Hangzhou, the most alluring was the world of foreign tourism, where young women could serve as the "Asian beauties" that foreign businessmen sought.

Cultural notions of gender thus construct work relations. Work relations, in turn, instill gender identities. Women and men participating in the dailiness of work activities come to embody gender distinctions as they imperceptibly take upon themselves the discursive regime of labor. In China, "labor" – rather than, say, family, sexual desire, the psyche, consumption, religion, or any number of other realms of human activity – under socialism served as the principal cultural site for the production of identities. The processes and practices associated with labor became infused with gender ideologies that, in turn, structured possibilities for women and men. Labor played such a critical role not because of its supposed objective materiality – after all, we are talking about a rather short period of history – but because of the party-state's success in discursively producing it as the critical site. That is, the state made labor the cultural arena in which women and men crafted the meaning of "liberation," proved their socialist moral worth, expressed their nationalist sentiments, and received their rewards – or punishments – from the state. Labor furnished the means by which the state measured its own modernity.

Political economy here becomes not the material ground of women's experiences, nor the objective framework for them; rather, it is a discourse like any other. It creates its object of knowledge and its construction of reality. That people labor and are exploited in the process is clear. But the meaning of labor is always contingent. Political economy, then, is a Marxist discourse that produces the meaning of labor and was, in socialist China, the primary means of producing modern identities. Because labor has provided such a vexed cultural site, in the post-socialist era it continues to be the focus of a number of cultural struggles – over "productivity," to be sure, but also over the meaning of socialism and capitalism, one's relationship to the state, one's identity as a woman or man, and one's future as a modern subject. Yet it now competes with other cultural realms. The state has enabled the "market" to become one such field for the intertwining of modernity and masculinity. The market – not construed as labor – is a new site for the cultural production of "liberated" modern subjects. Here, masculine men, not liberated women, transgress what people now call "traditional socialist" values. The invention of the psyche and of sexuality cultivate still other forms of modern identities. In the process, women workers became the feminized subjects of a reconceived state-run arena that, everyone complains, holds China back from reaching modernity.

NOTES

1. The wage system during the Cultural Revolution was actually much more complex. Those who entered the factory during those years received the same wages regardless of task, but those who were already in the factory had their wages frozen at the then-current hierarchical levels.
2. In 1986 weavers earned around ¥100 per month. At that time, they had to save their full salary for five months to buy a bicycle; in terms of food, ¥5 could buy a little over one pound of fish or several pounds of fruit. Five yuan also paid for one month's rent.
3. In state-run units, one can only leave the job with the permission of the unit's leaders – unless, that is, one is willing to risk abandoning the state's social security and benefits system. Most women looked for work in other state-run units, which had their own mappings of gender and work.

REFERENCES

Anangnost, Ann. 1997. *National Past-Times: Narratives, Representation, and Power in Modern China*. Durham, N.C.: Duke University Press.

Anderson, Benedict. 1991. *Imagined Communities*. New York: Verso.

Billeter, Jean-Francois. 1985. "The System of 'class Status' ", in *The Scope of State Power in China*, Stuart Schram (ed.) pp: 127–69. New York: St. Martin's Press.

Chan, Anita, Richard Madsen and Jonathan Unger. 1992. *Chen Village under Mao and Deng*. Berkeley: Berkeley University Press.

Dirks, Nicholas. 1990. 'History as a Sign of the Modern', in *Public Culture* 2(2): 25–32.

Hacking, Ian. 1991. 'How Should We Do the History of Statistics?', in *The Foucault Effect: Studies on Governmentality*, Graham Burchell, Colin Gordon and Peter Miller (eds.) 181–96. Chicago: University of Chicago Press.

Jeffery Lyn. 1995. 'Quian/Quan: Money and Power among China's Nouveaux Riches'. PhD, qualifying examination paper, University of California Santa Cruz.

Kraus, Richard. 1981. *Class Conflict in Chinese Socialism*. New York: Columbia University Press.

Lukács, Georg. 1971. 'Reification and Consciousness of the Proletariat', in *History and Class Consciousness: Studies in Marxist Dialectics*. Translated by Rodney Livingstone, 83–222. Cambridge, Mass.: MIT Press.

McClintock, Anne. 1995. *Imperial Leather: Race, Gender, and Sexuality in the Colonial Contest*. New York: Routledge.

Porter, Theodore. 1986. *The Rise of Statistical Thinking, 1820–1900*. Princeton: Princeton University Press.

Scott, Joan Wallach. 1988. 'A Statistical Representation of Work: La statistique de l'industrie à Paris, 1847–1848', in Joan Scott, *Gender and the Politics of History*. New York: Columbia University Press. Pp: 113–138.

Taussig, Michael. 1992. 'Maleficium: State Fetishism', in *The Nervous System*, 111–40. New York: Routledge.

Watson, James. (ed.) 1984. *Class and Social Stratification in Post-Revolution China*. Cambridge; Cambridge University Press.

White, Gordon. 1976. *The Politics of Class and Class Origin: The Case of the Cultural Revolution*. Canberra: Australian National University Press.

CHAPTER NINETEEN

Asking for and Giving *Baki*: Neo-bondage, or the Interplay of Bondage and Resistance in the Tamilnadu Power-loom Industry

GEERT DE NEVE

I. INTRODUCTION

Situated at the confluence of three rivers, the Cauvery, the Bhavani and the Saraswati, the ancient town of Bhavani has a long history both as a holy place visited by saints and devotees and as a centre for handloom weaving. Here, the *jamakkalam* carpet is woven and the weavers of the town are proud of their products which are well known all over India. On the other side of the Cauvery river and linked by a bridge, is the town of Kumarapalayam, which was a flourishing handloom centre up to the 1950s, when power-looms were introduced and the production of hand-woven carpets and saris was gradually replaced by the manufacturing of machine-made *lungis* and various types of cloth for the export market. Today, Kumarapalayam is a vibrant business and manufacturing centre, bustling with bullock-carts, vans, scooters and bicycles, all transporting yarn and cloth to factories and shops. The incessant rattling of the power-looms fills the town day and night with a deafening buzz which in many ways reflects the dynamics and vitality of Kumarapalayam. These two towns formed the location of my fieldwork in Tamilnadu, carried out between August 1995 and January 1997.

This paper will focus on Kumarapalayam and, more precisely, on relations between factory owners and wage labourers in its power-loom industry. I examine the practice of asking for and giving *baki*, that is, the advance which the labourers receive at the moment of recruitment. Over the last twenty-five years this practice of giving advances to labourers and thus binding them through debt, which has often been considered as characteristic of feudal or semi-feudal relationships, has been introduced within this capitalist, industrial and urban setting. I argue that the origins of this practice lie in the employers' attempts to attract, retain and discipline labour within a competitive market.

Labour shortage, in a highly fragmented labour market, combined with expanding demand, encourages capitalist entrepreneurs to pursue strategies that ensure a permanent labour force. The introduction of advances to workers will also be linked to the entry of the Vellalar Gounder, a caste of farmers, into this industry from the early 1970s onwards. I also explore the effects of this practice on labour relations and labour mobility within the power-loom sector. Some of the discourses surrounding the practice of asking for and giving *baki* will be addressed. Finally, I will indicate how the attempt of employers to reintroduce a form of labour attachment through debt within this small-scale power-loom industry is highly problematic and contradictory both for industrialists and for workers. Factory owners seek to impose their power but labourers resist it and repeatedly attempt to escape it. Their quiet resistance, though not fully successful, is nevertheless effective in preventing the unrestrained imposition of power from above.

II. THE ARRIVAL OF THE GOUNDERS, LABOUR SHORTAGE AND THE INTRODUCTION OF *BAKI*

When the power-looms were started up in Kumarapalayam during the late 1950s, Devangar Chettiyars and Kaikolar Mudaliyars, the two main handweaving castes of the area, were the first to purchase and install power-looms. They ran their small factories largely with family labour, or they employed people closely connected to them through kin and caste. Having been handloom weavers before, most families were used to engaging only domestic labour and their handloom production had been predominantly household based. With the rapid development of the power-looms, however, they were forced to employ labourers from outside and did so through localised networks of neighbourhood, kin and caste. Labour was abundantly available and advances were not given at the time of recruitment.

From the early 1970s onwards, however, the industry experienced explosive growth and numerous new factories arose in and around the town. It was during this period that Vellalar Gounders entered the industry. Coming from medium-sized farming families in the villages surrounding Kumarapalayam, these sons of relatively well-off farmers had been working for several years in the *patrai* (workshops) of Devangars and Mudaliyars and, with the experience gained there, now began setting up their own power-loom units. In 1972 nineteen Gounders started their own power-loom units and organised themselves in the Kongu Sangam (Kongu Vellalar Gounder Power-loom Association). Many other Gounders followed and many new factories were set up on the border of the town, where agricultural fields were converted overnight into industrial estates. Unlike the Devangars and Mudaliyars, the Gounders did not have to invest heavily in land, since that was an asset they already possessed. Most of them did not even have to take loans, since they had the money to construct buildings and to purchase looms. Gounders state that it was their economic surplus from agriculture that they transferred to this expanding and lucrative industry. Devangar and Mudaliyar owners confirm this by their envious observation that the Gounders were at an enormous advantage, compared to them, because of the wealth that the Gounders had accumulated in agriculture.

As newcomers in the industry, the Gounders faced a serious problem of labour recruitment. Unable to rely on family labour, because their kin stayed back in the villages where they took care of the fields, these young industrialists had to attract outside labourers from the very beginning to operate their looms. The majority of workers belonged to Devangar and Mudaliyar weaving castes and increasingly also to the Vanniyar caste (traditionally agricultural labourers). In order to attract labourers from these other castes, the Gounders employed an aggressive strategy of labour recruitment: they initiated the giving of *baki* (advance) or *munnpanam* (advance money) to the workers they engaged. Initially, only small sums were given and the advance seldom exceeded Rs 50 or Rs 100. Labourers were not given advances elsewhere and so were eager to join the Gounders' factories. In this way, the latter were able to secure a labour force and expand their factories. At this time, Devangar and Mudaliyar factory owners did not engage in this practice. They continued to rely on their established networks for labour recruitment and maintained good relationships with their workers.

Labour shortage, however, was not only caused by the expansion of the industry and the buoyancy of demand. The fragmentation of the labour market of the power-loom industry is due to a number of factors. First, there is the continued exclusion of untouchable castes from this occupation. Production is organised in small workshops and factories (*patrai*), often attached to the houses of owners who are Kaikolar Mudaliyars, Devangar Chettiyars or Vellalar Gounders. Most of these owners are unwilling to employ Harijans in their factories. This is partly because they want to avoid clashes between workers of different castes, and partly because they prefer to keep Harijan workers out of the 'domesticated' workshops where water is shared, food exchanged and close cooperation takes place on a daily basis. Secondly, the power-loom workforce is still predominantly male. Although employers are eager to recruit women workers, emphasising that they are more reliable and diligent than men, women still constitute only one-third of the workforce and are almost entirely confined to the winding and reeling sections of the workshops. The major restriction on women's access to the power-loom jobs lies in the control that fathers and husbands continue to exert over their labour. Men seldom allow their daughter or wife to operate looms in a system of alternating day and night shifts and in factories where men and women from different caste and kin backgrounds work side by side. In a study of textile employment in the Coimbatore District during the 1960s and 1970s, Isa Baud similarly pointed out how recruiting employers in the power-loom industry stated 'that they are completely indifferent to the gender of the person they employ,

because they cannot get enough workers to man the looms. . . . More often constraints
for the women workers come from their own families. Parents prefer to know the
employer, or even to have a male family member working in the same unit' (Baud
1991: 79). Up to this day, almost all female power-loom operators are chaperoned by
their fathers, husbands or brothers, who work next to them in the same shift.

   A third factor adding to the fragmentation of the labour market is the level of
skill required. In the reeling and winding sections of the workshops, skill is hardly
an issue. Today, these tasks are no longer manually performed as the winding and
reeling wheels are connected through a belt with an engine. The job involves little
skill as the worker only has to replace the wound cones and pins, and to fix broken
threads. These jobs are exclusively allocated to women, who can learn them in a
few days. The operating of looms, however, requires more skill. Here two factors
are crucial. First, skill develops out of on-the-job training and experience. There is
no formal education within the industry and young men learn the weaving and the
technical aspects of the looms at work. From the age of 14 or 15 onwards, boys start
accompanying their fathers, elder brothers or close relatives to the factories where
they get to observe the work process and have the various tasks explained to them.
As the transfer of skill is based on the willingness of elders to teach youngsters on
the job, skills are largely reproduced within circles of kin and caste relations. The
lack of formal training makes it difficult for outsiders to enter the occupation and to
acquire unnecessary skills. Power-loom operators are aware of these restrictions and
are seldom eager to expend the time and effort needed to train a person, unless they
know him or her personally. By introducing others into the occupation they know
that they are producing competitors for their own jobs. Labour supply is thus controlled by the nature of skill reproduction within the industry. Secondly, skills vary
considerably according to the products manufactured and the looms used. A man
who is experienced in the production of *lungis* or *dhotis* may not be able to work
on a loom which produces towels, handkerchiefs, or shirts for the export market.
This specialisation of skills further restricts the availability of skilled and experienced
labour. Finally, the problem of labour shortage, as I will discuss below, extends far
beyond the actual shortage of labour and is also manifest in the lack of stability of
the workforce, which the employers are so eager to obtain, but which they have been
patently unable to achieve.

   The decade of the 1980s was marked by a further boom in the power-loom industry and a massive increase in the demand for labour. Some of the factors which
account for this development include the introduction of new machinery which enhanced productivity and profitability, the introduction of a second shift which
doubled the demand for labour and the uninterrupted growth of market demand.
Although migration during this period provided a larger supply of labour to the
town and although women were increasingly attracted to work on power-looms,
the demand for labour was not matched by an equally steady rise in the labour supply.
This entailed increases in the overall level of wages, it also enhanced the competition
among the employers for labour and especially for skilled labour.

   The Gounders, eager to maintain a stable labour force, responded by augmenting the *baki* with which they attracted labourers. In their 'greediness', as they themselves admit today, they were willing to give whatever the workers asked for in order to get sufficient manpower to keep their looms running day and night and to secure their ever-growing profits. During this period, the practice of giving a substantial *baki* to newly engaged workers reached its peak in Pallipalayam, a small town about 5 km away from Kumarapalayam. There, the Gounders had entered the power-loom industry a few years earlier and dominated it. Giving large advances to attract labour was an established practice by then and its efficiency in securing a permanent labour force encouraged the development of the same practice in Kumarapalayam. Gounder factory owners today say that they were impressed by the way their caste fellows in Pallipalayam kept their looms running seven days a week, and therefore decided to pursue the same strategy. At the same time, this practice gained momentum because a number of labourers moved out of Pallipalayam in search of jobs in the rapidly expanding industries of Kumarapalayam. With them they brought debts which had to be repaid and therefore they asked for higher advances from their new employers. As one factory owner in Kumarapalayam put it, 'They would come to us and say that they had to return Rs 2,000 to their previous employer and therefore wanted a *baki* of Rs 3,000, while none of it was actually true. Nevertheless, we paid them the advance because we needed their labour.' During the 1990s the habit of giving and asking for *baki* became common practice in Kumarapalayam. Devangar and Mudaliyar owners also participated in this practice. In 1996–97, the majority of labourers employed on the looms had received *baki* from their employer, often amounting to several thousand rupees. Many labourers received advances of Rs 10,000 to Rs 15,000 and even more.

   Thus, since the 1970s, giving of *baki* has been used by owners in the power-loom industry as a strategy to secure a permanent labour force in a competitive labour market characterised by a diversified labour force and a continuing labour shortage. It was the Gounders who, at the beginning of this century, employed Madharis and Paraiyars as *pannaiyals* or permanent farm labourers on their fields (Cederlof 1997: 60). They provided advances to these farm labourers to secure a stable agricultural labour force. It seems that they are now transferring and reintroducing this previous model of agricultural labour recruitment into an expanding industrial and urban environment. However, the effectiveness of this practice in a new context remains in question.

III. THE REINTRODUCTION OF DEBT BONDAGE AND THE LIMITS OF PROFITABILITY

The outcome seems to be a system of dependent labour relations which has commonly been referred to as a system of debt bondage (Brass 1990, 1994; Breman 1993, 1996; Kapadia 1995; Vidyasagar 1985). When a labourer is employed by a factory owner, he receives what is locally referred to as *munnpanam* (money given before-hand), *baki* (an advance), or simply 'advance'. The advance which the labourer receives from his new employer is in fact a debt which he has to repay before he can leave the factory and search for a job elsewhere. In this way, the worker is bonded to his employer until the day he is able to repay the entire debt. It is through his indebtedness that the worker loses his freedom to leave his employer as he is obliged to work for him until the money advanced has been repaid. Recently, the giving of these advances has become a general custom in Kumarapalayam so whenever a factory owner employs a labourer he has to give *baki*.

A census conducted among a sample of 300 labourers employed in the power-looms of Kumarapalayam revealed that more than 75 per cent of the workers in the sample received *baki* and were, thus, indebted to their employers. Equally impressive is the extent to which workers were indebted. More than 67 per cent received Rs 1,000 or more, and more than 26 per cent received *baki* of over Rs 5,000. Sixteen workers out of 300 got an advance of more than Rs 10,000. Male and female power-loom operators and women engaged in winding and reeling received the highest advances. Children (classified here as those below the age of 18), who were engaged in reeling, winding and other side-jobs, received substantial *baki*, often amounting to thousands of rupees. The importance of these sums becomes evident when we relate them to the workers' income. A power-loom operator, for example, earns an average of around Rs 400 per week. *Baki* of Rs 5,000, therefore, represents about three months' gross income, while *baki* of Rs 10,000 is equivalent to half a year's income. For a woman worker who receives a weekly wage of less that Rs 200 for winding, an advance of Rs 5,000 amounts to more than half a year's income and Rs 10,000 to more than she can earn in an entire year. Thus *baki* represents not only a considerable amount of money in comparison with weekly wages, but also constitutes a unique opportunity for workers to get hold of a large sum.

The practice of giving advances is also related to the employers' aim to attract particular workers to their factories. They are willing to advance more money to skilled workers, and to female workers. Since the 1980s, factory owners have been increasingly eager to employ female workers not only as a response to an enhanced demand for labour, but also because, as they state explicitly, women are harder-working, easier to discipline and in many ways less troublesome than men. The often huge advances which they today hand out to women patently reflect the owners' preference for female workers and the crucial role of *baki* in attracting them. If, for example, a husband and wife with one or two children are employed in the same factory, the owner might also be prepared to give them a higher advance as he knows that a whole family cannot easily escape with the money and move to another factory. Advancing a larger sum of money for an entire family unit might enable him to hold onto the workers for a longer period of time. Husband and wife usually also prefer to be employed in the same factory, partly because they can then negotiate higher *baki*, and partly because it allows the husband to chaperon his wife and to discourage male co-workers from teasing, joking or taking advantage of her on the shopfloor. Moreover, if they are working together in the same shift, husband and wife can work side by side and a man can teach his wife how to operate looms as well, so that their joint income can be enhanced.

The sample data also reveal that workers who entered the factories most recently, within the last five years, received the largest advances. An advance of more than Rs 10,000, for example, was rare before 1990 and did not occur in my sample, while nine out of 109 workers who were employed in 1996 received an advance of more than Rs 10,000. Usually factory owners avoid giving newly recruited workers *baki* at the moment of employment. They ask them to first work for a few weeks, so that they can judge the person's skills, regularity and commitment, before giving an advance and thus guaranteeing employment for a longer period of time. The duration of the trial period varies according to the extent to which the employer knows the worker or needs more information about him or her. It usually does not extend beyond three to six months. During this period, repeated negotiations take place between owner and worker with the former trying to keep the advance as low as possible and the latter trying to get the maximum.

In Kumarapalayam, wages are paid weekly on Fridays, when all the factories close for half a day and the *varam sandai* (weekly market) attracts hundreds of people who buy their provisions for the week ahead. Although a number of workers stated that they repaid Rs 20 to Rs 50 weekly to the owner against the advance, regular repayment is definitely not a common practice. Factory owners do not ask their labourers to return *baki*. On the contrary, they openly state that they prefer to keep their labour force indebted. Many factory owners put it like this: 'Generally owners are successful in binding labourers to them. They prefer that labourers do not return their advances so that they remain indebted to them, and thus bonded. Moreover, if a weaver repays the money he received, he might ask for an even larger amount of money, or simply leave the factory and look for work elsewhere.' Employers realise that when advances are being paid back on a regular basis, the whole practice of giving *baki* loses its value. By settling their debts, workers consolidate their bargaining power and can demand higher advances. They regain their freedom to sell their labour power to any employer who offers them a better wage and the highest *baki*. Being aware that the repayment of an advance undermines their power over their labour force, owners prefer a status quo in which labourers do not return the advances they received, but do not ask for more money either. As long as the loan has not been repaid, owners retain a hold on the workforce. Simultaneously they can refuse to provide their labourers with any extra money by referring to their existing debts. In principle, the size of the debt is not so important. As long as a labourer is indebted, he is also dependent and unable to leave his employer. However, as we will see, this dependency is far from absolute, and the extent to which each individual employer is able to bind his workers to him, remains the issue that is at stake.

Before turning to the ambivalent effects of *baki* giving, let me briefly address the question of the profitability for the employers of giving advances and the relationship between the level of advances and wages. In Kumarapalayam piece-rate wages are paid to the power-loom operators and a fixed weekly wage is paid to women and children who do winding and reeling. The piece-rate wages vary according to the type of product manufactured (towels, handkerchiefs, *lungis*, etc.), the quality of the product (domestic market, export quality, etc.), the kind of loom operated (plain looms, drawbox looms, jaquard looms, automatic looms, etc.), the type of business the employer is engaged in (own trade and business, or jobwork), and a number of other variables. The level of payment also depends on the experience of the worker, so that younger power-loom operators are paid slightly less than experienced workers until they produce cloth of the required quality. So there is wide variation in wages between different factories. Each owner usually has only one type of loom and produces one type of cloth, so that within the factory itself the level of wages is much more homogeneous. A crucial point, however, is that within a factory, wages do not vary according to the *baki* one receives. If an owner pays Rs 1.50 per metre of *lungi* produced, this is paid both to a weaver who has not taken any advance and to a weaver who has received *baki* of Rs 10,000. This was stressed by owners and confirmed by labourers. In a recent article, however, Kapadia describes how in the gem-cutting industry of Tiruchi district (Tamilnadu) 'the amount of *baki* taken was indeed a crucial factor – among others – in determining wages' (Kapadia 1995: 461). Those workers who had taken a large advance would be paid a lower daily wage than those who had received a lower advance or no advance at all. The lower daily wages paid to a worker who has received a higher advance would then reflect the interest which the employers extract on the money they advanced to their labourers. In such a case, as indicated by Kapadia, the *baki* contains a 'hidden profitability' for the owners.

In Kumarapalayam, however, no 'hidden profitability' can be found behind the growing practice of giving *baki* and binding labourers within the power-loom industry. Firstly, within each power-loom factory the level of wages is determined by a number of variables, as I indicated above, which are unrelated to the amount of *baki* taken, Within the same factory, employers do not lower the wages of those workers to whom they provide a larger *baki*. Obviously there is some variation between factories and an employer who pays relatively high wages is much less likely to pay substantial *baki* advances. Secondly, on a practical level, the lowering and increasing of wages according to the levels of *baki* taken would result in an endless process of adjustment and readjustment of wages – which, my informants stressed, would simply be unfeasible. Not only do most workers get different advances from the outset, which would result in different wages for all of them, but some gradually pay back their debts while others get more advances and accumulate their outstanding debt over time. Thirdly, neither the employers nor the labourers implied the notion of loan or interest when discussing the practice of *baki* giving. The *baki*, my informants argue, was an advance given at the moment of recruitment (and often increased during the period of employment) to attract a sufficient supply of labour and to maintain a stable labour force over time. Often, the labourers were simply unable to repay the debt and the employers were aware that the money advanced would never be returned to them. Finally, any theoretical model which sees *baki* as a loan and focuses on the issue of interest payment neglects the importance of the main sum which makes up the *baki* itself. In Kumarapalayam, these sums, which today amount to thousands of rupees, are far more important to employers than the possible interest they could gain from them. They are much more concerned about reclaiming the principal than gaining interest from it. When I asked whether his employees paid interest on the *baki* they got, one Gounder factory owner answered laughingly, 'I probably will never see the money (the *baki*) itself back, so how could I expect to get interest on it?' And indeed his concern – like that of most of the other factory owners – was for tens of thousands of rupees which he had laid out in advances. Although long-term profit calculation is undoubtedly present in the minds of the power-loom owners, in Kumarapalayam there is no *direct* and *immediate* financial profit in giving advances to workers. Attracting a permanent supply of labour, selecting particular types of workers and disciplining the labour force are the primary concerns of the factory owners who, in a highly competitive and fluid environment, try to attain this goal by attempting to bind their labourers through debt.

IV. GIVING AND ASKING FOR *BAKI*

I now turn to the factors which push an employer to give and a worker to ask for *baki*. The eagerness and willingness of factory owners to give *baki* to a newly employed worker depend on the extent to which they need labour. As one Gounder said: 'When we came to the power-looms, during the 1970s, we needed a lot of labour and at that time, we would have given any amount to the workers in order to get them to work in our factories.' Or, as Palanisamy, a successful Gounder power-loom owner whose father started in the business about thirty years ago, confirmed: 'The Gounders who recently entered the industry had merely sold the lands of their fathers and invested in looms without knowing what the profits would be. Whenever a labourer came to them and asked for an extra Rs 5 or Rs 10, they gave it without properly calculating. Just to keep their looms running.' In 1996–97, however, export demand had seriously fallen, pushing a number of owners back into the production of *lungis* for the local market. During this period, owners were far more reluctant to give large advances than during earlier periods of high demand.

Factory owners look for 'good', 'skilled' workers. Skilled workers are those who have been operating looms for several years and who have gained experience on different types of looms, and so know how to manufacture various kinds of cloth with a minimum of damage. A 'good' worker (*nalla veelaikarar*), however, is more than just a skilled worker. He is the one who works regularly, arrives on time and does not take unnecessary breaks. He does not make trouble in the workplace, looks after his looms properly and shows respect towards his fellow workers and his employer. He is also the kind of man who saves some money, looks after his family and does not spend lavishly on cigarettes, alcohol or the cinema. Most importantly, he is the kind of person that the employer knows has not just come to get an advance and run away with it. Although this is the employers' stereotype image of a decent labourer, it is an important marker of how they judge their workers, and presents a picture of whom they might be willing to give a larger *baki* to.

When a new labourer turns up for a job, the owner will carefully inquire about his skills, where he has been working before and for how long, why he left the previous factory, and whether he still has to repay an outstanding debt to his previous employer. Besides inquiring about these issues, the owner will also try to contact the candidate's previous employer in order to confirm the information given. 'Many labourers', the owners complain, 'either still have debts which they have escaped from and therefore do not mention, or have no debts whatsoever, but say they do in order to get a higher advance from their new employer. If they do not mention a debt with a previous owner', they continue, 'then that owner might one day find out where his labourer escaped to and come to us to reclaim it.' Therefore owners try to retrace the recent work history of a candidate labourer before employing him or her in their own factory. In retracing the worker's past, the local sangams or power-loom owners' associations form an essential medium through which information about workers is exchanged between owners. In Kumarapalayam, these sangams, as they are locally referred to, are simultaneously caste based and neighbourhood based. The Kongu Sangam, for example, is the power-loom association of the Kongu Vellalar Gounders. It is situated to the south of the town where most Gounders have recently developed their new power-loom factories. In that area, the power-loom owners are closely related to each other through caste, the neighbourhood and the sangam itself. They regularly inform each other about the background of the labourers in the neighbourhood, wages and advances given and other issues related to their business. The same solidarity between owners exists in the Mudaliyar Sangam and the Devangar Sangam in the centre of the town. If an owner who is a member of the Kongu Sangam wants to inquire about a labourer who previously worked for an owner in another part of the town or in a nearby town, he will contact the sangam of that particular area and try to get information about that specific worker. These power-loom associations form tight networks of contacts through which crucial information for the owners is circulated, and in which their common interests are well protected.

The practice of giving advances in Kumarapalayam is closely related to the entry of factory owners from the Gounder community into the power-loom sector from the 1970s. Nevertheless, from the late 1980s onwards, employers belonging to the traditional weaving castes of Devangars and Mudaliyars also felt themselves increasingly forced to give advances to secure a sufficient labour force. The custom soon spread throughout the town and the area as a whole. However, Devangar and

Mudaliyar owners in Kumarapalayam still try to recruit labour without giving *baki* and, when they give *baki*, they try to limit it to a small amount. The Mudaliyars, who have a long history as a caste of Tamil weavers, continue to run smaller factories (with four to six looms) and to rely as much as possible on kin and caste for labour recruitment. As handloom weavers and home-based producers, the Mudaliyars of the past formed a closed community whose members were fairly independent from the relationships of agricultural interdependency which existed between for example, the Gounder landowners and their agricultural labourers. Just as the Gounders transferred their earlier practices of labour recruitment from agriculture to the power-loom industry, the Mudaliyars continued their practices of family labour organisation. But though they continue to rely largely on family labour, they have been unable to escape the new practice of giving advances. This was apparent from the many instances where fathers gave *baki* to their own sons and daughters who worked on their looms, or to cousins or nephews whom they had recently employed. The Devangars who have traditionally been as much engaged in business as in weaving, also give ever-increasing advances to their labourers, whom they recruit from a wide variety of communities. The factories of both Gounders and Devangars are the largest. While their *patrai* consist on average of ten to twenty looms, it is not unusual to find manufacturers who own forty to sixty power-looms and employ over a hundred labourers spread across two or three workshops. They also employ, apart from workers belonging to their own community, a heterogeneous group of Mudaliyars, Vanniyars, Nadars and Udaiyars.

Baki, however, is not only *given*, it is also *asked for*. In Kumarapalayam, power-loom workers are aware that their wages are relatively high compared to those of agricultural workers and handloom weavers in Bhavani, and that there is a constant and high demand for their labour. As they admit themselves: 'those who want work can always find a job in the *patrai* of this town.' If a husband and wife both operate power-looms and have one or two children working as well, they might indeed earn up to Rs 1,500 per week. Therefore, they find it difficult to ask openly for higher wages from their employer, as they know that the latter would immediately tell them how generously he is paying them. Nevertheless, in the informal sector – to which this small-scale industry belongs – there are no unemployment benefits, no health allowances or any other social benefits. Illnesses, festivals and life-cycle rituals are recurrent occasions of heavy spending and constitute moments at which most families do not succeed in making ends meet. Although they might approach their closest kin for help and assistance, the latter are usually not able to provide anything more than their own labour power to assist them. Since banks do not hide their reluctance to disburse money for these occasions and private moneylenders are infamous for asking usurious interest rates, the last and often only resort left to the poor is the *patraikarar* (factory owner) for whom they are working. Getting an advance at the moment of recruitment or asking for some extra advance later on, which is then usually added to the total outstanding debt, forms the only way in which poor labourers can obtain credit at short notice and on an interest-free basis. Moreover, workers in the Kumarapalayam power-loom industry constitute a highly differentiated workforce, consisting not only of families who get a good income but also elderly people, divorced and widowed women and single women with dependent children for whom power-loom labour in shifts of twelve hours yields an income on which their households can barely survive. The majority of workers emphasised that they used the advance for *dinamum selavu* (daily expenses) or *vitu selavu* (household expenses) since their weekly income fell short of their total expenditure. Since labourers find it difficult to ask openly for a pay rise and have no union in Kumarapalayam they resort to a more indirect strategy: they demand an ever-increasing amount of *baki* from their employers.

V. BONDS FORGED, BONDS ESCAPED

The discourses surrounding the practice of giving *baki* vary. Factory owners in Kumarapalayam do not hide the fact that the practice of giving advances is part of an often desperate attempt to attract labourers and to force them to work in their factories. *Maistries* and labourers recognise that their employers are trying to bind them and they describe their work relations as a situation of *kottadimai* or bonded labour. They describe themselves as being like bonded agricultural labourers or permanent farm servants of the past (*pannaiyal*). This comparison is an interesting one, since power-loom labourers usually refer to *pannaiyal* as a bonded labour relationship which existed in agriculture *in the past*. Even the term *adimai* (slavery) is recalled to stress their entrapment in debts and relationships which they cannot always easily escape. The question remains, however, whether the terminology of bondedness which has been transferred from a past agricultural context also mirrors actual power-loom labour relations today. The *patraikarar* do not deny that labour relations today contain features of bonded labour and they are eager to refer to the nearby town of Pallipalayam, where power-loom owners have succeeded in 'capturing' a labour force. They have done this by providing their workers with enormous advances and with cheap houses surrounded by large compound walls and under constant surveillance. This allows owners to keep a firm eye on their workers and to prevent them from escaping the compound with thousands of rupees. Moreover, keeping the workers close at hand, on their own premises, allows owners to discipline their labour force much more easily. They can check whether a worker is really ill when he does not turn up at the factory, or force him to work when he is absent without any valid reason. It is reported that the Gounders of Pallipalayam do not refrain from using physical force to coerce their labourers to pay back an advance or to work regularly. In short, factory owners of Pallipalayam (especially the Gounders) have been rather successful in binding their labourers, not only by distributing large amounts of *baki*, but also by devising and implementing a variety of economic and non-economic forms of coercion. In Kumarapalayam, too, a number of Gounder employers have started to build houses for their workers in an attempt to tighten their control and to facilitate labour disciplining. Many employers prefer to have their workers living close to the factory and to have their own house attached to it so that they can control labourers more easily. When the owner lives away from the factory, workers on the nightshift might sleep at the looms or simply return home before the end of the shift. Owners who live next to the factory will often get up two or three times during the night to check whether the production process is running smoothly and without interruption.

The dominant discourse among the *patraikarar* of Kumarapalayam centres on the so-called 'labour problem', which they describe partly as the problem of labour shortage and partly as the difficulty they have in disciplining workers and maintaining a stable labour force over time. Owners take every opportunity to complain about the unruliness of the workforce and the extent to which they have lost their hold over labourers. Or, as a successful Gounder *patraikarar* expressed it: 'What has been our greediness in the beginning has become our problem today.' This 'labour problem', as discussed by employers, seems to have many facets.

First of all, employers emphasise the huge amounts of money they have distributed as advances and which they consider as 'lost' capital, since, as they claim, it does not yield them any interest and they cannot invest it in any other part of their business. They also see it as a 'rotating' form of capital because it is transferred from worker to worker without being returned to them as long as they are in business: as soon as a worker leaves the factory and returns the money, it has to be given to the next worker who takes his place. Giving advances thus entails a huge loss of capital which could otherwise have been invested in the industry itself. Secondly, the breakdown of allegedly amicable relationships between employers and workers seems to be another dark side of the labour problem. Owners contend that, in the past, there was usually a good understanding between them and their workers: they had an open relationship and labourers who worked in their factories used to be almost a part of their own families. Today, they argue, there is no longer any respect for owners, nor for the work itself. 'Now the workers', the owners unanimously state, 'only want to make a lot of money and to work as little as possible.' A more critical Gounder, however, added: 'It is only because of the selfishness of the Gounders, who kept increasing wages and advances for the sake of their own business, that labourers have become ever less satisfied with what they get.'

Behind such a romanticisation of the past and contempt for the labour morality and commitment of today, however, lies a much sharper division between the conceptualisation of the labour problem by Devangar and Mudaliyar employers on the one hand, and Gounder factory owners on the other hand. Devangar and Mudaliyar owners claim to have had a reasonable hold over their labour force until the day that 'those violent Gounders aggressively entered the industry and started to spoil relations with the workers by giving huge advances.' Devangars and Mudaliyars, though they carefully avoid reproaching them openly, look upon Gounders as 'intruders' in the industry and are far from happy with the consequences of Gounder strategies to gain a labour force. They stress that Gounder owners are rough and do not refrain from using harsh language and even physical force to make labourers return debts. 'The Gounders will go in group to the labourer's house, drag him outside and beat him up until he repays the debt! They are used to being rough, since they have been working with agricultural labourers before. 'The Gounders' reputation has some substance, and violence is still really deployed to intimidate and 'discipline' their workers. Devangar and Mudaliyar owners, who do not have such a long history of working with (agricultural) labourers, have the reputation of being milder in deal-ing with labour problems. Workers themselves explain how the Devangar owners are friendly and cordial with their labourers and willing to discuss a problem when it arises. Devangars and Mudaliyars sincerely regret that the smooth relationships have vanished and that today they also have become caught in the vicious circle of giving ever-increasing amounts of *baki*.

The labour problem, finally, has been conceived of by all employers alike as a 'challenge to the balance of powers'. While they started to give advances in order to ensure a sufficient and permanent labour force and, thus, to impose their dominance upon their labourers, employers now realise that it is precisely this practice of giving *baki* which has increasingly problematised and complicated their hold on the labour force and their ability to discipline their workers, with the result that they claim to be 'trapped' or 'bonded' themselves by the advances given. A Jangamar *maistry* work-ing for a Gounder owner explained it thus: 'In the past, the labourers were working seriously, but now, because of this *baki*, they started to take things easier. They know that the owner is bonded to them because they hold his money as an advance.' And an Udaiyar owner added: 'The situation now is such that owners fear dismissing a labourer since they first of all might not be able to find another one and, secondly, if they want to dismiss the labourer, the latter might simply say: "If you dismiss me now, I cannot pay back the advance!" In this way, the owners themselves are trapped by their own practice of giving *baki*.' Employers complain that, because of *baki*, labourers have become more powerful: 'Once they have received an advance they will keep asking for more money. And if we refuse to give it, they will simply walk out and look for work in another factory, and on top of that they may not even return the advance which they previously took from us.' Moreover, owners are keen to mention the cases in which labourers escaped the factory and the town taking huge amounts of *baki* with them. The employers seem to be most powerless and desperate when they are confronted with various forms of foot-dragging. Labourers come late and leave early, they remain absent for days in a row and deliberately decelerate the work or walk to the *kadai* (shop) for a coffee or a snack whenever they like. According to employers, labourers are no longer properly committed to their work because they know that the owner cannot dismiss them as long as they still have to repay an out-standing debt. In short, owners find themselves confronted with the crucial problem of labour disciplining; or, having been able to secure a labour force, they now face the new problem of actually getting their workers to work. To curtail and control various forms of foot-dragging, owners now place a watchman at the entrance to their factories or employ managers to supervise labourers on a continuous basis. These managers check whether operators stay near their looms, whether women are winding the thread and that coffee breaks do not exceed fifteen minutes. When a labourer does not turn up in the morning, the manager might go to his house and call him to the factory. In smaller factories, the owner himself might go to the houses of his workers to 'drag' them to the looms. And, as I observed on several occasions, the managers did not hesitate to abuse the workers, and to shout at them to come imme-diately and look after their looms. It is also in this context that many Devangars and Mudaliyars state that they now prefer to subcontract their factories since they feel no longer able to cope with what they commonly refer to as 'the labour problem'.

Labourers, for their part, are very much aware that employers are attempting to bind them through debt. Although they express a dislike for the practice, realising that they are 'being captured like slaves' and 'being kept in bondage', power-loom workers did not explicitly express 'a strong dislike of attachment and a corresponding preference for non-bonded casual employment' as the agricultural workers in Haryana seem to do (Brass 1990: 37). The reason why they are not completely opposed to the practice and continue to ask for higher *baki* themselves may lie in the fact that they have learned how to get the best out of the advances and that they have devised their own partly effective strategies to escape personal bondage. A first way in which some labourers try to escape bondage is by repaying debt. This is illustrated by the case of Raju, a Mudaliyar power-loom operator:

> Initially, I was working in Pallipalayam where I received a large advance of Rs 10,000. Week after week I was paying back the advance and two. years ago I had already re-turned Rs 5,000. At the same time I had saved Rs 6,000 and when I got into trouble with the owner, I repaid the remaining Rs 5,000 and we moved to Kumarapalayam. On arriving here, we did not get any advance, but for my daughter's puberty ceremony I got Rs 3,500 from my employer and when my wife had to go to hospital I also got money from him. Like this, the advances are a good thing for us. The owners do not deduct interest from our wages, but week after week I try to pay back the debt.

Raju decided to repay the debt to his first employer in order to regain his freedom and to be able to move to another factory. If he had not been repaying the advance gradually over time, it would have been difficult for him to quit the job when he got into difficulties with his employer. Raju, however, is rather a rare case since labourers are seldom able to save sufficient money to 'buy their freedom'. Even though his eagerness to repay the debt discloses his awareness of being bonded and even though

he was able to escape the bonds imposed by an individual owner, Raju's poverty did
not allow him to escape the reimposition of indebtedness by his next employer. Given
the fact that he was later confronted with large and unexpected expenses within his
household, Raju had to ask his new employer for a new advance, and was once again
bonded by debt. Even though labourers might be able to escape long-term personal
bonds with one employer, they need to reattach themselves to another owner in another factory. This reattachment and the resulting entrapment seems to be as much
the outcome of poverty and the workers' need to obtain some additional money, as of
practical choice (or cultural choice?) dictated by workers' knowledge that their boss
is less likely to fire them if they owe him Rs 10,000.

There are only very few workers who are capable of putting sufficient savings
aside to repay an entire debt. Most workers, therefore, have recourse to a second
way of escaping bondage, that is, by shifting to another factory and transferring the
debt with them. This will only be possible if the new employer is willing to repay
the outstanding debt to the previous owner. In that case, the debt will be transferred
along with the worker to the new factory, and the worker will be bonded to his
new employer. The employers are usually unhappy and highly suspicious about these
shifts, but often have no choice other than to accept them. It is in their interest to avoid
frequent shifts because their main aim is to maintain a stable labour force and, moreover, on recruiting a replacement worker, they will have to provide a new and possibly
higher advance than the one which exists. The owner who takes on the worker who
has shifted will be particularly suspicious because he will seldom be able to trace the
'real' reason why the worker left his previous employer. Sometimes an owner simply
wants to get rid of a bad worker and dismisses him, while the new employer engages
him without being aware of the actual motive for the shift.

Workers have different reasons for shifting to another factory. First, they might
leave when they have a disagreement with the owner. It can be that they simply
do not like the owner or that they had some quarrel and therefore no longer want
to work for him. Or, there might have been some arguments with fellow workers or
with the *maistry*. Most often the disagreement is based on demands for extra *baki*
or for a hike in wages. If a worker asks for a higher piece-rate wage or for an advance
and the owner refuses, he or she might leave and approach another employer who
is willing to provide the money. In these cases the worker usually simply leaves his
previous employer and the latter has to approach the worker himself and urge him
to repay the outstanding debt; or alternatively, he has to approach the worker's new
employer and ask him for the money. Workers also move with the intention of getting
an extra advance from another owner. In this case, they approach an owner and
ask for an advance which is much higher than their outstanding debt, so that they
can repay their debt and still have a substantial amount of money left. In this way,
however, they once again attach themselves to a new employer, increase their total
outstanding debt, and, thus, enhance their dependency. Another reason for shifting is
when a worker has found a factory where the wages are higher and/or the working

conditions better, so that he does not have to bother asking his present owner for a wage increase or *baki*, but just shifts to the other factory. Or, good workers might also be attracted by employers by being offered a higher wage or substantial *baki* in a factory elsewhere. A final solution is to escape with a significant amount of unpaid *baki* to another part of the town or to another town altogether. This option is chosen when the total debt becomes so large that the worker has lost all hope of repaying it or of ever being engaged by any other employer. When an owner starts to harass a worker because of the poor quality of his work or his inability to return a debt, he might also escape with the money in an ultimate attempt to free himself from the burden of daily harassment and criticism. Usually workers will then flee to another town in order to avoid being traced by their employer. Although this is usually an act of despair, some workers seem to use it as a strategy to make some extra money or simply to survive and escape perpetual bondage.

I want to emphasise that these moves are not merely a marginal event at the fringes of the employer–worker relationship. Rather they form recurrent incidents which, generally initiated by workers, fundamentally shape – and simultaneously undermine – the organisation of labour, and the formation and disciplining of a labour force. The individual strategies pursued by power-loom workers clearly reflect a rather economising instrumental view on their part. In my sample of 300 workers, only thirty-five (less than 12 per cent) had been working in their current place of employment for longer than five years. The vast majority of labourers had been employed in one factory for less than five years, while more than one-third of the total labour force had been working for less than one year for the same owner. This high labour turnover indicates the extent to which labourers are frequently shifting factories and provides compelling evidence that from the employers' point of view, the strategy of securing labour through advances has been close to a failure.

VI. POWER AND RESISTANCE: A BALANCING ACT

To summarise, it seems to me that the growing practice of giving and asking for *baki* can be understood as follows. Within the small-scale power-loom industry of Kumarapalayam, the factory owners have attempted to attract 'good', 'skilled' workers (including increasingly also female workers) and to secure a stable labour force in the face of a fragmented labour market and a steady expansion of the market demand for their products over the past thirty-odd years. The strategy used by the capitalist entrepreneurs to secure this aim consists of a generalised practice of giving advances to workers whom they employ. Chandavarkar has described a parallel but inverse strategy used by capitalist employers and industrialists in the Bombay textile factories during the first half of this century. Industries in Bombay faced conditions of highly volatile market demand and were liable to sharp and arbitrary trade fluctuations. This encouraged capital to pursue flexible production strategies that resulted in the gener- ation of a small force of permanent labourers and a large pool of casual workers from which labourers could be drawn whenever required (Chandavarkar 1994: 72–122). Highly volatile market conditions for Bombay textiles encouraged employers to adopt strategies which ensured the maximum dispensability of labour, while steady and expanding demand for Kumarapalayam products encouraged manufacturers to pursue strategies designed to ensure its stability.

However, this practice of giving advances created the problem of disciplining the labour force, that is, of actually getting workers to work. Why should they work when they realise all too well that their boss cannot easily dismiss them given the thousands of rupees which they still owe him? One logical response to this problem is a system of piece-rate payment. The factory owners only pay the loom operators for the amount of cloth actually produced, thus trying to keep them at their looms. In other words, there is a 'fit' between the piece-rate payment system and the advance system. Not all workers are paid piece-rate wages, however, and, moreover, piece-rate payment *per se* does not seem to be sufficient to discipline the labour force, given the endless complaints of owners that workers are becoming lazier by the day. Additional extra-economic mechanisms of control are needed, of which the threat of physical force is the most important one. As I have described, the Gounders know how to get their workers to work and, on firing them, how to get their money back. Other coercive strategies are implemented as well, such as enhanced surveillance of the workers and attempts to control their housing.

How, then, can this material be incorporated into discussions on what is usually referred to as relations of 'bonded labour' and 'debt bondage' in India (see Breman 1993, 1996; Harriss 1982; Kapadia 1995; Prakash 1990; Rudra 1994)? Tom Brass (1990) has questioned the validity of the revisionist and increasingly influential theorisation of labour attachment in Indian agriculture, which has been reconceptualising attached labour in positive terms. Within this revisionist paradigm it is argued that the subjects enter these relationships freely and that attached labour is a form of subsistence guarantee which provides its subjects with economic security. Coercion is played down and the aspect of reciprocity in the relationship is stressed (Brass 1990: 36–42). Against this, Brass contends that 'worker attachment is a form of unfreedom, the object of which is to discipline (not habituate), control, and cheapen labour-power by preventing or curtailing both its commodification and the growth of a specifically proletarian consciousness' (ibid.: 37). Brass points to the coercive and exploitative side of unfree labour and situates it at the heart of the class struggle between landholders and agricultural labourers. In a later article he critiques the assumption that capitalist modes of production are incompatible with unfree labour by arguing that 'capitalism is not only compatible with unfree labour but in certain situations actually prefers this to a free workforce' (Brass 1994: 255). Capitalism actually 'aim(s) to bring about deproletarianisation, in the sense of diminishing or eliminating altogether the freedom of wage labour' (ibid.: 259). Deproletarianisation, then, 'corresponds to workforce restructuring by means of introducing or reintroducing unfree relations, a process of class composition/recomposition which accompanies the struggle between capital and labour' (ibid.: 271).

While Brass has classified Breman among the 'revisionists', the latter's work offers a far more subtle and interesting treatment of the issue of labour bondage than Brass might have us believe. Breman (1993) re-examines bondage and dependency, and points out how agricultural relations have changed in south Gujarat over a period of thirty years. The aspects of patronage and protection have increasingly fallen away and the labourers, still bonded out of economic necessity, are left with a situation of open but less personalised and more contractual exploitation. Bondage, he recognises, can continue to exist along with capitalist modes of agricultural production, after having undergone functional change (ibid.: 297–316). Instances of bonded labour in the textile factories of Surat, in the brickworks of Bombay and in the fields of south Gujarat today, lead Breman to conclude that there is some form of 'capitalist labour bondage' in which even today debt continues to play a crucial role:

> [N]otwithstanding the fact that the supply of labour seems to exceed demand, employers use force and oppression as tools with which to increase their hold on the workers. Such forms of neo-bondage result from the weak market position of the subordinated party, but are effected in a social framework based on capitalism. In other words, unfree labour may well and actually does go together with the drive towards capitalist accumulation dominating the economy of both rural and urban India (Breman 1996: 168).

Within the fast-growing urban textile industry of Kumarapalayam, the custom of giving and asking for *baki* is not a slowly disappearing remainder of a past feudal mode of production, but is indeed alive in a modern capitalist environment. The question remains, however, whether 'labour bondage' and 'unfreedom' effectively represent the situation in which the Kumarapalayam workers are caught. Have wage labourers lost their freedom, as suggested by Brass or, put differently, do factory owners succeed in tying labourers in lasting bonds of dependency? I argue that employers, as individuals, do not. They attempt to bind their workers to them, but the latter largely succeed in challenging the owners' power by continuous attempts to escape its yoke altogether. Workers' active strategies include repaying debts, shifting factories and employers, escaping from town and various forms of foot-dragging and indiscipline often successfully undermining their employers' desperate search for a sufficient and permanent labour force. It is paradoxically their bondage to their employers which allows them to resist them. If the employers were not bonded themselves by the advances given, they would have no hesitation to hire and fire labourers at will, and thus to impose their power without constraints. However, having left or escaped one employer, workers enter new bonds of debt and dependency with another employer. This seems to be as much a matter of material necessity as of a conscious choice to consolidate their grip on the employers.

Let me end with a brief reference to the neighbouring town of Bhavani, where a handloom industry has been characterised by the absence of 'giving and asking for advances', but has been affected by a long history of labour militancy. Both aspects of labour relations are clearly two sides of the same coin. In Kumarapalayam *baki*, being so individualised and variable in nature, divides the workforce and gives the

employer a certain leverage over each individual employee which inhibits their combination. While employers have to cope with the 'labour problem' which they created
for themselves by paying *baki*, they have arguably managed to avoid another kind
of labour problem – the union militancy experienced by owners in Bhavani. In other
words, the fragmented labour force of Kumarapalayam is largely shaped by the
system of *baki* giving. The few existing unions in Kumarapalayam complain about
the entire lack of interest among the power-loom workers in combined action and
their attempts to unite workers have repeatedly failed in the face of the workers'
preference for individual strategies. In Bhavani, on the other hand, where no custom
of giving *baki* has been institutionalised so far, workers have been eager to consolidate their power in a weavers' union and to pursue their shared interests through
militant action.

In this paper I have attempted to describe the ongoing tensions inherent in the
relations between employers and workers within an urban textile industry, to document the dynamics and instability of labour relations, and to bring out the internal
contradictions. Labour relations are never static, but always engulfed in a continuous
process of formation and reproduction in which all participants attempt to impose
whatever power is available to them. I therefore suggest that these relations should be
studied as formative processes and that their analysis may well be better understood
by situating more carefully the static concepts of 'bondage' and 'unfreedom' in their
dynamic context.

REFERENCES

Baud, I. 1991. In all its manifestations: The impact of changing technology on the gender
    division of labour. *In* N. Banerjee, ed., *Indian women in a changing industrial scenario*,
    pp. 33–132. New Delhi: Sage.
Brass, T. 1990. Class struggle and the deproletarianisation of agricultural labour in Haryana.
    Journal of peasant studies 18, 1: 36–67.
———. 1994. Some observations on unfree labour, capitalist restructuring and deproletarian-
    isation. *International review of social history* 39, 2: 255–75.
Breman, J. 1993. *Beyond patronage and exploitation: Changing agrarian relations in south
    Gujarat*. Oxford: Oxford University Press.
———. 1996. *Footloose labour: Working in India's informal economy*. Cambridge: Cambridge
    University Press.
Cederlof, G. 1997. *Bonds lost: Subordination, conflict and mobilisation in rural south India
    c. 1900–1970*. New Delhi: Manohar Publishers.
Chandavarkar, R. 1994. *The origins of industrial capitalism in India: Business strategies and
    the working classes in Bombay, 1900–1940*. Cambridge: Cambridge University Press.
Harriss, J. 1982. *Capitalist and peasant farming: Agrarian structure and ideology in northern
    Tamil Nadu*. Oxford: Oxford University Press.
Kapadia, K. 1993. Mutuality and competition: Female landless labour and wage rates in
    Tamil Nadu. *Journal of peasant studies* 20, 2: 296–316.

Kapadia, K. 1995. The profitability of bonded labour: The gem-cutting industry in rural south India. *Journal of peasant studies* 22, 3: 446–83.

Prakash, G. 1990. *Bonded histories: Genealogies of labour servitude in colonial India.* Cambridge: Cambridge University Press.

Rudra, A. 1994. Unfree labour and Indian agriculture. *In* K. Basu, ed., *Agrarian questions*, pp. 75–91. New Delhi: Oxford University Press.

Vidyasagar, R. 1985. Debt bondage in south Arcot district: A case study of agricultural labourers and handloom weavers. *In* V. Patnaik and M. Dingwaney, eds., *Chains of servitude: Bondage and slavery in India*, pp. 127–61. Madras: Sangam Books.

Part 5:
The Industrial Working Class?

SECTIONAL INTRODUCTION

Plainly, conditions of employment and rates of remuneration vary considerably between different industries in the same national economy, between regular and temporary workers, even within the same factory, and according to skill and experience. Generally, gender, ethnicity, regional origin and other forms of 'ascriptive' identity also differentiate the industrial workforce. Is it then useful to think of it as a single unitary 'working class'? To what extent can they all be said to share the same situation because of the way they are structurally located? Are they a class 'in itself'? If so, are they *conscious* of their common interests; are they, that is, a class 'for itself'? How does this consciousness manifest itself in the political realm? These are the questions that the readings in Part 5 are intended to raise; questions that have been most sharply posed by the Marxian tradition which, following its own teleological vision and in its classic formulation, predicted that the industrial proletariat would spearhead the revolutionary overthrow of the capitalist system. It is therefore fitting that our first selection is from Marx himself.[1]

Section 1 of *The Communist Manifesto* is a brilliantly succinct, accessible and powerful polemic that asserts the proposition that, while 'the history of all hitherto existing society is the history of class struggles', 'bourgeois society' has enormously simplified class antagonisms. 'Society as a whole is more and more splitting up into two great hostile camps directly facing each other: Bourgeois and Proletariat'. Though it has 'accomplished wonders far surpassing Egyptian pyramids, Roman aqueducts and Gothic cathedrals', and transformed the structure of society and revolutionized its values, the modern bourgeois is 'like the sorcerer, who is no longer able to control the powers of the nether world which he has called up by his spells', and is doomed to self-destruction. True, capital may in the short term manage to co-opt labour in its struggle against old class enemies, in its attempt to protect national industry and as a result of competition between workers, and may be able to turn the 'dangerous class', the 'social scum', into 'a bribed tool of reactionary intrigue'. But the inexorable historical logic is towards a homogenization of the working class, and a collision between it and the bourgeoisie. Unlike past oppressors, who guaranteed minimum conditions of existence to the oppressed, the bourgeoisie is 'incompetent to assure an existence to its slave', it creates 'masses of labourers crowded into factories, organized like soldiers', and so produces its own 'grave diggers'.

The fragment from Chandavarkar's *The origins of industrial capitalism in India* (1994) that follows pointedly calls this 'natural' propensity of the proletariat to class action into question. One issue it raises has to do with the dangers of writing a history (or sociology) of Indian (or Indonesian or Bolivian) industrialization that, on the one hand, represents it as a mere recapitulation of the historical experience of the West, or on the other hand emphasises its particularistic character. Either way, that history (or sociology) has little to offer a more general theory of industrial transformation. For present purposes, however, the more important issues have to do with class-consciousness and culture. During the period of which Chandavarkar writes (1900–1940), Bombay's biggest industry was its textile mills. Due to the way in which these were capitalized, and the strategies of their owners, the mills relied on cheap labour (much of it of rural origins) that could be hired and fired according to the current market demand for their product. The workers' apparent lack of 'commitment' to industrial employment and high rates of labour turnover were not therefore, as many earlier authors had supposed, a consequence of their atavistic commitment to their villages. It was in reality 'practical reason' not 'culture' that explained their behaviour. It was their poor wages and the chronic lack of security in the mills that forced them to rely on village, caste and kinship networks of support during hard times. Far from creating a united working class, industrialization in India has had the effect of reinforcing 'primordial' loyalties, strengthening the pre-industrial characteristics of the workforce and heightening its sectionalism. And elsewhere in the book, Chandavarkar shows how these divisions within it were exacerbated by the way in which labour was recruited; by the way in which workers were forced to compete with each other to get a job at all and then compete with each other for machines and raw materials. The real question, then, is 'not so much why the working classes have failed to realise the expectations theoretically imputed to them (by Marxists) but how and why at times they came together at all', as the history of the Bombay labour movement shows that they did. Between the two World Wars, Bombay experienced eight general strikes, each of which lasted at least a month. To explain how that came about the political context is crucial: the accumulated experience of previous strikes, state repression and the role of the communist leadership.

It was not only anthropological assumptions about the determining force of 'culture' that Chandavarkar was reacting against, but also those of other historians like Chakrabarty (1989: 218) who had concluded his study of migrant workers in the Bengal jute mills by observing that: 'In the jute worker's mind itself, the incipient awareness of belonging to a class remained a prisoner of his pre-capitalist culture; the class identity of the worker could never be distilled out of the pre-capitalist identities that arise from the relationships he had been born into.' Of these, caste, religious community and regional ethnicity are the most salient; and earlier (see Part 2, Introduction) we instanced Engleshoven's (1999) striking discussion of the way in which caste blunts class antagonism.

Such 'primordial' identities aside, the other major division in the Indian industrial labour force is between, on the one hand, the relatively privileged workforce employed by fairly large-scale, bureaucratically organized, capital intensive, 'organized' (formal) sector industry that is subject to state factory legislation covering minimum wages, working conditions, union recognition and the like, and, on the other hand, the much more down-trodden workforce employed in smaller-scale, informal, 'unorganized' sector units. Within the former, there is also a crucial distinction (manifest in terms of pay, security and working conditions) between regular company employees and contract labour. The issue is whether these different types of workers are realistically regarded as members of the same class. In the first of two monographs that addressed it, Holmström (1976) seemed to suggest not, and stressed the 'citadel' mentality of organized sector workers that divided them from others. In the second, however, he offered a revisionist account that proposed a less dualistic, and a more graduated, model (Holmström 1984). Is there an Indian working class? Have the labour aristocracy of the organized sector grown fat at the expense of unorganized sector workers? And do these class fractions think of themselves as having opposing interests? Holmström's answer was a qualified 'yes' to the first of these questions; and a clear 'no' to the second and third. Both the 'yes' and the 'no' were essentially explained by the kinship and neighbourhood ties that unite the two kinds of worker. Parry's ethnography (2009 and n.d.), however, suggests a rather less solidary picture, in which such ties have been progressively attenuated. As commonly as kin, steel plant workers are the employers of unorganized sector labour in the small-scale moonlighting enterprises they run; and the former have a clear sense of their difference from (and a rather more inchoate sense of the interests that oppose them to) those they refer to as 'the labour class'. Further, trade union politics reflect, and even (sometimes violently) exacerbate, these structural divisions within the industrial workforce.

Though the lines are differently drawn, divisions within China's industrial workforce seem no less entrenched. Writing of the period between the coming to power of the Communists and the mid-1980s, Walder (1986) describes a 'dual economy' made up of large-scale modern state industries on the one hand, and on the other, cooperative and smaller-scale government units formed in the 1950s by banding together previously privately owned workshops. In terms of pay, security and, above all, perks, a vast gulf separated the two workforces, and there was little mobility between them. At least in the case of 'primary sector' state enterprises, almost all welfare (including health care, housing and education) was administered by the factory, which was also the major channel for the distribution of consumption goods. That produced, Walder shows, a distinctive type of industrial authority system and also a major differentiation within the factory between party cadres and ordinary workers. For present-day China, Pun (2005) has emphasized the division between *gongren*, the old 'proletariat' who have secure jobs in large state-run industries and rights of permanent urban residence, and the *dagonmzei* and *dagonmei*, the 'boys' and 'younger sisters' who 'work for a boss' in the Special Economic Zones, and who are overwhelmingly flexible rural labour with only temporary (and always precarious) rights of urban residence.

In the case of both China and India (see also the case of the Mombasa docks referred to in the Introduction to Part 1 [Cooper 1992]), it is essentially state legislation and policies that have created these deep divisions within the industrial workforce. They may, however, arise without its direct intervention (witness the case of Japan referred to in the Introduction to Part 3). The chapter by Roberts reprinted below is a particularly interesting example in that it is drawn from his autobiographical account of a childhood spent during the first quarter of the twentieth century in the 'classic' Salford slum that Engels had written about in *The condition of the working class in England* (1987 [1845]). They are very different pictures. What Roberts portrays is a world in which 'the working class' was 'obsessed' with distinctions of status and material standing between its own members; where economic disparities were in fact considerable; where social and economic inequalities were regarded as 'the law of nature'; and where most of the inhabitants were completely apolitical. As described by Roberts, the Salford 'working class' showed no tendency towards the homogenization predicted by Marx, nor any inclination to embrace the historical destiny he assigned it.

Nor, again, have more recent ethnographies of labour activism in the West suggested much potential for united class action. Of Chicago union locals, for example, Durrenberger (2002:103) writes that 'under normal working conditions there is no space for working class solidarity'. Stewards and workers are swamped by the problems of everyday life on the shop floor, made up of grievances, fear of persecution and wearing physical labour, and are constrained by narrow and pragmatic world views. Beynon (1973) concluded his classic account of Ford's Halewood plant by identifying the narrow plant activism and focus on wage-bargaining, and the lack of any wider political vision, as what made the shop steward's movement ultimately ineffectual. Similarly Hayter and Harvey (1993) identified the 'militant particularism' of the workforce as responsible for the failure of the 1984 Rover workers' campaign against the closure of their Cowley plant. Addressing the problem of widening workers' horizons beyond the shop floor, however, Fantasia (1989) manages a more optimistic tone. Mollona's ethnography (2009) draws a revealing contrast between the dismal failure of the conventional union to protect the interests of workers in a modern, technologically sophisticated 'mini-mill', and the successful strategies of class resistance adopted by the non-unionized workforce in a smaller, technologically obsolete, engineering workshop; strategies based on neighbourhood and local informal networks, and the re-appropriation of non-work spaces.

The short extract from Nash's landmark ethnography on Bolivian tin-miners, reprinted as chapter 23, reinforces the point that it may be necessary to look beyond the workplace for the springs of class action and consciousness. As illustrated by the case of India, the pre-industrial culture and ascriptive identities of workers are often invoked to explain why it does not emerge. Nash turns this on its head. The central problem that her monograph addresses is the apparent contradiction between the Marxian theory of alienation and the theory that the industrial proletariat must arrive at revolutionary consciousness. If workers are alienated *from each other*, how is that possible? Nash's answer is that although Bolivian miners are alienated from the means of production, from the work process and from the products of their labour, they are not estranged from one another. The reason for that is their common commitment to a set of pre-Hispanic symbols and rituals that enable them to recreate their solidarity against management. These rituals mainly revolve around offerings (*cha'alla*) to *Pachamama*, now transmogrified into the Virgin Mary, who controls the fertility of the land; and to *Tio* (also known by the pre-Hispanic terms, *Supay* and *Huari*), now transmogrified into the Christian devil, who is the lord of the mountain and its mineral wealth. 'Culture', Nash claims, is what ultimately underpins class-consciousness. It might be noted, however, that even from the brief passage reproduced here it is clear that the *Cholo* culture of the miners, an unstable mix of the cultures of the dominant Spanish speakers and of Indian communities, is deeply riven by status distinctions based on whether one is more or less 'Hispanicized' or more or less 'Indian'. It seems more divisive than a bald statement of Nash's central argument would suggest, and she has to introduce the rider that a lid is kept on differentiation by the homogeneous housing conditions of the community and by the flagging economy of the mines. Without these material constraints, one wonders whether the capacity of ritual to recreate solidarity would seem quite so great.

The final reading is taken from Turner's monograph, *Japanese Workers in Protest* (1995), which documents and compares the labour struggles of two 'small sector' Japanese companies that declared bankruptcy. Both were taken over and run by their workers, who pursued campaigns against their former owners for unfair labour practices, unpaid wages, severance pay and, in one case, for rights to the brand name. In the chapter reproduced here, Turner describes the struggle of the Unikon workforce, a company producing camera equipment. It was in many ways a highly successful example of union mobilization, that attracted a good deal of support and solidarity from other unions, and from workers in other enterprises. What Turner also brings out with considerable sensitivity are the motivations of the rank-and-file workers: the contingency of their initial decisions to support a union takeover; the strong loyalties they developed with their work mates; and their sense of absolute outrage at the way they had been treated by their former employers. She convincingly shows how rank-and-file workers 'learn to protest' through praxis, and how the abstractions of class solidarity are turned into concrete class action. It is tempting to end this volume on that note, but it would not be quite honest. The depressing sequel, recorded later in Turner's account, was that although the Unikon workers eventually won, and the union leaders were able to restart the factory under their own direction, the terms of the deal required them to sell the existing factory premises and relocate outside Tokyo. Nearly all the rank-and-file workers were forced to leave, or were actually eased out of the jobs that they had spent the last two and a half years fighting to protect. All of the new labour taken on consisted of non-unionized part-timers and much of the company's production was 'put out' to off-shore operations in Taiwan and south China to save on labour costs. The former union President who had led the strike and was now the company chairman was finally forced to bow to the imperatives of the capitalist market place.

If what much of the literature seems to document is the defeat of conventional union activism, some put their faith in new community forms, such as the *Kilusang Mayo Uno* in the Philippines (Scipes 1992) and the Brazilian *Central Workers Union* (Ramalho and Santana 2001), that have emerged in the South, and in the North-South activist network (Anner 2003). These aim to open up new forms of radical politics that move away from class-based and factory-bound notions of labour and activism, and to articulate new democratic political identities across society. Of their long-term impact it is still too early to judge.

NOTES

1. Although *The Communist Manifesto* originally appeared under the names of both Marx and Engels, Engels subsequently made it clear that it was 'essentially Marx's work'.

RECOMMENDED FURTHER READING

Beynon, Huw. 1973. *Working for Ford*, London: Penguin Books.

Durrenberger, Paul. 2002. 'Structure, Thought and Action: Stewards in Chicago union locals', *American Anthropologist*, 104(1): 93–105.

Engelshoven, M. 1999. 'Diamonds and Patels: a report on the diamond industry of Surat', *Contributions to Indian Sociology*, 33(1-2): 353–77.

Holmström, Mark. 1984. *Industry and Inequality: The social anthropology of Indian labour*, Cambridge: Cambridge University Press.

Mollona, Massimiliano. 2009. *Made in Sheffield. An ethnography of industrial work and politics*, Oxford: Berghahn.

Parry, Jonathan. 2009. 'Sociological Marxism in Central India: Polanyi, Gramsci and the case of the unions'. In C. Hann and K. Hart (eds), *Market and Society: 'The great transformation' today*, pp. 175–202, Cambridge: Cambridge University Press.

Walder, Andrew. 1986. *Communist Neo-Traditionalism: Work and authority in Chinese industry*, Berkeley, CA: University of California Press.

OTHER WORKS CITED

Anner, Mark. 2003. 'Industrial Structure, The State, and Ideology: Shaping labor transnationalism in the Brazilian auto industry', *Social Science History*, 27(4): 603–34.

Chakrabarty, D. 1989. *Rethinking Working Class History: Bengal 1890–1940*, Princeton, NJ: Princeton University Press.

Chandavarkar, R. 1994. *The Origins of Industrial Capitalism in India: Business Strategies and the Working Classes in Bombay, 1900–1940*, Cambridge: Cambridge University Press.

Cooper, F. 1992. Colonizing Time: Work rhythms and labour conflict in colonial Mombasa. In N. Dirks (ed.), *Colonialism and Culture*, Ann Arbor, MI: University of Michigan Press.

Engels, Friedrich. 1987 [1845]. *The Condition of the Working Class in England*, London: Penguin Books.

Fantasia, Rick. (1989) *Cultures of Solidarity: Consciousness, Action, and Contemporary American Workers*, Berkeley, CA: University of California Press.

Hayter, Teresa and David Harvey. 1993. *The Factory and the City: the story of the Cowley Automobile Workers in Oxford*. London: Mansell.

Holmström, Mark. 1976. *South Indian Factory Workers: Their life and their world*, Cambridge: Cambridge University Press.

Parry, Jonathan. n.d. 'The Embourgeoisement of a "Proletarian Vanguard": Steel workers in Central India'. (Unpublished m.s.).

Pun, Nagai. 2005. *Made in China: Women factory workers in a global workplace*, Durham, NC: Duke University Press.

Ramalho, José Ricardo and Santana, Marco Aurelio. (2001). 'Tradição Sindical e as mudanças econômicas dos anos de 1990'. In J.R Ramalho and M. A. Santana (eds), *Trabalho e Tradição Sindical no Rio de Janeiro. A Trajectória dos metallurgicos*, Rio de Janeiro: De Paulo Editora.

Scipes, Kim. (1992). 'Understanding the New Labour Movement in the Third World: The emergence of social movement unionism', *Critical Sociology*, 19(2): 81–102.

Turner, Christena. 1995. *Japanese Workers in Protest: An ethnography of consciousness and experience*, Berkeley, CA: University of California Press.

CHAPTER TWENTY

Bourgeois and Proletarians[1]

KARL MARX

The history of all hitherto existing society[2] is the history of class struggles.

Freeman and slave, patrician and plebeian, lord and serf, guild-master[3] and journeyman, in a word, oppressor and oppressed, stood in constant opposition to one another, carried on an uninterrupted, now hidden, now open fight, a fight that each time ended, either in a revolutionary reconstitution of society at large, or in the common ruin of the contending classes.

In the earlier epochs of history, we find almost everywhere a complicated arrangement of society into various orders, a manifold gradation of social rank. In ancient Rome we have patricians, knights, plebeians, slaves; in the Middle Ages, feudal lords, vassals, guild-masters, journeymen, apprentices, serfs; in almost all of these classes, again, subordinate gradations.

The modern bourgeois society that has sprouted from the ruins of feudal society has not done away with class antagonisms. It has but established new classes, new conditions of oppression, new forms of struggle in place of the old ones.

Our epoch, the epoch of the bourgeoisie, possesses, however, this distinct feature: it has simplified class antagonisms. Society as a whole is more and more splitting up into two great hostile camps, into two great classes directly facing each other – Bourgeoisie and Proletariat.

From the serfs of the Middle Ages sprang the chartered burghers of the earliest towns. From these burgesses the first elements of the bourgeoisie were developed.

The discovery of America, the rounding of the Cape, opened up fresh ground for the rising bourgeoisie. The East-Indian and Chinese markets, the colonisation of America, trade with the colonies, the increase in the means of exchange and in commodities generally, gave to commerce, to navigation, to industry, an impulse never before known, and thereby, to the revolutionary element in the tottering feudal society, a rapid development.

The feudal system of industry, in which industrial production was monopolised by closed guilds, now no longer sufficed for the growing wants of the new markets.

The manufacturing system took its place. The guild-masters were pushed on one side by the manufacturing middle class; division of labour between the different corporate guilds vanished in the face of division of labour in each single workshop.

Meantime the markets kept ever growing, the demand ever rising. Even manufacturer no longer sufficed. Thereupon, steam and machinery revolutionised industrial production. The place of manufacture was taken by the giant, Modern Industry; the place of the industrial middle class by industrial millionaires, the leaders of the whole industrial armies, the modern bourgeois.

Modern industry has established the world market, for which the discovery of America paved the way. This market has given an immense development to commerce, to navigation, to communication by land. This development has, in its turn, reacted on the extension of industry; and in proportion as industry, commerce, navigation, railways extended, in the same proportion the bourgeoisie developed, increased its capital, and pushed into the background every class handed down from the Middle Ages.

We see, therefore, how the modern bourgeoisie is itself the product of a long course of development, of a series of revolutions in the modes of production and of exchange.

Each step in the development of the bourgeoisie was accompanied by a corresponding political advance of that class. An oppressed class under the sway of the feudal nobility, an armed and self-governing association in the medieval commune[4]: here independent urban republic (as in Italy and Germany); there taxable "third estate" of the monarchy (as in France); afterwards, in the period of manufacturing proper, serving either the semi-feudal or the absolute monarchy as a counterpoise against the nobility, and, in fact, cornerstone of the great monarchies in general, the bourgeoisie has at last, since the establishment of Modern Industry and of the world market, conquered for itself, in the modern representative State, exclusive political sway. The executive of the modern state is but a committee for managing the common affairs of the whole bourgeoisie.

The bourgeoisie, historically, has played a most revolutionary part.

The bourgeoisie, wherever it has got the upper hand, has put an end to all feudal, patriarchal, idyllic relations. It has pitilessly torn asunder the motley feudal ties that bound man to his "natural superiors", and has left remaining no other nexus between man and man than naked self-interest, than callous "cash payment". It has drowned the most heavenly ecstasies of religious fervour, of chivalrous enthusiasm, of philistine sentimentalism, in the icy water of egotistical calculation. It has resolved personal worth into exchange value, and in place of the numberless indefeasible chartered freedoms, has set up that single, unconscionable freedom – Free Trade. In one word, for exploitation, veiled by religious and political illusions, it has substituted naked, shameless, direct, brutal exploitation.

The bourgeoisie has stripped of its halo every occupation hitherto honoured and looked up to with reverent awe. It has converted the physician, the lawyer, the priest, the poet, the man of science, into its paid wage labourers.

The bourgeoisie has torn away from the family its sentimental veil, and has reduced the family relation to a mere money relation.

The bourgeoisie has disclosed how it came to pass that the brutal display of vigour in the Middle Ages, which reactionaries so much admire, found its fitting complement in the most slothful indolence. It has been the first to show what man's activity can bring about. It has accomplished wonders far surpassing Egyptian pyramids, Roman aqueducts, and Gothic cathedrals; it has conducted expeditions that put in the shade all former Exoduses of nations and crusades.

The bourgeoisie cannot exist without constantly revolutionising the instruments of production, and thereby the relations of production, and with them the whole relations of society. Conservation of the old modes of production in unaltered form, was, on the contrary, the first condition of existence for all earlier industrial classes. Constant revolutionising of production, uninterrupted disturbance of all social conditions, everlasting uncertainty and agitation distinguish the bourgeois epoch from all earlier ones. All fixed, fast-frozen relations, with their train of ancient and venerable prejudices and opinions, are swept away, all new-formed ones become antiquated before they can ossify. All that is solid melts into air, all that is holy is profaned, and man is at last compelled to face with sober senses his real conditions of life, and his relations with his kind.

The need of a constantly expanding market for its products chases the bourgeosie over the entire surface of the globe. It must nestle everywhere, settle everywhere, establish connexions everywhere.

The bourgeoisie has through its exploitation of the world market given a cosmopolitan character to production and consumption in every country. To the great chagrin of Reactionists, it has drawn from under the feet of industry the national ground on which it stood. All old-established national industries have been destroyed or are daily being destroyed. They are dislodged by new industries, whose introduction becomes a life and death question for all civilised nations, by industries that no longer work up indigenous raw material, but raw material drawn from the remotest zones; industries whose products are consumed, not only at home, but in every quarter of the globe. In place of the old wants, satisfied by the production of the country, we find new wants, requiring for their satisfaction the products of distant lands and climes. In place of the old local and national seclusion and self-sufficiency, we have intercourse in every direction, universal inter-dependence of nations. And as in material, so also in intellectual production. The intellectual creations of individual nations become common property. National one-sidedness and narrow-mindedness become more and more impossible, and from the numerous national and local literatures, there arises a world literature.

The bourgeoisie, by the rapid improvement of all instruments of production, by the immensely facilitated means of communication, draws all, even the most barbarian, nations into civilisation. The cheap prices of commodities are the heavy artillery with which it batters down all Chinese walls, with which it forces the barbarians' intensely obstinate hatred of foreigners to capitulate. It compels all nations, on pain of extinction, to adopt the bourgeois mode of production; it compels them to introduce what it calls civilisation into their midst, i.e., to become bourgeois themselves. In one word, it creates a world after its own image.

The bourgeoisie has subjected the country to the rule of the towns. It has created enormous cities, has greatly increased the urban population as compared with the rural, and has thus rescued a considerable part of the population from the idiocy of rural life. Just as it has made the country dependent on the towns, so it has made barbarian and semi-barbarian countries dependent on the civilised ones, nations of peasants on nations of bourgeois, the East on the West.

The bourgeoisie keeps more and more doing away with the scattered state of the population, of the means of production, and of property. It has agglomerated population, centralised the means of production, and has concentrated property in a few hands. The necessary consequence of this was political centralisation. Independent, or but loosely connected provinces, with separate interests, laws, governments, and systems of taxation, became lumped together into one nation, with one government, one code of laws, one national class-interest, one frontier, and one customs-tariff.

The bourgeoisie, during its rule of scarce one hundred years, has created more massive and more colossal productive forces than have all preceding generations together. Subjection of Nature's forces to man, machinery, application of chemistry to industry and agriculture, steam-navigation, railways, electric telegraphs, clearing of whole continents for cultivation, canalisation of rivers, whole populations conjured out of the ground – what earlier century had even a presentiment that such productive forces slumbered in the lap of social labour?

We see then: the means of production and of exchange, on whose foundation the bourgeoisie built itself up, were generated in feudal society. At a certain stage in the development of these means of production and of exchange, the conditions under which feudal society produced and exchanged, the feudal organisation of agriculture and manufacturing industry, in one word, the feudal relations of property became no longer compatible with the already developed productive forces; they became so many fetters. They had to be burst asunder; they were burst asunder.

Into their place stepped free competition, accompanied by a social and political constitution adapted in it, and the economic and political sway of the bourgeois class.

A similar movement is going on before our own eyes. Modern bourgeois society, with its relations of production, of exchange and of property, a society that has conjured up such gigantic means of production and of exchange, is like the sorcerer who is no longer able to control the powers of the nether world whom he has called up by his spells. For many a decade past the history of industry and commerce is but the history of the revolt of modern productive forces against modern conditions of production, against the property relations that are the conditions for the existence of the bourgeois and of its rule. It is enough to mention the commercial crises that by their periodical return put the existence of the entire bourgeois society on its trial, each time more threateningly. In these crises, a great part not only of the existing products, but also of the previously created productive forces, are periodically destroyed. In these crises, there breaks out an epidemic that, in all earlier epochs, would have seemed an absurdity – the epidemic of over-production. Society suddenly finds itself put back into a state of momentary barbarism; it appears as if a famine, a universal war of devastation, had cut off the supply of every means of subsistence; industry and commerce seem to be destroyed; and why? Because there is too much civilisation, too much means of subsistence, too much industry, too much commerce. The productive forces at the disposal of society no longer tend to further the development of the conditions of bourgeois property; on the contrary, they have become too powerful for these conditions, by which they are fettered, and so soon as they overcome these fetters, they bring disorder into the whole of bourgeois society, endanger the existence of bourgeois property. The conditions of bourgeois society are too narrow to comprise the wealth created by them. And how does the bourgeoisie get over these crises? On the one hand by enforced destruction of a mass of productive forces; on the other, by the conquest of new markets, and by the more thorough exploitation of the old ones. That is to say, by paving the way for more extensive and more destructive crises, and by diminishing the means whereby crises are prevented.

The weapons with which the bourgeoisie felled feudalism to the ground are now turned against the bourgeoisie itself.

But not only has the bourgeoisie forged the weapons that bring death to itself; it has also called into existence the men who are to wield those weapons – the modern working class – the proletarians.

In proportion as the bourgeoisie, i.e., capital, is developed, in the same proportion is the proletariat, the modern working class, developed – a class of labourers, who live only so long as they find work, and who find work only so long as their labour increases capital. These labourers, who must sell themselves piecemeal, are a commodity, like every other article of commerce, and are consequently exposed to all the vicissitudes of competition, to all the fluctuations of the market.

Owing to the extensive use of machinery, and to the division of labour, the work of the proletarians has lost all individual character, and, consequently, all charm for the workman. He becomes an appendage of the machine, and it is only the most simple, most monotonous, and most easily acquired knack, that is required of him. Hence, the cost of production of a workman is restricted, almost entirely, to the means of subsistence that he requires for maintenance, and for the propagation of his race. But the price of a commodity, and therefore also of labour, is equal to its cost of production. In proportion, therefore, as the repulsiveness of the work increases, the wage decreases. Nay more, in proportion as the use of machinery and division of labour increases, in the same proportion the burden of toil also increases, whether by prolongation of the working hours, by the increase of the work exacted in a given time or by increased speed of machinery, etc. ·

Modern Industry has converted the little workshop of the patriarchal master into the great factory of the industrial capitalist. Masses of labourers, crowded into the factory, are organised like soldiers. As privates of the industrial army they are placed under the command of a perfect hierarchy of officers and sergeants. Not only are they slaves of the bourgeois class, and of the bourgeois State; they are daily and hourly enslaved by the machine, by the overlooker, and, above all, by the individual bourgeois manufacturer himself. The more openly this despotism proclaims gain to be its end and aim, the more petty, the more hateful and the more embittering it is.

The less the skill and exertion of strength implied in manual labour, in other words, the more modern industry becomes developed, the more is the labour of men superseded by that of women. Differences of age and sex have no longer any distinctive social validity for the working class. All are instruments of labour, more or less expensive to use, according to their age and sex.

No sooner is the exploitation of the labourer by the manufacturer, so far, at an end, that he receives his wages in cash, than he is set upon by the other portions of the bourgeoisie, the landlord, the shopkeeper, the pawnbroker, etc.

The lower strata of the middle class – the small tradespeople, shopkeepers, and retired tradesmen generally, the handicraftsmen and peasants – all these sink gradually into the proletariat, partly because their diminutive capital does not suffice for the scale on which Modern Industry is carried on, and is swamped in the competition with the large capitalists, partly because their specialised skill is rendered worthless by new methods of production. Thus the proletariat is recruited from all classes of the population.

The proletariat goes through various stages of development. With its birth begins its struggle with the bourgeoisie. At first the contest is carried on by individual labourers, then by the workpeople of a factory, then by the operative of one trade, in one locality, against the individual bourgeois who directly exploits them. They direct their attacks not against the bourgeois conditions of production, but against the instruments of production themselves; they destroy imported wares that compete with their labour, they smash to pieces machinery, they set factories ablaze, they seek to restore by force the vanished status of the workman of the Middle Ages.

At this stage, the labourers still form an incoherent mass scattered over the whole country, and broken up by their mutual competition. If anywhere they unite to form more compact bodies, this is not yet the consequence of their own active union, but of the union of the bourgeoisie, which class, in order to attain its own political ends, is compelled to set the whole proletariat in motion, and is moreover yet, for a time, able to do so. At this stage, therefore, the proletarians do not fight their enemies, but the enemies of their enemies, the remnants of absolute monarchy, the landowners, the non-industrial bourgeois, the petty bourgeois. Thus, the whole historical movement is concentrated in the hands of the bourgeoisie; every victory so obtained is a victory for the bourgeoisie.

But with the development of industry, the proletariat not only increases in number; it becomes concentrated in greater masses, its strength grows, and it feels that strength more. The various interests and conditions of life within the ranks of the proletariat are more and more equalised, in proportion as machinery obliterates all distinctions of labour, and nearly everywhere reduces wages to the same low level. The growing competition among the bourgeois, and the resulting commercial crises, make the wages of the workers ever more fluctuating. The increasing improvement of machinery, ever more rapidly developing, makes their livelihood more and more precarious; the collisions between individual workmen and individual bourgeois take more and more the character of collisions between two classes. Thereupon, the workers begin to form combinations (Trades' Unions) against the bourgeois; they club together in order to keep up the rate of wages; they found permanent associations in order to make provision beforehand for these occasional revolts. Here and there, the contest breaks out into riots.

Now and then the workers are victorious, but only for a time. The real fruit of their battles lies, not in the immediate result, but in the ever expanding union of the workers. This union is helped on by the improved means of communication that are created by modern industry, and that place the workers of different localities in contact with one another. It was just this contact that was needed to centralise the numerous local struggles, all of the same character, into one national struggle between classes. But every class struggle is a political struggle. And that union, to attain which the burghers of the Middle Ages, with their miserable highways, required centuries, the modern proletarian, thanks to railways, achieve in a few years.

This organisation of the proletarians into a class, and, consequently into a political party, is continually being upset again by the competition between the workers themselves. But it ever rises up again, stronger, firmer, mightier. It compels legislative recognition of particular interests of the workers, by taking advantage of the divisions among the bourgeoisie itself. Thus, the ten-hours' bill in England was carried.

Altogether collisions between the classes of the old society further, in many ways, the course of development of the proletariat. The bourgeoisie finds itself involved in a constant battle. At first with the aristocracy; later on, with those portions of the bourgeoisie itself, whose interests have become antagonistic to the progress of industry; at all time with the bourgeoisie of foreign countries. In all these battles, it sees itself compelled to appeal to the proletariat, to ask for help, and thus, to drag it into the political arena. The bourgeoisie itself, therefore, supplies the proletariat with its own elements of political and general education, in other words, it furnishes the proletariat with weapons for fighting the bourgeoisie.

Further, as we have already seen, entire sections of the ruling class are, by the advance of industry, precipitated into the proletariat, or are at least threatened in their conditions of existence. These also supply the proletariat with fresh elements of enlightenment and progress.

Finally, in times when the class struggle nears the decisive hour, the progress of dissolution going on within the ruling class, in fact within the whole range of old society, assumes such a violent, glaring character, that a small section of the ruling class cuts itself adrift, and joins the revolutionary class, the class that holds the future in its hands. Just as, therefore, at an earlier period, a section of the nobility went over to the bourgeoisie, so now a portion of the bourgeoisie goes over to the proletariat, and in particular, a portion of the bourgeois ideologists, who have raised themselves to the level of comprehending theoretically the historical movement as a whole.

Of all the classes that stand face to face with the bourgeoisie today, the proletariat alone is a really revolutionary class. The other classes decay and finally disappear in the face of Modern Industry; the proletariat is its special and essential product.

The lower middle class, the small manufacturer, the shopkeeper, the artisan, the peasant, all these fight against the bourgeoisie, to save from extinction their existence as fractions of the middle class. They are therefore not revolutionary, but conservative. Nay more, they are reactionary, for they try to roll back the wheel of history. If by chance, they are revolutionary, they are only so in view of their impending transfer into the proletariat; they thus defend not their present, but their future interests, they desert their own standpoint to place themselves at that of the proletariat.

The "dangerous class", [lumpenproletariat] the social scum, that passively rotting mass thrown off by the lowest layers of the old society, may, here and there, be swept into the movement by a proletarian revolution; its conditions of life, however, prepare it far more for the part of a bribed tool of reactionary intrigue.

In the conditions of the proletariat, those of old society at large are already virtually swamped. The proletarian is without property; his relation to his wife and children has no longer anything in common with the bourgeois family relations; modern industry labour, modern subjection to capital, the same in England as in France, in America as in Germany, has stripped him of every trace of national character. Law, morality, religion, are to him so many bourgeois prejudices, behind which lurk in ambush just as many bourgeois interests.

All the preceding classes that got the upper hand sought to fortify their already acquired status by subjecting society at large to their conditions of appropriation. The proletarians cannot become masters of the productive forces of society, except by abolishing their own previous mode of appropriation, and thereby also every other previous mode of appropriation. They have nothing of their own to secure and to fortify; their mission is to destroy all previous securities for, and insurances of, individual property.

All previous historical movements were movements of minorities, or in the interest of minorities. The proletarian movement is the self-conscious, independent movement of the immense majority, in the interest of the immense majority. The proletariat, the lowest stratum of our present society, cannot stir, cannot raise itself up, without the whole superincumbent strata of official society being sprung into the air.

Though not in substance, yet in form, the struggle of the proletariat with the bourgeoisie is at first a national struggle. The proletariat of each country must, of course, first of all settle matters with its own bourgeoisie.

In depicting the most general phases of the development of the proletariat, we traced the more or less veiled civil war, raging within existing society, up to the point where that war breaks out into open revolution, and where the violent overthrow of the bourgeoisie lays the foundation for the sway of the proletariat.

Hitherto, every form of society has been based, as we have already seen, on the antagonism of oppressing and oppressed classes. But in order to oppress a class, certain conditions must be assured to it under which it can, at least, continue its slavish existence. The serf, in the period of serfdom, raised himself to membership in the commune, just as the petty bourgeois, under the yoke of the feudal absolutism, managed to develop into a bourgeois. The modern labourer, on the contrary, instead of rising with the process of industry, sinks deeper and deeper below the conditions of existence of his own class. He becomes a pauper, and pauperism develops more rapidly than population and wealth. And here it becomes evident, that the bourgeoisie is unfit any longer to be the ruling class in society, and to impose its conditions of existence upon society as an over-riding law. It is unfit to rule because it is incompetent to assure an existence to its slave within his slavery, because it cannot help letting him sink into such a state, that it has to feed him, instead of being fed by him. Society can no longer live under this bourgeoisie, in other words, its existence is no longer compatible with society.

The essential conditions for the existence and for the sway of the bourgeois class is the formation and augmentation of capital; the condition for capital is wage-labour. Wage-labour rests exclusively on competition between the labourers. The advance of industry, whose involuntary promoter is the bourgeoisie, replaces the isolation of the labourers, due to competition, by the revolutionary combination, due to association. The development of Modern Industry, therefore, cuts from under its feet the very foundation on which the bourgeoisie produces and appropriates products. What the bourgeoisie therefore produces, above all, are its own grave-diggers. Its fall and the victory of the proletariat are equally inevitable.

NOTES

1. By bourgeoisie is meant the class of modern capitalists, owners of the means of social production and employers of wage labour. By proletariat, the class of modern wage labourers who, having no means of production of their own, are reduced to selling their labour power in order to live. [Note by Engels, 1888 English edition]

2. That is, all *written* history. In 1847, the pre-history of society, the social organisation existing previous to recorded history, was all but unknown. Since then, August von Haxthausen (1792–1866) discovered common ownership of land in Russia, Georg Ludwig von Maurer proved it to be the social foundation from which all Teutonic races started in history, and, by and by, village communities were found to be, or to have been, the primitive form of society everywhere from India to Ireland. The inner organisation of this primitive communistic society was laid bare, in its typical form, by Lewis Henry Morgan's (1818–1861) crowning discovery of the true nature of the gens and its relation to the tribe. With the dissolution of the primeval communities, society begins to be differentiated into separate

and finally antagonistic classes. I have attempted to retrace this dissolution in *The Origin of the Family, Private Property, and the State*, second edition, Stuttgart, 1886. [Engels, 1888 English Edition and 1890 German Edition (with the last sentence omitted)]

3. Guild-master, that is, a full member of a guild, a master within, not a head of a guild. [Note by Engels, 1888 English Edition]

4. This was the name given their urban communities by the townsmen of Italy and France, after they had purchased or conquered their initial rights of self-government from their feudal lords. [Engels, 1890 German edition]

   "Commune" was the name taken in France by the nascent towns even before they had conquered from their feudal lords and masters local self-government and political rights as the "Third Estate". Generally speaking, for the economical development of the bourgeoisie, England is here taken as the typical country, for its political development, France. [Engels, 1888 English Edition]

CHAPTER TWENTY ONE

Perspectives on the Politics of Class

Rajnarayan Chandavarkar

In recent times, the conceptualization of class and social consciousness, culture and poverty, colonialism and industrialization has been in a state of flux. This enquiry into the processes which conditioned the formation of the working class in Bombay City seeks to address these broader questions and is offered as a contribution to a more general, comparative or 'theoretical' discussion of industrialization, class and labour movements. To a large extent, this discussion has thus far proceeded by generalizing from limited cases. The sociological and historical evidence of an 'Indian case' is not conventionally expected to provide material for thinking more generally about industrialization and its social consequences. Indeed, it is not often presented as if it might be. The interest of Indian society is assumed to lie in its 'agrarian' or 'pre-industrial' character, whose inwardness can only be properly comprehended in terms of its own particularisms. Alternatively, 'industrial development in India' is portrayed as 'part of the very broad movement which had its orgins in Western Europe'.[1] According to this evolutionary schemata, the patterns of social change and economic development in India were moving broadly along tramlines towards 'industrialism', or modern capitalism, familiar in the 'Western' experience. Thus, one historian of Indian labour was led to assure us that,

> group tensions and conflicts in Indian industry take on the characteristics of Western industrialization and do not require any analysis specifically developed to suit the requirements of a distinctively Indian situation ... The group tensions which will confront Indian industry will not be strange to the scholar. They will remind him very much of those which affected other regions in early periods of economic development.[2]

In this way, the historical experience of the West becomes the source of the conceptual frameworks and social theories by which the Indian working classes may be comprehended.

The assumption that Indian social history was essentially particularistic or that it simply followed patterns laid down by the West in earlier centuries has effectively withdrawn its study from an active role in the comparative discussion of social change and the wider discourse of social theory. The cost has often been either to attribute a cultural specificity to fairly general phenomena or to perceive as a general effect of a broader evolutionary development towards industrialism what is produced by a particular historical context and its contingencies. The cultural specificity of the jobber system or the characterization of indigenous patterns of entrepreneurship, averse to risk, prone to speculation, slow in its response to technology, is an example of the former. So perhaps is the readiness with which urban neighbourhoods are conceived primarily in oxymorons like 'urban villages'.[3] Conversely, historians have sometimes taken for granted that 'early industrial workers' or insufficiently industrialized or non-industrial urban labour were marked by their rural origins and peasant character.[4] Their attitudes to work and politics have often been read in the light of the perceptions of similar groups at what is deemed a comparable stage of industrialization in Britain or elsewhere in the West.

The term 'class' is used frequently in this book largely as a descriptive category. It was once taken for granted that since class and class consciousness presupposed the maturity of industrial capitalism, they could not be fruitfully applied to the study of the labour force in India. Indeed, it was argued, more generally, that the development of industrial capitalism would tend towards the increasing homogeneity and polarization of classes. From their concentration into factories, it was supposed, flowed the political solidarities of the working classes. On the other hand, peasants were in this view characterized by their 'low classness' – 'often lacking the discipline and leadership that would encourage opposition of a more organized sort'. This was why, as James Scott has recently argued, affirming an old orthodoxy, 'everyday forms of peasant resistance', individual and anonymous action, are 'eminently suited to the sociology of the class from which it arises'.[5] Factory workers by contrast are expected to manifest an inherent propensity to collective action. Yet the natural solidarities of the working class should not be taken for granted. The Indian working classes were highly fragmented. Their sectionalism has usually been perceived as a symptom of its pre-industrial economy. But their differentiation did not simply derive from the village and the neighbourhood, caste and kinship; rather, it was accentuated by the development of industry. At the same time, an increasing sensitivity among historians of the Western working classes to the competing and conflicting identities of ethnicity and gender, religion and nation, kinship and neighbourhood, has focussed attention upon the very issues which had in this perspective rendered Indian society exceptional in the first place and sometimes even demanded a culturally specific sociology for its proper analysis. It is one purpose of this book to investigate how far the factors which are deemed to make up the common experiences of the working class in the process of its formation have registered differences between them.

The notion that social groups have 'real' or objectively defined interests in common derived from theoretical assumptions about the effects of production and distribution. Class consciousness became the process by which classes recognized and realized the interests which they shared in common and in opposition to others. Yet the concepts of class and class consciousness were articulated by Marx and Engels before the emergence of the type of 'modern' working class in Europe to which they have been most frequently considered applicable. Significantly, these concepts were based upon philosophical, not sociological, assumptions about the ontological role of the working class in the transition to socialism.[6] They were fashioned from an already prevalent vocabulary of class in early-nineteenth-century England.[7] Moreover, they have never been easily transposed to the analysis of social conflict and political change within any other context in the West or the Third World. Yet, paradoxically, where the vocabulary of class reflected daily social reality less directly than in nineteenth-century England, it has more frequently and overtly informed an explicitly revolutionary ideology and inspired more sustained and effective radical political movements.

The assumption that social groups have common interests which derive from their broadly similar relationships to the means of production has led to the quest for its manifest consequences in the development of class consciousness: the processes by which classes recognized and realized the interests which they shared in common and in opposition to others. Not surprisingly, in some forms of social and cultural history, sociology and anthropology, an important, sometimes hidden, occasionally explicit, concern has been to explain the gulf between political expectations based upon class and their real shortcomings in practice: not only why revolutionary movements failed but also why they failed to occur. Recent attempts to direct attention away from revolutionary movements to 'the quiet, unremitting guerilla warfare that took place day-in and day-out' have nonetheless conceived social relations in terms of the distinction between 'exploiters' and 'resisters',[8] Similarly, some have depicted Indian society in terms of the fundamental divide between the subaltern classes and elites.[9] In these accounts, the working classes rather than peasants seemingly retain their status, attributed to them by Marx, as the most appropriate vehicle for the transition to socialism.

This book proceeds on a different set of assumptions about the conceptualization of class. It remains sceptical of the notion that exploiters and resisters were characterized by simply adversarial or consistently oppositional relationships. It would be misleading to suppose that 'resistance' flows naturally from the social situation of the subaltern classes. Moreover, the lines of exploitation, as we shall see, moved in diffuse and complex ways through society. The subordinate classes were drawn into competitive and exploitative relationships with each other; rivalries and factions within dominant classes limited their ability to exploit and weakened possibilities of hegemony or social control. Between subordinate and dominant groups were complex layers of intermediaries who, in changing situations, could be identified in either category and who, in any case, facilitated the processes of both exploitation and resistance. Their relationship was mediated by institutions which were driven by their own logic and subject to pressures not simply reflective of the prevailing sets of production relations and their attendant effects.

Furthermore, abstractions of apparently common interests based upon theoretical assumptions about the character and consequences of production relations will not necessarily match individual or even collective perceptions and calculations of self-interest. Perceptions of mutuality and indeed their notations, the language for their description, were produced by the specificities of a particular political and intellectual context. Moreover, the interests of social groups were shaped by and contingent upon specific historical circumstances, which were themselves constantly in flux. In turn, changing circumstances could serve to redefine the interests of the diverse elements which made up the working classes and reconstitute social identities. From this perspective, it would seem likely that the very processes which help to form and constitute social classes could also serve to fragment them. Our concern, therefore, should be not so much why the working classes have failed to realize the expectations theoretically imputed to them but how and why at times they came together at all.

Finally, the attempt to trace the subjective realization and expression through 'class consciousness' or 'culture' of objective and real interests based upon relations of production has tended to give class consciousness an essentialist meaning, as an expression and manifestation of a latent, concealed, perhaps even immanent reality within the working classes. In this light, scholars ask not only whether or how far a working class had achieved 'consciousness' but also seek to assess whether it matched qualitatively a given stage of social development: whether it constituted the 'consciousness' of a 'pre-industrial', 'early industrial' or 'fully mature' proletariat. There is an inherent tautology in such reductive reasoning. For social consciousness is first defined as the property of a given state of social being and then, in any particular case, described and measured according to its standard. As the unease among historians about the handling of 'consciousness' has increased, so the number of surrogates for the term have proliferated: culture, identity, mentality, in some usages, even ideology, ranking among the more common to have been wheeled in to do service. The theoretical vagueness of their conceptualization conceals the assumption of essentialism upon which they are constructed, whereby a single, essential way of thinking can be attributed to social groups or even whole societies.

Mounting scepticism about the definition of culture as an autonomous sphere of social action has cast into doubt the viability of attempts to recapture the mind and world of the common man and woman, and in particular, their prior assumption of the existence of a single popular mind or a homogeneous common world. Historians who set out to investigate 'popular culture' or delineate 'working-class culture' have sometimes either written its economic and social context out of the account or simply taken it for granted. Thus, Foucault's assumptions about and emphasis upon the 'industrial revolution' as a causative moment allowed him to structure around it his meditations on discursive practices in the cultural sphere. Conversely, assumptions about the cultural characteristics of the working classes at various stages of development have often informed the analysis of their attitudes to work and politics. It is often taken for granted that casual workers primarily sought temporary employment, rural migrants were unsuited to factory discipline and early industrial workers were inherently volatile:

as passive as peasants and, like peasants, prone to spasmodic bouts of violence.[10] These characterizations constituted the ideology of capitalists seeking a more firmly subordinated labour force and historians have often adopted them unwittingly.

There has been a similar propensity to attribute cultural characteristics to social groups defined by their relation to the means of production or to assume a simple and direct correspondence between social and economic status and behavioural traits and attitudes beyond the 'cultural' realm of the factory system. Casual labour is often distinctively set apart from 'industrial' or more permanent workers. They are assumed to display specific behavioural characteristics, marked especially by an aversion to work and political organization and a propensity to crime and violence, and to adopt lifestyles peculiar to themselves. Historians have frequently perceived 'peasant' mentalities characterizing the social action of proletarians, as if the rural and the urban formed generic social entities defined by the specificity, distinctiveness and coherence of their own particular cultures. Similarly, the quest for the culture of working-class 'communities' has been marked by a similar tendency to read cultural characteristics from class position. Thus, village characteristics are firmly etched into the foreground in portrayals of urban neighbourhoods while the romantic notion of 'community' has lent itself naturally to the exaggeration of homogeneity.

The relationship between social being and social consciousness is not overlooked in the following chapters but the issues are addressed from a somewhat different perspective. The emphasis rests not on the essential properties or generic character of migrant or casual workers, the neighbourhood or the workplace but upon the changing historical circumstances which shaped their formation and conditioned their development. The distinction between casual and permanent workers was not a function of individual choice but the result of business strategies, the mechanisms of the labour market and employer policies. More crucially, there was no permanent gulf between them. Indeed, the divide between the formal and informal sectors was entrenched and formalized only by changes effected in the legal framework and conditions of employment beginning in the late 1930s and gathering momentum after the Second World War. But this should not lead to the conclusion that because the divide between them was blurred and because they formed, in a sense, ideological constructs, the working classes were united and homogenous. Similarly, rural migrants were not the carriers and purveyors of a putative peasant culture. Indeed, they were deeply committed to the urban and the industrial, and often acted after the fashion or stereotype of urbanized and industrialized workers, more so than those who had no connection with the countryside. The urban working-class neighbourhoods neither formed rural cities nor urban villages; but, conversely, the experience of living together did not necessarily forge homogeneous bonds of community between residents. Moreover, the social organization of the working-class neighbourhood was constituted largely by its relationship to the workplace. Although it contributed in significant ways to shaping the political struggles of the working class, the neighbourhood also formed an arena of competition and conflict. The sectionalism of the working class did not arise from its ascriptive divisions, traditional roots or rural origins; even at the point of production, Bombay's workers entered into relationships which did not develop solidarities among them but often entailed divisions. By assuming that social groups, variously defined, possessed (or developed) a specific culture and a consciousness ascribed to their role, however ambiguous, in production relations, historians have perhaps played down the significance or ironed out the awkwardness of this sectionalism. The study of the social organization of Bombay's working class suggested that its cultural affinities, common interests and political solidarities formed within and were closely related to changing social and political contexts. Their presence at one moment did not necessarily ensure their persistence at the next.

The agenda of social history, as a specialism within the discipline, originally set in the 1960s, was characterized by a populist ambition to reconstruct the authentic social experience of ordinary men and women and their everyday lives and struggles.[11] Social historians tended to focus ever more closely upon the local community, yet their ambition was to grasp the 'total experience' of their subjects and they retained an increasingly tenacious determination not to leave the politics out. Slowly and unevenly, as research in social history developed, the contradictions inherent in these programmatic intentions rose more clearly to the surface. Totality was often found only in the eye of the beholder. Close attention to the local community made it difficult to grasp the larger play of political forces or to define the role of the state. Not only did the totality appear circumscribed but the 'social' seemed to lose its sanctity. Political conflicts and movements could not be explained adequately in terms of their social character or referred back to their roots in the local community. They also called to be located in their widest or most general political and ideological context. To explain political conflicts, it was necessary to look at politics and this search could not be satisfactorily confined to the local community.[12]

One response to this problem was to shift the focus of investigation towards politics and its role in determining social forms and social relationships. Another was to eschew social and economic explanation as unduly deterministic, reject implicit or explicit notions of its prior role in daily life and condemn its failure to grasp the symbolic forms, popular beliefs and cultural practices through which 'ordinary people' construed their experiences. This perspective had the merit of returning the study of popular experience to the wider currents of ideological discourse.[13] It also appeared to offer an alternative approach, running from the same direction as the social history of the 1960s and 1970s but by a different route towards the understanding of popular politics and its relationship with the dominant classes and the state. Along this route, historians were able to draw upon the insights of ethnography and cultural anthropology. Perhaps, to a greater degree than the sources of their inspiration, historians appreciated that this level of popular culture was defined in relation to its parts as well as to elite culture and by the participation of the masses in and their responses to wider social and political struggles. Nonetheless, the scope of this approach has been limited by the assumption that objective conditions inscribed a mutuality into particular social groups, whether defined by production relations, ascriptive or primordial categories, ethnicity or gender. By a different, often scenic and pleasurable route, it returns to a familiar destination. It adopts and projects the simplistic distinction between exploiters and resisters, the dominant and the subordinate, the elite and the subaltern. It assumes away the problem of explaining how social groups formed, whether in a material or ideational sense. Conversely, it assumes the existence of given social groups and categories and seeks to examine through their discursive practices how their preconceptions, beliefs and symbolic forms ultimately coincided with the prior definition of their objective status.

This book leans towards the 'political' rather than the 'cultural' interpretation of social history. The significance of Bombay City within India's political economy necessarily gave local events an immediate national importance. The formation of its labour force, conceived as a continuous process of social production, had inescapably political characteristics as well as consequences. It is scarcely possible to investigate Indian society in the twentieth century without reference to the state, whether in its colonial or national phase. The examination of the economy of labour, itself shaped and conditioned by political initiatives and conflicts, suggests that production relations, village, caste and kinship connections, the linkages of rural and urban communities, the social organization of the workplace and the neighbourhood, did not progressively increase the homogeneity of the working class; it often accentuated the divisions and heightened the conflicts between them. The scale and momentum of industrial action in the cotton-textile industry and more generally in the city as a whole cannot be explained in terms of the structure or material conditions of the working class, even as the latter could scarcely be grasped outside the context of the political struggles waged around them.

In the 1960s and 1970s, the significance of nationalism, the colonial state and the relationship between India and the world (or metropolitan) economy blunted in the case of the sub-continent the preoccupations of the old social history with recovering the total experience of local communities. Yet it is curious that the ambition to recapture the genuine experience of ordinary people, when it manifested itself in Indian history in the 1980s,[14] focussed at first upon the local community and local struggles before taking the form of investigating the mental and cultural universe of the populace and seeking to grasp the 'mind' of already given or assumed social groups.

To a large extent, the explanatory and conceptual frameworks for analysing industrialization and class have been upon the historical experience of the West, and especially the exceptional, even unique, case of Britain. Recent research, however, has suggested that these conceptual frameworks or models do not readily comprehend the particular cases upon which they were based.[15] It is time, therefore, to turn to the cases they regarded as exceptional, not only for their intrinsic interest, but also for the challenge they pose to the general arguments and received expectations. In particular, it is easy to see why evolutionary and developmental, almost Whiggish, conceptions of industrialization and class acquired such plausible meaning in British and European history. Industrialization, especially given the apparent disappearance of the peasantry in England, could signify the evolution from artisanal and domestic production to the factory and the production line. The development of the working class could be perceived in a trajectory from small peasant or rural pauper to factory proletarian and an increasingly homogenized (if at a very 'advanced' state, once again segmented) labour force. Class consciousness could be perceived in its early and developed manifestation and following its dissipation in the mid nineteenth century to receive expression once more in growing labour movements and political parties of the working class, gathered beneath the banner of socialism. In India, these trajectories of development were far less clear and far more complex. The differentiation of the peasantry, the expansion, decline and stabilization of artisanal industry and the emergence of large-scale factory production ran concurrently. Most factory workers, after a century of industrialization, remained rural migrants who retained their village base. Casual labour could scarcely be taken for the residue of the past or the social discipline of the factory as the signpost of the future. Trade unions were ruthlessly repressed in the workplace, often on the streets and sometimes by the state; yet working-class militancy exceeded the wildest expectations of a significantly casual, predominantly rural labour force, divided by caste, community and religion and in apparently an 'early' phase of industrialization. Yet this militancy received limited, indeed halting expression at the level of party politics and the state. Many of these developments will be familiar in the social history of industrialization elsewhere; some make it difficult to proceed on the assumptions and expectations of labour and social history. It is not intended to suggest that the burden of rethinking and re-casting social theory and the assumptions of social history could rest entirely upon the empirical investigation of Indian society. But it is probable that the scope and intellectual reach of the former has been significantly diminished by its neglect of the latter.

NOTES

1. M.D. Morris, 'The Growth of Large-Scale Industry to 1947', in Kumar (ed.), *CEHI*, II, 553.
2. M.D. Morris, 'The Effects of Industrialization on "Race Relations" in India, in G. Hunter (ed.), *Industrialization and Race Relations: A Symposium* (London, 1965), p. 160.
3. See, for example, O.M. Lynch, 'Rural Cities in India: Continuities and Discontinuities', in P. Mason (ed.), *India and Ceylon: Unity and Diversity* (Oxford, 1967), pp. 142–58; D.F. Pocock, 'Sociologies: Urban and Rural', *Contributions to Indian Sociology*, IV (1960), 63–81; W.D. Rowe, 'Caste, Kinship and Association in Urban India', in A. Southall (ed.), *Urban Anthropology: Cross Cultural Studies of Urbanization* (New York, 1973), pp. 211–49.
4. Chakrabarty, *Rethinking Working-Class History*, D. Arnold, 'Industrial Violence in Colonial India', *Comparative Studies in Society and History*, XIII, 2 (1980), 234–55.

5. J.C. Scott, 'Everyday Forms of Peasant Resistance', in J.C. Scott and B J.T. Kerkvliet (eds.), *Everyday Forms of Peasant Resistance in South-East Asia* (London. 1986), p. 28; J.C. Scott, *Weapons of the Weak: Everyday Forms of Peasant Resistance* (New Haven, 1985).

6. G. Stedman Jones, *Languages of Class: Studies in English Working Class History, 1832–1982* (Cambridge, 1983), pp. 1–24.

7. A. Briggs, 'The Language of "Class" in Early Nineteenth Century England', in A. Briggs and J. Saville (eds.), *Essays in Labour History* (London, 1960), pp. 43–73.

8. Scott, 'Everyday Forms of Peasant Resistance', p. 5.

9. Guha (ed.) *Subaltern Studies.* For an early manifesto, see R. Guha, 'Introduction', in *Subaltern Studies*, vol. I, pp. 1–8.

10. Arnold, 'Industrial Violence'; Chakrabarty, *Rethinking Working-Class History.* chs. 5 and 6; C. Joshi, 'Bonds of Community, Ties of Religion: Kanpur Textile Workers in the Early Twentieth Century', *IESHR*, XXII, 3 (1985), 251–80. But it should not be supposed that these lines of reasoning are confined to Indian social history.

11. For a programmatic statement, see E.J. Hobsbawm, 'From Social History to the History of Society', in M.W. Flinn and T.C. Smout (eds.). *Essays in Social History* (Oxford, 1974), pp. 1–22.

12. G. Stedman Jones, 'From Historical Sociology to Theoretical History', *British Journal of Sociology*, XXVII, 3 (1976), 295–306; E.F. and E.D. Genovese, 'The Political Crisis of Social History', *Journal of Social History*, X, 2 (1976), 205–21; T. Judt, 'A Clown in Regal Purple: Social History and the Historians', *History Workshop Journal*, VII (1979), 66–94.

13. For interesting examples, see W.H. Sewell, Jr., *Work and Revolution in France: The Language of Labour from the Old Regime to 1848* (Cambridge, 1980); S. Kaplan (ed.), *Understanding Popular Culture: Europe from the Middle Ages to the Nineteenth Century* (Berlin and New York, 1984); S. Kaplan and C. Koepp (eds.), *Work in France: Representations, Meaning, Organization and Practice* (Ithaca, 1986); R. Chartier, *Cultural History: Between Practices and Representation* (Cambridge, 1988).

14. For instance in the work of the 'subaltern' historians. See Guha (ed.), *Subaltern Studies.*

15. D. Cannadine, 'The Present and the Past in the English Industrial Revolution, 1880–1980', *Past and Present*, CIII, (1984), 131–71; C. Sabel and J. Zeitlin, 'Historical Alternatives to Mass Production: Politics, Markets and Technology in Nineteenth Century Industrialization', *Past and Present*, CVIII, (1985), 133–76.

CHAPTER TWENTY TWO

Class Structure in the Classic Slum

ROBERT ROBERTS

We are the mob, the working class, the proletariat
Song

No view of the English working class in the first quarter of this century would be accurate if that class were shown merely as a great amalgam of artisan and labouring groups united by a common aim and culture. Life in reality was much more complex. Socially the unskilled workers and their families, who made up about 50 per cent of the population in our industrial cities, varied as much from the manual élite as did people in middle station from the aristocracy. Before 1914 skilled workers generally did not strive to join a higher rank; they were only too concerned to maintain position within their own stratum. Inside the working class as a whole there existed, I believe, a stratified form of society whose implications and consequences have hardly yet been fully explored. Born behind a general shop in an area which, sixty years before, Frederick Engels had called the 'classic slum', I grew up in what was perhaps an ideal position for viewing the English proletarian caste system in all its late flower.

All Salford [wrote Engels in 1844] is built in courts or narrow lanes, so narrow that they remind me of the narrowest I have ever seen, in the little lanes of Genoa. The average construction of Salford is, in this respect, much worse than that of Manchester and so, too, in respect of cleanliness. If, in Manchester, the police, from time to time, every six or ten years, makes a raid upon the working-people's district, closes the worst dwellings, and causes the filthiest spots in these Augean stables to be cleansed, in Salford it seems to have done absolutely nothing.

For twenty years from 1850 Engels held interests in cotton mills on the western side of Manchester. This meant that on journeys between town and factory he had to pass through Salford; our 'village' lay the greatest slum *en route*. One of his early mills (Ermen and Engels) stood in Liverpool Street, which ran through the heart of it. This is how Engels described our area in 1844:

> The working-men's dwellings between Oldfield Road and Cross Lane (Salford), where a mass of courts and alleys are to be found in the worst possible state, vie with the dwellings of the Old Town in filth and overcrowding. In this district I found a man, apparently sixty years old, living in a cow-stable. He had constructed a sort of chimney for his square pen, which had neither windows, floor nor ceiling, had obtained a bedstead and lived there, though the rain dripped through his rotten roof. This man was too old and weak for regular work, and supported himself by removing manure with a hand-cart; the dung heaps lay next door to his palace.

Through a familiarity so long and close, this district must have become for Engels the very epitome of all industrial ghettos, the 'classic slum' itself. He died in 1895 having seen that little world change, develop, 'prosper' even, yet stay in essence the same awful paradigm of what a free capitalist society could produce. By 1900 the area showed some improvement; his 'cow-stable' had doubtless been demolished together with many another noisome den, but much that was vile remained.

Our own family was in the slum but not, they felt, of it: we had 'connections'. Father, besides, was a skilled mechanic. During the '60s of the last century his mother, widowed early with four children, had had the foresight to bypass a mission hall near the alley where she lived and send her three good-looking daughters to a Wesleyan chapel on the edge of a middle-class suburb. Intelligent girls, they did their duty by God and mother, all becoming Sunday school teachers and each in turn marrying well above her station, one a journalist, another a traveller in sugar and a third a police inspector – an ill-favoured lot, the old lady grumbled, but 'you can't have everything'. The girls adapted themselves smoothly to their new milieu, paid mother a weekly danegeld and Carter's Court knew them no more. My father, years their junior, stayed working-class; it was, in fact, always harder for a man to break into the higher echelons. At the age of eight, he took up education and, twelve months later, put it down, despite the newfangled 'Compulsion' Act, to find, his mother[1] said, 'summat a sight better to do at the blacksmith's'. At twenty-one Father married a girl from a cotton mill.

As a child my mother had been something of a prodigy and was hawked from one local school to another to display her talents; but, her father dying, she got work, at nine, helping in a weaving shed. Happily her family had 'expectations'. When the £900 legacy arrived it was laid out with skill and duly improved status: one sister married a clerk, and two elder brothers opened little shops, which prospered. They were on the way up! My father, a man given to envy, felt the call of commerce too and came home one evening twelve months after marriage to announce in tipsy triumph that he had, on borrowed money, just bought a grocery store for £40. Horrified, my mother inspected his 'gold mine' – in the heart of a slum – and refused point blank to go. But he cajoled and persuaded. In two or three years, he said, they could build it up, sell it for hundreds of pounds and buy a nice place in the country. She looked at the dank little premises and the grim kitchen behind. 'Two years,' she told him, 'and no more! This is no place to bring up a family.' Solemnly he promised. In the little bedroom above the kitchen she bore him seven children and stayed thirty-two years – a life sentence.

Every industrial city, of course, folds within itself a clutter of loosely defined overlapping 'villages'. Those in the Great Britain of seventy years ago were almost self-contained communities. Our own consisted of some thirty streets and alleys locked along the north and south by two railway systems a furlong apart. About twice that distance to the east lay another slum which turned on its farther side into a land of bonded warehouses and the city proper. West of us, well beyond the tramlines, lay the middle classes, bay-windowed and begardened. We knew them not.

In the city as a whole our village rated indubitably low. 'The children of this school', wrote one of King Edward VII's inspectors, commenting on our only seat of learning, 'are of the poorest class; so, too, is the teaching.' With cash, or on tick, our villagers, about three thousand in all, patronized fifteen beer-houses, a hotel and two off-licences, nine grocery and general shops, three greengrocers (for ever struggling to survive against the street hawker), two tripe shops, three barbers, three cloggers, two cook shops, one fish and chip shop (*déclassé*), an old clothes store, a couple of pawnbrokers and two loan offices.

Religion was served by two chapels (Primitive Methodist and Congregationalist), one 'tin' mission (Church of England and one sinister character who held spiritualist séances in his parlour and claimed from the window to cure 'Female Bad Legs'. (Through overwork innumerable women suffered from burst varicose veins.) Culture, pleasure and need found outlet through one theatre (and, later, three cinemas), a dancing room ('low'), two coy brothels, eight bookmakers, and a private moneylender.

The first of our public buildings reared its dark bulk near the railway wall. Hyndman Hall, home of the Social Democratic Federation (SDF), remained for us mysteriously aloof and through the years had, in fact, about as much political impact on the neighbourhood as the near-by gasworks. The second establishment, our Conservative Club, except for a few days at election times, didn't appear to meddle with politics at all. It was notable usually for a union jack in the window and a brewer's dray at the door.

Over one quarter of a mile industry stood represented by a dying brickworks and an iron foundry. Several gasholders on the south side polluted the air, sometimes for days together. Little would grow; even the valiant aspidistra pined.[2] We possessed besides two coal yards, a corn store, a cattle wharf and perhaps as closed an urban society as any in Europe.

In our community, as in every other of its kind, each street[3] had the usual social rating; one side or one end of that street might be classed higher than another. Weekly rents varied from 2s 6d for the back-to-back to 4s 6d for a 'two up and two down'. End houses often had special status. Every family, too, had a tacit ranking, and even individual members within it; neighbours would consider a daughter in one household as 'dead common' while registering her sister as 'refined', a word much in vogue. (Young women with incipient consumption were often thought 'refined'.) Class divisions were of the greatest consequence, though their implications remained unrealized: the many looked upon social and economic inequality as the law of nature. Division in our own society ranged from an élite at the peak, composed of the leading families, through recognized strata to a social base whose members one damned as the 'lowest of the low', or simply 'no class'. Shopkeepers, publicans and skilled tradesmen occupied the premier positions, each family having its own sphere of influence. A few of these aristocrats, while sharing working-class culture, had aspirations. From their ranks the lower middle class, then clearly defined, drew most of its recruits – clerks and, in particular, schoolteachers (struggling hard at that time for social position). Well before translation those striving to 'get on' tried to ape what they believed were 'real' middle-class manners and customs. Publicans' and shopkeepers' daughters, for instance, set the fashion in clothes for a district. Some went to private commercial colleges[4] in the city, took music lessons or perhaps studied elocution – that short cut, it was felt, to 'culture' – at two shillings an hour, their new 'twang' tried out later over the bar and counter, earning them a deal of covert ridicule. Top families generally stood ever on the look-out for any activity or 'nice' connection which might edge them, or at least their children, into a higher social ambience. But despite all endeavour, mobility between manual workers, small tradesmen and the genuine middle class remained slight, and no one needed to wonder why; before the masses rose an economic barrier that few men could ever hope to scale. At the end of the Edwardian period an adult male industrial worker earned £75 a year; the average annual salary of a man in the middle classes proper was £340.

That wide section beyond the purely manual castes where incomes ranged between the two norms mentioned was considered by many to be no more than 'jumped-up working class', not to be confused with the true order above: but the striving sought it nevertheless, if not for themselves, at least for their children. The real social divide existed between those who, in earning daily bread, dirtied hands and face and those who did not.

The less ambitious among skilled workers had aims that seldom rose above saving enough to buy the ingoing of a beer-house, open a corner shop or get a boarding house at the seaside. By entering into any business at all a man and his family grew at once in economic status, though social prestige accrued much more slowly. Fiascos were common; again and again one noticed in the district pathetic attempts[5] to set up shops in private houses by people who possessed only a few shillings' capital and no experience. After perhaps only three weeks one saw their hopes collapse, often to the secret satisfaction of certain neighbours who, in the phrase of the times, 'hated to see folk trying to get on'.

On the social ladder after tradesmen and artisans came the semi-skilled workers (still a small section) in regular employment, and then the various grades of unskilled labourers. These divisions could be marked in many public houses, where workers other than craftsmen would be frozen or flatly ordered out of those rooms in which journeymen forgathered. Each part of the tavern had its status rating; indeed, 'he's only a tap-room man' stood as a common slur. Nevertheless, whatever the job the known probity of a person conferred at once some social standing. 'She was poor but she was honest' we sang first in praise, not derision. I remember neighbours speaking highly of an old drudge, 'poor but honest', who had sought charring work with a flash publican new to the district. 'I dunno,' he told her, 'but come tomorrer and fetch a "character".' She returned the next day. 'Well, yer brought it?' he asked. 'No,' she said 'I got yours an' I won't be startin'!'

Many women and girls in the district worked in some branch of the textile industry. Of these, we accepted weavers as 'top' in their class, followed by winders and drawers-in. Then came spinners. They lacked standing on several counts: first, the trade contained a strong Irish Catholic element, and wages generally were lower than in other sections. Again, because of the heat and slippery floors, women worked barefoot, dressed in little more than calico shifts. These garments, the respectable believed, induced in female spinners a certain moral carelessness. They came home, too, covered in dust and fluff; all things which combined to depress their social prestige. Women employees of dye works, however, filled the lowest bracket: their work was dirty, wet and heavy and they paid due penalty for it. Clogs and shawls were, of course, standard wear for all. The girl who first defied this tradition in one of Lancashire's largest mills remembered the 'stares, skits and sneers' of fellow workers sixty years afterwards. Her parents, urgently in need of money, had put her to weaving, where earnings for girls were comparatively good. They lived, however, in one of the newer suburbs with its parloured houses and small back gardens. To be seen in such a district returning from a mill in clogs and shawl would have meant instant social demotion for the whole family. She was sent to the weaving shed wearing coat and shoes and thereby shocked a whole establishment. Here was a 'forward little bitch, getting above herself. So clearly, in fact, did headwear denote class that, in Glasgow, separate clubs existed for 'hat' girls and 'shawl' girls. Nevertheless, before 1914 even, continued good wages in weaving and the consequent urge to bolster status had persuaded not a few to follow the lone teenager's example. By the end of the war, in the big town cotton mills at least, coats and shoes could be worn without comment.

Unskilled workers split into plainly defined groups according to occupation, pos-sessions and family connection, scavengers and night-soil men rating low indeed. Following these came a series of castes, some unknown and others, it seems, already withered into insignificance in Professor Hoggart's Hunslet of the 1930s[6]: first, the casual workers of all kinds – dockers in particular (who lacked prestige through the uncertainty of their calling), then the local street sellers of coal, lamp oil, tripe, crumpets, muffins and pikelets, fruit, vegetables and small-ware. Finally came the firewood choppers, bundlers and sellers and the rag and boners, often whole fami-lies. These people for some reason ranked rock-bottom among the genuine workers.

It may have been that firewood sellers rated so very low socially because they competed in some districts with small teams of paupers who went about in charge of a
uniformed attendant hawking firewood, chopped and bundled at the Union. Workhouse paupers hardly registered as human beings at all. Even late in the nineteenth
century ablebodied men from some Northern poorhouses worked in public with a
large P stamped on the seat of their trousers. This not only humiliated the wearer
but prevented his absconding to a street market where he could have exchanged
his good pants for a cheap pair – with cash adjustment. The theft of 'workhouse
property' was a common offence among the destitute.

Forming the base of the social pyramid we had bookies' runners, idlers, part-time
beggars and petty thieves, together with all those known to have been in prison[7]
whatever might be their ostensible economic or social standing. Into this group the
community lumped any harlots, odd homosexuals, kept men and brothel keepers.

. . .

With us, of course, as with many cities in the North, until the coming of the coloured
people Irish Roman Catholic immigrants, mostly illiterate, formed the lowest socio-
economic stratum. A slum Protestant marrying into the milieu suffered a severe loss
of face. Such unions seldom occurred.

. . .

One or two proletarian authors, writing about these times and of the slump between the wars, appear to me to sentimentalize the working class: even worse, by too
often depicting its cruder and more moronic members they end by caricaturing the
class as a whole. In general, women in the slums were far from being foul-mouthed
sluts and harridans, sitting in semi-starvation at home in between trips to the pub
and pawnshop, nor were most men boors and drunken braggarts. People *en masse*, it
is true, had little education but the discerning of the time saw abundant evidence of
intelligence, shrewdness, restraint and maturity. Of course, we had low 'characters'
by the score, funny or revolting: so did every slum in Britain. Such types set no standards. In sobriety they knew their 'place' well enough. Very many families even in our
'low' district remained awesomely respectable over a lifetime. Despite poverty and ap-
palling surroundings parents brought up their children to be decent, kindly and
honourable and often lived long enough to see them occupy a higher place socially
than they had ever known themselves: the greatest satisfaction of all. It is such people
and their children now who deny indignantly (and I believe rightly) that the slum life
of the industrial North in this century, for all its horrors, was ever so mindless and
uncouth as superficial play and novel would have a later generation believe.

Position in our Edwardian community was judged not only by what one possessed but also by what one pawned. Through agreement with the local broker the
back room of our corner shop served as a depot for those goods pledged by the week
which owners had been unable to redeem before nine o'clock on Saturday, when the
local pawnshop closed. Our service gave women waiting on drunken or late-working

husbands a few hours' grace in which to redeem shoes and clothing before the Sabbath, and so maintain their social stake in the English Sunday. Towards our closing time there was always a great scurrying shopwards to get the 'bundle'. Housewives after washday on Monday pledged what clean clothes could be spared until weekend and returned with cash to buy food. Often they stood in the shop and thanked God that *they* were not as certain others who, having no clothes but what they stood in, had sunk low enough to pawn ashpans, hearth rugs or even the 'pots off the table'. Other customers tut-tutted in disgust. News of domestic distress soon got around. Inability to redeem basic goods was a sure sign of a family's approaching destitution, and credit dried up fast in local tick shops. Naturally, the gulf between those households who patronized 'Uncle', even if only occasionally, and those who did not gaped wide. Some families would go hungry rather than pledge their belongings.

The interest charged on articles pawned was usually a penny in the shilling per week, one half being paid at pledging time (Monday) and the other on redemption of the goods (Saturday). Much trucking went on among neighbours, and this often led to dispute. One woman, as a favour, would make up a bundle of her clothing for another to pawn. The pledger would then gradually gear her household economy to the certainty of hocking the same bundle every Monday morning. But the boon would be withdrawn with 'I don't know whose clothes they are – mine or hers!' Then came bitterness, recrimination and even a 'stack-up' street fight.

The great bulk of pledged goods consisted of 'Sunday best' suits, boots and clean clothing. Their lying with Uncle provided not only cash but also convenient storage for households with next to no cupboards and where the word 'wardrobe' was yet unknown. Among that body of 'white slaves', the washerwomen, there was always one notorious for pledging the clothes she had laundered professionally. Bold with booze from the proceeds of her crime, she would then send her client (usually a publican or shopkeeper) the pawn ticket and a rude verbal message ending her contract for ever. But even in those days washerwomen were hard to come by and the good one, though occasionally dishonest, could always find labour at two shillings *per diem*.

Behind his cold eye and tight lip our local broker, it was said, had a heart of stone. Only one customer, he boasted, had ever 'bested' him. An Irish woman he knew as a 'good Catholic' had presented him with a large bundle containing exactly the same washing week after week for months on end. At last he ceased to open it and paid her 'on sight'. Suddenly she disappeared and left the goods unredeemed. Weeks after a revolting smell from the store room forced him to open her pledge. He found, rotting gently among rags, an outsize savoy cabbage.

Few shopkeepers indeed would lend cash. Women customers at our shop very seldom asked for a loan but their husbands, banking on a wife's good name, would send children from time to time – 'Can yer lend me father a shilling, an' he'll give yer one an' three at the week end?'

'Tell him this is a shop,' my mother would snap, 'not a loan office.'

This usually happened on the day of some big race. If the would-be punter's fancy won, he blamed Mother bitterly for robbing him of his gains.

Only those in dire straits, and with a certainty of cash cover to come, patronized the local blood sucker; he charged threepence in the shilling per week. To be known to be in his clutches was to lose caste altogether. Women would pawn to the limit, leaving the home utterly comfortless, rather than fall to that level.

Though the senior members of a household would try to uphold its prestige in every way, children in the streets had the reprehensible habit of making friends with anyone about their own age who happened to be around, in spite of the fact that parents, ever on the watch, had already announced what company they should keep. One would be warned off certain boys altogether. Several of us, for instance, had been strictly forbidden ever to be seen consorting with a lad whose mother, known elegantly as the She Nigger, was a woman of the lowest repute. Unfortunately we could find nothing 'low' in her son. A natural athlete (he modelled his conduct on Harry Wharton of the *Magnet*), a powerful whistler through his teeth, generous, unquarrelsome, Bill seemed the kind of friend any sensible lad would pick. We sought him out at every opportunity but took very good care to drop him well away from home base. He accepted our brush-off meekly, but in the end protested with a dignity which left the other three of us in the group deeply embarrassed. 'Why', he asked, 'won't you be seen with me in the street?'

We looked at one another: 'It's – it's your old lady,' I mumbled at last – 'You know!'

'I can't help what the old lady does, can I?' he asked.

'It's not us,' we explained lamely. 'It's them – you know – them at home . . .'

He turned and walked away.

All of us were then within a few weeks of leaving school; no longer children. We went again to our common haunts but he came no more; the friendship was over.

Through our teens we saw him pass often, but he ignored us. The break would have come in any case, I told myself uneasily. He got a job after school as a mere chain horse lad; we had become apprentices of a sort; but a social barrier had risen for good.

The class struggle, as manual workers in general knew it, was apolitical and had place entirely within their own society. They looked upon it not in any way as a war against the employers but as a perpetual series of engagements in the battle of life itself. One family might be 'getting on' – two or three children out to work and the dream of early marriage days fulfilled at last. The neighbours noted it as they noted everything, with pleasure or envy. A second household would begin a slip downhill as father aged or children married. They watched, sympathetically perhaps, or with a touch of *schadenfreude*. All in all it was a struggle against the fates, and each family fought it out as best it could. Marxist 'ranters' from the Hall who paid fleeting visits to our street end insisted that we, the proletariat, stood locked in titanic struggle with some wicked master class. We were battling, they told us (from a vinegar barrel borrowed from our corner shop), to cast off our chains and win a whole world. Most people passed by; a few stood to listen, but not for long: the problems of the 'proletariat', they felt, had little to do with them.

Before 1914 the great majority in the lower working class were ignorant of Social-ist doctrine in any form, whether 'Christian' or Marxist. Generally, those who did come into contact with such ideas showed either indifference or, more often, hostility. Had they been able to read a *Times* stricture of the day, most would have agreed heartily that 'Socialist is a title which carries in many minds summary and contemptuous condemnation'. They would have echoed too its pained protests on the iniquities of the doctrine. 'To take from the rich', said a leader in 1903, *à propos* a mild tax pro-posal, 'is all very well if they are to make some more money, but to take from the rich by methods that prevent them replacing what is taken is the way to national im-poverishment from which the poor, in spite of all doles and Socialist theories, will be the greatest sufferers.'

Meanwhile, though the millennium for a socialist few might seem just around the corner, many gave up struggling. The suicide rate among us remained pretty high. There was Joe Kane, for instance, an unemployed labourer who was found by a neigh-bour blue in the face with a muffler tied about his neck. Some time previously he had taken carbolic acid and bungled that attempt too. But the magistrate didn't think much of Joe's efforts.

'If the prisoner', he said, 'is anxious to get to heaven, one would have thought he could have managed it by some better means than that. He could, now, have thrown himself into the river, or something else.'

The prisoner was discharged. But several months later Joe took up the magistrate's thoughtful suggestion and drowned himself in the canal.

Throughout a quarter of a century the population of our village remained gen-erally immobile: the constant shifts of near-by country folk into industrial towns, so common during the previous century, had almost ceased; though our borough was still growing at a diminished rate. A man's work, of course, usually fixed the place where his family dwelt; but lesser factors were involved too: his links, for instance, with local kith and kin. Then again, he commonly held a certain social position at the near-by pub, modest, perhaps, but recognized, and a credit connection with the corner shop. Such relationships, once relinquished, might not easily be re-established. All these things, together with fear of change, combined to keep poor families, if not in the same street, at least in the same neighbourhood for generations. There was of course some movement in and out, and naturally we had the odd 'moonlight' flit-ting when a whole household, to dodge its debts, would vanish overnight. Everybody laughed about it except the creditors. What newcomers we got were never the 'country gorbies' whom my grandfather remembered as the 'butt of the workshops' in his youth, but families on the way up or down from other slums of the city: yet new neighbours or old, all shared a common poverty.

Even with rapidly increasing literacy during the second half of the nineteenth century, years were needed, sometimes decades, before certain ideas common to the educated filtered through to the very poor. By 1900, however, those cherished prin-ciples about class, order, work, thrift and self-help, epitomized by Samuel Smiles and long taught and practised by the Victorian bourgeoisie, had moulded the minds of even the humblest. And slow to learn, they were slow to change. Whatever new urges might have roved abroad in early Edwardian England, millions among the poor still retained the outlook and thought patterns imposed by their Victorian mentors. For them the twentieth century had not begun. Docilely they accepted a steady decline in living standards and went on wishing for nothing more than to be 'respectful[8] and respected' in the eyes of men. For them the working-class caste structure stood natural, complete and inviolate.

NOTES

1. Grandma indeed seemed a realist all round. When, for instance, her husband, like Charles II, stayed lingering over his demise, solicitous neighbours were met with a cool 'I don't care how soon he's either better or worse'! She herself reached the age of ninety-three and died only moderately lamented.

2. To encourage the Adam in us our local park sold 'garden soil' at a penny a bucket. At home, expending twopence, we once tried a window box 'for flowers' in the back-yard. A few blooms struggled up then collapsed. 'So!' said my mother, loud in her husband's hearing, 'you can rear a child, it seems, on coal gas, but it does for geraniums!'

3. The railway company which owned most of our streets kept its houses in a moderate state of disrepair. Two workmen haunted the properties, a crabby joiner and, trailing behind him with the handcart, his mate, a tall, frail consumptive. This pair were known to the neighbourhood unkindly as 'Scrooge' and 'Marley's Ghost'.

4. Since the State educational system was doing little to train the mass of cheap female labour that commerce and the civil service drew upon after 1900, private 'colleges' sprang up in all the larger towns teaching shorthand, typing, book-keeping and foreign languages. One of these in the city, typical of many, opened in two small rooms, soared to prosperity through the inter-war years with more than a thousand students annually ('20 lessons, 20 shillings!'), then collapsed in the '60s when the State finally got round to providing commercial education for all who needed it.

   In the years of mass unemployment after the first world war some of these private establishments used to 'guarantee' their students a post after training. Many, desperate for work, borrowed or used savings to pay fees, only to be offered in the end one of those numberless jobs in commerce always to be had at starvation salaries.

5. 'Curran Cakes! 3 for 2*d*' advertised one neighbour on a little pile of grey lumps in her house window. Nobody bought. We children watched them growing staler each day until the kitchen curtain fell again on the venture like a shroud.

6. R. Hoggart, *The Uses of Literacy*. Penguin 1958.

7. Who, among the lowest orders, had just gone into or come out of Strangeways was of course a common topic of shop and beerhouse.

8. Harry Quelch, proletarian leader in the SDF, who knew the common people if ever a man did, called the English working class of that day the 'most reverential to the master class' of any in Europe. In London in 1889 at the time of the dockers' and gasworkers' strikes Engels wrote: 'The most repulsive thing here is the bourgeois "respectability" which has grown deep into the bones of the workers. The division of society into innumerable strata,

each recognized without question, each with its own pride, but also inborn respect for its "betters" and "superiors", is so old and firmly established that the bourgeoisie find it fairly easy to get their bait accepted.'

Engels seemed to find the workers' leaders little better. 'Even Tom Mann,' he complained, 'whom I regard as the best of the lot, is fond of mentioning that he will be lunching with the Lord Mayor.'-V. I. Lenin, *On Britain*.

CHAPTER TWENTY THREE

Community and Class Consciousness

JANE NASH

The assumptions underlying most analyses of the working class consistently underestimate the capacity for understanding and responding adaptively that exist among the people in less developed countries where industrialization has occurred late. The opposition of "traditional" and "modern" or "rational," of "heteronomy" and "autonomy,"[1] deny the potential for reinterpretation and growth in a cultural idiom different from that of the developed centers of the world but nonetheless capable of generating new understandings and adaptations, sometimes far in advance of the models we have from industrialized societies.

Eurocentric categories as to what constitutes rational behavior or what conduces to autonomy have little meaning for a marginal labor force in a dependent economy. The special characteristics of the work force in underdeveloped countries derive from the structural position of workers in the world economy as well as from ethnic differences defining the internal and external relationships. Bolivian miners are an extreme case of a work force linked to the international market and conscious of their role as producers in the global exchange system at the same time that they retain strong identification with prehispanic sources of cultural identity. As a result, their class consciousness is intrinsically tied to an awareness of the world division of labor, in which they feel themselves to be exploited not only as a working class in opposition to a managerial elite, but also as nationals of a dependent economy subject to domination by developed centers. As a class, they are more aware of international relations than are their counterparts in the United States. As a cultural enclave they are less alienated than the majority of the working class of industrial nations, since they are not cut off from the base of self-identification and communication that is still generated in the mining communities. The alienation of the working class takes on a more concentrated meaning in the tin mining community since it is related to the work scene, not to community or to self.[2] In this chapter I shall attempt to weave together some of the themes that I have touched on in relation to the problems of consciousness and ideology.

THE CULTURAL ROOTS OF WORKING-CLASS IDENTITY

The culture of transition in the industrial setting is that of the cholo. In studying such transitional cultures we discover that culture is not only something transmitted from the past to present and future generations. It is the generative base for adapting to conditions as well as for transforming those conditions. When we conceive of culture in this historical structural framework, it becomes a tool for analyzing processes of change rather than an ideology for confirming the status quo.

Miners are, as a group, very mobile, and many chose to go to the mines, since it was the only place where there were schools and the wages opened up at least the illusion of a better standard of living. However, becoming a cholo offered only a partial entry into the culture of the dominant Spanish-speaking group; it held the promise, but not the full admission, into the national society. Cholos[a] speak Spanish but are not always functionally literate. They wear an adaptation of the early Independence style of clothing, but the pollera, or voluminous skirt, worn by women, even when made of synthetics, is distinctly different from modern dress, and the derby hat is an emblem of ethnic identity. The cholos learn to despise the "ignorance and backwardness" of their Indian origins, but not to participate fully in the dominant culture. Women who have more than a primary school education often reject wearing the pollera that identifies them as cholas. Within the same family, sisters will often have different styles of dress and identify with an entirely different segment of the national culture because of educational differences. Children of the same parents may be labeled differently on their birth certificates as "blanco," "mestizo," or even "indio."[3]

The chola culture is, then, heterogeneous. Laymen and even social scientists often repeat the platitude that Bolivia's social problems result from its cultural and linguistic heterogeneity. However, when you have a sense of how the community functions, you realize that its strength derives from its ability to deal with differences not by suppressing them but by incorporating them. The miners are recruited from both Quechua – and Aymara-speaking communities as well as from mestizo populations of the altiplano and the Cochabamba valley. Since many are third-generation mine workers, they are often indirectly tied to a campesino background. Often parents are of different language groups and Spanish is the language of the home. Even when both parents speak the same Indian language, Spanish may be preferred in order to advance the children's opportunities. Quechua is more frequently spoken than Aymara, which is always combined with Quechua words. Language is not a basis for tribal identification, and whatever conflicts once existed have been worked out within family and neighborhood primary groups.

A gross measurement of the acculturation to a national pattern can be seen in the language used in the household. In sixty-one families for which we have language information in the household survey we found that in the households with parents between the ages of 21 and 30, Spanish was the only language spoken by the children, with only one adult speaking Quechua. In the remaining four cases with younger parents, the children were too young or their language was not recorded. In the household where the parents were from 31 to 40 years of age, the proportion was nearly even, with the children speaking an Indian language as well as Spanish in eleven cases compared to thirteen. In twenty-four households in which parents were from 41 to 50 years of age, the generation difference between older and younger children emerged, with six families in which older children spoke the Indian language and the younger spoke only Spanish. In one of these families, children spoke only Spanish. Finally, in the five households of the age group of parents 51 and over, in all but one case the children spoke the Indian language as well as Spanish.

For the most part, men have a higher acculturation rate than women, and this is reinfored by a specificity of tasks within the household. Women take responsibility for the old traditions with the house rituals to the Pachamama that give a sense of meaning and security to the men, while men bear the honor of the family, the root of which is providing with their wages the means of sustenance. If the family requires a loan or a favor of any kind, it is the woman who makes the approach in order to preserve her husband's honor. All the requests that I receive for loans or to become madrina of a cake for a birthday party, or a ring for a graduation ceremony (in effect a nonreciprocal loan, since the balance was maintained by the honor I received) were made by women. Men are typically more generous, and their wives limit this in the interest of the family. Thus the men have a stronger front and greater solidarity in the community, while the women have to preserve, out of a sense of family survival, what little resource base they have.

While men may be the primary modernizing agent, as Inkeles (1969), Kahl (1968), and others maintain, their position often depends on the strength of women who maintain the traditions that make life seem worthwhile and may even ensure survival. Women balance the tensions of penetrating into the modernizing sector of the society in a partial way, where the wage is insufficient to cover the new demands of living at a standard that is always beyond their family means, and where the modern health services are inadequate to their culturally felt needs, which were satisfied in the old system. They may maintain productive activities in the semi-subsistence areas of the economy that sustain the family in times of industrial layoffs and strikes.

As a result of this intrafamilial fragmentation of the culture, there is ambivalence about the chola/Indian identity, particularly in the first generation of transition. Basilia, a woman of 58 who worked inside the mines during the Chaco War[b], still retained the sense of contradiction between rural Indian and national chola cultures. She told me in Quechua:

> I understand Spanish, only I don't speak it. If I could speak at all clearly, I would have had another fate. If I knew how to read, if I understood the paper, I would have had another destiny. I would have taught them [the government agents from whom she was trying to get her pension] how to respect people.

She chose gente de vestido as padrinos for her children, and when her daughters grew up, they were de vestido.

> None of my children are chola. They wear only European dress, because people have more respect for such. For the cholas there is no respect. Whenever they want us, they just yell at us. They do not have the cross in their mouth [Quechua expression for Christian speech]. They don't have the standard that this brings. If one is a chola and doesn't know how to read, niñita, they don't have a good word. "The cholas don't know anything," they say. "They speak only ten words of Spanish."

Cholos often deprecate the Indians, even those who are their relatives. Manuel, who went into the mines to escape the poverty of his parents' home, says:

> My father was no more than an Indian with little capacity intellectually and with little vision. He was ignorant, my father, and I have tried to correct all that he did not have. And so have all my brothers and sisters who live tried to correct the errors and insufficiencies that our parents had.

Often the differential acculturation rates between husband and wife cause conflict in the home. Generally the man is the first to move away from the Indian or cholo culture. Petrona's mother was more acculturated than her father. She said:

> My mother fought a great deal so that I could go to school. My father was a brute who didn't understand. He didn't want it. "Why go to school? What is a woman going to learn in school?" he would ask. He fought that way with my mother. He didn't understand letters. He never went to school. He learned to speak Spanish when he went to work in the mines in Chile. My mother used to say, "Your father is an Indian and doesn't understand anything." My mother was well read, and she understood. She said that she was de vestido when she was young, but when she went to live with my papa she put on the pollera, because my father insisted on it. She cried when she changed her dress.

Men feel that they can control the mobility of their wives if they continue to wear the clothing that identifies them as cholas.

Becoming a chola is a continuous process of pendetration into national culture stimulated by educational advance and increasing consumption dependency. It was this process of becoming someone more advanced that kept the cholos tied to the mine and to the wage that gave them the promise if not the actuality of a better life. The tensions generated in this mobile strata are somewhat overcome in the family, work groups, and neighborhood compounds of the mining community. The homogeneous housing and life style limit the constant threat of invidious display that cannot be matched. While some think of the encampment as a trap, it offers some compensation in the communal sharing that overcomes the envy and divisiveness of other cholo subcultures. The mobility aspirations of the individual miner contradicts the ethic of communal sharing cultivated in the encampment. What shifts the balance in favor of solidarity in the class struggle is the inability of a flagging economy to permit social or economic advances for the vast majority of workers.

Within the chola culture of the mines, there is also a dialectical tension between egalitarianism and paternalism. The search for a patron is institutionalized in the com-padrazgo relationship and in the fiestas given to saints. Saints have varying degrees of luck that can be exploited by the lavishness of the fiestas offered to them. Since saints, like people, feel envy if one is not loyal to them, people tend to cultivate a single saint. Cholos often say of saints that they are "very evil," but this is taken as a sign of power, and people feel that this can be manipulated to one's advantage.

The chola culture in Bolivia differs from that of Peru and from the *rota* culture of Chile. Bourricaud (1970:79 et seq.) speaks of the cunning and violence of the cholos in Peru. He quotes José María Arguedas on the cholo who "no longer lives or belongs to the ayllu but he is constantly reminded of the fact that he comes from it" to capture the marginality of the cholo (Bourricaud 1970:71). Cotler (1969:68 et seq.) sees the cholo culture as a more positive product of the dislocation and migration that serves to break the monopoly of the mestizos in their control over Indian communities. By providing alternative sources of goods and services, the cholos open up new centers of social identity.

The difference in the Bolivian culture, at least in the mining community, is that cholos are the central figures here, not intermediaries between a subordinated Indian group and a superordinate ladino group. In their "centers of social identity" they have found a basis for social solidarity and collective action. This is based not on homogeneity, but on a cultivated ability to weave together the different cultural strands in the context of family and community.

The myths and rituals of the pre-conquest were an important means of transcending the culture shock of the Indian population that entered into the mines in the colonial period. The sense of fear that came with the violation of the earth and descending into the domain of Huari[c] the spirit of the hills, is dealt with explicitly in the myth set forth in chapter 1. The mythic time encompassed in this legend can be related to the Inca invasion merging into the Spanish conquest. The first invasion brought to an end the Garden of Eden, when the Uru Uru were pastorialists and agriculturalists, as the people turned from agriculture to work in the mines. They were delivered from the plagues brought upon them because of their indolence and vice by the Inca virgin, Ñusta. The return of the four plagues can be related to the Spanish conquest. This threat was overcome by the introduction of the Christian faith, symbolized by the church erected at the sites of the slain monsters. Each of the catastrophic events in the lives of the Indians was reworked into a thanksgiving for the merciful protection of the Ñusta, later identified with the Virgin of the Mine, who made it possible for life to go on. The Spaniards applied the term devil to the power of Huari, but this distorts the concept of this force as a potentially benevolent source of riches.

The ch'alla[d] for the Tío[e], or devil, inside the mines reenacts the strategy of appeasement and restoration. In the first place, the offering of blood and the palpitating heart of a sacrificed llama to the Tío satisfies his appetite and keeps him from unleashing destructive forces. Second, the offering of life is felt to restore the equilibrium of productive forces upset by mining. The foreign technicians were tolerant of these customs, but the national technicians, who replaced them after the nationalization of the mines, rejected them, possibly because of their own alienation and desire to separate themselves from the traditional culture. As one miner told me at a ch'alla I attended:

> Today the *jefes* that we have are nationals, and they are inattentive to the rituals. They believe themselves to be great señoritos who do not want to mix into the beliefs of the pueblo or of the workers. And because of this, the mines are declining. There is not as much production today.

Most of the miners feel that these beliefs are in no sense contradictory to the modernization and industrialization processes of which they are such an integral part in the country. A young miner who had completed his secondary school education said:

> The ch'alla this year was better than ever before. The miners are modernizing this kind of ch'alla; now the worker automatically goes to work on Tuesday, or Friday, prepares his coca, his cigarettes, his alcohol, his liquor, and whatever else he uses and makes his offering to the Tío.

In his view, this systematization of the ritual as part of an automatic work habit was the modernizing element and he saw no contradiction with the past. It reminded me of the Taylor principle in work process, where the modernizing aspect is the automatic performance regardless of content or whether the segmentation of the task structure actually means greater efficiency.

The cult of the Tío reinforces the solidarity of the work group. In the prenationalization days when the team operated collectively and was paid in proportion to its output, the inner solidarity of the cuadrilla was in opposition to the other work groups. The ch'alla was performed to wheedle more output from the devil, as each group competed with other cuadrillas. After nationalization, the individual worker was paid a basic wage regardless of the mineral produced, and solidarity included not only the entire work force of the mine but all nationalized mines. The ch'alla was more a recreation than a basis for solidarity in the productive work group. However, following the military takeover of the mines in 1965, the ch'alla was repressed along with unions and Worker Control. Workers continued to perform the ritual in secret, and these sessions become a focus for discussing the problems and struggles of the workers. Just as other pre-conquest rituals, such as the warming of the earth ceremonies at the fiesta of San Juan, became more explicitly the ritual expression of the desire to live, to multiply, and to enhance the reproductive and productive sources of life, so did the ch'alla. The resistance to military repression by men and women of the mining community came from these deep wells of cultural identity that gave them a sense of worth and the will to survive when they recognized the genocidal power of the Barrientos regime.

The separation of the indigenous customs in time and space from those of the Catholic religion imposed on the people gave a greater viability to the traditions in comparison to those cultures of Latin America where syncretism characterizes the relationship between Catholic and indigenous rituals. With the Virgin assigned to her niche in the church, the saints in their neon-lit boxes at level zero, the Supay[f] could maintain his dominion more effectively below ground and the Pachamama her identification with the earth and the riches thereof. The chola culture maintained this anchorage for the industrial workers who were only partially admitted into the industrial era.

Carnival remains the pinnacle in the yearly cycle of rituals that vindicate the chola culture and their means of dealing with their conditions of life. It is a dramatization of the occupational and ethnic roles into which Indians, blacks, and mestizos were thrust – llameras, morenadas, negritos, tobas, diablos – the polymorphous and perverse dance combinations where whites play blacks, men; play women, and all the contradictions of their lot in life are transformed into their opposite and transcended. Weaving in and around the dance figures are the condors, bears, hedgehogs – the totem of Oruro – which remind people that these enchanted figures can still make all their dreams come true.

Chola culture is an adaptive mode for adjusting to an industrial scene, but it does not provide a basis for changing the scenario. The fluid social ties, the coca chewing, the stress on commercialization are adjustive mechanisms to maintain humanity in inhuman working and living conditions. Even the mobility striving for self-improvement is adjustive, since it provides limited entry to a few top positions of influence in the dominant society and, by coopting the talented tenth, cuts off leaders from the masses of cholas. In the adjustment to the new, the technique of complementary distribution permitted cholos to retain elements of the old Indian culture that gave them the strength to resist the alienating effects of the industrial setting and to survive in the harsh physical and social environment of the mines. Instead of confronting the power structure that made the conditions of exploitation, it provided the myths that justified the polarized wealth and cultivated a desire on the part of workers to become a part of that dominant group. On the other hand, it is the milieu in which cholos become conscious of their class position and identify their frustrated mobility with a common understanding of their problems. Thus the chola culture stimulates the aspirations and desires that cannot be met for any but a small minority, and it is out of these frustrations that a class awareness is developed.

In the writing of political economists of the industrial age, there is a mystique about alienation as the human condition. This rests on the assumption that the sale of labor power universally results in estrangement culturally and socially because of the reification of the will and activity involved in work controlled by the owners of capital. Certainly industrialization does set the conditions for such alienation. But little has been said of the workers' resistance to that inner estrangement that reflects the social conditions imposed on them. Hobsbawm touched on it in *Primitive Rebels* (1959), when he saw in religion not just a pacifying illusion but the vindication of the self that was denied workers on the job. Anthony Wallace and others who have written about revitalization movements of colonized people touched by the industrialization process have captured some of the essential characteristics of such resistance. My experience living in mining communities taught me more than anything else, how a people totally involved in the most exploitative, dehumanizing form of industrialization managed to resist alienation. They did this in both a political and a religious idiom. For most miners, these were not contradictory expressions of commitment to proletarian struggle, although leaders of the institutions which promoted religious or political goals preached or polemicized that the aims and means of each sphere were dissonant. Huari, the devil, the Pachamama, Christ, and the Virgin Mary inhabited a unified world view where separate spheres of activity and timing enabled the miners to respond appropriately to each and all of these figures. Most miners did not oppose them to Marxist and Maoist teachings. What gave coherence to these prehispanic, Christian, and modern ideologies was a sense of self as members of a community sharing the sustenance offered by the Pachamama and occasionally taking advantage of the riches controlled by Huari. The ritual of the ch'alla – from the simplest reference to it in sprinkling liquor on the earth to the sacrifice of a llama in the k'araku – are a part of communal gatherings that collectively enable the miners to overcome the alienation in their lives.

. . .

EDITOR'S NOTES

(a) For an explanation of the term, see the Introduction to Part 5.
(b) The Chaco War was fought between Bolivia and Paraguay over the control of Gran Chaco region of South America.
(c) For an explanation of the term, see the Introduction to Part 5.
(d) For an explanation of the term, see the Introduction to Part 5.
(e) For an explanation of the term, see the Introduction to Part 5.
(f) For an explanation of the term, see the Introduction to Part 5.

NOTES

1. See, for example, a discussion of Weber's uses of concepts "traditional" and "rational" in H. H. Gerth and C. Wright Mills (1946:56). Alan Touraine and Daniel Pécaut reject the old dichotomies, but construct their own in the opposition of "heteronomy" and "autonomy." The so-called autonomy of the modern industrial working class is won at the expense of the semi-subsistent household production base. Given its condition of alienation from the means of production, the proletariat is even more dependent on capitalist enterprise and conditions of work over which they have little control.

2. D. Lockwood (1968:100–1) asserts that industries which concentrate workers in single-industry communities reinforce "proletarian traditionalism" and polarized class patterns. This view is supported by C. Kerr and A. Siegel (1954) and N. Dennis, F. Henriques, and C. Slaughter (1956).

3. For an interesting discussion of Indian and chola subcultures see Harris and Albó (1975).

REFERENCES

Bourricaud, Ferancois. 1970. *Power and Society in Contemporary Peru.* New York: Praeger.

Cotler, Julio. 1969. 'Actuales Pautas de Cambio en la Sociedad Peruana: Una Perspectiva Configuraciona', in José Matos *et al* (eds.) *Domacion y cambios en el Peru rural*, pp: 23–59. Lima: Instituto de Estudios Peruanos.

Dennis, N., F. Henriques and C. Slaughter. 1956. *Coal is Our Life.* London: Eyre.

Harris, Olivia and Javier Albó. 1975. *Monteras y guardatojos; Campesinos y mineros en el norte de Potosí.* La Paz: Bolivia: Centro de Investigación y Promoción del Campesinado (CIPCA).

Gerth, H. and C. Wright Mills, (trans and eds.) 1946. *From Max Weber: Essays in Sociology.* New York: Oxford University Press.

Hobsbawm, Eric. 1959. *Primitive Rebels: Studies in Archaic Forms of Social Movements in the Nineteenth and Twentieth Centuries.* New York: Norton.

Inkeles, Alex. 1969. 'Making Men Modern: On the Causes and Consequences of Individual Change in Developing Countries', *American Journal of Sociology*, 75: 208–25.

Kahl, Joseph A. 1968. *The Measurement of Modernism: A Study of Values in Brazil and Mexico.* Austin: University of Texas Press.

Kerr, Clark and Abraham Siegel. 1954. 'The Industrial Propensity to Strike: An International Comparison', in A. Kornhauser, R. Dubin, and A. Ross (eds.) *Industrial Conflict*, pp: 189–212. New York: McGraw-Hill.

Lockwood, D. 1968. 'Sources of Variation in Working Class Images of Society', in J. Kahl (ed.), *Comparative Perspectives on Stratification*, pp: 100–101. Boston: Little Brown.

CHAPTER TWENTY FOUR

Learning to Protest in Japan: Class Consciousness, Solidarity, and Political Action

CHRISTENA TURNER

By the time I came to Unikon, the union had been through three major labor disputes with their management and had struggled for sixteen years against strong opposition to form their union. The demonstration which I discuss in this chapter was for them a familiar action. That familiarity itself was a purposefully achieved goal of the leaders of Unikon and an accomplishment of some pride for the rank and file. It had evolved through a combination of explicit education and argument on the one hand and experiential learning on the other. Demonstrations and other acts of open protest are not ordinary in the lives of most workers. While the existence of such actions is known from the press or from union news or even from friends, they are not part of most people's personal experience. Consequently, when faced with a need to organize collective actions, the leaders of Unikon's union needed a strategy to build solidarity and to teach their rank and file to protest. That strategy included both plans for organizing collective action and plans for raising the consciousness of the membership so that their commitment would be deep enough to withstand a lengthy dispute. Moreover, the rank and file had to have personal strategies, including reasons for staying and fighting rather than quitting in favor of other employment. The collective history of the union and its disputes and protests is a history of several different strands of action, strategy, reason, and sensibility that together formed a series of unified struggles. Unity was a carefully and imperfectly constructed social form with divergent internal threads, formed as much from the sense people had of personal experiences as of arguments, analysis, or conversation.

HISTORY OF UNIKON'S MAJOR DISPUTES

There are two influential strands of history in Unikon's struggle: the history which had been shared by most of the workers still present and the history prior to their employment at the firm, providing stories which were a source of lessons, legends, and examples. At the end of the dispute there were 102 persons still working at Unikon. Of these between 80 and 90 had been with Unikon from the beginning of the organization of the labor union, about eleven years before. There were four major disputes in Unikon's history. The first three all involved struggles to form the union organization. In each case workers organized a union and in each case the company took action against it. Only in the third did a union survive, and that is the present Unikon union. The final and fourth dispute was the bankruptcy dispute which was ongoing when I worked there.

Unikon's First and Second Disputes

Unikon Camera was established in 1907 and operated without a union until 1956. After World War II, business expanded rapidly as the camera was sold to the U.S. military, and the work force of 150 increased by 1961 to 1500. It was during this period of growth that, in December 1956, an effort to organize a union was made. The new Japanese constitution and postwar labor laws guaranteed rights to organize, and the early postwar period saw an extraordinary rise in union organization and membership from just over 3 percent in 1945 to nearly 56 percent in 1949. From the mid-1950s rates dropped to about 35 percent, where they have remained ever since (Shirai 1983b). This first attempt at Unikon included about two hundred workers. The response by the owners was opposition. They formed a second union to divide workers, enlisted the help of police by charging union members with violence, and mobilized managers to threaten workers with dismissal if they joined the new organization. The union was dissolved within six months, and soon after the management-formed second union was also disbanded.

The company continued to grow, in particular with the expansion of the war in Vietnam and consequent increase in U.S. military personnel, the primary market for their cameras. The second Unikon dispute began in 1966 when five workers were dismissed. These two men and three women were preparing to organize a union once again, and they charged that their dismissal was for that reason. After their dismissal they organized a union anyway and carried on a struggle against unfair discharge and interference in their rights to organize. They brought suit on these charges and picketed outside the factory. The owners of Unikon responded with an uncompromising opposition, refusing to negotiate, and sending company employees to harass them. There were frequent incidents of minor violence. Workers reported being kicked, having lit cigarettes put to their skin, and being threatened with worse violence. Their homes were visited and their families embarrassed and intimidated, and anticommunist leaflets were distributed in their neighborhoods. After three years and nine months the workers were granted reinstatement by Labor Relations Commission mediators and the dispute ended.

These first two disputes continued to live in the minds of union members and were often cited as evidence of some basic characteristics of the Unikon union. They were seen, for instance, as early examples of the importance of women, the experience of victimization of workers trying to exercise legal rights to organize and bargain, and the persistence and determination of Unikon workers to overcome this opposition.

The Third Dispute

In February 1969, while the second dispute was still ongoing, five workers came together to try again to form a labor union. To avoid detection and further dismissals the five devised a strategy for recruitment of new members, which centered around the following rules: (i) union members should not interact with one another in the workplace; (2) new members are to be known only to the chairman and the secretary; (3) the existence of the union is to remain secret at the time of recruitment, so each individual is recruited as one of just two employees interested in the formation of a union; and (4) use of strict precautions when going to and from a meeting. This effort proceeded with great caution, and by December they had twenty members and began publication of a newsletter called *Phoenix*. In Japanese and Chinese mythology, this is a bird that cannot be killed, because it revives after each death to fly again. It seemed an apt image for their union's third attempt to become an official representative organization. The secrecy continued, and in fact instructions were given to burn this newsletter after reading it. By 1970 there were fifty members and by 1971 one hundred. In the fall of 1971 they made a flag and began preparations for going public, which they did on April 24, 1972. By this time they had 250 members; they joined the All-Japan Metalworkers Labor Union Federation and flew their red flag at the factory.

In May 1972 the union officers were dismissed from their jobs, and with this began the third dispute. Also in May, the owners formed a second union and sent letters to each of their employees introducing it, an act perceived as intimidation directed against all those who might join the union organized by the workers. There followed a variety of measures by management designed to discourage people from joining this union, including interruption of meetings, confinement of leaders, job transfers for workers, reduction in pay for members, visits to families of members, and forced discussions with members encouraging them to quit or join the other, company-approved union. This struggle continued through August 21, 1973, when the court rejected the dismissal of the union officials and ordered their reinstatement.

The Part-Timers Union

By 1974 the union had 102 members, the second breakaway union had 80, 70 employees were nonmembers, and there were 200 part-time workers. In the context of a company proposed reduction in employment, part-time workers, under the influence of the Unikon union, formed their own union and in May 1975 announced its existence publicly. Furthermore, this union decided to join the All-Japan Metalworkers Federation of which Unikon's union was a member, and with that decision, the balance of power between the original Unikon union and the breakaway union was won. The second union was dissolved, and the joint strength of the Unikon union and the part-timers union totaled just over 300 members. By 1977 a union shop agreement had been won, and the Unikon union became the representative of all workers within the company.

The Fourth Dispute

The fourth dispute is the bankruptcy struggle which Unikon was fighting at the time of my research there. This struggle began with three goals: (1) reconstruction of the company, (2) payment of unpaid wages, and (3) payment of debts to workers, including severance pay. Later a fourth was added, the recovery of rights to the Unikon brand, which were sold away during this time. It was only this final demand which was still entirely unmet at the time of the demonstration described below. The others were in the process of final resolution. This dispute took two and a half years to settle.

THE ORGANIZATIONAL PRACTICES OF STRUGGLE

It is of the period of the third dispute that most workers at Unikon have personal memories and experiences, and it is from this time that organizational practices of particular significance for nurturing solidarity became institutionalized. Of enduring importance were (1) formal study groups and educational activities, (2) individual participation in external union activities, (3) emphasis on strong personal ties between union members, (4) frequent meetings and communication among all members, (5) strong centralized leadership, and (6) cultivation of external labor movement networks of support. By the time of the fourth dispute nearly all workers, rank and file and leadership alike, were accustomed to participating in such an organization, and their own consciousness had been formed through such experiences.

Formal Study Groups

The Unikon union was a secret union for nearly three years. During that time, leaders decided that the long-term strength of their organization would be determined by the knowledge and education of each individual member. In particular, it was important to convince people that there were legal and constitutional guarantees for labor unions and collective bargaining, and that historically such action was justifiable. They formed five study groups: for history, literature, labor laws, economics, and U.S.-Japan Security Treaty issues. Each member was to belong to at least one, and they each met once a week. In addition there were training camps held in nearby resort areas once every four months. Here papers and lectures could be presented and members could study and have discussions together.

Since there was to be no socializing at work, due to the continuing secrecy of the union, these study groups and camps were the primary focus of energy and the primary form of the organization. They represent the most direct effort to affect the consciousness of the union members, stemming from a belief that workers had too little information about their own rights to be willing to fight for them and too little information about labor laws and the history of the labor movement in Japan to have confidence in their ability to have at least some success. The coincidence of this education effort with the origins of the union as an organization doubled the effectiveness of the groups in teaching new members about collective action, strength, and solidarity, because these workers were simultaneously participating in a new structure and explicitly learning a way to comprehend its utility and importance.

Individual Participation in External Union Activities

From the early days of the union, rank-and-file members were sent to other unions, to local organizations, and to the neighborhood associations to explain their struggle, to seek support from these groups, and to represent their union. Leaders of the Unikon union wanted all their members to be so identified with and knowledgeable about their union that any one of them could speak for the whole. Furthermore, they wanted each member to be fully conscious of the place of the union in the community and in the wider network of unions. Some of these concerns stemmed from a small company/small union consciousness on the part of the union leaders. Strength had to come from something other than great resources or large numbers; it had to be built through cultivating individual determination and external support. The explicit strategy was to cultivate these through the practice of having rank-and-file members do much of the external relations work which might otherwise be done as part of a leadership responsibility.

This practice, of course, reinforced the education efforts of the study groups. Workers later recounted how they had to study hard in order to answer questions and defend their union's position when they went out to other groups. In effect, they needed particular knowledge for particular ongoing practice. They also spoke with animation about the expansion of their own worldviews, talking about how much more of the world they understood after these experiences.

Emphasis on Strong Personal Ties Between Members

Having ties to one another as workers and as union members was not seen to be sufficient for real unity. Leaders of the Unikon union felt that they had to schedule a certain number of opportunities for people to socialize. In the early stages, before the union was public, the study retreats accomplished this by allowing time for drinking, walking, or bathing together. Dormitories also encouraged such socializing, as did various company-sponsored classes and events. At Unikon, however, there were relatively few such events, and as the union became public and larger they began organizing softball games, vacations, and various parties to improve personal ties of friendship and affection between workers. Commitment was believed to be fostered more effectively through such personal ties than through strictly formal ties of work or union membership.

Frequent Meetings and Communication Among Members

In the early months of union organizing when things were still secret, there were study group meetings at least once a week and a newsletter once every month or two. The newsletter was considered so risky that readers were asked to burn it after finishing it. Later, after going public, there gradually developed a regular schedule of meetings at various levels, beginning on the shop floor once a week and culminating in a general meeting once a month. During disputes, however, the general meeting convened once a week, and throughout the week there were informal gatherings on the shop floor with leaders present during lunches and at the end of the day or during breaks.

Constant contact between people was believed to be critical to a sense of unity and solidarity, and leaders of Unikon's union went to great lengths to keep everyone working together, even immediately after bankruptcy when people were not working on the same products or doing similar work. Immediately following the bankruptcy it was impossible to continue making cameras until the union leaders could reestablish smooth operations. Nevertheless, to enable workers to resist the order to vacate and disperse, their livelihood had to be secured. The solution of the Unikon union leaders was to pool unemployment checks and to have people seek piece work at other factories, bring it to the Unikon factory each morning, and do it there in the same room, thus sharing space and time if not work. The money each one earned was then pooled with the checks, and each worker was given a share at about 60 percent of their usual wage.

In hindsight, leaders claimed that had they not maintained the day-to-day contact of workers with one another in this way their struggle would have disintegrated. Rank and file looked back on this time as "inspiring," although harrowing, exhausting, and filled with uncertainties. Many reflected that it was an experience which built their commitment to each other and to their struggle. Organizationally, it built friendship through sharing of adversity and of resources, and it allowed union leaders to mobilize and communicate on an hourly basis with the entire membership.

Strong Centralized Leadership

The combination of strong centralized leadership with decentralized participation is certainly not unique to the Unikon union organization. It is a characteristic noted in many studies of large Japanese companies (Cole 1971 and 1979; Dore 1973, 1986, and 1987; Rohlen 1974). At Unikon it was a tradition from the earliest days of the union, due in part to the circumstances of these early times themselves. Since the union was organized by a handful of people who then became the core of the union's leaders and remained so through the fourth dispute, there was a sense of charisma, skill, and tradition to their leadership. Furthermore, the initial period, when no one but the president and the secretary even knew the names of the members, left its own legacy in the centralization of information, decision making, and control. The leaders of this union were skillful, dynamic, committed, and well respected in the labor union networks and in the community, in part for their success in organizing against what was considered to be an obstinate ownership. Rank and file were similarly proud of and supportive of them.

Frequency of meetings, agendas, strategies for protest, and programs for members were decided by leadership and presented as suggestions to members in meetings. Proposals were discussed, argued, and largely accepted and then implemented. Extensive programs for participation and discussion were implemented but with a strong centralized hand, one with every benefit of legitimacy and the confidence of its members.

Cultivation of External Networks of Support

Because Unikon was such a small union, there was a great effort to cultivate outside support from the Sōhyō federation, from the All-Japan Metalworkers Federation, from local union networks, and even from community organizations like neighborhood associations. Unikon was self-consciously modeling itself as an inspiration for workers in other largely unorganized small and medium-sized industries, to whom its leaders wanted to demonstrate that unions could be organized, disputes fought and won, and working conditions improved. This objective was part of the education campaigns for rank and file who were inclined to be more motivated by personal objectives than by wider social and political ones. It was also part of the motivation for sending all members out into the community and to other unions' meetings, to impress upon Unikon's membership that they were working for more than themselves and to educate others that even ordinary rank-and-file workers of a small company can get involved in the labor movement.

The negotiations and contacts with the Sōhyō and All-Japan Metalworkers federations were handled by leaders, and again the pattern of centralized leadership and decentralized participation emerges. In the hierarchy of significance and alliance, it was the higher-ranking affiliations that were handled by leaders alone, as were all negotiations about settlement, while lower-ranking network associations were visited by rank-and-file members.

UNIKON'S DEMONSTRATION

Of all the actions taken during their long struggle, the "Sōkōdō" demonstration described here brought workers into contact with the largest and most diverse population of workers. This demonstration was one of several types of demonstrations in which Unikon participated, and it was the largest and arguably the most important. About once every three months thousands of workers representing hundreds of labor unions engaged in disputes march through the financial district of Tokyo, combining their numbers and thus their strength to stage demonstrations in front of the financial institutions against which they are struggling. The event lasts from 7:30 in the morning until 8:00 at night. The organization responsible for these is Tōkyō Sōgidan (Tokyo Labor Dispute Association), and this action itself is called Sōgi Kōdō (Dispute Cooperative Action) and is often abbreviated in conversation as Sōkōdō.

Tōkyō Sōgidan comprises unions in the Tokyo region fighting labor disputes, most of which are from small and medium-sized firms. Their demonstrations have a history of about twenty years, and were initiated because of a need for strength through numbers. Small unions cannot make much of an impression if they demonstrate by themselves, but through Tōkyō Sōgi Kōdō they can muster thousands of people for a real show of strength. The purposes of the demonstration are to force the financial institution in question into negotiation and to maintain pressure on them while they negotiate. Typically, for example, while the demonstration is under way in front of a bank, there is a team of labor union negotiators trying to gain entry, or in some cases already inside negotiating.

My introduction to Sōkōdō was through the Unikon picture albums. One of the first things the union leaders did in familiarizing me with their union and its history was to take me on a tour of important events through these albums. They were carefully put together, and the pictures were shown and explained to me with a great deal of pride as well as enjoyment. The union leader who was describing these, a man named Tajima-san, explained that now that Unikon's own major struggle was coming to a positive conclusion, they would continue to participate in these partly because of their own still unresolved issues but also because they had a real "debt" to this organization for all the help they had received at critical times during their own dispute. In the spirit of reciprocity with affiliated unions, they would continue to participate to repay others who had helped them.

Unikon had been involved in a variety of actions, taking a very aggressive stance toward their owners. Their workers had staged protests on their own at banks, in their company's neighborhood, in front of train stations, and in front of the home of the owners. Because of the broader involvement of other unions and workers in large numbers, however, Sōkōdō demonstrations were particularly critical to raising the consciousness of their workers and to winning their dispute. Tajima-san even suggested that without these demonstrations, without this show of strength, it might have been impossible for them to succeed.

Among the pictures were scenes of brass bands with people assembled and singing, or in other cases Japanese *taiko* drum troops, also with people singing or chanting. I asked what they were singing, and he spoke with animation about the songs written by the Unikon union for each particular dispute, of which they had had four. The music was supplied by Sōhyō, which seemed to have a number of easily sung tunes on file, and the words were written by particular unions to suit their own particular struggle. Then the members learned the songs, and they were printed up to be distributed to nonmembers at demonstrations.

The scenes as he described them and showed them to me through pictures were extremely colorful, almost festive. People were wearing red and white headbands and chest signs painted in various colors, and were walking amid enormous red flags and banners. His description, which was reinforced repeatedly in conversations with other Unikon workers, was overall of a very important and exciting event, at once serious and fun.

Preparation

In April 1980, I was in a shop floor meeting where an upcoming demonstration was announced. The representative asked everyone to join, and as she announced the date people noted it in their open notepads or on scraps of paper. There was no more discussion of it at the time or for several weeks after. It seemed to have been taken for granted that everyone would go, and the mood around it was serious and casual. Not until the day before the demonstration was scheduled to take place did it come up again. I had nearly forgotten about it when at lunch people began discussing the time and meeting place. After lunch I noticed people talking about these details with one another and double-checking things with the shop floor steward. I checked with her to see if I might attend, and she discussed it with the union officials, who encouraged me to do so. We agreed that I should march with them but not wear either chest signs or head bands, since my doing so could get me into trouble with the police. As a foreigner my situation was a potentially risky one if I got involved in political activities.

Participation

The demonstration began early, with people gathering between 7:30 and 8:00 A.M. and continued until around 8:00 at night. There was a contingent of union leaders present from the morning throughout the day and into the night. Everyone else showed up in the late morning or after lunch, leaving a tiny staff to deal with telephones and necessary work. The assembly section, where I was working, went after lunch.

There was some anticipation in the air in the morning. People had brought snack foods like potato chips or homemade pickles to carry along and eat during the course of the demonstration. They were dressed nicely but not dressed up, and some women were talking about having worn comfortable walking shoes and wondering how far we would be walking today. A number of people took my presence as a chance to explain what was to be expected.

Several said that I'd be tired because we would walk several miles. Others asked me if I had ever been to Ginza or to Tsukiyabashi Park, from which the demonstration was to begin.

. . .

When we reached Ginza, we all disembarked and came out of the subway into a very crowded little park, a park from which all kinds of demonstrations frequently begin. People spoke of peace, anti–Security Treaty, and other kinds of demonstrations which traditionally center around this park. Entering, we found the statue which is its center, where a few union leaders were waiting for us with the chest signs and head-bands each person was to wear. People began putting these on, helping each other tie them securely. Small groups were doing the same everywhere. It was crowded, and while putting things on people were handing out and being handed leaflets describ-ing the various union struggles represented in the day's demonstrations. Among the leaflets were also ones for other, related causes and for movies shown by the Socialist and Communist parties. When the Unikon people were ready, we all walked to a nearby street, by this time filled with contingents ready to march, each holding red flags with white or black letters naming their union and proclaiming solidarity (*danketsu*), many preceded by a line of people carrying a banner announcing their union's particular grievance. The Unikon chest signs proclaimed support for all affiliated unions' struggles and demanded their brand be returned to them, a still-unresolved issue and a primary reason for their participation this day.

The Unikon workers lined up in their spot, and I separated from them a bit onto the sidelines, where I could take pictures and observe the march. There were police in obvious attendance all along the route and a number of onlookers standing watching the march go by. The majority of passersby, however, simply walked along minding their own business and showing little interest in the parade of marchers. At inter-sections there were police to help with the traffic, and of course that is where people gathered waiting to cross the street, becoming a sort of captive audience for the dem-onstrators. The comments I could hear were exclusively of the "I wonder what this is" variety. There was no leafleting along the march route.

We marched through the center of Ginza and in the direction of the financial dis-trict near Tokyo Station. At our first stop I was surprised to see the crowds of people waiting for us in front of the bank in question. There were people on every corner and in front of the bank giving out leaflets describing their grievance with the bank. The demonstrators began arriving by the hundreds. They lined up on the sidewalk, spilling over onto side streets and up and down the sidewalk in both directions. The most unexpected thing for me was that they lined up facing not the public passing by in the street, but facing the bank building, where no one stood facing them. I realized at that point that I had been expecting them to speak to the public, but what they intended was to speak to the bank, and in the absence of bank representatives, they spoke to the bank building itself, as a way of demonstrating quite literally their confrontation and thus communicating with the bank officers inside. The only attention paid directly to the public was the distribution of leaflets, and that was confined to the area immediately surrounding the building.

A truck pulled up, and the leaders of the involved union and a couple of supporting federation persons climbed on top and spoke, outlining their grievances and accusing the bank of being behind the management and not trying to protect the livelihood of the workers in their union. For ten minutes or so there were repeated accusations and chants of various kinds led by the leaders on top of the van and joined in by the hundreds of supporters on the sidewalk, all raising their fists in the direction of the bank as they proclaimed their determination not to give up in their fight.

There were some ten or so stops on our afternoon schedule, and the activities at each stop followed much this same pattern. The length of time spent varied somewhat, according to the stage of negotiation reached in the particular dispute. In the case of unions like Unikon, which had already been negotiating for some time, there was not even a stop at the bank in question. Instead, on this same day, there was a negotiation session under way. At the site of a demonstration against a bank which refused to negotiate, the time spent was longer, since a primary purpose of these demonstrations was to pressure the opposition into discussion and to keep them seriously negotiating. Once that purpose is served, the pressure is taken off.

The chants, which were led from atop the vans at each stop, were sometimes particular ones for the union involved, in which case they would not be repeated at other stops. A common one was "X Bank, Take responsibility for Y Company's bankruptcy!" There were also several chants that were repeated at many stops: "Victory in the 1980 Spring Labor Offensive!" "Oppose price rises! Oppose lay-offs!" "We demand a livable wage!" These themes came up at many stops, and at the end of each chant fists were raised toward the bank in question. The overall effect of hundreds of voices shouting out these statements and raising their fists was deafening for people inside the group and nearby. It created a very impressive show of strength and unity when viewed either from the midst of the demonstrators or from without.

The speeches from atop the trucks were done with microphones and so were very loud, audible for a couple of city blocks in either direction. The content was very specific to the case around which the particular demonstration was focused. Several of the speeches mentioned the Unikon union's recent success as an example for unions that persevere. Many speeches accused banks of conspiring with management to destroy a company in order to get rid of a strong union. Nearly all accused the banks of not taking responsibility for the livelihood of the workers in the companies with whose management they had financial ties. Every speech ended the same way, with a few chants and a final "We'll never give up!" (*Ganbarō*!) followed by applause.

When one demonstration had run its course people reassembled and marched to the next. There were several courses and at some points contingents would split up and join other marchers in another contingent. Only a few leaders seemed to know just how and when everything was to take place. The rest relied on them for instructions at the end of each demonstration. Between chants, while walking, there was a lot of talking. These conversations did not center around what was being done; they were more likely to be about the scenery of the area or how something had changed since last time they were downtown. The mood was relaxed and congenial. We had a break at one point where we were told to wait for a contingent to catch up to our Unikon group. We waited in front of a beautiful new bank, a skyscraper with elaborate landscaping and a modern architectural design. People walked unabashedly up to the side of the building, sat down on the ornamental walls surrounding the neatly trimmed shrubbery and flower beds and pulled out bags of potato chips, packages of homemade pickles, and other snacks to wait and enjoy a restful break. A few took off the head bands and chest signs, put them in their bags, and went into the bank building and downstairs to the bank's shopping and restaurant floor to use the restrooms. People joked about using the bank's facilities while preparing to demonstrate against them. "We have a lot of nerve, don't we [*Zūzūshii desu ne?*]?"

Everyone was tired by now. It was nearly 3:30 and some of the part-time women were planning to go home after the next demonstration. When the rest of the marchers got to this site there was a very large and noisy demonstration. After a couple more stops the women began going home. Part-time women workers were not asked to stay later than their usual quitting time, although many did remain for an extra hour or so. The leaders continued throughout the day, until about 8:00 that night. I went home with three young men and two women from the assembly section about 5:00. We talked about the incredible number of people who had turned up and about the length of the march and how tired everyone was. Again I was impressed that people did not seem to be as emotionally involved as the chanting, singing, and fist raising would have led an observer to suspect. The demonstrations were barely over and they were definitely not keyed up. Conversation centered on related topics, but it was not emotionally charged conversation. During one break young men even dragged out comic books they had brought along and squatted here and there reading them.

When I saw people at work the next day they were not talking about the demonstration very much. Some asked me what I had thought and asked me to compare the Japanese demonstrations to American ones. There was also discussion about how late everyone had gotten home and some comparing of notes about shopping and dinner preparation by the women who were also responsible for their families' evening meals regardless of the day's activities. There was a certain amount of discussion about the other unions' lengthy disputes and the likelihood of them settling in the near future or the long time that had passed without settlement. This discussion was interspersed with comments about how lucky Unikon was to have taken only two and a half years. Although that had seemed to be a very long time, clearly other unions were taking even longer.

The overall tone of conversation was again serious and subdued, involved but with some distance. People seemed very experienced. They had acted the day before and were commenting the following day in a way that showed them to be longtime veterans of labor movement demonstrations. The agility with which they slipped in and out of their chest signs and in and out of their demonstration behavior was something of which they were quite aware and quite proud. While many rank-and-file workers referred to it as part of their life experience (*jinsei keiken*), leaders spoke of it as an achievement, a carefully planned one. The common reference here was historical, to the years they had had together, to the other major disputes they had fought, and to their own personal, individual experiences within that history.

LEARNING TO PROTEST

Staying throughout this two-and-a-half-year dispute involved making sense of the struggle and deciding to join it oneself, both processes constituted by discursive thought and by experience. The struggle and its meaning were discussed at work and in conversation outside with family and friends as well. There were arguments about it. Not everyone, even those involved, thought it made sense all the time. There was a tacit, commonsensical side to it that was motivated in part by the action itself. As Victor Turner (1967, 1969) notes for rituals, doing something oneself creates a meaning that is experienced as well as thought through. So when the Unikon union leaders had rank and file go out to present their situation to other unions, they were not only convincing them through words but engaging them through their own actions. Consequently, what had to be made sense of was not just an external situation but one which these workers were themselves actively creating and responding to. Whereas the original causes and circumstances of the disputes were part of the work lives of all workers, the collective action that leaders instigated was not. That response, in order to grow out of this situation, had to grow through the actions and experiences of the rank-and-file workers. The Unikon workers in the final phase of their struggle spoke of these actions growing into and through their lives, creating a sensibility at once known and felt.

Why did over two hundred workers stay at Unikon and fight together in this struggle? What motivated them? How did they understand their own action and the meaning of their union's struggle? It is one thing to talk about participation in a demonstration or the history of union actions in which people participated, but the question remains: Why bother? Why not quit and go elsewhere as most workers do when companies go bankrupt, and as the majority of Unikon workers in this case did as well? Learning to protest is not something people go out of their way to do or arrange to do in their free time, and it isn't without risk and cost. The answers are multiple. There were several reasons that motivated commitment at Unikon, and each worker had his or her own combination of priorities and strategies which led them to stay. Furthermore, decisions to stay or quit, to participate or not in particular events or organizational practices were always made in specific institutional contexts which provided experiential constraints and encouragement. In other words, people were acting with particular structures both of thought and of experience. Their decisions, strategies, and ultimately their understandings were all well thought out and affectively compelling. Common sense and ideology, what felt right and what was believed to be right, what couldn't be helped and what were explicit goals – all were equally important in the process of interpreting situations, deciding upon strategies, and taking action.

Sometimes people had determined to stay out of anger. Most talked about this as the critical factor in the very beginning. They were angry at the "inhuman" treatment they received at the hands of the owners. After some time had passed, however, other factors compelled them to stay. Many talked about wanting to stay with their coworkers, saying essentially that because no one had quit once the dispute began, no one felt that they could quit. There were also elements of pride and excitement about being part of a very important labor movement event. Coming from such a small company, it was unusual to get such attention and support from the national networks of unions. Most people talked about the possibility of success, that all along there had been enough hope to sustain their efforts to win. And some workers talked about fear of trouble finding other employment. These factors had a fluid quality, some being more salient in early stages and others in later stages. Individual life courses intersected and pulled factors in and out of significance as well. And the organizational structures and practices were at all times forming a social arena within which people were weighing and balancing priorities and assessing and reassessing their own thoughts about their situation and their own actions. Comprehension and collective action were at all times integrally connected. The demonstration was not, of course, the only act of protest in which Unikon workers were engaged, but it was one of the most dramatic, most public, and politically most significant.

MAKING SENSE OF STRUGGLE

The demonstration itself was always a highly symbolic event, an occasion during which the fact of the struggle was brought front and center, made more visible, and its meanings addressed more explicitly. A lengthy dispute, and one carried out in the context of union-managed production like this one, tends to create a very matter-of-fact daily work life for rank and file. While leaders of the union, who are also managing the production of the factory, are still involved regularly with negotiations, labor networks, and strategy, the workers in the factory spend most days simply coming to work at 8:30 and leaving at 5:30 or 6:00, doing their own jobs, chatting with coworkers at breaks, socializing on their way to and from work, and attending meetings. While their situation is not forgotten, it is not primary in day-to-day consciousness at all times either.

Immediately before, particularly during, and then after demonstrations or other collective actions, such awareness of themselves as being involved in a protest is higher.

The very symbolic nature of the demonstration itself makes it particularly good at raising such issues. In the lives of the participating workers, the demonstration is set off from everyday life, clearly bounded by numerous symbolically rich actions, elements of dress, and patterns of movement. Virtually everyone who participates experiences this separation and views the involvement as something different, note-worthy, or special in contrast to the day-to-day, routine activities. The Unikon picture albums recording the history of the union, for instance, noted these demonstrations along with other special occasions like trips and festival celebrations, but had no pictures, until I took them, of people doing their everyday jobs or of regularly held union meetings and shop floor get-togethers. The movement between daily life and the demonstration was smooth for Unikon workers, and this agility in slipping into and out of their roles as protesters stands in sharp contrast to Universal workers, . . . Unikon workers had learned this agility, and it was an achievement of the union as a whole, planned and guided by leaders and experienced in a variety of ways by rank and file. The transition remains; that is, daily life is not a demonstration or protest when a dispute lasts two and a half years. Nevertheless, the transition, if it is made easily, is a sign that consciousness of collective interests and the sense that collective action is necessary have become strong and pervasive.

A Struggle for All Workers

The demonstration, their struggle, and all the protests in which they engaged rein-forced for them the importance of their own dispute for the strength and well-being of workers in general. At Unikon, words like *rōdōsha* (worker) and *rōdō undō* (labor movement) were very generously sprinkled throughout a day's conversation (given, of course, appropriate conversation topics), so there was a frequent linguistic reminder of a certain identity with other workers. By the time I saw them, the Unikon workers were already veterans of demonstrations of various kinds and of other labor movement activities, so they had in fact already learned to think of themselves and their struggle in this way. Both explicit arguments about such links and the structure of many activities influenced this process of learning to see their relationship to other workers. One woman put it this way: "In the beginning, I stayed with the union with-out a clear reason. Somehow I just didn't get around to quitting. Over the past two and a half years, though, I have been part of so many union activities like demonstra-tions. At first they were strange to me, but my consciousness as a worker has been strengthened. Now I work with a certain pride in myself as a *rōdōsha.*"

Perceiving oneself as a worker and one's actions as important to all workers involves sharing some characteristics with all other workers and identifying in a uni-versalistic sense with them. The existence of the Sōgidan organization itself is a state-ment of sorts about shared problems, shared conditions, and shared strategies for workers. Its role in promoting the collective action of unions in similar circumstances reinforces such an identity. Participation in these demonstrations rehearses in and of itself a communality of shared identities, interests, and collective action strategies.

The negotiations or speeches at each stop are led by Sōkōdō organizers accompanied by the officials of the union specifically involved. The membership watch as the same organizers and negotiators stand up for each of the individual unions involved. This, plus the thousands of demonstrators going from place to place in support of each union, is a very powerful statement arising out of the very structure of the event.

The colorful trappings of the event echo these themes as well. At the very least, for the duration of the demonstration all the participants share the same special attire, consisting of a headband and a chest sign. The exceptions are few, taking the form of substitutions by some contingents of arm bands for chest signs or headbands, for instance. Upon arrival at the demonstration site, everyone ties these on, and they mark them clearly as participants throughout, just as their removal marks clearly the end of the event. More specifically, their removal marks the end of the individual's participation, since if someone leaves in the middle it comes off and if they rejoin it goes back on. The color of the individual attire is echoed in the huge flags, banners, and signs of various sorts carried by members of each marching union and set up outside the institution against which each demonstration is to be held. The colors are primary – red, yellow, and blue – and the linguistic form of Japanese used in the written slogans is the direct command. These conventions are followed by each and every union, and the result is a tremendous feeling of sharing a language of power and struggle with thousands of other participants. The slogans chanted while marching and at each demonstration are, for the most part, designed to appeal to a common denominator for all workers. Slogans in support of the particular year's Spring Labor Offensive or in opposition to rising cost of living or demanding protection of the livelihood of workers are repeated throughout the day in unified chants. Even the chants specific to a particular union's struggle and chanted only at their demonstration are joined in by the thousands of accompanying workers from other unions, and the effect can be quite a strong sensation of solidarity.

Of course there is a powerful network of union affiliations supporting any union in dispute, and the union officials are always aware of these relationships. For the rank-and-file workers, however, the experience of these social relationships, of having some relationship with members of other unions, is not a frequent one. This is the source of a significant difference and sometimes of potential conflict between rank-and-file members and leaders. It was also a site of attention and efforts to educate by Unikon leaders.

In addition to the practice in demonstrations of these relationships of workers to other workers and of workers to particular institutions that structure their workplaces, Unikon workers also had study groups, meetings, the daily experience of work in their particular company and their particular union. The study groups, begun at the earliest stages of the union's history, gave instruction in such basics as labor law and constitutional provisions for worker rights. Many workers learned only through such groups that the constitution guaranteed to all workers their right to organize and that labor laws would protect certain of their interests. Study of the history of the Japanese and international labor movements made young workers aware of what they shared as workers with others. By the time of the demonstration recorded here, the Unikon workers took this identity for granted, just as they had learned to assume that their own struggle was of great inspiration and importance to workers in other firms, especially in smaller ones facing the problems associated with slowed growth. Demonstrations by now served to reinforce symbolically and experientially what Unikon workers already discursively knew.

. . .

The effectiveness of demonstrations in inspiring this consciousness of solidarity and shared interests varies from union to union. The nature of the struggle and the particular conditions of experience leading to the dispute set a certain social and political field within which the demonstration is enacted. Unikon's bankruptcy dispute began with workers occupying the factory to oppose liquidation and dispersal. They received the support of local residents and of unions in their regional federation. They also initiated a system of selling bonds to supporters to create an even broader network, a practice modeled after a union struggle at a French watchmaker, Lipp. The *Asahi Shinbun* labeled Unikon the "Eastern Lipp." The networks of unions helping them grew rapidly. Their small size and scarce resources made them extremely vulnerable, so the importance of the support of others was critical and more visible than it might otherwise have been. This visibility itself was enhanced for rank-and-file workers by the leadership policy of sending each and every member out to canvass neighbors and other unions for such support.

Once the bankruptcy dispute began, a Joint Struggle Committee was formed to oversee the struggle. That committee consisted of representatives from federation and affiliated unions and only the top leadership of the Unikon union. Formally, it was an advisory committee, but in practice it planned strategy and took over primary decision-making power. In a larger union the union itself often retains greater authority, but in such a small union the outside support was the core of their strength and became integrated very thoroughly with union activity. Rank and file were aware of this structure at every meeting, since these "outside" members would be present and their opinions valued and given precedence.

In short, the experiences of struggling in concert with other workers and unions and of having Unikon's own struggle managed by a committee of their own leaders and outsiders, combined with the participation in demonstrations of this kind, together forged a very strong sense of solidarity.

Capital, Labor, Inequality, and Injustice

The demonstration is both a vehicle for the experience of certain relationships of social inequality and a compelling force pushing many participants to reflect on and discuss their relationships with one another. Staying and fighting in the Unikon dispute meant for most struggling against forms of injustice associated with particular relationships, specifically those between capital and labor – also phrased as owners and workers, "the weaker" and "the stronger," protesters and institutions, and larger and smaller organizations.

The distinction between capital and labor was not in any sense introduced by the demonstration, but it was evoked and given dramatic experiential dimensions. The entire course of events at Sōkōdō demonstrations is designed around labor protesting against capital. This explicit opposition is discussed with a correspondingly explicit terminology in use throughout conversations surrounding the event. "Capitalists" (*shihonka*) and "workers" or "labor" (*rōdōsha*) were not only the common terminology used by leaders to rank and file and in speeches and pamphlets, but also in discussions by Unikon workers over tea, walking to the train after work, and during work-hour conversation having to do with disputes and grievances and events which are part of the demonstration. The identification of oneself and one's own union with *rōdōsha* as discussed above presumes this distinction. It is a distinction, however, that faces clear constraints.

In conversations about the struggle, its personal costs, and the personal sacrifices made, workers more frequently lament the distinction between capitalists on the one hand and common people (*futsū no hito*) or human beings (*ningen*) on the other. This distinction has less of the explicit ideological consciousness of relation to the means of production and more consciousness of a gap of wealth, power, and moral character. It calls to mind a distinction elegantly delineated by Tetsuo Najita between efficient, impersonal structures and an oppositional, idealistic, and caring human spirit. In his analysis of the intellectual foundations of modern Japan, he identifies an "elemental axis that is basic to an understanding of modern Japan" from the earliest formation of the nation and its industrial base into the postwar period, an axis constituted by "bureaucratism" (*kanryōshugi*) on the one hand and "purity of human spirit" (*ningensei* or *kokoro*) on the other (1974: 2). Capital, government, and bureaucracy are taken interchangeably and opposed as a system against "people." Furthermore the excesses of power and its uncaring use are conceptualized as "inhuman" and lacking in the moral character valued in human relations. This distinction is the most common one in conversations not specifically concerned with demonstrations and collective actions per se. It is this relationship of really blatant inequality and inhuman moral lapse which came to people's minds walking through the valleys of beautifully designed skyscraping financial buildings and which prompted comments about the incredible wealth of the "capitalists" who own such buildings.

On the other side of the coin are the "common people" living and working in small and crowded buildings not at all modern in design or convenience, what several Unikon workers liked to joke about as "rabbit hutches," borrowing a disparaging comment from a European journalist about Japanese housing. Unikon people were fond of saying that the capitalists and the Japanese government were anxious to object to that characterization, and to turn the eyes of the world toward their own lovely new urban structures and comfortable "Japanese" houses and gardens, in an attempt to hide the reality of the enormous gap between the average person and the capitalist. Demonstrations, taking place as they must in the territory of the elegant financial district, occasion this kind of observation and conversation about the economic inequality. The importance of buildings, both workplaces and homes, as symbols of both the wealthy and the poor ends of the spectrum shows up repeatedly.

Both the capital-labor and the capital-common folk distinctions represent relationships through which workers make sense of their struggle and structure their thoughts about injustice. Again, specific experience motivated certain feelings which were only later gradually given form and meaning. That process itself is an interesting interaction between consciousness and action in the conversations among coworkers, in organizational structures and incentives, and in explicit efforts to raise consciousness and motivate rank and file to join in collective action.

Most of the issues which made sense of the struggle for people took form later, after the fact. Action preceded carefully discussed and frequently considered thoughts on these issues. People were already fighting, already participating in the activities, had already decided – for the time being – to accept the personal sacrifices required, and of course they had already been working for years in companies structured as capitalist enterprises. As they organized, socialist ideology inspired much of the language and rationale for their struggle, but the great majority of rank and file did not decide to join or stay throughout these years primarily because they wanted to fight for socialism, for the right to own their own shops, or even for the sake of all Japanese workers.

They joined, they say, because they were angry, terribly and intolerably angry. They were being put out of work, without warning, without consultation, without an honest effort on the part of the Unikon owners to protect their jobs. The lack of effort in trying to save their jobs and the lack of enough consideration to at least discuss the situation with the union representatives prior to the bankruptcies left the workers feeling betrayed, feeling that they had been treated as less than human (*ningen to shite atsukawarete inai*). "Less than human," they explained, means that the managers and owners did not see them as human beings with lives to lead, a daily life and livelihood (*seikatsu*) to protect. These workers speak of a right to maintain a peaceful daily life, to a minimum livelihood. These rights are echoed in chants at demonstrations and in speeches at most union gatherings. The responsibility (*sekinin*) of the owners, financiers, and managers toward the workers was, they felt, sadly neglected.

The bankruptcy itself was not sufficient to inspire the anger they described. Bankruptcy may have been unavoidable, and some union members even suggest that the union itself may have gone too far and made bankruptcy inevitable by making too many demands without considering the fortunes of the company. It was more the way in which it was handled that angered people. There is a "responsible" and an "irresponsible" way to handle a crisis like this, a "human" and an "inhuman" way, a way that shows respect for workers' needs and a way that ignores them. At Unikon, people claim that their company was irresponsible, inhuman, and disrespectful, and it was here, in the realm of attitude and manner, that their anger was kindled and intensified.

Here is the nexus of concerns that reappears throughout this book because it reappeared through various activities and innumerable conversations. The content of their demand for "human" dignity and respect was a heartfelt belief that people have a fundamental right to some measure of control over their own livelihood. Livelihood here is not employment per se, but livelihood as employment linked to daily life, to family, to human existence at however modest a level. Control here is not an absolute concept existing outside the social relationships which define the company and the union relationships to rank-and-file workers. It includes the debate over the nature of control of labor which was ongoing at both Unikon and Universal. Union leaders were making concerted efforts to mobilize people around the idea that workers should control their own labor. Socialist and Communist Party resources and ideology reinforced this message. Rank-and-file workers were more convinced that they should have some measure of control than that they should have full control, and here the distinction between being managed and being controlled emerges and marks the unsettled issue for Unikon, Universal, and other worker-controlled struggles as well. Within this collective action were workers fighting for control of their own company and workers fighting for a stronger position within a structure of control which included managers.

The Unikon case involved fierce and even violent demonstrations in addition to the Sōkōdō events. The Unikon workers went to the home of the owner and harassed him and his family. They went to the local branch of the bank involved and stopped business for hours at a time by lining up single file and opening and closing accounts all day. These actions and others, like occupying their factory against court orders to evacuate, kept the workers constantly on the verge of illegality and in a state of uproar, not to mention financial sacrifice. The reason that the leadership was able to mobilize over two hundred rank and file to participate in this was explained to me by a union official:

> We were lucky, I suppose. It wasn't so hard to get people to do even the most outrageous things to fight against our owners and the bank. It's because of the way they [the owners] did it. If they had talked to us, made a sincere effort to maintain the solvency of the company, encouraged our cooperation or even insured our back wages and severance pay, we could never have enlisted enough support from the rank and file to fight against it.
> But they just deserted! They deserted the company, our contracts, and the workers. They didn't even think about the consequences their actions would have on us, about our lives and our families. It made everyone angry and they were ready to fight.

The Unikon workers and their leadership talked of their owners as having been militaristic and feudalistic, saying that their behavior had always been shocking and uncommonly lacking in compassion and respect for workers. Clearly, notions of inequality between capital and labor are involved here, but it is a particular dimension to that relationship which inspires a sense of injustice. For both Unikon and Universal workers, the injustice of the social structure which creates classes with unequal wealth and power was less moving personally than was the breach of basic human consideration appropriate to the treatment of workers by those with economic and political power.

People acted first on their implicit assumptions and a sense of outrage at offenses against those assumptions. The skill of the leadership at Unikon was in their ability to transform that highly emotional and largely unexamined action and outrage into a formulated collective act and a sensible struggle that would hold its rank-and-file participants together for two and a half years of sacrifice and extraordinary activities. That was accomplished with a combination of union organizing experience and education.

DECIDING TO JOIN, DECIDING TO STAY

Even given the anger and the sensibility of this struggle, not everyone stayed. Personal choices to stay or quit were based also on strategies for individual lives. The critical mass of workers who stayed and fought had in common a decision that it was worth it to them to do so. There are a cluster of factors which determined final decisions, a cluster from which each person pulled at least two or three factors to make a choice. These choices were made in the context of outsiders, with family and friends putting pressure on workers to stay or to quit. That pressure itself often became an important and sometimes determining force. Nearly everyone reported uncertainty about the decision to stay through this dispute. It was different from previous ones in that it concerned the total elimination of employment for all workers and the dissolution of the company itself. The odds of success were much harder to gauge and the risk of a lengthy and finally futile fight seemed high. Many workers talked frankly about their own decision as comprising a series of smaller decisions, revaluations, and calculated risks. The reasons people stayed in the beginning were generally different from reasons for persevering a year or two later. Reasons also flowed in and out of importance over this long time, and for all but a very few certainty was uncommon.

There were three kinds of concerns people could voice: affective ties and feelings, political purposes, and personal lifetime goals and constraints. In making the decision to join and stay through this struggle, individual workers had to feel that it was personally sensible and worthwhile. For them the solidarity which their own time and efforts constituted was a complex, changing, and uncertain phenomenon, and one upon which their own decisions could have a profound effect.

Affective Ties and Feelings

The two most important affective dimensions in workers' decisions were anger and closeness, anger at their owners and managers and feelings of closeness with coworkers. The notions of injustice which inspired this anger were discussed above. Here it is important to take note of its role in decision making for individual workers. The anger they felt upon initial news of the bankruptcy was a deciding motivation for many in joining, although no one recognized it as important in their staying beyond the first few weeks.

Closeness to other workers, ties of friendship and history were critical. People talked about working together through three previous disputes, about working at this factory with these same coworkers for ten or twelve years, and about sharing the extremely rough days and weeks immediately after the bankruptcy. Just as anger was the most commonly mentioned reason for joining, ties of closeness to other workers was the most common reason for staying through the two and a half years of the dispute. The sharing of demonstrations of all kinds, of building the union, of working day by day with one another, of trips, study-group retreats, year-end parties, spring cherry blossom viewing parties, and a host of other special occasions and daily life experiences came up over and over again in conversations about the effort and energy put into the struggle by the Unikon workers. Clearly one of the critical components of the union's political solidarity was this affective closeness, which was both explicitly cultivated by leadership and stumbled upon through routine practices as well. In the end, however, it was the remarkable solidarity of this union that prompted journalists and scholars in Japan to label them "advanced" and even the "avant-garde" of the labor movement.

This attention and these characterizations provided endless amusement for rank and file. The idea that they had "high class consciousness" or were at the cutting edge of the labor movement made people smile and laugh. It seemed distant and unfamiliar, as though the authors of such phrases were depicting some other group of people in some distant place. People insisted that they were "ordinary" and that ideology and labor movement goals had little to do with their own involvement in the struggle.

Political Purposes

While people did not talk in abstract terms about the politics of the labor movement when discussing personal decisions to quit or to stay, there were two political factors that came up frequently: the inspiration of their leaders and the defense of their own rights. The Unikon leadership was held in very high regard by rank and file. This too was contextualized in conversation by the proud recounting of history, the lengthy struggle of these men to form and sustain the union from its inception and through three other disputes. In essence, the respect for these individuals became one way of expressing a pride in the accomplishments of their union over the preceding ten years. People would say that they didn't want to "pull the rug out from under" their leaders by giving up. Once these leaders started a fight, many workers felt a strong sense of personal commitment to support them. Rank and file would also speak of the advances in working conditions under these leaders, which itself inspired a kind of obligation grounded in gratitude.

In comparison, defending workers' rights was infrequently mentioned, but nonetheless there were occasions when some people would talk about the feeling that they had to fight this battle to prove that workers could defend themselves against injustice. They related this to the anger they felt toward their owners and wanted to prove to them and to the public that workers couldn't be taken advantage of and dismissed in such a disrespectful way. The anger, which seemed to abate after a few weeks, appeared to have transformed itself into this commitment to stand up for a kind of justice for workers. This transformation itself showed the skill of the popular leaders in guiding the individual feelings and motivations of the workers into a more lasting solidarity. Practices like study groups, sending people out to speak on their own behalf to related groups, and frequent communication and education, especially in early stages, were extremely effective in accomplishing this transition.

Personal Circumstances

The factors people felt were most important to their own decisions were quite personal, having to do with their own desire to learn, to be part of something "larger," the difficulty of finding another job in the same kind of industry, or another job at all, and their own particular family circumstances, which determined whether or not they could afford to accept less pay for the duration of this struggle. I didn't have the opportunity to talk with people who had quit in the beginning, but those who stayed defended their decisions, saying that they were mostly men in their mid-thirties with children in school and higher expenses, thus unable to take the risk either of losing the dispute or of weathering many months of lowered income. Only younger men in their twenties and women with employed husbands could afford to stay. As the struggle wore on, it was this factor which most frequently caused people to reassess their own decisions and wonder if maybe they were being too optimistic. Many considered quitting, some did and then returned after a certain amount of encouragement from union leaders and coworkers.

Learning about the world, broadening horizons, and making this struggle into their own life experience were the attractive aspects of staying for many. Workers talked about seeing all parts of Tokyo, going places for demonstrations where they had never been and becoming familiar with the trains and subways that traverse the huge city and with its parks and downtown districts. The factory itself was located in the northeast section and most people lived farther east on the borders of Tokyo, whereas the owners' residences were in the wealthier western districts and the demonstrations against financial institutions were downtown in the financial district.

The long history of political protest in Japan was a factor for many. Some linked the Unikon struggle to struggles over the U.S.-Japan Security Treaty and other progressive causes supported by the labor movement. One young man laughed about learning to protest as a child playing in public housing playgrounds, where kids would dress up with handkerchiefs as headbands and handwritten signs pinned to their shirts and play "*anpo gokko*," or "pretend anti–U.S.-Japan Security Treaty demonstration." They would wind through the walkways between the apartment complex buildings, hands linked and chanting in playful imitation of the "snake dances" characteristic of the political demonstrations of the sixties. Many had parents in unions affiliated with Sōhyō and which had therefore been drawn into a variety of radical political actions through that federation. It was not unusual then or now for parents to take their children with them to peaceful demonstrations, and many of these Unikon workers recalled such experiences.

The larger social and political world experienced through Unikon and its federations broadened people's experience immeasurably. Since their small union was affiliated with many others and now actively utilizing those ties, each of them had visited other unions, some had gone to affiliated organizations' conventions or meetings, and they had Diet members and union federation officials at every one of their own general meetings. They were represented in the Sōkōdō demonstrations by Sōhyō officials and began to feel "larger," as many put it, that is, tied into something bigger and more important than just their own life or work with their limited boundaries. This expansion was in and of itself attractive. Many used the expression "life experience" (*jinsei keiken*) to describe the satisfaction of being involved in this fight, saying that the union's struggle had become their own life experience.

The very practical necessity of having a job was of utmost importance, and many were reluctant to quit because they were uncertain about their prospects for finding another job at all, or because they wanted to work in high technology and particularly in camera production and were afraid that they wouldn't be able to find such a job elsewhere. For virtually all the regular employees who stayed, this was their first full-time job. Most of these workers – nearly all men – came to Tokyo from the rural areas of northeast Japan to work at Unikon, and they were not eager to quit and look for other work. For the part-time women, a different factor was at work, the proximity to their own homes and the virtual nonexistence of labor unions for part-time workers. Unikon was one of the first anywhere in Japan to consider including part-time workers in their union, so finding another job with working conditions as good as this company, or with even a voice in the formation of working conditions was quite unlikely. Again history became important, in that these part-time workers had formed the union here and had a particular pride in its existence as well as in its strength. Several of these workers spoke of the impossibility of finding a job where there would be a union and admitted that while they could be active in one, they didn't feel they knew how to organize one from scratch by themselves.

CONSCIOUSNESS AND ACTION

The experience of the Unikon workers suggests several lessons: there is a very strong dialectical relationship between experience and consciousness; it is necessary to create a personal sensibility conducive to struggle; and learning and process are critical to taking and analyzing action. The bankruptcy of their company, their union activities, and their collective actions like the demonstrations were, as experience, part of their consciousness. Workers' thoughts, feelings, and actions are not segregated or compartmentalized, but rather contextualized and interdependent. The bankruptcy made them angry, but their anger had its own history; it was shaped and cultivated through previous experiences. Every individual had been through weekly meetings of study groups which taught them about legal and moral rights, discussed labor history, and promoted a sense of identity with organized unions and workers throughout Japan and the world. Each of these workers had also been through three labor disputes and all the collective actions and successes these had entailed.

Consequently, when their owners declared them bankrupt and neglected to consult with their union and to follow cautious legal procedures, they were angry. They felt angry, they knew why they were angry, and they took actions that expressed that anger. Their dignity as human beings was offended and their legal rights as organized workers were ignored. The organizational skill of Unikon leaders lay in weaving the threads of heartfelt offense against human dignity and ideological protest into collective actions which integrated goals of worker control and goals of worker participation into a single powerful movement.

Knowing that a struggle is for the benefit of all workers, finding it sensible to protest inequality and injustice, is still not enough to build motivations for action. A personal sensibility must develop, such that struggle seems reasonable, feels right, and matters to the individual worker. Such sensibility cannot be cultivated outside the experiences of social life and political action. For that, demonstrations and other organized union activities were critical. It was here that the merging of experience and thought were most obvious, and most reminiscent of the kind of ritual process discussed by Victor Turner. It is not necessary to have a ritual, however, to have a profoundly transformative experience. What is necessary is that an individual be personally participating in a socially constructed action while ideas about what those actions mean are presented in a coherent and convincing way. The reasons for this struggle, for instance, must become significant in explaining one's own behavior and action, not just the actions of others or of the union. While workers were angry and confused about what to do, the union sent them to explain and justify their cause. It sent them into demonstrations of various kinds. Within a few weeks efforts to understand the struggle of the Unikon union were efforts to understand their own personal experience and action. Their own participation created a personally felt sense of struggle, which shaped their motivation and commitment. Furthermore, this process had to be repeated. In the early stages it might be characterized as transformative. Later it was reinforcing. Throughout the two and a half years it was critical in rehearsing the personal importance of the meaning of their collective action.

The link between personal experience and purposeful political action is through a web of significance and feasibility. Decisions to take certain actions or stay in such a struggle were not made once and then left alone. They were themselves part of a process of learning that is just as concerned with experience and common sense, or implicit knowledge, as it is with ideas, interests, and explicit knowledge.

Both leaders and rank and file were involved in a fluid process of learning, teaching, experimenting, inquiring, explaining, reassessing, and deciding. Decisions, however, were not one-time events, taken and then followed through. They were sometimes actions taken with little thought, which just seemed natural, right, or inevitable. And sometimes they were agonized over and regretted and even resented. But always they were just points on a trajectory through the two-and-a-half-year period of time during which the 150 people who remained learned from one another and in each other's company how to construct both a convincing argument and a successful collective action to cope with the threat bankruptcy posed to their livelihoods.

REFERENCES

Cole, Robert. 1971. *Japanese Blue Collar: The Changing Tradition*. Berkeley and Los Angeles: University of California Press.

———. 1979. *Work, Mobility and Participation: A Comparative Study of American and Japanese Industry*. Berkeley and Los Angeles: University of California Press.

Dore, Ronald. 1973. *British Factory-Japanese Factory: The Origin of National Diversity in Industrial Relations*. Berkeley and Los Angeles: University of California Press.

———. 1986. *Flexible Rigidities: Industrial Policy and Structural Adjustment in the Japanese Economy, 1979–80*. Stanford: Stanford University Press.

———. 1987. *Taking Japan seriously. A Confucian Perspective on Leading Economic Issues*. Stanford: Stanford University Press.

Rohlen, Thomas P. 1974. *For Harmony and Strength: Japanese White-Collar Organization in Anthropological Perspective*. Berkeley and Los Angeles: University of California Press.

Shirai, Taishiro. 1983. 'A Theory of Enterprise Unionism', in *Contemporary Industrial relations in Japan*. Taishiro Shirai (ed.) Madison: University of Wisconsin Press.

Turner, Victor. 1967. *The Forest of Symbols: Aspects of Ndembu Ritual*. Ithaca: Cornell University Press.

———. 1969. *The Ritual Process*. Chicago: Aldine.

APPENDIX OF SOURCES

Grateful acknowledgement is made to the following sources for permission to reproduce material in this publication.

PART 1: INDUSTRIAL TIME AND WORK DISCIPLINE

1. 'Time, Work-Discipline, and Industrial Capitalism',
   E.P. Thompson
   Past and Present, 38 (Oxford University Press, 1967), 56–97.
   Reprinted by permission of Oxford University Press.

2. 'Peasant Time and Factory Time in Japan', *Thomas C. Smith*
   Past and Present, 111 (Oxford University Press, 1986), 165–97.
   Reprinted by permission of Oxford University Press.

3. 'Satanic Fields, Pleasant Mills: Work in a Indian Steel Plant', *Jonathan Parry*
   Contributions to Indian Sociology (new series), 33(1–2) (Sage Publications, 1999), 107–40.
   Copyright 1999 © Institute of Economic Growth, Delhi. All rights reserved. Reprinted in abridged form with the permission of the copyright holders and the publishers, Sage Publications India Pvt, New Delhi.

4. 'The Production of Possession: Spirits and the Multinational Corporation in Malaysia', *Aihwa Ong*
   American Ethnologist, 15 (University of California Press, 1988), 28–42.
   Published by Blackwell Publishing Ltd. Reprinted with permission of Blackwell Publishing Ltd.

PART 2: INDUSTRIAL WORK: SKILL, CONTROL AND CONSENT

5. 'Scientific Management', *Harry Braverman*
   Labour and Monopoly Capital: The Degradation of Work in the Twentieth Century (Monthly Review Press, 1974), 85–123.
   Published by Monthly Review Press.

6. 'Controlling the Line', *Huw Beynon*
    Working for Ford (Penguin Books, 1973), 139–61.
    Reprinted with kind permission of the author.

7. 'Thirty Years of Making Out', *Michael Burawoy*
    Manufacturing Consent (Chicago University Press, 1979), 46–73.
    Copyright © 1979. Reprinted with permission of University of Chicago Press.

8. 'The Nuclear Everyday', *Françoise Zonabend*
    The Nuclear Peninsula (Cambridge University Press, 1993), 101–20.
    © Cambridge University Press. Reprinted with permission.

PART 3: 'WORK', 'LIFE' AND GENDER

9. 'Emerging Alienation in Production: A Maussian History', *James Carrier*
    Man, 27(3) (Royal Anthropological Institute of Great Britain and Ireland, 1992), 539–58.
    Published by Royal Anthropological Institute of Great Britain and Ireland. Reprinted with
    permission of Blackwell Publishing Ltd.

10. 'Gendered Meanings in Contention: Anarchomex', *Leslie Salzinger*
    Genders in Production: Making Workers in Mexico's Global Factories (University of California
    Press, 2003), 128–55.
    Copyright © 2003 The Regents of the University of California. Published by the University of
    California Press. Reprinted with permission.

11. 'Local Despotism', *Ching Kwan Lee*
    Gender and the South China Miracle (University of California Press, 1998), 109–36.
    Copyright © 1998 Trustees of the British Museum. Published by the University of California
    Press. Reprinted with permission.

12. 'Femininity and Flexible Labor: Fashioning Class Through Gender on the
    Global Assembly Line', *Carla Freeman*
    Critique of Anthropology 18(3) (Sage Publications, 1998), 245–62.
    Extracts reprinted by permission of Sage Publications.

13. 'The Enterprise as a Community', *Ronald Dore*
    British Factory – Japanese Factory: The origins of national diversity in industrial relations
    (University of California Press, 1973), 201–15.
    Copyright © 1973 R.P. Dore. Reprinted by permission of University of California Press.

14. '*Yoseba* and *Ninpudashi*: Changing Patterns of Employment on the Fringes of
    the Japanese Economy', *Tom Gill*
    Globalization and Social Change in Contemporary Japan, (Trans Pacific Press, 2000), 123–42.
    Reprinted by permission of Trans Pacific Press.

PART 4: THE ROAD(S) TO INDUSTRIAL 'MODERNITY'

15. 'Anthropological Problems Arising from the African Industrial Revolution',
    Max Gluckman
    Social change in modern Africa, (Oxford University Press, 1961), 67–82.
    Copyright © 1961 International African Institute. Published by Oxford University Press. Extract
    reprinted by permission of the International African Institute.

16. 'Global Disconnect: Abjection and the Aftermath of Modernism'
    James Ferguson
    Expectations of Modernity: Myths and Meanings of Urban Life on the Zambian Copperbelt
    (University of California Press, 2002), 234–54.
    Copyright © 1999 The Regents of the University of California. Published by the University of
    California Press. Reprinted with permission.

17. 'Despair: The Decline of the Kanpur Textile Mills', *Chitra Joshi*
    Lost Worlds: Indian labour and its forgotten histories (Permanent Black, 2003), 313–29.
    Reprinted by kind permission of the author.

18. 'The Poetics of Productivity', *Lisa Rofel*
    Other Modernities: gendered yearnings in China after socialism (University of California Press,
    1999), 96–127.
    Copyright © 1999 The Regents of the University of California. Published by the University of
    California Press. Reprinted with permission.

19. 'Asking for and Giving *Baki*: Neo-bondage, or the Interplay of Bondage and
    Resistance in the Tamilnadu Power-loom Industry', *Geert De Neve*
    Contributions to Indian Sociology (new series), 33(1–2) (Sage Publications, 1999), 379–406
    Copyright 1999 © Institute of Economic Growth, Delhi. All rights reserved. Reprinted with the
    permission of the copyright holders and the publishers, Sage Publications India Pvt, New Delhi.

PART 5: THE INDUSTRIAL WORKING CLASS?

20. 'Bourgeois and Proletarians', *Karl Marx*
    Kindly translated by and reprinted with the permission of the Marxist Internet Archive.

21. 'Perspectives on the Politics of Class', *Rajnarayan Chandavarkar*
    The origins of industrial capitalism in India (Cambridge University Press, 1994), 11–20.
    © Cambridge University Press. Reprinted with permission.

22. 'Class Structure in the Classic Slum', *Robert Roberts*
    The Classic Slum: Salford Life in the First Quarter of the Century', (Manchester University Press,
    1971), 13–31.
    Reprinted with kind permission of the author's estate.

23. 'Community and Class Consciousness', *June Nash*
    We eat the mines and the mines eat us: Dependency and exploitation in the Bolivian Tin Mines
    (Columbia University Press, 1979), 310–20.
    Copyright © 1979 Columbia University Press. Reprinted with permission.

24. 'Learning to Protest in Japan: Class Consciousness, Solidarity, and Political
    Action', *Christena Turner*
    Japanese workers in protest: An Ethnography of Consciousness and Experience (University of
    California Press, 1995), 33–65.
    Copyright © 1995 The Regents of the University of California. Published by the University of
    California Press. Reprinted with permission.

LIST OF SERIES

33. **Chinese Lineage and Society**
    Fukien and Kwantung
    Maurice Freedman

32. **Kinship and Economic Organization in Rural Japan**
    Chie Nakane

31. **The Muslim Matrimonial Court in Singapore**
    Judith Djamour

30. **Saints and Fireworks**
    Religion and Politics in Rural Malta
    Jeremy Boissevain

29. **Malay Peasant Society in Jelebu**
    M. G. Swift

28. **Essays on Social Organization and Values**
    Raymond Firth

27. **A New Maori Migration**
    Rural and Urban Relations in Northern New Zealand
    Joan Metge

26. **Kinship and Marriage in a New Guinea Village**
    H. Ian Hogbin

25. **Conflict and Solidarity in a Guianese Plantation**
    Chandra Jayawardena

24. **Legal Institutions in Manchu China**
    A Sociological Analysis
    Sybille van der Sprenkel

23. **Marsh Dwellers of the Euphrates Delta**
    S. M. Salim

22. **Rethinking Anthropology**
    E. R. Leach

21. **Malay Kinship and Marriage in Singapore**
    Judith Djamour

20. **Social Status and Power in Java**
    L. H. Palmier

19. **Political Leadership among Swat Pathans**
    Fredrik Barth

INDEX